Francisco Pina Polo / Alejandro Díaz Fernández
The Quaestorship in the Roman Republic

KLIO
Beiträge zur Alten Geschichte

Beihefte. Neue Folge

Herausgegeben von
Hartwin Brandt und Martin Jehne

unter Mitarbeit von
Manfred Clauss, Peter Funke, Hans-Joachim Gehrke
und Christian Mann

Band 31

Francisco Pina Polo / Alejandro Díaz Fernández

The Quaestorship in the Roman Republic

DE GRUYTER

ISBN 978-3-11-076370-6
e-ISBN (PDF) 978-3-11-066641-0
e-ISBN (EPUB) 978-3-11-066374-7
ISSN 1438-7689

Library of Congress Control Number: 2019946391

Bibliographic information published by the Deutsche Nationalbibliothek
The Deutsche Nationalbibliothek lists this publication in the Deutsche Nationalbibliografie;
detailed bibliographic data are available on the Internet at http://dnb.dnb.de.

© 2021 Walter de Gruyter GmbH, Berlin/Boston
This volume is text- and page-identical with the hardback published in 2019.
Printing and binding: CPI books GmbH, Leck

www.degruyter.com

To Romana, as always and forever.
Someone like you makes it all worthwhile
Someone exactly like you

To Marina, Julia and María Jesús,
for their unconditional support,
infinite patience and daily love

Preface

This book is the fruit of the project 'The quaestorship during the Republic at Rome and abroad', sponsored by the Spanish Ministerio de Economía y Competitividad (HAR2013-43477-P).

The authors are very grateful to some individuals and institutions that have helped make this project a reality. Each author would like to express his gratitude separately.

Francisco Pina Polo took the first steps in researching the elusive quaestors in 2014, when he spent three months at Princeton's Institute for Advanced Study and enjoyed not only the wonderful atmosphere but also a place in its beautiful library overlooking the pond and woods. In 2015 and 2016, I was a guest for some weeks first at the Seminar für Alte Geschichte of Münster and then at the Institut für Geschichte (Lehrstuhl für Alte Geschichte) of Dresden, which are directed by two good friends and excellent colleagues, Johannes Hahn and Martin Jehne, respectively. Their hospitality and joviality truly helped me advance this project. Last but not least, in 2017 I had the privilege of being a Visiting Research Fellow at Merton College during Trinity term. Anyone who has ever spent some time working in the Sackler and Bodleian Libraries knows very well what this means for an ancient historian: paradise. For this privilege I am very much indebted to Jonathan Prag, Professor of Ancient History in Merton and himself a great expert on the Roman quaestorship. I would also like to thank other Oxonian colleagues who generously discussed some aspects of this book with me, including Fergus Millar and Henriette van der Blom (now in Birmingham). Some colleagues, including Werner Eck and Anne Kolb, have given their advice on various questions or have provided useful bibliographical items, for which I am very grateful. I owe a very special debt of gratitude to my colleague and friend Cristina Rosillo-López (University Pablo de Olavide, Seville), since she has patiently read substantial parts of the book and has always contributed invaluable advice and recommendations that have improved it. Needless to say, none of these colleagues and friends can be blamed for any infelicities or mistakes in the book.

Alejandro Díaz Fernández continued the work initiated by Francisco Pina Polo during two successive research trips in Rome (2016 and 2017) that were financed by the University of Málaga with the invaluable help of the Escuela Española de Historia y Arqueología of Rome (EEHAR-CSIC). I am sincerely grateful to Emma Chesterman for the translation and improvement of my text, as well as to my colleagues in the Department of Historical Sciences of the University of Málaga, my dear friend Francho and my family for their support and unconditional patience: completing this project would indeed have been impossible without the kind collaboration of so many people and institutions.

Finally, we want to thank Benjamin Jerue for the complete revision of the text and stylistic improvement.

Contents

Introduction —— 1

Chapter 1: The origin of the quaestorship —— 5
    The puzzle of the ancient sources —— 5
    Piecing the puzzle together: scholarly reconstructions —— 12
    Some conclusions and suggestions —— 19

Chapter 2: The development of the quaestorship and the so-called Italian quaestors —— 25
    The increasing number and functions of quaestors throughout the Republic —— 25
    The so-called Italian quaestorships —— 43

Chapter 3: The quaestorship within the political career: Age requirements and the *cursus honorum* —— 51

Chapter 4: Election, entry into office and allocation of quaestorian *provinciae* —— 64
    Election of quaestors and date of their entry into office —— 64
    Sortitio of quaestors and appointments *extra sortem* —— 69

Chapter 5: The urban quaestorship —— 79
    The administration of the *aerarium populi Romani* —— 84
    Diplomacy and accommodation of foreign guests —— 98
    Funerary honours —— 103
    Conservation of roads —— 105
    Minting of coins —— 107
    The urban quaestors as public notaries of the Roman Republic —— 112
    Oaths of magistrates and *imperatores* —— 115
    Selection of jurors for permanent courts —— 116
    The political role of urban quaestors —— 117
    List of urban quaestors in the Roman Republic —— 123

Chapter 6: The quaestor overseas: Development and role of the quaestorship in the provinces —— 125
    Provinces, sortitions, prorogations —— 131
    The quaestor in his province —— 163

Conclusions —— 196

Appendix 1: A prosopography of the Roman Republican quaestorship —— 205

Appendix 2: Chronological list of quaestors in the Roman Republic —— 336

Bibliography —— 348

Index of names —— 366

Index of subjects —— 374

Introduction

Some years ago in a paper in which he re-examined the quaestorship during the third and second centuries,[1] Jonathan Prag asserted that a monograph on this office was necessary: 'An assessment of the quaestorship on its own terms, and through the medium of the complete set of evidence, such as it is, for quaestors in the Republic, is long overdue... a comprehensive study remains a *desideratum*.'[2] This book aims to fill this gap in the scholarship. There are certainly good reasons why no monograph on the quaestorship has been published until now. The lack of evidence has not only proved to be the greatest obstacle involved in reconstructing the quaestorship but has also led to debates about nearly every particular detail concerning the institution and operation of the office. Indeed, the scarcity of evidence and the trend to focus on smaller questions have probably discouraged scholars from undertaking a large-scale study of the quaestorship. Coarelli put it plainly some years ago: 'nella storia delle istituzioni politiche romane, il caso della questura è forse il più intricate e controverso.'[3] In a different vein, historians at times have treated the quaestorship as a secondary office devoid of scholarly interest, even in ancient times. In 1983, for example, Badian wrote: 'Quaestors were essentially unimportant, especially before they came to be *ex officio* enrolled in the senate. No one transmitted lists of them to posterity, and no one felt politically or socially threatened by them.'[4]

Two German dissertations on the Roman quaestorship were written at the end of the nineteenth century and the beginning of the twentieth, respectively. To date, they are the only monographs that take the quaestorship as their main subject. Both dissertations, however, had a limited scope, since they were dedicated exclusively to assembling the prosopography of the Republican quaestors. In Chemnitz in 1893 Martin Bülz wrote his dissertation about the provincial quaestors between 82 and 44. In his book he ordered the quaestors chronologically, province by province. Some years later, in 1908, Bülz complemented his dissertation with a booklet entitled *Fasti Quaestorum*, in which he not only collected the quaestors between 414 and 83, but also amassed the ancient sources that provide evidence about the office. Friedrich Sobeck wrote his dissertation under the supervision of Conrad Cichorius in 1909. Although his work was intended primarily as a prosopography of the Roman quaestors, his objective was more ambitious than that of Bülz: Sobeck listed all the quaestors from the beginning of the Republic until 44, both those who performed their office in a province and those who stayed at Rome. Sobeck gathered the ancient sources for each magistrate along with any known details about each individual. His prosopography later served as one of the bases for Broughton's *The Magistrates of the*

---

1 All dates are BC unless expressly mentioned.
2 Prag 2014a, 208.
3 Coarelli 2014, 99.
4 Badian 1983, 168.

Roman Republic, which still remains the standard reference work on Republican prosopography.

Until now, Theodor Mommsen's nineteenth-century *Römisches Staatsrecht* provided the most comprehensive analysis of the quaestorship. As is often the case for those working on the Roman constitution, the shadow of Mommsen has continued to dominate the debate for better or for worse. Indeed, Mommsen has proven so influential that subsequent debates about the quaestorship sometimes appear to have been—or perhaps still are—little more than disputes among supporters and detractors of Mommsen's arguments, particularly with regard to subjects such as the origin of the quaestorship and its apparent relationship to the *quaestores parricidii*, the so-called Italian quaestorships, the place of the quaestorship in the development of the *cursus honorum* and the possible existence of a minimum age for holding the office.

In the context of more general reference works, only a few scholars have attempted to provide a global picture of the history and functions of the quaestorship. In his article on the quaestorship for the *Real-Encyclopädie Pauly-Wissowa* published in 1963, Wesener followed Mommsen's theses point-by-point. Kunkel and Wittmann did not go much further in 1995 in an article that adhered to the overly formalistic and legalistic framework inherited from Mommsen. At any rate, Kunkel and Wittmann did incorporate some of the new ideas—and questions—that had been generated during the debates of the twentieth century. Both Lintott in his 1999 book *The Constitution of the Roman Republic* and Covino in a 2013 article on quaestors for *The Encyclopedia of Ancient History* dealt very briefly with the office and merely summarised some of the well-known problems. In a 2014 article published in *Klio*, Muñiz Coello made the most recent attempt to analyse comprehensively the origin, history and function of the quaestorship, which unfortunately did not offer any answers to the main questions engulfing the office; furthermore, in some cases this article actually reverted to obsolete positions.

There is, therefore, no exhaustive monograph on the quaestorship. Nevertheless, a debate about this magistracy has certainly been taking place or at least arguments about specific aspects of the magistracy. Several articles that have been published on the topic deserve special mention here. In 1936, Latte challenged the main conclusions reached by Mommsen on the origin of the quaestorship and its relation to the *quaestores parricidii*, and hence he opened up a new way to understand the early characteristics of the office. Subsequently, questions about whether the quaestorship originated in the regal period or the early Republic, its apparent relation to the *quaestores parricidii* and the quaestor's initial duties at Rome have all been topics that have provoked discussion and led to a number of publications, as we shall see in the chapter that deals with these questions.

The other issue that has loomed large in scholarship on the quaestorship is the development of the magistracy throughout the Republic. In an important 1976 study of the office's history in the pre-Sullan age between 267 and 81, Harris used the meagre and contentious evidence available in an attempt to answer pressing questions such as how many quaestors existed in the pre-Sullan period and when new quaestorships were created. His reflections gave way to a series of new hypotheses about the so-called *quaestores classici* and Italian quaestorships, hypotheses that have challenged Mommsen's theories, which had largely remained unchallenged over the course of the twentieth century. Harris' article has indeed opened up new perspectives, advanced our knowledge and become a classic study on the office. However, it certainly did not bring the debate about the history of the quaestorship to a close. In fact, the discussion has been further propelled thanks to the discovery of some *rostra* belonging (in all probability) to ships that took part in the battle at the Egadi Islands, located off the western coast of Sicily, which put an end to the First Punic War in 241. Several of these *rostra* bear inscriptions that mention previously unknown Roman quaestors.[5] This discovery has provided food for thought and led to publications concerned with the development of the quaestorship in the third and second centuries. Consequently, the debate has received a new stimulus over the last years, and several articles on the subject have been published, among which Prag's 2014 article is especially significant.[6]

Along with these central issues, a sizable body of literature has accrued that deals directly or indirectly with many of the quaestors about whom the sources provide evidence. Many authors (Badian, Sumner, Ryan, etc.) have tried to establish the dating of their quaestorship and the actions that they undertook while in office. This bibliography together with the aforementioned works of Bülz and Sobeck and, of course, Broughton's monumental volumes provide the basis for reconstructing the prosopography of the identifiable Roman Republican quaestors.

This book contains a study of the quaestorship throughout the Roman Republic, from the fifth century to the year 44, both in Italy (particularly at Rome) and in the overseas provinces. It includes a history of the office, an analysis of its role within the *cursus honorum* and its larger importance for the Roman constitution. Chapters one to four focus on the institutional aspects of the quaestorship: its origins and its development; its incorporation into the *cursus honorum*; the conditions and procedures of selection; the assumption of the magistracy; and the allocation of tasks or *provinciae*. Chapter five examines the duties of the urban quaestors at Rome. A parallel analysis is found in chapter six where the focus turns to the position and functions of the quaestors within the Roman provincial framework. Finally, the book includes the prosopography of all quaestors known during the Republican period based on the literary, epigraphic and numismatic evidence. Unfortunately, the quaestors for whom we have any evidence are few and far between, and very often the precise dates during which they held the magistracy are uncertain or simply unknown.[7]

---

5 Tusa and Royal 2012; Oliveri 2012; Prag 2014b; 2014c; 2017.
6 Prag 2014a.
7 For the period between 200 and 91, Prag. 2014a, 193, has estimated that we only know about 10% of the total number of quaestors, of whom we can only identify a small number by name. This percentage is even lower for other periods of the Roman Republic, in particular the early Republic.

The number of quaestors for whom we have detailed information is, of course, even lower. These limitations in the sources, which especially pertain to the early Republic, have determined how far we can go in painting a definite picture of the Roman Republican quaestorship.[8]

---

[8] Francisco Pina Polo has written the chapters dedicated to the origin and development of the quaestorship at Rome and in Italy (chapters 1 to 5), while Alejandro Díaz Fernández has completed the book with the study of the quaestorship in the overseas provinces (chapter 6). The authors have collaborated on the prosopographical section, as well as on the completion of the entire book. Both authors accept the approaches and conclusions presented over the course of the book.

Chapter 1:
The origin of the quaestorship

In 1984 Adalberto Giovannini argued that the ideas found in present-day scholarship often reproduce the assumptions with which nineteenth-century scholarship has bequeathed us. At times, this adoption of a previous generation's preconceptions has been carried out unwittingly and in such cases it becomes incredibly difficult to free oneself from those ideas. Giovannini went on to suggest that if we hope to transcend the theories that have been debated for well over a century, we must critically re-examine the fundamental assumptions on which they rest. He reached these conclusions in an article on the origins of the Republican offices, a subject over which much ink had already been spilled, but which he claimed deserved a good deal more.[1] More than thirty years have elapsed since Giovannini wrote those words and yet his assertions about our relationship to past scholarship remain valid. As we shall argue throughout this book, the origin of the quaestorship is one such topic that requires a fresh and critical look. For decades scholars have analysed the quaestorship and proposed various solutions for solving the riddle of the office's origins. While these scholars have necessarily relied on the same set of primary sources, they have been greatly influenced by scholarship from the nineteenth and early-twentieth centuries. To a certain extent, anyone who seeks to understand and explain the origins of this office must enter into dialogue with Theodor Mommsen, whose presence is still felt in discussions of the Roman Republican constitution.

The puzzle of the ancient sources

Only a few late sources expressly mention the origin of the quaestorship, all of which are controversial and contradictory. Furthermore, it is striking that neither Livy nor Dionysus of Halicarnasus, our two main sources for the early Republic, specifically address the issues surrounding the creation of the quaestorship, although they speak of quaestors as a matter of fact from the very beginning of the Republic. As is always the case when dealing with archaic Rome, the difficulty lies not only in the lack of unanimity between the sources but above all in the dubious credibility of those very sources.

---

[1] Giovannini 1984, 15: 'Or nous sommes tributaires, souvent à notre insu, d'idées préconçues que nous ont léguées les savants du siècle dernier et dont nous avons la plus grande peine à nous libérer... ce sont précisément ces postulats fondamentaux que nous devons remettre en question si nous voulons aller au-delà des hypothèses défendues ou combattues avec plus ou moins de succès depuis plus de cent cinquante ans. Le problème des origines des magistratures républicaines, sur lequel on a tant écrit, est une bonne illustration de ce qu'il reste encore à faire dans ce domaine.'

Let us begin with Varro and Festus. Both antiquarians derive *quaestor* from *quaerere*, with the meaning of 'search', 'inquire' or 'investigate'.² Accordingly, Varro writes, 'the name quaestors derives from *quaerere*, and they were those who should enquire into public monies and crimes, which the *triumviri capitales* now investigate; from these, afterwards, those who pronounce judgement on matters of investigation were called *quaesitores*.'³ Whereas Varro includes the two functions —financial and judicial— that are usually attributed to quaestors, Festus, whose text is only partially preserved, only refers specifically to quaestors with judicial duties, the so-called *quaestores parricidii*.⁴

Some ancient authors dated the institution of the quaestorship to the regal period. The *Digest*, for example, preserves a passage from Ulpian's book on the quaestorship: 'the origin of quaestors is very old, almost previous to any other magistracy. Junius Gracchanus, in his seventh book *De potestatibus*, relates that Romulus himself and Numa Pompilius had two quaestors, who were appointed not by themselves but by the votes of the people. But even if there are doubts about whether there was any quaestor during the reigns of Romulus and Numa, it is certain that quaestors existed during the reign of Tullus Hostilius. And, certainly, the opinion of ancient writers is that Tullus Hostilius was the first to introduce quaestors in the government of the community.'⁵

Given that Junius Gracchanus must have been active in the second half of the second century BC, this passage indirectly offers the oldest preserved information about the origin of the quaestorship.⁶ According to Junius Gracchanus (provided

---

2 On *quaerere* and *quaestio* see Mantovani 2009.
3 Varr. *l.l.* 5.81: *Quaestores a quaerendo, qui conquirerent publicas pecunias et maleficia, quae triumviri capitales nunc conquirunt; ab his postea qui quaestionum iudicia exercent quaesitores dicti.*
4 Fest. 247 L: *Quaestores [dicebantur, qui quaererent de rebus] capitalibus, unde [iidem etiam quaestores parri]cidi appellantur.* Mommsen 1876–88, 525 n. 2, reconstructed Festus' text otherwise: *Quaestores [primum creabantur quaerendis rebus] capitalibus, unde [in XII tabulis quaestores parri]cidi appellantur.*
5 Dig. 1.13: *Origo quaestoribus creandis antiquissima est et paene ante omnes magistratus. Gracchanus denique Iunius libro septimo de potestatibus etiam ipsum Romulum et Numam Pompilium binos quaestores habuisse, quos ipsi non sua voce sed populi suffragio crearent, refert. Sed sicuti dubium est an Romulo et Numa regnantibus quaestor fuerit, ita Tullo Hostilio rege quaestores fuisse certum est. Et certe crebrior apud veteres opinio est Tullum Hostilium primum in rem publicam induxisse quaestores.*
6 Cicero (*de orat.* 1.256: *...a viro optimo et istis rebus instructissimo, familiari meo Congo mutuabor...*) mentions a Congus, *vir optimus*; on another Ciceronian passage, the Bobiensis scholiast speaks of him as *homo curiosus et diligens eruendae vetustatis. Nam historicus...* (Schol.Bob. p. 163 Stangl). In both Ciceronian passages Congus is presented as a prominent antiquarian. Curiously, no man by the name of Congus is actually ever cited as an authority either by Cicero or any antiquarian. He has been identified with a Marcus Junius known in the later sources as Gracchanus (Cichorius 1908, 123–127). Junius Gracchanus would have been born in the middle of the second century, and he wrote a work under the title *De potestatibus*. Since Ulpian mentioned his seventh book on the quaestorship, Cichorius (126) suggested that each book dealt with the history of one of the Roman magistracies (consul, praetor, etc., and finally quaestor). See also D'Orta 1993, 286. More re-

that Ulpian has accurately recorded his words), the quaestorship had existed in Rome since the very beginning of the *civitas*, if we accept that Romulus and Numa already had quaestors at their service. At any rate, he takes it is a fact (*certum est*) that the quaestorship had existed at least since the reign of Tullus Hostilius, which he claims was the position generally held by ancient writers. As a logical consequence, the quaestorship was among the most ancient magistracy in Rome (*paene ante omnes magistratus*). There were two quaestors when the office was created; furthermore, those that held the post were not directly appointed by the kings but rather elected by the people.[7]

A digression found in Tacitus' *Annals*, which provides one of the longest texts on the history of the quaestorship, also supports the thesis that the roots of the quaestorship lay in the Monarchy: 'With our ancestors, magistracy had been the reward of virtue, and all citizens who had confidence in their qualities could legitimately aspire to hold an office; and there was not even a distinction of age that prevented access to the consulate or to the dictatorship in early youth. The quaestorship was instituted while the kings still reigned, as shown by the curiate law that Lucius Brutus renewed. And the power of selection remained in the hands of the consuls until this office, like all others, passed into the bestowal of the people. The first election, precisely sixty-three years after the expulsion of the Tarquins, was that of Valerius Potitus and Aemilius Mamercus, in order to collaborate in military affairs. Then, as public business increased, two others were added to take care of their duties at Rome.'[8]

Here Tacitus clearly places the origin of the quaestorship in the time of the kings, while also referring to a supposed curiate law that Lucius Brutus renewed. He does not, however, provide a specific date for the creation of the office. Contrary to the

---

cently Rankov 1987 has accepted that Congus was the same as Junius Gracchanus and argued that he was a moderate Gracchan who was involved at some point in the reforms of C. Gracchus. This would explain Pliny's assertion: *ab amicitia eius [C. Gracchi] Gracchanus appellatus est* (Plin. *n.h.* 33.36). According to Rankov (90 n. 5), 'a democratic slant to Gracchanus' work' could be seen in his claim that quaestors were elected by the people as early as the regal period. On Junius Gracchanus see also Zucchelli 1975.

7 In the sixth century AD Lydus wrote his book *De magistratibus reipublicae Romanae*. It seems likely that Ulpian was Lydus' source, which would help explain why the Byzantine author places the origin of the quaestorship in the Monarchy and also claims that the people already elected quaestors at that time (Lyd. *de mag.* 1.24–26). Lydus is generally considered an inaccurate source, so his text does not add weight to the theory of the quaestorship's monarchical origin. See Cloud 2003, 95–96. Cf. Caimi 1984, 151–152; Cloud 1998. Nevertheless, some Lydus specialists have vindicated him as an accurate source (Dubuisson 1991 and 1992).

8 Tac. *ann.* 11.22: *Apud maiores virtutis id praemium fuerat, cunctisque civium, si bonis artibus fiderent, licitum petere magistratus; ac ne aetas quidem distinguebatur quin prima iuventa consulatum et dictaturas inirent. Sed quaestores regibus etiam tum imperantibus instituti sunt, quod lex curiata ostendit ab L. Bruto repetita. Mansitque consulibus potestas deligendi, donec cum quoque honorem populus mandaret. Creatique primum Valerius Potitus et Aemilius Mamercus sexagesimo tertio anno post Tarquinios exactos, ut rem militarem comitarentur. Dein gliscentibus negotiis duo additi qui Romae curarent.* On this digression see Dreyer – Smarczyk 2009, 151–154.

assertion of Junius Gracchanus (as reported in Ulpian), Tacitus assumes that the quaestors were initially chosen (*potestas deligendi*) by the consuls and, although he does not say so explicitly, presumably by the kings during the Monarchy; it was not until sixty-three years after the expulsion of the Tarquins, in 447–446, that quaestors began to be elected by the people. Additionally, Tacitus indicates that it was the quaestors' job to assist the consuls in military affairs. However, the exact thrust of Tacitus' sentence is not completely clear. It could be interpreted simply as meaning that Valerius Potitus and Aemilius Mamercus were the first quaestors who were elected by the people rather than selected by the consuls. But the passage could more specifically mean that only from 447–446 onwards quaestors acquired responsibilities in the field, and that this change explained why they were elected by the people and no longer selected by the consuls.[9] At any rate, Tacitus makes it clear that those who held the quaestorship were meant to collaborate closely with the consuls (and presumably earlier with the kings) and that their responsibilities in the field as the consuls' assistants predated their financial duties at Rome.

In contrast to Ulpian and Tacitus, Greek authors like Plutarch and Cassius Dio (preserved by Zonaras) represent a different tradition about the origins of the office: the quaestorship was created in the Republican age. The sources upon which Plutarch and Cassius Dio draw seem to have come from a common tradition, though each author tells a slightly different story with varied emphasis: whereas Plutarch focuses on the role played by Publicola in the foundation of the new magistracy, Cassius Dio is more interested in its institutional development.[10]

Here is what Plutarch has to say about the origin of the quaestorship in his biography of Publicola: 'He [Valerius Publicola] was also praised for his law concerning the quaestorship (τὸν ταμιευτικὸν νόμον)... Therefore, he made the temple of Saturn a treasury, as it is even today, and gave the people the power to appoint two men as quaestors (ταμίαι). And the first to be thus appointed were Publius Veturius and Marcus Minucius...' [11]

Plutarch links the institution of the quaestorship to the consul Valerius Publicola, and consequently to the very beginning of the Republic in 509. The date smacks of convenient guesswork: since he thought that the quaestorship was a Republican institution, what could be better than dating the office's inception to the very year in which the Republic itself was traditionally said to have been founded? Plutarch credits Publicola with the passing of a law to create the office as well as the related establishment of the temple of Saturn as the official treasury of the *civitas*. The function of the two quaestors was, therefore, the administration of public funds. Nothing is

---

9 Cloud 2003, 97 n. 11.
10 Urso 2005, 42.
11 Plut. *Publ.* 12.3: Ἐπῃνέθη δὲ καὶ διὰ τὸν ταμιευτικὸν νόμον. ἐπεὶ γὰρ ἔδει χρήματα πρὸς τὸν πόλεμον εἰσενεγκεῖν ἀπὸ τῶν οὐσιῶν τοὺς πολίτας, οὔτ' αὐτὸς ἅψασθαι τῆς οἰκονομίας οὔτε τοὺς φίλους ἐᾶσαι βουλόμενος, οὔθ' ὅλως εἰς οἶκον ἰδιώτου παρελθεῖν δημόσια χρήματα, ταμιεῖον μὲν ἀπέδειξε τὸν τοῦ Κρόνου ναόν, ᾧ μέχρι νῦν χρώμενοι.

said about a judicial function. According to Plutarch, the quaestors were elected by the people from the very start.

Cassius Dio's account is as follows: 'And the management of the funds he [Valerius Publicola] assigned to others in order that those who held the consulate could not have the enormous influence that would emanate from controlling all revenues. Now for the first time treasurers (ταμίαι) began to be appointed, and they were called quaestors (κοιαιστώραι). They first tried capital cases, and this was the reason why they had obtained that title, because of their questionings and their search for truth as the result of their investigations. But later they also acquired the management of public funds and received the additional name of treasurers (ταμίαι). After a time, the courts were put in charge of others, while these magistrates continued to manage the funds.'[12]

Like Plutarch, Cassius Dio dates the creation of the quaestorship—at least as an office concerned with finances—to the very beginning of the Republic, and also attributes its institution to the consul Valerius Publicola. Cassius Dio does, however, describe the development of the office in a new way. Although the exact phases of this development appear a little murky, he seems to distinguish three phases.[13] For Cassius Dio, quaestors were in charge of the management of public funds, but they also judged capital cases. Hence the name given to the office (κοιαιστώραι), Cassius Dio asserts, since the main task of a quaestor was to inquire (*quaerere*), that is, to investigate in order to establish the truth. Quaestors later received the additional duty of administering public funds, and at some point they ceased to be in charge of the courts. Eventually the quaestors were identified only as 'treasurers' and hence they continued to be called ταμίαι in Greek.[14] For Cassius Dio, consequently, the quaestorship was a unique magistracy that in its beginnings had two different functions: one judicial, the other administrative.[15]

As mentioned before, neither Dionysius of Halicarnassus nor Livy offer an account of the origin of the quaestorship, but implicitly both seem to advocate for its creation during the early Republic. This is certainly more dubious in the case of Dionysius. He mentions a quaestor for the first time at the very beginning of the Republic, in connection with the Etruscan king Lars Porsenna and his alliance with Tarquinius Superbus against Rome. According to Dionysius, the king 'made a

---

[12] Zon. 7.13.3: καὶ τὴν τῶν χρημάτων διοίκησιν ἄλλοις ἀπένειμεν, ἵνα μὴ τούτων ἐγκρατεῖς ὄντες οἱ ὑπατεύοντες μέγα δύνωνται. ὅτε πρῶτον οἱ ταμίαι ἤρξαντο γίνεσθαι· κοιαίστωρας δ' ἐκάλουν αὐτούς. οἳ πρῶτον μὲν τὰς θανασίμους δίκας ἐδίκαζον, ὅθεν καὶ τὴν προσηγορίαν ταύτην διὰ τὰς ἀνακρίσεις ἐσχήκασι καὶ διὰ τὴν τῆς ἀληθείας ἐκ τῶν ἀνακρίσεων ζήτησιν· ὕστερον δὲ καὶ τὴν τῶν κοινῶν χρημάτων διοίκησιν ἔλαχον, καὶ ταμίαι προσωνομάσθησαν. μετὰ ταῦτα δ' ἑτέροις μὲν ἐπετράπη τὰ δικαστήρια, ἐκεῖνοι δὲ τῶν χρημάτων ἦσαν διοικηταί.
[13] Urso 2005, 38.
[14] On the translation of the word *quaestor* in Greek, see Mason 1974, 91; Famerie 1999.
[15] Urso 2005, 38, connected the text of Cassius Dio / Zonaras to the tradition that appears in Tacitus and Junius Gracchanus (through Ulpian), defending the origin of the quaestorship during the Monarchy.

present to the community of no small value, as appeared from the sale made by the quaestors (ταμίαι) after the king's departure.'¹⁶ This passage clearly presents these quaestors as having financial duties. Dionysius says nothing at all about the history of the office. Perhaps he followed the same tradition that made Publicola the founder of the magistracy,¹⁷ but we cannot dismiss the possibility that Dionysius actually saw its origin in the regal period and simply thought that it had continued to exist in the Republic. Dionysius also speaks of quaestors with judicial functions, since he includes the story of Sp. Cassius being prosecuted for *perduellio* in 485 by the quaestors K. Fabius Vibulanus and L. Valerius.¹⁸ He also mentions the quaestor of 458 and ex-consul, T. Quinctius Capitolinus, who apparently had assisted the consul as a commander of some troops.¹⁹ Nothing is said about whether there were different types of quaestorships with distinct origins or, alternatively, whether these stories deal with the same office but stress its various functions.

Livy's approach is slightly different. That said, he also includes the story of Sp. Cassius' prosecution by quaestors in 485²⁰ as well as the prosecution of the tribune of the plebs M. Volscius Fictor in 459–458, whom the quaestors, including the previously mentioned T. Quinctius Capitolinus (whom Dionysius refers to as a military commander), prosecuted for bearing false witness.²¹ Like Dionysius, Livy explains nothing about the origin of the quaestorship. For Livy it is evident that the office already existed in the early Republic, and that it had a judicial function.

However, Livy reproduces a speech supposedly delivered by the tribune of the plebs C. Canuleius in 445 before the people, which contains some relevant information about the quaestorship.²² In defence of his bill to legalise intermarriage between patricians and plebeians, Canuleius argues that since the Roman state had always been willing to innovate when necessary in the past, nothing should preclude his proposed innovation now. In this context he adds: 'There were neither pontiffs nor augurs in the reign of Romulus: they were instituted by Numa Pompilius. There was no census in Rome, no distribution by centuries and classes: Servius Tullius did it. There had never been any consuls: when the kings were expelled, consuls were created. Neither the power nor the name of dictator had ever been known: in the time of our fathers they began to exist. There were no tribunes of the plebs, ae-

---

16 Dion.Hal. 5.34.4: οὐ μικρὰν τῇ πόλει χαρισάμενος εἰς χρημάτων λόγον δωρεάν. ἐδήλωσε δ' ἡ πρᾶσις, ἣν ἐποιήσαντο μετὰ τὴν ἀπαλλαγὴν τοῦ βασιλέως οἱ ταμίαι. The quaestors are mentioned again in 6.96, 7.53 and 10.21.6.
17 Cloud 2003, 99.
18 Dion.Hal. 8.77–80.
19 Dion.Hal. 10.23–25.
20 Liv. 2.41.11.
21 Liv. 3.24–25.
22 Liv. 4.3–5.

diles, or quaestors: it was decided to create them. Within ten years we have elected decemvirs to write our laws, and we have removed them from the community.'[23]

Canuleius' speech is obviously fictitious, but it contains a compelling internal logic that, in all probability, reflects what Livy thought about the creation and development of magistracies in the early Republic. It seems that there is a chronological organisation that determines the order in which Livy introduces the creation of Republican magistracies: first the consulship, then the dictatorship, and eventually the tribunes of the plebs, aediles and quaestors. Livy finally mentions the decemvirate, which, a short time before Canuleius' supposed discourse, had been tasked with putting Roman laws in writing. This chronological order seems to imply that Livy thought of the quaestorship as a Republican office that had been founded at some point after the institution of the consulship and dictatorship but before the decemvirate of 451–450. At any rate, the quaestorship already existed when Canuleius was supposedly delivering his speech in 445. We must remember that, according to Tacitus, the first quaestors elected by the people held office in 446. It should also be added that the first time Livy mentions quaestors in relation to the treasury (*aerarium*) is precisely in 446.[24] Of course, it is a separate question about what duties Livy thought came into the purview of the quaestorship in the first decades of the Republic.

Finally we should return to a portion of the *Digest* where Pomponius does not offer an alternative version of the quaestorship's origin, but does share some considerations about its different functions that indirectly shed some light on the office's origins: 'Then, when the public treasury had acquired a larger scale, in order to provide magistrates who could take care of it, quaestors were created to superintend financial matters, and they were so named because they were created for the purpose of inquiring into and guarding the money. And whereas, as has been mentioned, the consuls were not allowed to hold a trial of capital case against a Roman citizen without the consent of the people, quaestors were instituted by the people in order to preside over capital causes. These were called *quaestores parricidii*, and they were actually mentioned in the law of the Twelve Tables.'[25]

---

23 Liv. 4.4.2–3: *Pontifices, augures Romulo regnante nulli erant; ab Numa Pompilio creati sunt. Census in civitate et discriptio centuriarum classiumque non erat; ab Ser. Tullio est facta. Consules nunquam fuerant; regibus exactis creati sunt. Dictatoris nec imperium nec nomen fuerat; apud patres esse coepit. Tribuni plebi, aediles, quaestores nulli erant; institutum est ut fierent. Decemviros legibus scribendis intra decem hos annos et creavimus et e re publica sustulimus.*
24 Liv. 3.69.8: *haec omnia adeo mature perfecta accepimus ut signa, eo ipso die a quaestoribus ex aerario prompta delataque in campum, quarta diei hora mota ex campo sint, exercitusque novus, paucis cohortibus veterum militum voluntate sequentibus, manserit ad decimum lapidem.*
25 Dig. 1.2.2.22–23: *Deinde cum aerarium populi auctius esse coepisset, ut essent qui illi praeessent, constituti sunt quaestores, qui pecuniae praeessent, dicti ab eo quod inquirendae et conservandae pecuniae causa creati erant. Et quia, ut diximus, de capite civis romani iniussu populi non erat lege permissum consulibus ius dicere, propterea quaestores constituebantur a populo, qui capitalibus rebus praeessent: hi appellabantur quaestores parricidii, quorum etiam meminit lex duodecim tabularum.*

Without a trace of doubt, Pomponius clearly distinguishes between two different offices, both referred to as a quaestorship: one instituted to take care of the public treasury (*aerarium*) and, therefore, having financial and administrative duties; the other, the *quaestores parricidii*, created to try capital cases, and consequently having judicial functions. Pomponius' account does not seem to make any connection between the institutions beyond the similarity in their names.

Piecing the puzzle together: scholarly reconstructions

On the basis of these puzzling and contradictory ancient sources, modern historiography has attempted to reconstruct the early history of the quaestorship. Due to the elusive nature of the evidence, scholars have presented various solutions that have continued to fuel the controversy until the present day. Needless to say, no interpretation of the evidence has been unanimously accepted.

An often-overlooked essay published by Niemeyer in 1854 offered the first detailed analysis of the origin of the quaestorship. Niemeyer specifically focused on the intervention of quaestors in judicial affairs, during both the Monarchy and the Republic. He accepted that the word quaestor comes from *quaerendo / quaerere*, as the ancient sources state, with the meaning of 'judicial inquiry'. In his analysis, the *quaestores parricidii* already existed in the regal period and were appointed by the king. At that point, however, the quaestorship was not a permanent office, but rather an extraordinary one. There were regular quaestors only beginning with the first years of the Republic, and these were created to be in charge of the public treasury. While this financial duty was their main function, it was not their only one, since they also had the power to prosecute before the *comitia centuriata*.[26] According to Niemeyer, both Varro and Pomponius support the existence of the quaestors' dual judicial and financial functions. Finally, Niemeyer rejects the notion that two different magistracies with the same name but with different competencies existed in the Monarchy and in the Republic, on the grounds that the first quaestors were not actually magistrates per se, but were only called quaestors when they were carrying out an investigation.[27]

Niemeyer's ideas do not seem to have had much traction. Certainly, the publication of Theodor Mommsen's *Römisches Staatsrecht* came to eclipse all other approaches to problems of the quaestorship's origins. As has happened with other constitutional issues about which he wrote, Mommsen quickly became the main reference; indeed, he still provides the necessary point of departure for any debate.[28] According to Mommsen, the quaestorship was instituted in the Republican period in

---

[26] Niemeyer 1854, 526.
[27] Niemeyer 1854, 531.
[28] Mommsen 1876–88, esp. 2.511–515 and 2.525–531.

close connection with the creation of the consulship. Mommsen did not, however, give any credence to Plutarch's account, and consequently he did not accept the existence of a law promulgated by Publicola that would have given rise to the quaestorship. In his analysis, the quaestors acted specifically as assistants to the consuls. From the beginning, they were in charge of the *aerarium* as *quaestores aerarii*, but they also took care of judicial affairs as *quaestores parricidii*. There was, therefore, a single office with different functions. Mommsen had no doubt, following the ancient sources, that the word quaestor came from *quaerere*, and he saw a clear relationship between *quaestor* and *quaesitor*. Ultimately, this was sufficient evidence for the original criminal jurisdiction of the quaestors, who, nevertheless, merely acted as delegates of the consuls, since these magistrates were the only ones with *imperium*. The quaestors were therefore a kind of 'examining magistrate' ('Untersuchungsrichter') and hence their name. Mommsen took the quaestor's intervention in the trials of the archaic age against Sp. Cassius,[29] M. Volscius[30] and M. Camillus (in 396) as irrefutable proof of their judicial duties.[31] Nonetheless, Mommsen asserts that the financial function of quaestors was also very old —perhaps even as old as the judicial role, though always as assistants to the consuls. In his analysis, the *quaestores* may have been both *parricidii* and *aerarii* from the very moment when the office was created at the beginning of the Republic.

Mommsen's theses have obviously had enormous influence on the scholarship and it is no understatement to claim that at the very least they remain a force with which any serious scholar must reckon.[32] Accordingly, Mommsen has set the main contours of the debate that has endured since the nineteenth century: did the quaestorship already exist during the time of the kings, or was it a Republican office? Was the quaestorship a single magistracy with judicial and financial tasks, or were there two different types of quaestors with completely separate functions, the *quaestores parricidii* and the *quaestores aerarii*?

Some years after the publication of Mommsen's *Römisches Staatsrecht*, Fazio wrote an article specifically dealing with the origin of the quaestorship.[33] In his attempt to reconcile the different versions found in the ancient sources, Fazio came

---

29 Liv. 2.41; Dion.Hal. 8.77; Cic. *de rep.* 2.60.
30 Liv. 3.24–25.
31 Plin. *n.h.* 34.13.
32 Generally, most contemporary scholars of Roman law in Germany agreed with Mommsen. So Herzog 1884, 1.816; Karlowa 1885, 1.257: the genitive *parricidii* was dropped when the functions of the office changed. However, not all scholars of Roman law agreed with Mommsen: for instance, Madvig 1881, 1.438 n. 2, advocates the existence of two different offices, instead of the sole magistracy defended by Mommsen. Willems 1883, 303, argues that the *quaestores parricidii*, in all likelihood, already existed in the regal period. They continued to exist when the Republic was instituted, but the task of guarding the public treasury was then added to their functions, which led to them becoming *quaestores parricidii et aerarii*. They later lost their judicial function, most likely when the *quaestiones perpetuae* were created.
33 Fazio 1891–1892.

to some of the same conclusions as Mommsen, but he disagreed on other points. In his opinion, sources mentioning the existence of quaestors during the Monarchy refer exclusively to the *quaestores parricidii*. At that time the king held complete power, but probably had junior officers who helped him with political, religious and judicial affairs. The *quaestores parricidii* were some of these officers. Fazio was willing to accept that they were even elected by the people during the Monarchy, as suggested by Junius Gracchanus through Ulpian. The *quaestores parricidii* would have continued to exist in the Republic, but the duties performed by quaestors would have been extended to include financial tasks. Therefore, Festus' definition (*quaestores [dicebantur, qui quaererent de rebus] capitalibus*) refers to the regal period, whereas Varro's (*quaestores... qui conquirerent publicas pecunias et maleficia*) alludes to the subsequent Republican phase. Pomponius was unable to distinguish these two phases in the development of the office and only referred to the second. In short, for Fazio the Republican *quaestores parricidii et aerarii* evolved from the *quaestores parricidii* who already existed during the regal period.

In 1936 Latte published an article that challenged some of Mommsen's conclusions and offered a new way of understanding the office's history. Unlike Mommsen and Fazio, Latte follows Pomponius and completely rejects the identification of the *quaestores parricidii* with the later financial quaestors.[34] First, he reckons that it is difficult to explain how an occasional office, the *quaestores parricidii*, would have developed into an annual one, the *quaestores aerarii*. Second, Latte argues that there is no discernible link between the original judicial duties and the later financial functions.[35] According to Latte, Roman quaestorship may have been an imitation of an institution that existed in a certain number of Dorian cities of the Western Mediterranean, the μαστροί.[36] Their name meant 'searchers' and their function was to seek out goods belonging to the state.[37] The quaestorship would therefore be an adaptation from the Greek world; the function of quaestors as treasurers was financial in its origin and hence the office should be distanced from the *quaestores parricidii*. Furthermore, the quaestorship must be a Republican institution, since it would only make sense to have treasurers at a time when there was a public treasury. Consequently, the year 497, when the temple of Saturn was apparently built,[38] provides a *terminus post quem* for Latte: the quaestorship originated in the fifth century.

Latte therefore suggests an alternative reconstruction to that of Mommsen, according to which the quaestorship originated as an office concerned primarily

---

34 As noted, the same conclusion had been already pointed out very briefly by Madvig 1881, 1.438 n. 2. Latte's reconstruction also presents some similarities with Niemeyer's thesis.
35 Latte 1936, 28.
36 Arist. fr. 567 (Harp. s. v. Μαστῆρες): ἔοικεν ἀρχή τις εἶναι ἀποδεδειγμένη ἐπὶ τὸ ζητεῖν τὰ κοινὰ τοῦ δήμου, ὡς οἱ ζητηταὶ καὶ οἱ ἐν Πελλήνῃ μαστροί, ὡς <Ἀριστοτέλης> ἐν τῇ Πελληνέων πολιτείᾳ; SIG³ 671 A, l. 3; IG XII¹ 677, l. 35.
37 Latte 1936, 29.
38 Liv. 2.21.2.

with the management of the Roman public treasury and had nothing to do with the *quaestores parricidii*, a completely different office. While Latte agrees with Mommsen on dating the origin of the quaestorship to the Republican period, there are important differences between their theories: Mommsen considers it more likely that the office was created at the very outset of the Republic in close relation to the institution of the consulship, whereas Latte prefers a later date so as to connect the institution of the quaestorship to the development of the Roman state generally and to the foundation of the public treasury in the temple of Saturn in particular.

From that moment on, the debate has been polarised around these two competing positions. In their approaches to the question of quaestorship's origin, scholars have essentially taken up aspects of one of these two theses or mixed them together; only occasionally has someone contributed something new to the debate. What follows aims to be a brief reflection of the discussion throughout the 20th century and up to the present. We only emphasise publications in which the problem of the quaestorship's origin plays a prominent role or, at the very least, is a main ingredient for the larger argument.[39]

Accepting Latte's view as probable, Kunkel defends the existence of two different magistracies, the quaestorship in charge of criminal cases and the quaestorship focused on financial duties.[40] In a latter contribution, Kunkel and Wittmann maintain the same idea.[41] They reject the information provided by the ancient sources on the remote origin of the quaestorship, which they consider to be the speculation or even pure invention of the first annalists. They only find Tacitus' statement credible, according to which the people elected quaestors for the first time in 447–446. This could jibe well with the context of the post-decemvirate age, when the Roman state developed institutionally and became more complex.

In his article in the Real-Encyclopädie Pauly-Wissowa, Wesener accepts ancient sources' etymology of quaestor from *quaerere*, which in his opinion indicates that the initial duty of the quaestors, as *quaestores parricidii*, was the investigation of crimes.[42] The expression *quaerere* would subsequently have been transferred to the financial function of the quaestors, which ought to be understood as the search for money for the public treasury. Given that he finds Tacitus' account compelling, Wesener accepts the notion that the quaestorship already existed during the Monarchy: when needed, quaestors assisted the king if a *parricidium* had been committed; in like manner, they acted under the command of the consuls when the Republic was instituted. However, the number of two quaestors seems to belong to Republican age.

---

39 Even after the publication of Latte's article, a number of scholars have followed Mommsen' thesis in the 20th century without delving into its implications. See, for instance, De Sanctis 1907, 1.404–405; Kretschmer 1919; Siber 1952, 95–97; Staveley 1954–55, 425; De Francisci 1959, 618–619; Nicoletti 1967; De Martino 1960, 1.287–288; Jones 1972, 35; Santalucia 1989, 33.
40 Kunkel 1962, 37–45.
41 Kunkel and Wittmann 1995, 510–512.
42 Wesener 1963, 802–806.

Again following Tacitus, Wesener thinks that the quaestors were initially appointed by the kings and then later by the consuls; only at a later date were they elected by the people.

Magdelain explicitly puts aside the question of whether the *quaestores parricidii* should be distinguished from the *quaestores aerarii*; instead, he limits his analysis to the development of the magistracy.⁴³ Magdelain rejects the tradition according to which the quaestors were already elected by the people during the Monarchy, as well as the supposed law of Publicola that simultaneously instituted the public treasury and the quaestorship. In his opinion, the quaestors were initially nothing more than assistants to the consuls and were appointed directly by them. Following Tacitus' account, Magdelain claims that after the decemvirate the quaestors began to be elected by the people. He does not think that a law was necessarily promulgated to introduce the change in the way that quaestors were chosen.

In his contribution on the origins of Roman magistracies, Giovannini omits any reference to the financial quaestors and focuses exclusively on the *quaestores parricidii*.⁴⁴ In his view, these officers had already existed during the Monarchy as assistants to the kings, given that they could not assume all tasks derived from the government of the *civitas*, particularly in the judicial field. It is impossible to know, Giovannini asserts, whether these officers were appointed by the kings or elected by the people.

Garofalo, for his part, suggests that the consuls asked the people to nominate quaestors when a capital crime had been committed.⁴⁵ Quaestors were, therefore, in charge of trials before the people. This would indeed later be the case in the Republican age, but quaestors with judicial functions could already have existed in the regal period. In 446, these exceptional officers became regular magistrates elected every year, who could have multiple functions, among them the supervision of the *iudicia populi de capite civis*.

In the second edition of *The Cambridge Ancient History*, Drummond wrote a piece on the early history of the quaestorship within the context of the political and constitutional developments of Rome during the fifth century.⁴⁶ Drummond clearly saw the *quaestores parricidii*, who presumably were appointed on an *ad hoc* basis, and the financial quaestors as two different offices: 'there is unlikely to be any continuity between the *quaestores parricidii* and the financial quaestors since the transformation of an *ad hoc* judicial office into a regular magistracy of much wider purpose is not readily explained.' He suggests that the term could have initially applied to the financial quaestors and afterwards to the judicial commissioners. This would seem to contradict the generally accepted etymology of the word quaestor. In agreement with Tacitus, Drummond thinks that kings, and later consuls, appointed the

---

43 Magdelain 1968, 7–8.
44 Giovannini 1984, 21–26 and 29–30.
45 Garofalo 1985.
46 Drummond 1989, 195–197.

quaestors by themselves, instead of the magistrates being elected by the people. However, Tacitus' statement that a Valerius, probably the consul of 449, was among the first elected quaestors in 447–446 inspires no confidence in his accuracy, at least regarding the names of the magistrates. At any rate, whereas the *quaestores parricidii* still existed as a distinct office at the time of the Twelve Tables, the origin of financial quaestors should be dated no later than the fifth century.

Both Cornell and Forsythe, in 1995 and 2005 respectively, published books on archaic Rome in which they briefly tackled the problem of the quaestorship's origin. Cornell suggests that Tacitus could have been alluding to the judicial officers called *quaestores parricidii* who are mentioned in the Twelve Tables, when he asserted that there were quaestors in the regal period. However, Cornell avoids making a definitive pronouncement on whether these *quaestores parricidii* were the forerunners of the regularly elected quaestors or remained a separate institution.[47] On the contrary, Forsythe seems to draw a clear distinction between judicial and financial quaestors. Citing Tacitus, he dates 'the creation of the office of quaestor in 446', although Tacitus is actually talking about the first *elected* quaestors, not simply the first quaestors.[48] Forsythe sees the institution of the quaestorship in 446 as part of a more general reorganisation of the state.

Lintott's general compendium on the Roman constitution contains, of course, a chapter dedicated to the quaestorship. Lintott considers it 'a reasonable conjecture' that the *quaestores parricidii* antedated the Twelve Tables, in which they were mentioned, and thinks that they may have originated in the time of the kings. In any case, the *quaestores parricidii* were distinct from the administrative quaestors, independently of whether the consular or the urban quaestors were instituted first.[49]

In 1971, picking up on Latte's arguments, Cloud advocated a clear differentiation between criminal and financial quaestors. Consequently, we should speak of two completely different offices, not of one with multiple functions.[50] In 2003, Cloud published an article in which he thoroughly analysed the early history of the quaestorship, taking as his point of departure the study of the internal logic of the different ancient sources on the problem and the conflicts among them. Cloud emphasises that there is nothing in the annalistic record to link the prosecuting quaestors mentioned in the cases against Cassius, Volscius Fictor and Camillus with the so-called *quaestores parricidii*. As a matter of fact, these prosecuting quaestors are never termed parricide quaestors, a category that must be associated with Roman antiquarian research.[51] While these *quaestores parricidii* probably did exist, they should not be identified with the quaestors who assisted kings or consuls, as Latte had already suggested. Cloud's main justification for this position is that no ancient source makes

---

47 Cornell 1995, 265 n. 91.
48 Forsythe 2005, 236 and 238.
49 Lintott 1999, 134.
50 Cloud 1971, 18–24.
51 Cloud 2003, 107.

this identification. Moreover, there is no reason to think that the parricide quaestors evolved into the quaestors who prosecuted all capital offences before the assembly.[52] According to Cloud, it is impossible to judge definitively between the approach that asserts a Republican origin and the priority of financial quaestors (Livy and Plutarch) and that which places the office's origin in the time of the kings and defines quaestors as assistants to kings and consuls (Tacitus and probably Ulpian).

Cloud begins his article with the following vindicating and perhaps rather ironic words: 'It may be felt that there is no need for another essay on the origins of the quaestorship.'[53] The essay itself has proven that there was obviously a need for it. Despite its importance for the scholarly discussion, Cloud's contribution has not brought the debate to a definitive close, as can be seen from the series of articles that have subsequently appeared.

In a 2009 paper, Dementyeva focuses on the role played by the quaestors in criminal justice.[54] She considers the *quaestores parricidii* as 'assistants to major officials in the sphere of criminal justice', and, following Latte, rejects their identification with the *quaestores aerarii*. In the Republic, the parricide quaestors acquired further duties, so that they were able to prosecute not only murderers but also other criminals. For Dementyeva, the judicial function of quaestors in archaic Rome included the investigation of crimes, prosecution by trial and the doling out of punishment if necessary.

In a brief essay, Ralph Covino has summarised the fundamental progress in the debate on the early quaestorship.[55] He emphatically rejects the identification of the extraordinary parricide quaestors with the regular quaestors. As for the origin of the financial quaestors, Covino is sceptical of the accounts of Plutarch and Cassius Dio, which dated the magistracy to the beginning of the Republic in 509, when the official treasury did not yet exist in the Temple of Saturn. If the year 509 is too early, the date of 447–446, when Tacitus claims that the first quaestors were elected by the people, is too late. Covino argues that it seems likely 'that discussions concerning the institution of a regularized quaestorship were on-going well before 447.' Therefore, Covino sees the final institution of the quaestorship as the result of a prolonged process, which would be paralleled by other magistracies in the early Republic. On the basis of the speech of the tribune Canuleius found in Livy (see above),[56] the quaestorship may have been created at some point between the foundation of Saturn's temple and the Decemvirate of 451–450.

As testaments to the on-going nature of the debate, Kolodko and Muñiz Coello have provided the most recent attempts to cast light on the origin of the quaestorship in 2014. Kolodko finds no reason to reject the idea that the office originated in the

---

52 Cloud 2003, 119.
53 Cloud, 2003, 93.
54 Dementyeva 2009.
55 Covino 2011. See also Covino 2013.
56 Liv. 4.4.3.

time of the Monarchy. Rather surprisingly, he even accepts the information provided by Ulpian according to which king Tullus Hostilius may have been the inventor of the office.[57] However, the popular election of quaestors should be dated to later times, in particular to the Republic. Until that point, quaestors were appointed as assistants by the kings and then the consuls. Reproducing Latte's main arguments, Kolodko asserts that the *quaestores parricidii* cannot be identified with the regular quaestors (i.e. the administrative quaestors), since their duties were completely different. Moreover, there is no justification to derive the regular quaestorship from parricide quaestors; the name of the two offices is the only common point.[58]

For his part, Muñiz Coello has concluded that the investigation of capital crimes was already undertaken by regularly appointed quaestors under the Monarchy, or at least from the beginning of the Republic.[59] These quaestors were called *quaestores parricidii*, and were mentioned as such in the Twelve Tables. However, these quaestors were also in charge of the public treasury. Consequently, Muñiz Coello returns to Mommsen's idea of a single office with judicial and financial functions. In his view, the growth of the Roman state caused the later specialisation of the quaestors as financial magistrates in Rome and as provincial officers serving under the consuls. The investigation of criminal cases was then assigned by the senate to any of its members, who acted as extraordinary *quaestores* or *quaesitores*.

So far we have set out the ancient evidence and the main scholarly contributions to the debate over the past one hundred and sixty years. Despite these efforts, the question of the quaestorship's origin is far from being definitively resolved. On the basis of ancient sources and modern proposals, it is time to make a new attempt to reconstruct the early history of the quaestorship. That said, we acknowledge the unlikelihood of finding a definitive answer and rather seek to offer a reasonable, albeit hypothetical, solution.

Some conclusions and suggestions

Since Mommsen published his *Römisches Staatsrecht*, or even since the publication of Niemeyer's earlier article on the history of the quaestorship, the scholarly has moved forward considerably, although it has certainly sometimes moved in circles. Something that has been increasingly assumed and mostly accepted by scholarship—though, as we have seen, not universally—now seems clear: the judicial quaestorship should be dissociated from the financial and administrative quaestorship, since these were distinct offices with utterly different duties and functions; presumably, they also have different histories. We must address the fundamental questions of when the *quaestores*

---

[57] Kolodko 2014, 272: 'it seems that there are no obstacles to agree with the jurist in scope of contribution of King Tullus Hostilius to development of the quaestorship in Rome.'
[58] Kolodko 2014, 279–280.
[59] Muñiz Coello 2014, 500–512.

parricidii came into existence, whether there was any continuity of officers called quaestors with judicial duties between the Monarchy and the Republic and, finally, what these duties were. But these *quaestores parricidii*, whether regularly appointed or on a *ad hoc* basis, have, in all probability, nothing to do with the Republican quaestors who took care of the public treasury, acted as assistants to the consuls, and increasingly assumed other tasks at Rome, in Italy and in the provinces as the administration of the Empire became more and more complex. The administrative and financial quaestorship should not be understood as having evolved from an initially judicial office with the same name. In fact, the name quaestor is the only common point. And it was only because of this common name that the debate over the quaestorship was originally raised and has lasted so long. Indeed, it is incorrect to assume that offices with the same title should be identical or at least have a common origin. This is clearly not always the case, and particularly in Rome, where we find several offices with the title *tribunus* that have nothing to do with one another in terms of their functions or their history: tribunes of the plebs, military tribunes, *tribuni aerarii*, and even military tribunes with consular power.[60]

Nonetheless, the unanimous etymology that connects the word quaestor to the verb *quaerere* should be accepted. It seems to imply that the quaestorship originally had something to do with 'inquiring' or 'investigating', perhaps during the Monarchy. However, this does not necessarily mean that the term quaestor always had to refer to someone involved in investigation. In fact, it is not unusual for a word to lose its original meaning when applied to a different institutional reality. This may have happened to the term quaestor when it began to be applied to an office with administrative functions. Accordingly, it is not necessary to force the idea of 'searching' onto the administrative and financial quaestors as magistrates, as some have suggested.[61] Institutional terms sometimes have their own development throughout history, changing their meaning but maintaining their name. For instance, the term consul, which referred in ancient Rome to the two highest magistrates of the Roman republic, is now an official appointed by a government to reside in a foreign country in order to represent its commercial interests and to look after the welfare of its citizens living there.

Once this point has been made clear, we must consider when and how the administrative and financial quaestorship came into being, while trying not to mix in any discussion of the possible origin of the judicial quaestorship. The ancient sources are certainly confusing, as they came from different traditions (annalistic or antiquarian), were written in different periods, and betrayed different agendas. Indeed, some of the ancient authors wanted to build a coherent historical narrative, whereas others were instead interested in providing juridical explanations.[62] On one hand, Junius Gracchanus' dating of the creation of the quaestorship as a magistracy to the

---

60 Cloud 2003, 119.
61 Wesener 1963: searching for money.
62 In this respect, Cloud's remarks (2003, 94) remain relevant.

age of the kings, whether to the founder Romulus or to Tullus Hostilius, was a means of solidifying the legitimacy of the institution: in a sense, the more remote an institution's origin, the more prestigious it was.[63] On the other hand, there was an ancient tendency to see the creation of an institution as the result of a law passed in a given year, something that seemed to suggest constitutional planning and which would permit the fixing of a specific date for the founding of an institution. This occurs in Plutarch's account, which mentions the law that the consul Valerius Publicola supposedly promulgated in order to simultaneously found the public treasury in the temple of Saturn and the quaestorship in charge of the public finances. Plutarch therefore supplied the new magistracy with a legal background as well as with a symbolic date that, not by chance, coincided with the foundation of the Republic. In order to give more credibility to his account, Plutarch even provided the names of the first two presumed quaestors.

The idea of a permanent institutional order in Republican Rome, based on the promulgation of laws passed by popular assemblies, was inherent to Mommsen's systematic conception of the Roman constitution. According to Mommsen, there must have been foundational laws for Republican magistracies and consequently also for the quaestorship (though, we must note, he did not find Plutarch's account about Publicola's law and the creation of the quaestorship credible). However, it is very unlikely that there were any such laws in archaic Rome that established *ex novo* a given magistracy along with its functions and duties.[64] And this is certainly valid for the quaestorship.

On the contrary, the creation of the quaestorship should be understood in the context of the much longer process of development of Roman institutions. Romans were aware of the fact that their institutions were not the product of a single thinking mind that originally provided the community with a fully-fledged constitution, but rather the result of a prolonged process of experimentation.[65] Moreover, these institutions were not immutable; on the contrary, they were constantly modified and adapted to the changing circumstances of Rome's internal and foreign politics. There is no reason to suppose that this process of experimentation did not also apply to the quaestorship. As Drummond has rightly pointed out, 'specialized offices to relieve the consuls of individual responsibilities were slow to develop.'[66]

The quaestor could have initially been an assistant to the highest magistrates of the Roman republic regardless of whether these were the consuls, the *praetor maximus* or the dictator. Nevertheless, there is no need to rule out the possibility that quaestors already existed in the time of the Monarchy as assistants to the kings, since it is hard to believe that the monarch personally took control of all aspects

---

[63] See Ferrary 1984, esp.90. Of course, this also could be applied to Tacitus' account. Cf. Heuss 1944, 101.
[64] Mommsen's position was rightly criticised by Magdelain 1968, 5–6. See Jehne 2012, 407–408.
[65] Pina Polo 2016, 86–89.
[66] Drummond 1989, 195.

of government.⁶⁷ That said, the supposed creation of the institution by Tullus Hostilius is not at all credible, even less so its establishment by Romulus or Numa, as Junius Gracchanus had maintained. Ultimately, it is impossible to determine a specific date for the beginning of the quaestorship.

If we assume that quaestors were initially trusted advisors who assisted Rome's rulers, it seems reasonable that they were personally selected by the rulers themselves rather than elected by the people. However, the quaestorship may already have been a permanent office—though, strictly speaking, not a magistracy. The regularisation of the quaestorship as an administrative magistracy in charge of the state finances must have taken place when the public treasury and the public archive of the *civitas* were founded. This could have occurred in the context of the construction of the temple of Saturn (apparently at the beginning of the fifth century), which coincided with the outset of the conflict of the orders, when, according to ancient sources, a plebeian archive and some plebeian officers were created.⁶⁸ Livy refers to this process indirectly in the speech attributed to the tribune Canuleius, in which he seems to suggest that the quaestorship was instituted after the tribunate of the plebs and the aedileship but before the decemvirate (at any rate during the first half of the fifth century). The final step in the evolution of the historical quaestorship can be seen in the change from the selection of quaestors by the highest Republican magistrates to their popular election. According to Tacitus, this move from selection to election occurred in 447–446, soon after the Twelve Tables were put in writing and at a time when the Roman republic experienced a flurry of institutional innovation. This means that the quaestorship had been established definitively as a magistracy of the people almost at the same time that the censorship was created (in 443), which, it must be said, was also instituted to alleviate the duties of Rome's highest officers.⁶⁹ The popular election of quaestors should, therefore, be seen as a defining moment for the office.⁷⁰ It is precisely in 447–446 when Livy mentions quaestors for

---

67 Koptev 2005, 409 n. 156: 'In view of the fact that the office of quaestor was created only under the Republic, the word *quaestor* in the regal period could be used by annalists for defining auxiliaries of the king.'

68 Cornell 1995, 265, suggests that the plebs having two sets of elected magistrates perhaps inspired the innovations of electing two quaestors to assist the consuls in 447–446. According to Cornell, it is remarkable that plebeian institutions were 'more advanced and sophisticated' than those of the state. In fact, it was the plebeians who first established an archive in Rome: they 'pioneered the notion that official decisions should be systematically recorded and preserved.' That the 'patrician state' imitated a more sophisticated plebeian organisation is perhaps going too far. Nevertheless, the institutional changes throughout the fifth century should certainly be understood within the context of the social and economic uproar provoked by the conflict of orders.

69 Forsythe 2005, 236: when the creation of quaestors in 447–446, military tribunes with consular power in 445 and censors in 443 are all taken together, 'these three innovations constitute a strong indication of a major reorganization in the military structure of the Roman state during the decade of the 440's B.C.'

70 Stewart 1998, 30 and 69: the quaestors were established as political rather than personal appointees after the period of the decemvirate. Earlier, Ogilvie 1965, 521, already pointed out that the decem-

the first time in relation to the *aerarium:* a general levy had hastily been held and the men liable for service presented themselves in the Campus Martius, where the cohorts selected their own centurions and senators were placed in command. That morning, the quaestors took the standards (*signa*) from the *aerarium* and carried down to the Campus Martius.[71] Up to this point in his history, Livy had mentioned quaestors exclusively in relation to prosecutions and trials. Now, they clearly appear as the officers in charge of the public treasury.

Whereas Livy emphasises the quaestors' financial and administrative duties from the beginning, Tacitus speaks of their military tasks accompanying the consuls in the field. At first, the statements of Livy and Tacitus seem inconsistent, but they are not necessarily mutually exclusive. While there is good reason to be suspicious of the details found in our sources for the early Republic, it seems clear that the highest magistrates during the period (the consuls according to the ancient sources) were mainly commanders-in-chief of the Roman army. Consequently, they would have spent a substantial part of their time in office outside the city, fighting in seasonal campaigns around Rome against the peoples of central Italy. During the months in which the highest magistrates stayed away from the city, it seems feasible that their quaestors assisted them in military aspects in the field, given their role as men of confidence.[72] It should be kept in mind that in the following centuries quaestors certainly did play the role of right-hand men for commanders in the field both in Italy and the provinces. In the early Republic, however, the highest magistrates probably remained at Rome for nearly half of their mandate, namely the first months after taking office and the final ones after returning from the field.[73] Given that the highest magistrates carried out civil tasks during their stay at Rome, nothing would have prevented the quaestors, once again as their assistants, from assisting them. Once we accept that the highest magistrates in the early Republic were both administrative and military officers, it is perfectly logical that their assistants and trusted aides, the quaestors, also held the same types of responsibilities.

Livy dates the duplication of the number of quaestors to 421, twenty-five years after the first election of quaestors by the people, according to Tacitus' account. Livy explains that in addition to the two urban quaestors two others were needed to assist the consuls in war.[74] This measure had been proposed by the consuls and ac-

---

virs could have been responsible for the creation of the financial quaestorship: 'the function of the quaestors as financial officers is also a likely consequence of the Decemvirate.'

[71] Liv. 3.69.8: *Cohortes sibi quaeque centuriones legerunt; bini senatores singulis cohortibus praepositi. Haec omnia adeo mature perfecta accepimus ut signa, eo ipso die a quaestoribus ex aerario prompta delataque in campum...*

[72] Flach 1994, 253–254, asserts that Tacitus is right when he writes that quaestors initially only had military functions, accompanying the consuls in war. According to him, the first Republican quaestors had no duties in the city.

[73] Pina Polo 2011, 208–219.

[74] Liv. 4.43.3–4: *Quemadmodum bellum minore quam timuerant dimicatione erat perfectum, sic in urbe ex tranquillo necopinata moles discordiarum inter plebem ac patres exorta est, coepta ab dupli-*

cepted by the senate, but the tribunes of the plebs opposed it, claiming that plebeians could also be elected as quaestors.⁷⁵ In the end, the number of quaestors was increased from two to four that year and plebeians were also given the possibility of accessing the office—though only patricians were nominated until 409, when, according to Livy, the first three plebeian quaestors were elected.⁷⁶ The quaestorship was, therefore, the first regular magistracy to which plebeians gained access.⁷⁷

Livy's account is, on the whole, quite plausible. The increase in the number of quaestors can be understood as a necessary diversification and specialisation of functions within the magistracy.⁷⁸ Two of the quaestors (*quaestores urbani*) would remain in Rome during their mandate and would deal exclusively with financial and administrative matters. The other two would specifically assist the highest magistrates, both at Rome and in the field when they left the city. This new development in the office was the logical consequence of the increasing complexity of the state's administration, at Rome and outside the city. After decades of experimentation during the early Republic (and perhaps even earlier in the regal period), the quaestorship had reached its recognisable form: four magistrates elected by the people among patricians and plebeians, two of whom had administrative duties at Rome and were primarily in charge of the public treasury, while the other two assisted the highest magistrates in their civil and military tasks, at Rome and in the field.

---

cando quaestorum numero. Quam rem—praeter duos urbanos ut crearentur alii quaestores duo qui consulibus ad ministeria belli praesto essent... On the duplication of quaestors, see also Tac. *ann*. 11.22: *Dein gliscentibus negotiis duo additi qui Romae curarent.* According to Tacitus, the two new quaestors were in charge of the affairs in the city, since the two already existing ones assisted the consuls in military matters.

75 Ogilvie 1965, 598, considered the agitation for plebeian entry to the quaestorship 'pure fabrication.'

76 Liv. 4.54.2–3: *Eum dolorem quaestoriis comitiis simul ostendit et ulta est tunc primum plebeiis quaestoribus creatis, ita ut in quattuor creandis uni patricio, K. Fabio Ambusto, relinqueretur locus, tres plebeii, Q. Silius P. Aelius P. Papius, clarissimarum familiarum iuvenibus praeferrentur.*

77 Mommsen, Röm.St. II 1.516; Wesener 1963, 810.

78 See the reconstruction of Ogilvie 1965, 598: 'the quaestor was in origin an *ad hoc* assistant to the king or consul, in particular for the investigation of *parricidium*... The need for assistants to the consuls in other fields still remained, if anything the greater as Rome's commitments increased, and a logical consequence of the overhaul of the Roman constitution by Valerius and Horatius in 449 was the establishment in 446 of a parallel but separate pair of *quaestores*, regular magistrates charged above all with the control of military expenditure. Twenty-five years [i.e. in 421] is ample time for the tasks of government to have proliferated to such an extent that a further pair is required. The growth of the quaestorship should be compared with the gradual rise in the number of consular tribunes from three to six.'

Chapter 2:
The development of the quaestorship and the so-called Italian quaestors

The increasing number and functions of quaestors throughout the Republic

While the quaestorship reached its recognisable historical form by the end of the fifth century, almost nothing is known about how the office operated in the fourth century. In fact, only a few names of quaestors have been preserved before the beginning of the Hannibalic War, that is, for the period treated in Livy's (lost) second decade.[1] However, we do have a very limited number of texts that point to an increase in the number of quaestors at some point during the middle Republic. Once more, the lack of evidence has only fuelled scholarly controversy about the reason for establishing the new quaestorships, the date at which these new posts were introduced and, finally, the tasks that the new quaestors were assigned.

As usual, Mommsen put forth a theory on these topics that many subsequent scholars have accepted.[2] As Prag aptly puts it, 'the shadow of Mommsen looms particularly large in assessment of the quaestorship in the middle Republic.'[3] Accordingly, his reconstruction of the office in this period remains the necessary point of departure for any new analysis. The German scholar has exerted so great an influence throughout the decades and his ideas and terminology have pervaded the debate so deeply that even his detractors, despite the lack of evidence, have accepted a substantial part of his thesis, perpetuating a construct built on rather shaky ground.

Three ancient texts refer to the enlargement in the number of quaestors in the pre-Sullan age.[4] First, the Periochist of Livy's fifteenth book very concisely asserts that the number of quaestors was increased; the manuscript, however, frustratingly lacks the precise figure: *quaestorum numerus ampliatus est ut essent <—>*.[5] In the sixteenth century, Sigonius proposed completing the Latin text with *octo*, in which case Livy would have asserted that the number of quaestors had doubled from four to eight: 'the number of quaestors was increased, so that there were eight.'[6] Sigonius'

---

[1] The inscriptions from the Egadi's *rostra* have recently provides the names of three additional quaestors who held the magistracy in the middle of the third century. See Prag 2014b; 2014c; 2017.
[2] Mommsen, Röm.St. 2.556–559.
[3] Prag. 2014a, 207.
[4] See Harris 1976, 93–96; Loreto 1993, 494–496; Ferone 2003 (in particular on Lydus' text); Coarelli 2014, 100–101; Prag 2014a, 195–196.
[5] Liv. *per.* 15.
[6] Sigonius 1555.

emendation has generally been accepted.[7] Since the Periochist's mention of the expansion of the quaestorship follows news about the foundation of colonies in Beneventum and Ariminium in 268, the introduction of silver coinage at Rome in 269 or 268 and the surrender of the Umbrians and the Sallentini in 267–266, the change in the number of quaestors has been assigned to 267–266.[8]

Sigonius suggests reading eight as the new number of quaestors in the fragmentary text of the *Periochae*, an argument based on his interpretation of Tacitus' discussion of the quaestorship. When Tacitus speaks of the history of the quaestorship, he declares that two quaestors were elected for the first time in 447, and two other quaestors were added later on. The number of four quaestors was doubled at some point: 'The first election, precisely sixty-three years after the expulsion of the Tarquins, was that of Valerius Potitus and Aemilius Mamercus, in order to collaborate in military affairs. Then, as public business increased, two others were added to take care of their duties at Rome. Soon the number was doubled, when to the contributions of Italy were added revenues from the provinces. Later on, by a law of Sulla twenty were instituted to supplement the senate, to which he had transferred the courts.'[9] It is important to bear in mind that Tacitus' text does not necessarily imply that the number of quaestors was doubled in a certain year: another valid interpretation would be that there was a longer process during which the number of quaestors was progressively enlarged until reaching eight. In fact, Tacitus does not give any precise chronology; on the contrary, he only provides vague information alluding to Roman expansion in the Mediterranean. He certainly starts the sentence with the word *mox*, but this does not mean that the increase in the number of quaestors really occurred 'soon' after they had become four. For his part, Livy dates the first appointment of four quaestors to 421.[10] If we accept 267–266 as the date for the shift in the number of quaestors, the change would have happened about one hundred and fifty years later. *Mox*, then, is a rather loose term without any precise temporal implication; here it is used from the perspective of a much later writer, Tacitus, living in the first century AD. The number of quaestors had, at any rate, been doubled according to Tacitus before the Sullan age, at which point the number of quaestors finally increased to twenty. In this passage, Tacitus simply provides a snapshot of the long-term development of the quaestorship from its creation, that is, how the office had evolved from two quaestors in the early Republic to twenty by the end of the Republic.

---

7 Loreto 1993, 495, points out, with good reason, that the supplement has became perhaps 'too canonical.'
8 Cf. Zon. 8.7.3; Flor. 1.15.
9 Tac. *ann.* 11.22.4–6: *Creatique primum Valerius Potitus et Aemilius Mamercus sexagesimo tertio anno post Tarquinios exactos, ut rem militarem comitarentur. Dein gliscentibus negotiis duo additi qui Romae curarent. Mox duplicatus numerus, stipendiaria iam Italia et accedentibus provinciarum vectigalibus. Post lege Sullae viginti creati supplendo senatui, cui indicia tradiderat.*
10 Liv. 4.43.3–4.

The third text comes from the sixth-century antiquarian Joannes Lydus: 'In the two hundred and forty-third year of the consuls, during the consulship of Regulus and Julius, when the Romans had decided to wage war against those who had been allies of Pyrrhus the Epirote, a fleet was fitted out and the so-called *classici*, that is naval commanders, *quaestores*, namely treasurers and collectors of money, twelve in number, were advanced to office. How *quaestor* differs from *quaesitor*, I have already explained. In fact, such practice of collecting revenue was preserved by both the consuls and the *praetors* whenever they were abroad' (translation by Bandy).[11] Lydus clearly refers to the same event as Livy; furthermore, the date he provides is 267–266 (during the consulship of M. Atilius Regulus and L. Julius Libo), which essentially coincides with Livy's Periochist. Nevertheless, Lydus supplies different information from that found in Livy and Tacitus, since he claims that twelve new magistrates (δυοκαίδεκα κυαίστωρες) were now appointed, to whom he gives the name of *quaestores classici* (in Greek Lydus uses the word ναυάρχαι), meaning something like 'commanders of the fleet'.

There have always been doubts about Lydus' accuracy as a source for the period.[12] Accordingly, some scholars have sought to emend his text in order to make it better conform to other sources and mesh with scholarly opinions. This methodology, needless to say, has proven controversial.[13] At any rate, it seems clear that the idea of there being twelve quaestors beginning in 267–266 is untenable, particularly because it so strongly diverges from the more authoritative text of Tacitus.[14] Relying

---

[11] Lyd. *de mag.* 1.27: Τῷ δὲ τρίτῳ καὶ <τεσσαρακοστῷ καὶ> διακοσιοστῷ τῶν ὑπάτων ἐνιαυτῷ, ἐπὶ τῆς ὑπατείας Ῥηγούλου καὶ Ἰουλίου, κρινάντων Ῥωμαίων πολεμεῖν τοῖς συμμαχήσασι Πύρρῳ τῷ Ἠπειρώτῃ, κατεσκευάσθη στόλος καὶ προεβλήθησαν οἱ καλούμενοι κλασσικοί, οἷον εἰ ναυάρχαι, τῷ ἀριθμῷ δυοκαίδεκα κυαίστωρες, οἷον ταμίαι καὶ συναγωγεῖς χρημάτων. τίνι δὲ διαφέρει κυαίστωρ κυαισίτωρος προειρήκαμεν. καὶ διεφυλάχθη ἡ τοιαύτη συνήθεια καὶ συναγωγὴ τῶν πόρων τοῖς τε ὑπάτοις τοῖς τε πραίτωρσιν ἐκδημοῦσιν. On Lydus see Bandy 1983; Dubuisson – Schamp 2006.
[12] However, it must also be said that some Lydus specialists have defended him as a reasonably accurate source. In 1991 and 1992, Dubuisson refuted the established idea that Lydus was not an expert in Latin; on the contrary, he has shown that Lydus did have a good knowledge of this language and that his translations and explanations are essentially correct. Furthermore, the sources mentioned by Lydus are themselves reliable. A different matter is whether he really used them directly (which does not seem to be the case) and how accurately he used them. Cf. Ferone 2003, 74–75.
[13] Mattingly 1969, 509–510, has attempted to emend the text completely. According to Mattingly, Lydus mixed up two utterly different things: the election of the *duumviri navales* (supposedly the so-called *classici* in the text) in 267 and the increase in the number of quaestors. In his opinion, two new quaestors were certainly introduced at that point, but they had nothing to do with the fleet: one of them was stationed in Ostia, the other was in charge of the *calles*. Claudius had supposedly abolished these two quaestorships (Mattingly also emends Suet. *Claud.* 24.2). It must be taken into account that no other source supports Mattingly's hypothesis. Smith 1978 criticises Mattingly's theory (which Harris accepted in 1976) about Lydus' confusion between the *duumviri navales* and quaestors. Thus, Smith defends the internal logic of Lydus' text (see, however, the answer of Harris 1979b). Ferone 2003, 72, points out that Mattingly's reconstruction modifies the structure of text to such an extent that his proposed text is no longer linguistically correct.
[14] Harris 1976, 93: 'no modern scholar has even discussed the possibility that he [Lydus] was right.'

on a range of historical and linguistic arguments, some scholars have studied the Lydus passage and suggested that the number should be corrected to two, which is a reasonable conjecture.[15] Additionally, Lydus' connection of the so-called *quaestores classici* to the Roman fleet, which is not attested in any other ancient source, has also raised eyebrows.[16] Nevertheless, Lydus' phrase has found currency among some scholars. Furthermore, even though most scholars have rejected the name *quaestores classici* and scholarly consensus has gravitated toward Mommsen's concept of *quaestores Italici*, the debate over the creation of these new quaestors and their supposed relationship with the fleet remains an open one.

On the basis of these three texts, Mommsen assumes, first of all, that the quaestors were increased to eight in 267. He also initially accepts Lydus' name *quaestores classici*, although the section in which he discusses these new quaestors bears the title 'die italischen Quästoren', that is, 'Italian quaestors', a term that is not attested in the sources.[17] Mommsen, still following Lydus, directly associates the institution of the presumed four new quaestors with the construction of the fleet. Mommsen opts for the name 'Italian quaestors' because he thought they were stationed in four Italian cities: the first in Ostia at the mouth of the Tiber, the second in Cales in Campania and the third somewhere in Cisalpine Gaul (perhaps Ravenna).[18] There was no clear option for the fourth post, but Mommsen suggests Lilybaeum in Sicily, despite the fact that Roman administration did not arrive to the island until some decades later.

No ancient sources actually associate these cities with a quaestorship in the third century. However, Mommsen's proposal is based on late Republican and early imperial texts that mention—usually only once—a quaestor in Ostia, Cales (or *calles* in a more probable interpretation) and Cisalpine Gaul.[19] In the most charitable interpretation, Mommsen applies much later evidence to the third century—though, as we shall see, in some cases it is really more conjecture than fact—and hence implicitly assumes that these quaestorian *provinciae* were permanent and had been regularly allotted throughout the period between their supposed creation in the third century and the early Empire. Moreover, Mommsen argues that the functions of these so-called Italian quaestors were similar to those of provincial quaestors. In particular, their main task was apparently to supply allied troops for the Roman army and fleet—hence the name *quaestores classici*; additionally, in Ostia these quaestors were put in charge of the surveillance of the grain supply from different regions of

---

15 Mattingly 1969, 511, and Harris 1976, 94, have both suggested that the number was actually two. Especially important is the philological argument found in Smith 1978, where the figure of two is likewise reached with a simple and logical emendation of Lydus' text.
16 As Lintott 1999, 135, asserts there are no further traces of the so-called *quaestores classici* in our sources.
17 Mommsen, Röm.St. 2.556. Cf. Loreto 1993, 497 n. 15.
18 Mommsen, Röm.St. 2.557.
19 For the *quaestor Ostiensis*, Cic. Sest. 39; har.resp. 43; Mur. 18; Vell. 2.94; Suet. Claud. 24. For Cales (or *calles*), Tac. ann. 4.27 (year 24 AD). For Cisalpine Gaul, Plut. Sert. 4.1.

the Empire. Once again, Mommsen is only able to muster scanty evidence from the late Republic,[20] and there is no evidence from the time when these new quaestorships were supposedly instituted.

From a methodological viewpoint, Mommsen's reconstruction is clearly flawed and unreliable. The main issue is the absolute lack of evidence for the period in which Livy, Tacitus and Lydus mention new quaestorships. Despite this dearth of information, Mommsen proposes concrete headquarters for these new quaestors, which are only attested for certain years during the late Republic and/or the early Principate. In spite of the argument's patent difficulties, Mommsen's indisputable *auctoritas* overrode any doubts: scholarship unanimously adopted his hypothesis for decades, which was treated as definitive.[21]

The first scholar to impugn Mommsen's thesis, at least partially, was De Martino in his *Storia della costituzione romana*.[22] De Martino keeps the denomination of Italian quaestors for the four new quaestors, though he notes that there is no evidence for any such official title. Actually, the only attested title for a quaestor is *quaestor urbanus*. According to De Martino, this suggests that all the other quaestors carried out their functions outside the city, whether in Italy or the Empire's provinces. At any rate, he does not take it for granted that the new quaestors were assigned to the administration of Italy, especially for the period after the creation of the first provinces near the end of the third century. He does, however, accept that some quaestors could have been stationed throughout Italy with the purpose of carrying out financial administration.[23] Perhaps De Martino's most original contribution can be found in the suggestion that every year the senate determined the *provinciae* of the new quaestors according to changing political needs and circumstances.[24] This idea, which De Martino barely develops, deeply challenges Mommsen's static and perfectly structured system: for Mommsen the new quaestors' functions as well as their stations were decided in the third century and remained unchanged for centuries to come.

Some years later Mattingly suggested that only two new quaestorships were added in 267: one stationed in Ostia and another in charge of the Italian *calles* (trails

---

20 Plut. *Sert.* 4.1, for the quaestor Sertorius' recruitment of soldiers in Cisalpine Gaul; see Cic. *har.-resp.* 43, for Saturninus' quaestorship in Ostia.
21 A few examples are sufficient (see Harris 1976, 92 n. 2: 'the agreement among scholars makes a full bibliography unnecessary'): De Sanctis 1907, 2.453; Siber 1952, 200; Meyer ²1961, 86, 177 and 233; Wesener 1963, 809 and 818–819 (as a matter of fact, Wesener reproduces Mommsen's arguments almost verbatim); Toynbee 1965, 1.387–388. Perhaps the only criticism comes from Herzog 1884, 823–824, who emphasises the inconsistency of placing the stations of the new quaestors in cities such as Cales (an inland city), which would not match their supposed naval functions. However, Herzog does not challenge these headquarters; instead, he questions the duties of the new quaestors. In his opinion, their main task was to collect revenues in Italian towns for Rome.
22 De Martino 1960, 2.206–211.
23 De Martino 1960, 2.211.
24 De Martino 1960, 2.209.

for transhumance). He argues that these officials were in no way related to the fleet.[25] Mattingly's argument opened up a possibility that had not previously been considered: the increase of quaestors could have been more gradual than Mommsen had assumed. Some years later Harris adopted and developed this idea in the first article since Mommsen that specifically dealt with the history of the quaestorship down to Sulla. For Harris, Tacitus' text serves as the point of departure for a new interpretation. While Tacitus certainly claims that the number of quaestors was eight at some point before Sulla, he does not assert that the number of new quaestorships added in 267 was four. In fact, Tacitus' chronology is rather vague: he only places the change after Italy started paying taxes to Rome and when revenues were arriving from the provinces. As Harris has argued, Tacitus must have been referring to the time when Sicily and Sardinia were annexed.[26] The number of praetors was increased from two to four in 227 and an increase in the number of quaestors should have taken place simultaneously. Harris concludes, therefore, that Tacitus' account is more intelligible and compelling if we suppose that two quaestors were added in 267 and two more in 227.[27] Furthermore, Harris also rejects the idea, only found in Lydus, that these new quaestorships were in charge of the fleet.[28]

With respect to the specific tasks of the new quaestors, Harris argues that Ostia may have become the regular *provincia* for one of the two quaestors created in 267, but he recognises that this could also have happened later, perhaps during the Hannibalic War. In his opinion, the quaestorships for Sicily and Sardinia were created in 227. According to Harris, at some point a second quaestorship for Sicily was added, with 211 being the most plausible date, since this was when the eastern part of the island came under Roman control. Harris connects this fact to the creation of *triumviri monetales* by 211, which would have reduced the burden on the quaestors and hence freed up one of those who had been instituted in 267 for duty in Sicily.[29] In conclusion, Harris suggests the following reconstruction for the quaestorship in the middle Republic: two urban quaestors, two consular quaestors, one *Ostiensis*, two Sicilian and one Sardinian. However, Harris also partially accepts De Martino's suggestion and claims, 'the system remained flexible enough for the introduction of occasional *provinciae* such as the *calles* and the *aquae*.' That said, Harris argues that the *provinciae* of the quaestors were not as variable as De Martino had thought, since some of them were probably allotted regularly over very long periods, for example the *provincia Ostiensis*.[30]

Harris' article represented a fundamental step forward: for the first time, scholarship had a reconstruction for the history of the quaestorship that departed from

---

25 Mattingly 1969.
26 Harris 1976, 94.
27 Harris 1976, 94.
28 Harris 1976, 96–97. See now Harris 2017, 25–26.
29 Harris 1976, 104.
30 Harris 1976, 104 and n. 108.

Mommsen's rigid model. Nevertheless, not everyone was convinced: Mommsen continued to be exceedingly influential in subsequent analyses of the subject.

In a 1993 article, Loreto begins with an analysis of Tacitus that is essentially the same as Harris'. He argues that when Tacitus states that the number of quaestors was doubled (*numerus duplicatus*), he is not referring to a precise moment and specific event, but rather describes the total number of quaestors in office from a certain time until the Sullan law on the quaestorship.[31] According to Loreto, therefore, from 421 onwards the number of quaestors increased progressively to eight, a process about which Tacitus did not have sufficient information to determine exactly when any one alteration took place. For Loreto, there are two main issues to address: (1) the dates when the new quaestorships were instituted and (2) the functions that these officials assumed once in office. With respect to the latter question, Loreto unhesitatingly follows Mommsen's proposal and places the headquarters of the new quaestors in Cales, Ostia, Cisalpine Gaul (the station of this quaestor may have been at Rome, even if his responsibilities were in the *ager Gallicus*) and Lilybaeum in Sicily.[32] Loreto, nonetheless, rejects the idea that the new quaestors would have had any of naval responsibilities alluded to in Lydus, since this author was, in his opinion, quite unreliable; instead, he argues that the new quaestors carried out administrative tasks. When it comes to dating, Loreto, who has refused to call these new magistrates Italian quaestors, suggests ca. 267–264 for the quaestorship in Cales, ca. 240 for the one in Lilybaeum,[33] ca. 232 for the quaestor in Cisalpine Gaul and ca. 210 for the eighth and last quaestor in Ostia.[34]

In a 1995 article, Kunkel and Wittmann question some of Mommsen's assertions, though they nevertheless reproduce the main core of his theory about the so-called Italian quaestors.[35] Kunkel and Wittmann, who implicitly consider Tacitus' account the most plausible, reject the usual interpretation that four quaestors were created all together in one fell swoop. Instead, they argue that Tacitus' text better supports the theory that two new quaestorships were instituted in 267—as Lydus points out— and that the other two quaestors would have been added some thirty years later when eastern Sicily, Corsica and Sardinia came under Roman control.[36] Their conclusion essentially coincides with Loreto's in so far as they see the institution of new quaestorships as a more gradual development throughout the third century that re-

---

31 Loreto 1993, 496: 'il *duplicatus numerus* non si riferisce ad un momento puntuale e dunque ad un atto specifico bensì intende definire il numero complessivo di questori da un dato momento in poi fino alla *lex* di Silla.'
32 Loreto 1993, 497–500.
33 Loreto 1993, 498 n. 23, argues against Harris' proposal to date the creation of two quaestors to 227, one for Sicily and the other one for Sardinia.
34 Loreto 1993, 501.
35 Kunkel and Wittmann 1995, 529–531.
36 Kunkel and Wittmann 1995, 529.

sponded to the new and changing administrative needs of the growing Empire.[37] The rest of Kunkel and Wittmann's ideas, however, basically revert to Mommsen's reconstruction. Following Lydus, they argue that the two new quaestors were first responsible for the fleet that protected the Italian coast. As their tasks changed over time, they were put in charge of administrative functions in Italy, such as the control of the *ager publicus* as well as the supervision of woods and transhumance routes (*calles*).[38] By 240, the *quaestor Ostiensis*, who was responsible for the transportation and storage of grain, and the Sicilian quaestorship in Lylibaeum would have been instituted, which would have brought the total number of quaestorships from four to eight. Other quaestorships, such as the ones in Cisalpine Gaul and the so-called *provincia aquaria*, would also have been introduced at some point in the Republican period.

Despite some differences in the details, Loreto as well as Kunkel and Wittmann have maintained the substantial core of Mommsen's reconstruction, even with regard to the headquarters of the new quaestors and their functions. Accordingly, their analyses, in a sense, have actually constituted a step backwards, particularly given that Harris had tried to dispense with some of Mommsen's more questionable assertions. The only substantial disagreement concerns the moment when and the way in which the new quaestorships were introduced: according to Mommsen, all of them were simultaneously formed in 267, whereas the new proposals proffer a more gradual timeline. For more than one hundred years, Mommsen's strictly rational and immutable construct prevailed in the scholarship, despite a slew of both minor as well as more extensive criticisms levelled by De Martino, Loreto, Kunkel and Wittmann, and, most importantly, Harris. In so far as they maintain the idea of one or more of the so-called Italian quaestorships being a regular office, most of these scholars have merely quibbled with minor aspects of Mommsen's theory without truly challenging his overall construct. Indeed, scholarly discourse had been caught in Mommsen's web and had been unable to disentangle itself.

The debate remained more or less stagnant until 2014, when Prag published a groundbreaking and methodologically exemplary article that dared to call into question the foundations of Mommsen's theory and hence has led to a more productive discussion. First, Prag is absolutely right to highlight the dangers of using evidence related to a later period in order to reconstruct an earlier one. Such a scholarly manoeuvre wrongly implies that Roman institutions were immutable throughout the centuries. Prag emphasises that only one of the so-called Italian quaestorships, namely the *quaestor Ostiensis*, is actually attested in the pre-Sullan period. He correctly concludes: 'There is a fundamental methodological principle which deserves to be respected, namely that any argument concerning the organisation of quaestorian provinces in the middle Republic which is based solely upon the situation attested subsequent to the post-Sullan increase to twenty quaestors must be considered

---

37 Kunkel and Wittmann did not consider the aforementioned articles by Harris and Loreto.
38 Kunkel and Wittmann 1995, 530.

speculative; likewise, the assumption that a late Republican or even early Imperial *provincia* must have its origins in the third century can only ever be speculation.'³⁹ Prag convincingly exemplifies his argument with the Ostian quaestorship. The first *quaestor Ostiensis* mentioned in the sources is L. Appuleius Saturninus at the end of the second century.⁴⁰ Indeed, it borders on irresponsible to apply this solitary piece of evidence (particularly without more robust argumentation) to a time one hundred and fifty years earlier, especially since this would take for granted that this supposed *provincia* had already become permanent in the mid-third century.⁴¹

Thanks to Tacitus, we do know that at some point in the pre-Sullan age there were eight quaestors and that this number was likely reached during the course of the third century.⁴² There is no doubt that two of them were the urban quaestors and two others were consular quaestors. Additionally, Prag reasonably assumes that provincial praetors were normally attended by a quaestor during the second century and that this can also be applied to the third century.⁴³ If we bear these principles in mind and set aside all speculation about the so-called Italian quaestorships as regular offices, a totally different allocation of the annual quaestorian *provinciae* emerges. As a matter of fact, Prag uses a hypothetical reconstruction to demonstrate how it would have been possible to allocate eight quaestors throughout the second century to all the praetorian provinces that were gradually created without requiring any quaestor to serve more than a *biennium*.⁴⁴

Prag's reconstruction implies that the number of quaestors did not increase in the second century.⁴⁵ On the contrary, presumably there were already eight quaestors, who were assigned the following roles: two of them to the quaestorian *provinciae* at Rome (urban quaestors), two more under the command of the consuls and the rest to Empire's provinces. This system would have made frequent use of prorogation, as happened with governors in those provinces. This would mean that a new quaes-

---

39 Prag 2014a, 197.
40 Cic. *Sest.* 39; *har.resp.* 43.
41 Prag 2014a, 199, attributes this inappropriate methodology to what he has defined as 'historian's *horror vacui*: faced with the evidence that some increase in the number of quaestors took place in the period immediately prior to the First Punic War, we desperately want to be able to say why and where.'
42 Prag 2014a, 201.
43 Prag 2014a, 202.
44 Prag 2014a, 203–204.
45 Harris 1976, 106: 'in 197 the total was probably raised to ten, a figure not exceeded until Sulla.' Badian 1983, 167, has suggested (without giving a concrete figure) that the number of quaestors could have increased in the second century as the number of regular *provinciae* in the Empire increased. However, there is no trace of this enlargement in our sources. In a similar sense, D'Orta 1993, 288 n. 35: throughout the second century the number of quaestors increased as the number of provinces also increased, given that each governor had a quaestor as assistant (with two in Sicily). As a result, there would have been nineteen quaestors before Sulla, who would have simply added the twentieth, 'probabilmente con competenze di controllo sui rifornimenti idrici.' Again, nothing in our sources allows for such a reconstruction. Cf. Coarelli 2014, 102.

tor did not have to be appointed every year for each praetorian province, given that a quaestor could remain under his commander for a second year. In turn, this would have provided the system with the flexibility to allocate other tasks to quaestors whenever necessary. This policy of not increasing the number of quaestors without limits matches the senatorial policy regarding praetorships, whose number did not increase as new provinces were created across the Empire, in particular in 146 or during the 120s.[46]

Prag's article did not, of course, answer every question about the development of the quaestorship in the middle Republic. Certainly, the lack of evidence makes it unlikely that we will ever reach a definitive solution. However, by emphasising the limits of our knowledge and warning of the dangers inherent in speculation, his methodological approach does offer a new way to interpret the evidence. The preferable alternative is to use our very limited sources in a way that appreciates their historical context and avoids falling into anachronistic projections.

Let us summarise so far. According to Livy, from 421 four quaestors were elected each year in Rome, two in charge of the *aerarium* and the other two to serve under the command of the consuls.[47] Plebeians were then allowed to run for the office, but only in 409 were the first three plebeian quaestors elected.[48] Although Livy's account raises the usual questions about the reliability of the details found in any source dealing with the early Republic, his narrative is plausible. There is no further reference to the number of quaestors until the third century, when the *Periochae* of Livy, Tacitus and Lydus speak of the office's expansion. The new number of quaestors is lost in the text of the *Periochae*, whereas Lydus asserts that there were now twelve quaestors, a number that is not credible. Tacitus, who is the most reliable source on the matter, asserts that the number of quaestors was doubled (*numerus duplicatus*), implying that the total was increased to eight. The question is when this enlargement took place. Both the *Periochae* and Lydus date this increase to 267–266, whereas Tacitus does not give a precise date, but suggests that this process took place in connection with Roman expansion and prior to Sulla. Combining all these pieces of information, we can reasonably conclude that the quaestorship probably reached the number of eight sometime during the third century and remained stable throughout the second century until the Sullan age. Livy does not inform us of any change in his preserved books, and the *Periochae* do not add anything for the lost books. This absence of information from Livy is significant, though not definitive.

Consequently, the increase in the number of quaestors may have taken place in two or more stages. At first sight, it appears reasonable to suppose that a pair of new quaestors could have been added in 267–266 and that two more were added at some

---

46 Prag 2014a, 207.
47 Liv. 4.43.3–4.
48 Liv. 4.54.2–3.

other point during the third century. However, a one-by-one increase or even a combination of the two procedures cannot be completely discarded.

Due to the lack of evidence, the question of the functions assigned to these new quaestors is not easy to answer. Every proposed solution should be guided by the principle that Roman institutional innovations were based on pragmatic flexibility and were always a response to new demands. Accordingly, Mommsen's overly rigid theory—in essence followed by many subsequent scholars—that a series of fixed Italian quaestorships stationed in particular cities was created by 267 and remained unchanged for decades or even centuries should be abandoned. This is not to say that the *provincia* of a quaestor in the second or even third century could not have been Ostia, for instance, if this answered a real need. Indeed, it would be wrong to assume that Saturninus was necessarily the first *quaestor Ostiensis* simply on the grounds that he is the first one attested (see below). While other *quaestores Ostienses* may certainly have existed prior to him (if circumstances demanded it), there is no reason to assume that any quaestor whose tasks were carried out in Italy was every year (or even regularly) allotted the same *provincia* from the third century onwards.

As Harris has argued, one of the new quaestors created in the third century was likely stationed in Lilybaeum on a regular basis, probably from 227 but perhaps as early as 241 when the First Punic War ended. Harris also suggests that another quaestor may have been regularly assigned to Sardinia after 227. As we can deduce from Tacitus, these possible new quaestorships would have been closely related to Rome's expansion and would have been instituted in order to assist the higher magistrates with *imperium* who were allocated to these new provinces. It must be underscored, nonetheless, that Harris' suggestion for the allocation of quaestors in the newly minted provinces of Sicily and Sardinia is not based on any clear evidence in the sources (in fact there is no mention of this in the sources), but on the assumption that provincial praetors would have been attended by quaestors in their *provinciae* from the very moment when extra-Italian provinces were created.

While the quaestors in Sardinia and Sicily could have been created *ex novo* specifically for these posts, one or both of quaestorships could also have existed previously; in this case, an existing position would have been reallocated to meet new demands. This brings us back to the 260s, when Livy's Periochist and Lydus state, as we have already seen, that the number of quaestors was increased for the first time—if we accept the notion of a more gradual process throughout the third century. In the 260s, however, neither Sicily nor Sardinia could have been the headquarters for a quaestor, since these territories had not yet come under Roman control. The new quaestors, therefore, must have held other duties in the 260s. What could these duties have been? What new demands was the Roman state confronting in the 260s that could have led it to increase the number of quaestors, which had apparently remained stable since the fifth century?

The First Punic War began in 264. Prior to the outbreak of the war, however, the episodes of Rhegium in southern Italy and of the Mamertines in Messana had already entangled Rome in the affairs of Sicily and, therefore, brought them into increased tension with the Carthaginians.[49] In the early 260s, it would have been reasonable for Romans to foresee a future conflict with Carthage; indeed, it is hard to imagine that some senators were not already discussing a potential confrontation. As Polybius' account reveals, this does not necessarily mean that the senators—at least not a majority of them—wanted to wage a war against Carthage. According to Polybius, the appeal of the Mamertines for help, a request that, if met, would have likely led to war, gave way to an acrimonious debate among the senators, who rejected the call for assistance. In Polybius' telling, it was actually the assembled people who finally approved the Mamertines' request, which led to the consul Ap. Claudius Caudex being sent to Sicily in 264.[50]

If Rome foresaw war with Carthage, nothing would have appeared more necessary than obtaining a fleet, given that the Carthaginians were the great naval power in the central Mediterranean at that time.[51] So far, Rome had fought land wars in Italy and only a few known naval battles. In his seminal work on Roman sea power before the Hannibalic War, Thiel concludes that Rome had no real interest in naval power prior to the First Punic War, a viewpoint that has been widely accepted in the scholarship.[52] This idea, however, should be qualified. As Harris has recently shown, it is unlikely that Rome suddenly became a naval power in the early years of its first war against Carthage. On the contrary, it is reasonable to see an increase in Rome's interest in her naval capacities during the last years of the third century and the first quarter of the second century.[53] The appointment of the first *duumviri navales* in 311, following a tribunician law, reinforces this idea.[54] These *duumviri navales*, according to Livy, were to be 'in charge of preparing and repairing the fleet.' Indeed, if we accept Livy's claim, it only follows that there was a fleet for these *duumviri* to repair.[55] How big that fleet was, we do not know. That said, it is evident that Rome had not yet constituted herself as a Mediterranean naval power, and we can safely assume that Rome did not have a fleet that could truly compete with Carthage's. Was the construc-

---

49 Pol. 1.8–9.
50 Pol. 1.10–11.
51 Cassola 1962, 179, argues that Rome intentionally provoked the war and that the Romans made arrangements for it beforehand. Moreover, Cassola thinks that the creation of the so-called *quaestores classici* in 267 bears this out; accordingly, he is sceptical of the idea that the large Roman fleet of 260 was the result of an 'eroica improvvisazione', as Polybius asserts. See also Harris 2017, 26: 'leading senators knew that war outside the peninsula was coming and were preparing for it from 273 onwards, but Rome was not up to date with the latest developments in warship construction; so c.264...it had to adapt fairly rapidly to the construction not of its first warships but of quinqueremes.'
52 Thiel 1954.
53 Harris 2017, 16–20.
54 Liv. 9.30.4: *alterum, ut duumviros navales classis ornandae reficiendaeque causa idem populus iuberet.*
55 Harris 2017, 16.

tion, equipment and maintenance of a fleet the task entrusted to the new quaestors created in 267?

Polybius' account certainly pushes against such a theory. The Greek historian explicitly states that it was only in 261, once the war in Sicily had begun, that Rome decided to build her first fleet. Moreover, Polybius asserts that not only did the Romans have no capacity to construct ships, but they also did not even know how to row properly! Apparently, they were able to use a captured Punic prototype to help in the construction of their own fleet.[56] One of the main purposes of Polybius' narration was to emphasise the audacity and tenacity of the Romans, who dared to confront the Carthaginians despite their inferiority on the sea and, more importantly, were able to win all the same. Polybius' account is so rife with *topoi* and exaggerations that it becomes difficult to take the historian at his word.[57] In fact, the story found in Polybius is probably little more than the dressing up of a heroic legend, as Oakley has persuasively argued.[58]

On the contrary, Lydus' text supports the possibility that the new quaestors were put in charge of constructing a new fleet.[59] He provides some specific information: new quaestors were created during the consulship of M. Atilius Regulus and L. Julius Libo, consequently in 267–266. Lydus claims these new quaestors were twelve in number, which, as discussed above, clearly appears to be a mistake. He then relates that a new fleet was constructed when Rome had decided to wage war against the former allies of Pyrrhus. Accordingly, the new quaestors were called *classici*, in the sense of naval commanders, 'navarchs' according to Lydus. As noted above, scholars have generally not taken Lydus as a very reliable source. Moreover, his statement about the building of a fleet in 267–266 (or at least the beginning of that process) contradicts Polybius, who dates the construction of the fleet to 261.

However disputable Lydus' evidence might be, his assertion is perfectly plausible in the historical context of those years. Furthermore, Lydus clearly links the construction of the fleet with the institution of new quaestors and with the name he gives them, *quaestores classici*. Since the name is not attested in any other ancient source, it seems unlikely that was actually an official title. Moreover, Lydus' implication that these new quaestors were in command of the fleet is rather farfetched, since, as magistrates, quaestors never possessed *imperium*—although in exceptional circumstances they could take command of troops, if their commander died or was otherwise unavailable. In spite of all the problems posed by Lydus' passage, we are left to wonder whether there is a kernel of truth in it: were new quaestors instituted

---

[56] Pol. 1.20–21.
[57] Cf. Walbank 1970, 1.75, on the episode of a Punic warship captured by Rome and used as a prototype: 'it is a particular instance of the popular *communis locus* that the Romans were especially successful at learning from, and improving on, their foes.' See also Ferone 2003, 79 n. 60.
[58] Oakley 2005a, 394. In the same sense, see Souza 2015, 189–190. Cf. Harris 2017, 16: Polybius' main story 'reproduced a patriotic Roman fiction, presumably taken over from Fabius Pictor.'
[59] Lyd. *de mag.* 1.27 (see the translation of the text provided above n. 11).

in 267–266 with the main purpose of supervising the building of a fleet (*classis*), which would explain the name of *classici*? Given the evidence found in the *Periochae* of Livy, Lydus' chronology for the new quaestorships does appear to be accurate. Could Lydus also be correct, at least partially, with respect to the *provincia* of the new quaestors?

A few years ago we received valuable new information on the quaestorship: the recently discovered Egadi bronze rams (*rostra*) with Latin inscriptions have opened an interesting new perspective on the tasks that quaestors could have carried out in the third century.[60] The rams belonged to ships that presumably took part in the battle of the Egadi Islands in 241 at the end of the first Punic War. For Prag, the discovery of several *rostra* bearing Latin inscriptions precisely where the decisive Roman naval victory occurred would be explained if these rams originally came from Roman ships that had been captured by the Carthaginians in previous battles. This could have happened at the battle of Drepanum in 249, when the Carthaginians seized ninety-three Roman vessels and took them back to Carthage.[61] These ships and their rams may have been reused by the Carthaginians as part of their emergency fleet of 241, which the Romans finally defeated at the battle of the Egadi Islands. It cannot be completely ruled out, however, that the rams belonged to ships that were constructed in Rome in 242 (or perhaps earlier) specifically in preparation for the Egadi battle.

Some previously unknown quaestors are mentioned in the Latin inscriptions engraved on the rams: C. Papirius, M. Publicius Malleolus and L. Quinctius. The texts of the inscriptions record their names and their responsibilities in relation to the *rostra* and the ships, namely the *probatio*: L(ucios) Quinctio(s) C(aii) f(ilios) quaistor probavet (Egadi 10); M(arcos) Populicio(s) L(ucii) f(ilios) q(uaestores) p(robaverunt) C(aios) Paperio(s) Ti(beri) f(ilios) (Egadi 4); C(aios) Paperio(s) Ti(beri) f(ilios) M(arcos) Populicio(s) L(ucii) f(ilios) q(uaestores) p(robaverunt) (Egadi 6);[62] M(arcos) Populicio(s) L(uci) f(ilios) C(aios) Papeirio(s) Ti(beri) f(ilios) q(uaestores) p(robaverunt) (Egadi 11).[63] The approved objects to which the inscriptions allude are not explicitly named. As Prag points out, it seems reasonable that the rams themselves were approved by the quaestors, since it is on these very objects that the texts were inscribed.[64] While it remains uncertain whether the quaestorian approval (and as a consequence the previous contract) extended to the construction of the entire vessel, it seems very likely that it did.[65] The quaestors, then, certainly appear as the magistrates responsible

---

60 Oliveri 2012; Tusa – Royal 2012; Prag 2014a; 2014b; 2014c; 2017.
61 Pol. 1.51.12; 1.53.1. Tusa – Royal 2012, 45; Prag 2014b, 51.
62 Prag 2014b, 36–43; 2014c.
63 Prag 2017.
64 Prag 2014b, 57.
65 So Coarelli 2014, 109, who explains the fact that the inscription was placed on the *rostra* where it would have been more visible. For an opposing view, see Prag 2014b, 57: '[I]f the *probatio*… had ex-

for the casting and approval of the rams; in all likelihood, they were also in charge of building the entire ships to which these rams belonged.

The inscriptions do not specify which kind of quaestors they name: these could be urban quaestors, consular quaestors or the new quaestors created in 267–266. It appears unlikely that consular quaestors were assigned such tasks, given that they were in the service of the consuls and had other responsibilities. A more plausible theory is that the inscriptions refer to urban quaestors. Of course, the urban quaestors were in charge of the *aerarium* and consequently one of their main tasks was the administration of public funds. Considering that each of the *rostra*—and obviously each ship—was paid for with public money and required a considerable amount of high-quality bronze that may have come directly from the public treasury (if the rams were made in Rome and not in other parts of Italy),[66] it seems possible that the recorded magistrates were indeed urban quaestors. Whereas Papirius and Publicius are mentioned together, Quinctius appears alone. This does not prevent their identification as urban quaestors, since *quaestores urbani* could act together or individually (see the chapter on the urban quaestorship below).[67]

However, what if the quaestors mentioned in the Egadi inscriptions were the new quaestors created in 267–266? What if their *provincia* was specifically the construction and equipment of the fleet?[68] According to Polybius, Rome constructed warships

---

tended to the construction of the entire ship, that point would have been made explicit in the inscription.' However, it is not explicitly recorded in the inscriptions that the *rostra* were the objects of the *probatio*, though this could be understood implicitly. It seems just as likely that placing the inscription on a prominent part of the vessel could implicitly refer to the *probatio* of the ship as a whole. This would extend the contract signed by the quaestors to the construction of the ships and not only to the making of the rams.

66 Prag 2014b, 57: 'the act of *probatio* would then serve not only to confirm satisfactory production, but also to confirm that the full amount of the bronze had been used in the ram and no embezzlement had taken place.' Cf. Prag 2014a, 200.

67 Apart from these inscriptions, the only evidence of a possible relationship between urban quaestors and the construction of ships is found in Cicero. In his speech in favour of Flaccus, Cicero refers to the urban quaestors of 61, P. Sestullius (or Sextilius) and M. Curtius Peducaeanus and asserts that they expended money (*pecunia erogata*) on the fleet (Cic. *Flacc.* 30: *postero anno nonne M. Curtio et P. Sextilio quaestoribus pecunia in classem est erogata?*). Since Cicero does not provide any additional information, the sense of his statement is unclear. It is obvious that the urban quaestors extracted the money necessary to construct a fleet from the *aerarium*, but it remains unclear whether they also had something to do with its construction.

68 For Harris it was not necessary to create new quaestors specifically for the task of building warships: 'The urban and sometimes the consular quaestors played a part in operating the contract system, but there was scarcely any need to institute new quaestorships for the sake of ship-building contracts' (Harris 1976, 97). His conclusion could certainly be correct, but it must be borne in mind that the Egadi inscriptions were unknown when Harris wrote his article. However, also Prag 2014a, 200, has shown scepticism about the idea that the quaestors of the 260s were created for a specific naval role. On the contrary, Gnoli 2012, 86–97, considers that the inscriptions on the Egadi *rostra* confirm the veracity of the information given by Lydus. In his opinion, *classici* is not an official title, but just a description of their original naval duties. Cébeillac Gervasoni 2014, also accepts, though without pro-at several points during the First Punic War.⁶⁹ Although consular oversight of the construction of a fleet from the time of the first Punic War is regularly attested and the appointment of *duumviri navales* in 311 is well known (whether it was a permanent office from then on is uncertain),⁷⁰ the Egadi inscriptions prove that during the First Punic War quaestors were somehow involved in the construction of ships. If these arguments are correct, this implies that the new quaestors instituted in the 260s were responsible for tasks related to the building and equipment of ships, probably not only the *probatio* of the *rostra*, but also the larger process of making a vessel.⁷¹

Did these supposedly quaestorian duties overlap with those attributed to the *duumviri navales* in 311?⁷² Let us remember that Livy asserts that the *duumviri navales* were appointed to prepare and restore the fleet, the same tasks that the new quaestors may have implemented. However, the situation may have drastically changed be-

---

viding any discussion or further argument, that the quaestors mentioned in the inscriptions were *quaestores classici*. Furthermore, Cébeillac Gervasoni assumes, again without any supporting argumentation, that Lydus' *quaestores classici* were based in Ostia and that they were, therefore, identical to the *quaestores Ostienses*. She takes for granted that they had been appointed without interruption from 267 onwards. However, there is no evidence in Lydus or in any other source that suggests that *quaestores classici* and *quaestores Ostienses* were the same thing (cf. Prag 2017, 291 n. 8: 'the *rostra* themselves hardly provide 'evidence' for Mommsen's hypothetical Ostian quaestor in the third century BC'). Also Coarelli 2014, 106–108, openly assumes that the Egadi inscriptions demonstrate the existence of quaestors with naval competencies (not as naval commanders, but rather as those responsible for the construction of the fleet) and that these quaestors were the ones created in 267. Before the discovery of the inscriptions, Steinby 2007, 72, already linked the new quaestors created in the 260s with the preparation of the new Roman fleet: 'the new *quaestores* were probably involved in preparing the fleet. At this time, Rome had several cities supplying ships. It is therefore very plausible that the Romans needed officials to supervise the work of maintaining and equipping ships.' Finally, Harris 2017, 25, has argued that the 'navarchs' to whom Lydus refers were in fact *duumviri navales*, and not the new quaestors. Harris, however, makes no mention of the Egadi *rostra* in his article.

69 Tusa – Royal 2012, 45.
70 Prag 2014b, 44–47 and 55 with n. 78. Cf. Steinby 2007, 60–63; Dart 2012. It must be added that one of the Egadi inscriptions mentions an otherwise unknown sevirate in charge of the *probatio*. Coarelli 2014, 105–106 and 108, has proposed a different reading: *sexvir(i) q(uaistores) en[bolum] probave[ront]*. Coarelli concluded that a collegium of six 'military' (i.e. all existing quaestors except for the urban quaestors) existed, although they operated in pairs; this collegium apparently proves that the increase in the number of quaestors from four to eight took place in 267. Coarelli's reading, however, is far from certain; consequently, his interpretation is also very dubious. It is very unlikely that such a collegium of quaestors, including the two consular quaestors, ever existed. For another interpretation see Gnoli 2012, 94–95 and 97–114. On this inscription, see Prag 2014b 45–47 in particular.
71 The inscriptions on the Egadi *rostra* show that each set of *rostra* (and probably the ships themselves) were produced as part of a building programme under the responsibility of a pair of magistrates, and therefore within a single year. So Prag 2017, 290.
72 Ilari 1974, 116, has claimed that it would be problematic for quaestors to be in charge of the fleet, given that *duumviri navales* had already been created in 311.

tween 311 and 267: new demands could have led to the creation of new quaestorships and consequently either to the extinction of the *dummviri navales*[73] or to their transformation into naval commanders.[74] Naval preparations for the war against Carthage and the several known programmes for the building of ships during the First Punic War undoubtedly entailed a very complex process: ships had to be built (perhaps in more than one location)[75] and then decked out with the necessary equipment, all of which would have required coordination that the new quaestors could have provided. The quaestors were allowed to sign a contract and control the whole process of production from start to finish, since the same magistrate who signed a contract for a public work was usually in charge of verifying that the contract had been carried out satisfactorily.[76] As on other occasions, the quaestors must have acted in accordance with a senatorial decree, perhaps in response to a direct order from the consuls. The fact that two quaestors are mentioned jointly in three of the Egadi inscriptions seems to suggest that the number of quaestors increased by at least two in 267–266. As mentioned above, the fact that only one quaestor is mentioned in the other inscriptions indicates that these quaestors could act jointly or individually.

These quaestors were the so-called *quaestores classici*, to employ Lydus' terminology, who were initially associated with the fleet. This does not mean, however, that the *provincia* of these new quaestors was rigidly fixed over a long period of time.[77] On the contrary, we must account for the usual flexibility and pragmatism of Roman institutions, which were adaptable enough to respond to changing circumstances throughout the Republic. After the First Punic War, Rome controlled territories outside Italy for the first time; after the Hannibalic War, Roman expansion continued to grow rapidly across the Mediterranean. As a consequence, the quaestorship had to adjust to the new Roman reality. In all probability new quaestors were created at some point after the First Punic War for Sicily and Sardinia (see above). When circumstances and needs had changed, the quaestors who had once been responsible for the construction and equipment of the fleet would have become available for other functions. As can be deduced from Tacitus, eight quaestors existed in the final part of the third century, and this number remained unaltered throughout the second century and up to the Sullan reforms.

---

[73] Eckstein 2012, 67: 'it is possible that in 267 the *duumviri navales* were allowed to lapse, replaced by a board of four annually-elected Roman *quaestores classici* ('supervisors of the fleet'), but the evidence is disputed.'
[74] Ferone 2003, 80: the main duty of the *duumviri navales* was the 'tutela dell'*ora maritima*.' On the *duumviri navales* as naval commanders, see Potter 2004, 76; Gnoli 2012, 93.
[75] Prag 2017, 291, points out the possibility of multiple locations for the production of the ships.
[76] See Prag 2014a, 200: 'one of the most interesting aspects of these texts is the clear evidence which they provide of quaestors managing public contracts, as well as the very early date to which these attest for such public contracting.' Cf. Prag 2014b, 56.
[77] Gnoli 2012, 95–96, argues that the quaestors with naval duties continued to exist well after the First Punic War concluded; in his opinion, this went on probably throughout the second century.

While well aware of the caution required by the dearth of evidence, we propose the following reconstruction of the development of the quaestorship in the pre-Sullan age: the people elected two quaestors for the first time in 447–446. This number was doubled in 421 and plebeians were allowed to stand for the office. These four quaestors (two urban and two consular) remained the same throughout the fourth century and into the beginning of the third. In the aftermath of the war against Pyrrhus in 267–266, two more quaestors were added, as Lydus says, and their *provincia* was the construction and equipment of the fleet. These new quaestors would have been in charge of this *provincia* at least during the First Punic War, although it cannot be ruled out that they could temporarily have been assigned other tasks when necessary, especially once the war came to a close and Rome controlled extra-Italian territories. Two additional quaestors may have been added when Sicily and Sardinia became regular praetorian *provinciae* in 227, which would have reflected the existing institutional design for the consuls, according to which a quaestor, serving as his right-hand man, would accompany a higher magistrate with *imperium* to his *provincia*. At the same time, the quaestors in charge of the fleet could have assumed new tasks instead of their original duties. The third century ended, therefore, with eight quaestors elected every year, and the number remained steady until Sulla. During the second century there were two consular quaestors, two urban quaestors and four other quaestors who were assigned to the Empire's new provinces (Hispania Citerior and Ulterior, Africa, Asia, etc.) under the command of a higher magistrate with *imperium*, although they could also be given other tasks or *provinciae* in Italy, if need arose.

As we know from preserved fragments of the *lex Cornelia de XX quaestoribus* and from Tacitus' testimony, Sulla increased the number of quaestors to twenty in 81.[78] Later, Caesar further enlarged the number of quaestors in the context of his own institutional reforms.[79] While for the first century we know the names of more quaestors than for any other period of the Republic, we do not always have sufficient information about their *provinciae*; furthermore, we are often unable to reconstruct what kind of tasks these quaestors actually undertook. The consular quaestors provide a good example: as had been the case in earlier periods, each post-Sullan consul had a quaestor at his service, but we do not know exactly what these quaestors did.[80]

---

78 Tac. *ann.* 11.22.6: *Post lege Sullae viginti creati supplendo senatui, cui indicia tradiderat.* As we have seen, it is not easy to find such clear evidence for the history of the quaestorship. It is therefore difficult to understand the following statement from Badian: 'there is no evidence at all for the frequent implication that the number of quaestors jumped all at once from eight (or whatever other low number we like to imagine) to 20 in 81 BC' (Badian 1983, 168). On the *lex Cornelia de XX quaestoribus*, see Keil 1902; Gabba 1983; Varvaro 1995; Crawford 1996.
79 Suet. *Iul.* 41: *Senatum supplevit, patricios adlegit, praetorum aedilium quaestorum, minorum etiam magistratuum numerum ampliavit.* In the same sense Cass. Dio 43.47.2; 43.51.3. Cf. Jehne 1987, 372–373 and n. 6. On the presumed influence of the jurist C. Trebatius Testa on the institutional reforms that Caesar introduced, D'Orta 1993.
80 The consuls of the year 38 were the first to have two quaestors each: Cass. Dio 48.43.1.

Prior to Sulla, the consuls spent most of their magistracy outside Rome as the commanders-in-chief of their legions, and their quaestors accompanied them as right-hand men in the field, a job that included administrative and financial tasks in the provinces. In the post-Sullan age, however, consuls often spent most of their time at Rome; in fact, several consuls, such as Pompey, Cicero and Caesar, never even left the city while in office.[81] A quaestor continued to be attached to the consuls in the first century, but due to a lack of information we really cannot say what they did in the city. We can guess, of course, that they helped their consuls at Rome in whatever matter the highest magistrates happened to be involved (politics, legislation, etc.), that they accompanied the consuls if they left the city for their provinces, and that they were expected to become their confidants. Beyond that, there is little that we can safely assume.

Leaving aside the four consular and urban quaestors, another sixteen quaestors were in office every year between the Sullan and Caesarean reforms. Most of them were allocated to provinces across the Empire under the command of a magistrate with *imperium*. Other quaestors, however, were allotted *provinciae* that entailed duties to be carried out in Italy. Wiseman has suggested that the annual twenty quaestors after Sulla consisted of two consular assistants, two urban quaestors, thirteen serving in provinces and three entrusted with administrative tasks in Italy. The jurisdictions of these final three were the *provincia aquaria* (Ostia and the west coast harbours according to Wiseman), the *ager Gallicus* and the pastures of southern Italy.[82] Wiseman's reconstruction could be essentially accurate for most of the period between 81 and 44, but apart from the urban and consular quaestors, whose number was fixed, the senate determined the other quaestorian *provinciae* each year.[83] These quaestorian *provinciae* in Italy and in the provinces of the Empire were therefore not necessarily pre-determined, but could vary in number and tasks depending on changing circumstances.

The so-called Italian quaestorships

In his speech against Vatinius, Cicero provides the only mention of what he calls the *provincia aquaria*. Cicero tells us that in the year 63, when he himself was consul, Vatinius was quaestor and was assigned the *provincia aquaria* by lot. According to Cicero, he, as consul, sent Vatinius to Puteoli with the purpose of preventing the export of gold and silver from that Tyrrhenian seaport: *in eo magistratu cum tibi magno clamore aquaria provincia sorte obtigisset, missusne sis a me consule Puteolos, ut inde aurum exportari argentumque prohiberes?*[84] Cicero then accuses Vatinius both

---

81 Pina Polo 2011, 225–248.
82 Wiseman 1971, 156.
83 Cic. *Q.fr.* 2.3.1 (year 55).
84 Cic. *Vat.* 12.

of having acted dishonestly in order to keep part of the merchandise and also of having terrified the traders with his behaviour.[85] Cicero's accusations must be taken with a grain of salt and understood as a piece of rhetorical invective, in which an orator would do anything to discredit his opponent, including the use of half-truths and exaggerations. Since we only have the Ciceronian version of the events, it is impossible to determine how truthful the orator's claims really are. The text implies that Vatinius carried out his mission with extraordinary zeal and that his diligence led some merchants to complain. If he committed irregularities or even felonies during his time as quaestor, as Cicero would have us believe, we do not know of them. In any case, it does not seem that Vatinius was ever officially charged and brought to trial after leaving office.

More than Vatinius' honesty or dishonesty, it is his quaestorship in which we are interested. We know, according to Cicero, that Vatinius was allotted the *provincia aquaria* and that he spent at least a substantial part of his quaestorship in Puteoli in order to prevent the export of gold and silver, a job which the consul Cicero apparently assigned him. Mommsen, for his part, identifies control over Rome's water supply as the principle task pertaining to the so-called *provincia aquaria*; accordingly, he considers the dispatch of Vatinius to Puteoli as something out of the ordinary.[86] For Mommsen, the quaestor in charge of the *provincia aquaria* normally lived at Rome but could be sent to other places in Italy, as was the case with Vatinius. In short, Mommsen rejects the identification of the quaestor *aquarius* with the one established in Ostia or with the one who supposedly had his headquarters in Cales. While several scholars have taken up Mommsen's idea that the duties of the *provincia aquaria* involve Rome's water supply,[87] others have implicitly discarded Mommsen's reconstruction; instead, they identify the so-called *provincia aquaria* with the quaestorship in Ostia, despite the fact that there is no evidence of this.[88]

A text of Frontinus seems to lend support to the thesis that Vatinius' *provincia aquaria* should be associated with the water supply to Rome: *Tutelam autem singu-*

---

85 Cic. *Vat.* 12: *in eo negotio cum te non custodem ad continendas, sed portitorem ad partiendas mercis missum putares, cumque omnium domos, apothecas, navis furacissime scrutarere, hominesque negoti gerentis iudiciis iniquissimis inretires, mercatores e navi egredientis terreres, conscendentis morarere, teneasne memoria tibi in conventu Puteolis manus esse adlatas, ad me consulem querelas Puteolanorum esse delatas?*
86 Mommsen, Röm.St. 2.1.558 and n. 3.
87 Wesener 1963, 819, adds that this quaestorian *provincia* could have been created in the first century by the *lex Titia* mentioned in Cic. *Mur.* 18. Willems 1878, 305, already had suggested the relation of the *provincia aquaria* to the *lex Titia*. Along the lines that Mommsen had proposed, Kunkel and Wittmann 1995, 531, claim that the *provincia aquaria* related to Rom's water supply and that the *lex Titia* could have made it permanent in the first century.
88 Wiseman 1971, 156: 'the spheres of competence of the Italian quaestorships were Ostia and the west coast harbours (*provincia aquaria*), the *ager Gallicus*, and the upland pastures of southern Italy'; Lintott 1999, 135: 'one was the quaestorship at Ostia,…whose authority…might be exercised elsewhere on the Tyrrhenian coast: hence it was sometimes referred to as the *provincia aquaria.*'

larum aquarum locari solitam invenio positamque redemptoribus necessitatem certum numerum circa ductus extra urbem, certum in urbe servorum opificum habendi, et quidem ita ut nomina quoque eorum, quos habituri essent in ministerio per quasque regiones, in tabulas publicas deferrent; eorumque operum probandorum curam fuisse penes censores aliquando et aediles, interdum etiam quaestoribus eam provinciam obvenisse, ut apparet ex S. C. quod factum est C. Licinio et Q. Fabio cos.[89] For Harris, this passage is crucial to understanding the problem: 'correctly interpreted, this is the *cura aquarum*, i.e. of the city's water supply, more specifically the inspection of the work carried out by contractors on the aqueducts.'[90] Additionally, Harris sees no difficulty in assuming that Cicero was sending Vatinius on a special mission rather than accepting that he was performing his normal duties.[91]

Frontinus' text refers specifically to the year 116, when C. Licinius Geta and Q. Fabius Maximus Eburnus were consuls.[92] The passage reinforces the conclusion that the quaestorian *provinciae* were determined every year by the senate by means of a *senatus consultum*. Frontinus implies that these quaestorian *provinciae* could change every year at the senate's discretion. A senatorial decree in 116 designated the *tutela aquarum* as one of the quaestorian *provinciae* for that year specifically. According to Frontinus, this *tutela aquarum* particularly entailed the supervision of contractors' repairs and maintenance of the city's water conduits. It is evident from Frontinus' text that censors or aediles usually performed such duties and that putting a quaestor in charge of such work was rather exceptional.[93] This is why he specifically mentions the senatorial decree of 116, a year in which the senate took this decision due to unknown circumstances. Is Cicero referring to the *tutela aquarum* when he describes the *provincia* of Vatinius as *provincia aquaria* despite the fact that Vatinius' quaestorian duties had nothing to do with Rome's water supply?

An additional and far from insignificant problem is the name *provincia aquaria* itself. Was it the official title of a quaestorian *provincia* or was it a phrase that Cicero coined? Cicero used this designation in his speech against Vatinius, which, it must be stressed, belongs to the rhetorical genre of invective. In his speech, Cicero sought to criticise Vatinius and to damage his image as much as possible. In this context, it may be relevant that the word *aquarius* was usually applied to the servant who supplied water for domestic use, meaning a water-bearer.[94] Was Cicero subtlety discrediting Vatinius by using this word in relation to his quaestorian *provincia* in 63? Was it

---

89 Frontin. *aq.* 2.96. Cf. Schol.Bob. *In Vat.* 12 (p. 145 St.): *Hic igitur Vatinius aquariam sortitus erat, id est ut aquae curam sustineret.*
90 Harris 1976, 102. Also Badian 1974, 162 n. 11, rejects the identification of the *provincia aquaria* with any Italian quaestorship; furthermore, he saw its connection with the water supply to Rome as obvious.
91 Harris 1976, 102 n. 90.
92 Broughton MRR, 1.530.
93 Daguet-Gagey 2015, 386–390.
94 *Oxford Latin Dictionary*, s.v. aquarius.

a derogatory or mocking expression? While we cannot be sure since *provincia aquaria* is a hapax, the context of the speech does oblige us to be cautious. Consequently, *provincia aquaria* is not necessarily the official name of the quaestorian *provincia* that was allotted to Vatinius. Nevertheless, it is reasonable to suppose that his *provincia* had something to do with water—though not necessarily the water supply. In short, if Vatinius' post had nothing to do with water, Cicero could not have used the adjective *aquarius* to elicit the desired reaction from his audience.

If we do not see Vatinius' mission in Puteoli as an extraordinary assignment but rather as the task that had been originally allotted to him as quaestor, Cicero provides sufficient information to identify which *provincia* Vatinius held. While the orator's words do imply that it was the consul himself who personally decided Vatinius' assignment, we cannot discard Cicero's penchant for putting himself in the limelight. Besides, in the context of the invective against Vatinius, Cicero's alleged order seems calculated to humiliate him even further, by making of Vatinius little more than a water boy. However, it was in reality the senate that ultimately decided and allocated all quaestorian *provinciae*. This means that in all probability the consul Cicero was acting as no more than an intermediary who communicated to Vatinius the task that the senate had assigned him. Indeed, it would strain credulity that Vatinius' quaestorship depended on the consul's decisions: while a quaestor was certainly subordinated to a higher magistrate, his instructions came from the senate; once he had reached his destination, the quaestor had autonomy to take his own decisions.[95]

Therefore, the *provincia aquaria*, as Cicero calls it, probably had no relation to Rome's water supply or to the seaport of Ostia, as some scholars have suggested.[96] As a matter of fact, Vatinius' mission in Puteoli obviously had nothing to do with Ostia or with the supply of grain to Rome, a task that seems to have been a characteristic of the Ostian quaestor (see below). If anything, what we know about Vatinius' *provincia* distances it from the Ostian quaestorship. In fact, there are no discernible similarities between the two offices.

Given the preceding set of arguments, the most likely conclusion is that the Vatinius' *provincia* in 63 entailed nothing other than the prohibition of exporting gold and silver from the maritime town of Puteoli. Once more it is important to bear in mind the adaptability of Roman institutions to the needs of the moment. In 63 there was a real problem that was damaging the Roman economy.[97] As a conse-

---

[95] We have other examples of consuls being intermediaries between senate and quaestors: *S.C. de Asclepiade* ll.17–18 (= ll. 25–26 of the Greek text); Cic. *Phil.* 9.15–17; 14.38.
[96] So Lintott 1999, 135: 'the quaestorship at Ostia... was sometimes referred to as the *provincia aquaria*.'
[97] Verboven 2009, 108: the senatorial decree targeted both coins and bullion, and the implication is that merchants used uncoined gold to balance their affairs. Harris 2006, 18, points out, however, that one of the purposes of the mission undertaken by Vatinius could have been to prevent the export of coins.

quence, a senatorial decree prohibited the export of gold and silver and sent one of the year's quaestors, Vatinius, to oversee the implementation of the decree in Puteoli.[98] The assignment, then, provided a concrete answer to a specific problem. Therefore, Vatinius' quaestorship should not be used as evidence to reconstruct quaestorian *provinciae* of other years. That is, Cicero's text may be used neither to conclude that a *provincia aquaria* was allotted every year in the first century—let alone earlier —nor that Puteoli was the permanent station of a quaestor in the period. Vatinius' *provincia* in 63 was not a regular quaestorian *provincia*, but rather an occasional one.[99]

The Ostian quaestor is the only Italian quaestorship attested in the pre-Sullan age. According to Cicero, L. Appuleius Saturninus was *quaestor Ostiensis* in charge of Rome's food supply, probably in 105.[100] However, he was removed from this post by the senate and replaced by the *princeps senatus* M. Aemilius Scaurus. Such an important figure obviously did not assume the office of quaestor, but quite possibly was put in charge of the *cura annonae* to confront an exceptional situation.[101] Indeed, the fact that none other than the *princeps senatus* was called in to administer the food-supply speaks to the state of emergency at Rome. In any case, Cicero leaves no doubt about the task of the Ostian quaestor: this was the *frumentaria procuratio*, that is, the mission to guarantee the supply of grain to Rome from the port of Ostia.[102]

Another Ciceronian text refers to the Ostian quaestorship. Cicero asserts that Servius Sulpicius Rufus was a colleague of L. Licinius Murena in the quaestorship (presumably in 74) and calls him *quaestor Ostiensis*.[103] Cicero does not provide any precise information on the task that Sulpicius Rufus was supposed to undertake as Ostian quaestor, but he defines this quaestorian *provincia* as 'busy and annoying' (*negotiosa et molesta*), which he contrasts with the 'pleasant and distinguished' (*gratiosa et inlustre*) *provincia* that Murena received. This could be a general description of the Ostian quaestorship and its complicated duties: a quaestor's inattention or poor administration could provoke dissatisfaction among the population at Rome and consequently lead to the quaestor's unpopularity. But Cicero's words could

---

98 The senate had prohibited the export of gold on other occasions before 63: *Exportari aurum non oportere cum saepe antea senatus tum me consule gravissime iudicavit* (Cic. *Flacc.* 67). Cf. Rosillo-López 2010, 219.
99 Harris 1976, 100 n. 72 and 102, defends the occasional character of the *provincia aquaria*, which, as we have seen, he considered to be in charge of supervising Rome's aqueducts.
100 Cic. *har. resp.* 43: *Saturninum, quod in annonae caritate quaestorem a sua frumentaria procuratione senatus amovit eique rei M. Scaurum praefecit, scimus dolore factum esse popularem*; *Sest.* 39: *nec mihi erat res cum Saturnino, qui quod a se quaestore Ostiensi per ignominiam ad principem et senatus et civitatis, M. Scaurum, rem frumentariam tralatam sciebat...* Cf. Diodor. 36.12.
101 Cébeillac Gervasoni 2002, 63–64.
102 Harris 1976, 97. Cf. Chandler 1978, 330.
103 Cic. *Mur.* 18: *...tu illam cui, cum quaestores sortiuntur, etiam adclamari solet, Ostiensem, non tam gratiosam et inlustrem quam negotiosam et molestam.*

also allude to specific problems with the food supply in 74, when food shortages provoked riots in the city and the curule aedile M. Seius provided grain to the people in order to appease them.[104]

These two Ciceronian texts show that the Ostian quaestorship existed at least since the last years of the second century, although it obviously could have been created earlier.[105] These passages do not demonstrate, however, that this quaestorship was regular or allocated on a yearly basis, let alone that the *quaestor Ostiensis* existed since 267–266, when the number of quaestors was increased. Nevertheless, this has been a prominent and long-held opinion.[106] As in the case of the so-called *provincia aquaria* (it must be stressed that nothing indicates that they were the same

---

104 Sall. *hist.* 2.45 M.; Cic. *off.* 2.58. Cf. Ryan 1996f, 40 n. 19.
105 The only two known *quaestores Ostienses* until year 44 are the aforementioned Saturninus and Sulpicius Rufus. Cébeillac Gervasoni 2014, 57–58, includes in her prosopography of *quaestores Ostienses* the name of Novius Ofalius, a quaestor who dedicated an inscription to Liber in Ostia in the third or in the beginning of the second century (CIL I² 2440 = ILLRP 204: *No(merius) Ofalius No(meri) f(ilius) q(uaestor) pro sed et familia sova L[e]ibero donum dat meret(o)*). However, Novius Ofalus was in all probability a local quaestor, not a Roman quaestor.
106 This is Mommsen's view (Röm.St. 2.557–558), for whom the Ostian and the Gallic quaestorships were abolished by Claudius in 44 (Suet. *Claud.* 24: *Collegio quaestorum pro stratura viarum gladiatorium munus iniunxit detractaque Ostiensi et Gallica provincia curam aerari Saturni reddidit...*). Nevertheless, the changes introduced by Claudius were a response to the reforms established by Augustus (Harris 1976, 98). Suetonius' text cannot be used, therefore, to support the continuity of the Italian quaestorships as regular *provinciae* throughout the Republic up to the Principate. Other scholars, following in the footsteps of Mommsen, have defended the continuity of the Ostian quaestorship as a regular *provincia* (and of the other so-called Italian quaestorships) until the Principate: Wesener 1963, 819; Harris 1976, 98: 'the *provincia Ostiensis* may have been devised as early as 267' and it became a regular *provincia* (104); Chandler 1978, 328: it is reasonable to assume that the *quaestor Ostiensis* came into being when the number of quaestors was increased in 267, since the office is recorded before the time of Sulla, when the new increase of quaestors took place; the office was abolished in 44 by Claudius (333); Mattingly 1969, 509: the Ostian quaestorship was one of the two quaestorships instituted in 267; Kunkel and Wittmann 1995, 530: the *quaestor Ostiensis* may have been instituted by 240, when the regular transportation of Sicilian grain began. Also Loreto 1993, 498–499, connects the creation of a quaestorian *provincia* at Ostia in charge of the *res frumentaria* to the annexation of Sicily, in particular in 211–210, once Syracuse had been defeated. More recently, Cébeillac Gervasoni 2014, 55, confidently claims that the *quaestor Ostiensis* was created in 267, according to Lydus with the title of *quaestor classicus*, and that his function was to assure that the provisions reached naval troops (cf. Coarelli 2014, 108). According to Cébeillac Gervasoni, the *quaestor classicus* was based at Ostia because the Roman armies departed from this harbour. Finally, see the reconstruction of Meiggs 1973, 299: 'in the late Republic Rome's interests were safeguarded by a quaestor stationed at Ostia, whose primary function was to supervise the reception, storage, and reshipment of corn from the provinces. He had a tribunal in the forum at Ostia and perhaps his authority was backed by judicial powers greater than those normally associated with the quaestorship.' According to Meiggs, this seems a reasonable inference from a inscription set up, probably under Augustus, by the shipowners of Ostia: *Pacceio L.f. q(uaestori) pro p(aetore)* (CIL 14. 3603 = ILS 6171 = Inscr.It. 4, 1², 119; cf. AE 1955 no 178 and Di Stefano Manzella 1982), and he concludes: 'Perhaps all Roman quaestors at Ostia were given a praetor's judicial competence.'

provincia), it is much more probable that this Italian quaestorship was occasional and that Ostia was allotted as a quaestorian *provincia* only when the senate considered it necessary. This would certainly have been the case in times of crisis in the food supply, as seems to have been the case in 105 and 74 when Saturninus and Sulpicius Rufus held their quaestorships. In fact, Cicero asserts that Sulpicius Rufus was assigned the Ostian quaestorship by lot, and this means that the senate had included this *provincia* among the quaestorian *provinciae* for that year in advance. As a matter of fact, the demands and expectations of providing an adequate supply of food to the city probably made the office 'busy and annoying', to use Cicero's words, especially if any larger economic changes led to shortages and higher prices.[107] In such circumstances, the Ostian quaestorship would have been an unwelcome challenge and could have even provided a potential source of unpopularity.

Among the Italian quaestorships that he considered fixed quaestorian *provinciae* from the third century onwards, Mommsen also includes a quaestor in Cisalpine Gaul with Ravenna as a potential headquarters.[108] Other scholars, following Mommsen, have spoken more loosely of the *ager Gallicus* as one of the regular Italian quaestorships during the Republic; some have suggested other cities as their base such as Ariminium.[109] The only possible evidence for this quaestorship comes from a passage in Plutarch, who explains that Sertorius, after returning from Hispania where he had served as military tribune, became quaestor in Cisalpine Gaul.[110] According to Plutarch, Sertorius was quaestor on the brink of the *Bellum Sociale*. As quaestor, Sertorius levied troops and procured arms, which he did with determination and celerity, gaining prestige in the process. However, nothing in Plutarch's narration leads us to think that Sertorius was an autonomous quaestor who only answered to the senate or that he was in charge of Cisalpine Gaul as his province. Everything, in particular the deeds he accomplished, points to him rather as a quaestor serving under the command of a higher magistrate with *imperium* who had Cisalpine Gaul as his *provincia* and whose name we do not know.[111] In short, there is no reason at all to include Cisalpine Gaul—or the *ager Gallicus* for that matter—as a regular or even occasional

---

107 Chandler 1978, 331 n. 20.
108 Mommsen, Röm.St. 2.557. Cf. Wesener 1963, 819.
109 Chandler 1978, 333: Sertorius was quaestor at Ariminium or at Ravenna; Loreto 1993, 497–500; Lintott 1999, 135: 'we also hear of a *provincia Gallica*, perhaps connected with the public land in the *ager Gallicus*.' Kunkel and Wittmann 1995, 530–531: in the course of the second century an administrative quaestorship was probably established in Cisalpine Gaul, although Plutarch's text on Sertorius is not clear. It is also possible that this quaestorship was created by Augustus together with other Italian quaestorships.
110 Plut. *Sert.* 4.1: ἐκ τούτου Σερτώριος ἐν τῇ Ἰβηρίᾳ διεβοήθη, καὶ ὅτε πρῶτον ἐπανῆκεν εἰς Ῥώμην, ταμίας ἀποδείκνυται τῆς περὶ Πάδον Γαλατίας ἐν δέοντι.
111 Harris 1976, 100, argues that Sertorius may have served under a praetor or alternatively he could have been sent to Gallia as *quaestor pro praetore* 'in a period when senior magistrates were in short supply.' Cf. Mattingly 1969, 507; Prag 2014, 197 n. 14.

quaestorian *provincia* in the Republican period. Needless to say, there is consequently no reason for the quaestor's headquarters somewhere in the region.

Finally, Mommsen proposes Cales in Campania as one of the stations of the Italian quaestorships, which is again conceived of as a fixed assignment.[112] Mommsen's assumption is based on an unnecessary emendation of Tacitus, in which Lipsius proposed to read Cales instead of *calles*.[113] The emendation should undoubtedly be rejected. Moreover, Cales, which is located about twenty kilometres from the sea, would make no sense as the headquarters for a naval quaestor.[114] The *calles* were trails and tracks that were used by livestock for transhumance and connected distant regions. Given that these *calles* were highly in great use during the Republican period, their preservation and protection had important economic implications.[115] In the aforementioned text, Tacitus describes the intervention of a quaestor in a slave rebellion in 24 AD in the region of Brundisium. In this context, he refers to the *calles* as a *provincia ex more vetere*, a phrase that suggests the possibility that it was already a quaestorian *provincia* during the Republic. Nevertheless, it must be borne in mind that there is no evidence for this conclusion.[116] The existence of a Republican quaestorian *provincia* focused on the *calles* is no more than speculation, let alone the possible date at which it could have been instituted.[117] At any rate, if this *provincia* ever existed during the Republic, it was no doubt an occasional one like the other Italian quaestorships, rather than a regular one assigned to a quaestor each year.[118]

---

112 Mommsen, Röm.St. 2.557.
113 Tac. *ann.* 4.27: *et erat isdem regionibus Curtius Lupus quaestor, cui provincia vetere ex more calles evenerant*.
114 Harris 1976, 99.
115 Toynbee 1965, 2.286–295; Waldherr 2002.
116 Mattingly 1957, 114–115, proffers the very unlikely possibility that the *quaestor callium* was in charge of the coinage of victoriates. Mattingly places the quaestorian base in Brundisium. Nothing supports either supposition.
117 Skydsgaard 1974, 17–18: 'there is a great probability that it is older than 60 B.C., when the senate – to annoy the *consul designatus*, Caesar – makes *silvae ac calles* a consular province.' According to Skydsgaard, it is possible that this quaestorian *provincia* was established in 267, although not necessarily was filled every year from that moment on. Harris 1976, 100, thinks that the *provincia* was probably created after the Hannibalic War. Cf. Rolfe 1915; Mattingly 1969, 509–510; Pasquinucci 1979, 141–142.
118 Harris 1976, 100.

Chapter 3:
The quaestorship within the political career: Age requirements and the *cursus honorum*

The dictator Sulla seems to have devoted a lot of attention to the quaestorship. The so-called *lex Cornelia de magistratibus*, which Sulla put into effect in 81, established the sequence in which regular magistracies had to be held. The first was the quaestorship, which automatically granted access to the senate[1] (in the pre-Sullan age the quaestorship also could lead to membership of the senate, but only after the censors officially enrolled a quaestor in the *album senatus*[2]) and which had to be held before running for higher magistracies.[3] In the post-Sullan period, therefore, the quaestorship was the first magistracy a Roman politician had to hold within his *cursus honorum*.[4] When Sulla put this new requirement in place, he also increased the number of quaestors to twenty, as Tacitus and the *lex Cornelia de XX quaestoribus* show.[5]

---

[1] It seems that Tacitus thought that increasing the number of quaestors had the purpose of generating new senators: *post lege Sullae viginti creati supplendo senatui, cui indicia tradiderat* (Tac. *ann.* 11.22.6). Cf. Sumner 1971, 248; Develin 1979, 97; D'Orta 1993, 288; Kunkel and Wittmann 1995, 514; Lintott 1999, 136; Covino 2013; Steel 2014, 336.

[2] Harris 1976, 105, points out that 'few ex-quaestors were probably refused admittance in the immediately pre-Sullan period, and some who had not been elected quaestors were admitted.' Badian 1983, 168 n. 33, rejects this conclusion on the basis that there is not sufficient evidence to support it. We certainly have very weak evidence, so providing a conclusive statement for the pre-Sullan period would be irresponsible. However, Harris' deduction could be essentially correct.

[3] App. *b.c.* 1.100–101, is our main source. According to Appian, Sulla prohibited anybody from holding the praetorship until he had held the quaestorship, and from being consul before he had been praetor. Sulla put Q. Lucretius Ofella to death because Ofella wanted to become a candidate for the consulship before he had been quaestor and praetor. Cf. Cic. *Phil.* 11.11.

[4] It must be taken into account that Sulla increased the number of senators from 300 to 600 by direct appointment. This means that members of the Sullan senate might not have held the quaestorship or any other magistracy (Ryan 1998c, 86–87, suggests that the concept *pedarii* was coined 'to distinguish between *senatores* who had held office and *senatores* who had never held office'). How many of them, after being designated senators by Sulla, were later elected quaestors as part of a regular *cursus honorum* we do not know (Ryan 1998c, 86 n. 210, seems to imply that Sulla's nominees regularly sought the quaestorship and that most of the quaestors of the seventies were from this category; however, there is no evidence to confirm this conjecture). That said, it is likely that some of them were satisfied with entering the senate and never sought an office (or perhaps they were happy aspiring just to the quaestorship). On the senate in the post-Sullan period, see Steel 2014 (on this particular subject 327–328). Cf. Suolahti 1955, 32: in the first century it was not unusual, at least until 69, that some who were already senators became military tribunes, an office that usually was held at the beginning of a political career before becoming a senator.

[5] Tac. *ann.* 11.22.6: *Post lege Sullae viginti creati supplendo senatui, cui indicia tradiderat.* On the *lex Cornelia de XX quaestoribus*, Keil 1902; Gabba 1983; Varvaro 1995; Crawford 1996.

Ancient sources do not explain why Sulla made the quaestorship a compulsory first step before running for other magistracies.[6] Given that the number of quaestors suddenly increased, making the office obligatory for a political career could have been a way of guaranteeing that there were enough candidates to fill the twenty positions; alternatively, the change could also have been a response to already existing structural problems. Was there a regular lack of candidates for quaestorship that the new obligatory nature of the magistracy aimed to address? Had it previously been an unattractive office? Before it was obligatory, did young Romans usually prefer to be candidates for offices that afforded greater visibility, such as the aedileship or the tribunate of the plebs?[7] As a matter of fact, it is very likely that a substantial number of politicians never held the quaestorship before 81.[8] Yet, the magistracy existed throughout the Republic and required a certain number of candidates every year to fill the vacant positions. As a consequence, it is legitimate to ask whether in previous centuries members of minor families used the quaestorship as a sort of a springboard to launch their careers, whereas individuals from prominent families did not need to hold the office to mount a successful campaign for higher office. The very low percentage of quaestors about whom we have any information in the pre-Sullan age makes it impossible to reach any definitive conclusion on this matter. Among the small number of known quaestors, we find both members of prominent families that later reached the consulship as well as members of obscure families who do not seem to have progressed beyond the quaestorship. Moreover, not everybody necessarily had the same big aspirations to pursue a complete political career that culminated in holding the highest office; undoubtedly, for many individuals the quaestorship (or even a minor office) could have constituted personal success.[9] Whatever the role of the quaestorship within the political career had been up to that time, it is evident that Sulla made this magistracy more attractive and gave it more prominence, particularly by making it an automatic door to the senate.[10]

---

6 Flower 2010, 119–130, emphasises Sulla's general intention of replacing tradition (*mos maiorum*) with law (*lex*). Cf. Steel 2014, 324.

7 Cicero's quaestorship in Sicily serves as a good example of the little attention that quaestors could receive at Rome (Cic. *Planc.* 64–65). In this respect, being a quaestor outside the city could have been quite different from being a urban quaestor, since the latter's duties entailed being in constant contact with senators and higher magistrates as well as being in the spotlight of public life, at least to some extent.

8 Evans – Kleijwegt 1992, 182 n. 6.

9 Given the high number of military tribunes, Suolahti 1955, 170–171 concludes that only a small part of them (perhaps around a quarter or fifth) were subsequently able to be elected quaestors. Those who had the benefits conferred by a famous name and a prominent family obviously had greater chances. For many individuals from the countryside, a military tribunate could be seen as sufficient success. Suolahti offers similar conclusions about the *IIviri navales* (196–197).

10 Syme 1980, 404, argues that a *homo novus* was no doubt interested in being elected quaestor *suo anno* as a means of asserting his merit. However, a *nobilis* did not need to worry and could wait longer to hold his first office. Syme's assertion should be qualified. A member of a prominent family could certainly expect to have a successful political career even if he had a delayed start. Neverthe-

The Sullan reforms must also have included age limits for the praetorship (40) and the consulate (43). Was there an age limit for the quaestorship too? A Ciceronian passage may suggest that there was an age requirement for the quaestorship in the post-Sullan period. In his speech in favour of Caelius, delivered in 56, Cicero describes Caelius as a man who was able to run for office at that period of his life.[11] The text is rather vague: it could imply that indeed there was a minimum age necessary to hold an office,[12] but it could also be interpreted as a more general reference to the regular timeframe in which young men fulfilled their first magistracy, without implying a fixed age. A second Ciceronian passage seems more decisive. In his fifth *Philippica*, Cicero proposes a *senatus consultum* in favour of Octavian in gratitude for his recent achievements in defence of the *res publica*. Cicero suggested that the young Caesar should be granted exceptional privileges: he should become senator at once and subsequently speak in the turn of the *praetorii*; additionally, it should be considered legal that he seek whatever magistracy he pleased, as if he had been quaestor the preceding year, that is, in 44.[13] As the first magistracy to be held, the quaestorship legally opened the door to higher offices. Cicero's text implies that there was an age requirement for the quaestorship, but tells us nothing about what that age was.[14] While neither of the Ciceronian passages is conclusive, they do suggest the existence of an unmentioned minimum age for holding the quaestorship.

Despite the lack of decisive evidence, scholars have unanimously made an assumption that there indeed was a fixed minimum age for holding the quaestorship. Furthermore, it has been generally agreed that that age was thirty in the post-Sullan period and, therefore, the minimum age to become a senator as well.[15] Astin, following Mommsen, asserts so much without hesitation as did Sumner, following Astin:

---

less, it should be borne in mind that after Sulla the quaestorship granted instant access to the senate; therefore, it is easy to imagine how important it was for every young Roman, including *nobiles*, to become a member of the most prestigious and influential institution of the Republic as soon as possible. Cf. Steel 2014, 337: in the post-Sullan period, the senate was joined each year by twenty quaestors, 'who logic would indicate came from a wider sector of society than had been the case for the eight or twelve elected before Sulla.'

11 Cic. *Cael.* 18: ...*et per aetatem magistratus petere posset*...
12 So Ryan 1996f, 43.
13 Cic. *Phil.* 5.46: ...*ob eas causas senatui placere C. Caesarem C. f., pontificem, pro praetore, senatorem esse sententiamque loco praetorio dicere, eiusque rationem, quemcumque magistratum petet, ita haberi, ut haberi per leges liceret, si anno superiore quaestor fuisset.*
14 Ryan 1996f, 43: 'The collocation of the words *rationem...haberi* and *anno superiore quaestor* proves that there was a minimum age for the quaestorship.' Karlowa 1885, 1.182–183, interprets Cicero as saying that Octavian would be considered old enough to hold the quaestorship of 44, that is, as having the minimum age for the magistracy. After some hesitation, Astin 1958, 41, takes Karlowa's interpretation as the most probable.
15 Mommsen, Röm.St. 1.548–553.

neither bothers to muster any ancient source as evidence.¹⁶ The problem is twofold: first, we have knowledge of a limited number of quaestors for the period; second, we very seldom know both a given individual's birthdate and the date of his quaestorship, the two pieces of information needed to calculate the age at which he held the office. Despite these difficulties, Ryan has carried out a prosopographical analysis of all known quaestors from the post-Sullan period for whom he could collect certain—or at least reasonably secure—information about their dates of birth and offices.¹⁷ Ultimately, he reaches the same conclusion as previous scholars had: thirty was the minimum age to hold the quaestorship in post-Sullan times.¹⁸ Ryan has collected twenty-one instances in which, in his opinion, he can demonstrate that the quaestorship was held at or above the age of thirty. On the contrary, there is not a single example in which the quaestorship was assumed before the age of thirty.¹⁹ In short, despite the meagre information, the combination of prosopographical and literary evidence allows us to assume that the minimum age for the quaestorship was thirty throughout the post-Sullan period.²⁰ What about during pre-Sullan times? Was there an age requirement then as well?

If the scarcity of information complicates the study of the quaestorship in the first century, the scant, fragmentary and frequently dubious nature of the evidence for the early and middle Republic makes the task even more arduous. Between

---

16 Astin 1958, 39; Sumner 1973, 7. Cf. Badian 1959a, 86–87: there was a minimum age for the quaestorship and no fixed interval after it; Wesener 1963, 808; Develin 1979, 96: establishing the minimum age at thirty, 'Sulla wished the official career to begin later than had been possible before.' More recently, Covino 2013, has asserted that Sulla fixed the minimum age to hold the quaestorship at thirty for patricians and thirty-two for plebeians. However, he provided no evidence for this statement.
17 Ryan 1996f.
18 See for instance Afzelius 1946, 269–275. Cf. Lintott 1999, 145.
19 Ryan 1996f, 39–42. Some of Ryan's details are disputable, but his overall conclusions stand. These are the twenty-one quaestors Ryan identified (between brackets the number in RE, followed by the age at which they presumably or certainly held the quaestorship): C. Aelius Paetus Staienus (Staienus 1) at least 31 (he was quaestor in 78 rather than 77, but this does not significantly change things, provided that he was born by 110–109); L. Aemilius (*Lepidus) Paullus (81) at least 32; M. Antonius (30) 31, originally a candidate, at age 30, for a quaestorship in 52; P. Autronius Paetus (7) at least 32; C. Cassius Longinus (59) at least 30; P. Clodius Pulcher (48) at least 31; (*Q.) Cornelius (5) at least 45 (if Q. Cornelius, urban quaestor in 44, is the *scriba* who was active under Sulla's dictatorship); P. Cornelius Lentulus Spinther (238) at least 30 (the year 71 is preferable for his quaestorship rather than 70–69, but he could have been 30 if he was born by 101); P. Cornelius Lentulus Sura (240) 32 or 33; L. Domitius Ahenobarbus (27) at least 31; C. Julius Caesar (131) probably 32; M. Junius Brutus (53) at least 30; L. Licinius Murena (123) at least 30; C. Marcius Figulus (63) at least 31 (Ryan dates his quaestorship to 75–74, but the date is speculative); Cn. Plancius (4) at least 32; C. Scribonius Curio (11) at least 31; Ser. Sulpicius Rufus (95) at least 30; M. Terentius Varro Lucullus (Licinius 109) 35 (Ryan dates his quaestorship to 81, but Varro Lucullus may have been quaestor and proquaestor in 86–83; if he was born in 117, in any case he held the quaestorship when he was over 30); M. Tullius Cicero (29) 30; L. Valerius Flaccus (179) at least thirty-one; P. Vatinius (*2) at least 30.
20 Incidentally, Syme 1987, 323, points out that the age of marriage of Roman senators in the late Republic was close to the age they held the quaestorship.

446, when Tacitus claims that the quaestors were elected by the people for the first time, and the outbreak of the Hannibalic War in 218, we know the names of only eighteen quaestors, including those recently discovered in the inscriptions on the Egadi *rostra*. Little more than their names are known. The possibility of compiling any reliable statistics on the ages of the men who held these quaestorships is, unfortunately, absolutely out of the question. In this period of the Roman Republic, when a fixed *cursus honorum* did not exist as such and the holding of the quaestorship was not obligatory,[21] the only thing we can take for granted is that the quaestorship could serve as one of several possible initial steps in a political career, particularly for patricians.[22] While we can generally assume that young people held the magistracy, determining any magistrate's precise age is impossible. Furthermore, it must be kept in mind that plebeians also had the opportunity to launch a political career by holding one of the ten annual positions of tribune of the plebs. Therefore, plebeians could be quaestors or tribunes of the plebs. Furthermore, nothing would have precluded them from holding the two offices in close succession.

Again, the dearth of evidence precludes us to reaching any firm conclusion regarding the frequency with which plebeians preferred to hold one of these offices or both. We know of the apparently exceptional case of L. (?) Caecilius Metellus, who was quaestor in 214. That year, after Rome had suffered her worst defeats in the Hannibalic War, a group of Roman citizens planned to flee Italy. According to Livy, the quaestor was the most prominent among them.[23] Everyone who attempted to flee was brought to trial and found guilty of treason. The punishment for the quaestor Metellus consisted of his demotion to the rank of *aerarius* by the censors, thus losing part of his rights as a Roman citizen.[24] Nonetheless, Metellus became tribune of the plebs in 213 and tried to indict the censors for having demoted him the year before. Metellus, therefore, held the quaestorship and the tribunate of the plebs in two consecutive years, 214 and 213. Given the trouble that he encountered during his quaestorship, one should ask whether Metellus was especially—and per-

---

21 Given that there was not a legally structured *cursus honorum*, we find some 'anomalies' in the historical record: for instance, sources tell us that L. Valerius Poplicola Potitus was quaestor in 446 (hence he was apparently one of the first quaestors elected by the people) after having already held the consulship in 449 (Tac. *ann.* 11.22; Liv. 3.39–41). Supposedly, T. Quinctius Capitolinus was quaestor in 458 after having been consul three times. Obviously, we cannot uncritically accept these accounts, as is usual for the sources on archaic Rome. Nonetheless, they do demonstrate that such a political career in the early Republic was feasible for later authors.
22 Develin 1979, 28: 'There is no reason to believe that the holding of a quaestorship led quickly to other honours. It was easily obtained and was part of the training.'
23 Liv. 24.18.3: *Princeps eorum M. Caecilius Metellus quaestor tum forte erat.*
24 Liv. 24.43.2–4: *...quaestorem eum proximo anno adempto equo tribu moverant atque aerarium fecerant propter coniurationem deserendae Italiae ad Cannas factam...* Cf. Val.Max. 2.9.8: *M. enim Atilius Regulus et L. Furius Philus M. Metellum quaestorem conpluresque equites Romanos, qui post infeliciter commissam Cannensem pugnam cum eo abituros se Italia iuraverant, dereptis equis publicis inter aerarios referendos curaverunt.* Cf. Liv. 4.24.7; Cic. *Cluent.* 122. On this episode, see Tatum 1990b, 37.

haps unusually—interested in holding the tribunate, since it gave him the opportunity to take revenge on the censors.

The career of Q. Petillius Spurinus provides the other instance of a plebeian holding the quaestorship and the tribunate of the plebs successively. He was tribune in 187, and Livy shows that he also was quaestor at some point.[25] Assuming that it is likely that the quaestorship preceded his tribunate, he may have been quaestor by 189, although this date is only conjectural.[26] The important point is that he held both offices.

There are a very small number of other cases that shed light on an individual's political career. The *elogium* of Ap. Claudius Caecus, for instance, gives the following information: *Appius Claudius C. f. Caecus censor cos. bis dict. interrex III pr. II aed. cur. II q. tr. mil. III.*[27] According to the inscription, Ap. Claudius Caecus held the quaestorship (presumably at some point before 315) after having been military tribune (three times) and before being elected curule aedile. Caecus' *cursus honorum* resembles, perhaps suspiciously, the usual *cursus honorum* followed by politicians for subsequent eras. Nonetheless, the holding of the quaestorship at the very beginning of his career remains perfectly plausible.

Another *elogium* provides information about Q. Fabius Maximus Verrucosus, the Cunctator, who was consul, as well as dictator, several times before and during the Hannibalic War: *(Q. Fabius) Q. f. Maximus dictator bis cos. V ce(n)sor interrex II aed. cur. q. II tr. mil. II pontifex augur primo consulatu Ligures subegit...*[28] The *elogium* informs us that Fabius Maximus was, exceptionally, quaestor twice before becoming curule aedile and after having been military tribune twice. Again, his quaestorship took place towards the beginning of his political career, though the precise dates are unknown (certainly before 238–237) and there is no indication of how old Fabius Maximus was when he held his quaestorships.[29] Fabius Maximus may have held both quaestorships before his aedileship, but not necessarily.[30] At a time when the *cursus honorum* was not yet strictly fixed, it would have been possible for the second quaestorship to follow the aedileship. In any case, the repetition of the same office would not have implied a regression in Fabius Maximus' political career.[31] Furthermore, it must be noted that, according to his *elogium*, he was never praetor. Therefore, the

---

[25] Liv. 40.29.10: *et erat familiaris usus, quod scribam eum quaestor Q. Petilius in decuriam legerat*.
[26] Broughton MRR, 1.366 and 2.600: quaestor probably by 188; Develin 1978a, 143; 1979, 26.
[27] CIL I² 192 = Incr. Ital. 13.3.79. Cf. Ferenczy 1965; Humm 2005, 21–34 and 113–114.
[28] CIL I² 193 = Inscr. Ital. 13.3.80.
[29] Sumner 1973, 30–32, argues that Verrucosus' birthdate could not have been long before 265.
[30] Beck 2005, 274–275: both quaestorships must be dated to some point before his aedileship, which he held in 235 at the very latest.
[31] Referring to the first century in his speech against Piso, Cicero mentions a 'quaestor of aedilician rank' (*quaestor aedilicius*: Cic. *Pis.* 36), that is, a quaestor who had previously been aedile. We do not know any further details about this unusual late Republican *cursus honorum*.

second quaestorship, if he held it after his aedileship, could have substituted, so to speak, the praetorship in Fabius Maximus' *cursus honorum*.

The picture becomes a bit clearer between 218 and 167, since we have Livy's account for the period. Nevertheless, we know of only a very small portion of quaestors, and precious little is known about them beyond their names. In general, little has been preserved in relation to the role that the quaestorship played within the *cursus honorum*.

Some *elogia* again provide a snapshot of the *cursus honorum* of several politicians at the beginning of the second century. This includes L. Cornelius Scipio Asiaticus: *(L. Corneli)us P.f. S(cipio Asia)ticus (cos. pr. aed. cu)r. q. tr.(mil.).*[32] Scipio Asiaticus, who was consul in 190, must have been quaestor at some point before 196.[33] As happened with Ap. Claudius Caecus and Q. Fabius Maximus, Scipio Asiaticus also held his quaestorship after having served as military tribune and before becoming a curule aedile. The same occurred with L. Aemilius Paullus, the consul of 182 and 168: *L. Aemilius L. f. Paullus cos. II cens. interrex pr. aed. cur. q. tr. mil. tertio aug.*[34] His *elogium* provides the only evidence of Aemilius Paullus' quaestorship. Since Aemilius Paullus was aedile in 193 and triumvir for the foundation of the colony of Croton in 194,[35] he must have been quaestor before 194, perhaps in 195. Once again, we find that the quaestorship fell between a military tribuneship and curule aedileship.

Unfortunately, this series of *elogia* (Claudius Caecus at the end of the fourth century, Fabius Maximus at the end of the third century, Scipio Asiaticus and Aemilius Paullus at the beginning of the second century) does not allow us to establish with certainty the age at which these quaestors held the magistracy.[36] Although these men represent just a small sample of the total number of quaestors for such a long period, their *elogia* do reveal a certain degree of commonality in the quaestorship's role within the political career throughout the middle Republic: the quaestorship was very frequently the first regular magistracy to be held and was performed between the military tribuneship and aedileship.[37] At any rate, since the quaestorship was not compulsory at that point, we should not assume that every Roman politician held it. Indeed, the fact that a fixed *cursus honorum* did not exist would have allowed for the existence of very different kinds of political careers. While we have just stated

---

32 CIL I² 194 = Inscr. Ital. 13.3.15.
33 Sobeck 1909, 10–11; Broughton MRR, 1.336; Beck 2005, 359–360.
34 CIL I² 194 = Inscr. Ital. 13.2.81.
35 Liv. 34.45.3–5; 35.10.11–12. Cf. Plut. *Aem.* 3.1.
36 In his analysis of the ages of magistrates before 180, Develin 1979, 68, suggests that Cn. Tremellius Flaccus was quaestor in 206 when he was twenty-seven, before becoming aedile in 203 at thirty and praetor in 202 at thirty-one.
37 Cn. Cornelius Lentulus is another example of someone holding his quaestorship (in 212) after having been military tribune (in 216) and before the curule aedileship (in 205). According to Develin 1979, 68, he may have been quaestor at the age of 25. The same happened with M. Porcius Cato: military tribune in 214, quaestor in 204 and plebeian aedile in 199. If Cato was born in 234, he was quaestor at 30 (Sumner, 1973, 33; Develin 1979, 71).

that the aedileship usually appears to have followed the quaestorship,[38] C. Terentius Varro was quaestor before 222 and praetor in 218, without any hint that he was aedile between these offices. The same can be said of Q. Fabius Labeo, urban quaestor in 196 and praetor in 189.[39]

In the period that Scipio Asiaticus and Aemilius Paullus were quaestors, Livy also relates the extraordinary political career of T. Quinctius Flamininus. The historian raises the question of whether he could have been elected consul immediately after having been quaestor.[40] The exact meaning of the expression *consulatum ex quaestura petere* has proven controversial. While it seems clear that Flamininus held the consulship after the quaestorship without having held either the aedileship or the praetorship, what exactly does Livy mean beyond that? Did Flamininus become consul in 198 shortly after his quaestorship or directly after being quaestor in 199? Broughton notes that *ex quaestura* could indicate that Flamininus was quaestor in 199 and proceeded immediately to the consulship, but, in his opinion, this expression could also mean that some time had elapsed between two offices.[41] More emphatically, Badian asserts that *ex quaestura* does not mean 'straight after the quaestorship'; accordingly, he dates Flamininus' quaestorship to 206, after his military tribunate under the consul Marcellus in 208 and before he was placed in command at Tarentum in 205.[42] In contrast, Pfeilschifter has argued that Livy's text means that Flamininus moved directly from the quaestorship in 199 to the consulship in 198. In particular the phrase *transcendendo media summa imis continuare* seems to imply, in his opinion, a continuation between the two magistracies.[43]

While the expression *consulatum ex quaestura petere* cannot be rid of all ambiguity, the most probable interpretation is that it refers to the exceptional continuation between quaestorship and consulate. The extraordinary character of the transition from one office to the next would explain not only why the tribunes of the plebs opposed Flamininus' bid for the consulship, but also why Livy emphasises the con-

---

38 We can add to the aforementioned examples some additional cases. M. Valerius Falto was quaestor before 206 and curule aedile in 203 (Develin 1979, 70, supposes that he was quaestor at the age of twenty-five). C. Flaminius was quaestor in 210 and curule aedile in 196 (Develin 1979, 72, dates his quaestorship to 209 when he was probably twenty-seven years old). C. Laelius was quaestor in 202 and plebeian aedile in 197 (before his quaestorship, he had held several military offices during the Hannibalic War). P. Cornelius Scipio Nasica was quaestor at some point between 203 and 199, and afterwards he was curule aedile in 197. L. Cornelius Scipio Asiaticus was quaestor before 196 and curule aedile perhaps in 195. L. Aemilius Paullus was quaestor by 195 and curule aedile in 193.
39 Develin 1979, 74, suggests that he may have been quaestor when twenty-five.
40 Liv. 32.7.8–10: *quae ipsa per M. Fulvium et M'. Curium tribunos plebis impediebantur, quod T. Quinctium Flamininum consulatum ex quaestura petere non patiebantur: iam aedilitatem praeturamque fastidiri nec per honorum gradus, documentum sui dantes, nobiles homines tendere ad consulatum, sed transcendendo media summa imis continuare.*
41 Broughton MRR, 1.328 and 329 n. 2.
42 Badian 1971b.
43 Pfeilschifter 2005, 34–36.

frontation. At any rate, the senate considered Flamininus' candidacy for the consulship to be legal, although he had not held either of the intermediate magistracies, the aedileship or the praetorship. In the end, he was elected consul for 198.

The apparent irregularity committed by Flamininus—and authorised by the senate—had nothing to do with his quaestorship: he followed the normal pattern of holding the office at the beginning of his career after being a military tribune. The novelty was to hold the consulship directly after the quaestorship without first passing through the aedileship and praetorship. His behaviour, contrary to tradition, was ultimately possible because there was no strict legal regulation regarding the political career at that moment. This episode occurred in the first years of the second century, a period marked by especially fierce electoral competition,[44] when the senate was presumably first persuaded of the utility of regulating the political career. As a consequence, the *lex Villia annalis* was passed in 180. It marked a fundamental reorganisation of the political career and ushered in the fixed *cursus honorum*.[45] As the Sullan reforms later reasserted, the *lex Villia* established the order in which the magistracies were to be held and the minimum age for at least the higher offices.[46] Did it establish a fixed minimum age for the quaestorship too? This question has been much discussed.

Mommsen argues that the *lex Villia* established a minimum age for holding all magistracies. According to Mommsen, once a Roman citizen had accomplished the mandatory ten years of military service, he could then become quaestor at the age of twenty-seven.[47] However, two important points remain uncertain: was the quaestorship a compulsory step to aspire to the higher magistracies? Was there a minimum age to hold the quaestorship?

Mommsen' proposal of twenty-seven as the minimum age for the quaestorship is based on Polybius' assertion that nobody was eligible for any political office unless he had completed ten years of military service.[48] As usual, Mommsen constructs his argument on a strict and rigid legal framework: given that military service was compulsory for every Roman with political aspirations and that one could not begin those duties before being seventeen,[49] the minimum age to hold the quaestorship

---

44 Rögler 1962, 116–119; Develin 1979, 81–82; Evans – Kleijwegt 1992, 184; Beck 2005, 141–147.
45 On the *lex Villia* see Afzelius 1946; Astin 1958; Rögler 1962; Develin 1979, esp. 81–95; Evans – Kleijwegt 1992; Timmer 2005 and 2008, 84–95; Beck 2005, 57–61. Cf. Lundgreen 2011, 74–75, who argues that the *lex Villia* solidified a standing tradition.
46 Liv. 40.44.1: *Eo anno rogatio primum lata est ab L. Villio tribuno plebis, quot annos nati quemque magistratum peterent caperentque*. The text of Livy makes it clear that the *lex Villia* was the first law to set fixed ages for accessing the magistracies.
47 Mommsen, Röm.St. 1.544–548.
48 Pol. 6.19.4.
49 Liv. 25.5.8: *tribuni plebis, si iis videretur, ad populum ferrent ut, qui minores septendecim annis sacramento dixissent, iis perinde stipendia procederent ac si septendecim annorum aut maiores milites facti essent*; Gell. 10.28: *...pueros esse existimasse, qui minores essent annis septem decem, atque inde ab anno septimo decimo, quo idoneos iam esse reipublicae arbitraretur, milites scripsisse...* Cf.

should be set at twenty-seven. The fact that Polybius lived in Rome in the second century and was connected to aristocratic circles could very well lead us to assume that his account is correct.

There is indeed plenty of evidence for the tradition of fulfilling military service, and it is possible that ten years was the normal length of that service.[50] However, it is not evident that the completion of ten years of military service was obligatory for those who aspired to any political magistracy during the second century.[51] In addition, recruitment before the age of seventeen must have been quite common in the mid-second century, since Caius Gracchus introduced a law to forbid it.[52] Actually, both Tiberius and Caius Gracchus seem to have served in the military before turning seventeen: Tiberius, who was born in 163 or 162, was at Carthage with Scipio Aemilianus in 147–146, while Caius, born in 154 or 153, was quaestor in 126 after completing a twelve-year stint in the military.[53] The ten years required to qualify for candidacy for a regular office apparently included those who had served before the age of seventeen, though such a situation should not be taken as normal.

The problem, again, is the lack of evidence, since we know of just a limited number of second-century quaestors; within this already limited set, we know biographical details for only a few. This precludes any statistical approach to the question, which, in turn, makes it difficult to reach a truly convincing conclusion.[54] In his thorough study of the issue, Astin suggests that the evidence points towards the quaestorship not being a compulsory prerequisite for higher magistracies in the pre-Sullan period;[55] furthermore, he continues, there are reasons to doubt that a legally sanctioned minimum age for the quaestorship existed.[56] All in all, the meagre evidence that we have does suggest that Mommsen was right to place the usual age of quaestors in their late twenties. That same evidence, however, does not allow us to establish twenty-seven as the fixed legal minimum with any level of confidence, as he proposed. We have only a few quaestors in the second century whose age can possibly be deduced: Ti. Gracchus was twenty-four or twenty-five when he held the quaestor-

---

Astin 1958, 42: 'There is no doubt that seventeen was the age at which attendance at the levy became compulsory.'
50 See Harris 1979a, 11–12. Cf. Lintott 1999, 145.
51 Beck 2005, 57. However, Develin 1979, 59 and 88, assumes that the rule was generally followed. Develin accepts that military service normally began at 17, but it could begin two years earlier, as the case of Ti. Gracchus demonstrates.
52 Plut. *C.Gr.* 5.1. Cf. Astin 1958, 43.
53 Plut. *Ti.Gr.* 3.1; 4.4; *C.Gr.* 1.2; 2.5. Cf. Astin 1958, 43.
54 Astin 1958, 29.
55 This is the categorical conclusion offered by Timmer 2008, 90: '...weil die Quästur im 2. Jahrhundert v.Chr. nicht Voraussetzung für die Bekleidung anderer Ämter war.'
56 Astin 1958, 46. Evans – Kleijwegt 1992, 182 n. 6: 'The *lex Villia* cannot have enforced a legal minimum age for the quaestorship, since this office was not a pre-requisite for the consulship. If the quaestorship was not regarded as a political office then the military service might not necessarily have applied.' For a similar analysis, Timmer 2005, 57; 2008, 90 and n. 300.

ship in 137,⁵⁷ while his brother Caius was quaestor in 126 when he was twenty-six or twenty-seven; M. Antonius was quaestor in 113 at the age of twenty-nine; finally, Sulla held the quaestorship in 107 when he was thirty.⁵⁸

Astin is probably right to conclude that the question must remain undecided due to the lack of clear-cut evidence. If there was a minimum age for the quaestorship, it was in all probability introduced in the *lex Villia*. Nevertheless, we cannot determine whether that age requirement actually existed; even if we could make such a determination, there is no way of knowing whether the prescribed age would have been twenty-seven. Instead, it is preferable to accept that in the second century the *cursum honorum* was more flexible than Mommsen supposed and that this flexibility applied in particular to the quaestorship.⁵⁹ All in all, there is no reason to doubt that for young Roman aristocrats living in the second century (and the entire Republic for that matter), the quaestorship constituted the usual—but perhaps not obligatory—first regular office to be held within a political career. Furthermore, all evidence indicates that these young men usually held magistracy in their late twenties.

As in previous periods, the military tribunate must have preceded the quaestorship in the early political career of many Romans. So much is explicitly seen in a few cases, such as that of L. Manlius (Acidinus?) (military tribune in 171 and quaestor in 168) and L. Cornelius Scipio (military tribune by 168 and quaestor in 167). With the passing of the *lex Villia*, the aedileship became a compulsory office for those seeking the higher magistracies; accordingly, it became the office that usually followed the quaestorship: the cases of P. Licinius Crassus Dives Mucianus (quaestor in 151 and curule aedile by 142), Cn. Cornelius Scipio Hispanus (quaestor by 150 and curule aedile by 141) and C. Sempronius Tuditanus (quaestor in 145 and aedile by 135) attest to this fact. As in previous periods, the tribunate of the plebs provided plebeians another possible office to be held after the quaestorship, as several conspicuous examples demonstrate, including both Gracchi brothers (Tiberius was quaestor in 137 and tribune of the plebs in 133, while his brother Caius was quaestor in 126 and tribune in

---

57 According to Plutarch (*C.Gr.* 1.2.), Tiberius Gracchus held the quaestorship in 137 and had not yet turned thirty when he died in 133. It has been supposed that he was born around 162, hence his probable age when he was a quaestor. Nevertheless, the year 162 for his birthday has been called into question. See Rögler 1962, 79: if Ti. Gracchus was born in 162, he was 25 when he held the quaestorship; Evans – Kleijwegt 1992, 194; Timmer 2008, 86 n. 283.
58 See Astin 1958, 44–45.
59 Develin 1979, 59, implicitly rejects the existence of a fixed minimum age for the quaestorship in the pre-Sullan period and rather defends a flexible range: 'Thus we may safely assume a normal minimum age of 25 to 27 for quaestors.' Moreover: 'Thus, usually one's first office would be held at 27, perhaps at 25.' Furthermore, Develin establishes, not without hesitations, a hypothetical difference between patricians and plebeians: 'Patricians might be quaestors at 25 and so possibly aediles at an earlier age, but perhaps 25 was not usual; it was also possibly open to established plebeian families' (80). Finally, when Develin speaks about the period after the passage of the *lex Villia*, he asserts that '25 remained the minimum for candidacy for the quaestorship' (88), assuming that ten years' military service was required before public office.

123). The *elogium* of C. Marius shows that he was tribune of the plebs after having been quaestor: *C. Marius C.f. cos.VII pr. tr. pl. q. aug. tr. militum...*[60] The same career path is attested for L. Licinius Crassus, Q. Mucius Scaevola and C. Servilius Glaucia. However, C. Norbanus (Balbus?) was tribune of the plebs in 103, prior to holding the quaestorship, probably in 99. The order in which Norbanus held the lower offices may stand out as rather unusual, but merely confirms that during the period of Marius, Crassus, Scaevola and Glaucia nobody was obliged to be quaestor before becoming tribune of the plebs.

By the end of the second century and the beginning of the first century, we find evidence for a new pattern: the quaestorship alternating with the office of *monetalis* — and no doubt with the military tribunate and other minor offices — as the first magistracy held by young Romans.[61] As shown in his *elogium*, C. Claudius Pulcher (RE 302) began his political career by holding a quaestorship, probably shortly before 110, prior to a moneyership: *q. III vir a. a. a. f. f. aed. cur. iudex q. veneficis pr. repetundis curator vis sternundis cos. cum M. Perperna.*[62] For this period, this was hardly an extraordinary combination at the beginning of the *cursus honorum*. Around the same time, we find the same sequence in the career of L. Memmius, who was quaestor before 112 and *monetalis* in 109 or 108.[63] Finally L. Appuleius Saturninus may successively have been quaestor, moneyer and tribune of the plebs (see the Prosopography for the discussion of the dates). Other combinations of offices were also possible: Q. Minucius Thermus seems to have been moneyer in 103 before holding the quaestorship. According to Cicero, M. Fonteius was *triumvir monetalis* and quaestor at the beginning of his political career.[64] Apparently, Fonteius was a *monetalis* before hold-

---

60 CIL I² 195 = Inscr. Ital. 13.3.83.
61 Six boards of minor officers were collectively known as the *vigintisexviri*, among whom there were the *tresviri monetales* (Cic. leg. 3.6: *Minoris magistratus partiti iuris ploeres in ploera sunto. Militiae quibus iussi erunt imperanto eorumque tribuni sunto. Domi pecuniam publicam custodiunto, vincula sontium servanto, capitalia vindicanto, aes argentum aurumve publice signanto, litis contractas iudicanto, <quod> quodcumque senatus creverit agunto.* Cf. Dig. 1.2.2.29–31, according to Pomponius). On the vigintisexvirate see Purcell 1996. We only know the moneyers thanks to preserved issues that they struck; undoubtedly, other young Romans with political aspirations took charge of other duties included within this *collegium* of minor offices as a part of their training. Unfortunately, we have no evidence that allows us to determine specifically the role that these offices served in relation to the quaestorship or the *cursus honorum* more generally; presumably it was a similar role to that of a moneyership.
62 CIL I² 200 = ILS 45. Hamilton 1969, 187: this is the earliest surviving reference to the post of *monetalis*. It suggests that holding a minor office was not considered a necessary preliminary step to the *cursus honorum*. Actually, the quaestorship and moneyership of L. Memmius seem to have been contemporary to those of Claudius Pulcher. In any case, Hamilton's conclusion seems correct.
63 On the date of his coinage, see Crawford RRC 315 no. 304 (see the Prosopography for more details).
64 Cic. *Font.* 5: *Duorum magistratuum, quorum uterque in pecunia maxima tractanda procurandaque versatus est, triumviratus et quaesturae...*

ing the urban quaestorship.[65] In the post-Sullan age the quaestorship became compulsory as the first regular magistracy in the *cursus honorum*, but many young Romans at the beginning of a political career held the office of *monetalis* as a supplementary post that helped them raise their profiles within society.

To summarise, throughout the Republic the quaestorship was the first or one of the first regular offices in the political career of a Roman citizen, following military service. In the pre-Sullan age, before the passage of the *lex Villia annalis*, a fixed *cursus honorum* did not exist. Consequently, we should not assume that every politician in that period held the quaestorship, since they could begin their career with any other magistracy. Nevertheless, the quaestorship appears to have usually been the first office (often after being a military tribune) and to have normally preceded the aedileship or sometimes the tribunate of the plebs. That said, this was not always the case: in this period it was apparently possible to jump from quaestorship to a higher magistracy. There was no minimum age to access to the quaestorship, although quaestors must always have been youngsters, probably in their late twenties or around thirty years old.

The *lex Villia annalis* regulated the *cursus honorum* for the first time in 180. As a result, the minimum ages for aedileship, praetorship and consulship were established, but apparently not for the quaestorship. Quaestors throughout the second century continued to hold the office, nonetheless, in their late twenties or around thirty, as had previously been the case. The quaestorship does not seem to have become a prerequisite for reaching a superior magistracy, but it remained the normal office for an aspiring politician to hold before running for the aedileship; sometimes it was held in close conjunction with the office of *triumvir monetalis* or other minor offices included among the *vigintisexviri* and frequently with a military tribuneship. Finally, the dictator Sulla passed the so-called *lex Cornelia de magistratibus*, which updated the *lex Villia* confirming the sequence of the magistracies within the *cursus honorum* and introducing new regulations. From that moment forward, the quaestorship became the obligatory first magistracy in the political career and it automatically granted access to the senate. It was probably only at this point that a minimum age, 30 years, was established as a condition for holding the office.

---

[65] Crawford RRC, 361, dates his moneyership before 87.

Chapter 4:
Election, entry into office and allocation of quaestorian *provinciae*

Election of quaestors and date of their entry into office

As we have seen in chapter one, it is quite possible that early on quaestors were directly chosen by the highest Republican magistrates. According to Tacitus, quaestors were first elected by the people in 447–446.[1] Since the quaestorship was a lower magistracy, quaestors were elected in the *comitia tributa* from that time on, if we accept Tacitus' chronology.[2] The little evidence that we have suggests that the magistrates who presided over quaestorian elections were the consuls.[3] This is shown in the episode narrated by Cicero for the year 45. The consul Q. Fabius Maximus was in charge of overseeing the quaestorian elections, which in 45 were scheduled on the last day of the year. In preparation for the event, Maximus' consular chair was set out, but soon afterwards taken away, after word spread that he had suddenly died. As a consequence, Maximus was replaced at once by C. Caninius Rebilus, who held the consulship for just a few hours, until the new consuls entered office on the next day.[4]

The order in which Roman magistrates were elected was determined by each office's rank, beginning with the highest magistracy and finishing with the lower offices. Given that the quaestorship was the first magistracy within the *cursus honorum*, quaestors were the last magistrates to be elected each year.[5] On different occasions throughout the Republic, Livy betrays the existence of a specific order for elections, which always begin with the consuls. This had apparently been the case since early times, for example in 409 when the first plebeian quaestors were supposedly elected.[6] Cassius Dio provides definitive evidence for the late Republic: describing the confrontation between Milo and Clodius in 57, he specifies that the elections for the aedileship, the magistracy for which Clodius was running, had to be held before those for the quaestors.[7] Therefore, a law—or at least a standing tradition—must have existed at the time that regulated the order in which magistrates were elected. This law (or tradition) could already have been in force in previous centuries.

---

[1] Tac. *ann.* 11.22.
[2] Aulus Gellius reproduces the words of M. Messalla: *Minoribus creatis magistratibus tributis comitiis magistratus, sed iustus curiata datur lege; maiores centuriatis comitiis fiunt* (Gell. 13.15.4).
[3] Mommsen, Röm.St. II 1.517; Wesener 1963, 807.
[4] Cic. *fam.* 7.30. Cf. Broughton MRR, 2.304–305; Sumner 1971, 363.
[5] Mommsen, Röm.St. I 561; II 1.517.
[6] Liv. 4.54.1–3. Cf. 4.44.1–2.
[7] Cass. Dio 39.7.4.

Consequently, the date of quaestorian elections was directly connected to the dates on which the other magistrates were elected. Throughout the Republican age, the elections were usually held at the end of the consular year, as Livy repeatedly points out, in particular for the first decades of the second century.[8] In 187, the consular elections took place on the twelfth day before the Calends of March, approximately one month before the new consuls would enter office on the Ides of March. The praetorian elections were held the following day.[9] Nothing is directly said about the elections of the aediles and quaestors, which may have taken place soon afterwards (perhaps on the following day or within two days). In 186, the elections were once again held at the end of the consular year, either in late February or at the very beginning of March.[10] The situation changed once the consuls began to enter office on 1st January from 153 onwards. The elections of all magistrates obviously had to be transferred to another time of the year. In all likelihood, at first this continued to take place near the end of the consular year sometime in autumn.[11] Starting at some point in the first century, elections were usually held in the summer, apparently most often in July. This is well attested throughout the period,[12] although political instability could lead to exceptions, especially—but not solely—in the 50s and 40s.[13]

Some evidence for the post-Sullan age shows that quaestors entered office on the Nones of December, that is, on 5th December. The *lex Cornelia de XX quaestoribus*, issued by the dictator Sulla in 81, alludes several times to *apparitores* attending the new quaestors from 5th December: *co(n)s(ules) quei nunc sunt, iei ante k(alendas) Decembreis primas de eis, quei cives Romanei sunt, viatorem unum legunto, quei in ea decuria viator appareat, quam decuriam viatorum ex noneis Decembribus primeis*

---

8 See Pina Polo 2011, 16–17.
9 Liv. 38.42.1–2: *Exitu prope anni M. Valerius consul ex Liguribus ad magistratus subrogandos Romam venit nulla memorabili in provincia gesta re, ut ea probabilis morae causa esset, quod solito serius ad comitia venisset. Comitia consulibus rogandis fuerunt a. D. XII. Kal. Martias... Postero die praetores facti...*
10 According to Livy, Cn. Manlius Vulso celebrated his triumph on the third day before the Nones of March, once the new magistrates had been elected: *Extremo anni, magistratibus iam creatis, ante diem tertium nonas Martias Cn. Manlius Vulso de Gallis qui Asiam incolunt triumphavit* (Liv. 39.6.3). For other examples of elections taking place at the end of the consular year, see Liv. 39.23.1 (year 185); 42.28.1 (year 171).
11 Sallust (*Iug.* 27.4; 36–37; 44.3; 114.3) signals that during the last few decades of the second century the end of the year was the time when elections were usually held. The delay in holding the elections that Sallust mentions could be explained by his belief that the comitia took place during the summer, as was the case in his own lifetime. According to his account, however, the fact is that the elections of 112, 110 and 109 were held at the end of the year. See Pina Polo 2013, 424 n. 20. Cf. Paul 1984, 89, 108–109, 135 and 258: Paul assumes that consular elections at that time usually took place in the autumn, specifically in October or November.
12 Michels 1967, 58–59.
13 Pina Polo 2011, 284–287.

quaestoribus ad aerarium apparere oportet oportebit.[14] According to Cicero, P. Sulpicius was one of the jurors in the trial against Verres in 70, but he was obliged to give up his position on the Nones of December when he had to take up his new office. Although Cicero does not expressly identify this office as the quaestorship, there can be no doubt about the matter, since this was the only magistracy that began on that date during that period.[15] Sulpicius, therefore, held the quaestorship in 69, having entered office on 5th December 70. The Gronovian scholiast is unequivocal when commenting this passage: *quaesturam intellegimus. Nam omnes ceteri magistratus Kal. Ian. procedebant, soli vero quaestores Nonis Dec.*[16]

One more Ciceronian passage indirectly gives evidence for this date. In a passage from the fourth *Catilinarian* where Cicero emphasises the various groups that supported him against the plot, he singles out the scribes, who happened to be concentrated in large numbers around the *aerarium* during his speech.[17] The fourth Catilinarian was delivered in the senate on the Nones of December 63. The new quaestors had entered office that day, when it was also decided to which magistrate each scribe (as well as the other *apparitores*) would be attached for the following year. The drawing of lots took place *apud aerarium*, which explains why there were so many scribes at the treasury that day.[18]

No ancient source offers a rationale for why the quaestors entered office on this particular date. Indeed, this was earlier than the tribunes of the plebs, who began on 10th December, and the other magistrates, who assumed their offices on 1st January.[19] As a possible explanation for the peculiar date, Mommsen stresses that there would have been a good deal of necessary administrative preparation before the higher magistrates took office. This interpretation is as reasonable as it is conjectural.[20] Kunkel and Wittmann argue that the specific reason was that the new quaestors—really only the urban quaestors—were responsible for the allotment of the next year's jurors.[21] Since this was one of the tasks that the urban quaestors performed during

---

14 *Lex Cornelia de XX quaestoribus* ll. 7–11. Crawford 1996, 1.294 and 297: 'The consuls who are now in office, they before the Kalends of December next following are to choose, from those who are Roman citizens, one messenger who may attend as messenger in that group, which group of messengers it is or shall be appropriate that it attend on the quaestors at the treasury from the Nones of December next following.' See similar statements in *Lex Cornelia de XX quaestoribus* ll. 14; 18; 22; 26; and 30.
15 Cic. *Verr.* 1.30: *P. Sulpicius, iudex tristis et integer, magistratum ineat oportet Nonis Decembribus.*
16 Schol. Gronov. p. 337 Stangl.
17 Cic. *Cat.* 4.15: *scribas item universos, quos cum casu hic dies ad aerarium frequentasset, video ab expectatione sortis ad salutem communem esse conversos.*
18 Schol.Bob. *in Clod. et Cur.* fr.11 p.87 Stangl: *Aput aerarium sortiri provincias et quaestores solebant et scribae, ut pro certo appareret in quam provinciam vel cum quo praeside proficiscerentur.* Cf. Plin. *ep.* 4.12.2. Cf. David 2007, 42–43; 2019, 96.
19 Lintott 1999, 134 n. 52: 'Their date of entry into office is presumably of ancient origin, but remains mysterious.'
20 Mommsen, Röm.St. I 585.
21 Kunkel and Wittmann 1995, 87 n. 119.

the late Republic, Kunkel and Wittman may have correctly identified one of the reasons for the quaestors' earlier entry into office. There may also have been a connection with the end of the financial year: it appears that as one of their first orders of business, the urban quaestors had to scrutinise their predecessors' accounts as well as the accounts of the state in general. The final weeks of the year could have been dedicated to this task before the beginning of the new fiscal year. In addition, the new quaestors—again the urban quaestors in particular—could have used this time to get familiar with the administration of the treasury, relying on the help and expertise of the scribes who actually managed it every year.

More recently, Covino has suggested that this unusual date could be a vestige of ancient times. This would imply that quaestors had always entered office on 5th December throughout the Republic: 'their unusual date of entry to office, December 5, speaks to the antiquity of the position.'[22] However, this is highly unlikely. As a matter of fact, if we accept that throughout the Republic the quaestorian elections usually took place soon after the election of the higher magistrates, this would make 5th December an impossible date for new quaestors to take office until the year 153, since we know that the elections of higher magistrates were held at the end of the consular year, well after 5th December.[23] But even if this procedure for elections is not accepted, the date of 5th December remains quite implausible. According to the ancient sources, consuls did not take office on a fixed date during the early Republic.[24] On the contrary, sources show consuls taking office on a variety of different dates, namely in the months of May, Quinctilis, Sextilis, September, October and December.[25] While the fragmentary information on the early Republic certainly raises doubts about the credibility of the details found in our sources, in this case the general conclusion is quite palatable: consuls entered office on a variety of dates during the first centuries of the Republic, depending on historical circumstances; consequently, the duration of the consular year was variable. As Mommsen has maintained, the situation changed in the third century, when the consular year was regulated so that it

---

22 Covino 2013.
23 Kunkel and Wittmann 1995, 87 n. 119, point out that 5th December for the entry of quaestors into office is incompatible with the dates for elections before 153 and very problematic for the period between 153 and Sulla.
24 On consuls taking office throughout the Republic, see Pina Polo 2011, 13–15.
25 In the year 493 the consuls took office on the Calends of September (Dion.Hal. 6.49.1); in 476, in the month of Sextilis (Dion.Hal. 9.25.1); in 463, on the Calends of Sextilis (Liv. 3.6.1); in 462, three days before the Ides of Sextilis (Liv. 3.8.2); in 451 and 450 they entered office on the Ides of May (Liv. 3.36.3; 3.38.1); in 443, coinciding with the full moon of December (Dion.Hal. 11.63.1); in 423, on the Ides of December (Liv. 4.37.3); in 401, on the Calends of October (Liv. 5.9.8). For the fourth century only the date for 329 is known, when the consular year started on the Calends of Quinctilis (Liv. 8.20.3). In 321, both consuls abdicated and their substitutes took office on the very day that they were elected (Liv. 9.7.12–8.1), apparently kicking off a series of consulships that began at the end of autumn or at the beginning of winter.

would always begin on the Calends of May.²⁶ If Mommsen's hypothesis is correct, only from the beginning of the third century did the consular year have fixed dates. Moreover, consuls began to take office on the Ides of March around 218, coinciding with the outbreak of the Hannibalic War, if not slightly earlier.²⁷ This custom certainly endured until 153, when consuls began to enter office on 1ˢᵗ January, bringing the consular and official year into sync.²⁸ The length and dates of the consular year, therefore, varied throughout the Republican period, so it follows that the quaestorian year must have fluctuated as well.

From the very beginning the quaestorship had a close relationship with the Republic's highest magistracies: the quaestors' main function (or at least that of some of quaestors after their number increased) was to assist the consuls in Rome and outside the city. Consequently, it would be extremely implausible for the consuls to enter office on various dates throughout the Republic, but for the quaestors to have consistently entered office on 5ᵗʰ December.²⁹ It is far more reasonable to conclude that the consular and quaestorian years mirrored one another, so that consuls and quaestors entered office at the same time or at least in coordination.³⁰ The fact is that we only have evidence for quaestors taking office on 5ᵗʰ December in the post-Sullan age, when quaestors were regularly in office from 5ᵗʰ December to the following 4ᵗʰ December. It must remain a matter of speculation whether this date had already been established before Sulla and whether the choice of 5ᵗʰ December should be connected to 1ˢᵗ January, which had been the beginning of the consular since 153. It should not be dismissed that December 5ᵗʰ could have been a Sullan innovation, since it is perfectly possible that Sulla introduced the date in the context of a new general regulation of the quaestorship included in the *lex Cornelia de XX quaestoribus*.³¹

---

26 Mommsen 1859, 101–102, bases his hypothesis on the known dates of triumphs celebrated in the period between the war against Pyrrhus and the end of the First Punic War. Cf. Morgan 1977, 90–91.
27 According to Mommsen, Röm.St. I 599 (and later Broughton MRR, 2.638), the date of the Ides of March was designated as the beginning of the consular year some time between 233 and 217; based on the dates of consular triumphs reported by the *Fasti triumphales*, Mommsen argues specifically for the year 222 as the most likely starting point. More recently, Beck 2005, 409–411, has plausibly suggested that there may have been a military reason for beginning the consular year on 15ᵗʰ March; he suggests 218 as a possibility starting point, which would coincide with the beginning of the Hannibalic War. The first time Livy mentions the consuls taking office on the Ides of March is in his account for 217 (Liv. 22.1.5–7), and from then on he provides the same information on a good number of occasions, which indicates that this was indeed the norm until 153: 215: 23.30.17; 209: 27.7.7; 200: 31.5.2; 199: 32.1.1; 195: 33.43.1; 188: 38.35.7; 183: 39.45.1; 180: 40.35.2; 177: 41.8.4; 168: 44 19.1.
28 Liv. per. 47: *mutandi comitia causa fuit, quod Hispani rebellabant*. Cf. Cassiodor. Chron.: *Q. Fulvius et T. Annius. Hi primi consules kalendis ianuariis magistratum inierunt propter subitum Celtiberiae bellum*.
29 Mommsen, Röm.St. II 518–519.
30 Furthermore, all the quaestors had to take office at the same time, since, once this had happened, the sortition of their specific tasks took place immediately (see below).
31 Cf. Kunkel and Wittmann 1995, 87.

As has been argued in earlier chapters of this book in relation to Roman Republican institutions generally, the inauguration of the quaestors each year on 5th December, some weeks earlier than the consuls and the other magistrates, should not be seen as a long-standing or permanent tradition, but rather as the final stage of a more gradual development. In any case, the quaestorship was always, like the other regular magistracies except for the censorship, an annual magistracy. Nevertheless, as was the case with other magistracies during the late Republic, it became increasingly habitual for a quaestor to remain outside Rome in his province as a promagistrate for more than a year.

Sortitio of quaestors and appointments *extra sortem*

The responsibility or *provincia* of each of the elected quaestors was usually chosen by lot from a list of destinations that had been determined by the senate prior to the new quaestors taking office.[32] As the number of quaestors increased throughout the Republican period, the details of this procedure must have changed. Since the quaestorian *provinciae* were fixed at the beginning of the Republic, when there were only urban and consular quaestors, there was no need for the senate to decide on the *provinciae* in advance. In this period, the only business at hand was the allocation of these predetermined duties to the new quaestors. After Sulla, however, there were twenty quaestors, and it was necessary to determine at least some of their *provinciae*, depending on present circumstances. For the middle Republic, the question remains open as to whether or not there were some fixed Italian quaestorian *provinciae* (see above).

For the post-Sullan era, we do know about the process used to allocate the quaestorian *provinciae* for the year 56, which was exceptional from a political point of view: that year Pompey and Crassus' campaigns for the consulate aroused such opposition that the elections had to be postponed until the beginning of 55. Once elected as consuls, Pompey and Crassus took office immediately and the elections for the other magistrates of the year 55, which had also been deferred, went ahead.[33] The elections for aediles were set for 20th January 55,[34] so the elections for the year's quaestors would presumably have been held immediately after

---

[32] Greenidge 1901a, 213: the quaestorian *provinciae* 'were determined, before these magistrates entered on their office, by a decree of the Senate, and the individuals were then assigned to their several departments by lot; although, probably always by a special grace of the Senate, there are instances of commanders selecting their own assistants.' Cf. Prag 2014a, 201 n. 34. On procedure and significance of the quaestorian sortition, see Stewart 1987, 338–391 (but see below some criticisms of her arguments). For sortition more generally in Republican Rome, see Rosenstein 1995; Lundgreen 2011, 121–136.
[33] Pina Polo 2011, 285.
[34] Cic. *Q.fr.* 2.2.2.

these, at the end of January. In a letter written the day before the Ides of February, Marcus Cicero told his brother Quintus what had happened during a session of the senate four days before the Nones (i.e. 2nd February). Some of the issues under discussion during the senatorial session addressed the quaestorian *provinciae* and the outfitting of the praetorian provinces, topics that apparently superseded less urgent subjects such as legations.[35] According to this passage, the senate's determination of the quaestorian *provinciae* followed the elections and may have preceded the new quaestors' entry into office. This episode must be understood in the context of the exceptional historical circumstances at Rome in 56–55; consequently, its details should not necessarily be extrapolated to earlier Republican periods or even other post-Sullan years. Indeed, before the time of Sulla, the details surrounding the stages of the electoral process, the determination of quaestorian *provinciae* and new quaestors' entry into office could very well have been different. That said, the basic sequence of events must have always been the same.

At any rate, there is no doubt that it was the senate's responsibility to determine the quaestorian *provinciae* and that afterwards the senate had to validate the allocation of provinces by means of a *senatus consultum*, whether the distribution was made by lot or *extra sortem*.[36] In light of this, we can better understand a passage from Cicero's second *Philippica*, in which the orator was very keen to emphasise the extraordinary way in which Marcus Antonius became quaestor in 51 under Caesar's command: 'without a senatorial decree, without lot, without a law.'[37] In the context of invective, Cicero's statement was just one more way of accentuating Antonius' unusual and erratic behaviour, by making it clear that the usual procedure for determining a quaestorian *provincia* in the first century included a combination of *senatus consultum* and the drawing of lots. Similarly, Cicero asserts in his *Verrines* that Verres obtained his consular quaestorship by lot, which he held under the command of the consul Cn. Papirius Carbo, and that the assignment was made *ex senatus consulto*.[38]

---

35 Cic. *Q.fr.* 2.3.1: *A.d. IIII. Non. Febr. Milo affuit; ei Pompeius advocatus venit... Interim reiectis legationibus in Idus referebatur de provinciis quaestorum et de ornandis praetoribus.*

36 So Mommsen, Röm.St. II 520 n. 3. Cf. Lintott 1999, 136: 'The allocation of quaestors was supervised by the senate. The specific administrative posts at Rome and in Italy seem to have been settled by lot. We do not know within what limits this operated, nor can we elucidate the obscure references to a *lex Titia* and a *senatus consultum* of perhaps 137 BC which in some way regulated the sortition.' On senatorial supervision, see, for instance, the appointment *extra sortem ex senatus consulto* of C. Laelius in 202: *Laelium, cuius ante legati, eo anno quaestoris extra sortem ex senatus consulto opera utebatur...* (Liv. 30.33.2), or the designation of Cn. Calpurnius Piso as *quaestor pro praetore* in Hispania Citerior in 65: *Cn. Calpurnius / Cn. f. Piso / quaestor pro pr. ex s.c. / provinciam Hispaniam / citeriorem optinuit* (CIL I² 749 = ILS 875 = ILLRP 378).

37 Cic. *Phil.* 2.50: *Quaestor es factus; deinde continuo sine senatus consulto, sine sorte, sine lege ad Caesarem cucurristi.*

38 Cic. *Verr.* 2.1.34: *Quaestor ex senatus consulto provinciam sortitus es: obtigit tibi consularis, ut cum consule Cn. Carbone esses eamque provinciam obtineres.* We have even more evidence about quaestorian *sortitio* in the sources. Cicero makes clear that M. Pupius Piso Frugi was assigned by lot as quaestor of the consul L. Scipio Asiagenus in 83: *Quaestor cum L. Scipioni consuli obtigisset, non attigit pe-*

As we have seen in the aforementioned text, Cicero discredits Antonius for having performed his quaestorship under Caesar without a *senatus consultum*, without sortition, without a law. Was *sine lege* a general allusion, according to Cicero, to Antonius' unlawfully obtained *provincia*, or was Cicero referring to the option to secure a quaestorian *provincia* by means of a specific law? In his previous speech in favour of Murena, Cicero alludes to an otherwise unknown *lex Titia*, according to which the specific *provincia* of the quaestor designate Murena was allocated.[39] Murena probably held his quaestorship in 74, at the same time as Sulpicius Rufus. The meaning of Cicero's text, however, is not completely clear. In the sentence preceding the mention of the *lex Titia*, Cicero seems to imply that both Murena and Sulpicius Rufus were allotted their *provinciae* by lot, since both had similar luck. In the following sentence, though, it could be understood that Sulpicius obtained his quaestorship by lot, but that Murena did so according to the *lex Titia*. Did this *lex Titia* regulate the allocation of quaestorian *provinciae*, once the dictator Sulla had increased substantially the number of quaestors, and perhaps as a response to problems raised by the new organisation of the office? This is a possibility that must not be discarded, but it is a little surprising that such a supposedly general law is not mentioned by the sources. Perhaps this *lex Titia*, probably a tribunician law, had a more restricted goal and was specifically passed in order to assign a province to the quaestor Murena, 'a quiet and peaceable province' according to Cicero, but we do not know which that province was. If this is correct, a tribunician law could also have been a means to determine the *provinciae* of some specific quaestors under particular circumstances.

In any case, the evidence regarding the regulation of the quaestorian *sortitio* is quite elusive. Ulpian alludes to a *senatus consultum* passed under the consulship of Decimus Drusus (*sic*) and Porcina, according to which most quaestors were to

---

cuniam, non ad exercitum profectus est; quod de re publica sensit, ita sensit ut nec fidem suam nec morem maiorum nec necessitudinem sortis laederet (Cic. *Verr.* 2.1.37). Another example of sortition is known from Vatinius's quaestorship in 63: *in eo magistratu cum tibi magno clamore aquaria provincia sorte obtigisset...* (Cic. *Vat.* 12). Plutarch informs us that C. Gracchus was assigned by lot to the consul L. Aurelius Orestes in Sardinia (Plut. *C.Gr.* 1.4). Cicero makes it clear in his first preserved letter to his brother Quintus that a provincial governor received his quaestor by lot: *Quaestorem habes non tuo iudicio delectum, sed eum, quem sors dedit* (Cic. *Q.fr.* 1.1.11).

39 Cic. *Mur.* 18: *Sed quaestura utriusque prope modum pari momento sortis fuit. Habuit hic lege Titia provinciam tacitam et quietam, tu illam cui, cum quaestores sortiuntur...* Rotondi 1966 (¹1912) 333–334: 'Ne ignoriamo assolutamente l'autore e la data.' Broughton MRR, 2.2 tentatively attributes this law to Sextus Titius, a sympathizer of Saturninus and tribune of the plebs in 99: 'perhaps also author of a law regulating the assignment of quaestorian provinces' (cf. Harris 1976, 105). Here Broughton follows Münzer's thesis, for whom the tribune of 99 was the only candidate (RE 'Titius' no. 23). The author of the law, however, may have been another Titius who remains unknown. Actually, Broughton MRR, 2.473, includes a Titius with an unknown *praenomen* among the tribunes of the plebs of uncertain date, and attributes to him the authorship of this law: 'author of a law regulating the assignment of provinces to quaestors.' Among the known Titii, a possible candidate would be Q. Titius (Mutto) (RE 33), who was a *monetalis* by 90 according to Crawford RRC 344–346, no. 341 (cf. Broughton MRR, 3.206).

be allocated by lot to their provinces (except, Ulpian adds, for the *candidati principis*, which is a reference to his own time).⁴⁰ This *senatus consultum* has been dated to 138–137 BC on the grounds that Ulpian mistakenly combined the names of Decimus Junius Brutus, consul in 138, and M. Aemilius Lepidus Porcina, consul in 137.⁴¹ It is not easy to determine whether this senatorial decree introduced a new general regulation or was meant to address a specific situation at the time it was issued.⁴² In any case, the use of *sortitio* as the means of allocating quaestors seems to have already been put in pace long before 138–137; so much can be deduced from Livy's discussion of the quaestor C. Laelius in 202, who served as quaestor that year in Africa under Scipio Africanus by a special appointment that followed a senatorial decree (*extra sortem ex senatus consulto*).⁴³ The unusual method for designating Laelius makes it clear that *sortitio* was the standard procedure used for assigning quaestors, probably throughout the Republic; at the same time, Livy also demonstrates that an appointment *extra sortem* was indeed possible. Other examples confirm this view (see below).

Some quaestors were assigned specific tasks, such as the urban quaestors and those who were in charge of duties like the *provincia Ostiensis* (when this *provincia* existed). However, most quaestors were attached to a higher magistrate: a consul, praetor or promagistrate. Since provincial quaestors were responsible to their commanders, they were required to follow their superiors to the territories under their charge, once their provinces had been allotted.⁴⁴ This necessarily forged a

---

40 Dig. 1.13.1.2: *Ex quaestoribus quidam solebant provincias sortiri ex senatus consulto, quod factum est Decimo Druso et Porcina consulibus, sane non omnes quaestores provincias sortiebantur, verum excepti erant candidati principis: hi etenim solis libris principalibus in senatu legendis vacant.*

41 Mommsen, Röm.St. II 520 n. 3, had already suggested this date. However, Willems 1878, II 599, gave an erroneous imperial date that then was repeated by Thompson 1962b, 18. Cf. Harris 1976, 105 n. 114.

42 Harris 1976, 105: 'since the assignment of quaestors normally seems to have been achieved by *sortitio* even before 138, it is hard to see what this *s.c.* was for.' Cf. De Martino 1960, 2.209, n. 86: perhaps the *senatus consultum* fixed the quaestorian *provinciae* in order to avoid the need for the senate to reach a new decision on a yearly basis. More recently Gnoli 2012, 96, has suggested that the senatorial decree may have put an end to the practice of electing quaestors with naval competencies (the so-called *quaestores classici* from Lydus). This conclusion seems unlikely.

43 Liv. 30.33.2. See Broughton MRR, 1.316.

44 According to Stewart 1987, 344, it was the higher magistrate himself (rather than a specific territory) who was the *provincia* of a quaestor: 'in the late Republic the *provinciae* of the consular quaestors were not the consular geographical provinces but the consuls by name.' However, the sources do not make it clear that when deciding what the quaestorian provinces would be, senators were thinking of magistrates as *provinciae*. This is not apparent from the aforementioned text about the elections in 55 (Cic. *Q.fr.* 2.3.1). Likewise, when Cicero speaks of Verres' quaestorship, he asserts that Verres obtained a consular province by lot, and this finally meant that he served under the command of the consul Carbo, but Cicero never asserts that Carbo was Verres' *provincia* (Cic. *Verr.* 2.1.34). We know that in 50 the quaestor Marius replaced the proquaestor Caninius Sallustius in Syria (Cic. *fam.* 2.17.5: *Marium quidem successorem tarde video esse venturum, propterea quod senatus ita decrevit ut cum legionibus iret*) and that C. Coelius Caldus was sent as quaestor to Cilicia the same year (Cic.

close relationship between quaestor and commander, who was ultimately held accountable for his quaestor's behaviour.⁴⁵ Indeed, the circumstances of the consular quaestors were quite similar, since these magistrates assisted the consuls wherever they happened to be performing their duties, whether at Rome or in a territory outside the city.

The subordination of all quaestors to a superior magistrate (whatever their actual duties were) is an important feature of the magistracy. While this dependency is evident in the case of consular and provincial quaestors since they were attached to their commanders, the situation in which urban quaestors found themselves was different. Their *provincia* was the *aerarium* and they were not personally attached to another magistrate. Instead, they came under the senate's supervision. Urban quaestors were concerned with senatorial decrees that ordered, for instance, the minting of new coinage, the accommodation of prominent foreign guests or the implementation of honours for deceased individuals (see chapter 5 on the urban quaestorship). In all these cases, the urban quaestors were ultimately the magistrates responsible for carrying out senatorial decisions. In practice, however, it was actually the consuls, as the highest magistrates, who gave orders to the urban quaestors. This is clearly shown in the *senatus consultum de Asclepiade* of 78, according to which the consuls Q. Lutatius Catulus and M. Aemilius Lepidus were to instruct the urban quaestors to register Asclepiades, Polystratos and Meniskos in the official list of Rome's friends. They also had to take charge of organising the accommodation of honoured guests at public expense, as well as providing them with presents.⁴⁶ Another example illustrates the point. In 43, Cicero made a series of proposals in the senate: first to honour the deceased Servius Sulpicius Rufus and then two months later to honour the sol-

---

fam. 2.15.4: *Ego de provincia decedens quaestorem Coelium praeposui provinciae*). Coelius' *provincia* was assigned by lot (Cic. *fam.* 2.19.1: *Cum optatissimum nuntium accepissem te mihi quaestorem obtigisse, eo iucundiorem mihi eam sortem sperabam fore quo diutius in provincia mecum fuisses*), and he remained in command of Cilicia when Cicero went back to Rome at the end of July. Neither Marius nor Coelius could have been attached to their commanders, since the new governors had not been sorted out yet and Cicero's command in Cilicia was not going to be extended. They must, therefore, have been assigned to a certain territory as their quaestorian *provinciae* (in their cases Syria and Cilicia) and not specifically to a higher magistrate. Stewart 1987, 360–367, argues that this procedure was exceptional. According to Stewart (365), 'the quaestorian *provinciae* were only allotted as geographically designated *provinciae* when the senate realized the conflict over provinces would continue and decided not to prorogue the governors of 51.' However, it is far from evident that the procedure followed in the case of Marius and Coelius should be seen as unusual.

45 A close relationship between a quaestor and his commander is attested in the sources, a bond that could endure even years after the holding of the quaestorship. Nevertheless, this personal relationship can be easily explained by the collaborative relationship between the two magistrates during their mandate; consequently, it is not necessary to justify such a bond as the result of the supposed assignment of the quaestor to the higher magistrate as his *provincia*, as Stewart has argued (Stewart 1987, 443: 'In assigning a superior magistrate to a quaestor as his *provincia*, the lot sanctioned a personal relation, the quaestor's duty to his commanding officer').

46 *S.C. de Asclepiade* ll.17–18 (= ll. 25–26 of the Greek text).

diers who died while serving under the allied armies of Octavian, Hirtius and Pansa during their victorious campaign against Antonius' troops. In this circumstance it was the consuls Pansa and Hirtius (either one of them or both) who were to order the urban quaestors to contract the construction of Sulpicius Rufus' statue in the first case and to give the money necessary for the construction of a monument in the latter case.[47] The usual procedure, therefore, consisted of three distinct steps: the senate decreed, the consuls ordered, and the urban quaestors carried out the task.[48]

A similar process can be identified in 63 with respect to Vatinius and the so-called *provincia aquaria*, which had been assigned to him by lot. According to Cicero, he, as consul, sent the quaestor Vatinius to Puteoli to prevent the export of gold and silver.[49] We should not deduce from Cicero's words that he had personally decided what Vatinius' tasks should be during his quaestorship. Rather, the senate had taken the decision and the consul acted as intermediary to communicate the order to Vatinius (see above chapter 2).

Turning back to the regular procedure for the sortition of quaestorian *provinciae*, we know that the drawing of lots took place in the *aerarium* on the day the new quaestors took office. That said, ancient sources do not provide a detailed account of precisely how the sortition worked.[50] As we have seen, in the post-Sullan age quaestors entered office on 5th December, which was a few weeks before the higher magistrates to whom most of the new quaestors were to be attached took office. When the quaestorian *sortitio* took place on 5th December, the new quaestors learnt whether they were to remain at Rome as urban quaestors, to attend one of the new consuls wherever they spent their time in office (in the post-Sullan era mostly or entirely at Rome[51]) or to follow a governor to whatever province the latter would be assigned in January.

---

47 Cic. *Phil.* 9.15–17; 14.38.
48 In the first century, the consuls tended to be at Rome for most of their time in office. However, in previous centuries they were often far away from the city during a great part of the consular year. Accordingly, if the urban quaestors were assigned tasks by the senate and the consuls were absent, we can presume that the highest magistrate at Rome, the urban praetor, would have given them the order. This may have occurred in 168 when the urban quaestors L. Manlius and L. Sterninus were instructed to escort two sons of King Masinissa for the duration of their stay in Italy (Liv. 45.13–14; Val.-Max. 5.1.1).
49 Cic. *Vat.* 12: *in eo magistratu cum tibi magno clamore aquaria provincia sorte obtigisset, missusne sis a me consule Puteolos, ut inde aurum exportari argentumque prohiberes?*
50 Schol.Bob. *in Clod. et Cur.* fr.11 p.87 Stangl: *Tanto prius ad aerarium venit, ut ibi ne scribam quidem quemquam offenderet. Aput aerarium sortiri provincias et quaestores solebant et scribae, ut pro certo appareret in quam provinciam vel cum quo praeside proficiscerentur. Ardorem quendam nimiae cupiditatis volens exprimere festinasse ad aerarium dixit ut etiam scribarum praeveniret adventum.* The scribes who would be attached to every quaestor in the following year were also given their assignments on the day that the new quaestors took office (cf. Cic. *Cat.* 4.15; Plin. *ep.* 4.12.2). See Kunkel and Wittmann 1995, 514 n. 22; Lintott 1999, 136; David 2007, 42–43; 2019, 96.
51 Pina Polo 2011, 242–243.

We have seen above how in 202 C. Laelius was designated *extra sortem* quaestor under the command of Scipio Africanus in Africa. This is the oldest known example of a quaestor not receiving his *provincia* by lot, but we have evidence of others after him.[52] Although the sources do not confirm this, it has been supposed that Q. Fabius Maximus Allobrogicus, after his regular election, was directly nominated in 134 as quaestor in Hispania Citerior by his uncle Scipio Aemilianus.[53] The case of M. Junius Brutus is rather peculiar, since his own preferences seem to have determined his quaestorian assignment. Apparently, Brutus refused to serve under Caesar in Gaul and preferred to go with his father-in-law Ap. Claudius to Cilicia, probably in 54.[54] By that time, or at any rate during the fifties, Q. Cassius Longinus was allocated *extra sortem* Hispania Ulterior as his *provincia*, after Pompey had expressly nominated him for the office.[55] While we only know of a few certain examples of appointments *extra sortem*, there certainly could have been other unrecorded instances.[56] Whatever the actual number of cases is, it is clear that such direct assignments were very exceptional, as our sources (particularly Cicero when speaking of Antonius' quaestorship under Caesar's command) emphasise. All cases refer to quaestors serving under the command of an *imperator* and, hence, there is no example of an urban quaestor being appointed *extra sortem*. Given that a quaestor had to serve as an *imperator*'s right-hand man in the field during his mandate in a province, it is easy to understand why the appointments made *sine sorte* were based on friendship and trust or even in some cases on kinship between commander and quaestor; it is also likely that military prowess was also taken into account in such instances. We should resist the temptation, however, to see a relationship of patronage and *clientela* between the two magistrates.[57] We should suppose that ultimately the senate al-

---

52 On the subject see Thompson 1962b. Thompson is right to state that the *extra-sortem* appointment of quaestors was exceptional: 'No regular annual exemptions from *sortitio* occurred under the Republic' (18). Ulpian's assertion (*Dig.* 1.13.1.2), which certainly seems to suggest regular annual exemptions, was influenced by the situation under the Principate. See also Stewart 1987, 354–360.
53 Val.Max. 8.15.4; App. *Iber.* 84. The sources actually claim that Scipio Aemilianus 'commended' to the voters his nephew Fabius Maximus. After Fabius was elected, there is no evidence that he was appointed *sine sorte* as the quaestor of Aemilianus in Hispania, but it is difficult to believe that his assignment was simply the result of chance. See Thompson 1962b, 19.
54 *vir.ill.* 82.3–4: *Quaestor <Caesari> in Galliam proficisci noluit, quod is bonis omnibus displicebat. Cum Appio socero in Cilicia fuit, et cum ille repetundarum accusaretur, ipse ne verbo quidem infamatus est.*
55 Cic. *Att.* 6.6.4: *Pompeius, eo robore vir, iis radicibus, Q. Cassium sine sorte delegit, Caesar Antonium* (cf. Cass. Dio 41.24.2). In this passage, Cicero compares the similar ways in which Pompey and Caesar acted when they chose *extra sortem* Cassius Longinus and Antonius respectively as their quaestors.
56 So, Badian 1957, who points out that C. Norbanus may have been nominated quaestor *extra sortem* by M. Antonius, giving as his main argument the close relationship between the two men (cf. Thompson 1962b, 17–18). Thompson 1962b, 24–25, collects a number of quaestors that may hypothetically have been appointed without lot. Cf. Stewart 1987, 354 n. 50.
57 Stewart 1987, 354 n. 50: 'The total lack of supporting evidence in conjunction with the known evidence for the *clientela* relationship inherent in the *necessitudo* of quaestor and commander renders

ways had to authorise this kind of extraordinary appointment.⁵⁸ Such authorisations were probably preceded by a debate in the senate, although in the cases that we know of, the sources contain no hint of any opposition to such appointments.⁵⁹ In any case, an *extra-sortem* quaestorian appointment must not be seen as an honour bestowed on the quaestor, but rather as a concession made by the senate to the higher magistrate who would become the quaestor's commander.⁶⁰

In the first century we know of two instances in which quaestors-elect gave up their provinces. The first was M. Pupius Piso Frugi in 83: he was given the assignment to serve under the command of the anti-Sullan consul L. Cornelius Scipio Asiagenus, but according to Cicero he refused to join him.⁶¹ Piso's resolution must be understood in the context of the civil confrontation between pro- and anti-Sullans forces.⁶² We do not know whether Piso remained in Rome or undertook different quaestorian functions. Anyway, he does not seem to have been punished or even reprimanded for refusing to accept his initial assignment. As a matter of fact, Cicero warmly praises Piso's behaviour because he was faithful to his principles and, he adds, Piso neither betrayed his *fides*, the *mos maiorum* nor the obligations derived from the drawing of quaestorian provinces. Piso was later praetor by 72 and consul in 61.

In the year 58, the quaestor-elect C. Calpurnius Piso Frugi decided not to go to Pontus and Bithynia, the province that he had been given. According to Cicero, Piso Frugi, who was his son-in-law, chose to remain in Rome in order to help him to return from exile.⁶³ Cicero gives no further information. Apparently, Piso Frugi acted purely out of political motivations, but we know nothing about his activity in Rome in favour of Cicero, nor of the tasks he may have carried out as quaestor in Rome.⁶⁴ Again, his personal resolution reflects a certain ability to decide one's own destination as quaestor, though it seems problematic that this decision would not have required the senate's approval or at least its acquiescence. In the end, his decision not to go to Pontus and Bithynia presumably resulted in the nomination

---

all arguments of *extra sortem* appointment based on the criterion of political patronage highly unlikely.' Cf. Stewart 1998, 140 n. 5.

58 Thompson 1962b, 22: 'all appointments of quaestors *extra sortem*, in the period under consideration, were made *ex senatus consulto*.'

59 Thompson 1962b, 23, considers that the senate did not oppose an *imperator*'s expressed desire: 'Such appointments *sine sorte* must have been accepted without question and automatically sanctioned, on request, by the senate.'

60 Stewart 1987, 354–355.

61 Cic. *Verr.* 2.1.37 (see above n. 38).

62 Badian 1962, 60; Gruen 1968a, 169.

63 Cic. *p. red. Sen.* 38: *Alter fuit propugnator mearum fortunarum et defensor adsiduus summa virtute et pietate C. Piso gener, qui minas inimicorum meorum, qui inimicitias adfinis mei, propinqui sui, consulis, qui Pontum et Bithyniam quaestor prae mea salute neglexit.* Cf. Cic. *p. red. Quir.* 7.

64 His political career ended abruptly when he died suddenly in the first months of 57, before his father-in-law came back from exile (Cic. *Sest.* 68).

of another quaestor as his substitute and in Piso Frugi obtaining other functions as quaestor.

Even if there was an agreement between two quaestors for exchanging their *provinciae*,[65] the reorganisation of the quaestorian *provinciae* in 58 after they had already been assigned by lot must have required the senate's authorisation, just like the *extra sortem* allotment of *provinciae* necessitated.[66] In fact, the senate's use of an *extra-sortem* quaestorian appointment would provide the easiest solution for instances in which a quaestor renounced his province or refused his allotted province before taking office, and, consequently, a reassignment was necessary to nominate a substitute.[67] Is this what happened in 54? We have seen that Brutus refused to join Caesar in Gaul, and instead went to Cilicia under the command of his father-in-law Ap. Claudius. Either Brutus had been assigned to Gaul by lot or had been claimed as quaestor by Caesar himself. If the latter option is correct, Brutus simply refused to accept Caesar's invitation to serve under his command. However, if Brutus had been randomly assigned to Gaul initially, his later choice of Cilicia as his destination implies at least a certain ability to choose on his part, although the final decision rested with the senate, since an *extra-sortem* appointment would have been necessary. We know that M. Licinius Crassus was likely Caesar's quaestor in Gaul in 54 and that he remained in the province as proquaestor in 53. Was he likewise nominated *extra sortem* by the senate after Brutus' refusal?[68]

An *extra-sortem* appointment also seems to be the logical solution when a commander was dissatisfied with his quaestor' behaviour and dismissed him, although there is no evidence for how a replacement was appointed.[69] At any rate, the dismissal of a quaestor must have been very exceptional. Actually, we only know of one secure example of a quaestor having been discharged by his commander,[70] when M. Aurelius Cotta dismissed his quaestor P. Oppius from Bithynia, presum-

---

65 For 63 we know that the consuls Cicero and Antonius agreed to exchange their provinces. Antonius finally went to Macedonia in 62, whereas Cicero preferred to remain in Rome and then renounced his province. Was the exchange of *provinciae* between two quaestors also possible?
66 In the first century some consuls, like Pompey and Cicero, decided to give up their provinces and remain in Rome. Actually, a high proportion of magistrates, consuls and praetors, declined the governorship of a province. To a certain extent, such renunciations must have also implied a certain amount of reorganisation, since it meant a change to the senate's previous planning for provincial administration. See Blösel 2016, esp. 68–74. Cf. Pina Polo 2011, 239–241.
67 Stewart 1987, 357.
68 Stewart 1987, 359, claims that Brutus refused his quaestorian appointment to Caesar in 53. According to Stewart, Crassus, quaestor in 54, continued to serve under Caesar in 53. However, it is more probable that both Brutus and Crassus were quaestors in 54 (see Prosopography). Consequently, Crassus may have replaced Brutus as quaestor in Gaul, perhaps following an *extra-sortem* senatorial appointment.
69 Stewart 1987, 358.
70 The other possible example refers to a Q. Fabius who was dismissed by his father-in-law P. Rupilius for having neglegently lost the citadel of Tauromenium in Sicily (Val.Max. 2.7.3). However, it

ably in the year 73, after Oppius had been accused of bribery and suspected of conspiracy.[71] Nothing is known about how Cotta replaced Oppius, whether the senate sent a new quaestor (it must be borne in mind that Cotta remained in Bithynia as proconsul until 70), or whether the commander used a legate to perform the quaestor's duties.[72]

---

is not at all certain that Fabius was Rupilius' quaestor. He could also have been a *legatus* (see Prosopography).

[71] Cass. Dio 36.40.3; Sall. *hist.* 3.59–60 M.

[72] Stewart 1987, 359, suggests that Cotta could have named a legate to serve as *legatus pro praetore*, but she admits that there is no evidence for this.

Chapter 5:
The urban quaestorship

Throughout the Roman Republic, there is evidence for only a few *quaestores urbani*[1] who are expressly named as such in literary sources, inscriptions and coins.[2] At times, their tasks are specifically mentioned, while in other instances these can be deduced indirectly from the sources. As can be gleaned from a number of Republican legal documents, the *aerarium populi Romani* was the *provincia* of the urban quaestors,[3] who therefore were responsible for managing the public treasury[4]. The *lex repetundarum*, which was issued in the final decades of the second century, for instance, tells us the following:[5] *id quaestor [quei aerarium pro]vinciam optinebit.*[6] Another example is found in the following section of the *lex agraria* of 111:[7] *...quaestor,] quei aerarium provinciam optinebit in tableis [publiceis--].*[8] Finally, there is this passage from the *lex Cornelia de XX quaestoribus: q(uaestorem) urb(anum), quei aerarium provinciam optinebit, eam mercedem deferto, quaestorque quei aerarium provinciam optinebit, eam pequniam ei scribae scribeisque heredive eius solvito, idque ei sine fraude sua facere liceto, quod sine malo pequlatuu fiat, olleisque homini-*

---

[1] Apart from the general works on the Roman institutions (Mommsen, Kunkel and Wittmann, Lintott, etc.), where only a limited amount of space is dedicated to the urban quaestorship, there is no modern publication specifically dedicated to this magistracy. However, a venerable article exists, which C.-J. Revillout published in 1865 in the *Mémoires de la Societé des Sciences Morales*, under the title "Les questeurs urbains". In twenty-eight pages, Revillout analyses the tasks of urban quaestors and then turns to their *apparitores*; finally, he focuses on Cato Uticensis' quaestorship and his attempts to rescue the office from the corruption that dominated his time.
[2] The Greek translation was ὁ ταμίας κατὰ πόλιν (see *SC de Asclepiade* l.26. Cf. Mason 1974, 91). In general, we have knowledge of only a small number of quaestors throughout the Republic, and many times the sources do not allow us to determine whether they were urban quaestors. It is not necessarily true that urban quaestors were more likely to be mentioned in the sources, as Badian asserted: 'unfortunately quaestors hardly ever get into the record at all, and those in the city are more likely to than those *militae*' (Badian 1983, 164). In the Cicero's correspondence, for instance, we find much more information on provincial quaestors than on urban quaestors.
[3] On the *aerarium* in the Imperial period see Corbier 1974.
[4] On the meaning of the word *provincia* in the Republican age see Díaz Fernández 2015, 31–66; Dalla Rosa 2015.
[5] The epigraphic text has been identified as the *lex Acilia repetundarum* and dated to 123 (see among others Badian 1954). Ferrary prefers a date shortly before 111 rather than 123 (see Ferrary 2014).
[6] *Lex repetundarum* 69. See Crawford 1996, 1.72 and 93: 'the quaestor, [who] shall hold [the treasury] as his province.' Cf. Lintott 1992, 104; Stewart 1998, 96 n. 5.
[7] Cf. Crawford 1996, 1.53: 'The statute was probably passed some time between 15 March 111 BC and the harvests in the following autumn.'
[8] *Lex agraria* 46. See Crawford 1996, 1.118 and 146: '...the quaestor,] who shall hold the treasury as his province, in the [public] records...'

*bus eam pequniam capere liceto.*⁹ These passages obviously contain formulae that were repeated in official documents, either verbatim or with minor variations. They refer to the quaestor—or specifically to the urban quaestor—as he 'who will get the treasury as his duty.'

The aforementioned formulae always speak of the quaestor in charge of the public treasury in the singular. However, Rome had two urban quaestors each year. How should this fact be understood? Crawford argues that only one urban quaestor was the magistrate responsible for the *aerarium* at any one time.¹⁰ Prag concurs with this argument: 'it is likewise reasonably uncontroversial that two served as urban quaestors, of whom one was formally assigned to the *Aerarium*; as already noted, the other urban quaestor may well have been assigned a varying range of duties such as *curator viarum* or *res frumentaria* as the need arose.'¹¹ As we shall see later on, urban quaestors could certainly be assigned tasks other than the *aerarium*, such as looking after foreign guests as well as the other duties that Prag correctly mentions. That said, this fact does not imply that one of the two urban quaestors was excluded from the management of the *aerarium* during his time in office or that there was a rigid distribution of tasks between the two *quaestores urbani*. It seems more likely that they acted on collegial terms, officially assuming the same duties even though they did not necessarily have to act together.¹² This would explain the allusion to only one quaestor being responsible for the *aerarium* in the aforementioned formulae.

In the year 168 the urban quaestor L. Manlius was sent by the senate to meet Masgaba, a son of King Masinissa, who had landed at Puteoli. Manlius' mission was to escort Masgaba to Rome.¹³ Once Masgaba had intervened in the Curia and had received an answer from the senators, the quaestor Manlius was instructed to accompany him back to Puteoli. He had to attend to and honour the son of Masinissa during his entire stay in Italy. We do not know how long Masgaba remained in Italy, but we can certainly suppose that his stay lasted at least a few weeks. Most of that time Manlius was away from Rome, even though he was an urban quaestor. We can safely assume that the other remained at Rome during Manlius' absence.

---

9 *Lex Cornelia de XX quaestoribus* ll. 1–6. Crawford 1996, 1.294 and 297: '[---] he is to register [with] the urban quaestor, who shall have the treasury as his province, that fee, and the quaestor, who shall have the treasury as his province, is to pay that sum to that scribe, or (those) scribes, or to his heir, and it is to be lawful for him to do so without personal liability, in so far as it be done without wrongful enrichment, and it is to be lawful for those persons to accept that sum.'
10 Crawford RRC, 313; 330–331. Harris 1976, 103 n. 95, agrees with Crawford, 'at least in the late second century and under Sulla.'
11 Prag 2014a, 201.
12 Kunkel and Wittmann 1995, 515: 'Daß nicht beide Quästoren zusammen tätig werden mußsten, entspricht der eigentümlichen Natur magistratischer Kollegialität und wird durch zahlreiche Zeugnisse namentlich in inschriftlich erhaltenen Gesetzen und Senatsbeschlüssen erwiesen.'
13 Liv. 45.13.12.

The other urban quaestor in 168 was Lucius Stertinius. According to Livy, 'not long afterwards' (*haud ita multo post*) a letter reached Rome giving news about Misagenes, another of Masinissa's sons.[14] As had happened earlier with Manlius, the senate dispatched Stertinius to Brundisium to look after Misagenes and to accompany him to Rome. Although the text of Livy is lost at this point, Valerius Maximus provides further information: the quaestor was instructed to do anything necessary to assist with Misagenes' recovery—he was ill at the time—and to hire ships to take him and his entourage back to Africa.[15] Like Manlius before him, Stertinius must have been away from Rome for at least a few weeks.

If we accept that only one of the two urban quaestors was in charge of the public treasury during his entire year in office, it becomes rather difficult to explain the situation that is clearly laid out for 168 when both Manlius and Stertinius were at different times away from the capital; indeed, it seems rather unlikely that the magistrate responsible for the *aerarium* would have been away from Rome for an extended period of time. On the contrary, what happened in 168 is easier to comprehend if we assume that the two urban quaestors were both in charge of the treasury throughout their year of office. If the job was shared by the two, one of the urban quaestors would have been able to undertake other tasks on a temporary basis at the senate's request. What was important was that at least one of the two was always in Rome so that he could attend to the wide range of responsibilities related to the use of public money and the administration of official documents. Therefore, when Masgaba arrived in Italy, the quaestor Manlius was available to take care of him while Stertinius remained at the helm of the *aerarium* at Rome. When Misagenes came to Brundisium some time later, the quaestors simply switched roles.

Another telling occasion sheds further light on duties of the urban quaestors. According to Sallust,[16] the quaestor Cn. Octavius Ruso was sent to Africa in 105 in order to bring money (*stipendium*) to Marius' troops. Ruso was, in all probability, one of the two urban quaestors that year, which is why he was entrusted with this extraordinary mission (see below). After its completion, Ruso went back to Rome accompanying some legates of King Bocchus of Mauretania. Again, we do not know how long Ruso was away from Rome, but we can reasonably suppose that his absence from the city lasted longer than those of Manlius and Sterninus in 168, since he was dispatched to a more distant destination. Again, so long as Ruso was absent, the other urban quaestor must have been in charge of the public treasury at Rome.[17]

---

14 Liv. 45.14.9.
15 Val.Max. 5.1.1.
16 Sall. *Iug.* 104.3.
17 An alternation between the two urban questors in charge of the *aerarium*, either on a regular basis every month or every six months (as suggested by Muñiz Coello 2014, 514 n. 27), or based on a certain temporal flexibility depending on the circumstances, seems unlikely.

Mommsen claims that the urban quaestors were prohibited from leaving Rome, although he admits that there is actually no evidence for this in the sources.[18] He further ponders the possibility that there might have been a maximum period of time that an urban quaestor could be absent from the city. What happened in 168 with Manlius and Sterninus, as well as with Ruso in 105, shows that the urban quaestors could indeed leave Rome—and even Italy—if following an explicit order from the senate. Given that the period of time they remained outside of Rome would depend on how long it took to accomplish their task, hypothesizing a potential time limit seems somewhat unproductive.

In addition to the cases and arguments just discussed, an episode that occurred in 64 requires an explanation. That year Cato (Uticensis) and M. Claudius Marcellus, who had been close friends from boyhood, served as urban quaestors. According to Plutarch, on the last day of their term in office (namely 4th December 64) Cato had already been escorted to his house by a large group of citizens, although he was obviously still in office.[19] At the same time Marcellus, whom Plutarch depicts as a man of weak character who was inclined to please others and to grant any favour, was approached by some of his influential friends. In Plutarch's telling, these friends succeeded in pressuring Marcellus to register some remission of moneys due in the *aerarium*. In marked contrast to Marcellus, the integrity of Cato's character is proverbial, as his behaviour as quaestor and later on as praetor clearly demonstrated.[20] When Cato found out what had happened, he quickly leaped to action: he went to the treasury, asked for the tablets and erased the entries his colleague had just recorded, while Marcellus himself stood by and said nothing. Plutarch goes on to say that Cato led Marcellus out of the treasury and brought him to his house. Marcellus did not blame Cato for his actions and the two remained intimate friends.

Plutarch's account makes it clear that the two urban quaestors were simultaneously responsible for the *aerarium*, and consequently both had the capacity to register official documents there at any time. In the last day of their quaestorships, Marcellus legally entered some new records into the archive and then Cato, who possibly made use of his right to veto the decisions of his colleague,[21] legally erased those very same records. Moreover, we know for sure that Cato was responsible for the treasury throughout his quaestorship, since Plutarch makes this clear when speaking of his tough stance towards his scribes as well as his honesty during his time in office (see below).[22] Ultimately, this episode clearly reveals the collegiality of the magistracy.

Furthermore, the collegiality of the two urban quaestors and the resulting sharing responsibility are well demonstrated in several other cases. Livy uses the plural

---

18 Mommsen, Röm.St. II 523 and n. 3.
19 Plut. *Cat.min.* 18.3–4.
20 Plut. *Cat.min.* 16–18 and 44.
21 Fehrle 1983, 81.
22 Plut. *Cat.min.* 16.

when referring to the urban quaestors in several narrative passages, which provide further evidence for the collegial nature of the magistracy. In 205, for instance, the senate gave orders to the urban quaestors to sell a part of Capuan territory in order to raise funds for the war against Carthage.[23] In 187, the praetor Q. Terentius Culleo instructed the urban quaestors to confiscate Scipio Asiaticus's assets after he was convicted of embezzlement.[24] The following year after the senate allocated funds for rewarding informants, the urban quaestors paid a sum of money to the individuals who had provided early information about the Bacchanalia.[25]

Plautus, when speaking about the sale of prisoners of war as slaves at Rome, refers to the quaestors, again in the plural, as the magistrates responsible for the process.[26] The comic playwright does not specify whether he is alluding to the urban quaestors, but, given that the money raised from such sales went to the public treasury, there can be little doubt about it. Moreover, the plural *a quaestoribus* makes it absolutely clear that the sale was managed by the urban quaestors at Rome, not by a single provincial quaestor. Finally, when in 43 Cicero proposed in the senate that Ser. Sulpicius Rufus be honoured, he alludes to the urban quaestors, once more in the plural, as the magistrates responsible for commissioning Sulpicius' statue and then having it placed on the Rostra.[27]

The denarii minted jointly by the two urban quaestors Q. Servilius Caepio and L. Calpurnius Piso Caesoninus, probably in 103, offer a very good example of the collegiality that characterised the office (see below).[28] Both quaestors appear on the reverse sitting side by side on their stools, accompanied by the legend *AD · FRV(mentum) · EMV(ndum) / EX · S(enatus) · C(onsulto)* on the exergue. The two urban quaestors were responsible for the coinage, which was demanded by the senate in order to purchase grain due to the state of emergency at Rome. The iconography of the coin alludes to the tasks that the two quaestors executed together.

The urban quaestors, therefore, were entrusted with a wide set of duties pertaining to the *aerarium*, which they were expected to carry out during their term of office, as we shall see throughout in this chapter. These duties were the joint responsibility of the two magistrates who held the urban quaestorship every year, and as a result they sometimes acted together. In practice, however, some—if not most—of these tasks were actually carried out by a single urban quaestor. That is, while responsibil-

---

23 Liv. 28.46.4.
24 Liv. 38.60.8. In the same judicial process the quaestor C. Furius Aculeo and the legate A. Hostilius were also convicted. According to Livy, the confiscation of their properties was not necessary, because both gave the urban quaestors the required sureties on the day they were convicted (Liv. 38.58.1).
25 Liv. 39.19.4.
26 Plaut. *capt.* 1.2.111: *istos captivos duos, heri quos emi de praeda a quaestoribus, eis indito catenas singularias...*; 2.3.453: *... quom illos emi de praeda a quaestoribus.*
27 Cic. *Phil.* 9.16: *... quaestoribus urbis imperent, ut eam basim statuamque faciendam et in rostris statuendam locent.*
28 Crawford, RRC 330–331 no. 330.

ities were, in theory, shared, specific tasks related to the magistracy could be executed by a single quaestor.

The administration of the *aerarium populi Romani*

As has already been noted, the administration of the *aerarium populi Romani* was the main duty or *provincia* of the urban quaestors.[29] On the one hand, this entailed the management and the control of the money and metal reserves—particularly that of gold—which were deposited in the treasury. On the other hand, the urban quaestors, who always acted under the command of the senate,[30] found themselves in charge of supervising all public expenses and incomes at Rome as well as validating and archiving all official documents generated by the Roman bureaucracy. The quaestors were, of course, aided by assistants (*apparitores*), whose number increased considerably throughout the Republic as Rome's administration became increasingly complex.[31] The *Lex Cornelia de XX quaestoribus* offers information on the way the quaestorian *apparitores* (*scribae*, *viatores* and *praecones*) were nominated.[32] Among them, the *scribae* enjoyed an especially high status that corresponded to their greater responsibility.[33] As a matter of fact, the extensive range of complex tasks that the urban quaestors had to oversee during their term of office could not have been properly carried out without the continuous assistance of the scribes. It seems likely that these indispensible officials were appointed for several-year terms,[34] since this would have allowed them to become thoroughly familiar with the workings of the administration, or at the very least to become much more knowledgeable than the inexperienced young quaestors.[35]

---

[29] On the tasks performed by the urban quaestors generally, see Mommsen, Röm.St. II 523–541; Kunkel and Wittmann 1995, 515–523; Lintott 1999, 136–137; Muñiz Coello 2014, 512–520.

[30] See Pol. 6.13.2: 'the quaestors are not authorised to make any expenditure without a decree of the senate.' There is no doubt that Polybius is speaking at this point about the urban quaestors, whereas he refers to the consular quaestors in 6.12.8.

[31] On selection, functions and career of *apparitores*, see Purcell 1983; Muñiz Coello 1982 and 1983, esp.119–125; and especially David 2019.

[32] See Keil 1902; Gabba 1983; Varvaro 1995; Crawford 1996.

[33] Gabba 1983, 489. On the importance and outsize influence of the *scribae* working in the *aerarium*, see Plut. *Cat.min.* 16.2 (cf. David 2019, 63–65 and 224–225). Nonetheless, the *scribae* were of course subjected to control and they could be brought to trial for fraud. Cf. Plut. *Cat.min.* 16.3; Cic. *Mur.* 42: *scriba damnatus, ordo totus alienus.* On scribes brought to trial see Rosillo-López 2010, 127–131.

[34] Their longer tenure can be deduced from Plutarch's account (see below) of how Cato struggled against the corruption of the scribes of the *aerarium* (Plut. *Cat.min.* 16). Cf. Gabba 1983, 489; David 2007, 44.

[35] It seems that every year on the Nones of December (at least in the first century BC) the assignment of each scribe (as well as the other *apparitores*) to a particular magistrate for the following year was sorted out. This took place *apud aerarium* according to the Bobbio scholiast in a passage referring to Clodius: *Tanto prius ad aerarium venit, ut ibi ne scribam quidem quemquam offenderet. Aput aerarium*

Tacitus refers in general to the duties of the urban quaestors as *cura tabularum publicarum*.[36] Although he is speaking of the Principate, this terminology could no doubt be applied to the Republican age as well. Ultimately, all of these duties endowed the urban quaestors with an enormous amount of responsibility, given the sheer volume of public money that fell under their control. Cicero, at the beginning of his discourse in favour of Fonteius, wanted to emphasise the integrity of his client, who, according to Cicero, had demonstrated his honesty throughout his year as urban quaestor. This had a special significance, Cicero says, given the large sums of money that these magistrates regularly handled. In addition, he concludes, these operations were carried out openly, and everything had to be recorded in public and private registers.[37]

As a symbol of their control of public business, the urban quaestors apparently possessed the keys of the *aerarium*. We learn this detail from an episode in Polybius.[38] According to the Greek historian, there was an occasion when funds were urgently required for an unforeseen expenditure, but the urban quaestors did not dare open the treasury that day, since it was against the law to do so.[39] In response to this refusal, Scipio Africanus took the keys and declared that he would open the treasury's doors himself. We can wonder whether the urban quaestors actually had the keys to the whole building, where the *scribae* and other *apparitores* must have been responsible for the real day-to-day work, or whether, as seems more likely, they only controlled access to the area where the public money and assets were housed.[40]

The importance of the urban quaestorship can be further seen in the fact that the Rome's standards (*signa*) were also kept in the *aerarium*; accordingly, it was the

---

sortiri provincias et quaestores solebant et scribae, ut pro certo appareret in quam provinciam vel cum quo praeside proficiscerentur. Ardorem quendam nimiae cupiditatis volens exprimere festinasse ad aerarium dixit ut etiam scribarum praeveniret adventum (Schol.Bob. *in Clod. et Cur.* fr.11 p.87 Stangl). This fact explains why many scribes were around the *aerarium* on the Nones of December 63, when Cicero delivered his fourth *Catilinarian* (Cic. *Cat.* 4.15. See Chapter 4). Cf. David 2007, 42–43; 2019, 96.
36 Tac. *ann.* 13.28. Cf. Ps.-Ascon. p.226 Stangl: *Quaestores urbani aerarium curabant, eiusque pecunias expensas et acceptas in tabulas publicas referre consueverant.*
37 Cic. *Font.* 5: *Duorum magistratuum, quorum uterque in pecunia maxima tractanda procurandaque versatus est, triumviratus et quaesturae, ratio sic redditur, iudices, ut in eis rebus quae ante oculos gestae sunt, ad mu<l>tos pertinuerunt, confectae publicis privatisque tabulis sunt...* Fonteius was probably *triumvir monetalis*.
38 Pol. 23.14.5. Cf. Diodor. 29.21.
39 Both Polybius and Livy (*contra legem*) agree that the refusal of the urban quaestors to take money from the treasury was based on the law. Livy links Africanus' taking of the keys of the *aerarium* with the episode of the conviction of his brother Asiaticus: *Ab eadem fiducia animi, cum quaestores pecuniam ex aerario contra legem promere non auderent, poposcisse clavis et se aperturum aerarium dixisse, qui, ut clauderetur, effecisset* (Liv. 38.55.13).
40 In accordance with Kunkel and Wittmann 1995, 515, only the keys of the so-called *aerarium sanctius*, the special reserve fund of the *civitas*, seem to have been in hands of the consuls instead of the urban quaestors.

urban quaestors who were responsible for transferring them to the generals in command of the army at the gates of the city. The standards were to be returned to the *aerarium* whenever generals came back in Rome. This must have happened during the first centuries of the Republican period, when Rome's wars were fought seasonally and the number of legions was very limited.[41] In fact, this practice of depositing the standards in the *aerarium* may have fallen into disuse as the number of legions increased in step with Rome's expansion throughout the Mediterranean and as wars became semi-permanent and were waged farther and farther from the city.

Financial audits

Beyond the rather symbolic and secondary task concerning the *signa*, the urban quaestors were assigned a number of jobs in direct relation to the public finances. To begin with, they had to audit the accounts of all magistrates after they had completed their terms of offices, both in Rome and in the Empire's provinces. Let us take the auditing of Verres' accounts after his quaestorship as an example. Verres was quaestor in 84 and proquaestor probably in 83–82. After his return to Rome, he was obliged to present the urban quaestors with a detailed record of his accounts (*rationes*). Cicero reproduces the heading of Verres' report: 'Accounts related to the urban quaestors P. Lentulus and L. Triarius.'[42] Lentulus Sura and Triarius were the urban quaestors of 81.

The surrendering and inspection of accounts could sometimes result in political quarrels. In 187 the tribunes of the plebs Petillii launched an investigation against L. Cornelius Scipio Asiaticus for his conduct as proconsul in Asia. The tribunes specifically wanted to force Scipio Asiaticus to submit detailed records of the money and the spoils taken from Antiochus during the war (*pecuniae Antiochinae praedaeque*).[43] Scipio Africanus intervened on behalf of his brother. Africanus, who had acted as a legate under Asiaticus' command, showed the other senators the ledger (*liber*) in which, he claimed, all the money and booty had been recorded. The document had been written, he said, 'to be read publicly and deposited in the treasury' (*ut palam recitaretur et ad aerarium deferretur*). That said, Scipio Africanus went on, he was unwilling to do so. And at that very moment, he proceeded to tear the volume

---

41 Actually, the evidence in Livy is limited to the archaic period: *Haec omnia adeo mature perfecta accepimus ut signa, eo ipso die a quaestoribus ex aerario prompta delataque in campum...* (Liv. 3.69.8); *...cum omnes extra portam Capenam ad Martis aedem convenire armatos iuniores iussisset signaque eodem quaestores ex aerario deferre...* (7.23.3). Cf. Liv. 4.22.1: *Signa ex aerario prompta feruntur ad dictatorem.*
42 Cic. *Verr.* 2.1.37: *P. Lentulo L. Triario quaestoribus urbanis res rationum relatarum.* Unsurprisingly, Cicero uses the supposedly imprecise accounts presented by Verres to discredit him.
43 Gell. 4.18.7.

into pieces with his bare hands.⁴⁴ According to Livy, the investigation into Scipio Asiaticus and his staff did not stop there. As a matter of fact, Scipio Asiaticus, his legate A. Hostilius and also his quaestor C. Furius Aculeo were all found guilty of having embezzled large amounts of gold and silver, which presumably had not been registered in their official accounts.⁴⁵

This episode demonstrates that every magistrate who handled public money during his term in office was obliged to produce a detailed financial account and then bring it to the *aerarium* upon returning from his province.⁴⁶ After the *scribae* working in the treasury had checked them,⁴⁷ the urban quaestors were responsible for declaring whether or not the accounts were satisfactory.⁴⁸ The supposed inaccuracy of the *rationes* submitted by a magistrate could obviously provide fodder for a political attack or even judicial action, as became habitual in the last two centuries of the Republic. When referring to the shoddiness of Verres' accounts after his quaestorship, Cicero gives a hint of how these *rationes* were supposed to be structured. There were three major sections: the amount of money that the magistrate had when beginning of his office; the expenses incurred throughout his mandate; and the final balance.⁴⁹ Within these sections every element had to be described item-by-item, something that required, no doubt, a considerably sophisticated accounting skills.⁵⁰

The *lex Iulia de repetundis*, which was passed in 59, constituted a great effort to avoid the manipulation of public accounts (see chapter 6). Thanks to Cicero, who alludes to this law in letters written both during his term as governor in Cilicia and after his return to Rome, we have fairly good evidence for how this procedure

---

44 Gell. 4.18.8–12. Cf. Liv. 38.55.12: *...quod tantae summae rationem etiam ab ipso P. Scipione requisitam esse in senatu tradunt, librumque rationis eius cum Lucium fratrem adferre iussisset, inspectante senatu suis ipsum manibus concerpsisse indignantem...* Cf. Val.Max. 3.7.1d; Diodor. 29.21. See also the account of how Scipio Africanus destroyed the book of *rationes* in Pol. 23.14.7–11.
45 Liv. 38.55.1–7.
46 On the rules about bookkeeping in the late Roman Republic more generally, see Fallu 1979. Cf. Rosillo-López 2010, 110–111; Cuomo 2011, 198.
47 Cf. Cic. *Pis.* 25: *Ita enim sunt perscriptae scite et litterate ut scriba ad aerarium qui eas rettulit perscriptis rationibus secum ipse caput sinistra manu perfricans commurmuratus sit...*
48 According to Callistratus, a Roman jurist of second-third century AD, the accountability followed several stages: the review of the documentation (*legendas rationes*); the supervision of the calculations (*computandas rationes*) as well as the delivery of the remains (*reliqua solvere*); approval and closing of the accounts (*subscribere rationes*) (*Dig.* 35.1.82). These stages may also have existed during the Republic. See Rosillo-López 2010, 112 n.176.
49 Cic. *Verr.* 2.1.36: *Accepi...viciens ducenta triginta quinque milia quadringentos decem et septem nummos. Dedi stipendio, frumento, legatis, pro quaestore, cohorti praetoriae hs mille sescenta triginta quinque milia quadringentos decem et septem nummos. Reliqui Arimini hs sescenta milia.* Cf. Fallu 1979, 102.
50 Cicero reproaches Verres for the curt nature of his accounts, which is taken as unmistakable proof of his culpability; the orator rhetorically asks: 'Is this the way of presenting accounts?' (Cic. *Verr.* 2.1.36: *Hoc est rationes referre?*).

worked.⁵¹ In accordance with the *lex Iulia*, it was compulsory to deposit two copies of the accounts in two different cities of the province.⁵² This meant that accounts had to be put into their final form before the governor left his province and returned to Rome. A third copy had to be brought to the *aerarium* in Rome to be audited by the urban quaestors and their scribes.⁵³ This procedure was designed so that the different copies could be compared if necessary. The accounts could not be amended once deposited in the provincial cities.⁵⁴ Cicero touts the accuracy and integrity of his accounts, while simultaneously stressing his *scriba* M. Tullius' responsibility for the documents. For Cicero, this was obviously a way of distancing himself from any potential irregularity found in his accounts, though the anecdote also shows that in practice it was the *scribae* who took charge of such bureaucratic issues.⁵⁵

Cato Uticensis was sent to Cyprus in 58, shortly after the *lex Iulia de repetundis* was approved, as *proquaestor pro praetore*.⁵⁶ There, according to Plutarch, he got together nearly seven thousand talents of silver, which were safely transported to Rome.⁵⁷ Although Cato had produced two copies of the accounts relating to his administration of the island, neither was preserved. One of his freedman, Phylargirus, was in charge of bringing one copy along with part of the money to Rome by ship. However, the ship capsized after setting out to sea and the copy was lost. The other copy, which Cato kept on his own person, was destroyed when his ship caught fire in Corcyra.⁵⁸ In short, Cato's accounts in Cyprus were therefore lost forever, and only his sterling reputation protected him from possible accusations of misconduct (see chapter 6). The recent annexation of Cyprus and the temporary lack of a consolidated Roman administration on the island explain why Cato wanted to bring his accounts to Rome instead of leaving two copies in the provinces as the Julian law prescribed.⁵⁹

The booty gained by a general could constitute a substantial part of the accounts that a provincial governor delivered to the urban quaestors. A thorough catalogue of

---

51 See Cic. *fam.* 5.20.1, where Cicero contrasts the *ius vetus et mos antiquus* with the new regulations introduced in the Julian law. Cicero sent this letter to L. Mescinius Rufus, his quaestor in Cilicia. Cf. Venturini 1979, 471–477; Coudry 2009, 58–59; Rosillo-López 2010, 112.
52 Cic. *Att.* 6.7.2: *ego Laodiceae quaestorem Mescinium exspectare iussi, ut confectas rationes lege Iulia apud duas civitates possem relinquere*; *fam.* 2.17.4: *Rationes mei quaestoris nec verum fuit me tibi mittere nec tamen erant confectae. Eas nos Apameae deponere cogitabamus.*
53 Cic. *fam.* 5.20.2. It seems that the *scribae* of the *aerarium* made themselves an additional copy of the accounts, which suggests that the magistrate kept the original in his personal archives. Cf. Rosillo-López 2010, 112.
54 Cic. *fam.* 5.20.8.
55 Fallu 1979, 110; Cuomo 2011, 190.
56 See Díaz Fernández 2015, 205 n. 407.
57 Plut. *Cat.min.* 38.1.
58 Plut. *Cat.min.* 38.2–3.
59 Rosillo-López 2010, 111.

money, gold, silver and any other kind of asset had to be presented.[60] Failure to do so could result in prosecution.[61] Cicero forcefully contrasts the behaviour of Verres in Sicily with that of P. Servilius Vatia Isauricus. Not only had Verres plundered Sicily illegitimately, but he had also kept the spoils for himself and for his friends instead of giving them to the public treasury. On the contrary, Servilius had obtained his booty in accordance with the law of war (*imperatorio iure*), had brought it to Rome, had exhibited it in his triumph and eventually 'he took care of registering everything in public documents in the treasury.'[62] These documents, under the heading 'The accounts delivered by Publius Servilius', were actually available for consultation, since Cicero specifically mentions their contents: 'You see not only the number of the statues, but the size, form, and the state of each one accurately put down in writing.'[63]

Such honest behaviour was always expected from an *imperator*. According to the sources, Pompey had tried to create a good image of himself by acting with scrupulous honesty regarding the booty after his victory against Mithridates. Plutarch asserts that Pompey received from the king of Iberia splendid gifts such as a throne, a table and a couch, all of gold, but he preferred to deliver everything to the quaestors for the public treasury instead of keeping it for himself.[64] Likewise Pompey obliged King Tigranes to give him a large sum of money as punishment, all of which—as was Pompey's custom, according to Velleius Paterculus, and compulsory according to the law—was delivered to the quaestors and registered in public documents: *sicuti Pompeio moris erat, redacta in quaestoris potestatem ac publicis descripta litte-*

---

60 See Churchill 1999, 103: 'This document would serve as a concrete record of what the public had already seen (*during the ceremony of triumph), and would make it possible for those with access to the *aerarium* to confirm their recollections.' On the accounts of booty, see Coudry 2009, 52–60.
61 For example, Manius Acilius Glabrio was prosecuted because a part of the booty that had apparently been taken from Antiochus' camp was not exhibited in the triumphal procession and was not brought to the *aerarium*. See Liv. 37.57.12: *...quod pecuniae regiae praedaeque aliquantum captae in Antiochi castris neque in triumpho tulisset, neque in aerarium rettulisset.*
62 Cic. *Verr.* 2.1.57: *P. Servilius quae signa atque ornamenta ex urbe hostium vi et virtute capta belli lege atque imperatorio iure sustulit, ea populo Romano adportavit, per triumphum vexit, in tabula publica ad aerarium perscribenda curavit.* Cf. Coudry 2009, 53.
63 Cic. *Verr.* 2.1.57: *Rationes relatae P. Servili. Non solum numerum signorum, sed etiam unius cuiusque magnitudinem, figuram, statum litteris definiri vides.* Cf. Liv. 39.7.1, where a detailed list of what Cn. Manlius Vulso contributed to the treasury on the occasion of his triumph is given: 200 golden crowns, 220.000 pounds of silver, 2103 pounds of gold, etc. It is obvious that this information comes from the official report delivered by Manlius Vulso. According to Plutarch, Cato Uticensis paid five talents for a copy of the books containing accounts of the public business from the times of Sulla to his own quaestorship in 64 (Plut. *Cat.min.* 18.5). This seems to imply that public documents were available for private use.
64 Plut. *Pomp.* 36.7.

ris.⁶⁵ Cicero himself categorically declares in a letter written to Caninius Sallustius that the booty he had been able to acquire during his expedition was to be sent to the urban quaestors, that is, to the Roman people, without anyone else touching it. Cicero adds that in Laodicea he would take all necessary measures to ensure that the public money would reach Rome without any logistical mishaps.⁶⁶ At any rate, generals always had to deliver money to the urban quaestors after their return to Rome, though they gave other types of booty to other magistrates. After enjoying a victory in Sardinia in 215, for instance, T. Manlius Torquatus returned to Rome and transferred the money (*stipendium*) to the urban quaestors, the corn to the aediles and the prisoners to the praetor.⁶⁷

Every Roman general's final duty upon returning to the city, therefore, was to deliver to the urban quaestors a very detailed catalogue of spoils taken from the enemy. This documentation, kept in the *aerarium*, should be implicitly understood as a statement of public ownership. As in other cases, the duty of the urban quaestors was consequently to act as public notaries on behalf of the *civitas*.

The urban quaestors were the magistrates responsible for the general accounting of the Roman state, for its supervision, control and preservation. Presumably, they should also have been subject to oversight, since in practice they ultimately managed all public money. Plutarch provides an anecdote about Lentulus Sura in order to explain his *cognomen*.⁶⁸ When Lentulus Sura was *quaestor urbanus* in 81, he apparently wasted and lost large amounts of public money. The dictator Sulla then demanded that he present his accounts in the senate, to which Lentulus Sura arrogantly answered that he would not be handing over any such account. This episode must be understood in the context of the particular political circumstances of the Sullan dictatorship. That said, it could be indicative of a more widespread practice according to which the urban quaestors could be called to present their own accounts to the senate, if they were suspected of any wrongdoing. Nevertheless, it seems reasonable that the regular procedure would be that the urban quaestors delivered their accounts to the new urban quaestors when they left office and the official transfer of powers took place. The new magistrates would therefore scrutinize their predecessors' accounts, just like they would review the financial documents of any other magistrate who handled public money.

---

65 Vell. 2.37.5. There are, however, other versions of the episode. App. *Mith*. 105, asserts that Tigranes gave to Pompey 6000 talents as well as some extra money to the soldiers (cf. Plut. *Pomp*. 33.5); Str. 11.14.10 says that the money that Tigranes gave Pompey was distributed among the army.
66 Cic. *fam*. 2.17.4: *De praeda mea praeter quaestores urbanos, id est populum Romanum, terruncium nec attigit nec tacturus est quisquam. Laodiceae me praedes accepturum arbitror omnis pecuniae publicae, ut et mihi et populo cautum sit sine vecturae periculo.*
67 Liv. 23.41.7: *et stipendium quaestoribus, frumentum aedilibus, captivos Q. Fulvio praetori tradit.*
68 Plut. *Cic*. 17.2.

Public auctions

As previously discussed, the urban quaestors acted as public notaries when reviewing and keeping track of the booty that generals brought to Rome. Nonetheless, this was not the urban quaestors' only job related to war spoils. A portion of the booty, the *praeda*, was liable to be sold, in particular prisoners of war.[69] Although most war captives were sold by provincial quaestors in the territories where they had been captured, some were paraded before the Roman people during an *imperator*'s triumph. Once these captives entered the city, the urban quaestors were put in charge of selling them at public auction and raising as much money as possible for the *aerarium*.[70]

In his play *Captivi*, Plautus refers to this fact: 'Put a chain on each of the two prisoners whom I purchased yesterday out of the spoils from the quaestors.'[71] Of course, Plautus' plays takes place in a Greek setting, but they were addressed to a Roman audience and are chockfull of specific references to Roman institutions and daily life, which explains his mention of a well known type of auction specific to Rome. When speaking of the early Republic, both Livy and Dionysius of Halicarnassus take urban quaestor's auctioning of booty as a well-established practice, the proceeds of which would then be deposited in the public treasury.[72]

As the Empire expanded and more and more triumphs were celebrated at Rome, the sale of prisoners of war became a normal and increasingly common task that the urban quaestors had to conduct. However, other assets resulting directly from Roman expansion—but not from the spoils taken by an *imperator* in a war—could also be auctioned publicly. Attalus' treasure, for instance, was brought to Rome after the king of Pergamum had named the Roman people as his heir.[73] According to Pliny, 'the auction of the king's belongings' caused quite the frenzy at Rome.[74] This auction was, in all probability, conducted under the direction of one of the urban quaestors.

---

[69] See the diference between *praeda* and *manubiae* in Gell. 13.25.26: *Nam praeda dicitur corpora ipsa rerum, quae capta sunt, manubiae vero appellatae sunt pecunia a quaestore ex venditione praedae redacta*. Cf. Tarpin 2009.

[70] García-Morcillo 2005, 43–44. Cf. Mommsen, Röm.St. II 538; Kunkel and Wittmann 1995, 517.

[71] Plaut. *capt*. 1.2.111: *istos captivos duos, heri quos emi de praeda a quaestoribus, eis indito catenas singularias...* And again later in 2.3.453: 'when I purchased these men from the quaestors out of the spoils' (*quom illos emi de praeda a quaestoribus*). Cf. Leigh 2004, 59: 'the title of the play is not *Slaves* but rather *Prisoners* or even *Prisoners of War*.' See Leigh's chapter 3 on Plautus' *Captivi*.

[72] Liv. 4.53.10; Dion.Hal. 5.34.4–5. Cf. Liv. 6.4.2; 7.27.8–9: *magnam pecuniam in aerarium redegit*.

[73] According to Justin (36.4.9), it was M. Perperna (consul and proconsul in Asia in 130–129; cf. Broughton MRR 1.501–502) who put the treasure of Attalus on ships to be brought to Rome: *In huius locum missus Perperna consul prima congressione Aristonicum superatum in potestatem suam redegit Attalicasque gazas, hereditarias populi Romani, navibus inpositas Romam deportavit.*

[74] Plin. *n.h.* 33.148–149: *at eadem Asia donata multo etiam gravius adflixit mores, inutilioque victoria illa hereditas Attalo rege mortuo fuit. Tum enim haec emendi Romae in auctionibus regiis verecundia exempta est urbis anno DCXXII.*

The urban quaestors were also responsible for the auction of objects confiscated from citizens who either had debts to the state but were insolvent or those who had been condemned to pay a fine and were unable to do so. The assets of the victims of the Sullan and triumviral proscriptions were also sold at public auctions.[75] This legal process was called *bonorum sectio*.[76] Since the proceeds from the auction would go to the *aerarium* in such cases, there is no doubt that the urban quaestors were ultimately in charge of all these public auctions.[77] The auctions were managed in practice by one of their assistants, a *praeco*, who announced the items for sale and their prices.[78] The *bonorum sectio* constituted the distribution of the assets of the proscribed and convicted to a retailer or *sector* (the word *sectio* alludes specifically to the division of the auctioned assets for their private resale).[79] Next, the *sector* privately sold the acquired goods.[80] During the process of confiscation and sale, therefore, there was a close connection between urban quaestor and *sector*, as Cicero emphasises in his *Verrines*.[81] In his commentary on the Ciceronian text, Pseudo-Asconius specifies that a *sector* reached an agreement about payment with the Roman administration, which was obviously represented by the urban quaestor, and the sum of money was then delivered to the public treasury.[82]

Immediately after an individual was convicted and ordered to pay a sum of money, he was obliged to give to the urban quaestor guarantees (*praedes*) of the payment, since money ultimately had to be deposited in the *aerarium*. This is established in the *Tabula Bantina Latina* (*l*.10: *praedes praediaq]ue ad q(uaestorem) urb(anum)*

---

[75] When Cicero speaks of Sulla's proscriptions, he refers to the 'fatal auctions' in which the assets of the citizens who had been proscribed were sold off as if a sale of spoils (*praeda*) was being held: *L. Sulla cum bona indemnatorum civium funesta illa auctione sua venderet et se praedam suam diceret vendere...* (Cic. *leg.agr.* 2.56).
[76] Mateo 1999, 28–29. Cf. Mommsen, Röm.St. II 536.
[77] In the context of Sp. Maelius' conviction in 439 for supposedly having tried to become a tyrant, Livy includes as a punishment the sale of all his assets by the quaestors and the delivery of the money obtained to the public treasury: *Iubere itaque quaestores vendere ea bona atque in publicum redigere* (Liv. 4.15.8). The episode concerning Maelius is, in all probability, fictitious. However, the procedure to which Livy alludes is based on reality, and the quaestors mentioned can only be the *quaestores urbani*. Cf. Dion.Hal. 11.46.4, on the quaestors' confiscations of the estates belonging to the decemvirs, who had been put to death or had gone into exile.
[78] Schol. in Horatium, Sermonum libri 1.6.86: *praecones dicebantur qui stabant ad hastam et nuntiabant pretia allata*. Cf. Cic. *Phil.* 2.103: *quis hastam istius venditionis vidit, quis vocem praeconis audivit?*; *leg.agr.* 2.103: *publicus praeco*. See David 2019, 53.
[79] Gaius *inst.* 4.146: *Item ei qui publica bona emerit eiusdem condicionis interdictum proponitur, quod appellatur sectorium, quod sectores vocantur qui publice bona mercantur*.
[80] On the process of *bonorum sectio* see García Morcillo 2005, 48–49. Cf. Mateo 1999, 67.
[81] Cic. *Verr.* 2.1.52: *Quid tum hos de te iudicaturos arbitratus es, cum viderent te iam non contra accusatorem tuum, sed contra quaestorem sectoremque pugnare?* Cf. 2.1.61.
[82] Ps. Ascon. p.236 Stangl: *Sectorem autem dicit aestimatorem redemptoremque bonorum damnati atque proscripti, qui spem sectans lucri sui, id est secutus spem aestimationis suae, bona omnia re auctione vendit et semel infert pecuniam vela erario vel sociis*. Cf. Ps. Ascon. p.239 Stangl.

de taut bona eius poplice possideantur facito),⁸³ and in the *lex repetundarum* (*l*.57: *iudex... q(uaestorei) praedes facito det*).⁸⁴ The *lex repetundarum* makes it clear that the urban quaestors were involved in the entire process. They received the sureties from a condemned person along with a record of the amount given. They recorded the amount in the *tabulae publicae* and in the *aerarium*. Any damages were likewise to be delivered to the quaestors. The money collected by the quaestor for disbursement to the victims was gathered in baskets, sealed and labelled with the praetor's name as well as the source and the amount. Finally, the quaestors were responsible for overseeing payment to the relevant persons, in compliance with the praetor's orders.⁸⁵

In cases when a convicted individual refused to pay, the quaestor would proceed to confiscate his possessions and sell them at auction. Evidence of this procedure is found in the proceedings against Scipio Asiaticus in 187, which Livy narrates in detail. Scipio was convicted of embezzling funds from King Antiochus and as a consequence he was condemned to restore a significant sum of money to the treasury. The *praetor peregrinus*, Q. Terentius Culleo, who was in charge of the trial against Scipio, sent the quaestors to seize Scipio's property.⁸⁶ As Livy tells it, not only was the king's gold not found in Scipio's home but the amount obtained in the auction of his assets was also insufficient to cover the sum that he had been ordered to pay.⁸⁷ In this same judicial process, the quaestor C. Furius Aculeo and the legate A. Hostilius were also convicted, but in their cases it did not prove necessary to confiscate their properties, since they gave the urban quaestors the required guarantees on the day that their verdicts were delivered.⁸⁸

The urban quaestors were also in charge of selling public land (*ager publicus*). The Roman territory subject to sale by the urban quaestors received the name of *ager quaestorius*.⁸⁹ In accordance with Hyginus' definition, the *agri quaestorii* were lands that originally belonged to enemies who had been defeated and expelled, whose land thus became the property of the Roman people. At a given moment, a senatorial decree could instruct the quaestors to sell said property: 'Lands called quaestorian are those that the Roman people acquired after an enemy had been defeated and conquered, and which the quaestors were instructed to sell.'⁹⁰ Nonetheless, it must be borne in mind that the term *ager quaestorius* does not appear in Re-

---

83 Crawford 1996, 200.
84 Crawford 1996, 71 and 107.
85 *Lex repetundarum* ll.67–69. Cf. Crawford 1996, 72 and 108–109; Harries 2007, 63.
86 Liv. 38.60.8: *In bona deinde L. Scipionis possessum publice quaestores praetor misit*.
87 Liv. 38.60.9–10.
88 Liv. 38.58.1: *Iudiciis a Q. Terentio praetore perfectis, Hostilius et Furius damnati praedes eodem die quaestoribus urbanis dederunt*.
89 Roselaar 2010, 121–127, with additional bibliography.
90 Hyg.grom. *De condicionibus agrorum* 78: *Quaestorii autem dicuntur agri, quos populus Romanus devictis pulsisque hostibus possedit, mandavitque quaestoribus ut eos venderent*. Cf. Castillo Pascual 1996, 15–16; Hermon 1997.

publican sources, but only in the books of the land surveyors (*agrimensores*) dating to the Imperial period. Certainly the categories that the land surveyors of the Imperial age defined could already have existed under the Republic, but it is also possible that they were not yet strictly defined.[91] At any rate, it seems reasonable to use the term *ager quaestorius* for the land that was sold by the quaestors during the Republic.[92]

We have evidence of what happened in 205, when new funds were needed to continue the war against the Carthaginians. This needs raised by the war effort led the senate to instruct the urban quaestors to sell the part of Capuan territory that extended from the so-called Fossa Graeca to the coast.[93] Livy's account of this episode, which happens to be the only example of quaestors selling land that is preserved in the literary record, suggests that such a sale presented a possible remedy when Rome needed money quickly; more importantly for our purposes, Livy unequivocally shows that the urban quaestors were capable of selling public land at auction.[94] Moreover, in a passage from his second discourse against the Rullan agrarian bill where he criticises the overly wide-ranging powers of the commission, Cicero alludes to the (urban) quaestor as the magistrate whom the decemvirs, according to the new agrarian law, could appoint to delegate their functions. In accordance with Cicero, the urban quaestor could in turn delegate the responsibility of making a decision about the land that was to be distributed to a surveyor (*finitor*).[95] This text, then, supports the notion that the urban quaestors had the power to intervene in the distribution of public land.

---

[91] Roselaar 2010, 87.
[92] The concept *ager quaestorius* could have been created and developed in the third century; most of the lands under this name seem to have been in central Italy (see Roselaar 2010, 144).
[93] Liv. 28.46.4: *Et quia pecunia ad bellum deerat, agri Campani regionem a fossa Graeca ad mare versam vendere quaestores iussi...*
[94] Although the evidence is not conclusive, it is likely that *agri quaestorii* remained the property of the state, that is, *ager publicus* (Roselaar 2010, 122–123). The legal status of this land, however, is far from clear. See the conclusion of Campbell 2000, 474: 'In strict legal terms public land disposed of at auction remained in the property of the Roman people... But it remains unclear what status lands originally designated as quaestorian had, or if they were regularly subject to a *vectigal* denoting that they remained under public control. It is possible, however, that some quaestorian lands subject to *vectigal* existed, either as a temporary arrangement, or because they had subsequently been sold on and then rented out.'
[95] Cic. leg.agr. 2.34: *...singuli de maximis rebus iudicent, quaestori permittant, finitorem mittant, ratum sit quod finitor uni illi a quo missus erit renuntiaverit.* Cf. Walter 2013, 88, where *quaesitori permittant* is preferred to the usual reading *quaestori permittant*.

Public income and expenses

Through their assistants working in the *aerarium*, the urban quaestors acted as Rome's general accountants. One of their most important tasks, therefore, was the supervision of all public income and expenses, thus assuming the role of the Republic's comptrollers. We have already seen how the urban quaestors dealt with the public incomes derived from auctions in which different items were sold: part of the spoils, such as prisoners of war; the property of individuals who declared themselves insolvent or became outlaws due to a proscription; and public land. They were involved, additionally, in securing other resources for the *aerarium*.

The war reparations that defeated peoples or cities were obliged to pay Rome constituted one of the treasury's streams of income that the urban quaestors had to supervise. It was the senate's responsibility to take decisions about whether or not compensations had to be paid, while the actual amount sent to Rome was either imposed by Rome or was agreed upon by the two parties. Eventually, however, the quaestors had to ensure that the reparations were properly paid. In the year 199, Carthaginian legates brought to Rome the first instalment of the war indemnity, which was paid in silver. After assessing whether the amount was correct, the urban quaestors reported that a quarter was actually an alloy and therefore the required value was not reached. The Carthaginian envoys were forced to make up the missing amount, which they did by borrowing money in Rome.[96]

The Hannibalic War put a great economic strain on Rome, and part of the citizenship contributed towards financing the conflict. In 214, when the *aerarium* was empty, there was a sudden wave of solidarity among the Roman citizens, many of whom were willing to make financial sacrifices on behalf of the community: contractors asserted that they would not ask for money from the *aerarium* until the war was over; the owners of the slaves whom Ti. Gracchus had manumitted at Beneventum said that they would not claim the value of their slaves until the war ended.[97] In this context, there were actually sufficient funds to support orphans and widows preserved in the treasury, so that, according to Livy, 'whatever was bought or provided for orphans or widows, the [urban] quaestor gave the authorisation for payment.'[98] Once the war finished and Rome was in the process of recovery, the senate took the decision of giving back the money to all those who had contributed to the war effort. In 196 the last repayment was supposed to be made. In this context a serious quarrel erupted between the urban quaestors for that year, L. Aurelius and Q. Fabius Labeo, and the whole body of priests, since the augurs and pontiffs had not made

---

96 Liv. 32.2.1–2: *Carthaginienses eo anno argentum in stipendium impositum primum Romam advexerunt. Id quia probum non esse quaestores renuntiaverant experientibusque pars quarta decocta erat, pecunia Romae mutua sumpta intertrimentum argenti expleverunt.*
97 Liv. 24.18.10–12.
98 Liv. 24.18.14: *inde si quid emptum paratumque pupillis ac viduis foret, a quaestore perscribebatur.* Cf. Val.Max. 5.6.8. The term *perscribere* in this case specifically pertains to the language of banking.

any contribution during the war. At the request of the quaestors, the priests were compelled to pay their quota for each year of the war.[99]

Together with these extraordinary methods of raising income, the urban quaestors also supervised more normal means of doing so, such as the *tributum* paid by every Roman citizen. The amount paid by every citizen had to be registered in the *tabulae publicae*.[100] The fact that careful records were kept can be deduced from Livy's account of the events of 187: the urban quaestors, according to a senatorial decree, paid back some money to those who had paid more than their fair share to contribute to the *stipendium* of the soldiers. The funds used to reimburse these citizens were obtained from the money paraded in Manlius Vulso's triumphal procession.[101]

Just as the public income flowed into the *aerarium*, the money used to pay the state's expenses flowed out of the treasury. As a result, it was expected that the urban quaestors would monitor all expenses. To begin with, the urban quaestors were responsible for all regular public expenses, such as the payment of *apparitores* in the service of the various magistrates; the feeding of the Capitoline geese;[102] and the purchase of animals for official religious sacrifices performed by magistrates, since they acted in the name of the community.[103]

The urban quaestors did not take the initiative in paying a public expense, since they simply followed orders handed down by the senate or a higher magistrate in the name of the senate. Nevertheless, all public expenses required the urban quaestors' authorisation, since they were ultimately responsible the state's finances.[104] As a result, we can see a separation of specific duties among various magistrates who were involved in different aspects of a single project, such as the construction and maintenance of public buildings. The power to make a contract (*potestas locandi*) belonged primarily to the censors, although the consuls also possessed it.[105] The allocation of funds followed a certain procedure that began when the censors sent an official demand (*postulatio*) to the senate for money to be spent on public works.[106] If the request was accepted, a senatorial decree was issued authorising

---

99 Liv. 33.42: *Sed magnum certamen cum omnibus sacerdotibus eo anno fuit quaestoribus urbanis Q. Fabio Labeoni et L. Aurelio. Pecunia opus erat, quod ultimam pensionem pecuniae in bellum conlatae persolvi placuerat privatis. Quaestores ab auguribus pontificibusque quod stipendium per bellum non contulissent petebant... omniumque annorum per quos non dederant exactum est.*
100 Tributes brought by an embassy to Rome were also given to the urban quaestors for the *aerarium*, such as the *stipendium* of Antiochus brought by the leader of the king's envoys, Apollonius: *quaestores urbani stipendium, vasa aurea censores acceperunt...* (Liv. 42.6.11).
101 Liv. 39.7.5: *vicenos quinos et semisses in milia aeris quaestores urbani cum fide et cura solverunt.* Cf. Kunkel and Wittmann 1995, 518.
102 Cf. Kunkel and Wittmann 1995, 515.
103 Liv. 45.44.15.
104 Trisciuoglio 1998, 102. Cf. Mommsen, Röm.St. II 541.
105 Pina Polo 2011, 135–136.
106 Liv. 40.46.16: *censoribus deinde postulantibus, ut pecuniae summa sibi, qua in opera publica uterentur, <attribueretur,> vectigal annuum decretum est.* On the procedure see Trisciuoglio 1998, 118–121.

the urban quaestors to put a certain sum of money at the censors' disposal: this was the so-called grant of money (*adtributio*). The censors would then sign a contract, either jointly or separately. The same procedure was followed if the senate authorised the consuls or praetors to construct a building.

We have a good example of this process in 169, when Livy informs us of the senatorial decree by which the quaestors were instructed to give the censors half of the year's *vectigalia* for the construction of public works.[107] With these funds the censor Ti. Sempronius Gracchus purchased the house of Scipio Africanus on the state's behalf and then signed a contract for the construction of the building, which afterwards was known as the Basilica Sempronia.

The urban quaestors also dealt with any extraordinary expenses with which the Roman state was faced. In 186, once the Bacchanalia had been suppressed and the consul Sp. Postumius had returned to Rome, the question was raised about the rewards owed to the informers, on whose account the affair had been revealed. In accordance with a senatorial decree, the urban quaestors were instructed to pay P. Aebutius and Hispala Fecenia 100.000 asses each from the treasury.[108]

The unusual case of the quaestor Cn. Octavius Ruso raises some questions. According to Sallust, by 105 Ruso was entrusted to bring money (*stipendium*) for Marius' army in Africa. Once he had accomplished his mission, he returned to Rome with the legates of the king Bocchus of Mauretania (see above).[109] At first sight, he might appear to have been a consular quaestor joining his new commander (i.e. Marius) in the field.[110] However, this is highly unlikely. To begin with, it was Sulla who was serving at that moment under the command of Marius in Africa, first as quaestor and later as proquaestor. Second, it would make no sense for Ruso to join Marius, but then leave him immediately and go back to Rome. The fact that he was sent to Africa on a special mission to transport money taken from the *aerarium* as well as the subsequent detail that he escorted Bocchus' envoys on their trip to Rome suggest that Octavius Ruso was actually an urban quaestor. Given the circumstances of the war in Africa, the senate appears to have considered it convenient that one of the urban quaestors, the magistrates in charge of the *aerarium*, should personally be responsible for bringing the *stipendium* to Marius in the field.

---

[107] Liv. 44.16.9: *ad opera publica facienda cum eis dimidium ex vectigalibus eius anni attributum ex senatus consulto a quaestoribus esset...*
[108] Liv. 39.19.4: *...senatus consultum factum est, uti singulis his centena milia aeris quaestores urbani ex aerario darent.*
[109] Sall. *Iug.* 104.3: *Ceterum Mauri impetratis omnibus rebus tres Romam profecti duce Cn. Octavio Rusone, qui quaestor stipendium in Africam portaverat, duo ad regem redeunt.*
[110] Gruen 1966c, 106. Cic. *Verr.* 2.1.34 speaks of Verres as the quaestor of the consul Carbo in the year 84. As quaestor, Verres brought the money for the army to Gaul, where he joined his commander. This case could appear similar to Ruso's, but the difference rests in the fact that Verres stayed with his commander in the province, given that he was indeed a consular quaestor.

Diplomacy and accommodation of foreign guests

In one of his *Quaestiones Romanae*, Plutarch wonders why ambassadors, when arriving to Rome from any country, would immediately proceed to the temple of Saturn and register themselves with the treasury's prefects.[111] Plutarch, obviously speaking of his own time, refers to the *praefecti aerarii Saturni*, the magistrates that took charge of the *aerarium* under the Principate. Plutarch found the solution to his question in the historical record. Accordingly, his answer goes back to the Republican period and provides information about one of the tasks usually carried out by the urban quaestors: 'It seems that in early days the treasurers [i.e. the urban quaestors] used to give presents to foreign envoys, which were called *lautia*, and they took care of the ambassadors if they were sick, and buried them at public expense if they died; but now, because of the great number of embassies that come, this expensive practice has been interrupted; nevertheless, the preliminary meeting with the prefects of the treasury still exists as a kind of registration.'

The practices that Plutarch mentions are indeed attested for the Republican age in relation to the urban quaestors' duties. During the Republic, the consuls, if they were present at Rome, were in charge of introducing foreign legates to the senate. They then presided over the debate, and subsequently notified the envoys of the decision taken by the senators. The consuls also had to see to the adequate accommodation of the ambassadors, in accordance with their status. The urban praetor performed these functions if the consuls were absent from Rome.[112] Ultimately, a higher magistrate was always responsible—in the name of the senate—for the attention lavished on foreign legates at Rome. In practice, however, it was the urban quaestors had to implement this public show of respect.

Let us begin with the registration of foreign legates that Plutarch mentions at the end of his text. As with many other tasks that the urban quaestors carried out, there is no clear evidence in the sources. However, a Ciceronian text seems to allude to the role they performed. In his speech for Flaccus, Cicero refers in a deprecatory manner to three Greek legates who took part in the trial against his client. In particular, Cicero accuses them of having intended to falsify the documents filed in the *aerarium*: they declared they had come to Rome with nine slaves, when in fact they had trav-

---

111 Plut. *Quaest.Rom.* 43: 'διὰ τί δ' οἱ πρεσβεύοντες εἰς Ῥώμην ὁποθενοῦν ἐπὶ τὸν τοῦ Κρόνου ναὸν βαδίζοντες ἀπογράφονται πρὸς τοὺς ἐπάρχους τοῦ ταμιείου;' πότερον ὡς ξένου τοῦ Κρόνου γενομένου καὶ διὰ τοῦτο τοῖς ξένοις χαίροντος, ἢ καὶ τοῦτο λύεται τῇ ἱστορίᾳ; τὸ γὰρ παλαιὸν, ὡς ἔοικεν, οἱ ταμίαι ξένια τοῖς πρεσβεύουσιν ἔπεμπον ἐκαλεῖτο δὲ 'λαύτια' τὰ πεμπόμενα, καὶ νοσούντων ἐπεμέλοντο καὶ τελευτήσαντας ἔθαπτον ἐκ δημοσίου· νῦν δ' ὑπὸ πλήθους τῶν ἀφικνουμένων πρέσβεων ἐκλέλειπται τὸ τῆς δαπάνης, μένει δ' ἔτι τὸ τοῖς ἐπάρχοις τοῦ ταμιείου προεντυγχάνειν διὰ τῆς ἀπογραφῆς.
112 See Pina Polo 2011, 66–82.

elled without escort.¹¹³ This text seems to demonstrate that the foreign ambassadors were required to show the urban quaestors their credentials upon arrival and were likewise obliged to give information about their retinue. All relevant data were officially registered in the *aerarium*. Although Cicero is speaking of the first century, such a practice probably existed in earlier periods as well. This is easy to understand, since it provided a means of monitoring all legates who arrived in Rome as the representatives of a city, king or state.¹¹⁴ Additionally, these ambassadors might have been eligible to receive official hospitality, which included public accommodation for them and their entourage, and sometimes gifts, as we shall see.¹¹⁵ For this purpose, it was necessary to know exactly who the legates were, how many people were part of their entourage, and finally the social status of each member of the party. All of this information would be used to determine how much money their stay in Rome would cost to the *aerarium*. The urban quaestors were therefore directly interested in making sure that envoys were correctly registered and that all information, including any *senatus consultum* providing instructions for the ambassadors' stay and meetings, was recorded in the *aerarium*.

We do have clear evidence for urban quaestors escorting prominent foreign guests and generally being in charge of their accommodation.¹¹⁶ While the dedication of a quaestor's time and attention should obviously be seen as symbol of deference towards the guests, having the quaestors close at hand was also a means of control and provided a good way to keep the senate informed of guests' movements in Rome and Italy.¹¹⁷ In 168, L. Manlius was sent by the senate with a sum of money to meet Masgaba, one of the sons of King Masinissa, who had arrived in Puteoli.¹¹⁸ Manlius' assignment obliged him to escort his guest to Rome at the state's expense.¹¹⁹ Once in Rome, Masgaba was given an audience in the senate and spoke to the senators. After that, the senate instructed Manlius to spend 100 pounds of silver on gifts for the prince and then to escort him back to Puteoli. Manlius was to cover all of Masgaba's expenses as long as he was in Italy. Furthermore, Manlius

---

113 Cic. *Flacc.* 43: *Hi tres etiam aerari nostri tabulas falsas esse voluerunt; nam servos novem se professi sunt habere, cum omnino sine comite venissent.*
114 Cf. Coudry 2004, 533–534.
115 Coudry 2004, 535–536 and 538–539.
116 Mommsen, Röm.St. II 540; Kunkel and Wittmann 1995, 517; Muñiz Coello 2014, 520.
117 Coudry 2004, 547.
118 We have earlier evidence. In 173 envoys from Antiochus arrived in Rome under the leadership of Apollonius, who received a present of 100,000 ases as well as free hospitality as long as he remained in Italy (Liv. 42.6.11: *legato centum milium aeris munus missum et aedes liberae hospitio datae sumptusque decretus, donec in Italia esset*). Livy does not mention the urban quaestors as the magistrates responsible for the accomodation of Apollonius, but they surely were (Livy alludes to the urban quaestors in the previous sentence as accepting on behalf of the *aerarium* the presents that Apollonius brought in the name of King Antiochus).
119 Liv. 45.13.12: *Et Masgabae, regis Masinissae filio, Puteolis nave egresso praesto fuit obviam missus cum pecunia L. Manlius quaestor, qui Romam eum publico sumptu perduceret.*

was ordered to hire two ships in which Masgaba and his retinue were to be brought to Africa. Finally, clothes were given as presents to all members of his entourage, even including the slaves.[120]

Not long afterwards, a letter from Masinissa's other son, Misagenes, was received in Rome. After Perseus' defeat, L. Aemilius Paullus had sent Misagenes with his cavalry back to Africa. Unfortunately, his fleet had been dispersed during his journey, and he had ended up in Brundisium. Misagenes also informed the senate that he was ill. As had previously happened with Masinissa's other son, the senate reacted immediately by sending the other urban quaestor, L. Stertinius, to Brundisium with presents of equal value to those given to Masgaba. Likewise, Stertinius was instructed to provide Misagenes with accommodation, presumably in Brundisium.[121] Although Livy's account abruptly stops here since the text is corrupted, Valerius Maximus gives further details about this episode. The quaestor was to do everything necessary to encourage Misagenes' speedy recovery, to pay attention to him and to his entourage, and to hire vessels to transport the group back to Africa. In addition, each horseman received one pound of silver and 500 sestertii.[122]

Something similar happened the following year. In this case, when King Prusias arrived in Italy, the senate dispatched the urban quaestor L. Cornelius Scipio to meet the king in Capua. Once in Rome, Prusias was granted an immediate audience in the senate, but he asked for two days to visit the temples and the city before meeting with the senators. The quaestor Scipio was assigned to take him around the city and act as a sort of tourist guide. A house was also found for Prusias and for his retinue.[123] Valerius Maximus specifies that the senate decreed to rent Prusias the most beautiful house available in the city.[124] At the end of his stay in Rome, presents were given to Prusias, and also his son Nicomedes, which were equal in value to those given to Masinissa's son Masgaba. Animals for sacrifice were to be supplied to the king at public expense if he so desired. Back in Brundisium, twenty ships were set

---

120 Liv. 45.14.6–7: *munera ex senatus consulto emere regulo quaestor iussus ex centum pondo argenti et prosequi eum Puteolos omnemque sumptum, quoad in Italia esset, praebere et duas naves conducere, quibus ipse comitesque eius in Africam deveherentur; et comitibus omnibus, liberis servisque, vestimenta data.*
121 Liv. 45.14.8–9: *haud ita multo post de altero Masinissae filio Misagene litterae adlatae sunt... <ad> eum cum isdem muneribus, quae data Romae fratri eius erant, L. Stertinius quaestor Brundisium missus <iussus>que curare, ut aedes hospi<tio>...*
122 Val.Max. 5.1.1: *quod ubi senatus cognovit, continuo illo quaestorem ire iussit, cuius cura et hospitium adulescenti expediretur et omnia, quae ad valitudinem opus essent, praeberentur inpensaeque liberaliter cum ipsi tum toti comitatui praestarentur, naves etiam ut prospicerentur, quibus se bene ac tuto cum suis in Africam traiceret. Equitibus singulas libras argenti et quingenos sestertios dari imperavit.*
123 Liv. 45.44.7: *datus, qui circumduceret eum, <L.> Cornelius Scipio quaestor, qui et Capuam ei obviam missus fuerat; et aedes, quae ipsum comitesque eius benigne reciperent, conductae.*
124 Val.Max. 5.1.1: *...obviam illi P. Cornelium Scipionem quaestorem Capuam misit censuitque ut ei domus Romae quam optima conduceretur et copiae non solum ipsi, sed etiam comitibus eius publice praeberentur...*

aside for his use.¹²⁵ Throughout the time Prusias spent in Italy until he reached the fleet, the quaestor Scipio was told not to leave him alone and to pay for all expenses incurred by the king and the members of his entourage.¹²⁶ Presumably, the quaestor had to explain to the senate all the expenses incurred during the king's stay.

Some years later, in 164, Ptolemy VI Philometor was deposed from the throne by his younger brother and fled to Rome in search of support.¹²⁷ Because of his hasty escape, the Roman senate was not informed in advance of his imminent arrival to the city. In fact, the senate only learned of his presence when the dethroned king had already arrived in Rome and was staying at the house of an Alexandrian painter. The senators immediately summoned Ptolemy to the Curia, and apologised for not having sent a quaestor to meet him, according to the Roman custom, and for not having offered him public lodgings. Immediately after leaving the Curia, Ptolemy was taken to a house, in which he was accommodated at public expense. In addition, the urban quaestor was instructed to bring him presents (*munera*) every day.¹²⁸

We have information from the first century showing that the urban quaestors were still in charge of the accommodation of eminent foreigners. In 78 the so-called *senatus consultum de Asclepiade* was issued, a bilingual inscription engraved on a bronze tablet, with the Latin text on the upper half followed by a Greek translation on the lower portion of the tablet.¹²⁹ It contains a senatorial decree, according to which three Greek navarchs were granted some privileges as a reward for services rendered during the wars in Italy, which appears to be a reference to the Social War. The three beneficiaries were Asclepiades of Clazomene, Polystratos of Carystos and Meniskos of Miletus. They were declared 'friends of the Roman people' (*amici populi Romani*) and received Roman citizenship along with financial exemptions. In a similar way to the episodes narrated by Livy for 168 and 167, the senatorial decree instructed the urban quaestor to take care of the three honoured men:¹³⁰ 'the consuls Quintus Lutatius and Marcus Aemilius, one of them or both, if it seems good to them, are to take care that these men be entered on the roll (*formula*) of [Rome's] friends and that they be permitted to set up a bronze tablet of friendship on the Capitolium and to perform a sacrifice, and [the consuls] are to instruct the

---

125 Liv. 45.44.14–16.
126 Liv. 45.44.17: *donec ad classem dono datam ei rex pervenisset, L. Cornelius Scipio ne ab eo abscederet sumptumque ipsi et comitibus praeberet, donec navem conscendisset.*
127 Liv. per. 46. Ptolemy was restored the following year.
128 Val.Max. 5.1.1: *id postquam senatui relatum est, accersito iuvene quam potuit accurata excusatione usus est, quod nec quaestorem illi more maiorum obviam misisset nec publico eum hospitio excepisset... e curia protinus ad publicos penates deduxit hortatusque est ut depositis sordibus adeundi ipsius diem peteret. Quin etiam curae habuit ut ei munera per quaestorem cotidie darentur.*
129 See Raggi 2001.
130 The text mentions the *quaestor urbanus* in the singular but does not include his name; in contrast, the consuls' names are given.

quaestor urbanus to provide them with gifts according to the official roll (*formula*), to rent a lodging and to send furnishings.'¹³¹

The quaestors were to implement the senate's instructions. In turn, the text makes clear that the urban quaestors were directly dependent on the orders of the consuls, who acted as intermediaries between the senate and the executors. The urban quaestors' job in this case included several tasks. First, they had to register a copy of the *senatus consultum* in the *aerarium* (*in tabulas publicas referre*) to make the decree official.¹³² The first lines of the inscription date it to the month of May. Such a precise dating probably allowed for the documents to be categorized within the archive under the proper monthly sub-division.¹³³ The quaestors were also to register Asclepiades, Polystratos and Meniskos in the official list of Rome's friends. Finally, the urban quaestors were ordered to take charge of organising the accommodation for the honoured guests as well as providing them with the usual presents—all this, of course, at public expense. The implementation of this final task had to be carried out in accordance with procedural rules (*ex formula*), which means that there were established regulations related to the money that the urban quaestors were authorised to spend on honouring public guests; presumably, the level of approved expenses fluctuated depending on the importance of the guests. The quaestors were to provide the three Greeks with a *locus* and *lautia*, that is, 'lodging' and 'accommodation' (in Greek τόπος and παροχή, respectively). The text speaks specifically of *locare*, which means that the urban quaestors had to rent a house for them. This does not imply that they rented the house personally; indeed, it is quite likely that the quaestors left that process in the hands of a private contractor (*redemptor*).¹³⁴ The important point is that the urban quaestors were ultimately the magistrates responsible for overseeing the larger process.

---

131 S.C. de Asclepiade ll.17–18 (= ll. 25–26 of the Greek text): *[Uteiq]ue Q. Lutatiu[s M.] Aemilius co(n)s(ules) a(lter) a(mbove), s(ei) e(is) v(ideretur), eos in ameicorum formulam referundos curarent, eisq[ue tabulam aheneam amicitiae in Capitolio ponere] [rem]que deivina[m] facere liceret, munusque eis ex formula locum lautiaque q(uaestorem) urb(anum) eis locare mittere[q]ue iub[erent...]*. Text established by Raggi 2001, 80 (translation by Raggi 2001, 83).

132 Raggi 2001, 86–87: the *relator* of the senatorial decree handed over the original copy to the quaestors in the form of wooden tablets. The quaestors, through their *scribae*, copied the texts onto their own *tabulae*. As a result, it would appear that two official records of *senatus consulta* were stored in the *aerarium*.

133 Raggi 2001, 87–88. Cf. Willems 1878, 218 n.2: 'Il résulte de ces textes qu'il y avait un journal par année questorienne. Il allait donc du 5 décembre au 5 décembre de l'année suivante, et correspondait à deux colléges de consuls'; Sherk RDGE 131 n.10; Reynolds 1982, 64–66, claims that the copy of the document used by the engraver may have derived from the tablet which the *relator* of the decree deposited in the *aerarium*, instead of from the quaestorian archive; Coudry 1994, 67–70, believes that the consuls' records were not kept in the *aerarium* along with those of the quaestors, which were actually their copies.

134 Cf. Kunkel and Wittmann 1995, 517.

Funerary honours

The sources contain evidence for how the urban quaestors were instructed to organise and finance funerary honours for Roman citizens as well as foreigners. As in other cases, such a process was initiated by a senatorial decree;[135] next, the higher magistrates transmitted the order to the quaestors; and finally the urban quaestors would carry out the task.

We have already discussed honours that Cicero proposed on February 43 in the senate to commemorate the deceased Servius Sulpicius Rufus: a bronze statue should be erected on the *Rostra*, and the reason for this distinction should be inscribed on the pedestal; a space of five feet round this statue should be reserved for Rufus' children and descendants to attend the games and gladiatorial shows;[136] the funeral should be celebrated with great pomp, and the consul Pansa should designate a space of thirty feet in the Campus Esquilinus for the burial, a space which was to remain in perpetuity as the funerary property of Rufus' sons and descendants.[137] Cicero's *relatio* includes details about how the honours should be implemented and who was in charge of supervising the process. The consuls Pansa and Hirtius, one of them or both, would order the urban quaestors to contract the construction of the statue and its pedestal as well as its erection on the speaker's platform. Likewise, it was also the urban quaestors' responsibility to pay the contractor (*redemptor*) the required sum.[138] Based on Cicero's words, it seems reasonable to deduce that the state should also pay for the funeral (*funus publicum*) and the burial place (*locus sepulturae*).[139] If this was the case, the urban quaestors were to take care of these expenses too.

Two months later, Cicero again proposed in the senate to grant funerary honours, this time for the soldiers who had died in the victory of the allied armies of Octavian, Hirtius and Pansa over Antonius' army. According to Cicero's proposal, the consuls Pansa and Hirtius, one or both of them, should be in charge of the construction of a monument (*monumentum*) in their memory. However, although the consuls would ultimately be the magistrates responsible for the monument, they were to

---

135 Cf. Gregori 2007–2008: the epigraphy record allows us to explore who was commemorated and how often a *funus publicum* and/or a *locus sepulturae*, or even a monument, were granted to individuals in Latium. The inscriptions are dated almost exclusively to the Principate, although this does not mean that such honours were not conferred during the Republic. Such honours were always granted by the local *ordo decurionum*, which suggests that something similar could have taken place in Rome, and they are somewhat exceptional.
136 This meant a sort of circle with a radius of one meter and a half with the statue in the centre of the circle.
137 Cic. *Phil.* 9.15–17. Cf. Wesch-Klein 1993, 83–84.
138 Cic. *Phil.* 9.16: *utique C. Pansa A. Hirtius consules, alter ambove, si iis videatur, quaestoribus urbis imperent, ut eam basim statuamque faciendam et in rostris statuendam locent, quantique locaverint, tantam pecuniam redemptori adtribuendam solvendamque curent.*
139 Engels 1998, 175.

order the urban quaestors to give the money necessary for the construction and to pay the contractor (*pecuniam dare, attribuere, solvere*).¹⁴⁰ The procedure should, therefore, follow the usual protocol, according to which the senate decreed, the consuls ordered and the urban quaestors carried out the job.

Both Dionysius of Halicarnassus and, more concisely, Livy narrate what happened when Menenius Agrippa, who was supposedly consul in 503, died in 493.¹⁴¹ Since his assets were not sufficient to cover the expenses of a funeral and burial, the Roman people decided to contribute by way of a levy. According to Dionysius of Halicarnassus, upon being informed of the people's decision, the senate decided that the necessary finds should be taken from the public treasury, a matter which they entrusted to the quaestors. As a result, the quaestors spent a large sum of money on the contract for Menenius Agrippa's public funeral, resulting in a magnificent ceremony. While this story is in all probability fictitious, what is significant for our present purposes is how Dionysius of Halicarnassus is taking what had been happening in recent times and projecting it back onto archaic Rome. It is obvious that the urban quaestors were likewise presumably responsible for providing the money necessary for the public funeral of Sulla in 78, which is the first securely attested *funus publicum* in the history of Rome, and that of Caesar in 44.

It has been debated whether the Roman state, under certain circumstances, also organised public funerals for prominent foreigners, a process in which the urban quaestors would have also been involved. In the same paragraph in which Valerius Maximus speaks generally of the munificence and clemency of the Romans towards foreign rulers and in particular of the extraordinary reception given to King Prusias and to the two sons of Masinissa (see above), he also mentions the public funerals that were supposedly organised for Perseus and Syphax. According to Valerius Maximus, when the senators learned that Perseus had died around 165 in Alba Fucens, where he had been held as a prisoner after being paraded in Aemilius Paullus' triumphal procession,¹⁴² they decided to send a quaestor for the purpose of organising a public funeral worthy of a king.¹⁴³ While Valerius Maximus does not specify to which kind of quaestor he is referring, given that money from the *aerarium* had to be used, there should be no doubt that he is speaking about an urban quaestor.

Valerius Maximus tells a similar story about Syphax, the king of Numidia, who presumably was also honoured with a public funeral when he died in Tibur after

---

140 Cic. *Phil.* 14.38: *senatui placere, ut C. Pansa A. Hirtius consules, imperatores, alter ambove, si eis videatur… monumentum quam amplissimum locandum faciendumque curent quaestoresque urb. ad eam rem pecuniam dare, attribuere, solvere iubeant…*
141 Dion.Hal. 6.96.3 – 4; Liv. 2.33.10 – 11.
142 Liv. 45.42.4; Plut. *Aem.Paul.* 37. See Urso 1995.
143 Val.Max. 5.1.1: *consimilique clementia in Perse usus est: nam cum Albae, in quam custodiae causa relegatus erat, decessisset, quaestorem misit, qui eum publico funere efferret, ne regias reliquias iacere inhonoratas pateretur.*

having been taken prisoner by Rome.¹⁴⁴ This may have happened between 203 and 201.¹⁴⁵ On this occasion, Valerius Maximus does not mention the involvement of any quaestor as the magistrate in charge of the organisation of the funeral, though this seems exceedingly likely.

Scholars have cast doubt on the validity of these accounts about public funerals for Syphax and Perseus. Both had been formidable enemies of Rome, and Syphax could be even seen as a traitor to Rome. Neither Perseus nor Syphax, therefore, seem to qualify for receiving a public funeral from the Roman state; indeed, this was a great honour, which is first securely attested on the occasion of Sulla's death in the first century.¹⁴⁶ Nevertheless, the ancient sources may be partially right. Both Syphax and Perseus died in Italy, far from their homelands. Even though a public funeral may appear to be too great an honour for them, a dignified burial funded by the Roman state remains a plausible option.¹⁴⁷ If this is what happened, the urban quaestors certainly would have taken part in the process.

Conservation of roads

An epigraph found in Rome in the area of Porta Collina mentions an otherwise unknown Titus Vibius Temudinus (Temuudinus in the inscription), who was *quaestor urbanus* and *curator viarum*:¹⁴⁸

---

144 Val.Max. 5.1.1: *Syphacem enim, quondam opulentissimum Numidiae regem, captivum in custodia Tiburi mortuum publico funere censuit efferendum, ut vitae dono honorem sepulturae adiceret.* Liv. 30.17.1–2 asserts that Syphax was brought as a prisoner to Alba and was later transferred to Tibur. Livy also states that Syphax was given a public funeral: *Conspecta tamen mors eius fuit, quia publico funere est elatus* (Liv. 30.45.4). Cf. Zonar. 9.13.7.
145 Our sources do not agree about whether Syphax's death took place before or after Scipio Africanus celebrated his triumph in 201: Liv. 45.39.7; Val.Max. 6.9. ext.7; Pol. 16.23.6; Sil.Ital. 17.629–630; App. *Pun.* 28.
146 Blasi 2008, 4–9 and 2012, 235–253, discards the possibility of the celebration of a public funeral for both individuals, on the basis that conspicuous Romans of the same period did not receive such honours. Wesch-Klein 1993, 59 n.395, seems take the funerals of Syphax and Perseus as certain: 'Dagegen wurde dem 201 v.Chr. in römischen Gewahrsam verstorbenen König Syphax eine Bestattung aus der Staatkasse zuteil. Auch der nach Alba Fucens verbannte letzte König der Makedonen, Perseus, erhielt ein *funus publicum*.' Engels 1998, 175, does not doubt the *funus publicum* for Perseus, but does not even mention the supposed funeral of Syphax. See also Kunkel and Wittmann 1995, 518.
147 Blasi 2008, 9 and 11; 2012, 249: 'In considerazione di quanto detto, per i due re più che concessioni in senso onorifico, si potrebbe pensare a una *sepultura in loco publico* o *pecunia publica*, poiché essi erano deceduti lontano dalla loro patria e senza la famiglia che se ne potesse occupare.'
148 CIL VI 31603 = CIL I² 808 = ILS 5799 = ILLRP 465. See Kolb 2014, 658–659, with her translation: 'These works were contracted for repairs of the Via Caecilia out of a cash appropriation of [-] *sestertii*. Money appropriated for the repair of a bridge over the river Farfarus (?) at the 35th milestone; the people agree to pay [- *sestertii*] to Q. (?) [---]sius Pamphilus, freedman of Quintus, contractor and [director] of the works, while T. Vibius Temudinus, urban quaestor, was *curator viarum* [in charge of the roads]. The road to be paved with gravel from the [-] milestone to the [-] milestone and built across the

[haec] opera loc(ata)
[in refic(ienda) v]ia Caecilia de HS
[n(ummum)]—. ad refic(iendum) (?) a]d mil(liarium) XXXV pontem in fluio (!)
[Farfaro pecuni]a adtributa est populo const(at)
[HS n(ummum)—Q(uinto) (?) --]s(io) Q(uinti) <l(iberto)> Pamphilo mancupi(!) et ope[r(is)]
[magistro (?); cur(atore)] viar(um) T(ito) Vibio Temuudino q(uaestore) urb(ano).
[item via gla]rea sternenda af mil(liario) [--ad]
[mil(iarium)—et per Ap]pennium muunien[da est af]
[mil(iario)—ad mil(iarium) --] XX; pecunia adtributa
[est populo c]onst(at) HS n(ummum) CL L(ucio) Rufilio L(ucii et) L(ucii) l(iberto)
[-13/14?-]sti man[cu]pi; cur(atore) viar(um) T(ito) Vib[io]
[Temuudino q(uaestore) urb(ano]...

It is an exceptional inscription due to the unusual detail that it provides about the procedures and costs for repairing roads. Based on the inscription's palaeographic features, scholars have dated it to the 80s. It deals with the *via Caecilia* and refers to the renovation of a bridge, the arch of another bridge and a section of pavement along the road in particular. The contractors (*mancipes*) who were to execute the work as well as the amount of money they were to receive for their services are specified. The formula *pecunia adtributa est populo constat* appears several times throughout the inscription, referring precisely to the money that the contractors would receive from the *aerarium* (this explains the reference to the Roman *populus*).[149] The use of public funds to repair the road[150] explains why Vibius Temudinus is mentioned in the inscription, since he, as urban quaestor, was to authorize the expenses and pay out the agreed upon money. Nonetheless, he appears not only as urban quaestor, but also as 'supervisor of the roads' (*curator viarum*). This presumably means that during his tenure as urban quaestor he was specifically told by the senate either to repair the *via Caecilia* or to restore it and other roads in Italy. The supervision of Italian roads was not, therefore, a function implicitly included in the *provincia* of urban quaestors, but a task that could be assigned to them if the senate considered it necessary. Being responsible for the restoration of the *via Caecilia*, Temudinus was in charge of setting the price for project, selecting the contractors, making the contracts, verifying that the works had been performed in accordance with the agreements and finally paying the contractors.

Another inscription suggests that the urban quaestors undertook a very similar task at approximately the same time as Temudinus.[151] The epigraph appears to

---

Appennines from the [-] milestone to the [-] milestone. The money was appropriated; the community agreed to pay 150,000 *sestertii* to L. Rufilius, freedman of Lucius and Lucius, contractor, while Q. Vibius Temudinus, urban quaestor, was *curator viarum*...' (the fragmentary text continues). Cf. Giovagnoli 2012, for the complete text of the inscription, a commentary and a reconstruction of the road's trajectory. We would like to thank Prof. Werner Eck for his useful remarks on this inscription.
149 Trisciuoglio 1998, 92 n. 44.
150 On the use of public funds for major repairs of roads see Wiseman 1970, 145–147.
151 CIL I² 832 = IX 4541: *C. Pomponius C.f. L. Octavius Cn.f. q. d.s.s.*

refer to the road running from Nursia to Spoletium, though it does not give any details about the specific work that was required. However, it does mention the two quaestors, C. Pomponius and L. Octavius, whom the senate put in charge of the project (*de senatus sententia*). If this *L(ucius) Octavius Cn(aei) f(ilius)* is, as seems very plausible, the same as the later consul in 75, Pomponius and Octavius may have been quaestors by 90–88. The similarity with Temudinus' inscription suggests that they could have been urban quaestors at around the same time. Unfortunately, we do not have enough evidence to determine how frequently urban quaestors were put in charge of the repair and conservation of roads in Italy, but it is indeed interesting that the two inscriptions that prove their involvement in this sort of work both appear to date to the 80s.

Minting of coins

A board of three magistrates, the so-called *triumviri monetales*, regularly oversaw the production of coinage during the Republic, and their names usually appear on the coins. The institution of this board has been dated to 289 following Livy's *Periochae*, but the chronology remains uncertain.[152] Since the urban quaestors controlled the treasury, they were responsible for giving these moneyers the bullion necessary for coining silver and bronze. They were ultimately in charge of minting of coins in Rome, although the *triumviri monetales* carried out the task.[153] However, under special circumstances the senate could instruct one or both urban quaestors to take direct responsibility for issuing coins. In this case, the name or names of the *quaestores urbani* appear on the coins and are sometimes followed by the legend *S(enatus) C(onsulto)* or *Ex S(enatus) C(onsulto)*. There is no evidence, however, that all issues struck *senatus consulto* were struck by quaestors.[154]

An example that leaves room for no doubt is the coinage of the urban quaestor Cn. Nerius in 49. The legend *NERI. Q.VRB* appears on the obverse along with the head

---

[152] Liv. per. 15: *Tunc primum populus R. argento uti coepit*. On *triumviri monetales* see Pink 1952; Hamilton 1969; Gabrielli 2012, 61; Woytek 2016, 322.
[153] See Crawford RRC, 616–617: the censors were responsible for the issues from 280 to 225. They were probably executive officers of the senate, whereas the policy agreed on by the senate was presumably carried out by the quaestors. From the end of the third century, coinage was effectively left in the hands of three annually elected moneyers, which meant that the censors no longer had to concern themselves with such questions. Crawford (2.617) reconstructs the standard procedure as follows: 'At the beginning of the year the senate would meet to hear estimates of income and expenditure together with a statement on the surplus coinage in hand and to authorise the production of the required amount of coinage. The quaestors presumably handed bullion over to the moneyers and received it back in the form of coin.' Cf. Pink 1952, 58: 'the authorities who had charge of the coinage were from the beginning the highest financial officers, the quaestors.' See also Harris 1976, 103. On the mint of Rome see Gabrielli 2012, 55–61.
[154] Cf. Crawford RRC 88 n. 3.

of god Saturn. On the reverse there is a legionary eagle, with some standards, and the consular date (*L.LENT. C.MARC. COS*) alluding to the consuls C. Claudius Marcellus and L. Cornelius Lentulus Crus. The consular date is very unusual and should certainly be understood as a political message in the context of the outbreak of the Civil War. Indeed, it was necessary to make clear that the coins were minted at the order of the legitimate consuls of 49, who were then out of Rome. This could perhaps also explain the unusually complete reference to the urban quaestor in the legend, as *Q(uaestor) VRB(anus)*, which stands out from the more usual *Q(uaestor)*. According to Crawford, the eagle and standards allude to the fact that the issue was motivated by military needs, whereas the head of Saturn alludes to the fact that as urban quaestor Cn. Nerius had responsibility for the *aerarium*, which was located in the temple of Saturn.[155] However, Woytek has marshalled a series of compelling arguments and suggested that this issue was not actually struck at Rome, but rather when Pompey and a large part of the senate—including the consuls and urban quaestors—had already abandoned the city and were, perhaps, in Apollonia in Illyria. Since the responsibilities of the urban quaestors were limited to Rome, the mention of the consuls on the reverse would serve to legitimatise the coinage.[156]

The coins of P. Cornelius Lentulus Spinther and L. Plaetorius (Cestianus) provide a different case. The denarii of Spinther bear the legend *P. LENT P.F L.N* on the reverse, and *Q. S.C.* on the obverse, whereas those of Plaetorius present the legend *L. PLAETORI L.F. Q. S.C.*[157] Unlike the coins of Nerius, the two issues do not specify that Plaetorius and Spinther were urban quaestors, but simply that they were quaestors. Nonetheless, there is no doubt that both were urban quaestors. If, as has been suggested, the coins should be dated to 71,[158] it would mean that the two urban

---

[155] Crawford RRC 460–461 no 441. However, Crawford RRC 445–446 no 421 does not consider that the head of Saturn that appears on the coins issued by M. Nonius Sufenas implies that he was acting as urban quaestor. He may, rather, have been a moneyer (see Prosopography). Could the head of Saturn be an implicit symbol of Sufenas' quaestorship? Sobeck 1909, 54 accepts this interpretation. This conclusion, though, is problematic in so far as Sufenas did not mention his supposed quaestorship on his coins. It seems unlikely that Sufenas would not have signalled his office if he really were a quaestor. Consequently it seems more probable that he was a moneyer.
[156] Woytek 2003, 97–100.
[157] Crawford RCC 408 no 396 and 409 no 397. The type of Juno Moneta on the obverse of Plaetorius' coins, as well as the legend *MONETA*, who was the protecting goddess of the Roman mint, were the symbols of this official issue struck by the urban quaestor.
[158] Crawford RCC 408 no 396 and 409 no 397 dates the coins of Spinther and Plaetorius to the year 74 (see Sobeck 1909, 40; Broughton, MRR 2.103 and 2.554 for Spinther, 2.173 and 2.601 for Plaetorius: quaestor 74?; MRR 3.157: quaestor ca. 74–66). The discovery of the Mesagne hoard shifted the dating that had previously been accepted, and Hersh – Walker 1984, Table 2, date these denarii to 71. This date was followed by Hollstein 1993, 89–95. It is necessary to remember that Crawford's exemplary study was based on the analysis of the coin hoards for which evidence was available in the 1960s and that Crawford's chronology for most issues should be treated with caution. Indeed, new coin hoards that have surfaced since the publication of Crawford's book have required scholars to modify many of the dates that he gives. See Woytek 2016, 323.

quaestors of this year issued coins by senatorial decree—certainly separately, though perhaps in close succession. If this is correct, it supports the idea that throughout their year in office both urban quaestors held responsibility over the *aerarium*. According to Hollstein, who accepts 71 as the date for the quaestorian coins,[159] the issues were meant to finance the various celebrations of the year: Metellus and Pompey's triumph over Sertorius in Hispania and that of M. Terentius Varro Lucullus *de Bessis* as well as the *ovatio* for M. Licinius Crassus *de fugitivis et Spartaco*.[160] This explains the senate's order that the urban quaestor mint this special issue.

According to Hollstein, the extraordinary minting of coins in order to finance the celebration of a triumph finds another precedent in the issues struck by the urban quaestor C. Fundanius in 101. These coins were produced to supply money for Marius' triumph over Cimbri and Teutons, which was celebrated that year.[161] The reverse presents the legend *C. FVNDAN Q*. It therefore lacks the text *S.C.* or *EX S.C.*, but there should be no doubt that the coins were issued by Fundanius in his capacity as urban quaestor, and that the senate had previously ordered him to mint the coins.

Very likely in 75 we find another issue minted in all probability by an urban quaestor, in this case Cn. Cornelius Lentulus Marcellinus (see Prosopography).[162] Some denarii present the legend *CN. LEN. Q. EX S.C.*, while other coins of the same series read *LENT CVR. DEN. FL*, that is, *cur(ator) den(ariis) fl(andis)*. Initially, Crawford proposed that Marcellinus minted them in Hispania during the Sertorian War. However, Hollstein draws attention to the fact that in this period it was extremely unusual to mint coins outside Rome.[163] If these denarii were struck in Hispania, they would, in fact, be the only coins that were not minted in Rome between 78 and 50. Hollstein argues, therefore, that Marcellinus was *quaestor urbanus* in 76 and immediately after this office he was *curator denariis flandis*. The senate would have entrusted Marcellinus to mint coins in order to finance the Sertorian War. When he ended his term of office as quaestor, part of the silver that had been delivered to him to be minted still remained. To finish his task, he would have been designated *curator denariis flandis*. It seems certainly more acceptable, following Hollstein's argument, that Marcellinus minted the coins as urban quaestor, though the year 75 is preferable to 76 for his quaestorship. The coinage could be the senatorial

---

159 It cannot be proven, however, that Spinther and Plaetorius were urban quaestors at the same time; accordingly it remains possible that their coins were struck in different years.
160 Hollstein 1993, 84–88 and 89–95. In accordance with Hollstein, the types on the reverse, *Genius populi Romani* and Victory, should be seen as a symbol of the Roman triumph against Sertorius in Hispania.
161 Hollstein 1993, 87–88. Cf. Crawford RRC 328 no. 326. The reverse of the denarii shows a triumphator in a quadriga holding a laurel-branch in his left hand, while the quinarii depict Victory crowning a trophy and a kneeling captive with his hands tied behind his back.
162 Crawford RRC 407 no. 393, dates the denarii to 76–75, elsewere in his book he asserts that the issue 'still very fresh in the Pontecorvo hoard, belongs precisely in 75' (RRC 82). Hersh – Walker 1984, Table 2, give the same chronology.
163 Hollstein 1993, 63–73 esp.65.

response to the letter from Pompey, in which the *imperator* requested new funds for his army in Hispania.[164]

The coins of Q. Servilius Caepio and L. Calpurnius Piso Caesoninus pose a different problem.[165] While in the above-mentioned instances all the coins were minted by only one quaestor, in this particular case the moneyers were two quaestors, as is clearly indicated by the legend *PISO CAEPIO Q(uaestores)*, which is found on the obverse. This is not the only peculiarity, since the reason for the minting is specifically mentioned on the reverse: *AD FRV(mentum) EMV(ndum) / EX S(enatus) C(onsulto)*, that is, the coins were issued 'to purchase grain in accordance with a senatorial decree.' In addition, the reverse shows the two quaestors at work sitting on two individual chairs without arms or backrest, which look like stools. We know of Caepio's opposition as *quaestor urbanus* to the grain law that the tribune Saturninus intended to pass (see below).[166] This information seems to date Caepio's quaestorship—and consequently that of Piso Caesoninus—to 103 rather than 100 (see the arguments in the Prosopography). This quaestorian coinage and the subsequent acquisition of cereals by the Roman state were the senate's response to Saturninus' *lex frumentaria*.

But what kind of quaestors were Caepio and Piso Caesoninus? Since Crawford considered that only one urban quaestor was in charge of the *aerarium* at any particular moment, he argued that only one of the two moneyers was the urban quaestor, whereas the other could be the *quaestor Ostiensis*, since in his opinion this would be 'a likely combination for dealing with the corn supply.' As a result, Crawford identifies Caepio as urban quaestor and Piso as *quaestor Ostiensis*.[167] However, this argument is based on the two problematic assumptions: that only one urban quaestor was actually responsible for the treasury and that the Ostian quaestorship was regular office. As we have seen, both assumptions are highly unlikely. On the contrary, it is more probable that both Caepio and Piso were acting as urban quaestors. This is probably the reason why the abbreviation *Q(uaestores)* alone was used on the denarii, since there was no the need to distinguish between the different offices that Crawford has suggested for the two quaestors. It probably also takes for granted the usual relationship between minting and the urban quaestorship at Rome: as seen in previous examples, only the abbreviation *Q(uaestor)* appears on the issues, with the exception of Nerius' coins.

During the state of emergency that seems to have taken place in 103 during which a lack of grain in the city led to the mobilisation of the plebs, who had been roused by the tribune Saturninus, the senate may have decided, exceptionally, to instruct the two urban quaestors jointly to mint coins 'to purchase grain' immediately and perhaps in large quantities, in an attempt to pacify social and economic tensions. This would explain the exceptional nature of this issue, which not only

---

164 Sall. *hist.* 2.98 M.
165 Crawford, RRC 330–331 no. 330.
166 *Rhet.Her.* 1.21.
167 Crawford RRC 331.

met a financial need but clearly also played the propagandistic purpose of highlighting the senate's role in responding to the crisis. This solution seems more compelling than Crawford's, since there is no other evidence of the so-called *quaestores Ostienses* minting coins;[168] indeed, even if such quaestors had regularly existed, they would presumably have had nothing to do with the management of the treasury, which was the sole responsibility of the urban quaestors. As discussed elsewhere in this chapter, it would not have been unusual for the urban quaestors to carry out a particular task jointly in response to the senate's orders.

This leads to a final question that likewise revolves around a possible allusion to two urban quaestors. The issue was struck at the end of the second or at the very beginning of the first century,[169] and reads *T. MAL.* (or *T. MANL.*) *AP. CL. Q. VR.* Since Mommsen, it has generally been assumed that *Q.VR.* is the abbreviation of *Q(uaestores) VR(bani)*; accordingly, the two names would belong to the urban quaestors who had coined the issue, presumably Ap. Claudius Pulcher and perhaps T. Maloleius (alternatively T. Mallius or T. Manlius. See the Prosopography). This interpretation appears to be reinforced by the fact that the order of the names is not always the same in the series, sometimes with *AP.CL* appearing first, while on other occasions *T. MAL.* comes first. What is consistent is that *Q. VR* is always placed at the end of the legend. Contra Mommsen, Crawford argues that *Q. VR.* should be read as a third name, namely Quintus Urbinius, who would be otherwise unknown. Again, Crawford's interpretation is based on the questionable assumption that only one urban quaestor was in charge of the *aerarium* at any given time. Accordingly, in his opinion, it would have to be explained why the two urban quaestors issued these coins exceptionally and why their names appeared together. As a result, Crawford offers a different explanation: the coins were issued by three moneyers, whose names were abbreviated in the legend.

While Crawford is certainly right to assert that a historical explanation for the unusual joint coinage of the two urban quaestors is needed, Mommsen's explanation remains the easiest and most logical interpretation. We have seen that the urban quaestor's role as moneyer is, rather exceptionally, indicated on coins. However, this should not come entirely as a surprise, since abbreviations such as *S.C.* or *EX S.C.* appear only occasionally, even though coinage was always under senatorial control. The moneyers seem to have had a free hand over the design of their issues, including the legends inscribed on their coins.

Under the supervision and direction of the senate, the urban quaestors, who were the magistrates ultimately responsible for coinage, were sometimes directly in charge of the minting of coins. In such instances, they recorded the role they

---

[168] Some coins have been attributed to L. Appuleius Saturninus. They present the legend *L. SATVRN*. Bennes 1991, 58–59, suggests that Saturninus could have minted the issue as *quaestor Ostiensis*, even if there is no mention of the office of the moneyer. Nevertheless, it seems more likely that Saturninus minted the coins as moneyer and not as quaestor (Crawford 1969, 1.37–38; RRC 1.324).
[169] On the date see Broughton, MRR 2.2: year 99; Crawford RRC 1.312–313 no 299; 111 or 110.

played by including their names and a reference to their office in the issue's legend. Since only the *quaestores urbani* were responsible for the public treasury, it seems exceedingly unlikely that other quaestors would have had a hand in issuing coins at Rome's mint (the case of provincial quaestors is obviously different); as a result, the abbreviation Q. in coins should always be seen as referring to the urban quaestorship.[170]

The urban quaestors as public notaries of the Roman Republic

All official documents generated by the Roman Republican administration (senate, magistrates, assemblies, courts, etc.) were recorded and kept in the *aerarium*; as a consequence, they came under the direct responsibility of the urban quaestors, the magistrates who had to ensure both their accuracy and preservation. As a matter of fact, it was the very act of depositing a document in the *aerarium* that turned it into a public record. In this way, the urban quaestors became the general public notaries of the Republic. To provide a complete inventory of documents registered in the public treasury is beyond the purpose of this section.[171] However, some of them will be discussed in order to illustrate the vast volume of documentation and the complexities that the state bureaucracy generated for the urban quaestors or, more accurately, their assistants in the *aerarium*.

To begin with, senatorial decrees were to be registered in the *aerarium*; the resulting record had to include the name of the proposer as well as the decree's content and date.[172] As a matter of fact, the date of a *senatus consultum* was probably the data point that was used to archive decrees in chronological order (see above on the *SC de Asclepiade*). Josephus attests to the existence of this register, when he quotes a senatorial decree from 44 that had been copied from the treasury's *tabulae publicae*, which belonged to the urban quaestors of that year, Quintus Rutilius and Caius Cornelius.[173] Cicero, for his part, accuses Antonius of depositing ficticious *senatus consulta* in the *aerarium*.[174] Moreover, in a letter to Atticus, Cicero alludes to the volume (*liber*) containing the senatorial decrees approved during the consulship of Cn. Cornelius and L. Mummius, which suggests that the decrees of each year were compiled and archived in a book.[175]

---

170 The coins of M. Sergius Silus in 116 or 115 with the legend *M. SERGI SILVS Q* (Crawford RRC 302 no. 286), as well as the issues of A. Manlius (Torquatus) in 80 with the legend *A. MANLI A.F. Q* (Crawford RRC 397 no. 381) should consequently be included among the coinage of urban quaestors at Rome.
171 See Mommsen, Röm.St. II 532–535; Kunkel and Wittmann 1995, 518–521.
172 A general reference is found in Liv. 39.4.8: *senatus consultum factum ad aerarium detulerit*.
173 Ios. AJ 14.219.
174 Cic. Phil. 5.12: *senatus consulta numquam facta ad aerarium deferebantur*. Cf. Cic. fam. 12.1.1.
175 Cic. Att. 13.33: *reperiet ex eo libro, in quo sunt senatus consulta Cn. Cornelio, L. Mummio coss.*

Based on a passage from Diodorus Siculus,[176] some scholars have argued that urban quaestors had the capacity to veto a senatorial decree by refusing to register a *senatus consultum* in the *aerarium*. This is, however, highly unlikely. According to Diodorus Siculus, a Cretan embassy arrived in Rome in an attempt to recover the senate's lost favour towards the island. The legates intervened before the senators and were initially successful, since a senatorial decree declaring the Cretans to be friends of the Roman people was going to be issued. However, Lentulus Spinther opposed the *senatus consultum*, which apparently was never passed, and the Cretan legates left. Mattingly argues that Lentulus Spinther, as urban quaestor, could have invalidated the *senatus consultum* by refusing to register it in the *aerarium*, a task for which he was responsible: if it was not properly registered, a senatorial decree could not be enforced.[177] More recently, Ryan has taken up this thesis: the senatorial decree in favour of the Cretans and Lentulus' urban quaestorship should be dated to the same year; Lentulus, as urban quaestor, had the opportunity to render decrees invalid, which was exactly what he did so in this case.[178]

However, this hypothesis is riddled with problems. In the first place, the date of the Cretan embassy that occasioned the senatorial decree is itself uncertain. The Cretan legates may have come to Rome in 70 or 69,[179] in all probability one or two years after Lentulus had held his quaestorship, since he was probably urban quaestor in 71. In fact, there is no evidence to support dating the Cretan embassy and Lentulus' quaestorship to the same year. Moreover, although urban quaestors were certainly in charge of registering *senatus consulta* in the *aerarium*, they always followed the orders handed down by the consuls, who in turn were following the senate's instructions (see above for the procedure regarding the application of the *SC de Asclepiade*). The urban quaestors' task was merely to record previously issued senatorial decrees. Indeed, a quaestorian capacity to veto senatorial decisions is not attested and seems to be totally beyond the urban quaestors' *potestas* given their status as lower magistrates. In short, the proposal is utterly implausible. The text of Diodorus, nonetheless, is certainly mysterious regarding the exact nature of Lentulus Spinther's intervention. Here it is important to note that Diodorus does not actually allude to Lentulus holding any office at the time. It is probable that Lentulus opposed the *senatus consultum* while it was under debate during a meeting of the senate, in which case he would have been acting in his capacity as a senator and not as an urban

---

176 Diodor. 40.1.2: ἡ δὲ σύγκλητος ἀσμένως τοὺς λόγους προσδεξαμένη δόγμα ἐπεβάλετο κυροῦν δι' οὗ τῶν ἐγκλημάτων τοὺς Κρῆτας ἀπολύουσα φίλους καὶ συμμάχους τῆς ἡγεμονίας ἀνηγόρευεν ἄκυρον δὲ τὸ δόγμα ἐποίησε Λέντλος ὁ ἐπικαλούμενος Σπινθήρ. οἱ δὲ Κρῆτες ἀπηλλάγησαν. See the Prosopography on P. Cornelius P.f. Lentulus Spinther.
177 Mattingly 1956, 200 n. 1: 'Spinther in 70 BC invalidated an *SC de Cretensibus*; he could well do this as *quaestor urbanus*, the official responsible for registering Senatus Consulta at the *aerarium*, by which alone they gained force.'
178 Ryan 1996 g, 83–84.
179 Marshall 1985, 218; Linderski 1990, 163 and n.33.

quaestor. The dismissal of the decree must have followed a vote in the senate and must not have been the result of a quaestorian veto, which would have constituted a serious confrontation between a lower magistrate and the senate.

The exact texts of the laws that were passed in the popular assemblies were also registered in the *aerarium*. This procedure was designed to ensure the impossibility of someone falsifying or altering a law's content.[180] This legal provision was supplemented in 62, when the *lex Iunia Licinia*, sponsored by the consuls Junius Silanus and Licinius Murena, was passed. Although its content has been the subject of debate, the law probably made it mandatory to submit to the *aerarium* a copy of every bill (*rogatio*) when it had been made public, before being discussed in *contiones* and being voted on in the *comitia*.[181]

Lists of the allies and friends of the Roman people (*formula sociorum* and *formula amicorum populi Romani*) were also kept in the *aerarium*.[182] The aforementioned *SC de Asclepiade* clearly attests to the existence of such a list of friends: *[Uteiq]ue Q. Lutatiu[s M.] Aemilius co(n)s(ules) a(lter) a(mbove), s(ei) e(is) v(ideretur), eos in ameicorum formulam referundos curarent...*[183] Livy also implies so much in a passage referring to 170. An embassy from Lampsacus brought a crown weighing eighty pounds to Rome: they declared that they had revolted against Perseus as soon as the Roman legions appeared in Macedonia and had given all possible assistance to the Roman commanders. As a reward for their behaviour, they made a request to the senate to be counted amongst the friends of Rome. As a result, the senate instructed the praetor Q. Maenius to enrol the Lampsacans amongst the states allied to Rome: *Lampsacenos in sociorum formulam referre Q. Maenius praetor iussus.*[184] In addition, each of the legates was to receive 2000 asses as a gift. Livy does not mention the urban quaestors, but it is clear that they were implicated in both recording the Lampsacans in the list of allies in the *aerarium* and giving them the money from the treasury.

Even though direct evidence does not always exist in the sources, the *aerarium* must have contained many other documents: lists of the census;[185] perhaps records written by various magistrates;[186] public contracts;[187] lists of the state's debtors and creditors;[188] certificates of property;[189] lists of citizens which specified their tax obli-

---

[180] Cf. Sisenna fr. 117 P.: *idemque perseveraverunt, uti lex perveniret ad quaestorem ac iudices quos vellent instituerent praefestinatim et cupide.*
[181] See Gagliardi 2009, with supplementary bibliography. Cf. Mommsen 1858, 186 (294).
[182] Kunkel and Wittmann 1995, 521.
[183] *S.C. de Asclepiade* l.17 (= l. 25 of the Greek text).
[184] Liv. 43.6.10.
[185] Kunkel and Wittmann 1995, 518.
[186] Mommsen, Röm.St. II 533.
[187] Mommsen, Röm.St. II 532.
[188] Plut. *Cat.min.* 17.
[189] Cic. *Flacc.* 80: *illud quaero sintne ista praedia censui censendo, habeant ius civile, sint necne sint mancipi, subsignari apud aerarium aut apud censorem possint.*

gations; probably the minutes from the comitia;[190] minutes from trials or legal proceedings that included fines to be paid to the state or rewards for informers; etc.

Oaths of magistrates and *imperatores*

Within a period of five days after entering office, magistrates were obliged to swear to follow the law and at the end of their term of office that they had indeed fulfilled the law.[191] The importance of such ceremonies should not be underestimated, since a magistrate was barred from holding office if he had not taken the oath: *magistratum autem plus quinque dies, nisi qui iurasset in leges, non licebat gerere*.[192] Some laws also specifically required the year's magistrates to swear that they would observe them. The oaths were taken before an urban quaestor, who acted as public notary on behalf of the community, and the oaths were subsequently recorded in the *aerarium*. When speaking about the legislation of the tribune of the plebs Saturninus, which included an oath of loyalty, Appian asserts that the (urban) quaestors were accustomed to administering oaths before the temple of Saturn. Saturninus and his friends, Appian goes on, were the first to swear their adherence to this new legislation.[193]

The *Tabula Bantina Latina* provides a good evidence of this procedure.[194] According to the preserved text, which is dated to the late second century, the magistrates were to take the oath publicly before the temple of Castor and Pollux while facing the forum: *Eis consistunto pro ae[d]e Castorus palam luci in forum vorsus et eidem in diebus (quinque) apud q(uaestorem) iouranto per Iovem deosque [Penateis sese quae ex h(ace) l(ege) oport]ebit facturum...*[195] Next, the text specifies that the oath must be taken before the urban quaestor, who would register the names of the magistrates that had sworn on *tabulae publicae* in the *aerarium*: *Quei ex h(ace) l(ege) ioudicaverit, is facito apud q(uaestorem) urb(anum) [utei nomen in taboleis pobliceis sc]riptum siet; quaestorque ea nomina accipito et eos quei ex h(ace) l(ege) apud sed iourarint*

---

190 Cic. *Pis*. 15.
191 On oaths of magistrates see Rosillo-López 2010, 107–109. Cf. Mommsen, Röm.St. II 533; Kunkel and Wittmann 1995, 520.
192 Liv. 31.50.7. It is well known that Cicero used his oath at the end of his consulship as a chance to vindicate his behaviour in 63 (Plut. *Cic*. 23.1; Cic. *fam*. 5.2.7).
193 App. *b.c*. 1.31.
194 The discussion on the *Tabula Bantina* has generated a huge bibliography without solving all the problems about its chronology, content and meaning. Debating such points is, in any case, beyond our present purpose. See Hinrichs 1970; Galsterer 1971; Lintott 1978; Brunt 1988; Crawford and Coleman 1996; Richardson 1996.
195 CIL I² 582 *ll*. 17–18. Crawford 1996, 200 and 203: 'They – in front of] the temple of Castor, openly, before the light of day, facing the forum, and they are to swear within the same five days, in the presence of the quaestor, by Jupiter and the [ancestral] gods, [that he] will do [what shall be appropriate according to this statute,]...'

facito in taboleis [pobliceis utei scriptos habeat].[196] The oath of loyalty to the law was extended to the senators, who were also obliged to swear before the urban quaestor: *[quei senator est erit queive in senatu sententi]am deixerit post hance legem rogatam eis in diebus (decem) proxsumeis quibus quisque [eorum sciet] / [hance legem populum plebemve iosisse i]ouranto apud quaestorem ad aerarium palam luci per Iovem deosque Penat[eis seese quae ex hace lege]...*[197]

Every *imperator* had to deliver a report upon his return to Rome (see above). This report had to include information about his military operations, his own casualties as well as the enemy's, details of booty and so on. All this information was essential for deciding whether or not he would receive a triumph. In 62, the tribunes of the plebs M. Porcius Cato (Uticensis) and L. Marius carried a law regarding the requirements for triumphs. According to Valerius Maximus, the law demanded that every *imperator* expecting a triumph must take an oath about the accuracy and veracity of the information that a general gave to the senate about the number of the enemy killed and his own losses. The oath had to be taken before the urban quaestors.[198] The introduction of this new law suggests that false information was sometimes included in the reports and that the formal oaths were intended to discourage such a practice or, at the very least, to make the fabrication of details a punishable offense. Whether a similar obligation already existed in connection with triumphal regulations is not attested, but it seems unlikely.[199] As in other cases, the oaths were recorded in the *aerarium*.

Selection of jurors for permanent courts

Each year, the urban quaestors were in charge of selecting the jurors that would take part in upcoming trials. This procedure, of course, applies only to the late Republican

---

196 CIL I² 582 *ll.* 20–22. Crawford 1996, 200 and 203: 'Whoever shall have (sworn) according to this statute, he is to see that [his name] be written down [in the public records] in the presence of the urban quaestor; and the quaestor is to receive those names and is to see [that he keep] those who have sworn in his presence according to this statute [written down] in the [public] records.'
197 CIL I² 582 *ll.* 23–25. Crawford 1996, 200–201 and 203–204: '[Whoever is or shall be a senator or whoever] shall have spoken [his opinion in the senate] after the (successful) proposal of this statute, in the ten days next after any [of them shall know that the people or plebs have passed this statute,] they are to swear in the presence of the quaestor at the treasury, openly, before the light of day, by Jupiter and the ancestral gods, [that he will do what shall be appropriate according to this statute...'
198 Val.Max. 2.8.1: *legis alterius adiutorio fulta est, quam L. Marcius et M. Cato tribuni plebei tulerunt: poenam enim imperatoribus minatur, qui aut hostium occisorum in proelio aut amissorum civium falsum numerum litteris senatui ausi essent referre, iubetque eos, cum primum urbem intrassent, apud quaestores urbanos iurare de utroque numero vere ab iis senatui esse scriptum.* Cf. Bastien 2007, 293–296 and 303–304.
199 According to Orosius (5.4.7), a law establishing the number of enemies killed, but also of Rome's own losses, already existed in the second century. Nevertheless, nothing is said about an oath confirming the information. Cf. Develin 1978.

period, when permanent courts were instituted. A passage from Cassius Dio relating to the conflict between Clodius and Milo in 57 makes this clear.[200] Milo indicted Clodius, but was unable to bring him to trial. This was because the (urban) quaestors, who were responsible for forming the following year's jury, had not yet been elected. This was in December 57. According to the regular procedure, the quaestors who had begun their term of office on 5th December 58 would step down on 4th December 57 and transfer their power to the new quaestors; in this instance, however, the election for the quaestors of 57 had not yet been held. Additionally, the consul Metellus Nepos had forbidden the (urban) praetor from allowing any trial to go forward before the new jurors were selected, a policy which led to delays.

The procedure for choosing jurors can be reconstructed as follows. Every year, the urban praetor was provided with a total pool of jurors that could take part in trials,[201] according to their condition as senators, knights or *tribuni aerarii*. The Sullan reforms, of course, which put the courts solely in the hands of senators, greatly restricted the number of possible jurors. At the beginning of every year, seats on the juries for all courts (*quaestiones de peculatu, de ambitu, de maiestate*, etc.)—not specifically for each trial—were allocated. The urban quaestors presided over this process, which must have taken place shortly after the new quaestors entered office on 5th December and presumably before the new praetors did so on 1st January.[202]

The political role of urban quaestors

Throughout the Roman Republic the urban quaestors played a very prominent role within the public administration; their political role, in contrast, was apparently much more limited. We know from the sources of only a few instances in which an urban quaestor actively intervened in politics during his term of office.

The most conspicuous example is that of Quintus Servilius Caepio, who was urban quaestor during one of Saturninus' tribunates of the plebs. It is known that as *quaestor urbanus* he opposed in the senate the grain law that Saturninus intended to pass, by arguing that the treasury would not be able to endure such great largesse.[203] It is exceptional to hear of a quaestor speaking during a senatorial session,

---

200 Cass.Dio 39.7.4. Cf. Cic. *Q.fr.* 2.1.2.
201 The list of potential jurors seems to have been kept in the *aerarium* along with every other official document regarding the Roman administration: *Hos ille demens iudices legisset, horum nomina ad aerarium detulisset...?* (Cic. *Phil.* 5.15). Cf. Greenidge 1901b, 446.
202 On this subject see Lengle 1933, 291–292, who first established the doctrine that other scholars have since followed. Cf. Kunkel 1963, 749–755: the lot may have been made by *tribus* and not individually (754); Santalucia 1999, 144–145. Jones 1972, 68: the urban praetor drew the names for a jury, while the urban quaestor made an official record of the names.
203 *Rhet.Her.* 1.21: *Cum Lucius Saturninus legem frumentariam de semissibus et trientibus laturus esset, Q. Caepio, qui per id temporis quaestor urbanus erat, docuit senatum aerarium pati non posse largitionem tantam.* Cf. *Rhet.Her.* 2.17; Cic. *Brut.* 162.

and it was indeed his office as urban quaestor that explains Caepio's intervention in this case.²⁰⁴ His statement no doubt carried particular weight, since he was in charge of the *aerarium* and consequently knew the state of the public finances very well. The dating of Caepio's quaestorship depends on the date accepted for Saturninus' *lex frumentaria*, something that has been a continual subject of debate. Nonetheless, the year 103, when Saturninus held the tribunate of the plebs for the first time, is the most probable date. As Schneider rightly argues, Saturninus' grain law should be linked to the slave revolt that began in Sicily in 104.²⁰⁵ The rebellion on the island must have resulted in a food shortage at Rome. Saturninus' bill would therefore have been responding to this situation.

Caepio was highly vocal in his hostility to the grain law to the point that it could be even said that he led opposition the Saturninus' bill. In spite of the senatorial opposition, Saturninus went forward with his motion. Other tribunes of the plebs then interposed a veto, which Saturninus ignored. He then summoned the comitia for a vote on his bill. Caepio, together with others (*cum viris bonis*), reacted by bursting violently into the assembly and blocking the process. As a result, Caepio was later brought to trial for treason (*de maiestate*).²⁰⁶ This was not the only action undertaken by Caepio as urban quaestor. Together with Piso Caesoninus (see above), he issued some denarii that, besides their names and the abbreviation *Q(uaestores)*, included the legend *AD FRV EMV / EX S.C* (*ad frumentum emundum ex senatus consulto*).²⁰⁷ According to this legend, the coins were specifically minted 'to purchase grain in accordance with a senatorial decree.' This, then, is one of the few examples of coins issued by urban quaestors, an exceptional event that always resulted from a senatorial decree. The coinage, and ultimately the purchase of grain by the state, should be understood as the senatorial response to Saturninus' attempt to pass his *lex frumentaria*.

If an urban quaestor confronted Saturninus fiercely in 103, some years later the quaestor C. Saufeius was one of the most prominent supporters of Saturninus during his extremely brief final tribunate. Actually, Saufeius was assassinated along with the tribune Saturninus and the praetor Glaucia during the riots on 10ᵗʰ December 100, the day on which the new tribunes of the plebs entered office.²⁰⁸ As for the

---

204 The attendance of urban quaestors at senatorial meetings may have been habitual, since they usually remained at home for their term in office. On the contrary, the consular and provincial quaestors stayed away from Rome for a large part of their term of office. Cf. Taylor and Scott 1969, 535.
205 Schneider 1982–83, 209. The date 103 has been proposed and accepted by other scholars, among them Last 1932, 165; Passerini 1934, 113–115; Badian 1964, 63 n.9; Gruen 1966a, 44 n.71 and 57 n.151; Broughton, MRR 3.21; Benness 1991, 38.
206 *Rhet.Her.* 1.21: *Caepio, ut illum, contra intercedentibus collegis, adversus rem publicam vidit ferre, cum viris bonis impetum facit, pontes disturbat, cistas deicit, inpedimento est quo setius feratur. Arcessitur Caepio maiestatis.* Cf. Alexander 1990, 45–46.
207 Crawford, RRC 330–331.
208 App. *b.c.* 1.32. Cf. Cic. *Rab.perd.* 20; Oros. 5.17.8.

kind of quaestorship Saufeius held, he might certainly have been urban quaestor as Hinrichs has supposed,[209] though this is not confirmed by our sources.

In a letter sent to C. Trebonius, Cicero praises him for his actions when he was quaestor. [210] In all probability, Cicero has the year 58 in mind, when he left Rome to go into exile. Trebonius was one of the magistrates who most actively tried to bring about Cicero's return from his banishment. According to Cicero, Trebonius opposed the tribune (an obvious reference to Clodius) and, in the orator's opinion, acted openly, as the consuls should have done. This does not mean that Trebonius assumed the duties of the consuls, which would have been legally impossible, but that he worked politically as would have been expected from the Republic's highest magistrates.[211] In addition, the quaestor Trebonius defended Cicero, speaking in assemblies before the people (*cum me contionibus tuis defendisti*). Cicero also contrasts Trebonius' conduct with that of his colleague, whose name he does not mention and who did not oppose Clodius. The allusion to Trebonius' colleague in the quaestorship strongly suggests that he was one of the two urban quaestors that year.

Cicero's allusion to Trebonius' intervention in *contiones* is particularly interesting, since there is very little evidence of quaestors speaking during a *contio*. C. Gracchus apparently spoke in 126 against the proposal of the tribune M. Junius Pennus to prevent non-citizens from settling in Roman towns and to remove those who had previously done so.[212] In 126 Gracchus was quaestor in Sardinia under the consul L. Aurelius Orestes. He must therefore have spoken in the assembly before departing for Sardinia. It is very likely that he was given the floor by the tribune Junius Pennus in one of the *contiones* that he summoned while his bill was being discussed. We also know that Clodius spoke in a *contio* in February 61. [213] Clodius was quaestor that year in Sicily under the command of C. Vergilius Balbus. His departure for the island was delayed by the Bona Dea trial, and his intervention in the assembly must be understood in this context. Clodius might have called for the *contio* himself,[214] but another magistrate could also have convoked it for him.[215] Finally, Caesar

---

209 Hinrichs 1970, 482.
210 Cic. *fam.* 15.21.2: *Nam, ut illa omittam, quae civitate teste fecisti, cum mecum inimicitias communicavisti, cum me contionibus tuis defendisti, cum quaestor in mea atque in publica causa consulum partes suscepisti, cum tribuno plebis quaestor non paruisti, cui tuus praesertim collega pareret...*
211 For this argument see Ryan 1997a.
212 Cic. *Brut.* 109; *off.* 3.47; Fest. p. 362 Lindsay: *Resp. multarum civitatum pluraliter dixit C. Gracchus in ea, quam conscripsit de lege p. Enni et peregrinis, cum ait: eae nationes, cum aliis rebus, per avaritiam atque stultitiam, res publicas suas amiserunt.* Cf. Broughton MRR 1.508; Stockton 1979, 94–95.
213 Cic. *Att.* 1.14.5: *Clodius contiones miseras habebat, in quibus Lucullum, Hortensium, C. Pisonem, Messallam consulem contumeliose laedebat...* (cf. Cic. *Att.* 1.16.1; Schol.Bob. *in Clodium et Curionem* p.21,14 H; p.24 H).
214 Pina Polo 1989, 295.
215 Moreau 1982, 121–122, suggests the tribune of the plebs Fufius was the summoner of the assembly.

delivered the funeral orations for his aunt Iulia and for his wife Cornelia while he was quaestor, before departing for Hispania.[216]

The question of whether quaestors had *potestas contionandi* (i.e. whether they were able to summon and preside over popular assemblies), as the other regular magistrates did, remains an open one.[217] If quaestors did indeed have the power to convoke a contio, it is quite possible that Trebonius organized the public meeting in which he took the sort of political initiative that Cicero praised so highly. That said, we cannot discount the possibility that another magistrate might have been the summoner of that *contio*. At any rate, this is the only evidence of an urban quaestor intervening as an orator in a popular assembly, since C. Gracchus, Clodius and Caesar were all provincial quaestors.

The urban quaestorship of Cato Uticensis

Cato Uticensis' urban quaestorship in the year 64 is well known, thanks to the information found in Plutarch's biography.[218] Above all else, Plutarch emphasises Cato's integrity, highlighting particular points: how carefully he prepared himself before holding the quaestorship, how vehemently he fought against the corruption of the scribes who worked for the public treasury and against irregular practices of earlier quaestors, and how honestly he acted throughout his office.

Having served as military tribune in the East, Cato returned to Rome. According to Plutarch's account, although Cato might have already canvassed for the quaestorship, he preferred to read in advance all the laws related to the office as well as to form a general picture of the magistracy worked from those who had already held it.[219] Once Cato considered himself adequately prepared, he was elected to the quaestorship and became urban quaestor by lot. During his term of office, Cato intended to put an end to the excessive influence of the assistants and scribes working in the *aerarium*. As Plutarch asserts, after several years of performing their job these clerks were much better versed in the workings of the institution than the inexpert quaestors, who changed every year. This fact led to the risk of the scribes considering themselves superior to the quaestors instead of serving under their command, as they were obliged to do.[220] Cato endeavoured to put assistants and *scribae* in their place and he did not hesitate to confront them if necessary: he expelled the chief

---

216 Suet. *Iul.* 6; Plut. *Caes.* 5.
217 In his definition of *contio*, Festus seems to include all magistrates as potential summoners: *Contio significat conventum, non tamen alium, quam eum, qui <a> magistratu vel a sacerdote publico per praeconem convocatur* (Fest. p.38 L.). See Pina Polo 1989, 48 and 1995, 205, defending the idea that the quaestors did indeed have the *potestas contionandi*. Cf. Tan 2008, 181.
218 See Fehrle 1983, 76–81; Morrell 2017.
219 Plut. *Cat.min.* 16.1.
220 Plut. *Cat.min.* 16.2. See David 2019, 64 and 151.

among them from the treasury, after he was found guilty of committing an irregularity with an inheritance; another was brought to trial for fraud.[221] This man was acquitted despite the confrontation between Cato and Q. Lutatius Catulus during the trial. However, Cato did not approve of the verdict; on the contrary, he refused to employ the scribe after he was acquitted.[222]

According to Plutarch, Cato acted with incredible diligence in demanding payment from those with long-standing debts to the *aerarium* and in making prompt payment to the state's creditors.[223] He eliminated the sort of bad practice and fraud characteristic of previous quaestors, who were apparently even willing to enter false senatorial decrees into the *aerarium* in order to please others.[224] Plutarch asserts that on one occasion when Cato did not believe that a senatorial decree had actually been passed, he only agreed to archive it in the treasury after the consuls took an oath and swore to its validity.[225] Cato also accused many to whom Sulla had granted a reward for killing men under proscription of having received public money by unjust means. They were charged with murder, brought to trial and punished.[226]

In short, during the time in which Cato was in charge of the public treasury, he managed it—at least according to Plutarch—with the utmost probity and strictness that came characterise him more generally. It is not appropriate to speak of Cato introducing reforms to the administration of the public treasury during this term of office, but rather of his determination for correctly running the *aerarium* with a strict adherence to the rules. With a treasury full of money and without corruption, Plutarch says, Cato 'taught men that a city can be rich without treating its citizens unjustly.'[227] By way of conclusion, Plutarch states that Cato 'brought the quaestorship into greater esteem than the senate, so that everybody thought and said that Cato had given the quaestorship the dignity of the consulship.'[228]

Plutarch depicts Cato's urban quaestorship as something extraordinary, an exception to the rule: for most other quaestors, the quaestorship was little more than the first step in the *cursus honorum*. It must be taken into account, though, that Plutarch selectively chose information with the main purpose of constructing an image

---

221 Plut. *Cat.min.* 16.3.
222 Plut. *Cat.min.* 16.4–6.
223 Plut. *Cat.min.* 17.1–2.
224 See above the incident that occurred on the final day of his quaestorship, when he confronted his colleague and friend Marcellus for having committed fraud.
225 Plut. *Cat.min.* 17.3.
226 Plut. *Cat.min.* 17.4–5. According to Cassius Dio, Cato demanded those who had murdered anyone in the time of Sulla return anything that they had received for their work (Cass.Dio 47.6.4. Cf. 37.10.2).
227 Plut. *Cat.min.* 18.2.
228 Plut. *Cat.min.* 17.1. Plutarch emphasises that Cato was the first to arrive at the *aerarium* and the last to leave the building (18.1). Even after leaving the quaestorship, Cato took an interest in the proper management of the treasury, and even bought himself a copy of the books containing accounts of the public business from Sulla to his own quaestorship, in order always to have them at hand (18.5).

of Cato as an honest and incorruptible politician, as he was thought to have been throughout his entire life. There is no reason to doubt the veracity of this information in general, but caution is also necessary.[229] In any case, Plutarch's account points to some features that occasionally or regularly must have formed part of the urban quaestorship, such as tensions with scribes, who were the real experts in the nitty-gritty of the Roman administration, pressures from friends or prominent citizens to introduce irregularities in the *tabulae publicae*, and ultimately the more general temptation of corruption and fraud. While in every public administration, then and now, corruption must obviously have existed, one can doubt whether Cato was really the sterling exception that Plutarch paints and whether the *aerarium* was really so rife with scoundrels. Indeed, Plutarch may be exaggerating the contrast in order to accentuate Cato's exceptionality. Given the duties that it entailed in the city, the urban quaestorship provided an excellent chance for young and ambitious politicians to showcase their talents to the people and, in particular, to members of the senate; this would have increased their chances of progressing up the *cursus honorum*. A *quaestor urbanus* had in his hands the great political responsibility of the administration of public money and public documents. Lack of attention to his duties and dishonest behaviour could stop a politician's career dead in its tracks.

---

[229] Fehrle 1983, 77.

List of urban quaestors in the Roman Republic[230]

196[231]	L. Aurelius (RE 18)
	Q. Fabius Labeo (RE 91)
168	L. Manlius (Acidinus?) (RE 26)
	L. Stertinius (RE 6)
167	L. Cornelius Scipio (RE 324)
116 or 115?	M. Sergius Silus (RE 42)
111–110? (or 99?)	Ap. Claudius Pulcher (RE 296)
	T. Maloleius? (or Mallius? or Manlius?)
by 105	Cn. Octavius Ruso? (RE 82)
103?	L. Calpurnius Piso Caesoninus (RE 89)
	Q. Servilius Caepio (RE 50)
101	C. Fundanius (RE 1)
by 90–88?	L. Octavius? (RE 26)
	C. Pomponius? (not in RE)
80s?	T. Vibius Temudinus (not in RE)
86	Hirtuleius (RE 1)
83	M. Fonteius (RE 12)
81	P. Cornelius Lentulus (Sura) (RE 240)

---

[230] Obviously, some of the quaestors recorded in the sources since the fifth century (see the general list of quaestors in chronological order) must have been urban quaestors, although this information is not given explicitly. Ap. Claudius Sabinus Inregillensis (cos. 495; RE 321) was supposedly urban quaestor at some point at the beginning of the Republican age, according to his *elogium*: *Ap. Claudius q. urb. cos. cum P. Servilio Pr(isco)* (CIL 1² p. 199 = VI 1279 = Inscr.Ital. 13.3.65). Claudius Sabinus was allegedly consul in 495. In accordance with his *elogium*, the quaestorship preceded his consulship, which is of an uncertain date. Everything about him, however, is highly doubtful. See Sobeck 1909, 1–2; Broughton MRR, 1.12; Ogilvie 1965, 274.

[231] L. Aurelius and Q. Fabius Labeo are the first quaestors to which Livy (33.42.2) refers expressly as urban quaestors.

	C. (Valerius) Triarius (RE 363, 366)
80	A. Manlius [Torquatus] (RE 13, cf. 70 and 76)
75?	Cn. Cornelius Lentulus Marcellinus (RE 228)
71?	P. Cornelius Lentulus Spinther (RE 238) L. Plaetorius (Cestianus) (RE 14)
64	M. Claudius Marcellus (RE 229) M. Porcius Cato (Uticensis) (RE *20)
63?	C. Cornelius Cethegus?[232] (RE 89)
61	M. Curtius Peducaeanus (RE 8) P. Sestullius (RE Sextilius 13)
58?	C. Trebonius (RE 6)
by 54	T. Ligarius (RE 5)
49	Cn. Nerius (RE 3)
44	Q. Cornelius (RE 5 and 52; cf. 51) Q. Rutilius (RE 11)

---

[232] Ryan 1994d, proposes that C. Cornelius Cethegus, one of the leaders of the Catilinarian plot, may have been an urban quaestor in 63. Ryan's proposal is ultimately speculative and is not supported by the evidence.

Chapter 6:
The quaestor overseas:
Development and role of the quaestorship in the provinces

Like with all Roman institutions and magistracies, the characteristics, importance, role and responsibilities of the quaestorship evolved over the decades. This has been demonstrated in previous chapters, which focus on the evolution of the quaestorship in Rome and Italy. This chapter, in turn, will discuss the changes and adaptations that the magistracy underwent overseas in the provinces during the Republic. At a time when Rome began to make its presence permanent in various territories across the Mediterranean, these changes can largely be seen as the result of a process of adaptation in which the magistracy had to meet the particular needs found in the provinces. After the regular assignation of two praetors to the provinces of Sicily and Sardinia beginning in 227, the number of Rome's permanent provinces grew continually, though at an uneven pace.[1] It is well known that the increase in the number of *provinciae*, which were divvied up each year to magistrates with *imperium* (i.e. consuls and praetors), caused the number of praetorships to increase: first to four in 227, next to six in 197 and then to eight under Sulla. Despite these rising numbers, it was the increasingly common practice of proroguing a magistrate's command that sustained the system of provincial governance, a system whose principal virtue can be seen in its malleability and capacity to adapt to the circumstances that the maintenance of Roman *imperium* generated in each moment.[2]

In the same way, the quaestorship was also shaped by the changing situation and the need to govern Rome's provinces properly. So such is seen in the well known passage from Tacitus: *mox duplicatus numerus, stipendiaria iam Italia et accedentibus provinciarum vectigalibus.*[3] As we have seen in chapter 2, from at least 421 two of the quaestors were assigned to assist the consuls. These quaestors became the right-hand men of the supreme magistrates of the Republic, not only in matters concerning the administration of the city, but also when it came to waging war outside Rome, as both Tacitus and Livy observe. Although the sources do not specify exactly when, it appears that this dynamic was also extended to the praetorship, the magistracy that shared with the consulship the exercise of *imperium* and the administration of the provinces. It thus became standard that every *imperator* who left Rome

---

[1] Solin. 5.1; Liv. *per.* 20; cf. App. *Sic.* 2.6; Brennan 2000, 91–95; Prag 2013, 53–54. For a recent overview of the historical development of the Roman provinces during the Republic, see Díaz Fernández 2015, 109–275; see also Letta and Segenni 2016, 87–273; cf. Richardson 2008, 12–62; Ferrary 2010, 34–38; Drogula 2015, 235–255. For a more traditional approach, see Luzzatto 1985, 46–209.
[2] Brennan 2000, 239–241; Díaz Fernández 2015, 66–85.
[3] Tac. *ann.* 11.22.

for his *provincia* had to be accompanied by a quaestor *ad ministeria belli* ('to administer war') or *ut rem militarem commitaretur* ('to collaborate with military tasks'), as Livy and Tacitus make explicit in the case of the consular quaestors.[4] Immediately after the disaster at Cannae in 216, for instance, M. Claudius Marcellus (the praetor initially destined for Sicily) was assisted by an unnamed quaestor in Nola. This fact seems to corroborate the idea that praetors were already assigned a quaestor in the late third century.[5] Accordingly, the fact that quaestors were traditionally expected to collaborate with the consuls in theatres of war could very well explain why every magistrate who was dispatched to a particular destination had a mandatory quaestor in his service. Over time, the quaestor—who was the right-hand of the consuls and praetors, and hence he ranked second in the provincial hierarchy—thus became another component of the provincial administration.[6]

When Rome decided to make its presence in Sicily and Sardinia permanent by regularly sending a praetor to each of the islands (an action that constituted a decisive step in the political and institutional evolution of Rome), the senate perhaps understood that those magistrates also should be accompanied by a quaestor, as had become common practice in the case of the consuls.[7] As we have already argued in chapter 2, it is plausible that the number of quaestorships increased to eight in 227, which would have been in step with the attested increase in the number of praetors from two to four that took place in the same year.[8] This number remained unchanged until the Sullan period. As Prag has demonstrated,[9] having four quaestors seems to have been sufficient to meet the needs of the Roman provinces until the beginning of the second century, when the increase in the number of Rome's permanent provinces made it necessary to incorporate more quaestors into the Republic's annual roll call of magistrates. As in the case of the praetorship, the prorogation of the quaestors could, in principle, have been sufficient for covering the seven permanent provinces under Roman control at the end of the second century, if we remember that the consuls could also have been sent to provinces that were usually praetorian. Such an arrangement would have freed up praetors and quaestors who would have initially been destined for these provinces to carry out other assignments.[10] The provinces in Hispania, for instance, were a normal destination of consuls throughout much of the second century, just like Sardinia and Macedonia were in certain peri-

---

[4] Liv. 4.43.3–4; Tac. *ann.* 11.22.
[5] Liv. 23.15.15: *laetoque iuveni promissis equum eximium dono dat bigatosque quingentos quaestorem numerare iubet; lictoribus imperat ut eum se adire quotiens uelit patiantur*; cf. Plut. *Marc.* 10.1–9.
[6] Johnston 2008, 8–9.
[7] Prag 2014a, 202–204.
[8] Liv. *per.* 20: *praetorum numerus ampliatus est ut essent IIII*.
[9] Prag 2014a, 201–207; cf. Harris 1976, 104.
[10] Prag 2014a, 206–207. We must keep in mind that the number of praetors was not increased from 197 to 81, despite the creation of several permanent provinces like Africa, Macedonia, Asia or Cilicia; see Badian 1979, 793–794; Brennan 2000, 239–241; Barrandon and Hurlet 2009, 36–39; Díaz Fernández 2015, 66–73.

ods. Apparently, the Roman constitution must have been sufficiently versatile to sustain the provincial administration throughout the second century.

Some scholars have suggested that the Romans must have stationed a quaestor in Lilybaeum after the end of the First Punic War in 241.[11] According to the proposals found in chapter 2, two new quaestorships might have been created in 267 (as the *Periochae* of Livy and Lydus suggest) in order to finance and arm a navy that could fight the Carthaginians; that said, quaestors were no longer needed to fulfil that function once the war ended in 241. As a result, it is certainly possible that one of those two quaestors would have been available to be stationed in Sicily after the close of the war. But as Harris himself admits, there is not a single piece of concrete evidence to support the notion that there was a quaestor (or a praetor, as has also been suggested[12]) permanently in Sicily before 227.[13] Such a proposal, then, is largely a vestige of the tendency to assume that Sicily must have been placed under the control of a Roman commander after the Carthaginians were expelled in 241. However, it is perfectly possible that the Romans simply left a military detachment on the island, perhaps supported by the troops of their ally, Hiero of Syracuse.[14] It is only from 227 that we can be sure that the senate sent a praetor to Sicily every year, and, given the considerations discussed above, it is likely that the praetor was accompanied by a quaestor, whose office was quite plausibly created that same year for that very purpose.[15]

While it appears that the number of eight quaestors was sufficient (at least at first) to cover the various Roman provinces thanks in large part to the increasingly

---

11 As Mommsen proposed in Röm. St. II 571–572; see more recently Dahlheim 1977, 30–35; Harris 1976 104; 1979, 136, n. 2; Marino 1988, 25–26; Loreto 1993, 496–498; Brennan 2000, 139; Serrati 2000, 122–123; Prag 2013, 61–62, n. 13. Pinzone 1979, 172–173 identifies the *quaestor Lilybitanus* as direct successor of the quaestor supposedly sent to Sicily from 241; cf. Pinzone 2000, 859–861; 875, n. 55.
12 According to Kienast 1968, 357–359, n. 89, a passage from Appian (*Sic.* 2.6: Σικελίας δὲ οὕτω τοῦ πλέονος Ῥωμαῖοι κατέσχον, ὅσον Καρχηδόνιοι κατεῖχον, φόρους τε αὐτοῖς ἐπέθεσαν καὶ τέλη τὰ θαλάσσια ταῖς πόλεσι μερισάμενοι στρατηγὸν ἐτήσιον ἔπεμπον ἐς Σικελίαν) may suggest that a praetor was already stationed in Sicily in 241; the proposal has been partially accepted by Brennan 2000, 87–89, who suggests that the praetor *inter peregrinos* was created in 242 with the possible aim of governing Sicily. See, however, Prag 2007b, 72: 'If the *stratēgos* referred to by Appian existed, he cannot regularly have been a praetor prior to 227 B.C., and was not necessarily so afterwards. If he existed pre-227, then he was perhaps, as some scholars have speculated, a *privatus cum imperio*'; see also Crawford 1990, 92–94; cf. Barrandon and Hurlet 2009, 36–37; Prag 2013, 61; Díaz Fernández 2015, 111–118; 2017a, 71–75.
13 Harris 1979, 136, n. 2: 'It is possible, but quite uncertain, that a quaestor was regularly stationed at Lilybaeum even before 227.'
14 This is a proposal found in Richardson 1986, 7–8: 'A more plausible guess is that the Romans relied on their ally, Hiero of Syracuse, supported at most by a naval squadron which may have been stationed at Lilybaeum; but there is no trace of such a force, nor of its commander, who would presumably have been a *duovir navalis*'; Prag 2007a, 96–99; Díaz Fernández 2015, 116–118; cf. Serrati 2000, 115–119.
15 Harris 1976, 104; cf. Prag 2014a, 201–202.

common use of prorogations, this could not have been the case by the beginning of the first century, when the provinces of Cilicia and probably Gaul were incorporated into the Empire. Such an addition almost certainly would have strained the system, which in turn must have prompted Sulla to increase the numbers of praetorships to eight and quaestorships to twenty.[16] The *lex Cornelia de XX quaestoribus* of 81 permanently relieved the quaestorship of the pressures that must have been since the beginning of the first century, since the law created such a large pool of magistracies that the use of prorogation would no longer have been necessary to ensure that each of the provinces had the needed number of quaestors each year. In fact, if the limited number of quaestors before the Sullan period has generated some scholarly debate about how Rome managed to furnish its provinces with quaestors[17], the new number of quaestors created by Sulla presents historians, paradoxically, with the opposite problem: what could the function of each of those twenty magistrates possibly have been?[18] As we will see below, even accepting that mandates such as the *provinciae Ostiensis, aquaria* and *Callium* could have been included occasionally or even often in the list of Roman quaestorian *provinciae*, we still have some serious difficulty in assigning a *provincia* to each of these twenty magistrates every year, especially for the period immediately following the passage of the Sullan law.

If we are correct that the number of quaestorships was raised to eight in 227, this decision would have established a precedent in the administrative workings of the Roman overseas territories and also would have further bound the quaestorship to the exercise of *imperium*, a process that began with the long-standing allocation of two consular quaestors (see above). Although there is no explicit evidence in the sources that neatly lays this out, everything seems to point in this direction: from 227 onwards, whenever a magistrate with *imperium*—whether a consul or a praetor—was sent somewhere, that magistrate was accompanied by a quaestor.[19] By becoming the close confidant of the magistrates sent overseas, the quaestors, whose responsibilities until then had principally been financial and administrative, began to play an active role in the duties assigned to their superiors, that is, in the military and jurisdictional responsibilities entrusted to those higher magistrates. This indeed

---

16 See Stewart 1987, 342–343: 'The Sullan increase in the number of quaestors to twenty likewise reflected the further increase in the number of Rome's overseas provinces and the concomitant need for more administrative officials.'
17 Harris 1976, 104–105; see Badian 1983, 167–168; Prag 2014a, 202–207; Stewart 1987, 342–343, n. 19.
18 Badian 1983, 167–169.
19 Prag 2014a, 201–202: 'From 227 praetors were sent to Sicily and Sardinia with regularity. From 197 two praetors were usually sent to *Hispania Citerior* and *Ulterior*. There was of course some variation to that general pattern. I think it is uncontroversial to assume that provincial praetors were normally attended by a quaestor during the second century. Quaestors attending on a 'regular' praetorian governor (rather than a consul on campaign in the same area) are attested in at least one instance for every 'regular' *prouincia* of the second century with the sole exception of Africa'; cf. Stewart 1987, 342–343.

would mesh with the type of collaboration *ad ministeria belli* outlined in Livy. As a consequence, the quaestors considerably broadened their field of action in the provinces, even to the point of assuming *imperium* at the discretion of their superiors or following a senatorial decision.

We must assume that the system adopted in 227 was upheld in 197, when the senate decided to add two more praetorships to the *cursus honorum* with the intention of sending both to what would become the permanent provinces of Hispania Citerior and Hispania Ulterior. In this case, Livy informs us of the decision to create the two new praetorships, though his account is quite terse: that year (198) the Romans chose for the first time six praetors *crescentibus iam provinciis et latius patescente imperio*, that is, since the number of *provinciae* had increased and the *imperium* had grown.[20] There is not a single allusion to the procedures by which this decision was taken, nor to what extent this decision affected the quaestorship. Nevertheless, today it is taken for granted that two of the eight quaestors elected each year must have been sent to Hispania from then on.[21]

In fact, the main problem for those trying to reconstruct the role of the quaestorship in the Republican provinces is the same issue that has been discussed repeatedly throughout this book: the lack of sources. As a result, we modern historians have tried our best to fill in the gaps: we have tended think that the first praetors sent to Sicily, Sardinia, or the two Hispaniae must have been accompanied by a quaestor, although there is no actual evidence to substantiate this theory. In fact, besides the dispatch of M. Claudius Marcellus' quaestor to Sicily in 216 (and it is by no means certain that he disembarked on the island),[22] it is not until 185 that the sources cite the first quaestor in the service of a praetor in a province: Q. Fabius, about whom we simply learn that he was charged with depositing in the *aerarium* part of the extensive booty from Hispania Citerior that L. Manlius Acidinus, praetor and proconsul in that province during the years 188–185, had obtained.[23] Livy tells us noth-

---

20 Liv. 32.27.6; on the creation of two praetors for the Hispanian provinces in 197, see Richardson 1986, 75–76; Salinas de Frías 1995, 42–44; Brennan 2000, 163–164; Díaz Fernández 2015, 125–131.
21 Despite Livy's silence on the quaestorship, Harris 1976, 104–105 suggests that the number of quaestors was also increased to ten in 197: 'When mentioning the increase in the number of praetors from four to six in 197, Livy ignores the quaestors, which favours the view that the number of quaestorships remained unchanged—at least for a while. Tacitus' concise account passes directly from eight to twenty. On the other hand, since it was probably the unvarying practice to send a quaestor to every province, it is reasonable to assume that there was an increase at some date. And Livy's failure to mention an increase in 197 is not a decisive argument. It is true that he mentioned the increase in 267, but no law was necessary for such an increase, and it may have gone unnoticed by annalists who were interested in recording the names of all praetors and aediles but not of quaestors'; cf. also 106: 'In 197 the total was probably raised to ten, a figure not exceeded until Sulla.' See, however, Badian 1983, 168, n. 33.
22 Liv. 23.15.15; Plut. *Marc.* 10.1–9.
23 Liv. 39.29.6–7: *tulit coronas aureas quinquaginta duas, auri praeterea pondo centum triginta duo, argenti sedecim milia trecenta, et pronuntiauit in senatu decem milia pondo argenti et octoginta auri Q. Fabium quaestorem aduehere: id quoque se in aerarium delaturum*; Broughton MRR, 1.366.

ing more. We do not know if he accompanied Acidinus from the start of his command in Hispania (which would place his quaestorship in 188 and imply that, like his praetor, he was successively prorogued), or if he was later dispatched to Hispania. Since Livy calls Fabius *quaestor*, at first glance it appears that he was occupying the quaestorship in that year; it is well known, however, that classical authors did not always use these denominations in their strict sense; hence, it is not totally clear whether or not the man in question actually held that magistracy or was serving *pro quaestore*.[24]

As we have already highlighted in the introduction, this is another of the problems inherent to the study of quaestorship in the provinces: not only are we lacking information, but what little we have is often quite vague. Accordingly, we cannot confidently date the quaestorships of many of the magistrates sent to the provinces, nor can we specify at what point they joined the governor's retinue. Besides the example of Q. Fabius, the sources provide many more examples of so-called *quaestores* who, in reality, were actually *proquaestores*, since they had already completed their year of office. L. Cornelius Sulla is a case in point: he is consistently cited by Sallust as Marius' quaestor, despite the fact that he remained serving him in Numidia from 107 (the year of his quaestorship) to 105, by which stage he was actually a proquaestor.[25] Likewise in his letters, Cicero does not speak of L. Mescinius Rufus as his proquaestor, although we know that he was with him in Cilicia from 51–50 and that he must have been prorogued.[26] It is thus impossible to determine the duration of the majority of quaestors' stint in the provinces, since in most cases we do not know whether they had been prorogued or not. There are very few occasions when the sources speak about the quaestor from the moment he left for his province accompanying his superior, as in the cases of Sulla and L. Mescinius Rufus. On the other hand, it is inscriptions and coins (rather than the literary record) that usually specify the magistrate's actual rank and determine whether he was in reality a quaestor or a proquaestor during a particular year of his stay in a province, as well as whether he had *imperium* or not.[27] In fact, most of the time, quaestors appear in the sources coincidentally, in a

---

24 Syme 1955a, 131–132; see also Badian 1983, 158–159; Konrad 1995, 186–187.
25 See Sall. *Iug.* 103.7: *igitur quaestori mandata Bocchi patefaciunt*; 106.1: *Volux adveniens quaestorem appellat dicitque se a patre Boccho obviam illis simul et praesidio missum*; 113.5: *cum paucis amicis et quaestore nostro quasi obvius honoris causa procedit in tumulum facillumum visu insidiantibus*. Sulla is nevertheless reported as proper quaestor in 95.1: *ceterum, dum ea res geritur, L. Sulla quaestor cum magno equitatu in castra venit*; cf. also Diodor. 34.39 (συνέλαβε τὸν Ἰογόρθαν καὶ δήσας παρέδωκε Λευκίῳ Σύλλᾳ τῷ ταμίᾳ τῷ πρὸς τὴν παράπεμψιν ἐκπεμφθέντι); Liv. *per.* 66; Vell. 2.12.1; Eutr. 4.27.4; Broughton MRR, 1.554 and 1.556). Since, in 105, Marius left Sulla in charge of the Roman troops of Numidia as *propraetor* (Sall. *Iug.* 103.4: *ad Sullam profugiunt, quem consul in expeditionem proficiscens pro praetore reliquerat*), we should suppose that his proper title was *proquaestor pro praetore*.
26 Cic. *fam.* 13.26.1: *L. Mescinius ea mecum necessitudine coniunctus est quod mihi quaestor fuit*; Att. 6.4.1: *nihil minus probari poterat quam quaestor Mescinius*; 6.7.2: *ego Laodiceae quaestorem Mescinium exspectare iussi*; cf. *fam.* 2.17.4; 16.4.3. Broughton MRR, 2.242; Thompson 1965; cf. Muñiz Coello 1998, 198–206.
27 See Badian 1983, 158–159.

specific episode, a commemorative inscription, or a coin whose date ranges between several years if not decades. Nevertheless, and despite the difficulties discussed just outlined, this chapter will try to provide a picture of the role of the quaestorship in the provinces that is as complete and faithful to the sources as possible, always bearing in mind that its conclusions will be proposed cautiously, as the condition of the sources demands.

Provinces, sortitions, prorogations

While Livy's account allows us to know the names of almost all the praetors and consuls chosen by the *comitia* between 217 and 166 as well as their respective *provinciae*, there is no such detailed information available for the quaestorship.[28] Indeed, there is not a single year from 227 (when Sicily and Sardinia became permanent provinces) until the death of Caesar for which a complete list of quaestors and their corresponding *provinciae* is preserved. Our knowledge of the procedures for selection and assignation of quaestorian provinces during the Republic is, as a consequence, inevitably partial and limited. In the same way, we do not know each of the provinces assigned every year to the quaestors, although the question is intimately connected with the annual distribution of consular and praetorian assignments.

As in the case of consular and praetorian provinces, the senate appears to have decided in advance *ex senatus consulto* which duties would be assigned to the incoming quaestors, among whom there always had to be two *quaestores urbani*, charged with the *aerarium provincia*, and two consular quaestors who were attached to their superiors' *provinciae*. When the senate decided to make Sicily and Sardinia permanent provinces under the control of respective praetors, it may be supposed that both of these places were incorporated into the annual sortition of quaestorian provinces. Perhaps the same thing occurred with the provinces of Hispania years later. Once the quaestors were chosen, the distribution of provinces was normally made following the same procedure that was used for superior magistrates, namely by sortition, although there was also the possibility of designating a province *sine sorte* (either by senatorial decree or via a tribunician law). As discussed in chapter four, the official assignation of *provinciae* to the quaestors appears to have been sanctioned *ex senatus consulto* as well, regardless of whether it was done by sortition or *sine sorte*:[29] in 202, C. Laelius was named Scipio Africanus' quaestor *extra sortem*

---

28 Harris 1976, 104–105; Badian 1983, 168–169.
29 According to the sources, the senate was ultimately responsible for granting *provinciae* to the quaestors: cf. particularly *Dig.* 1.13.1.2: *Ex quaestoribus quidam solebant provincias sortiri ex senatus consulto...*; also Front. *de aq.* 2.96; *eorumque operum probandorum curam fuisse penes censores aliquando et aediles, interdum etiam quaestoribus eam provinciam obvenisse, ut apparet ex S. C. quod factum est C. Licinio et Q. Fabio cos.*; Cic. *Verr.* 2.1.34 (see below); CIL I² 749. Several instances attest to the fact that quaestors could receive their *provinciae* without sortition: in *Phil.* 2.50 Cicero signifi-

ex senatus consulto, in the same way as Verres became quaestor for the consul Cn. Papirius Carbo via a sortition *ex senatus consulto*: *Quaestor ex senatus consulto provinciam sortitus es: obtigit tibi consularis, ut cum consule Cn. Carbone esses eamque provinciam obtineres.*[30]

As mentioned above, we believe that in principle every *imperator* sent to a *provincia* had a quaestor *ad ministeria belli:* whether it was temporary or permanent, every *provincia* under the command of an *imperator* had a corresponding quaestor. When L. Anicius Gallus received the command of the *provincia Illyricum* during his praetorship in 168, the senate would probably have assigned him a quaestor to pursue his mission in the war against Gentius, even though Illyricum stopped being considered a province after Anicius Gallus' victory in 167: we therefore assume that Illyricum was one of the *provinciae* assigned to one of the quaestors.[31] We know for certain that P. Varinius, one of the praetors sent to fight Spartacus in 73, had C. Toranius as quaestor during his campaigns in Campania: P. Varinius was a praetor with a clearly military mission, for which reason he was given a quaestor *ad ministeria belli*, regardless of the fact that his *provincia* (perhaps Campania or *Bellum Spartacum*) was not a permanent province.[32] Moreover, even Roman citizens granted *imperium* by special concession were provided with quaestors, as we see with Pompey's various commands during his career: during his campaigns in Hispania, the Mediterranean and the East, when fighting against Sertorius, the pirates and Mithridates respectively, Pompey had several quaestors under his command even though he did not at the time hold any magistracy.[33] Likewise, Scipio Africanus had C. Flaminius

---

cantly stresses the unusual way in which M. Antonius became Caesar's quaestor in 51 (*quaestor es factus; deinde continuo sine senatus consulto, sine sorte, sine lege ad Caesarem cucurristi*). Lintott 1999, 136.

30 Cic. *Verr.* 2.1.34; on C. Laelius' quaestorship, cf. Liv. 30.33.2: *Laelium, cuius ante legati, eo anno quaestoris extra sortem ex senatus consulto opera utebatur, cum Italico equitatu ab sinistro cornu, Masinissam Numidasque ab dextro opposuit.*

31 Liv. 44.21.4: *L. Anicius praetor, cuius inter peregrinos iurisdictio erat; eum in provinciam Illyricum circa Lychnidum Ap. Claudio succedere placuit*; Broughton MRR, 1.428; on the *provincia Illyricum* allotted to L. Anicius Gallus, see Dzino 2010, 57–58.

32 Sall. *hist.* 3.96 M.: *at Varinius, dum haec aguntur a fugitivis, aegra parte militum autumni gravitate neque ex postrema fuga, cum severo edicto iuberentur ullis ad signa redeuntibus et qui reliqui erant, per summa flagitia detractantibus militiam, quaestorem suum C. Thoranium, ex quo praesente vera facillime noscerentu<r, Roma>m misera[n]t*; cf. Broughton MRR, 2.110; Brennan 2000, 431–432; 925, n. 439; Vervaet 2014, 414–418.

33 According to the sources, Pompey successively had his brother-in-law C. Memmius and C. Cornelius (tr. pl. 67) as quaestors during the Sertorian War in Hispania; cf. Cic. *Balb.* 5: *ut Pompeius in Hispaniam venerit Memmiumque habere quaestorem coeperit*; Oros. 5.23.12; Plut. *Sert.* 21.2; Broughton MRR, 2.93; 98; Konrad 1994, 175; 1995, 184–186; on C. Cornelius' quaestorship see Ascon. 57 C: *fuerat quaestor Cn. Pompei, dein tribunus plebis*. During the Mithridatic War in the East, Pompey had M. Aemilius Scaurus as his quaestor: cf. Ios. *AJ* 14.79; *BJ* 1.157; App. *Syr.* 51; IGRom. 3.1102. Asconius (35C) points out that P. Plautius Hypsaeus was Pompey's quaestor at some point, probably during the latter's command against the pirates in 67 or in the East; Broughton MRR, 2.153; see Ioannidopoulos 2017, 98–

in his service as quaestor during his command in Hispania in 210 and probably 209.[34] Therefore it appears beyond doubt that the exercise of military *imperium* implied the company of a quaestor *ad ministeria belli*,[35] which would be decisive, as we will see, in the development of the duties granted to overseas quaestors.

As De Martino compellingly argues, it appears that the senate decided on the list of quaestorian provinces every year depending on Rome's needs and circumstances.[36] When, therefore, the number of *provinciae* to share among the Roman magistrates in any particular year was more than the number of magistrates available, the senate usually prorogued the magistrates who were already in office at that time, in order to distribute the tasks needed for that year among the incoming magistrates. This is what also happened with the quaestors, who—perhaps in the majority of cases—must also have been prorogued when the senate extended their superiors' commands.[37] Based on this consideration, we could conclude that the sortition of *provinciae* for the quaestors usually took place in conjunction with the distribution of *provinciae* among the consuls and praetors.

All evidence suggests that in the last decades of the Republic, the quaestors started their role on the Nones of December (5th December), despite being chosen last: that is, the quaestors took office weeks before the consuls and praetors did. We do not know the reasons that led the senate to structure things this way, nor do we know with certainty when 5th December was adopted as the start of the quaestors' term of office, but the fact is that we only have evidence for quaestors taking office on 5th December in the post-Sullan age (see chapter 4). Livy reveals that the senate usually distributed the consular provinces after the consuls' inauguration; the praetorian provinces were designated after that. Once the senate had taken these decisions, the *provinciae* were distributed by *sors* or (sometimes) *comparatio*, and the relevant prorogues were assigned.[38] This system did not change in essence

---

105. Plutarch (*Pomp.* 26.2) states that Pompey had two quaestors during his campaigns against the pirates.
34 Liv. 26.47.8: *haec omnia C. Flaminio quaestori appensa adnumerataque sunt*; cf. 26.49.10; Broughton MRR, 1.286.
35 According to Velleius, M. Porcius Cato also received a quaestor for his command in Cyprus as *proquaestor propraetore*: cf. Vell. 2.45.4: *quippe legem tulit, ut is quaestor cum iure praetorio, adiecto etiam quaestore, mitteretur in insulam Cyprum*; Broughton MRR, 3.171; Badian 1965, 110–111.
36 De Martino 1960, 2.244–245: 'riteniamo che la magistratura fosse unitaria e che, salvo i questori urbani, che furono una magistratura stabile, per gli altri incarichi si provvedesse secondo i bisogni più o meno contingenti, mediante il solito sistema della determinazione annuale da parte del Senato delle rispettive competenze (provinciae), e con l'attribuzione ai singoli eletti per mezzo del sorteggio oppure in casi assai rari per mezzo della scelta del Senato'; see Prag 2014a, 201–205; cf. Harris 1976, 104, n. 108. See Cic. *Q. fr.* 2.3.1: *prodicta dies est in VII Id. Febr. interim reiectis legationibus in Idus referebatur de provinciis quaestorum et de ornandis praetoribus.*
37 A discussion can be found in Badian 1983, 158–168; cf. Prag 2014a, 205–208.
38 For an overview of the allotment and prorogation of provincial commands, see Schulz 1997: 53–71; cf. also Brennan 2000, 239–246; Ferrary 2010, 38–41; Drogula 2015, 255–263; Díaz Fernández

until the approval of the *lex Sempronia* in 123, which established that the senate had to choose the consular provinces every year before the election of the consuls.³⁹

Despite the lack of information on the subject, we can assume that, before Sulla, the sortition of quaestorian *provinciae* also took place in the first few days of the consular year, once the *provinciae* had been distributed among the higher magistrates. Accordingly, the sortition of quaestors would conform to the roles assigned to the consuls and praetors. We can take the years 188 and 187 as an example: when M. Valerius Messalla and C. Livius Salinator were elected consuls for 188, the senate decided that they would share the *provinciae* of Gaul and *Pisa cum Liguribus*, while the six new praetors would draw from among the usual options: *iurisdictio urbana*, *iurisdictio peregrina*, Sicily, Sardinia, Hispania Citerior and Hispania Ulterior.⁴⁰ We therefore can assume that the eight quaestors elected that year had to share the two urban quaestorships (*aerarium provincia*), Gaul and *Pisa cum Liguribus* (the consular provinces), as well as Sicily, Sardinia, and the two Hispaniae. The following year, however, during the consulate of M. Aemilius Lepidus and C. Flaminius, both consuls were assigned the *provincia Ligures* while the provinces drawn among the praetors were the two *iurisdictiones* of Rome (*urbana* and *peregrina*), two provinces outside Italy (Sicily and Sardinia), and two provinces in Italy (Tarentum and Gaul): *Comitiis perfectis, quas provincias praetoribus esse placeret, retulit ad senatum consul. Decreverunt duas Romae iuris dicendi causa, duas extra Italiam, Siciliam ac Sardiniam, duas in Italia, Tarentum et Galliam; et extemplo, priusquam inirent magistratum, sortiri iussi.*⁴¹ L. Manlius Acidinus and C. Atinius, the praetors sent to Hispania in 188, were presumably prorogued. Despite Livy's silence, we should assume that the quaestors of 187 divided between them the two urban quaestorships (*aerarium provincia*), the two consular provinces (*Ligures*) and the other four military provinces in Italy and overseas that were assigned to the praetors. It is likely that the two quaestors stationed in Hispania for 188 must have been prorogued in the same way as their superiors, though there is no explicit account that confirms this.⁴² In

---

2015, 66–85; on the prorogation, see the classic study of Jashemski 1950, 17–94. For the assignment of quaestorian provinces, see Stewart 1987, 338–353.

39 For the *lex Sempronia* see the following: Cic. *dom.* 24; *Balb.* 61; *Prov. Cons.* 3; 17; *fam.* 1.7.10; Sall. *Iug.* 27.3. Schulz 1997: 42–45; Vervaet 2006, 627–656; Ferrary 2010, 40; Drogula 2015, 298–304; Rafferty 2019.

40 Livy. 38.35.7–10: *M. Valerius Messala inde et C. Livius Salinator consulatum idibus Martiis cum inissent, de re publica deque provinciis et exercitibus senatum consuluerunt. De Aetolia et Asia nihil mutatum est; consulibus alteri Pisae cum Liguribus, alteri Gallia provincia decreta est. Comparare inter se aut sortiri iussi et novos exercitus, binas legiones, scribere, et ut sociis Latini nominis quina dena milia peditum imperarent et mille et ducentos equites. Messalae Ligures, Salinatori obtigit Gallia. Praetores inde sortiti sunt: M. Claudio urbana, P. Claudio peregrina iurisdictio evenit; Q. Marcius Siciliam, C. Stertinius Sardiniam, L. Manlius Hispaniam citeriorem, C. Atinius ulteriorem est sortitus.* Broughton MRR, 1.365.

41 Liv. 38.42.5–6; Broughton MRR, 1.367–368.

42 See Liv. 39.7.6; 39.21.2–6; Broughton MRR, 1.369.

any case, regardless of when the quaestors may have taken office in this period, it is clear that the sortition of their provinces had to wait until the senate had decided which would be the tasks given to the senior magistrates for that year: for the years covered by Livy's account, this moment only took place once the consuls had taken office on the Ides of March.

After the *lex Sempronia* of 123 took effect, the senate had to decide before the election of the consuls which provinces the high magistrates would be assigned once in office: this obliged the senate to have decided the upcoming consular duties by the end of each year, although the consuls would not distribute the provinces between them until the start of their commands. In principle, the introduction of the *lex Sempronia* did not affect the distribution of provinces for the quaestors, who probably continued to take office and draw their *provinciae* at the start of the consular year. More important was perhaps the successive incorporation of a series of *quaestiones* into the catalogue of praetors' *provinciae* after the creation of the *quaestio repetundae* in 149.[43] This brought about a gradual accumulation of tasks put into the praetors' hands and inevitably delayed the date of their departure for their provinces. As a result, it seems that some praetors left for their posts near the end of the year of their magistracy or, in some instances, even once it was finished. A parallel process occurred with the consulship.[44] We do not know to what extent these new circumstances impacted the exercise of quaestorian duties, but all indications suggest that some of them stayed in Rome for several months, waiting for the praetors to able to set out for their provinces. While this process became more and more common during the Late Republic, we do already have some examples from the last decades of the second century: the praetorship of C. Marius, who was *praetor urbanus* in 115 and governor of Hispania Ulterior μετὰ τὴν στρατηγίαν (that is, 'after the praetorship'),[45] and that of L. Licinius Lucullus, who was sent to Sicily after completing his praetorship in Rome in 104.[46]

According to Plutarch, Marius received the command of Hispania Ulterior by lot, after his praetorship (μετὰ δὲ τὴν στρατηγίαν κλήρῳ λαβὼν τὴν ἐκτὸς Ἰβηρίαν), which seems to suggest that he left for his province once he had completed his year's magistracy in Rome (i.e. at the start of 114) either as propraetor or as proconsul.[47] In this case, we can assume that the quaestor assigned to Marius in 115 (whose name we do not know) must have remained in Rome throughout his quaestorship until, finally, he moved to Hispania as proquaestor—unless we think that Marius obtained his quaestor in 114, which does not seem to correspond to the standard pro-

---

[43] Brennan 2000, 235–246; cf. Díaz Fernández 2015, 79–82.
[44] See Pina Polo 2011, 208–222; cf. Brennan 2000, 239–241; Díaz Fernández 2015, 79–82; Rafferty 2019.
[45] Plut. *Mar.* 6.1–2; Broughton MRR, 1.534–535, n. 3; Brennan 2000, 498.
[46] Diodor. 36.2.5; 36.9.1; Broughton MRR, 1.559; 564; Brennan 2000, 478–479.
[47] Vervaet 2012, 58–79; cf. Brennan 2000, 619–621; Barrandon and Hurlet 2009, 36–41; Díaz Fernández 2015, 74–78.

cedures followed before Sulla. It remains a matter of debate whether Marius received his two provinces (*iurisdictio urbana* and Hispania Ulterior) in a single draw at the start of his praetorship in 115 or, alternatively, in two successive draws. In an analysis of the allotment of praetorian provinces of 63, Hurlet suggests the possibility that the praetors may have received their overseas provinces in a second draw (perhaps held at the end of the summer) which must have determined the distribution of these commands for the following year (62) for the praetors currently in office.[48] Once this selection was completed, according to Hurlet, the praetors usually left for their provinces in December.[49] If this is the case, it is possible that during the last decades of the Republic quaestors were assigned to their praetors only after this second lot was drawn, when the latter were about to set out for their provinces. That being so, this may arguably have been the reason that quaestors took possession of their office on the Nones of December, the same day (as the Gronovian scholiast seems to imply) that the drawing of lots took place for quaestorian provinces at the end of the Republic.[50] The sortition for the quaestors would thus happen in conjunction with this supposed second draw for praetorian provinces, and the praetors would then depart for their destinations in December, accompanied by their recently chosen quaestors.

The lack of evidence, however, makes it difficult to accept this possibility: in fact, we know that these time frames were not always adhered to, since there were years in which the political situation provoked considerable delays in the election of the provincial praetors, such as in 62; in the same way, we also lack certainty that there were two sortitions for provincial praetors every year during the Late Republic.[51] The cases in which Livy describes the concession of two successive missions to the same praetor, furthermore, refer to a single sortition. It is quite possible that a similar process was in place until the end of the Republic.[52] In reality, we do not

---

48 Hurlet 2010, 58–61; cf. Schulz 1997, 48–49; Brennan 2000, 498; Vervaet 2006, 636–637, n. 45; see however Giovannini 1983, 92–93.

49 Hurlet 2010, 60: 'Le recours à un tirage au sort des provinces prétoriennes extra-urbaines dans le courant de l'année 63 – en mai-juin tôt, en octobre au plus tard – suffit à écarter l'idée, défendue par Giovannini, selon laquelle 'il n'y pas de trace, dans les sources antiques, de double *sortitio*'. Les événements liés à la conjuration de Catilina permettent de préciser qu'il y avait chaque année pour les préteurs deux tirages au sort: un premier à leur entrée en fonction ou peu Avant quand ils étaient préteurs désignés pour se répartir les provinces urbaines; un second qui avait pour objet d'attribuer les provinces extra-urbaines et qui se déroulait d'ordinaire dans le courant de l'année de la magistrature, sauf quand les circonstances ne l'ont pas permis comme ce fut le cas en décembre 62 avec l'affaire de la *Bona Dea*. À l'issue de la seconde *sortitio*, ils quittaient Rome dans un délai plus ou moins court, mais si possible avant la fin du mois de décembre.'

50 Schol. Gronov. p. 337 Stangl: *quaesturam intellegimus. Nam omnes ceteri magistratus Kal. Ian. procedebant, soli vero quaestores Nonis Dec.*; cf. *Lex Cornelia de XX quaestoribus* ll. 7–11; Cic. *Verr.* 1.30.

51 So Giovannini 1983, 92–93; for the provincial allotment of 62, cf. Cic. *Q. fr.* 2.3.1; Hurlet 2010, 57–58.

52 See Liv. 27.7.8 (*L. Veturius Philo peregrinam cum Gallia...*); 29.13.1 (*L. Scribonio Liboni peregrina et eidem Gallia...*); 39.38.3: (*Q. Naevius Matho Sardiniam et ut idem quaereret de veneficiis...*). Cf. 40.19.9:

know if the praetors' accumulation of tasks influenced the decision to move the quaestors' inauguration and the sortition for the provinces to the Nones of December. In any case, if the distribution of *provinciae* for the praetors continued to be carried out in a single sortition during the Late Republic and, consequently, if the praetors sent to overseas provinces received their quaestors at the start of their praetorships (once the quaestorian assignments had been drawn the previous December), this would certainly imply that those quaestors remained in Rome for the majority of their magistracies waiting for their superiors to conclude their duties in the city before leaving for the provinces. It is possible, during these months, that the quaestors kept themselves busy by preparing for the administration of their provinces or that they assisted the praetors with their duties at Rome, as the consular quaestors most likely did. Again, we cannot be certain on this matter and there are more questions than answers.

At any rate, we can venture that in the final decades of the Republic, the senate decided *ex senatus consulto* at the end of every year which provinces would be drawn for the quaestors on the Nones of December. This decision would be made in the context of which provinces would be distributed later (at the start of the consular year) to the consuls and praetors, including those provinces in which the senate had opted to replace the sitting quaestor while nevertheless proroguing his governor (see below). The senate, therefore, not only decided the two consular provinces before the elections (as was required by *lex Sempronia* of 123), but also the praetorian provinces and the prorogations of command. We may thus assume that after Sulla's dictatorship the assignments drawn among the quaestors on the Nones of December were the *aerarium provincia* of the two urban quaestors, the two quaestorships attached to the consuls for the following year (at that point, *consules designati*), the *provinciae* that the senate determined that year depending upon the needs of the *res publica* (*provincia Ostiensis*, etc.) and each of the overseas provinces that were to receive a new governor the following year or that would require a new quaestor.

A few examples reveal beyond a doubt that quaestors did not always stay in the provinces during the same period as their senior magistrates, who could have several different quaestors in their service throughout their time in the provinces. C. Sempronius Gracchus, who was sent to Sardinia as quaestor in 126 under the command of the consul L. Aurelius Orestes, returned to Rome in 124 to run in the elections for tribune of the plebs for 123; Aurelius Orestes continued there possibly until 122.[53] It is

---

L. Duronio praetori, cui provincia Apulia evenerat, adiecta de Bacchanalibus quaestio est; 43.2.3: *L. Canuleio praetori, qui Hispaniam sortitus erat, negotium datum est, ut in singulos, a quibus Hispani pecunias repeterent, quinos recuperatores ex ordine senatorio daret patronosque, quos vellent, sumendi potestatem faceret*; 44.17.10: *L. Anicius peregrinam et si quo senatus censuisset…*; 45.16.4: *A. Manlio Torquato Sardinia obvenerat: <at> nequiit ire in provinciam, ad res capitalis quaerendas ex senatus consulto retentus*; Brennan 2000, 106–107; 127–128; 204–205; cf. 239–242.

[53] Plut. *C.Gr.* 2.3–5; cf. particularly 2.4: ὁ δὲ τούτων αὐτῷ προσπεσόντων εὐθὺς ἐξέπλευσε πρὸς ὀργήν, καὶ φανεὶς ἐν Ῥώμῃ παρ' ἐλπίδας οὐ μόνον ὑπὸ τῶν ἐχθρῶν αἰτίαν εἶχεν, ἀλλὰ καὶ τοῖς πολ-

well known that Caesar also returned to Rome early (perhaps at the end of 68) during his quaestorship in Hispania Ulterior; as a result, it is quite probable that his praetor, Antistius Vetus, received a second quaestor to serve as Caesar's replacement for the remaining duration of his command.[54] C. Verres had at least four quaestors in his service during his command in Sicily: M. Postumius and Q. Caecilius Niger, in 73, and P. Caesetius and T. Vettius ca. 72–71, corresponding respectively with the two Sicilian quaestorships of Lilybaeum and Syracuse, which we will discuss below.[55] Sex. Peducaeus (pr. 77) must also have had several quaestors under his command—one of them being Cicero (q. 75)—during his two years as governor in Sicily (76–75).[56] These cases demonstrate that the distribution of consular and praetorian provinces was not the only factor that determined the allocation of quaestorian provinces. Despite the connection that linked the quaestor to his senior magistrate, quaestors were apparently not obliged to remain in the province throughout the same period of time as their seniors, which means that a consul or praetor might end up having several quaestors in his service over the course of his tenure.

There is, however, no evidence that the opposite could take place: as far as we know, there is no evidence that a quaestor could remain in a province longer than his superior—except in very exceptional circumstances—and serve under two different magistrates.[57] The case of C. Verres, who was quaestor to the consul Cn. Papirius Carbo in Gaul and then proquaestor in Cilicia under Cn. Cornelius Dolabella, does not support the theory that quaestors could serve consecutively under two different commanders: Verres went to Cilicia initially as a legate to Dolabella, who later named him proquaestor after his quaestor C. Malleolus died.[58] As we will see, a governor could leave the command of his province in the hands of a quaestor until his substitute arrived, as Cicero and Q. Minucius Thermus did when they respectively left Cilicia and Asia in 50, though it is probable that the quaestor was also replaced after the

---

λοῖς ἀλλόκοτον ἐδόκει τὸ ταμίαν ὄντα προαποστῆναι τοῦ ἄρχοντος. According to the *Fasti Triumphales*, L. Aurelius Orestes celebrated his triumph in 122; cf. Díaz Fernández 2015, 332–333.

54 Suet. *Iul.* 8: *decedens ergo ante tempus colonias Latinas de petenda ciuitate agitantes adiit, et ad audendum aliquid concitasset, nisi consules conscriptas in Ciliciam legiones paulisper ob id ipsum retinuissent*; Plut. *Caes.* 5.6; cf. Taylor 1941, 122–123; Broughton MRR, 2.132; 136, n. 7; 3.105–106.

55 Cic. *div. in Caec.* 4; *Verr.* 2.2.44; 2.3.168; 2.4.146; 2.5.63; 2.5.114; Ps. Ascon. p. 185; 195 Stangl; cf. Prag 2007b, 306; Brennan 2000, 486–490.

56 Cic. *Verr.* 2.3.216 (*biennium provinciam obtinuit*); *div. in Caec.* 2; Ps. Ascon. p. 185 Stangl; Brennan 2000, 484–485; Díaz Fernández 2015, 312–313; sources in Broughton MRR, 2.98; Prag 2007b, 304–305.

57 Despite Lintott's assertion that 'a quaestor might remain through more than one governorship' (Lintott 1999, 135), there is no evidence to support such a possibility. Lintott marshals the cases of C. Sempronius Gracchus and Sulla as evidence; although they certainly remained in their provinces during more than one year, they did so under the same governor; cf. Lintott 1999, 135–136, n. 58.

58 Cic. *Verr.* 2.1.41: *Itaque idem iste, quem Cn. Dolabella postea C. Malleolo occiso pro quaestore habuit, – haud scio an maior etiam haec necessitudo fuerit quam illa Carbonis, ac plus iudicium voluntatis valere quam sortis debeat, – idem in Cn. Dolabellam qui in Cn. Carbonem fuit.* Broughton MRR, 2.80; 85; 3.176.

new governor arrived.⁵⁹ It is also possible that a quaestor may have stayed in the province and held command there after the death of his superior, as M. Annius and C. Cassius Longinus both did after the death of Sex. Pompeius (ca. 119) and M. Licinius Crassus (53) in Macedonia and Syria, respectively. However, these were obviously exceptional circumstances.⁶⁰

As we have seen, the quaestorship was essentially linked to a higher authority and, in the case of quaestors assigned to consuls and praetors, to the *imperium* of those magistrates. It is therefore possible that their provincial duties could only be performed under the *imperium* and auspices of the commander to whom they had been assigned and to whom that province had been allocated. That is to say that is was probably inconceivable for a quaestor who had been sent to a province under the command of a particular consul or praetor to stay in that province after the departure of his superior and continue to serve under the command of a different magistrate. Unlike the quaestors who were given solo assignments, such as the abovementioned *provincia Ostiensis*, for example, or Cyrene and Cyprus, as we will see below, a quaestor assigned to a provincial commander exercised his duties in a province under the *imperium* and auspices of that commander: he was subject to his superior's authority and, therefore, his role in the province was inextricably linked to that higher authority. This basic system is not at all challenged by the fact that a quaestor could leave his post early or be dismissed from his duties before the governor left the province. Furthermore, there is no evidence for an individual holding two successive quaestorships, though we do know that this could happen with praetors: in other words, there is no evidence that a *quaestor urbanus*, for example, could be prorogued and sent to an overseas province once he had finished his duties in the *aerarium*.⁶¹

In the cases of M. Annius and C. Cassius Longinus, their continued tenure in the province was should be seen in light of an exceptional situation: the death of the governor. As we will see, this was precisely the reason Cassius took over command of Syria with *imperium*, as Annius possibly did in Macedonia. When Q. Minucius Thermus left L. Antonius in command of Asia as proquaestor propraetor, Antonius remained in the province under the auspices and *imperium* with which Thermus had invested to him. In this respect, we should remember Cicero's own concern

---

59 Cic. *fam.* 2.15.4: *ego de provincia decedens quaestorem Coelium praeposui provinciae*; Att. 6.6.3; 7.1.6; cf. Thompson 1965. Q. Minucius Thermus left his quaestor L. Antonius Pietas in charge of Asia in 50; cf. Cic. *fam.* 2.18.2; IGRom. 4.400; Ios. *AJ* 14.235.
60 M. Annius took command of Macedonia after Sex. Pompeius' death in 120–119; SIG³ 700, *ll.* 3–6; Broughton MRR, 1.526; 527 n. 3; Brennan 2000, 521–522; Díaz Fernández 2015, 422–423. C. Cassius Longinus saved the rest of M. Licinius Crassus' troops after the battle of Carrhae in 53; Liv. *per.* 108; Vell. 2.46.4; Cass.Dio 40.25.4–5; cf. Cic. *fam.* 15.14; Broughton MRR, 2.229; Díaz Fernández 2015, 66–67; 486–487. According to Cassius Dio (40.30.1), Cassius Longinus was replaced in the command of Syria when M. Calpurnius Bibulus arrived to the province in 50: ἅμα δὲ οὗτος ἀνεκεχωρήκει καὶ ὁ Βίβουλος ἄρξων τῆς Συρίας ἀφίκετο.
61 Prag 2014a, 205. On the controversial case of L. Sestius Quirinalis Albinianus (q. 45), see above.

over whom he should entrust with the command of Cilicia after his departure from the province; the choice was important: the decisions that that person would take between Cicero's departure and the arrival of his successor were ultimately Cicero's responsibility since they were acts carried out under his auspices and *imperium*.[62] When the *legatus pro praetore* A. Postumius Albinus was censured for his disastrous intervention in the Jugurthine War, ultimate responsibility for the events fell upon his brother, the consul Sp. Postumius Albinus, who was commander of the province of Numidia and the person under whose auspices the legate had acted.[63]

According to Plutarch, when C. Sempronius Gracchus left Sardinia after spending over two years in the service of L. Aurelius Orestes (who remained on the island), both the senate and public opinion roundly condemned the fact that the quaestor had left the province before his commander. C. Gracchus was denounced before the censors; in his defense, Gracchus mustered a series of arguments, including that the law allowed a quaestor to return to Rome after a year of service, that is, after having completed his quaestorship.[64] Plutarch's quote shows that in the Late Republic quaestors could turn down a prorogation of their mandates once their magistracy had ended, even if their commanders remained in the province. According to Suetonius, during his quaestorship in Hispania Ulterior Caesar returned to Rome *ante tempus*, that is, before completing his mandatory year of service or, at least, before Antistius Vetus ended his term of office. It is possible that Caesar had to ask permission from his praetor before leaving the province. [65] The law quoted by C. Grac-

---

62 Cic. *Att.* 5.21.9; 6.3.1–2; 6.5.3; 6.6.3–4; Thompson 1965, 375–381.

63 A. Postumius Albinus was forced by Jugurtha to accept a treaty of peace under severe conditions and to pass under the yoke with the Roman army: Sall. *Iug.* 37.3–38.10. When the disaster was announced in Rome, a strong feeling of discontent seized the public. According to Sallust, Sp. Postumius Albinus, fearing the consequences of his brother's action, laid the question of the peace before the senate, but the senators decided to reject the proposal; cf. Sall. *Iug.* 39.2–4: *ob ea consul Albinus ex delicto fratris invidiam ac deinde periculum timens senatum de foedere consulebat, et tamen interim exercitui supplementum scribere, ab sociis et nomine Latino auxilia arcessere, denique omnibus modis festinare. Senatus ita, uti par fuerat, decernit suo atque populi iniussu nullum potuisse foedus fieri. Consul inpeditus a tribunis plebis, ne quas paraverat copias secum portaret, paucis diebus in Africam proficiscitur.* We do not know if A. Postumius Albinus was prosecuted for his misconduct as legate, but his brother Spurius was condemned under the *rogatio* proposed by the tribune of the plebs C. Mamilius Limetanus; Cic. *Brut.* 128: *nam invidiosa lege [Mamilia quaestio] C. Galbam sacerdotem et quattuor consularis, L. Bestiam C. Catonem Sp. Albinum civemque praestantissimum L. Opimium, Gracchi interfectorem, a populo absolutum, cum is contra populi studium stetisset, Gracchani iudices sustulerunt*; cf. Sall. *Iug.* 40.1: *interim Romae C. Mamilius Limetanus tribunus plebis rogationem ad populum promulgat, uti quaereretur in eos, quorum consilio Iugurtha senati decreta neglegisset, quique ab eo in legationibus aut imperiis pecunias accepissent, qui elephantos quique perfugas tradidissent, item qui de pace aut bello cum hostibus pactiones fecissent.* See Alexander 1990, 28–29; Rosenstein 1990, 135–137; Clark 2014, 188–191; Díaz Fernández 2019, 127–129.

64 Plut. *C.Gr.* 2.4: ἐστρατεῦσθαι μὲν γὰρ ἔφη δώδεκα ἔτη, τῶν ἄλλων δέκα στρατευομένων ἐν ἀνάγκαις, ταμιεύων δὲ τῷ στρατηγῷ παραμεμενηκέναι τριετίαν, τοῦ νόμου μετ' ἐνιαυτὸν ἐπανελθεῖν διδόντος.

65 Suet. *Iul.* 8; cf. Taylor 1941, 123–124.

chus to justify his departure must have opened up (or, more likely, normalised) the possibility that a quaestor could leave his province before his superior, although it is probable that political influences played a decisive role when it came to deciding the duration of a term of office. This is also suggested by the actions of P. Sestius, proquaestor of C. Antonius Hybrida, who wrote to Cicero asking him to intervene with the senate so that he was not replaced in his position in Macedonia.[66]

In any case, the usual scenario must have been that the quaestor was prorogued at the same time as his senior magistrate. Livy demonstrates that the senate decided on the *prorogationes* of *imperium* and the provinces (*prorogata imperia provinciaque*) after the annual sortition of provinces for the incoming consuls and praetors had taken place, although all evidences suggests that the senate decided beforehand which provinces would keep their governor. Although Livy gives no information on the subject, it may be assumed that quaestors were also prorogued at that time. As we have already commented, it is likely that the prorogation of the consul or praetor designated to Sicily, Hispania, Macedonia or any other province would generally entail the prorogation of its quaestor, who thus became proquaestor. This is what Plutarch seems to suggest in his discussion of the prorogation of L. Aurelius Orestes and C. Gracchus in Sardinia: '[the senators] passed a decree that fresh troops should be sent to relieve the soldiers in Sardinia, but that Orestes should remain, with the idea that Caius also would remain with him by virtue of his office.'[67]

In fact, although there were only eight quaestors when Rome created its first overseas provinces, prorogation allowed Rome to keep a quaestor in each of its permanent provinces every year—at least until the number of provinces grew to such a point that Sulla increased the number of quaestors to twenty at the same time that he raised the number of praetors to eight. When the *provinciae* of Africa, Macedonia (145), and Asia (126?) became permanent, Rome controlled a total of seven provinces with only two consuls (one of whom usually stayed in Italy), six praetors (of whom at least one had to take responsibility for Rome's *iurisdictiones*) and eight quaestors, of whom two were committed to the *aerarium provincia*, while another two were under the command of the consuls. The use of prorogation, which had been common for some time in the provinces of Hispania, must have become even more widespread in the second half of the second century, not only in Hispania, but also in other equally belligerent provinces: C. Sempronius Gracchus, for instance, spent over two years in the service of the consul Aurelius Orestes in Sardinia, which gives us a good idea of the increasing delay of governors' commands as well as those of their quaestors in certain provinces. Despite our lack of information, tenures as protracted as that of C. Gracchus' must have become increasingly common. Indeed, the

---

66 Cic. *fam.* 5.6.1; cf. Rosillo-López forthcoming.
67 Plut. *C.Gr.* 2.3: ἔπειτα δόγμα ποιοῦνται τοῖς μὲν στρατιώταις διαδοχὴν ἀποσταλῆναι, τὸν δ' Ὀρέστην ἐπιμένειν, ὡς δὴ καὶ τοῦ Γαΐου διὰ τὴν ἀρχὴν παραμενοῦντος (trans. by B. Perrin, Loeb).

case of Sulla seems to indicate so much: he remained in Marius' service as quaestor in Numidia from 107 until he returned to Rome in 105.⁶⁸

When Sulla decided to increase the number of quaestors to twenty, the Republic must have been struggling to meet the growing demands presented by the Roman Empire.⁶⁹ The incorporation of Cilicia and, possibly, Gaul into the list of Rome's permanent provinces at the beginning of the first century increased the number of provinces with a consul or praetor (along with a quaestor) to at least nine. As we will see later, it is unlikely that Sicily could have had two permanent quaestors before the approval of the Sullan law, since there would not then have been enough magistrates to oversee the rest of the provinces.⁷⁰ Apart from the political interests that this measure might have served, it is undeniable that one of the priorities of the *lex Cornelia de XX quaestoribus* was to provide a sufficient number of quaestors to cover all the provinces each year, thus avoiding the need for magistrates to stay there for long stretches of time. It is not a coincidence that from Sulla onwards, it is much less common to find a quaestor serving in a province for longer than two years; it becomes increasingly unusual to find cases such as that of C. Cassius Longinus, quaestor in 55 with the consul M. Licinius Crassus, who spent several years in Syria until he was replaced in 51 by the proconsul M. Calpurnius Bibulus and his quaestor, Caninius Sallustius.⁷¹ A large number of the quaestors about whom we have information after Sulla, moreover, seem to have spent only a year in their province. Cicero provides a case in point: he was quaestor in 75 in Lilybaeum under Sex. Peducaeus, who was praetor in 77 and governor of Sicily from at least 76 until 75. The dates suggest that the orator only stayed in the province as a quaestor for a single year; furthermore, it seems that there was (at least) one other quaestor on the island in the service of Peducaeus before Cicero.⁷² The lack of concrete data on the actual duration of quaestorian appointments nevertheless requires caution: in fact, the mention of proquaestors (ἀντιταμίαι) in certain Late Republican inscriptions (particularly those from the eastern provinces) demonstrate that quaestors continued to be prorogued, although it seems that they generally remained in office for only one more year.⁷³

As mentioned above, the increase in the number of quaestors to twenty in the Sullan period poses the paradoxical question of what role of all these new quaestors could have had, a problem that, to our knowledge, has not yet attracted scholarly attention. Yet, given the state of the available evidence, the only certainty is that convincingly answering this question is a tall order. When the civil war broke out in 49,

---

68 Broughton MRR, 1.551; 554; 556; cf. Badian 1983, 167–168.
69 See Badian 1964, 71–104; Brennan 2000, 583–596.
70 See however Prag 2014a, 201–208.
71 Cass.Dio 40.30.1: ἅμα δὲ οὗτος ἀνεκεχωρήκει καὶ ὁ Βίβουλος ἄρξων τῆς Συρίας ἀφίκετο; Broughton MRR, 2.229; 237; 242. On Caninius Sallustius, Cic. *fam.* 2.17.
72 See Cic. *div. in Caec*, 2; Plut. *Cic.* 6.1; Broughton MRR, 2.98; cf. Fallu 1973a, 31–53.
73 Badian 1983, 158–168.

Rome controlled no fewer than twelve permanent provinces; as mentioned several times throughout this book, when identifying the quaestorian *provinciae*, we must add the *aerarium provincia* of the two urban quaestors, the two consular quaestorships and, finally, other quaestorian *provinciae*, permanent or otherwise, such as the second Sicilian quaestorship, Cyrene and Ostia. Taking all of these posts into consideration, it is possible to reach the figure of twenty *provinciae* without much difficulty. This would, in principle, still have allowed the annual rotation of quaestors in all the provinces;[74] as previously noted, however, the senate continued to confer prorogations upon some quaestors, and in such cases those provinces would have been removed from the annual sortition of duties. More problematic is determining what were the twenty *provinciae* granted to the quaestors in the years immediately following the approval of the Sullan law, when provinces such as Bithynia, Cyrene, and Syria were not being assigned to a Roman magistrate. Undoubtedly, the question becomes even more complex when we consider Caesar's decision to increase the number of quaestors to 40 in 45. Such a dramatic expansion of the office suggests that the duties conferred upon quaestors had greatly grown by 45 and had come to encompass a new range of assignments that far surpassed those initially entrusted to quaestors.

Undoubtedly, each of the twenty quaestors appointed after the Sullan law—and later each of the forty quaestors established by Caesar—had their own role or *provincia*. Given our current state of knowledge, however, it is impossible to determine what each of these *provinciae* would have been every year. In any case, although it is not our intention here to discuss all the *provinciae* that were allocated to the quaestors from Sulla's dictatorship onwards, it is apposite to spend some time discussing a series of particularly interesting *provinciae*. This will allow us to highlight the distinctiveness of certain duties with the list of quaestorian provinces and also determine their impact upon the development of the Roman provincial system. First, we will turn to the controversial question of the two Sicilian quaestorships (Lilybaeum and Syracuse), a case with no known parallels in the Republican provincial landscape. Then, we will focus on the designation of Cyrene and Cyprus as quaestorian provinces at the end of the Republic.

Sicily as two *provinciae quaestoriae* (Lilybaeum and Syracuse)

Among the many questions raised by the study of the quaestorship in the provinces, undoubtedly one of the most controversial has centred on the presence of two quaestors in Sicily, a phenomenon that is unparalleled in the other Roman provinces.[75] The only sources on this subject are two brief comments made by Cicero in his *Verrines* as

---

74 Lintott 1999, 135–136.
75 Harris 1976, 102; 104; Pinzone 2000, 859–861; Brennan 2000, 139; Prag 2013, 61; 2014a, 202, n. 38.

well as two annotations on those passages found in the commentary of Pseudo-Asconius, who appears to have been a fifth-century Latin grammarian.[76] According to the latter (who provides the most complete information on the subject), Sicily had two quaestors, one in Lilybaeum and the other in Syracuse, who were called *Lilybitanus* and *Syracusanus*, respectively. The author adds that although Sicily was one single praetorian province, the island nevertheless was divided into two quaestorian provinces: *duos quaestores habet Sicilia, Lilybitanum et Syracusanum; nam praetori una provincia est, quaestoribus duae*.[77] Pseudo-Asconius' second passage claims that Cicero was in fact *quaestor Lilybitanus* during the command of the praetor Sex. Peducaeus (pr. 77), though in this case the grammarian is a bit more cautious in so far as he says that Sicily 'tended to be' governed by two quaestors (*cum enim a duobus quaestoribus Sicilia regi soleat*). This begs the question of whether there were always two Sicilian quaestors or only in certain years.[78]

Neither of the two quotes from the *Verrines* helps us resolve these uncertainties. Indeed, they simply reiterate that Sicily had two distinct quaestorian provinces, associated with the command of the island's praetor (*quaestores utriusque provinciae qui isto praetore fuerant*). Beyond the Romans' reasons that would motivate maintaining two quaestors in Sicily, there is the additional problem of when this measure was first put in place: we neither know when this began nor under what the circumstances. As we have seen, we assume that there was a quaestor in Sicily serving a praetor from at least 227 since this was the prevailing pattern in the provinces at that time; we cannot, however, be completely certain of this, since there is no record of a quaestor on the island until 211, when the consul M. Claudius Marcellus moved a quaestor (whose name we do not know) to the island of Nassus, accompanied by a *praesidium*, so that he could take charge of the royal treasury after the conquest of Syracuse.[79] Some years earlier, in 216, as we have already mentioned, Livy places a quaestor in Nola in the service of the then-praetor Marcellus, whose province had initially been Sicily. However, we do not know if both happened to move to the island as a result of the disastrous situation unleashed in Italy after Cannae.[80] In fact, it is not until 102 that we find a quaestor under the command of a praetor in Sicily: this was L. Philo, who, according to Cicero, held the quaestorship under the command of C. Servilius, praetor in Sicily during the Second Slave War.[81]

---

76 Cic. *Verr.* 2.2.11: *quaestores utriusque provinciae qui isto praetore fuerant cum fascibus mihi praesto fuerunt*; cf. 2.2.156; Ps. Ascon. p. 187; 259 Stangl.
77 Ps. Ascon. p. 259 Stangl.
78 Ps. Ascon. p. 187 Stangl: *cum enim a duobus quaestoribus Sicilia regi soleat, uno Lilybitano, altero Syracusano, ipse vero Lilybitanus quaestor fuerit Sex. Peducaeo praetore*; Broughton MRR, 2.98.
79 Liv. 25.31.8: *inde quaestor cum praesidio ad Nassum ad accipiendam pecuniam regiam custodiendamque missus*; Prag 2007b, 291.
80 Liv. 23.15.15.
81 Cic. *div. in Caec.* 63; Ps. Ascon. p. 203 Stangl. Broughton 1951, 569; Prag 2007b, 301.

As pointed out above, some scholars have assumed that Sicily was under the command of a quaestor (installed in Lilybaeum) starting in 241, after the Roman victory in the *Egadi Islands* and the end of the First Punic War. Theorizing aside, we must remember that the sources are silent about this matter.[82] This assumption is based largely upon the unfounded assumption that Sicily must have remained under the command of a Roman magistrate after the end of the war in 241. However, other examples, such as Macedonia and Illyria after the victories of L. Aemilius Paullus and L. Anicius Gallus over Perseus and Gentius in 168, demonstrate that Roman domination did not always entail the sending of Roman magistrates to said territory; that is, *imperium* did not necessarily result in a *provincia*, as several authors have rightly stressed.[83]

On the basis of events in Sicily, it is clear that this supposed second quaestorship must have been incorporated into the Roman institutional system at some point after M. Claudius Marcellus' conquest of Syracuse in 211;[84] the issue is to determine when and why this decision was taken. Given the state of the sources, it is not easy to give a clear answer. We also need to ask, moreover, how far we must accept that the two quaestorships in Sicily were permanent, when one of Pseudo-Asconius' passages tellingly says that the island 'tended to be governed' (*regi soleat*) by two quaestors. As we have emphasised throughout this book, the Roman provincial system could be adapted to the specific needs of a given moment; accordingly, the most likely scenario is that the destinations of the quaestors were decided on a yearly basis in the senate depending on the circumstances on the ground—though the senate always allocated a single quaestor for each of the permanent provinces. Given the notable increase in the number of Rome's permanent provinces from 146, when Africa and Macedonia were newly minted as provinces, it strains credulity that the senate would always decide to send two quaestors to Sicily. Indeed, if we remember that at the beginning of the first century Rome had to assign a quaestor to no fewer than eight other *provinciae* (despite there only being four quaestors available each year), the idea of there always being two quaestors in Sicily starts to look even more far-fetched. Prag rightly highlights the fact that the few references to the presence of two quaestors in Sicily all date from after Sulla (specifically to the years 75–72), although it is obvious, as Prag himself recognises, that the period immediately after the conquest of Syracuse (i.e. in the middle of the Second Punic War)

---

82 Cf. App. *Sic.* 2.6. See the discussion in Prag 2013, 61–62, n. 13; cf. Brennan 2000, 87–89; 88: 'it would be surprising if Sicily did not receive a regular Roman magistrate in (or soon after) 241'; also, Harris 1976 104; 1979, 136, n. 2; Marino 1988, 25–26; Pinzone 1979, 172–173; 2000, 859–861; 875, n. 55; Loreto 1993, 496–498; Díaz Fernández 2015, 109–118. See also Richardson 1986, 7–8.
83 Liv. 45.1.9; 45.18.1–2; Just. 33.2.7. Also see, for instance, Gruen 1984, 423–436; Kallet-Marx 1995, 18–29; Díaz Fernández 2015, 114.
84 Harris 1976, 104: 'the most plausible date for the creation of the second quaestorship is clearly 211 when the province had just been enlarged by the addition of Syracuse, which is known to have been the base of one of the two'; Pinzone 1979; 2000, 859; Brennan 2000, 139.

would have been the most opportune moment to create the Syracusan quaestorship.[85]

It is the numerical question, however, that is decisive in this case. Allowing that, every year, the senate allocated *ex senatu consulto* two quaestors to the two new consuls, two urban quaestors for the *aerarium provincia* and one quaestor for each praetor who would be sent that year (*suo anno*) to an overseas province,[86] it is mathematically impossible for Sicily to have regularly had two quaestors, at least, during the second century. As we know, in 197 the senate incorporated two new praetorships into the Roman magistrate system so that Rome could maintain two praetors in Hispania from that point onwards; by that time, it is quite plausible that the number of quaestors was already eight, so that the new praetors in Hispania could also have had a quaestor. That year, the elected consuls were C. Cornelius Cethegus and Q. Minucius Rufus, who were allocated Italy as their province with their respective quaestors. Two more quaestors (the *quaestores urbani*) must have been put in charge of the *aerarium*, while the four remaining quaestors must have been assigned to the praetors L. Manlius Volso, L. Atilius, C. Sempronius Tuditanus, and M. Helvius, who were sent to Sicily, Sardinia, Hispania Citerior, and Hispania Ulterior, respectively. It is therefore difficult to see how Sicily could have had two quaestors that year, one in Lilybaeum and the other in Syracuse.[87]

Let us now take the years 174, 173 and 172 as a case study. Thanks to Livy's account, we know that between the years 174–172, six consuls and eighteen praetors were elected, as well as (probably) twenty-four quaestors (i.e. eight per year).[88] Twelve of those quaestors were assigned to the consuls and the *aerarium provincia* as urban quaestors, which leaves twelve additional quaestors available for other *pro-*

---

85 Prag 2014a, 202, n. 38: 'There is formally no pre-Sullan evidence for the double quaestorship, but I would concede that it is very difficult to imagine any context for its creation except the period of the First and Second Punic Wars.'
86 See Prag 2014a, 201–202.
87 Liv. 32.27.5–28.3: *Sex. Aelius consul ex Gallia comitiorum causa Romam cum redisset, creavit consules C. Cornelium Cethegum et Q. Minucium Rufum. Biduo post praetorum comitia habita. Sex praetores illo anno primum creati crescentibus iam provinciis et latius patescente imperio; creati autem hi: L. Manlius Volso C. Sempronius Tuditanus M. Sergius Silus M. Helvius M. Minucius Rufus L. Atilius, Sempronius et Helvius ex iis aediles plebis erant; curules aediles Q. Minucius Thermus et Ti. Sempronius Longus. Ludi Romani eo anno quater instaurati. C. Cornelio et Q. Minucio consulibus omnium primum de provinciis consulum praetorumque actum. Prius de praetoribus transacta res quae transigi sorte poterat: urbana Sergio, peregrina iurisdictio Minucio obtigit; Sardiniam Atilius, Siciliam Manlius, Hispanias Sempronius citeriorem, Helvius ulteriorem est sortitus. Consulibus Italiam Macedoniamque sortiri parantibus L. Oppius et Q. Fuluius tribuni plebis impedimento erant...*; cf. 32.28.8: *permittentibus utrisque liberam consultationem patres consulibus ambobus Italiam prouinciam decreverunt*; Broughton MRR, 1.332–333. In his useful survey of the allocation of quaestors in the second century, Prag 2014a, 203, removes Hispania Citerior from the table of quaestors of 197, which allows him to include the second Sicilian quaestorship in the allotment of quaestorian provinces of that year.
88 N. Fabius Buteo (pr. 173) died in Massilia on his way to Hispania (Liv. 42.4.1), but he had undoubtedly received his quaestor before leaving Rome.

vinciae. We know from Livy that the command of the four permanent provinces usually assigned to praetors (Sicily, Sardinia, and the two Hispaniae) rotated annually during those three years:[89] that is, leaving to one side the two praetors put in charge of the *iurisdictio urbana* and the *iurisdictio inter cives et peregrinos*, each of the four remaining praetors was destined for one of these four provinces *suo anno*, each of whom took his quaestor to his province. This implies that the twelve praetors sent over those three years to the provinces of Sicily, Sardinia, and the two Hispaniae needed the twelve quaestors left over in the above calculation, which again raises the possibility that the Sicilian praetor had two quaestors serving him during those years.

Table 1: Allotment of quaestorian provinces for the years 174–172 BC, according to the sortition of consular and praetorian provinces (Livy).

174	Sp. Postumius Albinus (*cos.*)	Q. Mucius Scaevola (*cos.*)	–	–	L. Claudius (*pr.*)	M. Atilius (*pr.*)	P. Furius Philo (*pr.*)	Cn. Servilius Caepio (*pr.*)
	?	?	*aerarium provincia*	*aerarium provincia*	Sicilia	Sardinia	Hispania Citerior	Hispania Ulterior
	quaestor	*quaestor*	*quaestor urbanus*	*quaestor urbanus*	*quaestor*	*quaestor*	*quaestor*	*quaestor*
173	L. Postumius Albinus (*cos.*)	M. Popillius Laenas (*cos.*)	–	–	M. Furius Crassipes (*pr.*)	C. Cicereius (*pr.*)	N. Fabius Buteo (*pr.*)	C. Matienus (*pr.*)
	Liguria	Liguria	*aerarium provincia*	*aerarium provincia*	Sicilia	Sardinia	Hispania Citerior	Hispania Ulterior
	quaestor	*quaestor*	*quaestor urbanus*	*quaestor urbanus*	*quaestor*	*quaestor*	*quaestor*	*quaestor*
172	C. Popillius Laenas (*cos.*)	P. Aelius Ligus (*cos.*)	–	–	C. Memmius (*pr.*)	Sp. Cluvius (*pr.*)	M. Junius Pennus (*pr.*)	Sp. Lucretius (*pr.*)
	Liguria	Liguria	*aerarium provincia*	*aerarium provincia*	Sicilia	Sardinia	Hispania Citerior	Hispania Ulterior
	quaestor	*quaestor*	*quaestor urbanus*	*quaestor urbanus*	*quaestor*	*quaestor*	*quaestor*	*quaestor*

Earlier in this chapter, we dismissed the extremely unlikely hypothesize that a quaestor could be prorogued and stay in a province, if his superior had already left. The notion that a quaestor could serve two different magistrates (except in the most ex-

---

89 Liv. 41.21.1–3; 41.28.4–5; 42.1.1–6; 42.9.8; 42.10.10–14; cf. Broughton MRR, 1.403–404; 407–408; 410–411.

traordinary of circumstances) is quite implausible. If we are correct to reject this theory, it would then be impossible for Rome to have maintained two quaestors in Sicily on a permanent basis. Loreto doubts that Sardinia routinely received a quaestor from 227, on the grounds that Rome would not have needed one. Although there is no direct evidence for the presence of quaestors on the island until many years later during the quaestorship of C. Sempronius Gracchus in the service of the consul L. Aurelius Orestes (126 – 124), the Italian scholar's argument from silence is not particularly convincing.[90] In conclusion, bearing in mind the numbers, we should dismiss the idea that Rome routinely had two provincial quaestors stationed in Sicily before the Sullan law that increased the number of quaestors to twenty. However, this does not mean that in particular circumstances Rome did not choose to deploy two quaestors to the island. [91] If, however, Sicily had two quaestors permanently during Cicero's career (or perhaps only habitually, if we accept Pseudo-Asconius' *soleat*), we should conclude that this practice was instituted only after the Sullan law. As indicated, that law unclogged the Roman institutional system to the point that it allowed for the annual rotation of quaestors in the provinces—and perhaps also the presence of two quaestors in Sicily.

It is more difficult to determine the causes that could have prompted the Romans to decide to assign two quaestors to Sicily. Scholars have usually proffered reasons connected with the grain supply or to issues related to the idiosyncrasies of the island's population (i. e. there were Punic and Greek populations there) in order to explain the presence of two quaestors.[92] The only certainty, however, is that it is ultimately difficult to specify the reasons that made it necessary for the praetor of Sicily to have two quaestors in his service. Caius Verres, who spent no fewer than three years in the province, had four quaestors under his command at least during the years 73 and 72, which must have further complicated the already-complex administration in Sicily, since there would have to have been four different financial ledgers.[93] Further, it is striking that the information that we have about the presence of two quaestors in Sicily is limited to the short interval between the years 75 – 72, which run from Cicero's quaestorship in Lilybaeum (75), under the praetor Sex. Peducaeus (76 – 75),[94] to Verres' governorship. Those years constituted a particularly difficult period, since a grain shortage in Italy coincided with a series of important mili-

---

90 Loreto 1993, 498, n. 23. Given the state of the sources, the proposal is clearly suspect; cf. Prag 2014a, 202, n. 36.
91 See Ps. Ascon. p. 187 Stangl. A passage from Plutarch points out that the *lex Gabinia* apparently allowed Pompey to have two quaestors during his command in the war against the pirates; see *Pomp.* 26.2: ἡγεμονικοὶ δὲ καὶ στρατηγικοὶ κατελέγησαν ἀπὸ βουλῆς ἄνδρες εἰκοσιτέσσαρες ὑπ' αὐτοῦ, δύο δὲ ταμίαι παρῆσαν. Ioannidopoulos 2017, 104 – 105. Nevertheless, the fact that Plutarch stresses Pompey having had two quaestors shows this was an exceptional situation.
92 Pinzone 1979, 172 – 173; 2000, 859 – 860.
93 Prag 2007b, 306.
94 Cic. *div. in Caec.* 2; *p. red. sen.* 21; Ps. Ascon. p. 185 Stangl; Broughton MRR, 2.98; Prag 2007b, 304 – 305; cf. 2014a, 202, n. 38.

tary campaigns. This was a consequence of the many wars that Rome was waging throughout the Mediterranean, as Appian indicates.[95] While Pompey and Q. Caecilius Metellus Pius tried to end Sertorius' adventure in Hispania, the East witnessed the start of a new war between Rome and Mithridates after the death of king Nicomedes of Bithynia in 75; in Macedonia, the consul C. Scribonius Curio (76–73) and then later the consul M. Terentius Varro Lucullus (73–71) fought against the ever-rebellious Thracians, while the praetor M. Antonius received *imperium infinitum* to take on the pirates throughout the entire Mediterranean (74–71).[96]

A passage in Sallust's *Historiae* mentions a speech that the consul C. Aurelius Cotta made before the Roman people (75) in which he highlights the many difficulties that Rome was facing at that time: while in Hispania the *imperatores* demanded *stipendium*, soldiers, arms, and grain (*namque imperatores Hispaniae stipendium milites, arma, frumentum poscunt*) for the war against Sertorius, the Republic had to feed both armies in Asia and Cilicia (*exercitus in Asia Ciliciaque ob nimias opes Mithridatis aluntur*) and fight against different enemies in Macedonia, the coasts of Italy and the provinces, even though taxes covered scarcely a fraction of the costs incurred (*cum interim vectigalia parva et bellis incerta vix partem sumptuum sustinent*).[97] As mentioned above, at the same time as Rome fought her enemies overseas, Italy suffered from a serious grain shortage that quickly unleashed chaos in the capital: Sallust, again, discusses the riots that took place in Rome in 75 as a consequence of the city's hunger. The situation was so tense that the two consuls, C. Aurelius Cotta and L. Octavius as well as Q. Caecilius Metellus, a candidate for the praetorship, were attacked by the masses on the Via Sacra and were forced to take refuge in Octavius'

---

95 App. *B. Civ.* 1.111: τοῦ δ' ἐπιόντος ἔτους, ἕκτης ἑβδομηκοστῆς καὶ ἑκατοστῆς ὀλυμπιάδος οὔσης, δύο μὲν ἐκ διαθηκῶν ἔθνη Ῥωμαίοις προσεγίγνετο, Βιθυνία τε Νικομήδους ἀπολιπόντος καὶ Κυρήνη Πτολεμαίου, τοῦ Λαγίδου βασιλέως, ὃς ἐπίκλησιν ἦν Ἀπίων, πόλεμοι δ' ἤκμαζον οὗτός τε ὁ Σερτωρίου περὶ Ἰβηρίαν καὶ Μιθριδάτου περὶ τὴν ἀνατολὴν καὶ ὁ τῶν λῃστῶν ἐν ὅλῃ τῇ θαλάσσῃ καὶ περὶ Κρήτην πρὸς αὐτοὺς Κρῆτας ἕτερος καὶ ὁ τῶν μονομάχων ἀνὰ τὴν Ἰταλίαν, αἰφνίδιος αὐτοῖς καὶ ὅδε καὶ σφοδρὸς ὁμοῦ γενόμενος. διαιρούμενοι δ' ἐς τοσαῦτα, ὅμως καὶ ἐς Ἰβηρίαν ἔπεμψαν ἄλλα στρατοῦ δύο τέλη, μεθ' ὧν ἅμα τῷ ἄλλῳ παντὶ Μέτελλός τε καὶ Πομπήιος αὖθις ἀπὸ τῶν Πυρηναίων ὀρῶν ἐπὶ τὸν Ἴβηρα κατέβαινον. Σερτώριος δὲ καὶ Περπέννας αὐτοῖς ἀπήντων ἀπὸ Λυσιτανίας (cf. trans. by H. White, Loeb: 'The following year, which was in the 176th Olympiad, two countries were acquired by the Romans by bequest. Bithynia was left to them by Nicomedes, and Cyrene by Ptolemy surnamed Apion, of the house of the Lagidae. There were wars and wars; the Sertorian was raging in Spain, the Mithridatic in the East, that of the pirates on the entire sea, and another around Crete against the Cretans themselves, besides the gladiatorial war in Italy, which started suddenly and became very serious. Although distracted by so many conflicts the Romans sent another army of two legions into Spain. With these and the other forces in their hands Metellus and Pompey again descended from the Pyrenees to the Ebro; and Sertorius and Perpenna advanced from Lusitania to meet them').
96 Sources in Broughton MRR, 2.96–124; cf. Kallet-Marx 1995, 292–311.
97 Sall. *hist.* 2.47.6–7 M. For a commentary on the passage, see McGushin 1992, 211–217.

house, the walls of which were then stormed.⁹⁸ In the same year, the quaestor Cicero made an important shipment of corn from Sicily to Rome that coincided—as the orator himself tells us—with an alarming need for supplies in Rome.⁹⁹ Only two years later, in 73, Verres received *ex senatus consulto* the order to buy Sicilian grain in significant quantities, in accordance with the *lex Terentia et Cassia frumentaria* which, quite unusually, was approved that same year on the motion of the two consuls. All of this seems to underscore the Republic's continuing need for corn (and money).¹⁰⁰ Besides all this, piracy continuously caused problems for the navigation and transit of goods throughout the Mediterranean, as a passage from Appian reveals,¹⁰¹ while the revolt sparked by Spartacus in 73 naturally further complicated the situation in Italy.¹⁰²

As Cotta's speech in Sallust highlights, Rome did not only have to supply the ever-impoverished Roman plebs, but also a large number of soldiers distributed across various active fronts during those years.¹⁰³ The taxes from the provinces, how-

---

98 Sall. *hist.* 2.45 M.; Oost 1963, 20–21; Kallet-Marx 1995, 367; Pina Polo 2011, 301–302. As McGushin 1992, 208–210, stresses some decades later (in 40) a similar incident that took place in Rome when Octavian and Antonius had to escape from the mob as a consequence of a severe shortage of corn; cf. App. *b.c.* 5.67–68; Cass.Dio 48.31.5–6; for the historical circumstances of this episode, see Rickman 1980, 61.
99 Cic. *Planc.* 64: *frumenti in summa caritate maximum numerum miseram*; cf. Plut. *Cic.* 6.1: ἀποδειχθεὶς δὲ ταμίας ἐν σιτοδείᾳ καὶ λαχὼν Σικελίαν, ἠνώχλησε τοῖς ἀνθρώποις ἐν ἀρχῇ, σῖτον εἰς Ῥώμην ἀποστέλλειν ἀναγκαζομένοις. According to Cicero, in 75 the curule aedile Q. Hortensius made a distribution of corn to the Roman people to reduce the food shortage; Cic. *Verr.* 2.3.215: *quod nisi omnis frumenti ratio ex temporibus esset et annona, non ex numero neque ex summa consideranda, numquam tam grati hi sesquimodii, Q. Hortensi, fuissent, quos tu cum ad mensurae tam exiguam rationem populo Romano in capita descripsisses, gratissimum omnibus fecisti; caritas enim annonae faciebat ut istuc, quod re parvum videtur, tempore magnum videretur*. The shortage of corn lasted into 74, to the point that the curule aedile M. Seius supplied corn to the people at very low cost; cf. Cic. *off.* 2.58; Plin. *n.h.* 15.2; 18.16. See Rickman 1980, 166–168; McGushin 1992, 210–211.
100 Cic. *div. in Caec.* 32: *emptum est ex senatus consulto frumentum ab Siculis praetore Verre, pro quo frumento pecunia omnis soluta non est*; *Verr.* 2.3.163: *frumentum emere in Sicilia debuit Verres ex senatus consulto et ex lege Terentia et Cassia frumentaria*; 3.173; 5.52; Sall. *hist.* 3.48.19 M.; Rickman 1980, 166–168; Pina Polo 2011, 302–303.
101 App. *Mith.* 93. During C. Verres' governorship in Sicily the pirates launched devastating attacks on the port of Syracuse (Cic. *Verr.* 2.5.95–101); Oros. 5.6.3; cf. Plut. *Pomp.* 24.6; Cic. *leg. Man.* 32–33; De Souza 1999, 155–157; cf. Rickman 1980, 49–52. Cicero (*leg. Man.* 34) praises Pompey for having protected the coasts of Sicily, Africa and Sardinia—*tria frumentaria subsidia*—during his command against the pirates: *qui nondum tempestivo ad navigandum mari Siciliam adiit, Africam exploravit, inde Sardiniam cum classe venit atque haec tria frumentaria subsidia rei publicae firmissimis praesidiis classibusque munivit*.
102 According to the sources, Sicily was also threatened by Spartacus' slave revolt: a fragment of Sallust (*hist.* 4.32 M.) says that Verres fortified the Sicilian coastline close to Italy: *C. Verres litora Italia propinqua firmavit*; see McGushin 1994, 151; cf. also Cic. *Verr.* 2.5.5. During Verres' praetorship in Sicily, the fleet commanded by the quaestor P. Caesetius (q. 72) and the legate P. Tadius seized a pirate vessel off the coast of Sicily; cf. Cic. *Verr.* 2.5.63.
103 Sall. *hist.* 2.47.6–7 M.

ever, were insufficient to cover all the costs that those campaigns generated. It is perhaps for this reason that those same years coincide with the dispatch of various quaestors to a series of destinations that seem to be related to the problem of supplying the Republic with direly needed supplies. The port of Ostia, one of the principal supply routes into Rome, was under the authority of the quaestor Ser. Sulpicius Rufus in 74 as the *provincia Ostiensis*, a task that Cicero describes as *non tam gratiosam et inlustrem quam negotiosam et molestam* (see chapter 2).[104] Only a few months before, in 75, the Romans had sent Q. Pompeius to Bithynia, who was later called Bithynicus (possibly a quaestor), with the likely mission of seizing Nicomedes' royal treasury and then auctioning it off to raise money for the *aerarium*;[105] the quaestor P. Cornelius Lentulus Marcellinus was possibly sent to Cyrene during these same years (ca. 75–74) for a similar purpose, as we will see below.

In short, we should not rule out that the presence of two quaestors in Sicily in 75–72 might have responded to Rome's demand for grain and the need for supplies at that time. If this was indeed the case, we could consider it a temporary arrangement, prompted by the needs of those years, contrary to the usual interpretation of Pseudo-Asconius' comments. It may also be worth considering whether the presence of two quaestors in Sicily should be related to the supplementary tithes raised during those years on the island (for there is evidence in the *Verrines*), although we must admit that Cicero never says that the dispatch of two quaestors to Sicily constituted an interim solution to temporary problems.[106] In any case, as we have argued above, it is improbable that the island had two permanent quaestorian provinces before the Sullan period; once Sulla had raised the number of quaestors to twenty, the ever growing need to supply Rome with food and money could have led the senate to establish a second quaestor in Sicily as a way to acquire grain from the island, particularly during the tense period between 75–72. It is even possible that that decision became common from then on, as Pseudo-Asconius' comments may suggest.[107] That said, in this case as in others, the state of the evidence requires us to be cautious.

---

104 Cic. *Mur.* 18; on the date of Ser. Sulpicius Rufus' quaestorship, see below.
105 Festus p. 320 L.; cf. Kallet-Marx 1995, 299–300, n. 33; Ballesteros Pastor 2009, 127–133; Díaz Fernández 2015, 476–477; 562, n. 232. Kunkel and Wittmann's proposal that Q. Pompeius was sent to Bithynia as *quaestor pro praetore* is not supported by the sources and, furthermore, seems unnecessary; cf. Kunkel and Wittmann 1995, 360, n. 210.
106 See Cic. *Verr.* 2.3.163. According to Cicero (*Verr.* 2.3.47), Sicily was in a rather sorry state when the orator visited the island after C. Verres' governorship. Beyond Cicero's dramatic commentary, we cannot dismiss that such a situation was the consequence of the repeated collection of supplementary tithes during those years. On the importance of Sicily for the corn supply in the Late Republic, cf. Rickman 1980, 104–106; Ñaco del Hoyo 2003, 86–95; Erdkamp 2005, 214–218.
107 Ps. Ascon. p. 187 Stangl.

Cyrene as *provincia quaestoria*

According to a short passage from Sallust's *Historiae*, which is partially preserved in an early mediaeval manuscript,[108] around the year 75 or 74 the senate decided to send the quaestor P. Cornelius Lentulus Marcellinus *in novam provinciam Curenas*.[109] Sallust tells us nothing more: neither how much time the quaestor spent in Cyrene nor what work he did there; we do not even know for certain what motivated the senate at that time to send a quaestor to Cyrene. In all likelihood, this quaestor was sent alone to carryout a particular mission there and did not go in the company of a higher magistrate, as was customary. Sallust's text tells us that Ptolemy Apion had bequeathed Cyrene to the Roman people in his will in 96. Apparently, according to Livy's *Periochae*, the senate's response was then limited to declaring that the cities that had previously been under royal rule were to be free. While the senate's actions may have complied with Apion's own desires, there are doubts on this point.[110] There is no evidence that a senatorial commission (or any Roman magistrate for that matter) went to Cyrenaica.[111] In fact, the city does not seem to have played any further role in Rome's affairs until 86, when L. Licinius Lucullus, Sulla's quaestor in 87, ap-

---

108 Deutsche Staatsbibliothek lat. Qu. 364. Scholars have concluded that the manuscript was written in Italy in the fifth century; the codex was in Fleury Abbey (Saint-Benoît-sur-Loire) until part of it was separated in the seventh or eighth century to replace Sallust's text with Hieronymus' *Commentarii in Isaiam*.
109 Sall. hist. 2.43 M.: *P.que Lentulus Marcel[linus] eodem auctore quaest[or] in novam provinci[am] Curenas missus est, q[uod] ea mortui regis Apio[nis] testamento nobis d[ata] prudentiore quam [illas] per gentis et minus g[lo]riae auidi imperio co[nti]nenda fuit*. Perl 1970, 321, n. 3, proposes another version: *P.que Lentulus Marcell[inus] eodem a<u>ctore quaest[or] in novam provinci[am] Curenas missus est, c[um] ea mortui regis Apio[nis] testamento nobis d[ata] prudentiore quam [adu]lescentis et minus q[uam] ille avide imperio co[nti]nenda fuit*. See the commentary in McGushin 1992, 206–208; cf. Kallet-Marx 1995, 364–365. See also App. b.c. 1.111: οὗ δ' ἐπιόντος ἔτους, ἕκτης ἑβδομηκοστῆς καὶ ἑκατοστῆς ὀλυμπιάδος οὔσης, δύο μὲν ἐκ διαθηκῶν ἔθνη Ῥωμαίοις προσεγίγνετο, Βιθυνία τε Νικομήδους ἀπολιπόντος καὶ Κυρήνη Πτολεμαίου, τοῦ Λαγίδου βασιλέως, ὃς ἐπίκλησιν ἦν Ἀπίων.
110 Liv. per. 70: *Ptolemaeus, Cyrenarum rex, cui cognomen Apionis fuit, mortuus heredem populum R. reliquit et eius regni ciuitates senatus liberas esse iussit*; Iust. 39.5.2–3: *dum haec aguntur, frater eius ex paelice susceptus, cui pater Cyrenarum regnum testamento reliquerat, herede populo Romano instituto decedit. Iam enim fortuna Romana porrigere se ad orientalia regna, non contenta Italiae terminis, coeperat. Itaque et ea pars Libyae prouincia facta est*; Iul. Obseq. 49; cf. Braund 1983, 23–24; Díaz Fernández 2016, 229–234; see, however, Oost 1963, 11–12. Attalus of Pergamum bequeathed his kingdom to the Roman people on the condition that several Greek cities were declared *liberae*. Liv. per. 59: *Aristonicus, Eumenis regis filius, Asiam occupavit, cum testamento Attali regis legata populo R. libera esse deberet*; OGIS 338, ll. 3–5; CIL I² 588, ll. 1–3; Flor. 1.35.2; Val.Max. 5.2 ext.3; Vell. 2.4.1; Str. 13.4.2; App. Mith. 62; see Braund 1983, 21–23; Kallet-Marx 1995, 101–104.
111 An inscription from Cyrene (AE 1967, no. 532) honours the consul C. Claudius Pulcher (cos. 92) as εὐεργέταν καὶ πάτρ[ωνα], but the dedication is not apparently related with an alleged command in Cyrenaica; cf. Broughton MRR, 3.57–58; Gasperini 1967, 53–57; Badian 1971, 134–136; Brennan 2000, 364; Canali de Rossi 2001, 27–28. We cannot, however, dismiss the possibility that a senatorial commission visited Cyrene after Appion's death in 96; see Díaz Fernández 2016 231–233.

peared there with the intention of raising ships for the siege of Athens.¹¹² Appian, Plutarch and other sources agree in highlighting the delicate political and social situation in which the Libyan cities found themselves when Lucullus docked in Cyrene —so much so that the quaestor himself saw the need of providing the Cyrenians with a series of laws according to which they could govern themselves and hopefully ameliorate a situation that bordered on civil war.¹¹³

It seems at first surprising that the senate did not decide to send a magistrate (a quaestor, in this case) to Cyrenaica for over two decades after Apion's death; several scholars have seen this delay as proof of Rome's lack of interest in taking charge of royal estates, which would also be reflected in the declaration that the cities of Pentapolis were free; this seems, however, too bold an interpretation. In fact, Rome initially acted in the same way when they discovered that Attalus III of Pergamum had left all his possessions and kingdom to the Roman people. Furthermore, we know that the senate conceded ἐλευθερία to the cities of Ephesus and Pergamum, in accordance with the conditions specified in Attalus' will.¹¹⁴ In this case, the senate sent a delegation of five senators to Asia to ratify the will, but it was not until 131, when the commission became aware of the state of conflict into which Pergamum had been plunged, that the senate decided to grant the *provincia Asia* to a consul, with the intention of asserting their authority over the former Attalid realms.¹¹⁵

It is very possible that the senate took the same steps when it learned that Apion had left his kingdom to the Roman people. From that moment on, Cyrenaica became another realm under the Roman aegis, regardless of whether or not there was a Roman magistrate in charge, or whether its cities had been declared *liberae:*¹¹⁶ in

---

112 Plut. *Luc.* 2.2–5; cf. App. *Mith.* 33; 51; Ios. *AJ* 14.114; *vir.ill.* 74.1–2; Broughton MRR, 2.55–56.
113 Plut. *Luc.* 2.4–5; cf. Ios. *AJ* 14.114; Oost 1963, 18–19; Díaz Fernández 2016, 242–243.
114 Liv. *Per.* 59; OGIS 338, *ll.* 3–5: [ἐπεὶ βασιλεὺς Ἄτταλος / φιλομήτωρ καὶ εὐεργέτη[ς μεθισ]τάμενος ἐξ ἀν/θρώπων ἀπολέλοιπεν τὴμ [πατρ]ίδα ἡμῶν ἐλευθέραμ; see also CIL I² 588, *ll.* 1–3; Val.Max. 5.2 ext.3; Vell. 2.4.1; Flor. 1.35.2; Eutr. 4.18; App. *Mith.* 62; Str. 13.4.2. Braund 1983, 21–23; Kallet-Marx 1995, 101–104; 111, n. 61; cf. Díaz Fernández 2016, 230–232.
115 See the following sources on the senatorial commission: Str. 14.1.38; Plut. *Ti.Gr.* 14.1–6; Liv. *per.* 58; on the role of P. Cornelius Scipio Nasica, cf. Broughton MRR, 1.499. See Sherwin-White 1977, 66–69; Kallet-Marx 1995, 106–108. P. Licinius Crassus Mucianus was the consul who received the *provincia Asia* to combat Aristonicus: Gell. 1.13.11–13; Liv. *per.* 59; Vell. 2.4.1; Eutr. 4.20; Oros. 5.10.1–2; Iust. 36.4.7–8.
116 Díaz Fernández 2016, 233–234. See Laronde 1988, 1008: 'Autrement dit, la solution adoptée par Rome ne signifiait en aucun cas un désintérêt pour la Cyrénaïque. Les cités, bien loin d'être abandonnées à elles-mêmes, entretenaient des rapports étroits avec Rome, et recherchaient pour des raisons fiscales le patronage des hommes politiques en vue.' See the revision of the concept of *imperium* in Lintott 1981a, 63–64; 1993, 36–42; see 41: 'Such are the forms by which the Romans defined their relationship with those whom they regarded as their subordinates (even if they generally termed them friends and allies). The multiplicity of the typology is confusing and tends to obscure the fundamental homogeneity in the *imperium Romanum*—the fact that the Romans expected their commands to be obeyed, even when they allowed a great deal of *de facto* autonomy and frequently exercised power by indirect means'; also Kallet-Marx 1995, 335–341; Richardson 2008, 66–79.

fact, it was Rome's very authority that guaranteed this *libertas* and ensured that this freedom was respected. As allies ultimately subjected to Rome's authority, the Cyrenians had to remain loyal to the Republic and, possibly, fulfil certain commitments to it. We can perhaps glimpse what such commitments might have entailed in the testimony about when Lucullus came to Cyrenaica to raise ships during the Mithridatic War.[117] The senate, however, did not think it necessary to send a consul or praetor to Cyrene to cement their rule, much less to maintain a permanent magistrate there, which would amount to making the kingdom into a province. In any case, it is clear that the situation changed around 75–74, though we do not know exactly why.

In reality, Sallust's passage presents more interpretative problems than it solves: to start with, it is unclear why the senate changed its policy towards Cyrenaica and sent a magistrate there for the first time. Several sources indicate that the cities of Cyrenaica endured a slew of tyrannies and internal upheavals after Apion's death in 96. This already bad situation was apparently aggravated by the incursions of Libyan peoples. This explains why Lucullus tried to improve the situation by imposing a series of laws upon the Cyrenians during his short visit there as quaestor.[118] Additionally, we must take the increasing presence of pirates off the Libyan coast into consideration. Indeed, it is hardly a coincidence that the praetor M. Antonius was conceded a special command against piracy in the Mediterranean (74), perhaps in conjunction with the dispatch of P. Cornelius Lentulus Marcellinus to Cyrenaica.[119] We can therefore understand the decision to send a magistrate to Cyrene as Rome's attempt to recover control and consolidate its authority in the area: if this was the motive, however, it is surprising that the mission was entrusted to a quaestor—a junior magistrate —devoid, in principle, of *imperium*. Indeed, such a job would have been more fitting for a praetor or consul, as was standard practice in analogous cases.[120] In 75 the con-

---

[117] Plut. *Luc.* 2.2–5. A shipment of *silphium* was sent from Cyrene to Rome in 93: Plin. *n.h.* 19.40; Oost 1963, 12–13. Pliny's passage shows that Romans immediately established business relationships with the cities of Cyrenaica after Appion's death in 96. An inscription from Cyrene (CIL I² 2958) mentions the *[cives Romani] qui Cyrenis negotiantur*, which supports the presence of Roman *negotiatores* in the Cyrenaica in the Late Republic.

[118] Plut. *Mor.* 255e-257e; Polyaen. 8.38; Str. 17.3.22; cf. Plut. *Luc.* 2.4–5; Ios. *AJ* 14.114. See Braund 1985, 319–320.

[119] Cic. *Verr.* 2.2.8; 2.3.213–216; Liv. *per.* 97; Sall. *hist.* 3.5–6 M.; Broughton MRR, 2.101–102. On M. Antonius' command against piracy, see Kallet-Marx 1995, 304–311; De Souza 1999, 141–148; Brennan 2000, pp. 406–407.

[120] See Badian 1965, 120: 'In Cyrene, then, it seems that in 74 a quaestor (almost certainly with *imperium propraetore*) had organized the revenues accruing to Rome from the estate of a Ptolemy, at a time when money was urgently needed in Rome. The reason was evidently the Senate's unwillingness to appoint a senior man with a dangerous imperium for the task'; cf. Brennan 2000, 409: 'A praetorian or consular commander was apt to go off triumph hunting. But above all it was dangerous for the public finances. A well-connected senior magistrate might feel bold enough to keep a substantial portion of the royal wealth for himself—for example, to cover (whether prospectively or retrospectively) his own electoral expenses—and not worry too much about the consequences of being haled into court on his return before a jury of his peers'; Díaz Fernández 2016, 234–235.

suls C. Aurelius Cotta and L. Octavius were sent to the provinces of Gallia Citerior and Cilicia, respectively (in the latter case in the face of imminent war against Mithridates). As we have already seen, before departing for their destinations they had had to confront serious disturbances in Rome (to which they themselves fell victim) because of the grain shortage from which the city was suffering.[121]

It is therefore possible, as we anticipated in the previous section, that the decision to send a quaestor to Cyrene was principally meant to secure grain (or money directly) at a time when the plebs and Roman troops were clambering for solutions and needed provisions were increasingly harder to obtain due to multiple wars and the plague of piracy.[122] This could explain why a quaestor was selected for this task instead of another magistrate. This does not negate the possibility that Marcellinus might have taken advantage of his time in Cyrene to establish certain measures to address the tumultuous political situation and attempt to impose order. If that was the case, however, he does not seem to have been exceedingly successful: an interesting collection of inscriptions found in Cyrene and Ptolemais reveal that only a few years after Lentulus Marcellinus' quaestorship, in 67, Cn. Cornelius Lentulus Marcellinus (who, incidentally, was probably his brother) was in Cyrene where he prescribed a series of measures to settle internal disputes in his capacity as Pompey's *legatus pro praetore*.[123]

This situation poses the question of what happened in Cyrenaica after Lentulus Marcellinus' quaestorship. It is indeed surprising that a Pompeian legate (and not a praetor in the role of governor) mediated the political conflicts that continued to roil the Cyrenian cities after 74. The sources' silence on this question is absolute: leaving aside the report of the visit by Pompey's legate in 67, there is no evidence for the presence of more Roman magistrates in Cyrenaica until 62, when we encounter another quaestor there, in this case M. Juventius Laterensis.[124] We know little of his mission: whether Laterensis was sent to Cyrene alone, as appears to have been the case with P. Lentulus Marcellinus, or whether he was serving a higher magistrate (perhaps a praetor) is unknown. An inscription found in the forum of Ptolemais seems to mention Laterensis ([---]τίου Λατερα[---]) alongside a [-- στρα]τηγοῦ (one line beneath), whose name is not preserved: it could refer to the quaestor himself, and therefore Laterensis would have been invested with *praetorium imperium* as *quaestor pro praetore*

---

121 C. Aurelius Cotta's and L. Octavius' *provinciae* in Sall. *hist.* 2.98 M.; cf. 2.45; 2.47.6 – 7; McGushin 1992, 208 – 209.
122 Oost 1963, 20 – 21; Badian 1965, 119 – 120; Kallet-Marx 1995, 364 – 367; Brennan 2000, 408 – 409; cf. Braund 1985, 321 – 323.
123 Reynolds 1962, 97–103; cf. SEG 20.730: Γναῖον Κορνήλιον Λέντολον Ποπλίω υἱὸν Μαρκελλῖνον πρεσβευτὰν ἀντιστράταγον τὸν πάτρωνα καὶ σωτῆρα Κυραναῖοι; sources for Cn. Cornelius Lentulus Marcellinus' command under Pompey in Flor. 1.41.9; App. *Mith.* 95.
124 Cic. *Planc.* 12; 63; cf. Perl 1970, 330 – 331; 1971, 371 – 373; Díaz Fernández 2015, 490 – 491.

([-- ταμίας καὶ ἀντιστρα]τηγοῦ), but it could also refer to the praetor (or propraetor) whom Laterensis accompanied as quaestor.[125]

P. Lentulus Marcellinus' mission also raises the question of whether or not he had *imperium* to undertake the task entrusted to him by the senate, whatever that job may have been. Sallust tells us nothing about this and there is not a single piece of evidence that indicates that this was in fact the case, although scholars have generally accepted this possibility.[126] In principle, if Lentulus Marcellinus' remit was limited to undertaking an extraordinary levy of wheat or money for the Roman treasury (perhaps by auctioning off the property of Ptolemy Apion), there is no need to suppose that the senate invested him with *imperium*, since he could have completed his mission without such authority. As we will see below, however, only a few years after Marcellinus was sent to Cyrene, in 58, M. Porcius Cato, who had been *quaestor urbanus* in 64, was assigned to Cyprus as *[pro]quaestor pro praetore* to take charge of Ptolemy's treasure and take control of it from the island's government.[127] If the mission entrusted to Lentulus Marcellinus was similar to Cato's, the senate could have given him *imperium praetorium ex s. c.*, which would have put troops at his disposal and allowed him to make a military intervention, if necessary. The lack of concrete evidence means that we can only consider this proposal as a possibility.[128]

It is even more difficult to determine whether Cyrene continued to be a *provincia* after the quaestorship of P. Lentulus Marcellinus. As we observed above, there is no evidence of there being more magistrates in Cyrene until the quaestorship of M. Juventius Laterensis. All this makes some scholars doubt whether Cyrene continued to be a province after Marcellinus' departure. Joyce Reynolds, for example, considers that the role played in Cyrenaica by the Pompeian legate Cn. Lentulus Marcellinus was an indication that it was not at that time (i.e. 67) under the command of a Roman magistrate and, therefore, it was not actually a province.[129] In fact, the only attestation of Cyrene being granted as a province to a praetor dates to the period immediately following Caesar's death in 44: the praetor C. Cassius Longinus, one of the participants in the Ides of March, received Cyrene as a province with the obvious intention of removing him from Rome as quickly as possible. However, he did not

---

125 Pugliese Carratelli 1963, 338, no. 211, *ll*. 16–17; Laronde 1988, 1013, n. 46; Díaz Fernández 2015, 242; 2016, 235–239.
126 Jashemski 1950, 78–79; Broughton MRR, 2.103; 2.554; 3.69; Oost 1963, 21; Balsdon 1962, 134–135; Badian 1965, 119–121; cf. McGushin 1992, 206–207; Kallet-Marx 1995, 364–367; Brennan 2000, 408–409; Díaz Fernández 2016, 234–235, n. 25.
127 Cic. *dom.* 20–21; Vell. 2.38.5–6; 2.45.4–5; Flor. 1.44.1–5; Plut. *Cat.min.* 34.2–4; Cass.Dio 39.22.1–23.4.
128 Badian 1965, 118–121.
129 Reynolds 1962, 101–103; cf. 102: 'The wide range of action taken by Pompey and his legate might even suggest that the government authorized and presumably established in 75 had never been effective or had broken down'; also Kallet-Marx 1995, 366, n. 113. See, however, Brennan 2000, 409.

even manage to assume that command, due to the outbreak of the Civil War.¹³⁰ This evidence suggests (in principle) that the *provincia Cyrenae* was an occasional command during the Republic, only conceded in special circumstances and usually to quaestors, as would have been the case with P. Lentulus Marcellinus in 75 or 74 and M. Juventius Laterensis ca. 62.¹³¹

Several historians, nevertheless, have also maintained that Cyrene became a permanent province following Marcellinus' command with the peculiarity that it was governed exclusively by quaestors, unlike any other province: this would explain why we only have quaestors attested in Cyrene during the Republic.¹³² Other scholars have attributed Cyrene's conversion into a province to Pompey: according to this theory, Pompey created this new province once his campaigns had ended against the pirates and against Mithridates in the East, which would explain the presence of Juventius Laterensis in Cyrenaica around 62.¹³³ In any case, it should be clarified that speaking of a *nova provincia* Sallust does not point to anything like its 'provincialization' at that time, but simply that Cyrene had not previously been assigned as a *provincia* to a magistrate.¹³⁴ The possibility that Cyrene constituted a permanent

---

130 App. *b. c.* 3.8; cf. 3.12: ἀγγέλλεται Κάσσιός τε καὶ Βροῦτος ἀφῃρημένοι πρὸς τῶν ὑπάτων Συρίαν καὶ Μακεδονίαν καὶ ἐς παρηγορίαν βραχύτερα ἕτερα Κυρήνην καὶ Κρήτην ἀντειληφότες; 3.16; 3.36; 4.57; Plut. *Brut.* 19.5; cf. Perl 1970, 333–334; Díaz Fernández 2015, 492–493.
131 See the discussion of the so-called 'provincialization' of Cyrene in Díaz Fernández 2015, 239–247; also 2016, 236–244. See Kallet-Marx 1995, 367: 'Cyrene was 'reclaimed' in 75 in order to supplement from one of the great cereal regions of the Mediterranean the grain supply of Rome, which, it is surely no accident, was severely strained precisely in 75, when a consul was actually attacked by an angry mob. The interest of the Senate in Cyrene was on this view extremely restricted in scope in the 70s and 60s, and it is therefore no surprise that signs of Rome's presence are so scarce and sporadic in subsequent years, for the crisis had receded—due surely to Antonius' efforts in the West as well as to the exploitation of Cyrene—by 73, when the state could again offer subsidized grain'; cf. Laronde 1988, 1011–1014; Brennan 2000, 408–409.
132 For Cyrene as permanent quaestorian province, see Romanelli 1943, 56–58; Jashemski 1950, 153; Luzzatto 1985, 149, n. 2; cf. Perl 1970, 336–342; Laronde 1988, 1011–1013; Kallet-Marx 1995, 319, n. 119; cf. Reynolds 1962, 102: 'It is pertinent that the whole of Cyrenaica fell within an area of fifty miles from the sea to which those powers were confined, and that the normal governor was probably a comparatively junior man, perhaps no more than a quaestor.'
133 Reynolds 1962, 101–103; see Badian 1965, 120: 'Cyrene probably, like so many other provinces, owes its real organization to Pompey. It is very likely that the documents concerning Cn. Marcellinus show us part of the actual event'; Brennan 2000, 364; 409; cf. Eutr. 6.11.2–3: *ad id missus Q. Caecilius Metellus ingentibus proeliis intra triennium omnem provinciam cepit appellatusque est Creticus atque ex insula triumphavit. Quo tempore Libya quoque Romano imperio per testamentum Appionis, qui rex eius fuerat, accessit, in qua inclutae urbes erant Berenice, Ptolomais, Cyrene*; Diodor. 40.4. See, however, Harris 1979a, 267; Díaz Fernández 2016, 241–242.
134 Kallet-Marx 1995, 366: 'Sallust's reference to Cyrene as a *nova provincia* need hardly imply that the quaestor organized the 'permanent annexation' of the area… As usual here again the 'organizing' of a 'province' at 75, 67, or any other time passes without direct attestation in our evidence, and such a conception is singularly unhelpful for understanding the peculiar character of Roman intervention in Cyrene at this time'; also Badian 1965, 119–120; Díaz Fernández, 2015, 239, n. 528. There are similar uses of *nova provincia* in Liv. 28.40.1; 25.3.6.

quaestorian *provincia* is problematic because it lacks parallels within the Roman *imperium* (possibly the senate would have perceived a need to concede *imperium* systematically to the quaestors destined for Cyrene so that they could successfully complete their mission). Furthermore, this would appear to contradict the evidence that points in precisely the opposite direction. Both Strabo and Cassius Dio include Cyrenaica with Crete among the provinces assigned by Augustus to the senate and Roman people in 27, which suggests that Cyrene had already become a permanent province before the Principate.[135] Furthermore, a passage from Diodorus, which supposedly transcribes an inscription commemorating Pompey's campaigns in the East, specifically mentions Cyrenaica as a *provincia* (Κυρηναϊκὴ ἐπαρχία), a denomination that the text also assigns to Asia and Bithynia, both of which had been permanent Roman provinces for years.[136]

A letter from M. Caelius Rufus to Cicero, dated October 51, includes a *senatus consultum* pertaining to the distribution of provinces for 50, in which he speaks of a total of nine provinces (Cilicia included) *quas praetorii pro praetore obtinerent*.[137] As Shackleton Bailey points out, given the number of praetorian provinces mentioned and taking into account that Gaul, Syria, and both Hispaniae would have continued under consular command in 50, we should assume that both Cyrene and Crete were two of those provinces assigned to the propraetors. Though Shackleton Bailey's argument is compelling, we cannot completely rule out the possibility that some other occasional province was included for 50.[138] In any case, these passages suggest that Cyrene might have received a permanent praetor after the quaestorship of P. Lentulus Marcellinus, which means that assigning it to C. Cassius Longinus in 44 would not have been an exceptional circumstance. In fact, it is likely that P. Lentulus Marcellinus was initially sent to Cyrene on a special mission, which was perhaps determined by Rome's need for grain and money, in the same way that M. Porcius Cato would be sent to Cyprus some years later. Once his mission was completed and he had returned to Rome, it is possible that Marcellinus made the senate aware of the increasing instability of the Cyrenian cities and of the danger of losing control of Pentapolis because of the pirates and Libyan populations. In such a case, the sen-

---

135 Str. 17.3.25; Cass.Dio 53.12.4.
136 Diodor. 40.4: Πομπήιος Γναΐου υἱὸς Μέγας αὐτοκράτωρ τὴν παράλιον τῆς οἰκουμένης καὶ πάσας τὰς ἐντὸς Ὠκεανοῦ νήσους ἐλευθερώσας τοῦ πειρατικοῦ πολέμου, ὁ ῥυσάμενός ποτε πολιορκουμένην τὴν Ἀριοβαρζάνου βασιλείαν, Γαλατίαν τε καὶ τὰς ὑπερκειμένας χώρας καὶ ἐπαρχίας, Ἀσίαν, Βιθυνίαν, ὑπερασπίσας δὲ Παφλαγονίαν τε καὶ τὸν Πόντον, Ἀρμενίαν τε καὶ Ἀχαΐαν, ἔτι δὲ Ἰβηρίαν, Κολχίδα, Μεσοποταμίαν, Σωφηνήν, Γορδυηνήν, ὑποτάξας δὲ βασιλέα Μήδων Δαρεῖον... καὶ τὴν κατὰ Κιλικίαν Συρίαν, Ἰουδαίαν, Ἀραβίαν καὶ τὴν κατὰ Κιλικίαν Συρίαν, Ἰουδαίαν, Ἀραβίαν, Κυρηναϊκὴν ἐπαρχίαν... See the commentary on the passage in Díaz Fernández 2015, 239–243.
137 Cael. *fam.* 8.8.8: *senatui placere in Ciliciam provinciam in VIII reliquas provincias quas praetorii pro praetore obtinerent eos qui praetores fuerunt neque in provincia cum imperio fuerunt, quos eorum ex s. c. cum imperio in provincias pro praetore mitti oporteret*; Perl 1970, 331–332; Shackleton Bailey 1977, 405–406; Brennan 2000, 409.
138 Shackleton Bailey 1977, 405: 'Sicily, Sardinia, Africa, Macedonia, Asia, Bithynia, Crete, Cyrene...'

ate could have decided to send a permanent praetor to Cyrene, thus converting Cyrenaica into another of Rome's provinces. This is what happened with Syria after Pompey conquered it: once Antiochus XII Asiaticus was deposed, Pompey temporarily entrusted the command of Syria to his quaestor, M. Aemilius Scaurus, who remained in charge there *pro praetore* until the senate assigned the province of Syria to the praetor L. Marcius Philippus (pr. 62) in 62 or 61.[139]

In spite of the dearth of available evidence, the considerations discussed here lead us to think that, although Cyrene was perhaps a *provincia* assigned on a one-off basis to P. Lentulus Marcellinus in 75 or 74, the circumstances there could have led the senate to change its mind at a later date and hence to incorporate Cyrenaica into the list of permanent provinces assigned to Roman praetors.[140] If this is correct, M. Juventius Laterensis would have served his quaestorship under a praetor, in accordance with what seems to have been the usual custom in Republican provinces. The intervention of the Pompeian legate, Cn. Lentulus Marcellinus, in the internal convulsions of the Cyrenian cities in 67 does not therefore prove the absence of a praetor in Cyrene, since we do not know with certainty how the Pompeian legates dealt with the provincial authorities. Once Q. Caecilius Metellus (cos. 68) had completed the conquest of Crete in 66, the island could nominally have remained under the authority of the praetor of Cyrene; in fact, a passage from Cicero seems to indicate that M. Juventius Laterensis' province also encompassed the island of Crete, a possibility that is further bolstered by the *Scholia Bobiensia*.[141] In particular circumstances, nevertheless, it is possible that the command of Cyrene and Crete could have been divided, as might have taken place in the year 50. In any case, the inclusion of Crete and Cyrene among the provinces entrusted by Augustus to the senate and the Roman people in 27 would not therefore have done anything other than follow what was already an established custom, as was the case for all the other provinces.

Cato Uticensis' command in Cyprus

Among the many policies that P. Clodius Pulcher proposed in 58, the tribune of the plebs brought forward a law that required that Cyprus and the inheritance from Ptolemy (the younger brother of Ptolemy XII Auletes, king of Egypt) would pass to the Roman people. A passage from Livy's *Periochae* cites this law as *lege lata de redigenda in provinciae formam Cypro et publicanda pecunia regia*, that is, the law that turned Cyprus into a *provincia* of a Roman commander and the royal treasury into a

---

139 App. *Syr.* 51; cf. *b. c.* 5.10; Ios. *BJ* 1.157; *AJ* 14.79.
140 Díaz Fernández 2015, 243–247; 2016, 240–243; cf. App. *b.c.* 1.111.
141 Cic. *Planc.* 85; cf. Schol. Bob. p. 167 Stangl: *constabat enim Laterensem fuisse in Creta provincia, et solebant omnes candidate alba creta oblinire cervicem, ut populo notabiliores essent*; Díaz Fernández 2015, 247–249.

public inheritance.¹⁴² According to the terms of the law or perhaps via a *senatus consultum*—as Velleius Paterculus seems to suggest¹⁴³—the *provincia Cyprus* was immediately allocated to the senator M. Porcius Cato, who had been *quaestor urbanus* years earlier in 64.¹⁴⁴ While Velleius Paterculus suggests that Clodius' purpose was specifically to remove Cato from Rome through the allocation of 'a most honourable mission' (*sub honorificentissimo ministerii titulo*), all indications suggest that the law's main priority was to finance the tribune's expensive *lex frumentaria*; in this case, Cato's absence would have been an added bonus to his political adversaries.¹⁴⁵

One way or another, Cato was sent to Cyprus with the mission of depriving Ptolemy of his rule over the island and royal treasury. In addition, various other tasks were tacked on, such as returning the exiles from Byzantium to their native city.¹⁴⁶ Velleius Paterculus again provides us with the useful information: Cato was sent to Cyprus *cum iure praetorio* and that he was even allocated a quaestor to help with his mission (*quippe legem tulit, ut is quaestor cum iure praetorio, adiecto etiam quaestore, mitteretur in insulam Cyprum ad spoliandum regno Ptolemaeum*).¹⁴⁷ This detail is of particular interest, since it not only reveals that Cato was granted *imperium* (*praetorium*), but also that he was assigned a quaestor. This gave rise to a peculiar and, as far as we are aware, unparalleled situation: a quaestor serving under the orders of someone who was no more than a *quaestorius*.

In fact, the sources usually refer to Cato simply as 'quaestor', and no author other than Velleius refers to him being invested with *imperium*. There is, nevertheless, no reason to doubt the historian's version, since—as Balsdon and Badian both explain—everything seems to point to his true title being *proquaestor pro praetore*, a position that is recorded in Greek inscriptions dating to the final years of the Republic.¹⁴⁸ We should not forget that Cato had been quaestor several years previ-

---

142 Liv. *per.* 104; see also Cic. *dom.* 20–21; 52–53; 65; *Sest.* 56–57; 59–61; Vell. 2.45.4 (cf. 2.38.6); *vir.ill.* 80.2; Str. 14.6.6; App. *b.c.* 2.23; Plut. *Cat.min.* 34.1–4; Cass.Dio 38.30.5; 39.22.1–2; cf. Broughton MRR, 2.198. Badian 1965, 110–121; Díaz Fernández 2015, 205–206.
143 Vell. 2.38.6: *Cypro devicta nullis adsignanda gloria est; quippe senatus consulto, ministerio Catonis, regis morte quam ille conscientia acciverat facta provincia est*; Badian 1965, 115–117.
144 Sources for M. Porcius Cato's quaestorship in 64: Plut. *Cat.min.* 16.3–6; Cass.Dio 47.6.4; cf. Broughton MRR, 2.163.
145 Vell. 2.45.4; cf. Cic. *dom.* 65; Plut. *Cat.min.* 34.1–4. Badian 1965, 117–118, suggests that the mission was initially given to the consul A. Gabinius as governor of Cilicia, but this proposal is merely conjectural; also Brennan 2000, 428–429. 573. On P. Clodius' grain law, cf. Cic. *dom.* 25; *Sest.* 55; Ascon. 8 C; Schol. Bob. p. 132 Stangl; Cass.Dio 38.13.1. See Badian 1965, 116–117: 'it will appear even more clearly that the traditional interpretation of them, inherited from ancient biographical romance—that the two tasks in Cyprus and Byzantium were thought up chiefly in order to remove Cato from Rome—must be entirely abandoned. Even Cicero, amid rhetorical distortion, makes it perfectly clear that the confiscation of Cyprus was a measure important to Clodius for its own sake: the choice of Cato for the mission was a happy afterthought.'
146 Cic. *dom.* 52–53; *Sest.* 56; *har.resp.* 59; Schol. Bob. p. 132 Stangl; Plut. *Cat.min.* 34.4.
147 Vell. 2.45.4.
148 Balsdon 1962, 134–135; Badian 1965, 110–113; Broughton MRR, 3.171.

ously, so the references that the sources make to him as quaestor must necessarily be understood as an imprecise use of the term; when Clodius passed his law, Cato was in reality a citizen who held no public responsibility beyond being a senator. In this respect, the conditions of his command in Cyprus are not essentially different from those of the successive commands conceded to Pompey throughout his career, for example. When Sulla sent Pompey to Sicily in 82 to fight M. Perperna as *propraetor*, Pompey was no more than a young man (*privatus*) from the *nobilitas* who had not yet been admitted to the senate.[149] Some years later, as a consular senator of undisputed standing, Pompey received special commands from the *leges Gabinia* and *Manilia* to fight the pirates (67) and Mithridates in the East (66), respectively; both commands, which were *proconsulares*, were, however, conceded to him as a senator, since he did not occupy any magistracy at that time.[150]

In the same way, although Cato may be cited in the sources as a quaestor, we should conclude that he was, in reality, *[pro]quaestor propraetor*. In any case, given the character of the mission, which was predominantly fiscal, it was decided to allocate the *provincia Cyprus* to a senator of quaestorian rank. We can perhaps find some precedents years earlier when the Romans sent P. Cornelius Lentulus Marcellinus to Cyrene and Q. Pompeius Bithynicus to Bithynia. We do not know the reasons why the mission was entrusted to a *quaestorius* instead of a serving quaestor (as happened in the earlier cases), but it is possible that the political circumstances on the ground made it desirable to put the command of Cyprus into the hands of a senator like Cato. A possible parallel for the *quaestorius* Cato can be seen in the nomination of Verres as proquaestor to the consul Cn. Cornelius Dolabella (pr. 81) in Cilicia: Cicero tells us that, after the death of his quaestor, C. Publicius Malleolus, Dolabella decided to fill the vacancy by naming Verres proquaestor; Verres had been quaestor in 82 under the consul Cn. Papirius Carbo and at that point was serving as a legate in the cohort of the proconsul of Cilicia.[151] As Badian points out, the flexibility of the Roman institutional system apparently made it possible that a *quaestorius* could be empowered to perform the duties of a quaestor if need be, just like a senator of consular rank could be empowered to perform the duties of a consul (as Pompey's successive commands demonstrate).[152]

---

[149] See Cic. *leg. Man.* 61: *Quid tam novum quam adulescentulum privatum exercitum difficili rei publicae temporare conficere?*; Liv. *per.* 89; App. *b.c.* 1.96; Plut. *Pomp.* 10.1–2; *Sull.* 28.8; cf. Badian 1965, 110–111; Brennan 2000, 481–482; Girardet 2001, 162–165; bibliography in Díaz Fernández 2015, 310–311.

[150] Sources in Broughton MRR, 2.144–146; 153; 155; see Kallet-Marx 1995, 311–323; Girardet 2001, 171–187. More recently Morrell 2017, 57–97.

[151] Cic. *Verr.* 2.1.41; 90–91; Broughton MRR, 2.81.

[152] Badian 1965, 110–111; cf. Balsdon 1962, 134, n. 3. See also the case of L. Sestius Quirinalis Albinianus, who (according to an interpretation of Cic. *Att.* 13.2a) could have been urban quaestor in 45 and proquaestor in Macedonia in 44–42.

Cicero points out that *honos* and *imperium* were conceded to Cato *extra ordinem nominatim*, given his particular status: *ad hunc honorem et imperium extra ordinem nominatim rogatione tua detulisti*.[153] Precisely because he had received *imperium*, moreover, Cato had to have a quaestor in his service, as was the custom every time a Roman commander (*imperator*) assumed the command of a *provincia*. As noted above, Velleius is unequivocal on this point: Cato received a quaestor to carry out his mission in Cyprus, even though we do not know anything about that quaestor's identity. Plutarch indicates that Clodius refused to provide Cato with ships, soldiers, or assistants, putting at his disposal only two secretaries of dubious reputation.[154] This does not necessarily negate Velleius' report, however, above all because it was possibly the senate who would have had to nominate *ex senatus consulto* the quaestor who would be sent to accompany Cato (see above).

Despite Clodius' desires, it is likely that the senate did indeed appoint a quaestor to Cato (since he had been invested with *imperium* over the *provincia Cyprus cum iure praetorio*) and that they gave him ships to undertake his mission. A passage in Cicero reveals that in fact Cato was well prepared for battle in case Ptolemy resisted (*si ius suum defenderet, bello gerendo M. Catonem praefecisti*).[155] Plutarch indicates that Cato sent his friend Canidius ahead to Cyprus so that he could convince Ptolemy not to resist and could offer him a priesthood in Paphos as a reward for his cooperation. In the meantime, Cato made his way to Rhodes, perhaps to add more ships to his fleet.[156] In the end, Cato did not have to intervene militarily in Cyprus, since Ptolemy committed suicide before his arrival: once the king's death was known and while he himself was travelling to Byzantium, Cato sent his nephew M. Junius Brutus (one of the members of his cohort) to Cyprus, since he did not have complete confidence in Canidius, according to Plutarch.[157] This Canidius, Cato's frequent collaborator in Cyprus, could very well have been the quaestor to whom Velleius referred, but this is not certain.[158] Once in Cyprus and after resolving the issue concerning the Byzantine exiles, Cato meticulously compiled an inventory of all Ptolemy's property before selling it off (possibly by auction) to convert the royal treasure into cash. As Plutarch comments, Cato acted with such integrity during the sale of the treasure that he apparently scolded the majority of the friends who were accompanying him, on the grounds that they evidently had hoped to benefit from the operation.[159]

---

[153] Cic. *dom.* 21.
[154] Plut. *Cat.min.* 34.3: ἐξιόντι δ' οὐ ναῦν, οὐ στρατιώτην, οὐχ ὑπηρέτην ἔδωκε, πλὴν ἢ δύο γραμματεῖς μόνον.
[155] Cic. *dom.* 20.
[156] Plut. *Cat.min.* 35.1–2.
[157] Plut. *Cat.min.* 36.1: ὁ δ' ἐν Κύπρῳ Πτολεμαῖος εὐτυχίᾳ τινὶ τοῦ Κάτωνος ἑαυτὸν φαρμάκοις ἀπέκτεινε. πολλῶν δὲ χρημάτων ἀπολελεῖφθαι λεγομένων, αὐτὸς μὲν ἔγνω πλεῖν εἰς Βυζαντίους, πρὸς δὲ τὴν Κύπρον ἐξέπεμψε τὸν ἀδελφιδοῦν Βροῦτον, οὐ πάνυ τι πιστεύων τῷ Κανιδίῳ. τοὺς δὲ φυγάδας διαλλάξας καὶ καταλιπὼν ἐν ὁμονοίᾳ τὸ Βυζάντιον, οὕτως εἰς Κύπρον ἔπλευσεν.
[158] Wiseman 1964, 123; Broughton MRR, 3.49.
[159] Plut. *Cat.min.* 36.2–3.

We do not know much more about Cato's mission. Once his job was completed, it seems that Cyprus became part of the provincial command of Cilicia, as Cicero's letters suggest.[160] One of these letters, sent to the proconsul P. Cornelius Lentulus Spinther (cos. 57), clearly states that he had *Ciliciam Cyprumque* under his command, which demonstrates that the administration of Cyprus had been immediately added to the portfolio of the governor of Cilicia.[161] It seems that this same Lentulus Spinther, moreover, approved a *lex* during his command that was intended to regulate the administration of the island: Cicero recommends the use of that law in a letter sent in 49 to C. Sextilius Rufus, who was, according to Cicero, the *primus quaestor* sent to Cyprus.[162] Cicero's comment has provoked some controversy, since he does not make clear whether Sextilius was sent only to Cyprus or, alternatively, he was simply the quaestor sent with the governor P. Sestius to run the province of Cilicia; in the latter case, Cicero's comment would have to be understood in the sense that none of the quaestors sent to Cilicia had until then travelled to Cyprus, despite the fact that the island had been considered part of that province since Lentulus Spinther' mandate (57–54). Although Cicero offers us no further information about this mission, we nevertheless cannot dismiss the possibility that Sextilius may have only been sent to Cyprus with a particular objective (e.g. the extraordinary collection of money). In any case, we know that Caesar ceded Cyprus to the Ptolemies in 47, which was scarcely a decade after Cato took control of the island.[163] According to both Strabo and Cassius Dio, only a few years later Cyprus again fell into Roman hands and became one of the ten praetorian provinces assigned by Augustus to the people.[164]

The quaestor in his province

As has already been pointed out at the outset of this chapter, the longstanding link between the consulship and the quaestorship as well as the latter's eventual incorporation into the command structure of the Roman provinces (possibly as early as 227) were defining factors when it came to conferring a range of duties upon the overseas quaestors that went well beyond those traditionally attributed to the quaestors

---

160 Cic. *fam.* 1.7.4; 13.48; *Att.* 5.21.6–12; 6.3.5; cf. 6.1.5–6; 6.2.7; cf. Badian 1965, 114–115; Brennan 2000, 429–430; 811, n. 365; see also Marshall (1964) 206–215.
161 Cic. *fam.* 1.7.4: *tantam vim habet ut magis iratorum hominum studium quam constantis senatus consilium esse videatur, te perspicere posse, qui Ciliciam Cyprumque teneas, quid efficere et quid consequi possis...*
162 Cic. *fam.* 13.48: *cum primus in eam insulam quaestor veneris, ea te instituere quae sequantur alii. quod, ut spero, facilius consequere si et P. Lentuli, necessari tui, legem et ea quae a me constituta sunt sequi volueris. quam rem tibi confido magnae laudi fore.* See the discussion of the passage in Marshall (1964), 209–215; cf. Badian 1965, 113–115; however, Díaz Fernández 2015, 208.
163 Cass.Dio 42.35.5; also Str. 14.6.6; cf. Marshall (1964), 207–208.
164 Str. 17.3.25; Cass.Dio 53.12.7.

who served in Italy. During his command in a province, the praetor or consul was practically a plenipotentiary agent upon whom each and every aspect of government associated with that *provincia* depended: responsibilities ranged from the maintenance of Roman power to the resolution of any legal problem and, of course as, the supervision of all fiscal activity. Many of these tasks were limited in practice (and legally), since a magistrate's experience conformed to a more or less clear administrative model. As the governors' main and closest assistants in the provinces, quaestors could also define and even augment their own competencies as the circumstances in the province dictated. In fact, provincial quaestors did not limit themselves to executing duties associated with management or financial administration, but expanded their functions to legal and even military matters, in accordance with the same principle of collaboration *ad ministeria belli* by means of which the quaestors were linked to their superiors.

Indeed, one feature that characterises the role played by quaestors in the provinces and distinguishes them from the majority of their colleagues based in Italy is the office's association with *imperium*. This relationship with military power was at times made explicit when a quaestor ended up holding that authority, which he received either through delegation from a superior or directly from the senate: such an arrangement conferred extensive powers on a quaestor, comparable, to a point, with those of the province's highest commander.[165] Accordingly, it was the quaestor who would assume command of the province if the governor was absent. Apart from the praetor or consul, the quaestor was ultimately the only Roman magistrate present in a province, which automatically made him the second highest authority there. The power and responsibility that a quaestor could potentially yield is even clearer in those cases in which a quaestor was assigned an overseas *provincia* alone, as sometimes occurred in Cyrene or Cyprus at the end of the Republic; in those cases, the quaestor was simply Rome's most senior representative in that place. This was how a quaestor could come to discharge a series of duties that covered all areas of government associated with the command of the provinces. Needless to say, this greatly increased a quaestor's responsibility beyond the tasks with which his office was usually endowed.

Financial responsibilities

We cannot overlook the fact that financial matters constituted the majority of the duties allocated to quaestors, including those who found themselves in the provinces. In this respect, the kind of tasks that overseas quaestors discharged did not essentially differ from those undertaken by their colleagues in Italy. In his analysis of Roman institutions, Polybius undeniably attributes to quaestors the leading role in

---

165 Lintott 1999, 136; Johnston 2008, 8–10.

managing a consul's economic resources for his campaign (i.e. the command of a *provincia*). Polybius indicates that the senate assigned public funds to the consuls to be handled at their own discretion (ἐξουσίαν δ' ἔχουσι καὶ δαπανᾶν τῶν δημοσίων ὅσα προθεῖντο), and it appears that the quaestors were in charge of administering those funds, always under the orders of the consul (παρεπομένου ταμίου καὶ πᾶν τὸ προσταχθὲν ἑτοίμως ποιοῦντος).[166] Although Polybius only speaks of the role undertaken by the quaestors in the service of the consuls, we should assume that essentially the same mechanism applied in the case of praetors sent overseas, who were also given a sum of money and troops. This sum included, in principle, the money required to pay the Roman soldiers, a fund that the quaestors also managed. This is what Polybius suggests when he says that the Roman troops' salaries were administered by the quaestors, who deducted from their wages the sum required to maintain and clothe them and eventually to repair their arms.[167]

Apparently, once the quaestor received his task *ex senatus consulto* and was assigned to a consul or praetor, the quaestor received and then oversaw the transportation of the public money (*pecunia publica*), which the senate gave both to defray the expenses incurred during the command of the province and also to acquire any provisions needed to maintain the army. Polybius' account suggests that the quaestor used this money to supply the Roman troops in almost every respect: both in the payment of the soldiers' wages, as well as in their personal upkeep, usually represented by the purchase of grain. In his account of the Jugurthine War, however, Sallust records that the quaestor Cn. Octavius Ruso was the man who transported to Africa the *stipendium* of the soldiers, who had previously been sent to Numidia under the command of the consul Marius.[168] Whether Octavius Ruso was the quaestor sent to the province of Africa at that time or was the *quaestor urbanus* is something that we do not know with certainty (Marius' quaestor was still Sulla); the fact that he returned again to Rome after delivering the money to Africa and that he did so accompanying Bocchus' envoys, leads us to prefer the second option (see chapter 5). In this case, Sallust's evidence reveals that, under certain circumstances, the urban quaestors could also be dispatched to the provinces with the *stipendium* for the troops stationed there.

In addition to administering the public funds granted by the senate, the quaestor was also in charge of accumulating all the resources and provisions that the Roman army might have needed in their province, especially in terms of foodstuffs. Sallust, for example, remarks that Sextius (probably C. Sextius Calvinus), L. Calpurnius Bestia's quaestor (111), was sent by the consul to the city of Vaga in Numidia where he

---

166 Pol. 6.12.8; cf. 6.13.2; cf. Walbank 1970, 677–678.
167 Pol. 6.39.15.
168 Sall. *Iug.* 104.3; Broughton MRR, 1.556; on the concept of *stipendium* in the Republic, cf. Ñaco del Hoyo 2003, 28–56.

was to collect the grain that Jugurtha's envoys had promised to pay the Romans.[169] A passage in Plutarch records that, some years earlier, in 129, the Numidian king Micipsa had sent cereal to Sardinia out of regard for C. Sempronius Gracchus, then quaestor to the consul L. Aurelius Orestes on the island, which suggests that it was possibly the quaestor who requested these supplies from the Numidian king.[170] It was not, however, always a question of obtaining food: indeed, Caius Gracchus' powers of persuasion also allowed the Romans to collect clothes from a series of provincial cities for the soldiers who wintered in Sardinia, despite the complaints that the Sardinians initially made to the senate about L. Aurelius Orestes' requisitions.[171]

Far from being limited to managing the resources assigned to them, therefore, quaestors also had the responsibility of obtaining all kinds of additional resources for Roman troops, whether by hook or crook. Usually, as was the case with Caius Gracchus, the province's inhabitants subsidized the acquisition of these provisions, since they were obliged to make all kinds of contributions to the Roman authorities. Given his responsibility for financial management, the quaestor also had to oversee the efficient extraction of tribute in his province. Some reports indicate that quaestors were somehow involved in the provincial tax system, but we do not know to what extent this was the case. According to a passage in Cicero, for example, until the consulate of L. Octavius and C. Aurelius Cotta (75), it was the quaestors in Sicily who sold the *decuma* of wine, oil, and grain to the companies of *publicani* which later collected these products; starting in 75, however, the senate allowed the consuls to make such arrangements in Rome.[172] In fact, although the presence of two quaestors in Sicily was possibly only occasional, that circumstance seems to be linked to the increased taxes that Rome demanded from the island, for which the quaestor was possibly also responsible.

During his term in Cilicia as legate and proquaestor to Cn. Cornelius Dolabella, Verres extracted a series of cash payments in lieu of cereal and clothing from certain communities in Asia. All indications suggest that these were isolated requisitions rather than tribute per se.[173] In any case, Cicero's testimony makes it clear that it

---

[169] Sall. *Iug.* 29.4 : *ceterum interea fidei causa mittitur a consule Sextius quaestor in oppidum Iugurthae Vagam. Quoius rei species erat acceptio frumenti, quod Calpurnius palam legatis imperaverat, quoniam deditionis mora indutiae agitabantur.*
[170] Plut. *C.Gr.* 2.2–3; see below.
[171] Plut. *C.Gr.* 2.2–3: ἰσχυροῦ δὲ καὶ νοσώδους ἅμα χειμῶνος ἐν Σαρδόνι γενομένου, καὶ τοῦ στρατηγοῦ τὰς πόλεις ἐσθῆτα τοῖς στρατιώταις αἰτοῦντος, ἔπεμψαν εἰς Ῥώμην παραιτούμενοι. δεξαμένης δὲ τῆς βουλῆς τὴν παραίτησιν αὐτῶν καὶ τὸν στρατηγὸν ἄλλοθεν ἀμφιέζειν τοὺς στρατιώτας κελευούσης, ἀπορούντος δ' ἐκείνου καὶ τῶν στρατιωτῶν κακοπαθούντων, ἐπελθὼν τὰς πόλεις ὁ Γάιος αὐτοὺς ἀφ' ἑαυτῶν ἔπεισεν ἐσθῆτα πέμψαι καὶ βοηθῆσαι τοῖς Ῥωμαίοις; cf. Ñaco del Hoyo 2003, 104; 229.
[172] Cic. *Verr.* 2.3.18: *L. Octavio et C. Cottae consulibus senatus permisit ut vini et olei decumas et frugum minutarum, quas ante quaestores in Sicilia vendere consuessent, Romae venderent, legemque his rebus quam ipsis videretur dicerent*; cf. Ñaco del Hoyo 2003, 241–248.
[173] Cic. *Verr.* 2.1.95–96.

was Verres, as [pro]quaestor, who initiated the requisition of this money. A passage from Plutarch points out that L. Licinius Lucullus, Sulla's quaestor during the Mithridatic War, was also charged with seizing the twenty thousand talents that the dictator demanded from the populations of Asia as damages for their support of Mithridates. Apparently, the quaestor undertook this task with great honesty and restraint, to the provincials' utter relief.[174] A series of inscriptions from Asia are preserved, in which Lucullus is celebrated as proquaestor (ἀντιταμίας), with titles such as εὐεργέτης, πάτρων and σωτήρ, perhaps bestowed because of his amenable disposition towards the provincial communities during the collection of taxes.[175] The same reasons seem to lie behind the fact that certain *pagi stipendiariei* from Africa (that is, communities liable for the payment of *stipendium*) paid homage to the quaestor Q. Numerius Rufus with a statue,[176] a fact that seems to indicate that the quaestors undeniably played a central role in the tax administration of some provinces. Given that tax requirements could vary significantly between one province and another, it may be assumed that the quaestors' role in these matters could also vary greatly between one province and another.

When necessary, quaestors also had the option of minting money in the province, either to supplement the soldiers' wages, to pay for an expense or fund an operation. In fact, we have many coins minted by quaestors in their provinces, the majority of which appear to have financed expenses that arose during conflict: for example, the series issued by the quaestor Aesillas (q. ca. 95–94) in Macedonia, where the Roman governors engaged in frequent battles against the Thracians, or the coins minted by Fabius Hispaniensis and C. Tarquitius, quaestors to Caius Annius in Hispania, during the Sertorian War.[177] Plutarch stresses that L. Licinius Lucullus issued so much money minted in the Peloponnese during the Mithridatic War that the coins came to be called 'Lucullan' (Λευκόλλειον) and remained in use for a long time among the soldiers.[178] As the evidence provided by Plutarch suggests, the main purpose of the coins issued by provincial quaestors was to pay the soldiers' stipendium during periods of military activity. Even so, the work by Frey-Kupper on the coinage issued in Sicily in the late second century (possibly during the Slaves

---

174 Plut. *Luc.* 4.1: ἐπεὶ δὲ συνθηκῶν γενομένων Μιθριδάτης μὲν ἀπέπλευσεν εἰς τὸν Εὔξεινον πόντον, Σύλλας δὲ τὴν Ἀσίαν δισμυρίοις τάλαντοις ἐζημίωσε.
175 MAMA 4.52: ὁ δῆμος/ Λεύκιον / Λικίννιον / Λευκίου / υἱὸν / Λεύκολλον / ἀντιταμίαν / πατρῶνα / καὶ / εὐεργέτην; cf. also IG 9.2.38; TAM 5.2.918 ; I. Ephesos 2941; IG 12.1.48; cf. Cic. *acad.* 1.1: *in Asiam quaestor profectus ibi per multos annos admirabili quam laude provinciae praefuit*; see also Plut. *Cim.* 2.2. Payne 1984, 256–258.
176 CIL I² 2513 = ILS 9482 = ILLRP 388: Q. *Numerio Q. f. Rufo q. stipendiariei pagorum Muxsi Gususi Zeugei*; Zucca 1994, 1446–1447.
177 Aesillas, in Head 1911, 240; Broughton MRR, 2.13. L. Fabius Hispaniensis and C. Tarquitius: Crawford RRC, 381–386 no. 366; Broughton MRR, 2.77; 3.86; 3.203; cf. Antela-Bernárdez 2012, 37–47.
178 Plut. *Luc.* 2.2: δι' ἐκείνου γὰρ ἐκόπη τὸ πλεῖστον ἐν Πελοποννήσῳ περὶ τὸν Μιθριδατικὸν πόλεμον, καὶ Λευκόλλειον ἀπ' ἐκείνου προσηγορεύθη καὶ διετέλεσεν ἐπὶ πλεῖστον, ὑπὸ τῶν στρατιωτικῶν χρειῶν ἐν τῷ πολέμῳ λαμβάνον ἀμοιβὴν ταχεῖαν. Marsura 2015, 43–59.

Wars) warns against identifying all the magistrates who issued coins in the provinces as quaestors.[179] As Frey-Kupper has shown, only two of the names attested in the Sicilian series (M'. Acilius and L. Alp[ius]) actually bear the Q that unmistakeably identifies them as quaestors. As a result, it is possible that the remaining names on the coins are associated with other offices besides the quaestorship (see the Prosopography).

Wherever the funds came from, the quaestor had to manage and record carefully all the sums of money handled by the Roman authorities during their provincial term. According to Cicero, when Verres obtained the *provincia Gallia ex senatus consulto* as quaestor under the command of the consul Cn. Papirius Carbo, he received a sum of money in cash (*pecunia attributa numerata est*) with which he travelled to Cisalpine Gaul to join the consular army (*profectus est quaestor in provinciam: venit exspectatus in Galliam ad exercitum consularem cum pecunia*).[180] Cicero indicates that this sum reached 2,235,417 sesterces, of which Verres assigned 1,635,417 sesterces for *stipendium*, the purchase of grain, the legates, the proquaestor (perhaps to square his predecessor's accounts?) and the *cohors praetoria* (*dedi stipendio, frumento, legatis, proquaestore, cohorti praetoriae HS mille sescenta triginta quinque milia quadrigentos decem et septem nummos*), while the remaining six hundred thousand sesterces were supposedly deposited in Ariminum.[181] According to Cicero, however, Verres never deposited this sum in Ariminum and he never transferred it to Carbo or Sulla; in fact, Cicero continues, he did not even deposit the money in the *aerarium* in the presence of the urban quaestors, P. Lentulus and C. Triarius. Instead, he kept this sizable sum for his own profit. In Cicero's opinion, Verres alleged that he had deposited the money in the city of Ariminum precisely in order to hide his embezzlement, since the city was sacked shortly afterwards by Sulla's army.[182]

Leaving aside for the moment Verres' possible reasons for depositing the sum in Ariminum, this Ciceronian passage sheds light on the destination of the part of the budget entrusted to a quaestor during his stay in a province: in addition to paying the abovementioned soldiers' *stipendium*, the quaestor had to deduct from the allocated money the cost of importing grain to feed the army and a series of unspecified expenditures incurred by the governors' associates and subordinates, such as legates and members of the *cohors praetoria*. In principle, it can be supposed that the latter largely corresponded to the subsistence costs of the governor's associates, budgeted apart from the costs of feeding the soldiers. A passage from Cicero's famous letter to his

---

[179] Frey-Kupper 2013, 248–253.
[180] Cic. *Verr.* 2.1.34 ; cf. Cuomo 2011, 184–185.
[181] Cic. *Verr.* 2.1.34–36.
[182] Cic. *Verr.* 2.1.36 : *Illa tamen HS sescenta milia, quae ne falso quidem potuit quibus data essent describere, quae se Arimini scribit reliquisse, quae ipsa HS sescenta milia reliqua facta sunt, neque Carbo attigit neque Sulla vidit neque in aerarium relata sunt. Oppidum sibi elegit Ariminum, quod tum, cum iste rationes referebat, oppressum direptumque erat: non suspicabatur, id quod nunc sentiet, satis multos ex illa calamitate Ariminensium testis nobis in hanc rem reliquos esse.*

brother Quintus during his command in Asia specifically alludes to the outlay that a governor and his companions would incur during their stay in a province, a matter that Cicero would re-emphasise in several of the letters that he sent to his friends from Cilicia.[183] Plutarch also alludes to the expenses both the governors and their companions habitually generated for the public treasury when he highlights M. Porcius Cato's moderation during his praetorship in Sardinia in 198. Apparently as praetor, Cato went so far as dramatically reducing subsistence costs.[184] According to Plutarch's testimony, it was common practice for provincial commanders to squander public money on accommodation expenses, such as tents, couches or clothing, not to mention expensive furnishings for banquets. Furthermore, officials were often accompanied by numerous servants and friends, which, understandably, significantly increased the strain on the public purse. A fragment of Sallust's *Historiae*, for example, records the expensive splendours lavished by the quaestor C. Urbinus and his inner circle upon Q. Caecilius Metellus Pius (cos. 80) during his proconsulship in Hispania Ulterior: presumably, such luxury was subsidized with public funds.[185]

The fact that Verres handed over a sum of public money to an unknown proquaestor raises further questions:[186] Cicero does not indicate the identity of the person in question, but it was quite possibly the quaestor who had served until then under the command of Cn. Papirius Carbo, who had been consul in 85.[187] As discussed above, Verres may have handed over a portion of the public money to this individual at the start of 84, so that he could square his accounts and settle any debts that had accrued during his term in Carbo's service, though this is only a possibility. In any case, in a letter that Cicero sent to Caninius Sallustius (q. 51?), proquaestor to M. Calpurnius Bibulus in Syria, the orator implies that he had asked Cicero (still proconsul in Cilicia) for a loan of a hundred thousand drachmas, which the orator refused to give him, on the grounds that all the money that Cicero had at his disposal in the province was either war booty that was in the hands of his prefects or part of the budget controlled by his quaestor (*omnis enim pecunia ita tractatur ut praeda a praefectis, quae autem mihi attributa est a quaestore curetur*).[188] Apparently, Caninius

---

183 Cic. *Q. fr.* 1.1.9–14. Also note the moderation shown by Cicero and his companions during their stay in Asia and Cilicia: cf. Cic. *Att.* 5.10.2; 5.16.3; 5.21.5.
184 Plut. *Cat.mai.* 6.2: ἐπαρχίαν δὲ λαβὼν Σαρδόνα, τῶν πρὸ αὐτοῦ στρατηγῶν εἰωθότων χρῆσθαι καὶ σκηνώμασι δημοσίοις καὶ κλίναις καὶ ἱματίοις, πολλῇ δὲ θεραπείᾳ καὶ φίλων πλήθει καὶ περὶ δεῖπνα δαπάναις καὶ παρασκευαῖς βαρυνόντων, ἐκεῖνος ἄπιστον ἐποίησε τὴν διαφορὰν τῆς εὐτελείας. δαπάνης μὲν γὰρ εἰς οὐδὲν οὐδεμιᾶς προσεδεήθη δημοσίας, ἐπεφοίτα δὲ ταῖς πόλεσιν αὐτὸς μὲν ἄνευ ζεύγους πορευόμενος, εἷς δ' ἠκολούθει δημόσιος, ἐσθῆτα καὶ σπονδεῖον αὐτῷ πρὸς ἱερουργίαν κομίζων; cf. Liv. 32.27.3–4: *Sardiniam M. Porcius Cato obtinebat, sanctus et innocens, asperior tamen in faenore coercendo habitus; fugatique ex insula faeneratores et sumptus quos in cultum praetorum socii facere soliti erant circumcisi aut sublati.*
185 Sall. *hist.* 2.70.1–4 M.; cf. Plut. *Sert.* 22.2–3.
186 Cic. *Verr.* 2.1.36.
187 Broughton MRR, 2.57.
188 Cic. *fam.* 2.17.4; cf. Shackleton Bailey 1977, 458–460.

Sallustius even asked Cicero for a copy of the accounts (*rationes*) of his quaestor, L. Mescinius Rufus, which the orator also flatly refused (*rationes mei quaestoris nec verum fuit me tibi mittere nec tamen erant confectae*). Despite Cicero's rejection, it seems clear that quaestors could authorise this sort of loan, possibly in order to settle the accounts from their terms in office: in fact, Cicero's letter indicates that Caninius Sallustius was at that time preparing the *rationes* for his stay in Syria.[189]

All the accounts kept by quaestors in their provinces had to be registered in their *tabulae publicae* and later presented in Rome (*rationes referre*).[190] Plutarch reveals the importance of these *rationes* and, more specifically, of the *tabulae publicae* in a passage about Ti. Sempronius Gracchus' quaestorship in Hispania Citerior in 137. Tiberius had the dubious fortune of being assigned as quaestor to the consul C. Hostilius Mancinus, undoubtedly one of the most scorned characters in Roman historiography due to his disastrous defeat and peace agreement with the Numantines. According to Plutarch, after the Numantines surrounded Mancinus' army and forced him to make peace on dishonourable terms (apparently negotiated by the quaestor, as we will see below)[191], Tiberius asked the Numantines to return some tablets (πινακίδες) that they had taken while sacking Mancinus' camp.[192] It seems that the tablets contained the records and accounts from Tiberius' administrative term (γράμματα καὶ λόγους ἔχουσαι τῆς ταμιευτικῆς ἀρχῆς), so their preservation was particularly important for the quaestor: in fact, Tiberius knew that if the tablets were lost, his political enemies could bring accusations against him and he would be unable to defend the accounts dating from his time in the province (ἐκκαλέσας δὲ τῶν Νομαντίνων τοὺς ἄρχοντας, ἠξίου κομίσασθαι τὰς δέλτους, ὡς μὴ παράσχοι τοῖς ἐχθροῖς διαβολήν, οὐκ ἔχων ἀπολογίσασθαι περὶ τῶν ᾠκονομημένων[193]). As an acknowledgement of the ties that the quaestor's father had with the Numantines, they returned Tiberius' tablets, while also demonstrating their courtesy.

Apart from other details, Plutarch demonstrates the particular importance of these public tablets for how a provincial term in office was later judged, since they were supposed to record all movements of funds resulting from the administra-

---

189 Cic. *fam.* 2.17.2: *De rationibus referendis, non erat incommodum te nullam referre, quam tibi scribis a Bibulo fieri potestatem; sed id vix mihi videris per legem Iuliam facere posse, quam Bibulus certa quadam ratione non servat, tibi magno opere servandam censeo.*
190 Apparently, these *tabulae* and *libri* are quoted in the *lex Acilia repetundarum* of ca. 123: cf. Crawford 1996, no. 1 (CIL I² 583), l. 34: *quai ita conquaesiverit, et sei qua tabulas libros leiterasve pop[licas preivatasve pos]cere proferrequ[e volet...]*; cf. Cic. *Font.* 2 (*eodem modo Hirtuleium dissolvisse publicae tabulae coarguunt*); Cic. *Verr.* 2.1.36; Fallu 1973b, 209–211; Berrendonner 2014, 178–179.
191 Plut. *Ti.Gr.* 5.1–4. See Broughton MRR, 1.84; Wikander 1976, 85–104; Rosenstein 1986, 230–252; Richardson 2000, 168–169; García Riaza 2002, 159–171.
192 Plut. *Ti.Gr.* 6.1–3; cf. 6.1–2: Τὰ δ' ἐν τῷ χάρακι λειφθέντα χρήματα πάντα κατέσχον οἱ Νομαντῖνοι καὶ διεπόρθησαν. ἐν δὲ τούτοις καὶ πινακίδες ἦσαν τοῦ Τιβερίου, γράμματα καὶ λόγους ἔχουσαι τῆς ταμιευτικῆς ἀρχῆς, ἃς περὶ πολλοῦ ποιούμενος ἀπολαβεῖν, ἤδη τοῦ στρατοῦ προκεχωρηκότος, ἀνέστρεψε πρὸς τὴν πόλιν, ἔχων μεθ' ἑαυτοῦ τρεῖς ἢ τέτταρας ἑταίρους.
193 Plut. *Ti.Gr.* 6.2.

tion of the province, especially the use of public funds that the senate had granted. When he lost his tablets, Plainly, Tiberius's fear shows how the disappearance of accounts could arouse immediate mistrust among the Roman public (especially among the political class) and lead to the suspicion that a quaestor might have diverted some of the public money for himself. We should not forget that quaestors had to submit these tablets to the senate and urban quaestors to be inspected. Accordingly, their loss could become to be a serious problem when it came to justifying the sums of money that had been disbursed. The accounting books, furthermore, could be requested as evidence in a trial: Cicero, for example, recalls that P. Albius (q. 120) had to present his *tabulae* in the trial *de repetundis* against Q. Mucius Scaevola Augur for his term of office in Asia, although it seems that the judges dismissed the documents in this case.[194]

According to Cicero's discussion of a certain *lex Iulia*, once their term of office was over, the governor and his quaestor had to agree on the *rationes* and deposit two copies of their ledgers in two cities within their province (*ut confectas rationes lege Iulia apud duas civitates possem relinquere*).[195] A third copy had to be presented to the senate and the urban quaestors for approval and subsequent registration in the *aerarium* (*quoniam lege Iulia relinquere rationes in provincia necesse erat easdemque totidem verbis referre ad aerarium*),[196] where the quaestor had to deposit any leftover money as well as all additional sums or goods obtained during his stay in the province.[197] Cicero, for example, deposited the *rationes* of his proconsulate in Apamea and Laodicea, as he had agreed with his quaestor, L. Mescinius Rufus, since they were the most important cities in Cilicia. This implies that the decision was left to the governor and quaestor's judgment and that the chosen cities were not always the same: *illud quidem certe factum est quod lex iubebat, ut apud duas civitates, Laodicensem et Apamensem, quae nobis maxime videbantur quoniam ita necesse erat, rationes confectas collatas deponeremus*.[198] Likewise, the fact that Verres deposited the money that was left over after his stewardship in the service of Cn. Papirius Carbo in Ariminum suggests that quaestors also deposited his *rationes* in the same

---

194 Cic. *de orat.* 2.281; Alexander 1990, no. 32; on the use of these *tabulae* in trials *de repetundis*, cf. Cic. *Font.* 3: *Nemo, nemo, inquam, iudices, reperietur qui unum se in quaestura M. Fonteio nummum dedisse, aut illum ex ea pecunia quae pro aerario solveretur detraxisse dicat; nullius in tabulis ulla huius furti significatio, nullum in eis nominibus intertrimenti aut deminutionis vestigium reperietur*; Scaur. 18; *Att.* 1.16.4; Val.Max. 2.10.1. See Fallu 1973b, 209–213.
195 Cic. *Att.* 6.7.2.
196 Cic. *fam.* 5.20.2; 2.17.2; cf. 2.17.4: *rationes mei quaestoris nec verum fuit me tibi mittere nec tamen erant confectae. Eas nos Apameae deponere cogitabamus*; *Att.* 6.7.2: *ego Laodiceae quaestorem Mescinium exspectare iussi, ut confectas rationes lege Iulia apud duas civitates possem relinquere*. Sources for the *lex Iulia de pecuniis repetundis*: Broughton MRR, 2.188; cf. also Cic. *Rab. Post.* 8; 12; *Vat.* 29; *Sest.* 135. Fallu 1973b, 211–213; Gruen 1974, 239–241; Lintott 1981b, 202–207; Berrendonner 2014, 183–187.
197 See Cic. *Verr.* 2.1.57; *Font.* 3.
198 Cic. *fam.* 5.20.2; cf. 2.17.4.

place. Given that Ariminum was in effect one of the main bases for Roman operations in Cisalpine Gaul,[199] it actually appears quite logical for Verres to have chosen that city to deposit both the unspent money from his term as well as a copy of his accounts; this, of course, did not stop Cicero from levelling accusations of corruption against his opponent. In the majority of cases, however, we do not know the names of the cities in which governors used to deposit their accounts.

While we do not know with certainty to which Julian law Cicero refers in his letters, scholars have assumed that it is the *lex Iulia de repetundis* published during Caesar's consulship in 59.[200] Furthermore, we do not even know if the requirement of depositing the *rationes* in two different cities and of submitting a copy in the *aerarium* was first imposed by that law from 59 or, alternatively, if it was already an established custom. In fact, as Cicero says in a letter to his quaestor, L. Mescinius Rufus, tradition (*mos*) dictated that the governor should render accounts of his provincial command in conjunction with the quaestor (*dein, si rationum referendarum ius vetus et mos antiquus maneret, me relaturum rationes nisi tecum pro coniunctione nostrae necessitudinis contulissem confecissemque non fuisse*).[201] The governor, therefore, shared with the quaestor the responsibility of presenting an appropriately detailed and substantiated financial statement in Rome, but this was not always an easy task: for example, Cicero's abovementioned letter reveals the mistrust that existed in this case between the orator and his quaestor. According to the contents of the letter, it seems that Rufus had asked Cicero to explain a series of dubious accounts, responsibility for which (at least according to the quaestor) fell upon Cicero's *scriba*, M. Tullius. Ostensibly, Cicero had limited himself to ratifying the budget produced by Rufus and M. Tullius; the *scriba* later delivered the *librum* containing the accounts to the proconsul (*ita accepi librum a meo scriba...*), while two copies were deposited in Laodicea and Apamea, pursuant to the *lex Iulia*.[202]

Cicero's quaestor, nevertheless, was not satisfied with some sections of the accounts, which could call his stewardship in Cilicia into serious question. The crux of the issue was rooted in three million sesterces, which one P. Valerius (possibly a representative of a *societas*) should have credited as *mancipes* ('purchaser') in order to be granted an unspecified public enterprise. However, this sum was never paid in full. Apparently, the matter also compromised some of the proconsul's associates in Cilicia, such as Q. Volusius (son-in-law of an Atticus' friend) and (per-

---

199 Ariminum is sometimes mentioned by Livy as a praetorian *provincia*: see Liv. 28.38.13: *tum praetoriae provinciae in sortem coniectae. Urbana Cn. Servilio obtigit, Ariminum—ita Galliam appellabant—Sp. Lucretio*; also 24.44.2–3; 30.1.9; 32.1.1–2; cf. 21.63.1–2; 27.7.11; Brennan 2000, 183.
200 Gruen 1974, 239–241.
201 Cic. *fam.* 5.20.1; cf. Fallu 1973b, 210–213.
202 Cic. *fam.* 5.20.1–4; Fallu 1973b, 217–223. On M. Tullius, Cuomo 2011, 196–198; David 2019, 167–168.

haps) his legate M. Anneius,²⁰³ possibly as guarantors of said enterprise. Cicero, however, claims that he had personally paid a large portion of the sum, while he had recorded the rest in his accounts (*erat enim curata nobis pecunia Valeri mancipis nomine, ex qua reliquum quod erat in rationibus rettuli*). He even goes on to remind Rufus that he, Cicero, was aware of each and every movement of funds.²⁰⁴

Cicero also refers to certain money which was handed over to Pompey and P. Sestius (his successor in Cilicia), in this case as a deposit made by the quaestor himself (*qua pecunia Pompeius est usus, ut ea quam tu deposueras Sestius*), although it seems that this transfer was made with the agreement of the proconsul and in accordance with a *senatus consultum*.²⁰⁵ Cicero gives us no further details on the subject, but it is likely that this deposit was part of the mandatory process of handing over the provincial command and that, therefore, it was a sum left in Cilicia to be managed by P. Sestius during his term in office.²⁰⁶ In a letter to Atticus dated October 50 after his term in Cilicia had ended, Cicero points out that he decided to return to the *aerarium* around a million sesterces of the annual budget granted by decree and hand over a year's allowance to C. Coelius Caldus, the quaestor left in Cilicia after his departure from the province (*ex annuo sumptu qui mihi decretus esset me C. Coelio quaestori relinquere annuum, referre in aerarium ad HS <M>*). As was to be expected, the members of his *cohors* were not pleased with this decision, since they thus lost the opportunity to divide up funds that remained—much to their chagrin—in the province.²⁰⁷

Returning to Cicero's letter to L. Mescinius Rufus, the orator's words give us a glimpse of Rufus' fear, when faced with the prospect that the possible irregularities perpetrated by his proconsul could damage his own reputation and, ultimately, implicate him in an extortion trial in Rome. In the end, as quaestor, Rufus had to present the accounts of his administration in Cilicia before the senate (the quaestor could even render accounts of his stewardship in the absence of his superior²⁰⁸),

---

203 Cic. *fam.* 5.20.4: *sed sic me et liberalitatis fructu privas et diligentiae et, quod minime tamen laboro, mediocris etiam prudentiae: liberalitatis, quod mavis scribae mei beneficio quam meo legatum meum <M. Anneium> praefectumque, Q. Leptam, maxima calamitate levatos, cum praesertim non deberent esse obligati*; Q. Volusius: *Att.* 5.21.6; Broughton MRR, 2.254; cf. Muñiz Coello 1998, 206–213.
204 Cic. *fam.* 5.20.3.
205 Cic. *fam.* 5.20.5 ; Fallu 1973b, 223–226.
206 See Fallu 1973b, 223–225.
207 Cic. *Att.* 7.1.6: *cum enim hoc rectum et gloriosum putarem, ex annuo sumptu qui mihi decretus esset me C. Coelio quaestori relinquere annuum, referre in aerarium ad HS <M>, ingemuit nostra cohors, omne illud putans distribui sibi oportere, ut ego amicior invenirer Phrygum et Cilicum aerariis quam nostro*.
208 Cic. *Verr.* 2.1.98–99: *Audistis quaestoriam rationem, tribus versiculis relatam; legationis, non nisi condemnato et eiecto eo qui posset reprehendere; nunc denique praeturae, quam ex senatus consulto statim referre debuit, usque ad hoc tempus non rettulit. Quaestorem se in senatu exspectare dixit, proinde quasi non, ut quaestor sine praetore possit rationem referre,—ut tu, Hortensi, ut omnes—eodem modo sine quaestore praetor.*

so it could be assessed whether or not he had perpetrated any irregularity. In fact, we know that quaestors, like governors themselves, also exploited their tenures in provinces for their own advantage, either by misappropriating funds (as Verres supposedly did during his quaestorship under Cn. Papirius Carbo) or by using their time in the province to get involved in all kinds of business schemes. For example, in some of Cicero's letters in which he requests the support of a quaestor for particular enterprises that certain individuals (usually equites and members of *societates*) ran, we see how quaestors could also partake in opportunities for their own enrichment.[209]

We know, for example, that Verres did not hesitate to take advantage of his tenure in Cilicia to make money once the praetor Cn. Cornelius Dolabella named him proquaestor after the death of the quaestor, C. Malleolus (q. 80).[210] It seems that during his term Malleolus had devoted himself to advancing money to the province's towns and had made them sign promissory notes (*praeterea pecunias occuparat apud populos et syngraphas fecerat*), investments that, like his substantial personal wealth, passed into the hands of Verres when he became proquaestor. Verres conveniently exploited the windfall for his own personal gain.[211] But his greed did not stop there: first as legate and later as proquaestor, Verres looted Asia and burdened the inhabitants of Cilicia with excessive levies of wheat and money. Apparently, Dolabella, whom the legate blamed for all the abuses committed in the province during his famous trial in Rome, was also in on the scheme.[212] As a result, Dolabella was punished with a fine of three million sesterces, since he was ultimately responsible for the actions taken in his province, even though the majority of the excesses had been committed (according to Cicero) directly by Verres: *te haec coegisse, te aestimasse, tibi pecuniam numeratam esse dico, eademque vi et iniuria, cum pecunias max-*

---

209 See Cic. *fam.* 13.9 (Furius Crassipes in Bithynia); 13.45 (P.? Appuleius in Asia); cf. also 13.48 (C. Sextilius Rufus in Cyprus). An inscription from Aigion shows the *Italicei quei Aegei negotiantur* honouring the quaestor P. Rutilius Nudus (ILLRP 370); the inscription suggests that, as quaestor in Macedonia (ca. 87?), Rutilius Nudus collaborated in one way or another with these *negotiatores*; Broughton MRR, 3.182. See also SIG³ 745 = ILLRP 369.
210 Broughton MRR, 2.81.
211 Cic. *Verr.* 2.1.91–92.
212 See the sources in Alexander 1990, no. 135. See Cic. *Verr.* 2.1.41: *Nam quae in ipsum valebant crimina contulit in illum, causamque illius omnem ad inimicos accusatoresque detulit; ipse in eum cui legatus, cui pro quaestore fuerat, inimicissimum atque improbissimum testimonium dixit. Ille miser cum esset Cn. Dolabella,—cum proditione istius nefaria, tum improbo ac falso eiusdem testimonio,—tum multo ex maxima parte istius furtorum ac flagitiorum invidia conflagravit*; 2.1.95–97; cf. 95: *pro quaestore vero quo modo iste commune Milyadum vexarit, quo modo Lyciam, Pamphyliam, Pisidiam Phrygiamque totam frumento imperando, aestimando, hac sua, quam tum primum excogitavit, Siciliensi aestimatione adflixerit, non est necesse demonstrare verbis: hoc scitote, [his nominibus—quae res per hunc gestae sunt] cum iste civitatibus frumentum, coria, cilicia, saccos imperaret, neque ea sumeret proque iis rebus pecuniam exigeret—his nominibus solis Cn. Dolabellae HS ad triciens litem esse aestimatam. Quae omnia, etiamsi voluntate Dolabellae fiebant, per istum tamen omnia gerebantur.*

imas cogeres per omnis partis provinciae te tamquam aliquam calamitosam tempestatem pestemque pervasisse demonstro.[213]

Even more striking is the case of C. Furius Aculeo, quaestor to the consul L. Cornelius Scipio Asiaticus (cos. 190) during the war against Antiochus III in Asia.[214] According to Livy who follows Valerius Antias' account, Furius Aculeo was found guilty alongside Scipio Asiaticus and the legate Aulus Hostilius Cato under the *rogatio Petillia* on the charge of *peculatus* ('misappropriation of money').[215] Apparently, they had taken large sums from Antiochus, who then asked them to advocate for a more advantageous peace deal after the battle of Magnesia: specifically, Furius Aculeo had retained a hundred and thirty pounds of gold and another two hundred of silver, while Scipio had supposedly received six thousand pounds of gold and four hundred and eighty of silver, none of which was handed over to the *aerarium*.[216]

What is undeniable is that the behaviour of quaestors did not always comply with the administrative obligations of the office, regardless of whether they could count on their superiors' acquiescence. The quaestor and his commander did not always collude when it came to committing financial crimes: P. Oppius, quaestor to the consul M. Aurelius Cotta (cos. 74) in Bithynia, was denounced and expelled from the province by the latter 'because of bribery and suspicion of conspiracy' (τοῦ γοῦν Κόττου τοῦ Μάρκου τὸν μὲν ταμίαν Πούπλιον Ὄππιον ἐπί τε δώροις καὶ ἐπὶ ὑποψίᾳ ἐπιβουλῆς ἀποπέμψαντος), according to Cassius Dio.[217] A passage in Quintilian furnishes some more details: Oppius was accused of having appropriated particular resources intended to maintain the army and of trying to bribe the soldiers (*obicitur Oppio quod de militum cibariis detraxerit: asperum crimen, sed id contrarium ostendit Cicero, quia idem accusatores obiecerint Oppio quod is voluerit exercitum largiendo corrumpere*).[218] This demonstrates that the quaestors were not always choirboys who were unfamiliar with corruption in the provinces. So much is also indicated by the laments of C. Asinius Pollio, governor of Hispania Ulterior, over the questionable management of money by his quaestor, L. Cornelius Balbus, during his term in that province (ca. 44–43).[219]

Despite Cicero's indignation over Verres' disloyalty displayed during the trial against Dolabella, this is not the only case in which we find a quaestor denouncing

---

213 Cic. *Verr.* 2.1.96: cf. 2.1.98–102.
214 Sources in Broughton MRR, 1.356.
215 Liv. 38.55.1–13.
216 Liv. 38.55.5–7: *Scipio et A. Hostilius legatus et C. Furius damnati: quo commodior pax Antiocho daretur, Scipionem sex milia pondo auri, quadringenta octoginta argenti plus accepisse, quam in aerarium retulerit, A. Hostilium octoginta pondo auri, argenti quadringenta tria, Furium quaestorem auri pondo centum triginta, argenti ducenta.*
217 Cass.Dio 36.40.3.
218 Quint. *inst.* 5.13.17; cf. Sall. *hist.* 3.59; McGushin 1994, 102–103. See also Shatzman 1972, 197–198.
219 Cic. *fam.* 10.32.1: *Balbus quaestor magna numerata pecunia, magno pondere auri, maiore argenti coacto de publicis exactionibus, ne stipendio quidem militibus reddito duxit se a Gadibus et triduum tempestate retentus ad Calpem Kal. Iun. Traiecit sese in regnum Bogudis plane bene peculiatus.*

or testifying against his superior for wrongful conduct in a province. When he reproached Q. Caecilius Niger (one of Verres' quaestors) for having the presumption of taking over the prosecution against Verres in the trial for his term in Sicily, Cicero mentions several examples of quaestors who attempted to denounce their superiors after their term in a province, an action which constituted a violation of the close connection (*necessitudo*) that bound a quaestor to his commander: *neque fere umquam venit in contentionem de accusando qui quaestor fuisset, quin repudiaretur. Itaque neque L. Philoni in C. Servilium nominis deferendi potestas est data, neque M. Aurelio Scauro in L. Flaccum, neque Cn. Pompeio in T. Albucium; quorum nemo propter indignitatem repudiatus est, sed ne libido violandae necessitudinis auctoritate iudicum comprobaretur.*[220] We will return to this point later.

Apart from the duties already discussed, one of the most important tasks quaestors could undertake in the provinces was to inventory and manage the valuables obtained there and subsequently to deposit them in the *aerarium* in Rome (see chapter 5). It is significant that the only thing that we know of the abovementioned Q. Fabius, the first quaestor attested in a province under the command of a praetor, was that he was tasked with transporting to the *aerarium* a portion of the spoils obtained during campaigns undertaken by the proconsul L. Manlius Acidinus (pr. 188) in Hispania Citerior in 186.[221] Discussing Acidinus' request for a triumph (the senate later authorised the celebration of an *ovatio*), Livy recounts that during the *ovatio*, the proconsul brought *coronas aureas quinquaginta duas, auri praeterea pondo centum triginta duo, argenti sedecim milia trecenta* as well as the *decem milia pondo argenti et octoginta auri* which, according to his declaration in the senate, the quaestor Q. Fabius had to deposit in the *aerarium* once he returned to Rome.[222]

As stewards of the financial aspects of provincial administration, quaestors were effectively responsible for keeping track of war spoils or any other material assets that Romans acquired by 'right of conquest'. Despite Livy's silence, Q. Fabius possibly had to inventory all the goods that L. Manlius Acidinus obtained during his campaigns in Hispania Citerior, regardless of whether or not Acidinus personally transported part of this booty to Rome. When M. Claudius Marcellus' troops took Syracuse in 211, Livy indicates that a quaestor was sent immediately to the island of Nassos with troops (*cum praesidio*) to take possession of Hieron's royal treasury and safeguard it, while the Roman troops devoted themselves to sacking the city.[223] Only two years later, in 209, it would also be a quaestor, C. Flaminius, who remained in charge of the booty taken by Scipio after the capture of Carthago Nova.[224] Livy points out that the considerable amount of gold and silver pieces that the Roman troops

---

[220] Cic. *div. in Caec.* 63; cf. Badian 1957, 332; Thompson 1962a, Thompson 1962a, 350–355.
[221] Liv. 39.29.7.
[222] Liv. 39.29.5–7; Broughton MRR, 1.373; cf. 1.366. Richardson 1986, 117–121.
[223] Liv. 25.31.8: *inde quaestor cum praesidio ad Nassum ad accipiendam pecuniam regiam custodiendamque missus*; cf. Prag 2007b, 291.
[224] Liv. 26.47.1–10; Broughton MRR, 1.286.

seized in this case was presented to the *imperator* Scipio, before being weighed and inventoried by Flaminius (*haec omnia C. Flaminio quaestori appensa adnumerataque sunt*), who in all likelihood also recorded in his accounts the grain confiscated and, perhaps, the immense arsenal of arms and ships captured from the Carthaginians.²²⁵ We could even wonder whether the detailed account of assets given by Livy—not only in this case, but in others as well—could perhaps be based on the actual accounts that the quaestors compiled at the conclusion of their terms in office and later deposited in the *aerarium*.

As in the case of Fabius, it was possibly Flaminius who brought the booty (or a part of it) to Rome in order to deposit it in the *aerarium*. As the example of Acidinus demonstrates, however, the commanders themselves could also transport the spoils acquired during their commands: in the case of Cicero, it seems that the proconsul himself personally oversaw the transport of public funds to Rome, regardless of the fact that his quaestor also had to register all the sums generated in his ledgers and then deposit those documents in the *aerarium*. Cicero even accepted guarantors in Laodicea for the amount of money that would be transferred to Rome (*Laodiceae me praedes accepturum arbitror omnis pecuniae publicae...*) in an attempt to insure the value and avoid the dangers of transit.²²⁶ Apparently, the *pecunia publica* that Cicero was to deposit in the *aerarium* was composed both of the money left over from the allocated budget (possibly those million sesterces mentioned above) and also of the spoils from his campaigns.²²⁷ In one of his letters to Atticus, the orator recalls that he gave his soldiers all the booty obtained when Pindenissus was taken, except for the prisoners, who were sold as slaves over the following days.²²⁸ Despite Cicero's silence, it may be assumed that it was his quaestor, L. Mescinius Rufus, who oversaw the sale of those slaves, most likely at auction; the profits of the sale reached no less than a hundred and twenty thousand sesterces.²²⁹

As the sources demonstrate, it was traditionally the quaestor who oversaw the sale (usually at auction) of the goods obtained as a result of a campaign, in order to convert the spoils (*praeda*) into liquid assets (*manubiae*) which were deposited in the public coffers in Rome:²³⁰ Gellius explicitly indicates so much when clarifying that *manubiae* means 'not booty, but money collected from the sale of the booty by a quaestor of the Roman people' (*manubiae enim sunt, sicuti iam dixi, non praeda, sed*

---

225 Liv. 26.47.8.
226 Cic. *fam.* 2.17.4; cf. the case of Q. Servilius Caepio (cos. 106) who lost the booty from his victory at Tolosa under compromising circumstances, while transporting it to Massilia: Cic. *nat. deor.* 3.74; Iust. 32.3.9 – 11; *vir.ill.* 73.5; Gell. 3.9.7; Oros. 5.15.25; Str. 4.1.13; see Alexander 1990, no. 65.
227 Cic. *fam.* 2.17.4.
228 Cic. *Att.* 5.20.5: *hilara sane Saturnalia militibus quoque, quibus exceptis <captivis> reliquam praedam concessimus*.
229 Cic. *Att.* 5.20.5.
230 See García Morcillo 2005, 41–48.

pecunia per quaestorem populi Romani ex praeda vendita contracta).²³¹ That is possibly why the *hasta* (spear) appears in certain coins minted by quaestors, since they wielded them during this kind of sale.²³² It is possible, furthermore, that Q. Fabius, L. Manlius Acidinus' quaestor, returned to Rome after his superior for the simple reason that he had to remain in Hispania to finish auctioning off the assets acquired in the war against the Celtiberians and then complete his *rationes*; in this case, it is possible that the ten thousand pounds of silver and eighty of gold (*decem milia pondo argenti et octoginta auri*) that Fabius apparently deposited in the *aerarium* corresponded—at least in part—to the sale of the booty that had Acidinus captured, but other options cannot be dismissed.²³³

The essentially financial nature of the tasks traditionally perceived as belonging to quaestors (both in Italy and also in the provinces) certainly made them the most suitable magistrates for confiscating and selling wealth abroad. As pointed out above, Livy comments that it was a quaestor (whose name is unknown) who took charge of the treasury of Hieron when M. Claudius Marcellus took Syracuse in 211.²³⁴ We have also seen in this chapter that when the Romans decided to take possession of the kingdom of Cyrene, which Ptolemy Apion had left to the Roman people years earlier, they sent the quaestor P. Cornelius Lentulus Marcellinus to Cyrenaica. Among other activities, Marcellinus might have confiscated the royal treasury before inventorying and then selling it at auction, with the intention of replenishing the funds of the ailing public coffers in Rome.²³⁵ In that very year, 74, word spread that Nicomedes IV Philopator, who was king of Bithynia, had also bequeathed his kingdom to the Roman people in his will.²³⁶ According to a passage in Festus, a certain Q. Pompeius, called *Bithynicus*, was sent to Bithynia in order to transport the royal assets to Rome, (*quod signum Pompeius Bithynicus ex Bithynia supellectilis regiae Romam deportavit*).²³⁷ It is not known whether this Pompeius was quaestor to M. Junius Juncus, proconsul of Asia (75–74), who intervened immediately in Bithynia once the death of Nicomedes became known,²³⁸ or if he was sent directly from Rome *ex senatus consulto* for this particular mission.²³⁹ It should be borne in mind that the abovementioned P. Cornelius Lentulus Marcellinus was sent that same

---

231 Gell. 13.25.29; cf. Shatzman 1972, 179–188.
232 See Longpérier 1868, Schäfer 1989, Ryan 2015.
233 Liv. 39.29.7. Ñaco del Hoyo 2003, 153–154.
234 Liv. 25.31.8.
235 Sall. *hist.* 2.43 M.
236 Liv. *per.* 93: *Nicomedes, Bithyniae rex, populum R. fecit heredem, regnumque eius in provinciae formam redactum est*; Sall. *hist.* 4.69.9 M.; Eutr. 6.6.1; App. *Mith.* 71; Magie 1950, 302–320; 1200–1201, n. 49; Kallet-Marx 1995, 299–302; Díaz Fernández 2015, 209–211.
237 Fest. p. 320 Lindsay. Brennan 2000, 879, n. 276; Ballesteros Pastor 2009, 127–133; Díaz Fernández 2015, 476–477; 562, n. 232.
238 Vell. 2.42.3; cf. Gell. 5.13.6; Plut. *Caes.* 2.3. On M. Junius Juncus' proconsulship, cf. Magie 1950, 1201–1202, n. 51; Brennan 2000, 559–561; Díaz Fernández 2015, 209, n. 418; 454–455.
239 Kunkel and Wittmann 1995, 360, n. 210.

year expressly to Cyrene with an apparently similar aim. Perhaps the something similar occurred with Q. Pompeius Bithynicus.

In any case, it seems clear that both P. Lentulus Marcellinus and Q. Pompeius were tasked with appropriating the royal treasuries and, therefore, with writing their inventories and transferring them to Rome, as Festus suggests when speaking of Q. Pompeius' mission in Bithynia. In neither of these cases is there evidence that the quaestors sold off the royal heritage; it is likely, however, that at least a part of the treasure was auctioned and converted into liquid assets. According to Plutarch, during his mission in Cyprus (58), M. Porcius Cato minutely inventoried Ptolemy's assets with the intention of fetching the maximum profit from the sale of the royal furnishings (like beakers, tables, jewels and purple clothing) and hence converting the property into cash at auction (ἣν ἔδει πραθεῖσαν ἐξαργυρισθῆναι).[240] To that end, Plutarch adds, Cato personally supervised both the inventory as well as the sale of the assets, while keeping those who were accustomed to participate in this type of operation (such as criers, friends, assistants of the governor himself) at an arm's length in order to prevent any embezzlement. As a result, Cato enraged those around him.[241] Despite the lack of information on the subject, it is likely that the missions undertaken by P. Lentulus Marcellinus and Q. Pompeius in Cyrene and Bithynia were similar to Cato's. Consequently, the majority of the property belonging to Ptolemy Apion and Nicomedes Philopator was likely sold as well, just like Ptolemy of Cyprus' assets. It is probable, furthermore, that the treasury of Attalus III of Pergamum met the same fate after the king's death in 133, in which case it could also have been a quaestor who was tasked with managing the Attalid assets after the kingdom of Pergamum had been inherited by the Roman people.[242]

Despite the scrupulousness with which Cato oversaw the sale of these goods and the careful detail he paid to his accounts, which were also preserved in two copies (in accordance with the abovementioned *lex Iulia?*), he lost both documents, apparently through a series of accidents. This led to some reasonable eyebrow-raising among certain Romans.[243] Plutarch notes that one copy was lost by Phylargirus, one of Cato's *liberti*, when he sailed from the port of Cenchreae (near Corinth), while the other copy was burnt in Corcyra while it was being transported by Cato himself, who perhaps intended to present this book (τὸ βιβλίον) to the senate and deposit it in the *aerarium* after the mandatory audit of his accounts. Cato was nonetheless met with acclaim on his return to Rome for being able to deposit almost seven thou-

---

240 Plut. *Cat.min.* 36.2–3: οὔσης δὲ πολλῆς καὶ βασιλικῆς ἐν ἐκπώμασι καὶ τραπέζαις καὶ λίθοις καὶ πορφύραις κατασκευῆς, ἣν ἔδει πραθεῖσαν ἐξαργυρισθῆναι, πάντα βουλόμενος ἐξακριβοῦν καὶ πάντα κατατείνειν εἰς ἄκραν τιμὴν καὶ πᾶσιν αὐτὸς παρεῖναι καὶ προσάγειν τὸν ἔσχατον ἐκλογισμόν...
241 Plut. *Cat.min.* 36.3–4.
242 For Attalus' will, see the following: Liv. *per.* 58–59; Flor. 1.35.2; Vell. 2.4.1; Val.Max. 5.2 ext. 3; Iust. 36.4.5; App. *Mith.* 62; Str. 13.4.2; cf. Kallet-Marx 1995, 97–99.
243 Plut. *Cat.min.* 38.2: τὰ μὲν οὖν χρήματα πλὴν ὀλίγων τινῶν ἀσφαλῶς διεκομίσθη, λόγους δὲ πάντων ὧν διῴκησε γεγραμμένους ἐπιμελῶς ἔχων ἐν δυσὶ βιβλίοις, οὐδέτερον ἔσωσεν...

sand talents of silver in the *aerarium*, which Plutarch says were transported in large chests that were sealed and bound with pieces of cork so that they could be spotted floating on the sea in case of shipwreck.[244]

Beyond the details of Cato's mission, his term in Cyprus perfectly reflects the primary duty for which quaestors were responsible when they took up their post: the procurement and management of assets. Above any other task, quaestors were mandated to obtain supplies for the Roman state, whether they were in Italy or in the provinces, whether in the form of grain or money; this explains why we encounter quaestors like P. Cornelius Lentulus Marcellinus and (possibly) Q. Pompeius Bithynicus taking charge of royal legacies which they could convert into money to help fill the public coffers in Rome. Although the sources are not as explicit as we would like, the evidence analysed here demonstrates that, apart from the management of resources (including those assigned by the senate), one of the main functions of a quaestor sent to a province was the extraction of whatever material assets the Roman military apparatus might need. For this reason, their role was necessary for sustaining an *imperium* that, in essence, sustained itself by means of military force.

Provinces, quaestors, and the high command

We have seen how exercise of the quaestorship in Rome in large part determined the responsibilities given to quaestors in the overseas provinces; likewise, it would be a quaestor's role as his governor's principal associate with the resulting association with the governor's *imperium* that would justify a quaestor's involvement in almost all aspects of provincial administration. As Lintott stresses, given their status as their superiors trusted confidant, quaestors could deal with all aspects of provincial government:[245] from military obligations—in accordance with the principle *ad ministeria belli* with which the quaestors had been assigned to the consuls—to more diplomatic tasks as well as administrative and legal tasks. Cicero, in fact, emphasises that Verres was sent as quaestor to the army of the consul Cn. Papirius Carbo 'not only as guardian of the money, but also of the consul, as well as the sharer in all his business and of all his counsels' (*particeps omnium rerum consiliorumque fueris*).[246] Like his mag-

---

[244] Plut. *Cat.min.* 38.1; cf. Badian 1965, 116–117.
[245] Lintott 1999, 136: 'The quaestors attached to major magistrates were their assistants in all kinds of activity. Those of the consuls seem in effect to have held the post of private secretary or aide-de-camp at home and abroad with particular responsibility for money, including army pay. The same was true of those appointed to serve a magistrate or promagistrate abroad, though these quaestors had a wider remit, being deputy to the commander or governor and usually his temporary replacement, if he left his post for any reason'; Johnston 2008, 8–10; cf. 9: 'In addition to his financial duties, the provincial quaestor clearly also served as military aide-de-camp. He was probably next in official rank to the commander.'
[246] Cic. *Verr.* 2.1.40: *tu cum quaestor ad exercitum missus sis, custos non solum pecuniae sed etiam consulis, particeps omnium rerum consiliorumque fueris.*

isterial colleagues who held the quaestorship in Italy in the service of the consuls, the quaestors who performed their duties in overseas provinces were also subordinate to the *imperium* of a consul or praetor with whom he had to collaborate at all times, except in cases where the quaestor was sent to a certain province alone.

This situation apparently remained unaltered from the moment when two praetors were first sent to Sicily and Sardinia in 227 and were each, in all likelihood, accompanied by a quaestor *ad ministeria belli*. As discussed at the outset of this chapter, the decision to station a praetor in Sicily and Sardinia—an act that converted each island into a permanent *provincia*—constituted the Roman manner of placing the islands beneath the control of these two magistrates invested with *imperium*. The responsibilities related to military command always constituted the main priority of the magistrates who were assigned to a province's governorship. Consequently, this responsibility also trickled down to the quaestors who were designated as a higher magistrate's close associates. In fact, the majority of the sources that allude to quaestors' duties in the provinces depict them as military officials subordinate to the authority of their superior; as such, they took on a role that was analogous to—or at least not totally different from—that which other members of the governor's entourage, such as his legates, could execute.

In reality, apart from the financial tasks inherent in the quaestor's job, many of the assignments that the quaestor would have carried out in the province were not exclusively reserved for someone of his rank; instead, such duties were granted to him in his capacity as a member of the governor's retinue:[247] many of the functions that the quaestors exercised could also be discharged by legates, for example. We know, furthermore, that tensions could arise between legates and quaestors, quite possibly as a result of rivalry between them. This dynamic can be seen in the controversy involving C. Flavius Fimbria, who was probably a legate, and the unnamed quaestor to the consul L. Valerius Flaccus (cos. 86) in Asia: the two bickered over the accommodation of Roman soldiers in Byzantium, a dispute which ultimately triggered the riot that cost Flaccus his life: when he was assassinated by Fimbria in Nicomedia.[248] Although we do not have a clear picture of all the details related to this episode, it is safe to assume that relations between the quaestor (usually a young man around thirty years old) and the legates along with other members of the governor's retinue (people sometimes of consular rank) were not always amicable and could even give rise to tense confrontations. We should stress that, despite his youth, the quaestor in reality was higher up the chain of command than the other members of the senior commander's staff: indeed, besides the governor, he was the only magistrate and therefore representative of the senate and the Roman people.

---

247 For a survey of the role of the governor's *consilium* in a Roman province, see Johnston 2008, 113–131.

248 App. *Mith.* 52; Cass.Dio 30–35, fr. 104.4–6; cf. Liv. *per.* 82; Vell. 2.24.1; Broughton MRR, 2.56; 3.92. On C. Flavius Fimbria, see particularly Lintott 1971, 696–701; Kallet-Marx 1995, 261–264; also Muñiz Coello 1995–1996, 257–275.

This effectively converted the quaestor into the second Roman authority in the province. The quaestor, then, had greater authority than legates in all areas of provincial command, including the military.[249]

Indeed, the sources include many passages in which we encounter the quaestors directing all kinds of troops and military operations in the provinces. As seen above, when M. Claudius Marcellus took Syracuse in 211, the consul sent his quaestor to the island of Nassus to safeguard the royal treasury with a contingent of troops (*cum praesidio*).[250] Only a few years later, C. Laelius, Scipio Africanus' quaestor, even led the Italian cavalry in the battle of Zama (202),[251] while Q. Fabius Maximus, quaestor to his uncle, the consul Scipio Aemilianus, was placed at the forefront of the consul's well known φίλων ἴλη, which consisted of his clients and friends from the Numantine War in Hispania (134–133).[252] According to the sources, neither C. Laelius nor Q. Fabius Maximus was assigned as quaestor to the two Scipiones during the usual sortition, but instead by direct senatorial designation, possibly at the instigation of the consuls involved.[253] This may suggest that the important military responsibilities discharged by these quaestors resulted from the close ties that bound them to their superiors. However, we know of many other quaestors who took on military responsibilities in the provinces (many during the first century),[254] which demonstrates that this was a relatively common practice, regardless of whether personal ties could also have exerted any influence in cases of C. Laelius and Q. Fabius Maximus. Quaestors not only led cavalry and infantry, moreover, but could also command a fleet:[255] for example, P. Caesetius, one of Verres' quaestors in Sicily, apparent-

---

249 See Johnston 2008, 9. According to Polybius (6.35.4), the Roman commanders appointed three guards (φυλακαί) to the tent of the quaestor, while each of the legates serving on the council received two: τὰς δὲ λοιπὰς ὁ στρατηγὸς ἀποτάττει. γίνονται δ᾽ ὡς ἐπίπαν τρεῖς φυλακαὶ παρὰ τὸν ταμίαν, καὶ παρ᾽ ἕκαστον τῶν πρεσβευτῶν καὶ συμβούλων δύο.
250 Liv. 25.31.8: *inde quaestor cum praesidio ad Nassum ad accipiendam pecuniam regiam custodiendamque missus...*
251 Liv. 30.33.2: *Laelium, cuius ante legati, eo anno quaestoris extra sortem ex senatus consulto opera utebatur, cum Italico equitatu ab sinistro cornu, Masinissam Numidasque ab dextro opposuit.*
252 App. *Iber.* 84; cf. Val.Max. 8.15.4; Richardson 2000, 172; on Scipio Aemilianus' φίλων ἴλη, cf. Pina Polo 2001, 89–98.
253 Liv. 30.33.2; Val.Max. 8.15.4; cf. Astin 1967, 82 n. 4; 135, n. 5; Richardson 2000, 172. On the appointment of provinces *sine sorte*, cf. Thompson 1962b; Stewart 1987, 354–356.
254 For the military activities of quaestors during the civil wars, consider the following: C. Memmius (q. 77?) died in battle during Pompey's stay in Hispania (cf. Plut. *Sert.* 21.1–2; Oros. 5.23.12: *Memmius, quaestor Pompei idemque vir sororis eius, occisus est*; Konrad 1994, 175); L. Hirtuleius played an important military role as Sertorius' quaestor in Hispania (Liv. *per.* 90–91; Plut. *Sert.* 12.3; Konrad 1994, 131–132); see also C. Plaetorius (*bell. Alex.* 34.5.); Cinna (Cic. *Phil.* 10.13; Plut. *Brut.* 25.1); P. Cornelius Lentulus Marcellinus (Caes. *civ.* 3.62.4); L. Egnatuleius (Cic. *Phil.* 3.7).
255 See, for instance, C. Laelius, Scipio's quaestor in Hispania, who commanded the Roman fleet against Mago's vessels in the battle of Carteia (Liv. 28.30.3–31.1); Marcius Rufus, C. Scribonius Curio's quaestor in Africa (cf. Caes. *civ.* 2.23.5); Ti. Claudius Nero during the Alexandrian war in 48–47 (Suet. *Tib.* 4); D. Turullius in Bithynia in 44–43 (Cic. *fam.* 12.13.3).

ly led a fleet of ten ships with the legate P. Tadius, possibly to protect the island from pirates—though it seems likely that Verres used these ships for his own gain.[256]

Sulla also led some troops during his quaestorship in Numidia in the service of the consul C. Marius: Sallust records that Sulla joined Marius' camp with a significant contingent of cavalry (*cum magno equitatu*) that the quaestor had raised in Latium and among the Italian allies.[257] This anecdote demonstrates that quaestors could occasionally raise troops and transfer them to a province. Cicero, for example, indicates in his letter to Caninius Sallustius that the quaestor Marius, Caninius' successor in Syria, had received an order from the senate to take the legions that had been destined by decree for Syria from Italy to that province (*senatus ita decrevit ut cum legionibus iret*) in order to fight the Parthians.[258] The fact that these troops never managed to leave Italy is besides the point: the story shows that quaestors were not only responsible for transferring public funds granted by the senate to the provinces, but also that in some cases they were the ones who raised soldiers for the army and then led them to their respective destinations. No less interesting is the story that as quaestor Sertorius took charge of recruiting soldiers and amassing arms in Cisalpine Gaul when the Social War broke out in 91.[259] Be that as it may, this job was not exclusively carried out by quaestors: Scipio Aemilianus was sent to Numidia as legate to the consul L. Licinius Lucullus (cos. 151) to raise auxiliary troops for the war in Hispania Citerior. This final example suggests that in such cases the quaestor was simply acting as one more of the governors' associates.[260]

A well known passage in Plutarch also emphasises the important task of raising ships undertaken by L. Licinius Lucullus, when he was Sulla's quaestor during the siege of Athens: determined to recruit naval support for Sulla's army, Lucullus travelled the coasts of Egypt, Crete, Cyprus, Rhodes and other Aegaean islands as well as the city of Cyrene, where he also tried to ease the political tension found there.[261] Lucullus' mission did not stop there: among the many actions that he undertook later on as proquaestor during the final stages of the Mithridatic War, Plutarch highlights various episodes such as the overthrow of Epigonus, tyrant of Colophon, the attack on Neoptolemus' fleet off the coast of Troas and the capture of the city of Mytilene, the conquest of which yielded Lucullus a total of six thousand prisoners and considerable spoils. Despite Plutarch's silence on the matter, it can be safely assumed that Lucullus sold off the slaves and assets obtained from conquests and thus added to

---

256 Cic. *Verr.* 2.5.63.
257 Sall. *Iug.* 95.1.
258 Cic. *fam.* 2.17.5; cf. Caes. *Gall.* 8.54.1.
259 Plut. *Sert.* 4.1–2: …ταμίας ἀποδείκνυται τῆς περὶ Πάδον Γαλατίας ἐν δέοντι. τοῦ γὰρ Μαρσικοῦ πολέμου συνισταμένου, στρατιώτας τε προσταχθὲν αὐτῷ καταλέγειν καὶ ὅπλα ποιεῖσθαι, σπουδὴν καὶ τάχος προσθεὶς τῷ ἔργῳ παρὰ τὴν τῶν ἄλλων νέων βραδυτῆτα καὶ μαλακίαν ἀνδρὸς ἐμπράκτως βιωσομένου δόξαν ἔσχεν. Konrad 1994, 53–55.
260 App. *Pun.* 71; cf. *Iber.* 49.
261 Plut. *Luc.* 2.2–3.3; cf. App. *Mith.* 33; 51; Keaveney 1992, 18–28.

his accounts a notable sum of money that he had to deposit in the *aerarium*, in compliance with the law.²⁶² As already mentioned above, Lucullus was also entrusted with levying and minting the twenty thousand talents that Sulla demanded from the cities of Asia as damages, a sum that Lucullus would also have recorded and deposited in the public treasury.²⁶³

Plutarch's comprehensive portrait of Lucullus' quaestorship constitutes a valuable picture of the important role that quaestors could play in their provinces: in addition to the administrative and financial obligations demanded by the office, quaestors could fulfil a range of functions that greatly exceeded those responsibilities. Aside from managing public accounts and collecting the sanctions imposed by Sulla, Lucullus had to take on the missions that the circumstances of war demanded, even to the point of undertaking military operations of some importance, which he apparently did at his own initiative. As quaestor and representative of Roman authority, manifested in Sulla's *imperium*, furthermore, Lucullus also had to intervene in internal political matters in some of Rome's allied cities, such as Cyrene and Colophon. If we had to define quaestors' functions at the end of the Republic solely on the basis of Lucullus' career under Sulla (and taking into account that many aspects of his command are overlooked by Plutarch), it would be very difficult to determine which particular competencies were specifically related to the quaestorship.

Of course, not all the quaestors had as eventful a term of office as Lucullus. Given the complexity of the circumstances and the variety of tasks that he had to undertake during that time, Lucullus' quaestorship under Sulla represents a unique example of the form that the exercise of the magistracy in a province could possibly take. That said, his case clearly illustrates how far a quaestor's responsibility could stretch in a province. In fact, as the example of Lucullus further suggests, it was possible for a quaestor to intervene directly in battles fought by Roman troops and to lead some operations personally, if commanded to do so by his superior. Leaving aside the examples dating to the civil wars, whose circumstances can be considered exceptional, there are several quaestors who took an active part in military campaigns during their term in the provinces, as we have seen with C. Laelius' participation in the battle of Zama. In his account of the wars in Hispania, for example, Appian places several quaestors within the Roman troops' theatres of war: besides the abovementioned Q. Fabius Maximus, quaestor to Scipio Aemilianus during the siege of Numantia, Appian mentions Terentius Varro, quaestor to Calpurnius Piso in Hispania Ulterior (154), who fell in battle along with six thousand Roman soldiers at the hands of the Lusitanian chief Punicus;²⁶⁴ he also tells of an unnamed quaestor

---

262 Plut. *Luc.* 3.3–4.3; cf. 4.3: ἐπεὶ δ' ἀτάκτως καὶ μετὰ θράσους ὡς ἔρημον ἀναρπασόμενοι τὸ στρατόπεδον οἱ Μιτυληναῖοι προῆλθον, ἐπεισπεσὼν αὐτοῖς ἔλαβέ τε παμπόλλους ζῶντας καὶ τῶν ἀμυνομένων πεντακοσίους ἀπέκτεινεν, ἀνδραπόδων δὲ χιλιάδας ἓξ καὶ τὴν ἄλλην ἀναρίθμητον ἠλάσατο λείαν; Keaveney 1992, 30–31.
263 Plut. *Luc.* 2.2; Marsura 2015, 43–59.
264 App. *Iber.* 56; Richardson 2000, 151.

who gathered the six thousand Roman soldiers who fled Viriathus' ambush of the army of C. Vetilius (who died in the incident) near city of Tribola 146 (the city is otherwise unknown).²⁶⁵

Even more interesting is the case of the quaestor L. Tremellius Scrofa (q. 143 or 142): various sources record his victory in Macedonia over a usurper (cited as Pseudophilippus or Pseudoperses) who passed himself off as the son of Perseus and aspired to become king of Macedonia. Furthermore, Varro points out that the quaestor's victory led to his praetor, Licinius Nerva, being hailed as *imperator* (*nam eo proelio hostes ita fudit ac fugavit, ut eo Nerva, praetor imperator sit appellatus*).²⁶⁶ The episode has come under the scrutiny of several scholars who have underscored the fact that the credit for the victory was in fact given to the *imperator* (in this case the praetor), since the quaestor acted under his *imperium* and auspices.²⁶⁷ Varro's evidence perfectly demonstrates the extent to which the quaestors' role was linked to his commander's *imperium*. In reality, apart from specific cases (such as P. Cornelius Lentulus Marcellinus' command in Cyrene), quaestors were sent to overseas provinces as the close collaborators of their *imperatores* (consuls, praetors or citizens *cum imperio*) who had been granted the command over a *provincia* where they could exercise their *imperium*: we should remember that even the *quaestorius* M. Porcius Cato had a quaestor in his service during his mission to Cyrene, as a consequence of his *praetorium imperium*.²⁶⁸ Their subordination to their commanders' *imperium* was such that all the actions that quaestors undertook in their *provinciae* ultimately relied on the authority of their superiors, both the good—such as Scrofa's victory in Macedonia—as well as the cases when the quaestors' actions seriously harmed their *imperatores*, such as the abuses committed by Verres in Cilicia under Cn. Cornelius Dolabella.

Additionally, Varro claims that Licinius Nerva left L. Tremellius Scrofa in charge of the province.²⁶⁹ As second in command in the province and their superiors' closest collaborators, quaestors were usually the ones who temporarily assumed high command when their governors were away or left the province.²⁷⁰ However, things did not always pan out this way: As the end of Cicero's provincial command and his departure from Cilicia approached, he contemplated various candidates among the

---

265 App. *Iber.* 63; Richardson 2000, 155.
266 Var. *r.r.* 2.4.2; cf. also Liv. *per.* 53; Eutr. 4.15. Broughton MRR, 1.472; Kallet-Marx 1995, 33, n. 92; Brennan 2000, 226–227; for the chronology, cf. Morgan 1974, 198–199.
267 See recently Vervaet 2017, 121–122; Berthelet 2015, 167–168.
268 Vell. 2.45.4.
269 Var. *r.r.* 2.4.1: *avus meus primum appellatus est Scrofa, qui quaestor cum esset Licinio Nervae praetori in Macedonia provincia relictus [esset], qui praeesset exercitui, dum praetor rediret, hostes, arbitrati occasionem se habere victoriae, inpressionem facere coeperunt in castra.*
270 Johnston 2008, 9–10: 'Also in support of the quaestor's preeminece is the general tendency for a magistrate of consular *imperium* to appoint his quaestor to serve *pro praetore* (that is, with the delegated *imperium* equal to that of a praetor) in his absence'; cf. Lintott 1999, 114–115; 136. Also Jashemski 1950, 89–91; Balsdon 1962, 134–135; Thompson 1965, 375–376.

members of his entourage, such as the legate C. Pomptinus, or his brother Quintus, not only because they were men of praetorian rank, but also because of his known reservations about his quaestor, L. Mescinius Rufus.[271] Ultimately, the orator decided to leave the command of Cilicia to the quaestor C. Coelius Caldus, who was Rufus' successor, 'in accordance with how everyone proceeds',[272] just as the quaestors L. Antonius Pietas and T. Antistius were also left in command of Asia and Macedonia after their respective governors departed for Rome in 50.[273] In fact, Cicero himself had strongly recommended Q. Minucius Thermus, L. Antonius Pietas' commander (in this case, his propraetor), to leave the province in the hands of the quaestor, particularly when there was no one of higher rank in his retinue.[274]

Judging from Cicero's comments, it seems that the most common practice (and, perhaps, the one least likely to compromise the governor) was to cede authority temporarily to the quaestor once the commander had left his province, although he also had the option of entrusting the command to a legate, who usually was of high rank, in light of his superior status. According to Sallust, for example, the consul Sp. Postumius Albinus (cos. 110) left his brother and legate, Aulus Postumius Albinus, in charge of the camp *pro praetore* when he returned to Rome to preside over the *comitia* (*Albinus Aulo fratre in castris pro praetore relicto Romam decessit*), a decision that was evidently made due to the family connection and, perhaps, his brother's rank.[275]

---

271 Cic. *fam.* 2.15.4: *ego de provincia decedens quaestorem Coelium praeposui provinciae. 'Puerum' inquis. At quaestorem, at nobilem adulescentem, at omnium fere exemplo. Neque erat superiore honore usus quem praeficerem...* See especially Thompson 1965, 376–386.

272 Cic. *fam.* 2.15.4: *at omnium fere exemplo...*; cf. 2.18.2; *Att.* 6.6.3. See Balsdon 1962, 134.

273 See Balsdon 1962, 134: 'Minucius Thermus, Propraetor of Asia in 51–50, left his quaestor in charge of the province when he came home, and we have inscriptional and documentary evidence of his titles—'quaestor pro praetore' for the remainder of 50, 'pro quaestore pro praetore' after 1st January, 49. No appointments of provincial governors having been made since June, 51, it is unlikely that on the first day of January, 49, there was any province in the Empire, apart from the Spains, the Gauls and Illyricum, which had as its governor a man with any other title than 'pro quaestore pro praetore'; such men were T. Antistius (Macedonia), L. Antonius (Asia), C. Coelius Caldus (Cilicia), T. Furfanius Postumus (Sicily).' See the following sources for L. Antonius Pietas (q. 50): IGRRP 4.400–401; 4.1346; TAM 5.2.1365; Ios. *AJ* 14.235; cf. Cic. *fam.* 2.18.2. T. Antistius (q. 50): Cic. *fam.* 13.29.3–4; Sarikakis 1971, 182–183. See also T. Furfanius Postumus (q. 50?) in Sicily: Cic. *Att.* 7.15.2. Cicero (*Att.* 7.3.5) asserts that M. Calpurnius Bibulus left a certain Veiento in command of Syria in 50 (*Bibulus de provincia decessit, Veientonem praefecit*), but the passage does not specify his rank. According to Broughton MRR, 2.253 he was a legate; cf. Díaz Fernández 2015, 564, n. 242.

274 Cic. *fam.* 2.18.2: *sed mihi magis magisque cottidie de rationibus tuis cogitanti placet illud meum consilium quod initio Aristoni nostro, ut ad me venit, ostendi, gravis te suscepturum inimicitias si adulescens potens et nobilis a te ignominia adfectus esset. Et Hercule sine dubio erit ignominia. Habes enim neminem honoris gradu superiorem; ille autem, ut omittam nobilitatem, hoc ipso vincit viros optimos hominesque innocentissimos legatos tuos, quod et quaestor est et quaestor tuus. Nocere tibi iratum neminem posse perspicio, sed tamen tris fratris summo loco natos, promptos, non indisertos, te nolo habere iratos, iure praesertim*; Thompson 1965, 376.

275 Sall. *Iug.* 36.3; Liv. *per.* 64. Sumner 1973, 82–84, proposes that A. Postumius Albinus was the cos. 99 (RE 33) and was already a senator of praetorian rank when he became Spurius' legate in

Only a few years later, C. Marius decided to cede command of the *hibernia* of the Roman troops in Africa to his quaestor L. Cornelius Sulla, also *pro praetore*, while he spearheaded a campaign in the interior of Numidia.[276] Likewise, Pompey entrusted the command of the Roman troops in Syria to his quaestor, M. Aemilius Scaurus, as ἀντιταμίας ἀντιστράτηγος, when he left for Rome in 63.[277]

What is most striking, however, are the instances when a governor died.[278] We have already alluded to the quaestor who assumed leadership of the Roman troops in Hispania Ulterior after the assassination of C. Vetilius at the hands of Viriathus' soldiers in 146. Appian says that the quaestor fled with the survivors to the city of Καρπησσός (sic), where he received the support of a contingent of Hispanian auxiliaries and hoped to resist Viriathus' army, while waiting for military backup from Rome;[279] the quaestor, therefore, had to take charge of the province until the praetor C. Plautius arrived in Hispania at the head of ten thousand soldiers and one thousand three hundred horsemen, while Viriathus sacked Carpetania.[280] Only a few decades later, in 119, the situation was repeated in Macedonia after the praetor (στρατηγός) Sex. Pompeius fell in battle at the hands of a Γαλατῶν ἔθνος (possibly the Scordisci) near the Macedonian city of Argos.[281] According to an inscription from Lete, M. Annius, ταμίας ὑπὸ τοῦ δήμου τοῦ Ῥωμαίων ἐπὶ τὰ κατὰ Μακεδονίαν πράγματα, assumed the command of the remnants of the Roman army, reclaimed the bodies of the fallen and fought the enemy valiantly until he defeated them in successive assaults during which he obtained vital spoils in the form of horses and arms.[282] In thanks for his decisive intervention, the βουλή and the δῆμος of Lete paid tribute to M. Annius with a series of honours, among which stand out a civic crown and the annual celebration of an equestrian competition.[283]

---

110. As Broughton MRR, 3.173 stresses, no source attests that Aulus was condemned by the *rogatio Mamilia* in 109, so it is unnecessary to think that his political career ended after his stay in Numidia.
276 Sall. *Iug.* 103.4: *illi mature ad hiberna Romanorum proficiscuntur, deinde in itinere a Gaetulis latronibus circumventi spoliatique pavidi sine decore ad Sullam profugiunt, quem consul in expeditionem proficiscens pro praetore reliquerat.*
277 App. *Syr.* 51: Συρίας δ' εὐθὺς ὁ Πομπήιος Σκαῦρον, τὸν ἐν τοῖς πολέμοις ἑαυτῶ γενόμενον ταμίαν; Ios. *BJ* 1.157; *AJ* 14.79; *IGRRP* 3.1102. See Díaz Fernández 2015, 221–224.
278 According to Livy (25.19.4), the quaestor Cn. Cornelius (Lentulus) was the one who assumed the command of Ti. Sempronius Gracchus' troops after the death of the latter in 212: *ita equestre proelium erat, cum procul visus Sempronianus exercitus, cui Cn. Cornelius quaestor praeerat.*
279 App. *Iber.* 63.
280 App. *Iber.* 64; cf. Richardson 2000, 155–156.
281 *SIG*³ 700, *ll.* 8–12; cf. Sarikakis 1971, 48–49; Kallet-Marx 1995, 38–39; Brennan 2000, 521–522; Díaz Fernández 2015, 422–423.
282 *SIG*³ 700, *ll.* 3–6: ἐπεὶ Μάαρκος Ἄννιος Πο/πλίου υἱός, ἀνὴρ καλὸς καὶ ἀγαθός, ἀποσταλεὶς ταμίας ὑ/πὸ τοῦ δήμου τοῦ Ῥωμαίων ἐπὶ τὰ κατὰ Μακεδονίαν πράγμα/τα...; cf. *ll.* 15–36.
283 *SIG*³ 700, *ll.* 36–40: διὸ δεδόχθαι Ληταίων τῆι βουλῆι καὶ τῶι δή/μωι, ἐπαινέσαι τε Μάαρκον Ἄννιον Ποπλίου ταμίαν Ῥωμαίων καὶ στεφα/νῶσαι αὐτὸν χάριν τῶν πεπραγμένων θαλλοῦ στεφάνωι καὶ τίθεσθαι αὐτῶι / ἀγῶνα ἱππικὸν καθ' ἔτος ἐν τῶι Δαισίωι μηνὶ ὅταν καὶ τοῖς ἄλλοις εὐεργέ/ταις οἱ ἀγῶνες ἐπιτελῶνται...; cf. Payne 1984, 207.

Beyond the concession of this type of honour, of which we have already seen some other interesting examples,[284] the inscription sheds light on the role that quaestors took on in the absence of the governors. In the end, as magistrates of the Roman people, quaestors were the only authority apart from the governor who legitimately could hold a *provincia:* that is, as well as being their superiors' closest collaborators, quaestors were the only ones who had been assigned that province *ex senatus consulto* as a 'mission', so it was up to them to assume supreme command immediately— including that of the Roman troops—if the governor disappeared. Aside from the cases discussed, the most telling example of this situation is that of C. Cassius Longinus, the quaestor who took over the command of the soldiers who survived the battle of Carrhae in 53. After the death of the proconsul M. Licinius Crassus (cos. 55) and a large proportion of his troops at the hands of the Parthian king Orodes, Cassius withdrew with the remnants of the army to the city of Antioch, where the Romans resisted the Parthians. Despite everything, Cassius was able to defend his position and even to quell an uprising in Judaea. He did all of this before being relieved of his command of Syria by the proconsul M. Calpurnius Bibulus in late 51.[285]

As in the case of M. Annius, the fact that C. Cassius Longinus assumed the command of the Roman army and actively fought the enemy suggests that the quaestor had *imperium*, probably *praetorium imperium*.[286] As we have seen, when Marius left Sulla at the head of the *hibernia* of Numidia, the quaestor remained in command of the troops *pro praetore*. In fact, classical authors as well as the epigraphic and numismatic records collect a considerable number of quaestors who are cited as *propraetores* or ἀντιστράτηγοι, that is, as having *praetorium imperium*; only in the triumviral period do we find M. Junius Silanus cited on some coins as *Q. PRO COS* (i.e. with *consulare imperium*), but this is a late example that quite possible should be explained in light of unusual circumstances.[287] Despite all that, in the cases of Annius, Cassius and C. Vetilius' quaestor, there is no reference to the quaestors possessing *imperium*. The inscription from Lete only refers to Annius as ταμίας ὑπὸ τοῦ δήμου τοῦ Ῥωμαίων, while none of the sources that allude to Cassius speak of his as *pro praetore*, but rather as quaestor or proquaestor. Cicero, for example, addresses C.

---

284 For honours bestowed on quaestors in provinces, see the following: AE 1983, 920; CIL I² 2513; VI 14446a/b; I. Délos 1603; 1632; 1659; 1694; 1858bis; I. Ephesos 2941; IG V 2, 146–147; IX, 1, 143; X 2,1 135; XIV 356; ILLRP 370; ILS 8775; I. Olympia 328; I. Priene 121; 244; OGIS 452; SEG 37.959. See Badian 1983, 158.
285 Liv. per. 108: *C. Cassius, quaestor M. Crassi, Parthos qui Syriam transcenderant, cedicit*; Vell. 2.46.4: *reliquas legionum C. Cassius, atrocissimi mox auctor facinoris, tum quaestor, conservavit Syriamque adeo in populi Romani potestate retinuit*; cf. Cic. fam. 15.14; Eutr. 6.18.2; Oros. 6.13.5; Cass.Dio 40.25.4–5. Broughton MRR, 2.229.
286 Balsdon 1962, 134–135; Kondratieff 2015, 438–439.
287 CRRBM 2.522; cf. IG II-III² 4114 = SIG³ 767; Broughton MRR, 2.412; 416; Jashemski 1950, 82, 91.

Cassius Longinus himself as proquaestor in a letter written in October 51; if he had held *imperium*, perhaps Cicero would have addressed Cassius in those terms.²⁸⁸

This circumstance raises the question not only of how this *imperium* was granted to quaestors, but also how common it was for them to be invested with *imperium* in the provinces, above all in the absence of the governor. Not even in the case of L. Tremellius Scrofa, moreover, is there evidence that the quaestor earned his victory in Macedonia with *imperium*. This poses the further question of whether a quaestor really needed *imperium* to undertake military action in his province. The same applies to L. Licinius Lucullus, whose actions as Sulla's quaestor have already been discussed, and of P. Cornelius Lentulus Marcellinus, to whom some scholars have ascribed *imperium* on the grounds that the quaestor must have been invested with that power to undertake his mission in Cyrene. In neither case is there any evidence that suggests that they possessed *imperium*.²⁸⁹ The sources' silence in these instances contrasts with the numerous examples in which they describe quaestors with *praetorium imperium*, particularly in inscriptions and coins: perhaps one of the best known examples is a Latin inscription (now lost) which records that Cn. Calpurnius Piso (q. 65) received the province of Hispania Ulterior as *quaestor pro pr. ex s. c.*, which corroborates a passage in Sallust (*postea Piso in citeriorem Hispaniam quaestor pro praetore missus est adnitente Crasso*).²⁹⁰ Sallust associates Piso's dispatch to Hispania with the political tensions that preceded the Catilinarian conspiracy of 63, but does not explain why the quaestor received *imperium* as *pro praetor:* the author simply comments that the senate sent Piso to Hispania Ulterior with the intention of keeping him away from Rome and that he was later assassinated in his province by Hispanian horsemen serving in his army, a detail that clearly points to the military nature of his mission in Hispania.²⁹¹

---

288 Cic. *fam.* 15.14 (*M. CICERO IMP. S. D. C. CASSIO PRO Q.*); cf. also the case of Marcius Rufus (q. 49), who was quaestor of C. Scribonius Curio in Africa and, apparently, assumed the command of the *castra* after the death of Curio; cf. Caes. *civ.* 2.43.1.
289 Balsdon 1962, 134–135; Badian 1965, 119: 'What the Senate did, perhaps in 75 and certainly for 74, was to send a P. Lentulus Marcellinus to Cyrene, quite probably (though Sallust does not say so explicitly) as quaestor pro praetore. That he had imperium may be assumed without hesitation (as indeed it generally is—Sallust is often wrongly cited as asserting it): in view of what we know of the state of the province he could not do without it'; Jashemski 1950, 79: 'Most scholars are agreed that Lentulus was the first governor to Cyrene, for such would be the natural influence from the phrase 'in novam provinciam'. Nor is his imperium mentioned, but the fact that Lentulus was sent to organize a new province certainly implies imperium, and such a grant would be consistent with Roman practice. But whether it was propraetorian or proconsular, we cannot say for sure. Since Lentulus was only a quaestor he probably had only propraetorian imperium'; see, however, Kallet-Marx 1995, 366–367; McGushin 1992, 206–207.
290 CIL I² 749: *Cn. Calpurnius / Cn. f. Piso / quaestor pro pr. ex s.c. / provinciam Hispaniam / citeriorem optinuit*; cf. Sall. *Cat.* 19.1.
291 Sall. *Cat.* 19.2–4: *neque tamen senatus provinciam invitus dederat, quippe foedum hominem a re publica procul esse volebat, simul quia boni complures praesidium in eo putabant et iam tum potentia Pompei formidulosa erat. Sed is Piso in provincia ab equitibus Hispanis, quos in exercitu ductabat, iter*

An interesting passage from Livy might shed some light on this matter: in 186, the senate received a letter from Hispania Ulterior which notified them of the death of the propraetor C. Atinius (pr. 188), who had been wounded during the siege of Hasta.[292] Upon learning the news, the senate ordered the immediate dispatch of an emissary *ad Lunae portum* to urge C. Calpurnius Piso, the praetor then assigned to that province, to leave as soon as possible for Hispania so that the province should not remain any longer *sine imperio: litteris de morte propraetoris recitatis senatus censuit mittendum, qui ad Lunae portum C. Calpurnium praetorem consequeretur, nuntiaretque senatum aequum censere, ne sine imperio provincia esset, maturare eum proficisci.*[293] A few years later, in 183, Hispania Ulterior once again found itself *sine imperio*—to use Livy's phrase—after illness killed the proconsul P. Sempronius Longus, who happened to be C. Calpurnius Piso's successor in the province.[294] Livy does not tell us who remained provisionally in charge of Hispania Ulterior after the deaths of Atinius and Sempronius, but, in any case, it seems clear that whoever assumed command at that point did not do so *cum imperio*. Livy's words perhaps suggest that when a subordinate remained in charge of a province in the governor's absence, he did not necessarily assume *imperium*, even if he was a quaestor.

Like legates, moreover, quaestors assumed *imperium* in the provinces by direct delegation from their superiors through a process that is unknown to us, as Marius and Pompey apparently did when they ceded their respective commands in Numidia and Syria to their quaestors L. Cornelius Sulla and M. Aemilius Scaurus. When a commander fell in combat, this concession by delegation was clearly impossible, so either we should assume that quaestors were automatically invested with *imperium* after the death of a governor[295] or, alternatively, we have to admit that quaestors did not really need *imperium* to command troops and take interim charge of the province. Of course, this does not negate the possibility that some quaestors could have been delegated *praetorium imperium* by their superiors and subsequently retained command of the province as propraetors after their superiors' deaths. A letter sent in 43 by P. Cornelius Lentulus Spinther to the magistrates, senate and people of Rome records that he took charge of Asia as *proquaestor pro praetore* after the death of the proconsul C. Trebonius (cos. 45) at the hands of P. Cornelius Dolabella,

---

faciens occisus est. sunt qui ita dicant imperia eius iniusta superba crudelia barbaros nequivisse pati. See Brennan 2000, 515–517; here we follow Seguí Marco 2001, 401–410.

292 Liv. 39.21.1–4.
293 Liv. 39.21.4; cf. Vervaet 2014, 55–56.
294 Liv. 40.16.7.
295 So Balsdon 1962, 134: 'If the governor of a province died, his quaestor (or 'pro quaestore') automatically became acting-governor ('pro praetore'), and was attended probably by six fasces, until a replacement arrived; and if a governor left his province before the arrival of his successor, he appointed an acting-governor to fill the gap'; also Johnston 2008, 9–10: 'Also in support of the quaestor's pre-eminence is the general tendency for a magistrate of consular *imperium* to appoint his quaestor to serve *pro praetore* (that is, with the delegated *imperium* equal to that of a praetor) in his absence. In the event of the magistrate's death, the quaestor might replace him'; cf. Badian 1983, 158–159.

which clears up any doubts about that particular scenario.²⁹⁶ It is therefore also possible that the same happened when M. Annius and C. Cassius Longinus took command of Macedonia and Syria, but the sources' silence invites caution in both cases and means that we cannot discuss these quaestors' supposed *imperium* in a conclusive manner.

As we saw above, the same caution should be exercised over the possibility that P. Cornelius Lentulus Marcellinus received *imperium* to complete his mission in Cyrene in 75 or 74. Responding to the example of M. Porcius Cato and his command as *[pro]quaestor pro praetore* in Cyprus, the majority of scholars have accepted that Lentulus Marcellinus also had *praetorium imperium*, a supposition that, though possible, finds no support in the sources. It should also be taken into account that, despite his status as *quaestorius*, Cato was actually just a senator who was granted *imperium* through the *lex Clodia* so he could act in the *provincia Cyprus* as a propraetor; Cato received a quaestor in accordance with his status as *imperator*. P. Lentulus Marcellinus, however, was a serving quaestor, as Sallust indicates, so parallels between the two cases should be drawn with some circumspection. Like the vexed question of the *consulare imperium* that the praetors could come to exercise as proconsuls,²⁹⁷ it is likely that the circumstances and needs of each province and each governor would ultimately determine the decision of whether or not to concede *imperium* to a quaestor. In any case, taking into account the number of quaestors *pro praetore* attested in the sources (especially in certain provinces), it is possible that, with the passage of time, it became somewhat common for governors to invest their quaestors with *imperium* and later to cede command of the province to them, as suggested by the late Republican cases of Sulla, M. Aemilius Scaurus and L. Antonius Pietas, whom the propraetor Q. Minucius Thermus left to lead Asia as ταμίας καὶ ἀντιστράτηγος in 50.²⁹⁸

Despite the importance of military duties, a quaestor's role in the administration of the province was not restricted just to these military and financial matters, as we have already mentioned: quaestors also collaborated and took an active part in a range of aspects of provincial governments, such as diplomacy and jurisdiction. Some passages in Cicero's *Verrines* confirm, for example, that quaestors could participate in provincial court proceedings over which their provincial governor was presiding; not without reason did Cicero reproach Verres for not drawing upon the *con-*

---

296 Cic. *fam.* 12.15.1–4.
297 See Barrandon and Hurlet 2009, 45–47; Vervaet 2012, 73–79; Hurlet 2012, 98–101; Díaz Fernández 2015, 73–78; 2017a, 69–73; cf. Marshall 1972, 903–904; Kallet-Marx 1995, 343–345; Brennan 2000, 398–400; 619–621.
298 See Badian 1983, 158. Also C. Plantius had lictores during his quaestorship in Macedonia; cf. Cic. *Planc.* 98 (*Nam simul ac me Dyrrachium attigisse audivit, statim ad me lictoribus dimissis, insignibus abiectis, veste mutata profectus est...*). L. Antonius Pietas (q. 50) as ταμίας καὶ ἀντιστράτηγος: IGRRP 4.400–401; 4.1346; Ios. *AJ* 14.235.

silium of his quaestor, T. Vettius during the trial of the Sicilian navarchs in 71,[299] which demonstrates that quaestors held an important role as advisors for their commanders' judicial duties. It seems that quaestors' functions in judicial matters were not, however, limited only to advisory roles within the governor's *consilium*. Suetonius suggests so much when he describes the work that Caesar undertook in the *conventus* in Hispania Ulterior, where as quaestor he presided over judicial matter, which he had been commanded to do by his praetor, Antistius Vetus (*cum mandatu pr[aetoris] iure dicundo conventus circumiret*);[300] that is, like in so many other tasks, an *imperator*, as the sole individual legitimately empowered to exercise jurisdiction in his *provincia*, could delegate such tasks to his quaestor.

The same may be said of the work that quaestors did in diplomatic matters at the behest of their superiors. As quaestor to the consul C. Hostilius Mancinus in Hispania Citerior, Ti. Sempronius Gracchus took personal responsibility for negotiating the terms of peace with the Celtiberians after the Roman troops' humiliating capitulation before the Numantines in 137.[301] According to Plutarch, when the Romans saw that they were surrounded by the enemy, Mancinus sent heralds to the Numantines asking for peace, but the Hispanians demanded that they speak directly with Gracchus, not only because of the quaestor's good reputation, but also because of their memory of his father, who had reached settlements with the Hispanian populations during his praetorship in Hispania Citerior.[302] Apparently, Gracchus' mediation saved the lives of over twenty thousand Roman citizens who had been surrounded by the Numantines, although the peace treaty was later invalidated by the senate because it was considered unworthy of Roman authority.[303] No less notable was the role that Sulla played in the capture of Jugurtha, an episode that was immortalised in the coins later minted by his son Faustus. Sallust, in fact, directly credits Sulla with convincing king Bocchus to hand Jugurtha over to him, who in turn brought the Numidian king before Marius in chains and ready to be transported to Rome.[304]

---

299 Cic. *Verr.* 2.5.114; cf. 2.2.44: *Deinde ceteras dicas omnis illo foro M. Postumius quaestor sortitus est.*
300 Suet. *Iul.* 7.
301 Plut. *Ti.Gr.* 5.2–4.
302 Plut. *Ti.Gr.* 5.2–3: ἀπογνοὺς τὴν ἐκ τοῦ βιάζεσθαι σωτηρίαν ὁ Μαγκῖνος ἐπεκηρυκεύετο περὶ σπονδῶν καὶ διαλύσεων πρὸς αὐτούς. οἱ δὲ πιστεύειν ἔφασαν οὐδενὶ πλὴν μόνῳ Τιβερίῳ, καὶ τοῦτον ἐκέλευον ἀποστέλλειν πρὸς αὐτούς. ἐπεπόνθεσαν δὲ τοῦτο καὶ δι' αὐτὸν τὸν νεανίσκον – ἦν γὰρ αὐτοῦ πλεῖστος λόγος ἐπὶ στρατιᾶς – καὶ μεμνημένοι τοῦ πατρὸς [Τιβερίου], ὃς πολεμήσας Ἴβηρσι καὶ πολλοὺς καταστρεψάμενος εἰρήνην ἔθετο πρὸς τοὺς Νομαντίνους καὶ ταύτην ἐμπεδοῦντα τὸν δῆμον ὀρθῶς καὶ δικαίως ἀεὶ παρέσχεν; cf. Wikander 1976, 93–97; García Riaza 2002, 284–286.
303 Plut. *Ti.Gr.* 5.4: οὕτω δὴ πεμφθεὶς ὁ Τιβέριος καὶ συγγενόμενος τοῖς ἀνδράσι, καὶ τὰ μὲν πείσας, τὰ δὲ δεξάμενος, ἐσπείσατο καὶ δισμυρίους ἔσωσε περιφανῶς Ῥωμαίων πολίτας, ἄνευ <τῆς> θεραπείας καὶ τῶν ἔξω τάξεως ἐπομένων; cf. 7.1–4; App. *Iber.* 80; Liv. *per.* 55. See Wikander 1976, 93–94; García Riaza 2002, 282–284; Díaz Fernández 2019, 121–124.
304 Sall. *Iug.* 113.1–7; Vell. 2.12.1; Oros. 5.15.18; Diodor. 34–35.39; Plut. *Sull.* 3.2–3; on Faustus Sulla's coins, cf. Crawford RRC, 449–451 no. 426; see Plut. *Sull.* 6.1; Val.Max. 8.14.4; Plin. *n.h.* 37.8.

Beyond the individual circumstances of each case, it is very striking that both Tiberius Gracchus and Sulla took on such a decisive role in resolving these conflicts, despite being quite young; Tiberius Gracchus was perhaps twenty six years old when he went to Hispania Citerior as Mancinus' quaestor, so it is not surprising that Plutarch stresses the youth of the magistrate who took responsibility for negotiating peace with the Numantines at a time of utmost delicacy.[305] The fact that the quaestors were usually young men is somewhat shocking when we consider the important responsibilities that they took on during their tenures as quaestors in the provinces. A man, who started his *cursus honorum* with the quaestorship when he was around thirty, was not only responsible for the detailed administration of funds given to his superior for the exercise of the command, but also of gathering every kind of resource needed to maintain the Roman army; furthermore, he could even lead troops in combat if needed; indeed, it was this young man who would have to assume command of the province in the event that his superior was absent or died, even over and above the governor's other associates who, like legates, could very well be of praetorian or consular rank. In short, undertaking the quaestorship in a province put the young Roman before all kinds of responsibilities that made this magistracy a fundamental part of the Roman provincial system.[306]

It should be emphasised, however, that ultimate responsibility for the wide range of duties that a quaestor could discharge in his province fell on his commander, that is, on the person under whose *imperium* and *auspicia* he acted. We have already discussed the consequences that this could have for the senior magistrate: at times, this was welcomed, like when Licinius Nerva was called *imperator*, while in other instances a senior magistrate could even be prosecuted; it should not surprise us, then, that Sallust should have judged Sulla so highly for not damaging the *fama* of the consul C. Marius during his quaestorship, as those who allowed themselves to be consumed by ambition often did.[307] This is perhaps why the sources, and Cicero in particular, give such weight to the close relationship (*necessitudo*) that the governor and his quaestor should foster between them, even to the point of comparing it to the relationship between father and son; Cicero emphatically claims that the consul Cn. Papirius Carbo considered his quaestor C. Verres as one of his own children: *habitus sis in liberum loco, sicut mos maiorum ferebat*.[308] From this standpoint, Verres' disloyalty in abandoning Carbo in the middle of his command was doubly serious, since it not only violoated the *mos maiorum*, but also the *necessitudo* that joined the quaestor to his superior with an almost paternal bond.

---

305 Plut. *Ti.Gr.* 5.3: ...ἐπεπόνθεσαν δὲ τοῦτο καὶ δι' αὐτὸν τὸν νεανίσκον...
306 For quaestors' accounting knowledge, see Berrendonner 2014, 180–183.
307 Sall. *Iug.* 96.3–4: *neque interim, quod prava ambitio solet, consulis aut quoiusquam boni famam laedere, tantummodo neque consilio neque manu priorem alium pati, plerosque antevenire. Quibus rebus et artibus brevi Mario militibusque carissumus factus*.
308 Cic. *Verr.* 2.1.40.

Cicero, as we know, repeats the same argument in his *Divinatio in Caecilium*, when he reproaches Q. Caecilius Niger for wanting to take over the prosecution against Verres after having been his quaestor in Sicily: once again, Cicero recalls that, according to *maiores nostri*, a praetor should be like a father to his quaestor (*praetorem quaestori suo parentis loco esse oportere*). Accordingly, for Caecilius to join the prosecution of Verres almost amounted to impiety (*id pie facere non posses*), even though it could be undertaken in accordance with *ius*.[309] In a letter sent to C. Coelius Caldus from Cilicia, nevertheless, Cicero celebrated the fact that Coelius was to be sent to his province as quaestor, in this case distinguishing between the *consuetudo* that had led fortune (*fors*) to unite them in the province and the *necessitudo* that also united quaestors with their commanders.[310] In fact, Thompson demonstrates that the *necessitudo* of which Cicero so often speaks in his works held more of the formal courtesy and respect proper to the discharge of a public office than a truly paternal connection. This *necessitudo*, furthermore, was not at all exclusive to the relationship between commanders and their quaestors, but also extended to all the commander-in-chief's associates and subordinates.[311]

In reality, behind the paternalistic overtones with which Cicero portrays the relationship between the governor and his quaestor (quite possibly for rhetorical purposes), there was the need to maintain the most cordial relationship possible between the two magistrates who represented the Roman people in the province as well as the need to avoid tensions that could threaten the government of the province. Cicero's letters in effect show us a glimpse of a certain degree of complicity that was necessary between both parties for the administration to run smoothly and even to conceal anything that could compromise the magistrates' reputations—a task that was not always easy, as we have seen.[312] After all, despite being the governor's main associate in the province, quaestors were normally assigned to their superior by

---

309 Cic. *div. in Caec.* 61–62: *nullam neque iustiorem neque graviorem causam necessitudinis posse reperiri quam coniunctionem sortis, quam provinciae, quam offici, quam publici muneris societatem. Quam ob rem si iure posses eum accusare, tamen, cum is tibi parentis numero fuisset, id pie facere non posses; cum vero neque iniuriam acceperis et praetori tuo periculum crees, fatearis necesse est te illi iniustum impiumque bellum inferre conari.*

310 Cic. *fam.* 2.19.1: *cum optatissimum nuntium accepissem te mihi quaestorem obtigisse, eo iucundiorem mihi eam sortem sperabam fore quo diutius in provincia mecum fuisses. Magni enim videbatur interesse ad eam necessitudinem quam nobis fors tribuisset consuetudinem quoque accedere.*

311 Thompson 1962a, 347–349; cf. 349: 'the relationship between quaestor and commander-in-chief, as prescribed by public policy and custom, was an entirely official relationship. The quaestor was required to show a certain reverence, courtesy, and loyalty towards his superior during their official connexion. This held good also for other members of the commander's staff who did not happen to be friends or clients of the commander. Public policy and custom also imposed on the commander the moral obligation to treat his juniors correspondingly'; see also 354–355; Johnston 2008, 8–10.

312 See the above-mentioned case of P. Oppius, M. Aurelius Cotta's quaestor in Bithynia, who was dismissed by the consul because of his innappropriate conduct (cf. Cass.Dio 36.40.3; Quint. *inst.* 5.13.17). A more striking case is that of Q. Fabius, perhaps P. Rupilius' quaestor in Sicily, who was sent home by his commander for having lost Tauromenium during the Slave War: cf. Val.Max. 2.7.3.

lot. That meant that in principle there was no reason for the parties to have an already established rapport; this explains the interest demonstrated by some eminent personalities in Roman politics in choosing their quaestors personally *sine sorte* from within their closest circle, as Scipio Africanus did, for example, when he took his friend C. Laelius as his quaestor for his command in Africa in 202.[313] Possibly, the relationship between the governor and his quaestor could be compared with that of a father and son insofar as the senior magistrate was responsible for everything that his quaestor did under his auspices and *imperium*, while the quaestor was subordinate to every decision and order that his commander gave him. Beyond the personal ties that could bond the governor and his quaestor, it was an essentially institutional relationship enforced not only by the obligations and responsibilities that each of them assumed when they entered office, but also by the consequences that their respective actions could have for the other.[314]

---

313 Liv. 30.33.2; cf. also Cic. *Phil.* 2.50: *Quaestor es factus; deinde continuo sine senatus consulto, sine sorte, sine lege ad Caesarem cucurristi.* See Thompson 1962b, 19–24.
314 Thompson 1962a, 354–355.

Conclusions

The lack of sources makes the study of the quaestorship during the Republic, both at Rome and in the provinces, a challenge. Throughout this book we have endeavoured to provide answers to the key questions on the subject, knowing full well that finding a definitive answer for many of them is close to impossible. Indeed, we expect debate about the Republican quaestorship to continue over the coming years and even decades.

The first central question discussed in this book concerns the origin of the quaestorship, both the chronology and the original characteristics of the office. In order to determine when and how the quaestorship was created, the study of the judicial quaestors ought to be separated from that of the financial and administrative quaestors, since they were different offices with completely different functions; as a result, they presumably developed along different lines. In fact, the name 'quaestor' is the only common point between them. In other words, the *quaestores parricidii* had nothing to do with the quaestors who dealt with the public treasury, acted as assistants to the consuls and progressively assumed other functions at Rome, in Italy and in the provinces: this administrative and financial quaestorship should not be seen as an outgrowth of what was originally a judicial office of the same name.

The creation of the administrative and financial quaestorship should be understood in the context of the prolonged developmental process of Roman institutions. While quaestors could very well have initially been assistants to the highest magistrates of the Roman Republic, we cannot rule out the possibility that quaestors already existed during the Monarchy as the kings' auxiliaries. At any rate, the institutionalisation of the quaestorship as the magistracy in charge of the state finances must have occurred when the public archive and treasury were founded, which appears to have taken place at the beginning of the fifth century. If we accept that quaestors were originally trustworthy persons who assisted those who ruled Rome, it seems reasonable that they would have been selected personally by the rulers themselves rather than elected by the people. A decisive step in this progressive shaping of the historical quaestorship was the change from the selection of quaestors by the highest Republican magistrates to their popular election, which Tacitus dates to 447–446.[1]

According to Livy, the number of quaestors was doubled in 421.[2] This change should be seen as a response to the increasing complexity of the Roman state machinery, which in turn required the office's functions to be specialised and diversified. From that moment on, two of the quaestors (*quaestores urbani*) would exclusively take charge of administrative and financial matters and would remain at Rome throughout their whole mandate. The other two quaestors would assist the highest

---

[1] Tac. *ann.* 11.22.
[2] Liv. 4.43.3–4.

magistrates, who in the early Republic were both administrative and military officers. The consuls performed civil task at Rome for at least half of their mandate and spent the rest of their time in office away from the city commanding the army. As assistants to the highest magistrates, the quaestors presumably also participated in these civil and military duties.

Therefore, after decades of experimentation and evolution, the quaestorship had reached its recognisable form: four magistrates elected by the people from patricians and plebeians—only in 409 were the first plebeian quaestors elected—two of whom had administrative duties at Rome and were primarily in charge of the public treasury, while the other two assisted the highest magistrates in their civil and military tasks at Rome and in the field.

Virtually nothing is known about how the quaestorship operated in the fourth century, in large part because only a few names of quaestors have been preserved for the period before the Hannibalic War. Nonetheless, some texts have been preserved which indicate that there was an increase in the number of quaestors at some point in the third century: a single sentence in the *Periochae* of Livy's fifteenth book; Tacitus' excursus on the quaestorship; and a paragraph of the sixth century antiquarian Joannes Lydus.[3] Tacitus, the most reliable source on the matter, claims that the number of quaestors was doubled (*numerus duplicatus*), which implies that the number of quaestors was increased at some point to eight. The question is when this enlargement took place: both the *Periochae* and Lydus date it to 267–266, whereas Tacitus does not give a precise date, but seems to imply that this was a more gradual process that occurred in connection with Roman expansion across the Mediterranean before the time of Sulla. Taking into account these elusive details, there is no reason to exclude the possibility that the enlargement in the number of quaestors could have taken place in two or more stages: two new quaestors may have been instituted in the aftermath of the war against Pyrrhus in 267–266, while two more may have been added at some other point in the third century. However, it remains possible that the number of quaestors was increased one by one or, alternatively, that the number was increased by two at one point and by one on two further occasions. We can reasonably conclude, therefore, that the number of quaestors probably reached eight during the third century and remained constant at this number throughout the second century and the beginning of the first, until the dictator Sulla increased the number of quaestors to twenty in 81, as we know from Tacitus and the *lex Cornelia de XX quaestoribus*.[4]

If it is difficult to determine how the quaestorship developed and precisely when the number of quaestors increased, it is no less complicated to determine which tasks these new quaestors were assigned. In this respect, Mommsen's rigid model, in which several fixed Italian quaestorships were created by 267 and remained un-

---

[3] Liv. *per.* 15; Tac. *ann.* 11.22.4–6; Lyd. *de mag.* 1.27.
[4] Tac. *ann.* 11.22.6.

changed for decades or even centuries, should be abandoned. Methodologically, every proposal for reconstructing the office's history ought to be based on an analysis of our very limited and fragmentary sources in their historical context. In other words, we must resist the urge to fall back on anachronisms and to use details pertaining to one historical period to reconstruct another. Simultaneously, every hypothesis should be guided by the principle that Roman institutions were innovative, pragmatic and flexible, since they were capable of responding to new demands.

If we assume that 267–266 may have been the date when new quaestors were created, we must ask what new demands Rome was then facing that would have required an increase in the number of quaestors. At that moment, a war against Carthage could have been seen as more than probable, especially when we take into account that the First Punic War broke out just a few years later in 264. In that context, nothing could have appeared more necessary for Rome than the construction of a fleet to confront the great naval power in the central Mediterranean. If we understand the changes to the quaestorship in this context, we reach the conclusion that the construction, equipping and maintenance of a fleet could very well have been the *provincia* entrusted to the two new quaestorships, which were probably created by 267. This theory jibes with Tacitus, who links the new quaestorships with Roman expansion in general, and more specifically it coincides with Lydus, who connects the construction of a fleet with the institution of new quaestors in 267 whom he calls *quaestores classici*, a name that is not attested in any other ancient source and was unlikely to have been an official title. The recently discovered Egadi bronze *rostra* with Latin inscriptions prove that during the First Punic War quaestors were responsible for tasks related to the building and equipping of ships. Indeed, this discovery seems to provide further support to this hypothesis about the new quaestors' original duties. This does not mean, however, that the *provincia* of these new quaestors necessarily remained the same forever: once the war was over, these quaestors—if they continued to exist as permanent magistrates—could have continued to perform the same tasks or could have been allocated other functions.

After the First Punic War, extra-Italian territories began to be kept under Roman control. As a consequence, when Sardinia and Sicily became regular praetorian *provinciae* in 227, two more quaestors may have been added in order to assist the praetors who were sent to these new provinces. This would mirror the standing tradition in which a higher magistrate or private citizen with *imperium* was to be accompanied to his *provincia* by a quaestor as his right-hand man, just as the consuls annually received quaestors *ad ministeria belli* or *ut rem militarem commitaretur*, according to Livy and Tacitus.[5] Again, this new enlargement in the number of quaestors was closely related to Roman expansion, as Tacitus asserts. By the end of the third century, therefore, Rome probably elected eight quaestors every year. During the second century there were two consular quaestors, two urban quaestors, and four other quaes-

---

5 Liv. 4.43.4; Tac. *ann.* 11.22.

tors who were assigned to the Empire's new provinces and always served under the command of an *imperator*. As a consequence of the progressive increase in the number of *provinciae* allotted to Roman magistrates, the use of prorogation became standard not only among consuls and praetors, but also among the quaestors who accompanied them.

Nevertheless, on the basis of the aforementioned institutional pragmatism and flexibility of the Roman state, these quaestors could also be appointed for other tasks or *provinciae* in Italy whenever necessary. These so-called Italian quaestorships, of which only the Ostian quaestorship is attested in both the pre- and post-Sullan age, should not be seen as permanent assignments but rather as occasional offices. Given that the senate determined the quaestorian *provinciae* on a yearly basis, these quaestorships in Italy—such as the Vatinius' assignment in Puteoli that Cicero (mockingly?) dubbed *provincia aquaria* and perhaps the *calles*, among other possible *provinciae*—must have been allocated as quaestorian *provinciae* only when the senate considered it necessary. In other words, the quaestorian *provinciae* were not necessarily fixed and could vary in number and responsibilities according to the changing circumstances and needs.

Throughout the Republic, the quaestorship was always the first—or one of the first—regular offices in the political career of a Roman citizen. There were, nonetheless, some slight developments over this period of Roman history. Since a fixed *cursus honorum* did not exist before the passage of the *lex Villia annalis* of 180, we should not assume that every politician in that period held the quaestorship: in fact, the quaestorship was not compulsory at that point, and so a citizen could begin his political career with any other magistracy. The big problem is that between 446 and 180 we know of only twenty-three quaestors, whose names, in most cases, are the only preserved information. All in all, it is reasonable to conclude that in this period the quaestorship was very often the first regular magistracy to be obtained and that it was held between the military tribuneship and the aedileship (or sometimes the tribunate of the plebs). The dearth of evidence does not allow us to establish with certainty the age at which quaestors usually held the office. Still, it seems clear that, although there was no minimum age to access the quaestorship, quaestors must always have been young, probably in their late twenties or around thirty years old.

The *lex Villia annalis* regulated the *cursus honorum* for the first time. Although we know of a very limited number of quaestors during the second century and have details about only a few of those magistrates, we can come to the likely conclusion that the quaestorship did not become a prerequisite for reaching a higher magistracy at this point. As in previous periods, the quaestorship remained the normal initial office in a political career before a politician would hold the aedileship (now compulsory for candidacy for the higher magistracies) or the tribunate of the plebs in the case of plebeians. At times, the quaestorship was held in close combination with the office of *triumvir monetalis*, which could precede or follow the quaestorship, or other minor offices including the *vigintisexviri*. With respect to the age at which the quaestorship was held during the second century, it does not seem that the *lex Villia* established a minimum age, as it certainly did for the aedileship, praetorship and consulship. The situation, nonetheless, did not change substantially in the second century: quaestors continued to hold the office in their late twenties or around thirty, just as they had done previously. The scarce sources do not, however, allow us to establish twenty-seven as the fixed legal minimum age, as Mommsen proposed.

In 81 the dictator Sulla promulgated the so-called *lex Cornelia de magistratibus*, which updated the *lex Villia* and confirmed the sequence of magistracies to be held in a political career and also introducing additional regulations. From that moment on, the quaestorship became the compulsory first regular magistracy of the *cursus honorum*. Additionally, and no less importantly, holding the quaestorship automatically granted an individual access to the senate. This fact no doubt made the quaestorship much more attractive for young men who wanted to build a political career. In all likelihood, the Sullan law was the first to establish a minimum for holding the office (thirty years).

Throughout the Republic the quaestorship was an annual magistracy. Quaestors were elected in the *comitia tributa* and were apparently the last magistrates to be elected each year. We only have evidence of quaestors taking office on the Nones of December (i.e. 5th December) in the post-Sullan period. This means that they were in office from 5th December to the following 4th December. No ancient source explains why the quaestors entered office on such an unusual date, which fell some weeks earlier than the consuls and the other magistrates. Moreover, it is unlikely that this system was previously in use, at least not before 153, when consuls began to enter office on 1st January. Quaestors always had a close relationship with the highest magistrates of the Republic, as can be seen in the fact that some quaestors attended the consuls in and outside of Rome. Therefore, it seems implausible that while the consuls took office on very different dates throughout the Republic, the quaestors always had the fixed date of 5th December for taking office. It is much more logical to assume that the consular and quaestorian years developed in tandem, so that consuls and quaestors entered office, if not simultaneously, at least on dates close to one another. In other words, both the consular and the quaestorian years fluctuated during the first centuries of the Republic. The inauguration of the quaestors in the post-Sullan age on 5th December should be seen as the final stage of a process of institutional development, and not as a permanent tradition.

Once elections had been held, the senate established the quaestorian *provinciae* for the next year. This was not necessary in the early Republic, when there were only two urban quaestors and two consular quaestors per year. As the number of quaestors increased over time and their duties diversified, it became necessary for the senate to determine the quaestorian *provinciae*.[6] Since quaestors became the assistants of the praetors sent to the provinces from (probably) 227 onwards, we can deduce

---

6 See Cic. *Q.fr.* 2.3.1.

that the setting of quaestorian *provinciae* was always determined by the allocation of the higher magistrates' *provinciae*, in such a way that each magistrate *cum imperio* who was sent to a *provincia* had to have a quaestor at his service. The quaestors were usually assigned to their *provinciae* by lot (*sortitio*), but a special appointment (*extra sortem*) was also possible. The sortition of the *provinciae* took place in the *aerarium* on the day that the new quaestors took office, at least in the post-Sullan period. An *extra sortem* quaestorian appointment was a concession made by the senate to the higher magistrate who would be the quaestor's commander. These appointments, made directly by a higher magistrate without the drawing of a lot, were based on friendship, trust, kinship and even military abilities (when applicable). In any case, the senate validated *a posteriori* the allocation of provinces *ex senatus consulto*, whether the distribution had been made *extra sortem* or by lot.

The urban quaestorship came into being in the fifth century, and from then on there were always two urban quaestors elected annually in the Republic. However, only a few are expressly named as such in the literary sources, inscriptions and coins. As attested by literary sources and some legal documents, the care and management of Rome's public treasury (*aerarium populi*) was the *provincia* of the urban quaestors, although urban quaestors could occasionally and temporarily be assigned tasks other than the *aerarium*, if the senate so required. The two urban quaestors were simultaneously responsible for the public treasury and their shared responsibilities were characterised by collegiality. In practice, however, some or even most of their tasks were carried out individually. That is, the two urban quaestors shared a joint and collegial responsibility, but that does not mean that they did not individually execute the functions associated with the magistracy.

With the support of a large permanent team of assistants (*apparitores*), the *quaestores urbani* took care of a very wide range of tasks, including the following: the management and supervision of money and metal reserves, in particular of gold, which were deposited in the treasury; the supervision of all public expenses and income in Rome, which meant that these quaestors become the Republic's de facto comptrollers; and the validation and archiving of all official documents generated by the Roman bureaucracy and administration.

In particular, the urban quaestors were responsible for the general accounting of the Roman state, including its supervision, control and preservation. They had to supervise the accounts of all magistrates after they had concluded their offices, both in Rome and in the Empire's provinces. It was compulsory for every magistrate who handled public money to put down in writing and bring to the *aerarium* detailed accounts when they returned from his province. This included a detailed catalogue of spoils taken from the enemy. The *scribae* who worked in the treasury had to check these accounts before the urban quaestors gave their approval.

The urban quaestors were involved in securing resources for the public treasury. Consequently, the *quaestores urbani* had to supervise the regular income of the *civitas*, in particular the *tributum* paid by every Roman citizen, which had to be registered in the *tabulae publicae*. The urban quaestors were also responsible of controlling occasional extraordinary types of income. They therefore took charge of some public auctions carried out to raise money on behalf of the *aerarium*, such as the sale of public land, booty and prisoners of war brought to Rome for the celebration of a triumph; they also oversaw the sale of the properties of citizens with debts to the state who had been declared insolvent. Likewise, they oversaw the payment of war reparations that defeated peoples or cities were obliged to pay Rome. As was the case for public income, all public expenses were also controlled by the urban quaestors and required their authorisation, always by order of the senate.

The urban quaestors also carried out other functions on behalf of the *civitas* that indirectly entailed the use of public expenses from the *aerarium*. For instance, we know of some cases in which, following orders from the senate, the urban quaestors escorted prominent foreign guests and were also put in charge of their accommodation in Italy and, in particular, at Rome. Likewise, when the senate gave precise instructions, urban quaestors were ordered by a higher magistrate to organise and procure public money for funerary honours for eminent Roman citizens as well as prominent foreigners. We even have an example of an urban quaestor who in the first century was instructed to renovate the *via Caecilia* with public funds. Moreover, during the late Republic the urban quaestors were also put in charge selecting the jurors who would take part in the year's upcoming trials held in the permanent courts.

The close relationship between the urban quaestors and Roman finances is reflected in their involvement in the minting of coins. The *quaestores urbani* were ultimately responsible for the coinage at Rome, although in practice the *triumviri monetales* carried out the task. As the magistrates in charge of the public treasury, the urban quaestors were responsible for giving the moneyers the bullion necessary for minting silver and bronze coins. Under special circumstances the senate could instruct one or both urban quaestors to issue coins directly. If this was the case, the name (or names) of the *quaestores urbani* appeared on the coins along with an abbreviation referring to their office (Q or Q.VRB) and sometimes the legend *S(enatus) C(onsulto)* or *EX S(enatus) C(onsulto)*. There is no evidence at all, however, that all issues struck *senatus consulto* were coined by quaestors.

All official documents generated by the Roman administration (senate, magistrates, assemblies, courts, etc.) were recorded and kept in the *aerarium:* the act of depositing a document in the *aerarium* turned it into a public record. The urban quaestors were therefore responsible for ensuring their accuracy and preservation; in this way, they became the general public notaries of the Republic. Among those official documents were: senatorial decrees; text of laws; lists of allies and friends of the Roman people; public contracts; census documents; etc.

The quaestorship was always an office for beginners who aspired to follow a political career. In this regard, it is striking how confident the Roman system was in its young citizens, given that the quaestorship was far from being an office with minor responsibilities. Urban quaestors had to control the finances of the Roman state and serve as public notaries. Their integrity was therefore important for the proper functioning of the administration, given that a huge volume of public money was under their control. The same was true for provincial quaestors, who also had important financial duties as administrators of the public money granted to their superiors for their commands; furthermore, the overseas quaestors had to manage all supplies and goods obtained during their terms of office in a province, which in turn had to be registered meticulously in their *rationes* and later presented in Rome.

A quaestor serving under a consul at Rome or under an *imperator* in an overseas province was much more than merely his accountant or assistant: he was his trusted right-hand man, to the point that he worked at all times under the *imperium* and auspices of his commander. Licinius Nerva's acclamation as *imperator*, as a result of the military victory of his quaestor in Macedonia, shows the link between the quaestor's role in a *provincia* and the *imperium* of his commander.[7] Apart from his superior (usually a consul or praetor), the quaestor was the only other magistrate who was present in a *provincia*, which made him the second authority in the province. This bestowed upon the quaestorship a series of duties that exceeded the responsibilities traditionally assigned to the magistracy and made it a key part of the Roman system of provincial administration. Additionally, although the quaestorship was never given *imperium*, a quaestor was expected to assume military command in place of his commander in case of his absence, death or disability (we must keep in mind that, from the fifth century onwards, a quaestor was allocated to each consul to assist in administering war, as Livy points out).

Whether quaestors necessarily required *imperium* on such occasions is, however, far from certain. Whereas it is well known that Sulla was left *pro praetore* in charge of the Roman troops in Numidia during Marius' absence, quaestors who assumed the command of their provinces after the death of their superiors, like M. Annius or C. Cassius Longinus, are not said to have been invested with *imperium*. Likewise, P. Cornelius Lentulus Marcellinus, the quaestor sent *in novam provinciam Curenas* in 75, is not mentioned as propraetor. In contrast, a number of quaestors are attested as *propraetores* or ἀντιστράτηγοι in the sources, making it difficult to determine to what extent the grant of *imperium* to quaestors was common in the provinces. It seems that *imperium* did not need to be directly delegated for quaestors to participate in military duties. There is no clear evidence for a systematic practice: possibly it depended on the circumstances (as well as on the controversial investiture of *consulare imperium* to praetors), but it is probable that in the last decades of the Republic it became usual for commanders to grant their quaestors *imperium*, especially in certain provinces.

As the trusted man of his superior and the second-in-command of his provinces, a quaestor's duties were not restricted to financial and military competencies: these magistrates took part in such diverse aspects of provincial administration that we can conclude that quaestors were able to assume every task linked to the provincial

---

7 Varr. *r.r.* 2.4.1.

command, including, as our sources stress, juridical and diplomatic matters. The role of a quaestor was consequently decisive for the success of a provincial commander, so that a well disposed relationship between him and his superior was not only advisable but even necessary; hence, Cicero emphasised in his speeches the importance of this *necessitudo*, to the point of comparing it to the relationship between father and son. Given that during their terms of office in a province, senior commanders certainly had to share their responsibilities with young citizens who began their political careers as quaestors and were no more than thirty years old, Cicero's comparison seems particularly appropriate.

In short, the quaestorship remains an obscure magistracy, given the scarce number of quaestors about whom we have information and the relatively few and elusive sources providing information about the office. That said, the office was a prominent part of the Roman administration, both at Rome and abroad, and it was endowed with truly significant tasks and responsibilities. Ultimately, quaestors were far from being 'unimportant', as Badian claimed decades ago. On the contrary, they have long deserved a book about them. We can only hope that this book is deserving of them.

Appendix 1:
A prosopography of the Roman Republican quaestorship

C. Aarcellus. See **C. (Claudius) Marcellus**

M'. Acilius (q. in Sicily in the second century) (RE 11):
See **L. Alp(ius)? De(-).** Some issues from Sicily (Panormos) bear on the reverse the inscription *MAN(ius) ACILI(us) Q(uaestor)*. Sobeck 1909, 85, includes Acilius among the list of quaestors who minted coins in Sicily in the first century. Sobeck has been followed by Broughton MRR, 2.478, who assumes that Acilius was a quaestor before 50 (cf. Gruen 1974, 517). Grant 1946, 17 and 26, identifies him with M. Acilius Caninus, who was Caesar's legate in 48 and proconsul in Sicily in 46–45. However, Frey-Kupper 2013, 267, has shown that these coins were minted in the second century. On only two of them (see L. Alpius) is the magistracy of the moneyer expressed with the abbreviation Q. On the coin and on the moneyer, see Frey-Kupper 2013, 212–213, 248–249, 253–255.

Fig. 1: M'. Acilius, quaestor second century. Æ As. Sicily. Laureate head of Janus. MAN. ACILI. Q within laurel wreath.

P. Aelius (q. 409) (RE 9):
See **P. Papius** and **Q. Silius**. According to Liv. 4.54.2–3, P. Aelius was one of the first three plebeian quaestors in the history of Rome, elected in 409. There are serious

doubts about the historicity of the quaestors' names and even the episode itself. So Ogilvie 1965, 616: 'yet the trio as a whole cannot be viewed with equanimity. It is suspicious that the Aelii could also claim the first plebeian augur (10.9.2)...' Cf. Sobeck 1909, 4; Broughton MRR, 1.78.

C. Aelius Paetus Staienus (q. 78, proq. 77?) (RE Staienus 1):

According to Cicero, Staienus was quaestor under the command of the consul M. Aemilius Lepidus: *cum quaestor esset, in exercitu seditionem esse conflatam* (Cic. *Cluent.* 99). He encouraged sedition within Lepidus' army and was later charged with treason. Since Lepidus was consul in 78, the year in which his revolt began, it seems reasonable to date Staienus' quaestorship to the same year. He may have stayed as proquaestor in 77 under Lepidus. As far as his name is concerned, he became C. Aelius Paetus Staienus through adoption, although his complete name is not attested. Cicero's comment in *Cluent.* 72 (*hoc enim sibi Staienus cognomen ex imaginibus Aeliorum delegerat*) seems to imply that he usurped the name Aelius Paetus without undergoing formal adoption; see also Cic. *Brut.* 241: *et C. Staienus, qui se ipse adoptaverat et de Staieno Aelium fecerat*. See Shackleton Bailey 1976, 65; 1992, 10). Cicero refers to him once as C. Aelius Staienus (Cic. *Cluent.* 65), but usually prefers to name him simply as C. Staienus (*Cluent.* 70; *Brut.* 241). See Sobeck 1909, 35–36: quaestor in 78; Broughton MRR, 2.89: quaestor in 77. Cf. Wiseman 1971, 262 no. 410.

Q. Aelius L. f. Tubero (q. by 46?) (RE 156):

He was the famous jurisconsult and son of L. Aelius Tubero (RE 150). His quaestorship is not attested in the sources. Broughton MRR, 3.5. supposed that he was 'almost certainly a senator before 31.' Taking into account the institutional irregularities of the triumviral age, this does not necessarily imply that he had held the quaestorship before gaining access to the senate. Ryan 1999, 244–245, suggests that Aelius Tubero may have been quaestor by 46, 'and probably in 47–46.' Aelius Tubero prosecuted Q. Ligarius in 46. Cicero's speech in his defense (*Pro Ligario*) was delivered towards the end of that year. Ryan bases his argument on a passage from Cicero's speech: *Sed parum est me hoc meminisse, spero etiam te, qui obliuisci nihil soles nisi iniurias... te aliquid de huius illo quaestorio officio, etiam de aliis quibusdam quaestoribus reminiscentem, recordari* (Cic. *Lig.* 35). With the phrase 'certain other quaestors' (*de aliis quibusdam quaestoribus*), Cicero is seeking to respond to an argument made by the prosecution; among these quaestors he includes Aelius Tubero. Ryan recognises, nonetheless, that Aelius Tubero's quaestorship must remain speculative, since it is not certain that he was one of the Caesarian quaestors attested in Cicero's speech. Despite this, Ryan argues that 'this queried quaestorship should fall after 48,' since Aelius Tubero was then still an enemy of Caesar, but 'it cannot be later than 46,' since the *Pro Ligario* was delivered at the end of that year.

Aelius Tubero's quaestorship is certainly possible, but there is no clear evidence for it, and its dating is speculative.

Aemilius (q. in the third century?) (not in RE or RE 66?):
According to Plutarch, the first stone bridge in Rome was built by the otherwise unknown quaestor Aemilius: ἡ δὲ λιθίνη πολλοῖς ὕστερον ἐξειργάσθη χρόνοις ὑπ' Αἰμιλίου ταμιεύοντος (Plut. *Numa* 9.3. Cf. Sobeck 1909, 74: late second century; Broughton MRR, 2.474: quaestor of uncertain date). Coarelli, s. v. Pons Aemilius, 106–107: if Plutarch is speaking of the first stone bridge, it should precede the *pons Mulvius*, probably dated to 220. The *pons Aemilius* would have been built between 292 (when the preserved text of Livy ends) and 220, perhaps linked to the opening of the *via Aurelia* probably in 241. According to Coarelli, the quaestor Aemilius, mentioned by Plutarch, could be the same man as M. Aemilius Lepidus, consul in 232 (RE 66). More doubtful is the interpretation of the monument depicted on a coin dated to 114–113 (Crawford RRC 305–306, no. 291) with the inscription *MN·AEMILIO LEP(ido)* as the *pons Aemilius* (the construction of the bridge was supposedly commemorated by a descendant of the quaestor Aemilius). Crawford RRC, 305–306, identifies the arches represented on the reverse as a part of the aqueduct that M. Aemilius Lepidus and M. Fulvius Nobilior began in 179 when they were censors. Regarding our quaestor, Crawford adds: 'The bridge-building Aemilius of Plutarch, *Numa* 9 does not get one very far' (305 n. 1).

M'. Aemilius M'. f. Lepidus (proq. in Asia between 84 and 78) (cos. 66) (RE 62):
Two inscriptions from Delos (I. Délos 1659: Ἀθηναίων καὶ Ῥωμαίων καὶ / τῶν ἄλλων Ἑλλήνων οἱ κα/τοικοῦντες ἐν Δήλωι καὶ / οἱ παρεπιδημοῦντες ἔμ/ποροι καὶ ναύκληροι Μάνιον Α[ἰ]/μύλιον Μανίου υἱὸν Λέπεδον / ἀντιταμίαν ἀρετῆς ἕνεκεν / καὶ δικαιοσύνης καὶ τῆς πρὸς / τοὺς θεοὺς {ευσ} εὐσεβε<ί>/ας) and Priene (*I. Priene* 244: ὁ δῆμος ὁ Πριηνέω[ν] / [Μ]ᾴ[ν]ιον Αἰμύλιον [Μ]ανίου υἱὸν / Λέπ[ι]δον ἀντι[τ]α[μί]α̣ν / ἀρετῆς ἕνεκεν καὶ εὐνοίας / καὶ εὐεργεσίας τῆς εἰς ἑαυτὸν / καὶ τοὺς ἄλλους Ἕλληνας) mention a M'. Aemilius M'. f. Lepidus as proquaestor. He must be identified as one of the consuls of 66. Cf. Sobeck 1909, 32; Broughton MRR, 2.86.

P. Aemilius Lepidus (q. 44? proq.? 43 in Crete) (not in RE):
According to Appian (*b.c.* 5.2), Lepidus won Crete for Brutus and joined his troops with Cassius Parmensis' fleet in 43 (προσλαβόντες δὲ καὶ Λέπιδον μεθ' ἑτέρας δυνάμεως, ᾗ Βρούτῳ καθίστατο Κρήτην). See Broughton MRR, 2.342; 3.8. Since he is mentioned as proquaestor on some bronze coins from Crete, Brutus might have been sent him to the island as quaestor in 44 and held it as proquaestor in 43. See Grant 1946, 35–36; Perl 1970, 336–338; Buttrey 1978, 168 and 173 n. 7; Weigel 1978, 42–45; Crawford 1985, 253.

L. Aemilius M. f. Lepidus Paullus (q. 60 and proq. 59 in Macedonia) (cos. 50) (RE 81):
Cic. *Vat.* 25: *L. Paulum, qui tum quaestor Macedoniam obtinebat… in idem Vettii iudicium congregasti.* Cf. Cic. *Att.* 2.24.3: *Vettius… dixerat… in eo principem Paulum fuisse, quem constabat eo tempore in Macedonia fuisse.* L. Aemilius Lepidus Paullus probably went to Macedonia as a quaestor in 60 with the proconsul C. Octavius. He remained under Octavius as proquaestor in 59. Cicero's reference to him as quaestor in 59 should be understood as proquaestor. See Bülz 1893, 27–28; Sobeck 1909, 54–55; Broughton MRR, 2.190; 3.9; Badian 1959a, 83; Sarikakis 1971, 177–179; Sumner 1973, 137: 'quaestor 60 (or 59)'; Syme 1987, 321: 'he is to be presumed quaestor in 60.' More recently, Ryan 1988a, reasserts the dates (q. 60 and proq. 59) on the basis of Cicero's letter to Atticus (2.24.3). According to Ryan, Cicero's words (eo tempore) indisputably show that Paullus was no longer in Macedonia when Cicero wrote the letter. Paullus may have returned to Rome, perhaps in July 59. Cf. Ryan 1996 f, 41: Paullus was at least thirty-two when he became quaestor.

Mam. Aemilius (Mamercinus) (q. 446) (tr. mil. c. p. 438) (RE 16, 97):
See **L. Valerius Poplicola Potitus.** Tac. *ann.* 11.22: *Creatique primum Valerius Potitus et Aemilius Mamercus sexagesimo tertio anno post Tarquinios exactos, ut rem militarem comitarentur.* He is one of the two first quaestors elected by the people in 446. Sobeck 1909, 3 (Aemilius Mamercus); Broughton MRR, 1.51; 2.527 (Mamercus Aemilius Mamercinus). Livy usually calls him Mamercus Aemilius (4.16.8; 4.17.8; 4.23.5; 4.30.5; 4.31.5; 4.32.3; 4.41.11) or simply Mamercus (4.24.7 and 9).

L. Aemilius L. f. Paullus (q. 195?) (cos. 182 and 168) (RE 114):
CIL I^2 p. 194 = Inscr. Ital. 13.2.81: *L. Aemilius L. f. Paullus cos. II cens. interrex pr. aed. cur. q. tr. mil. tertio aug.* The elogium offers the only evidence of L. Aemilius Paullus' quaestorship. He was aedile in 193 (Liv. 35.10.11–12; cf. Plut. *Aem.* 3.1) and triumvir in 194 for the foundation of the colony of Croton (Liv. 34.45.3–5). Consequently, he ought to have been quaestor before 194, perhaps in 195. See Sobeck 1909, 11; Broughton MRR, 1.340.

M. Aemilius M. f. Scaurus (q. 67 or 66, proq. 66–64 or 65–64, proq. pro pr. 63–61 in Syria) (pr. 56) (RE 141):
See **P. Plautius Hypsaeus.** Marcus Aemilius Scaurus may have been quaestor in 66 and may have been under Pompey's command in Syria this same year (against this dating Ryan 1996 g, 84: his aedileship shows that he was born in 96 or 95, and his praetorship proves that he was born precisely in 96; it follows that he could not have been quaestor before 65). However, he may have been one of Pompey's quaestors already in 67 (according to the *lex Gabinia*, which apparently allowed Pompey to have

two quaestors) and may have remained under his command once the *lex Manilia* was passed in 66 (Ioannidopoulos 2017). Scaurus remained in Pompey's service during the following years as proquaestor. When Pompey returned to Rome in 63, Scaurus took charge of Syria as *proquaestor pro praetore* (ILS 8775 = IGRom. 3.1102: ἡ βουλὴ καὶ ὁ δῆμος / Μᾶρκον Αἰμύλιον Μάρκου υἱὸν / Σκαῦρον ἀντιταμίαν ἀντι/στράτηγον τὸν ἑαυτῶν / πάτρωνα εὐνοίας ἔνεκε[ν]) until the arrival of his substitute in 61, the *praetorius* L. Marcius Philippus (στρατηγικός, according to App. *Syr.* 51). See Bülz 1893, 63–65; Sobeck 1909, 48; Broughton MRR, 2.153; 2.159; 2.163; 2.168; Balsdon 1962, 134; Thonemann 2004, 81; Kondratieff 2015, 437. For his position in Syria, see Sartre 2005, 44; Díaz Fernández 2015, 222–224; 484–485.

Aesillas (q. and proq. in Macedonia in 95–94?) (not in RE):

Aesillas is only known through some silver coins minted at the beginning of the first century in Macedonia (Bauslaugh 2000, 21). On the reverse we find the Latin name *AESILLAS*, together with the letter Q of q(uaestor), but some issues also bear on the obverse the inscription *CAE(sar) · PR(aetor) · ΜΑΚΕΔΟΝΩΝ* (Head 1911, 240): the praetor might be L. Julius Caesar (cos. 90) or his son and namesake (cos. 64). Scholars have compared Aesillas' issues with that of a certain *SVVRA LEG · PRO · Q*, perhaps P. Cornelius Lentulus Sura (cos. 71), the brother-in-law of L. Julius Caesar, the consul of 64 (see for this option Mattingly 1979, 147–155) or more probably the Βρέττιος Σούρρας πρεσβευτὴς (Plut. *Sull.* 11.4) under C. Sentius (*pr.* 94) in Macedonia (Broughton MRR, 3.34; Thonemann 2015, 176). As a consequence, Aesillas may have been active in Macedonia before C. Sentius' praetorship, perhaps in 95–94, first as quaestor and then as proquaestor of the praetor L. Julius Caesar (cos. 90). See Bültz 1908, 24–25; Sobeck 1909, 27–28 (quaestor 93); Broughton MRR, 2.13 (quaestor 94; proquaestor 93–92); Evans 1994, 214 (quaestor 94?); Wiseman 1971, 209–210; Sarikakis 1971, 174; De Callataÿ 1996, 113–151; 1998, 113–117; Bauslaugh 2000, 111–115; Thonemann 2015, 175.

P. Albius (P. f.) (q. 120 in Asia) (RE 2):

Q. Mucius Scaevola the Augur was prosecuted by T. Albucius for *repetundae*, presumably in 119 (Gruen 1968b, 115–116; 305, Alexander, 1990, 17, no. 32). During the trial P. Albius, who had been his quaestor during his government in Asia, was required to present the account books (Cic. *de orat.* 2.281). Albius' records were dismisssed and Scaevola was acquitted. The quaestorship of Albius in Asia under Scaevola can probably be dated to 120 (Cf. Evans 1994, 212: Albius may have been quaestor soon after 120. For Scaevola's command in Asia, see Brennan 2000, 547; Díaz Fernández 2015, 442–443). This Albius must be the same man who appears eleventh on the *S.C. de agro Pergameno* (Sherk, RDGE, no. 12, *l.* 27) as Πόπλιος Ἄλβιος Ποπλίου Κυρίνα. Albius' *praenomen* has been subject to discussion. See Sobeck 1909, 18–19, who accepts the *praenomen* Publius suggested by Cichorius 1908, 246; Broughton MRR, 1.524; 3.14: the

Fig. 2: L. Julius Caesar, praetor, and Aesillas, quaestor 95–94? AR Tetradrachm. Macedonia. ΜΑΚΕΔΟΝΩΝ, diademed head of Alexander the Great right. AESILLAS Q, *capsa*, club and chair, all within wreath.

praenomen Publius must be rejected because the *S.C. de agro Pergameno* is dated to 129, and consequently before the quaestorship of Albius. However, Broughton MRR, 3.24, seems inclined to accept 101 as the date of the senatorial decree. This date, 101, is now generally accepted by the scholarship (see Brennan 2000, 348 n. 80 and 671–673, with supplementary bibliography; especially Magie 1950, 1055–1056 n. 25; Mattingly 1972a, 412–423; Badian 1986, 14–16). The *praenomen* Publius should definitely be accepted for the quaestor Albius.

C. Alfius Flavus (q. by 64?) (tr.pl. 59) (RE 7):
Ryan 1997b: it must be concluded from Cic. *Vat.* 38 that Alfius Flavus' defeat in the elections for the praetorship happened in 58. He is mentioned as a member of Cicero's *consilium* in 63 (Cic. *Planc.* 104). This makes it likely that Alfius Flavus was then a senator and already been quaestor (Willems 1878, 1.484). Since he was able to present his candidature for the praetorship in 58, he was born ca. 97. Ryan concludes that C. Alfius Flavus 'was quaestor by 64.' Cf. Wiseman 1971, 211.

A. Allienus (q. in Macedonia by 62?) (pr. 49) (RE 1):
According to Shackleton Bailey 1977, 2.439, A. Allienus may have been quaestor in Macedonia by 62. He based this suggestion on a letter in which Cicero asks Allienus to support financially one of his Greek friends, Democritus of Sicyon (Cic. *fam.* 13.78). According to Shackleton Bailey, this could imply that Allienus was quaestor in Macedonia before he became a legate under Q. Cicero in Asia in 61 (Cic. *Q.fr.* 1.1.10). Cf. Broughton MRR, 3.14. The text in Cicero's letter is too vague to infer firmly that Allienus held the quaestorship in Macedonia.

L. Alp(ius)? De(-) (q. in Sicily in the second century) (not in RE):
See **M'. Acilius.** Frey-Kupper 2013, 213 – 214 (cf. 218; 248; 253 – 255), proposes to interpret the inscription on a Sicilian coin as *L. ALP(ius)? DE(-) Q(uaestor)*. The name Alpius is otherwise unknown. According to Frey-Kupper, these coins were issued in the second century. The inscription had usually been read as *L(ucius) AP(p)ul(eius) DE(cianus) Q(uaestor)* and the coin dated to the first century (cf. Broughton MRR, 2.474). Sobeck 1909, 85, wrongly reads it as *L. APU(leius) DE(signatus) Q(uaestor)*.

M. Ampudius N. f. (q. late first century, perhaps in the 40s) (RE 1):
CIL I² 812 (= CIL X 6082): *M. Ampudius N. f. q. tr. pl. aid*. This inscription from Formiae provides the only evidence for Ampudius' quaestorship. He may have been active during the late Republic and/or the early Augustan period (Sobeck 1909, 75; Broughton MRR, 2.474). Mommsen Röm. St., I 555 n. 1, suggests that his political career began under Caesar's dictatorship. If this is the case, M. Ampudius may have been quaestor before 44, although this remains conjectural. Cf. Wiseman 1971, 212. Cichorius 1922, 285 – 286, identifies Ampudius with an Ἀπούδιος (or Σέξτος τις Πακούουιος, ὡς δ' ἕτεροι λέγουσιν Ἀπούδιος) mentioned by Cassius Dio (53.20.2) for 27, but the proposal is far from secure.

Q. Ancharius Q. f. (q. 74 and proq. 73 – 71 in Macedonia?) (pr. 56) (RE 3):
A Q. Ancharius, Q. f. is honoured in an inscription from Olympia as patron and benefactor by the koinon of the Achaians (I. Olymp. 328: τὸ κοινὸν τῶν / Ἀχαιῶν / Κόϊντον Ἀγχάριον / Κοΐντου υἱόν, / ἀντ[ι]ταμίαν, τὸν / αὐτ[ῶ]ν πάτρωνα καὶ /εὐεργέταν). He must be identified with the praetor of 56, and not with the praetor of ca. 88 (Tanner 2000, 37 n. 101, dates the inscription before 90, making Ancharius proquaestor of Macedonia-Achaia in the 90s); see Sarikakis 1971, 175 – 176. Ancharius was honoured as proquaestor (this title excludes the possibility of the inscription referring to Ancharius' proconsulship in Macedonia 55 – 54). Sobeck 1909, 56, very prudently places his proquaestorship in Macedonia before his praetorship in 56 (it should also have predeced his tribunate in 59). Broughton MRR, 2.158, gives 65 as the conjectural year of his quaestorship on the basis of the dates of his tribunate and praetorship. However, in MRR, 2.480, Broughton proposes placing his proquaestorship in Macedonia 'probably before 66.' See Eilers 2002, 192: Q. Ancharius served under M. Antonius Creticus (pr. 74, propr. 73 – 71) against the pirates in the late 70s. He was presumably quaestor and then proquaestor, rather than legate. Broughton 2.112 and 115 n. 5, includes in 73 Q. Ancharius as a legate serving under Antonius Creticus, although this title is not preserved. Eilers' proposal is reasonable: Ancharius could have served under Antonius Creticus, not as a legate, but first as quaestor in 74 and then as proquaestor in 73 – 71. The inscription from Olympia would have belonged to this time. This hypothesis certainly implies that Ancharius held the praetorship not *suo anno*, but later.

Q. Anicius (q. by 86? in Sicily) (not in RE):
CIL I² 2951 was completed by Manganaro 1989, 178–181. In this inscription the Italian scholar restores the name Anicius as quaestor of C. Norbanus (Prag 2007b: pr. in Sicily 90?, pro pr. 89–85?), with the following reading (*ll.* 1–3): *C. Norb[anus – f. – n. Balbus] / anno [extremo praeturae] / [Q. A]nic[ius--] / [quaestor pro pr(aetore) –] / [vias in] cl[inatas et angustas a] / Syracuss[is ad Acras vorsum].* Consequently, Q. Anicius may have been quaestor (or/and proquaestor) in Sicily under Norbanus at any point during his stay on the island, around 86. Further speculation, such as the cognomen Gallus or Balbus (for Anicius Gallus and Anicius Balbus see Broughton 2.529), or that Anicius was later quaestor pro praetore (Manganaro 1989, 179) lacks all foundation (Prag 2007b, 303).

C. Annaeus C. f. (q. by 75?) (not in RE):
C. Annaeus (Γάϊος Ἀνναῖος Γαΐου υἱὸς Κλυτομίνα) is mentioned in the *S.C. de Oropiis* of 73 (SIG³ 747 = FIRA I² 36 = RDGE 23) as a member of the senatorial *consilium*. Broughton MRR, 2.115, includes him within the *aedilicii* under the name *C. Annaeus C. f. Clu. (Brocchus?)* (RE 3) (cf. 2.529: senator before 70, aed.? before 73; cf. Taylor 1960, 190). However, Ryan 1995d, rejects this identification and thinks C. Annaeus to be a new senator, who was previously unidentified (not in RE). In the list of senators in the *S.C. de Oropiis*, M. Tullius Cicero is mentioned immediately after Anneus. Since Cicero was quaestor in 75, but not the first elected (Cic. *Pis.* 2), Ryan concludes that all that can be said is that Annaeus 'was quaestor by 75' (p. 306).

C. An(n)ius (q. third century?) (RE 8):
CIL I² 20: *[M. Aim]ilio M.f. C. An[io C. f.] / [quais?]toris pro po[plod] / [vic. par?]ti Diove dede[re].* The inscription must be dated before the Hannibalic War. The fragmentary text *[---]toris* could be reconstructed either as *[prai]toris* (as in CIL I² 20) or as *[quais]toris*. If the second reconstruction is correct, C. Annius would have been a quaestor at some point in the third century. See Sobeck 1909, 82; Broughton MRR, 2.474.

M. Annius P. f. (q. 120–119) (not in RE):
In a Greek inscription from Lete, Macedonia (SIG³ 700, *ll.* 3–6: ἐπεὶ Μάαρκος Ἄννιος Πο/πλίου υἱός, ἀνὴρ καλὸς καὶ ἀγαθός, ἀποσταλεὶς ταμίας ὑ/πὸ τοῦ δήμου τοῦ Ῥωμαίων ἐπὶ τὰ κατὰ Μακεδονίαν πράγμα/τα), a quaestor (not a proquaestor) M. Annius is thanked for having repelled a military attack (probably by the Scordisci) after the defeat suffered by the στρατηγός Sex. Pompeius, who was killed by the same enemies. Sex. Pompeius may have been praetor in 121 or 120 and promagistrate in Macedonia until 120 or 119 (Broughton MRR, 1.526 and 527 n.3; Brennan 2000, 521–522; Díaz Fernández 2015, 422–423), or just praetor in 120 (see Sarikakis 1971, 170–172). M. Annius may have been his quaestor in the province, taking command after Pompeius'

death until his successor arrived in Macedonia (Bültz 1908, 14–15; Sobeck 1909, 19; Broughton MRR, 1.526 and 527 n.4). Cf. Evans 1994, 208: quaestor in 119; Sarikakis 1971, 170–172.

T. Antistius (q. 50, proq. pro pr.? 49, in Macedonia) (RE 22):
According to Cicero, T. Antistius was still in Macedonia in 49 when Pompey entered the province where Antistius had been quaestor in 50. Cicero did not know whether Antistius had been involved in the minting of provincial coins (Cic. *fam.* 13.29.4: *Huius propinquus fuit T. Antistius, qui quum sorte quaestor Macedoniam obtineret neque ei successum esset, Pompeius in eam provinciam cum exercitu venit... Quum signaretur argentum Apolloniae, non possum dicere eum praefuisse neque possum negare affuisse, sed non plus duobus aut tribus mensibus*). Some denarii were certainly minted in Apollonia for the consuls of 49. Some of them bear the abbreviation *Q(uaestor)* on their reverse (Crawford RRC 462 no. 445.1–2). According to Crawford, this anonymous quaestor should be identified as T. Antistius (RRC 89), and the issue should be regarded as military and irregular (RRC 462).

The combination of this evidence allows us for the conclusion that T. Antistius was first quaestor in 49 in Macedonia. Since no appointments of new provincial governors had been made since June 51, Antistius was forced to remain as *proquaestor* (perhaps *pro praetore*) in 49 (Balsdon 1962, 134). As *proquaestor* he would reluctantly have been in charge of the minting in Apollonia. Cf. Bülz 1893, 30–32; Sobeck 1909, 62; Broughton MRR, 2.249 and 260; Sarikakis 1971, 182–183; Gruen 1974, 200–201.

C. Antistius Vetus (proq. pro pr.? 45–44? in Syria) (cos. suff. 30) (RE 47):
Plutarch states that Caesar served as quaestor in 69 in Hispania Ulterior under Antistius Vetus, whose son, in turn, Caesar later made his own quaestor (Plut. *Caes.* 5.3: καὶ τὸν υἱὸν αὐτοῦ πάλιν αὐτὸς ἄρχων ταμίαν ἐποίησε). The question of when this happened has been debated (Sobeck 1909, 75: he was a Caesar's quaestor in an undetermined year). Klebs in RE assumes that C. Antistius Vetus served under Caesar in Hispania Ulterior in 61, and Badian 1969, 202–203, also considers a date probable. Sumner 1971, 361 n. 49, proposes that Plutarch's statement that Caesar made Antistius quaestor could simply have meant that Caesar chose him as his quaestor in Gaul *sine sorte*, in 51 or 50. According to Sumner, Antistius cannot have been old enough for a quaestorship in 61.

However, it is much more likely that Antistius was appointed by Caesar as proquaestor in Syria in 45–44 (against Sumner, who argues that Antistius is not attested as a quaestor at that time) and that he was the same person who was later *consul suffectus* in 30 (see Broughton 2.308; 2.327; 3.18; cf. Shackleton Bailey 1976, 8–9; 11–13. Cf. Cass.Dio 47.27.2–4). His title was probably *proquaestor pro praetore*.

C. Antonius M. f. (q. 51?) (pr. 44) (RE 20):

There is no evidence in the ancient sources for the quaestorship of C. Antonius. However, Broughton MRR, 2.241, links a letter sent by Cicero to Q. Thermus in 50 (Cic. *fam*. 2.18.2–3) with the presumed quaestorship of C. Antonius. In his letter Cicero alludes to the three brothers who were soon to become tribunes of the plebs. In 50 L. Antonius was the quaestor of Thermus. M. Antonius had been quaestor in Gaul under the command of Caesar in 51 (Broughton favours the year 52). Broughton thinks that the third brother, C. Antonius, could have been quaestor in 51 (see, however, MRR, 2.531: quaestor? in 51?). Cicero's letter provides no evidence for C. Antonius' quaestorship. He presumably held this office, but the date is unknown.

L. Antonius M. f. Pietas (q. 50, proq. pro pr. 49 in Asia) (cos. 41) (RE 23):

Q. Minucius Thermus, propraetor in Asia in 50, left his quaestor L. Antonius in charge of the province when he returned to Italy that year (cf. Cic. *fam*. 2.18). Consequently, Antonius was *quaestor pro praetore* for the rest of 50 (or just from the beginning of 49), and he remained in Asia in 49 as *proquaestor pro praetore*. There is sufficient evidence of his rank in the sources: some honorific inscriptions from Magnesia (IGRom. 4.1346), Ephesus (Merkelbach 1978, 36 = SEG 28.856: Λεύκιον Ἀντώνιον Μάρκου υἱὸν [ταμίαν κ]αὶ ἀντιστράτηγον, πάτρων[α καὶ εὐεργέτην τῆς] / Ἀρτέμιδος καὶ τῆς πόλεως) and Pergamun (IGRP 4.400: ὁ δῆμος [ἐτίμησεν] / Λεύκιον Ἀντώ[ν]ιον Μ[αάρκου υἱόν] / ταμίαν καὶ ἀντιστράτη[γον, τὸν πάτρω]/να καὶ σωτῆρα; 4.401: ὁ δῆμος / Λεύκιον Ἀντώνιον Μαάρκου υἱόν, ταμί/αν καὶ ἀντιστράτηγον, πάτρωνα καὶ σω/τῆρα; TAM 5.2. 1365) mention Antonius as *quaestor pro praetore*, and he described himself with this title in a letter to Sardis (Ios. *AJ* 14.235: Λούκιος Ἀντώνιος Μάρκου υἱὸς ἀντιταμίας καὶ ἀντιστράτηγος Σαρδιανῶν ἄρχουσι βουλῇ δήμῳ χαίρειν). See Bülz 1893, 44–46; Sobeck 1909, 63; Broughton MRR, 2.249; 2.260; Merkelbach 1978; Ryan 1994b, 596; Thonemann 2004, 81; Kondratieff 2015, 437.

M. Antonius M. f. (q. 113 in Asia, proq. pro pr. in Asia 112) (cos. 99) (RE 28):

According to Valerius Maximus (Val.Max. 3.7.9: *M. Antonius ille disertus… quaestor proficiscens in Asiam, Brundisium iam pervenerat…*), M. Antonius was quaestor in Asia in 113. Presumably he stayed in this province in 112 as *proquaestor pro praetore*, since he was honoured at Delos under this title by the Pisidian town of Prostaenna (I. Délos 1603: ὁ δῆμος ὁ Προσταεννέ/ων Πισιδῶν Μάαρκον / Ἀντώνιον Μαάρκου υἱὸν / ταμίαν ἀντιστράτηγον / Ῥωμαίων, ἀρετῆς ἕνεκεν / καὶ εὐνοίας τῆς εἰς ἑαυ/τόν). See Bültz 1908, 16–17; Sobeck 1909, 20; Broughton MRR, 1.536; 1.539; Sumner 1973, 96; Tanner 2000, 38 n. 102; Eilers 2000, 213–214. Antonius was quaestor at the age of thirty (Evans 1994, 184).

M. Antonius M. f. (q. 51 in Gaul) (cos. 44 and 34) (RE 30):
Cicero provides evidence of Antonius' quaestorship: *venisti e Gallia ad quaesturam petendam...postea sum cultus a te, tu a me observatus in petitione quaesturae* (Cic. *Phil.* 2.49; cf. *Att.* 6.6.4). However, the date is uncertain. The year 52 was first proffered by Sobeck 1909, 61, who argues that Antonius remained in Gaul after his quaestorship as a legate of Caesar (cf. Bülz 1893, 23–25; Broughton MRR, 2.236: quaestor in 52). Currently, there is consensus that Antonius' quaestorship should be dated to 51 (see especially Linderski and Kaminska-Linderski 1974). Antonius was certainly eligible for 52 as he was born in 83. He returned to Rome in 53 intending to run for the quaestorship for 52, but the murder of Clodius and the subsequent disturbances made him change his mind and wait for better political circumstances. Presumably in the summer of 52 Antonius was a candidate in the elections for 51. Once elected quaestor, he hurried to join Caesar in Gaul before the lots were drawn and apparently without waiting for legal procedures to be fully conducted (Cic. *Phil.* 2.50: *Quaestor es factus; deinde continuo sine senatus consulto, sine sorte, sine lege ad Caesarem cucurristi*). Antonius joined Caesar in autumn 52. Since he had not yet taken office, Caesar called him *legatus* (Caes. *Gall.* 7.81.6). Once Antonius officially became quaestor in December, Caesar referred to him regularly as quaestor throughout 51 (*Gall.* 8.2.1; 8.24.2; 8.38.1) and then went back to calling him legate in 50 (*Gall.* 8.46.4). For the acceptance of Linderski and Kamiska-Linderski's arguments and 51 as the date of Antonius' quaestorship, see Broughton MRR, 3.19–20; Bengtson 1977, 45; Lacey 1985; Chamoux 1986, 52–53; Dettenhofer 1992, 66–68; Ryan 1996f, 42: since Antonius was born on 14 January 83, he was thirty-one years, ten months, and twenty days when he took up the quaestorship.

M. Appuleius (q. 45? proq. in Asia 44?) (RE 13):
The problem consists in identifying the correct Appuleius (see following entry). He must be different from the proquaestor Appuleius to whom Cicero addressed a letter, because this was written in 46 (Cic. *fam.* 13.45. Cf. Bülz 1893, 62–63; Sobeck 1909, 69–70). According to Broughton this M. Appuleius could be a brother of Sex. Appuleius (RE 16a), and therefore not the consul of 20, but his uncle (see the stemma in Sumner 1971, 361–362). Sumner provides supplementary arguments against the identification of this Appuleius with the consul of the year 20. He may be the proquaestor in Asia who in 44 gave his forces and public funds over to Marcus Brutus at Carystus; in this case he was presumably a quaestor in 45 (Broughton MRR, 2.308; 2.327; 3.20).

P.? Appuleius (q. 48 or 47 in Asia? proq. in Asia 47 or 46?) (tr. pl. 43?) (RE 2? 15?):
As in the previous entry, the problem is in identifying this Appuleius, to whom Cicero apparently wrote a letter in 46 (Cic. *fam.* 13.45 [cf. 13.46]: *Cicero Appuleio proquaestori*). Cicero does not mention his *praenomen*. Initially Broughton MRR, 2.288, included him

among the promagistrates in 47 as a proquaestor in Asia. But he later clarified this, considering him a quaestor in 48 or 47 and identifying him most probably with P. Appuleius, tribune of the plebs in 43 (Broughton MRR, 3.20; cf. Sumner 1971, 363). If the Ciceronian letter is to be dated to 46, Appuleius was obviously a proquaestor in this year.

Cn. [Appuleius] Saturninus: see Cn. Saturninus

L. Appuleius Saturninus (q. Ostiensis 105?) (tr. pl. 103 and 100) (RE 29):

Cicero is the main source on Saturninus' quaestorship: *Saturninum, quod in annonae caritate quaestorem a sua frumentaria procuratione senatus amovit eique rei M. Scaurum praefecit, scimus dolore factum esse popularem* (Cic. har. resp. 43); *nec mihi erat res cum Saturnino, qui quod a se quaestore Ostiensi per ignominiam ad principem et senatus et civitatis, M. Scaurum, rem frumentariam tralatam sciebat...* (Cic. Sest. 39). According to Cicero, Saturninus was *quaestor Ostiensis* in charge of Rome's food supply (Chandler 1978, 330). He was removed from this task by the senate and replaced by the *princeps senatus* M. Aemilius Scaurus, who obviously did not assume the quaestorship but most likely an exceptional *cura annonae* in order to address the difficult situation (Cébeillac Gervasoni 2002, 63–64). This affront impelled Saturninus to become a *popularis*. Cicero's information is supplemented by Diodorus (36.12). The Greek author adds that after his quaestorhip Saturninus adopted a more sober way of life, which caused him to be elected by the people as tribune of the plebs. Diodorus' text suggests that an interval (of undetermined length) passed between his quaestorship and tribunate. In addition to these literary sources some coins are atributed to L. Appuleius Saturninus. They depict the god Saturn in a chariot with the inscription *L · SATVRN* (Crawford RRC, 323–324 no. 317). According to Crawford, Saturn alluded to the *cognomen* of Saturninus, who had acted as a moneyer and not as a quaestor (cf. also Crawford 1969). Crawford dates Saturninus' moneyership between his quaestorship and his first tribunate from December 105 to December 104 (Mattingly 1977, 205–206, gives 102 or 101 as a date for the coins, but this is really only a *terminus ante quem*). However, Benness 1991, 58–59, suggests that Saturninus could have minted the issue as *quaestor Ostiensis*, although there is no mention of this office on the coins. In fact, Benness proposes that the minting of coins without senatorial authorization could have been the reason behind Saturninus' removal from office. This hypothesis is not corroborated by the sources, which suggest, rather, a problem related to the food supply (Cicero) or Saturninus' misconduct (Diodorus).

The date of Saturninus' quaestorship has been widely debated. Some scholars have taken 104 as the most likely date (Bültz 1908, 19; Sobeck 1909, 24–25; Broughton MRR, 1.560; Sumner 1973, 119–121; Rickman 1980, 47; Schneider 1982–83, 208; Garnsey 1988, 198; Benness 1991; Evans 1994, 212). Given that Saturninus held his first tribunate in 103, this would mean that he committed a legal irregularity according to the *lex Villia*, since he had probably been a candidate for the tribunate while still serving as quaestor (the sources speak of the removal of Saturninus' duties relating to the food supply, the *procuratio frumentaria*, but not of his dismissal as quaestor; cf. Prag 2014a, 198). Seeking an explanation, Sumner 1973, 119–121, proposes the possibility of the elections for tribunes 103 taking place between 5th and 9th December 104, once Saturninus had left the quaestorship. This argument, however, is rather forced and finds no support in the sources (moreover, we do not know whether the quaestors entered office on 5th December at that time). If we follow Crawford and accept that Saturninus was a moneyer before holding the tribunate for the first time and after his quaestorship, the sequence of events might have been as follows: quaestor 105, moneyer 104, and tribune of the plebs 103 (Crawford RRC, 75; cf. Mattingly 1969, 506; Gruen 1968b, 163, n. 35: 104 could be the date of Saturninus' quaestorship, but 105 cannot be ruled out; Broughton MRR, 3.20–21, summarises the arguments for 105 or 104 without committing himself to either date). It was not unusual at that time to hold the quaestorship before being a moneyer. This reconstruction does not contradict Cicero, because he is not necessarily talking about an immediate transformation from quaestor to *popularis*. On the other hand, it fits well with Diodorus' text, which suggests a process, a certain interval between quaestorship and tribunate (cf. Badian 1974, 160 n. 5). At any rate, the fact that the *princeps senatus*, the most prestigious politician of the time, took over the tasks of a quaestor, a lower magistrate, points to an exceptional situation in Rome (Cicero just says *in annonae caritate*). The city certainly lived through critical times in 105 (Gran. Licin. 33.25–27 C), but the situation must not have been much better in 104. Finally, according to Evans 1994, 184, Saturninus may have been born in 135, and consequently, held the quaestorship when he was thirty.

C. Appuleius M. f. Tappo (q. late first century, perhaps in the 40s) (RE 31):
CIL I² 814 = V 862 = ILS 906: *C. Appuleius M. f. Tappo pr. aed. tr. pl. q. iudex quaestionis rerum capital(ium)*. His quaestorship is known only through this inscription. He may have been active in the late Republic and/or the early Augustan period (Sobeck 1909, 75; Broughton MRR, 2.474. Cf. Wiseman 1971, 213). According to Mommsen Röm.St., I 555 n. 1, his political career may have begun under Caesar's dictatorship. If this hypothesis is accepted, C. Appuleius Tappo may have been quaestor before 44.

M'. Aquillius M'. f. (q. before 136?) (cos. 129) (RE 10):
There is no specific evidence for Aquillius' quaestorship. However, Ascon. 24C (*ac neque illius Crassi factum superioris isdem honoribus usus, qui fortissimus in bellis fuisset, <M'.> Aquilius potuit imitari* [the praenomen *M'* was added by Manutius]) makes a comparison between M. Aquillius and P. Licinius Crassus Dives Mucianus, the consul of 131 (Ascon. 25C identifies him; cf. Marshall 1985, 142). Asconius states that both politicians held the same offices throughout their cursus honorum (isdem ho-

noribus usus). Since Crassus' quaestorship and aedileship are securely attested (see his entry), Aquillius must also have been quaestor and aedile. Aquillius may have held the praetorship by 132. Consequently, the latest possible date for his aedileship is 134, and the latest possible date for his quaestorship is 136 (Ryan 1996b). More recently, Lewis has suggested that this M'. Aquillius is not the consul of 129 but rather his son of the same name, consul in 101 (Lewis 2006, 225). Nevertheless, the identification with the consul of 129 is much more likely: he and Crassus Dives Mucianus were contemporaries and were both in command in Asia. That makes a comparison between their political careers all the more reasonable (see the contrast between the honourable Mucianus and the disreputable Aquillius in Flor. 1.35).

L. Aquillius M'. f. Florus (q. in Asia by 70?) (not in RE):

Three bilingual Latin and Greek milestones from the ancient road Ephesus-Sardis (CIL III 479 – 14201[11]; 14202[4] = ILS 5814) record a restoration made by the quaestor L. Aquillius Florus (*M'. Aquilli[us M'. f. cos.]* / [Μ]άνιος Ἀκύλλι[ος Μα]νίου υἱός [ὕπατος] / *[L.] Aquillius [M'. f.] M'. n. Floru[s q.] / restitu[it XXI]III* / [Λε]ύκιος Ἀκύιο[ς Μ]ανίου υἱός / [Μ]ανίου δὲ υἱ[ωνὸς Φλῶ]ρος ταμίας / ἀποκατέσ[τησεν] / ΚΔ). He was presumably a son of M'. Aquillius (cos. 101) and a grandson of M'. Aquillius (cos. 129). According to the inscriptions, he probably restored (*restituit*) the milestones, not the road built by his ancestor, the consul of 129, as Haussoullier initially proposed (Haussoullier 1899, provided the first interpretation of the milestone and has been followed by Bültz 1908, 11– 12, Sobeck 1909, 76 and Broughton MRR, 2.475). The restoration of the milestones may have been connected to a reorganisation of the roads in the area at an uncertain time. It is impossible to fix the date of Aquillius Florus' quaestorship (Sobeck 1909, 76, includes him among the quaestors of uncertain date; Broughton MRR, 2.533, just dates his quaestorship to the late Republic). However, Haussoullier suggests a period around 70, a rather speculative date that has been accepted by French 1995, 99 – 101, who emphasises that financial reforms were initiated in 70 in Asia Minor (cf. Broughton MRR, 2.129), and by Thonemann 2004, 81.

M. Aquinius (or Aquinus) (q. by 51?) (RE Aquinius 2; cf. Aquinus 5):

Bell. Afr. 57: *Scipio mittit ad Aquinium... Usu venisse hoc civi Romano et ei qui ab populo Romano honores accepisset... M. Aquinium hominem novum parvumque senatorem* (cf. *bell. Afr.* 89). According to this text, M. Aquinius was a senator in the Pompeian forces in Africa in 46, probably a legate (Broughton MRR, 2.300; cf. 3.25). By then he had held plural *honores* in his *cursus honorum*, in other words at least two offices. As a senator, he must have begun his political career with the quaestorship. Ryan 1996a, 214 – 215, points out that Aquinius could have been quaestor by 51 and perhaps tribune of the plebs by 49, taking into account that the Pompeians in Thessalonica held no elections for 48 (Cass.Dio 41.43.1– 3). Accordingly, 49 was the last year in which Pompeians held office. As a senator M. Aquinius certainly held the quaestorship. The year 51 is the latest possible date, but it could of course have been earlier.

Asullius (q. by 130) (not in RE):
Diodorus (37.8.1–4) praises a Λεύκιος Ἀσύλλιος (sic) for having reconstructed Sicily when he was στρατηγός, presumably after the Second Slave War (104–100). Broughton MRR, 2.9 and 2.614, identifies him as L. (Sempronius) Asellio (RE 18), and dates his praetorship in Sicily by 96 (MRR, 3.188: his governorship in Sicily is subsequent to that of Mucius Scaevola in Asia). Prag 2007b, 302, accepts the identification and places his praetorship sometime between 96 and 92 (see also Brennan 2000, 480). Additionally, Diodorus asserts that this Λεύκιος Ἀσύλλιος was the son of a man who only reached the rank of *quaestorius* (πατρὸς μὲν ὑπάρχων τεταμιευκότος). If the date of Asullius's praetorship in Sicily is correct, the quaestorship of his father should presumably be dated to around 130 (Sobeck 1909, 80–81, claims that the Asullius in Diodorus was in reality an Aquillius and vaguely dates his quaestorship to the second half of the second century). At that moment we only know of a Sempronius Asellio (RE 16), who was military tribune in 134–133 in Numantia under Scipio Aemilianus and was the historian (Broughton MRR, 1.491). Münzer in his article in RE suggests that the praetor of Sicily at the beginning of the first century could have been the brother or son of RE 16. Badian 1968a [1970], argues that the praetor in Sicily was the historian's eldest son, and he proposes the *praenomen* Lucius for the historian, who would have been born, in his opinion, by 159–158. Provided the identification of the praetor of Sicily is correct, the historian L.? Sempronius Asellio may have been quaestor by 130 after his return from Numantia. However, Pobjoy in Cornell (ed.) 2013, 1.275, asserts that nothing is recorded of Asellio's career after the Numantine War, not even whether or not he became a senator. Pobjoy dates his birth to around 160.

However, a mistake between Ἀσύλλιος (to which all the manuscripts point) and Ἀσελλίων seems very unlikely, though not impossible from the paleographical point of view. As a matter of fact, 'Asullius' is a well-attested *nomen* both in later Latin epigraphy (for instance AE 1981, no. 334; 1993, no. 200; CIL II² 14.2236; VI 21379) and Cassius Dio, who mentions a στρατηγός named Λούκιος Ἀσύλλιος in the manuscripts, who was replaced in the praetorship by his son in 33 (49.43.7). According to the evidence, the praetor mentioned by Diodorus could also be a Lucius belonging to this missing *gens Asullia*, which was perhaps introduced into the Roman senate by Asullius' quaestorship in the 130s; see Díaz Fernández 2017b.

L. Ateius L. f. Capito (q. 53 or 52) (pr. date uncertain) (RE 9):
See **M. Eppius** and **C. Scribonius Curio**. L. Ateius Capito is mentioned by Caelius (Cic. *fam.* 8.8.5–6: ...*C. Scribonius C. f. Pop. Curio, L. Ateius L. f. An. Capito, M. Eppius M. f. Ter.*) as one of the senators present at the session in which a *senatus consultum* was approved. Assuming that Caelius mentions the senators in hierarchical order, Ateius

and Eppius would have been among the newest members of the senate; consequently, they were in all probability *quaestorii* in 51. C. Scribonius Curio (RE 11), who is mentioned inmediately before Ateius Capito, had been quaestor in Asia, perhaps in 55, and proquaestor in 54 and 53. Ateius Capito was, therefore, quaestor before 51 and after 54 (or 55), presumably in 53 or 52. See Broughton MRR, 2.236; 2.246–247; 2.533: quaestor by 52. Cf. Wiseman 1971, 215–216.

L. Atilius (q. 216) (RE 13):
See **L. Furius Bibaculus.** L. Atilius and L. Furius Bibaculus were the quaestors of the consuls C. Terentius Varro and L. Aemilius Paullus in 216 (Liv. 22.49.16: *in his ambo consulum quaestores, L. Atilius et L. Furius Bibaculus…*). Both died in the battle of Cannae. See Bülz 1908, 4; Sobeck 1909, 7; Broughton MRR, 1.249.

Sex. Atilius Serranus Gavianus (q. 63) (tr. pl. 57) (RE 70):
As a tribune of the plebs in 57, Sextus Atilius Serranus Gavianus opposed a motion in the senate in favour of Cicero's return to Rome. Later on in his speech to the people after his return, Cicero states that Serranus was quaestor in the same year as Cicero was consul, in 63 (Cic. *p. red. Quir.* 12: *Atque eo die confecta res esset, nisi is tribunus plebis, quem ego maximis beneficiis quaestorem consul ornaram…*). See Sobeck 1909, 51; Broughton MRR, 2.168.

L. Aurelius (q. urb. 196) (RE 18):
See **Q. Fabius Labeo.** Lucius Aurelius and Q. Fabius Labeo were the *quaestores urbani* in 196. They had a serious quarrel with the augurs and pontifices over the payment of their quota throughout the Hannibalic War (Liv. 33.42.2: *Sed magnum certamen cum omnibus sacerdotibus eo anno fuit quaestoribus urbanis Q. Fabio Labeoni et L. Aurelio*). See Sobeck 1909, 10; Broughton MRR, 1.336.

M. Aurelius Scaurus (q. by 103?) (RE 215):
See **M. Aurelius Scaurus** (RE 216); also **Cn. Pompeius Strabo** and **L. Philo.** According to Cicero, a Marcus Aurelius Scaurus unsuccessfully tried to prosecute L. Flaccus, under whose command he had served as quaestor: *Neque fere umquam venit in contentionem de accusando qui quaestor fuisset, quin repudiaretur. Itaque neque L. Philoni in C. Servilium nominis deferendi potestas est data, neque M. Aurelio Scauro in L. Flaccum, neque Cn. Pompeio in T. Albucium* (Cic. *div.in Caec.* 62–63). The date of Scaurus' quaestorship depends on when this L. Flaccus was praetor or proconsul, which remains an unresolved question. Sobeck 1909, 22, identifies this Scaurus with the *consul suffectus* of 108, and merely places his quaestorship before 108. Broughton MRR, 1.529 and 2.536 (cf. 3.32) also proposes this Scaurus to be the *consul suffectus* of

108, and dates his quaestorship to ca. 117; however, he concedes that the date is a conjecture based on the supposed interval between the quaestorship and the consulship in this period (Sumner 1973, 52, shows, however, that in the period before the Sullan legislation the interval between the two magistracies was longer than Broughton supposes). Broughton's assumption seems too speculative and it forces the invention of a Flaccus as praetor or proconsul perhaps around or before 120 rather than ca. 117.

The situation changes if Scaurus is not identified with the consul of 108 but with his son. Badian 1964, 86–87 with nn. 96–98, proposes that the Valerius Flaccus to whom Cicero refers was the consul of 100. He may have been praetor by 103, and consequently this would also be the date of Scaurus' quaestorship. Gruen 1968b, 178–179, basically accepts Badian's suggestion: Flaccus was the consul of 100; his praetorship should be dated to around 104; the attempt at prosecution by Scaurus would immediately follow the praetorship; Scaurus would be a son of the consul 108 and is otherwise unknown (Crawford RRC, 299, states that the moneyer M. Aurelius Scaurus, who issued coins in Narbo in 118, is the quaestor of Cic. *div. in Caec.* 63 and of Cic. *Verr.* 2.1.85, son of the consul 108). However, Sumner 1973, 79–82, chooses to deny the existence of the proposed quaestor Scaurus in 103. Instead, he is inclined to see the same quaestor in Cic. *div. in Caec.* 63 and in Cic. *Verr.* 2.1.85 (this hypothesis was already put forth by Münzer in RE 8 A 26–27, Valerius 178). According to Sumner, this quaestor Scaurus would have served under Flaccus in Asia around 95–90, and this Flaccus was later *consul suffectus* in 86; the proposal has also been accepted by Badian 1984b, 299. Ferrary 2000b, 337–339, concludes that L. Valerius Flaccus governed Asia ca. 91–90; see also Brennan 2000, 553–554.

If we follow Sumner (and Münzer), there would be only one quaestor with the name M. Aurelius Scaurus. The problem in accepting this thesis is that Cicero (*Verr.* 2.1.85) states that Scaurus had been quaestor not long before (*nuper*) the trial against Verres (see the following entry). This Ciceronian claim seems to suggest that there were indeed two different quaestors named Marcus Aurelius Scaurus. The elder was probably a son of the consul suffectus 108, and he may have served under Flaccus by 103, as Badian proposes.

M. Aurelius M. f. Scaurus (q. in the 70s in Asia) (RE 216):
See **M. Aurelius Scaurus** (RE 215). According to Cicero, a Marcus Aurelius Scaurus was quaestor in Asia not long before (*nuper*) Verres' trial: *Nuper M. Aurelio Scauro postulante, quod is Ephesi se quaestorem vi prohibitum esse dicebat quo minus e fano Dianae servum suum...* (Cic. *Verr.* 2.1.85; see I. Délos 1858bis = CIL I^2 816 = ILLRP 373: *M. Aurelius M. f. Scaurus q.*). The interpretation of the word *nuper* is the key. Badian 1963, 133, points out that the term *nuper* is elastic, and does not necessarily imply that Scaurus' quaestorship should be dated shortly before 70 (cf. Badian 1984b, 298–299). Actually, Badian suggests that Scaurus was quaestor by 80, taking Q. Hortensius' political career as similar: Cic. *Verr.* 2.3.182, refers to Hortensius' quaestorship as *nuper*

despite having been held by 80, according to Badian (Hortensius was aedile in 75). If this Scaurus was a member of the *consilium* of Pompeius Strabo in Asculum (CIL I² 709 = CIL VI 37045 = ILLRP 515 = ILS 8888) and consequently a military tribune in 89 (cf. Broughton MRR, 2.35 and 38 n. 12, from Cichorius 1922, 149), he certainly may have been quaestor around 80 as Badian proposes. In any case, the word *nuper*, although ambiguous, suggests that Scaurus was quaestor closer to Verres' trial in the seventies. The exact year is, however, impossible to determine. See Bültz 1908, 25; Sobeck 1909, 45: shortly before 70; Broughton MRR, 2.475: quaestor in Asia before 70; 3.32: 'quaestor in Asia of uncertain date'; Gruen 1974, 194: 'a quaestor in Asia before 70'; 529: quaestor in the latter part of the seventies.

P. Autronius L. f. Paetus (q. 75) (cos. desig. 65) (RE 7):
Cicero states that Publius Autronius Paetus was his colleague in the quaestorship in 75: *Veniebat enim ad me et saepe veniebat Autronius... et se meum... conlegam in quaestura commemorabat fuisse* (Cic. *Sull.* 18). See Sobeck 1909, 38; Broughton MRR, 2.97. Cf. Badian 1959a, 87: Autronius got his quaestorship two years later than the minimum age, but he was elected for the consulship *suo anno* for 65, two years before Cicero. Cf. Ryan 1996f, 40: he was at least thirty-two when he became quaestor.

Q. Axius M. f. (q. 75 or 74) (RE 4):
Quintus Axius (Κόϊντος Ἄξιος Μαάρκου υἱὸς Κυρίνα) is included in the list of senators in the *SC de Oropiis* of year 73 (SIG³ 747 = RDGE 23). The names of the list appear in order of rank. Axius is one of the *quaestorii* and is mentioned immediately after Cicero, who had been quaestor in 75. As a result, Axius must have held the quaestorship before 73, either in 75 as a colleague of Cicero, or in 74. See Broughton MRR, 2.475; 2.537 as well as 3.33: 'Q. before 73'; Ryan 2005.

Q. Baebius Q. f. (pro[q.?] at the beginning of first century in Macedonia?) (RE 20a, suppl. 1.236 / 53, suppl. 3.192):
A Q. Baebius is known through two honorific inscriptions in Greek from Tegea. He is mentioned as ἀντι[ταμίας], patron and benefactor of Tegea (IG 5.2.146: πόλις Τεγεατᾶν / Κόϊντον Βαίβιον Κοΐν/ του υἱὸν Ῥωμαῖον / τὸν αὐτᾶς πάτρωνα / καὶ εὐεργέταν; 147: [πόλις] / [Τεγεα]τᾶν Κόϊντον [---] / [Κοΐ]ντου υἱόν, ἀντι[ταμίαν] / [τὸν α]ὐτᾶς πάτρω[να καὶ] / [εὐεργέταν]). Sobeck 1909, 81, simply considers Baebius a proquaestor in the Republican age, but a restoration of ἀντι[στράτηγος] could be also possible (cf. IG 12.5.722, ll. 6–7: ὑπὸ Γναίου Αὐφιδίου Γναίου υοῦ ἀντι/στρατήγου). Broughton MRR, 2.480: dates his proquaestorship in Greece speculatively to the second century. Harmand 1957, 74, provides a more specific date, since he identifies the patron of Tegea as the tribune of the plebs who in 200 opposed the motion to declare war against Philip (cf. Broughton MRR, 1.324). Nevertheless, as Eilers 2002, 196–197, points out, nothing

suggests that this tribune was ever in Greece or had any Greek contacts. Harmand's identification is therefore pure speculation without basis. Eilers challenged the dating of Baebius' proquaestorship to the second century, which in his opinion was little more than a guess; instead he proposes to date the inscriptions towards the beginning of the first century. This Baebius could have been, in his opinion, the brother or some other relation of Baebia, the mother of L. Valerius Flaccus, praetor in 63. See also Canali de Rossi 2001, 68–69.

C. Billienus C. f. (q. by 120–115?) (RE Bellienus 3–4):

A C. Billienus is mentioned as quaestor in a Greek inscription from Delos (I. Délos 1632, ll. 3–4: Βιλλιῆνον [---] / ταμίαν [---]). Cicero alludes to a man of the same name who could not reach the consulate because his attempts coincided with the consecutive consulships of Marius at the end of the second century (Cic. Brut. 175). If the quaestor mentioned in the inscription from Delos is the orator of Cicero's Brutus, his quaestorship may be dated to the last decades of the second century. If he really competed with Marius for the consulate in the final years of the century, he could have been a quaestor some fifteen years earlier, perhaps at some point between 120 and 115. See Broughton MRR, 2.475: quaestor of uncertain date; 2.538: quaestor before 100; Sumner 1973, 21 and 105: Billienus was a candidate for the consulship during the period 105–101 (perhaps more than once) and consequently must have been of consular age by 101 and born no later than 143. Cf. Wiseman 1971, 217.

However, note that the lost part of the inscription seems to be large enough to include the terms στρατηγός or ἀνθύπατος after the name of Billienus (he was proconsul in Asia by 107; see I. Délos 1854) as well as the name of an unknown quaestor. In this case, the inscription might belong to Billienus' proconsulship and the quaestor would be an unknown Roman citizen.

Caecilius (q. 59) (RE 1):

It can be deduced from a letter sent by Cicero from Antium that a Caecilius was quaestor in 59, the date of the letter (Cic. Att. 2.9.1: *subito cum mihi dixisset Caecilius quaestor puerum se Romam mittere...* Cf. Att. 2.19.5 and 2.20.1, where a Caecilius is also mentioned; this Caecilius, however, seems to be different from the quaestor). He is otherwise completely unknown. Mommsen Röm.St., II 557 n. 2, wagers that Caecilius was probably the quaestor of Cales. Mattingly 1969, 506, suggests that he was the *quaestor Ostiensis*. Both suggestions are based on the unproven assumption that these two quaestorian *provinciae* existed every year. Caecilius seems to have been staying at Antium when Cicero wrote his letter, but nothing is said about his presumed official activities in the town. He could have been there enjoying some days of rest on a private trip. See Harris 1976, 101. Cf. Sobeck 1909, 55; Broughton MRR, 2.190; Shackleton Bailey, *Ep.Att.* 1.369.

C. Caecilius Metellus (q. shortly before 82?) (RE 71):

Plutarch (*Sulla* 31.1–2; cf. Schol. Gron. 337 Stangl) asserts that C. Caecilius Metellus was one of the youngest senators in 82. He dared to ask Sulla in the Curia for details of the proscriptions. Plutarch adds that other sources assert that it was Fufidius who asked the question. Given that Metellus was one of most junior senators in 82, it is reasonable to assume that he may have been a quaestor shortly before, although his quaestorship is not explicitly attested. See Broughton MRR, 2.475.

L.? Caecilius Metellus (q. 214) (tr. pl. 213) (RE 73):

In 214 some Roman citizens planned to flee from Italy after the defeat at Cannae. The quaestor Metellus was the most prominent among them: *Princeps eorum M. Caecilius Metellus quaestor tum forte erat* (Liv. 24.18.3). As a punishment for his betrayal, Metellus was demoted by the censors to the rank of *aerarius* (Liv. 24.43.2–4: *quaestorem eum proximo anno adempto equo tribu moverant atque aerarium fecerant propter coniurationem deserendae Italiae ad Cannas factam...* Cf. Val.Max. 2.9.8: *M. enim Atilius Regulus et L. Furius Philus M. Metellum quaestorem conpluresque equites Romanos, qui post infeliciter commissam Cannensem pugnam cum eo abituros se Italia iuraverant, dereptis equis publicis inter aerarios referendos curaverunt*). On this episode, see Tatum 1990b, 37. Livy and Valerius Maximus give three different *praenomina* for this man, but Münzer in RE, Sobeck and Broughton agree on Lucius as the correct one. See Sobeck 1909, 7; Broughton MRR, 1.260–261 n. 2; Develin 1979, 68.

L. Caecilius L. f. Metellus (q. by 52? in Sicily) (tr. pl. 49) (RE 75):

A Greek inscription from Eryx records L. Caecilius Metellus as ταμίας (IGRom. 1.501 = IG 14.282 = CIL 10.7258: ἐπὶ ταμία Λευκίου Καικιλίου / Λευκίου υἱοῦ Μετέλλου). It has therefore been deduced that he was quaestor at Lilybaeum in Sicily. There is no evidence of the exact year of Metellus' quaestorship, but it should be obviously dated a few years before his tribunate in 49, probably by 52 (Sobeck 1909, 55; Broughton MRR, 2.236; 2.478; Prag 2007a, 82; 2007b, 308). Brennan 2000, 844 n. 158, suggests that he was *quaestor pro praetore*, but this proposal is conjectural.

Q. Caecilius Q. f. Metellus Pius Scipio Nasica (q. 62?) (cos. 52) (RE 99):

See **M. Favonius.** In May 60 Metellus Scipio and M. Favonius competed in a special election to choose a substitute to fill a regular magistracy (Cic. *Att.* 2.1.9). Metellus Scipio was the winner (Favonius prosecuted him unsuccesfully after the election, probably for *ambitus*) and so he became a magistrate *suffectus* for the rest of 60. But for which magistracy? Broughton MRR, 2.189, supposes that this magistracy was the tribunate of the plebs. However, Sumner 1973, 112–113, denies that the magistracy could be the tribunate and proposes instead the quaestorship. According to Sumner, Metellus Scipio was a quaestor *suffectus* in 60. Broughton MRR, 3.41–42, has declared that the election 'remains a puzzle,' but has changed his mind to follow Sumner: a quaestorship in 60 seems too late for a man born around 95, but it is the most convenient magistracy for Metellus Scipio in that year. Wiseman again proposes the tribunate of the plebs in his review of Sumner's book (*JRS* 65, 1975, 198). More recently, Ryan 1994c, has tried to refute thoroughly all previous arguments to make a new proposal: the magistracy Metellus Scipio won in May 60 must indeed have been the suffect tribunate of the plebs; he had already held the quaestorship in 62. Nevertheless, Konrad 1996, 108, rejects Ryan's argument as 'untenable' in favour of a tribunate sought in 60, and argues that 'the supplementary election in which Favonius ran unsuccessfully against Metellus Pius in 60 was almost certainly for the curule aedileship' (cf. Pina Polo 2012, 67 and 82 n. 61). This scholarly ping-ponging demonstrates the difficulty of reaching a conclusive answer. Given what is currently known, it seems necessary to discard Metellus Scipio's position as quaestor *suffectus* in 60; his quaestorship by 62 is plausible, though not secure.

Q. Caecilius Niger (q. 73 in Sicily) (RE 101):
See **M. Postumius.** Q. Caecilius Niger was quaestor under Verres in Sicily at Lilybaeum in 73 (Cic. *div. in Caec.* 4: *Dicebam habere eos actorem Q. Caecilium, qui praesertim quaestor in eadem provincia post me quaestorem fuisset*). See Marinone 1965–66, 252; Broughton MRR, 3.43, follows Marinone and corrects 2.117: Niger was probably among those of his staff who left Verres at the end of this first year (Cic. *Verr.* 2.2.49); Prag 2007b, 306: he was running for the aedileship or at least was capable of doing so, in 70, which further implies that he was quaestor in 73, given the normal intervals between offices. Cf. Brennan 2000, 840 n. 94. Sobeck 1909, 44, wrongly dates Niger's quaestorship to 72.

L. Caecilius L. f. Rufus (before 64) (pr. 57) (RE 110):
An inscription recording the *cursus honorum* of Lucius Caecilius Rufus includes the quaestorship among his magistracies: *L. Caecilio L. f. Rufo q. tr. pl. pr. pro cos. dis manibus L. Caecili Rufi* (CIL I^2 761 = ILS 880). He was tribune of the plebs in 63 (Broughton MRR, 2.167), before which he had held the quaestorship. Taking into account the compulsory interval between two offices, Caecilius Rufus was a quaestor before 64, 65 being the latest possible date. Broughton MRR, 2.153, includes him among the quaestors of 66, but makes clear that the date is conjectural (cf. MRR, 2.540: 'Q. ca. 66').

L. Caecina L. f. (q. in the late first century, perhaps in the 40s) (not in RE):
Lucius Caecina's *cursus honorum* is mentioned in an inscription from Volsinii: *L. Caecina L. / q. tr. p. p. pr. cos. / IIIIvir i. d. / sua pecu/nia vias / stravit* (CIL I^2 2515). This otherwise unknown man was probably active in the late Republic, but the date of his

quaestorship is impossible to determine. It could be earlier or later than 44. See Broughton MRR, 2.475: 'probably in the late Republic.' But MRR, 2.468: 'held office [i.e. the tribunate of the plebs] in the late Republic or the Early Augustan period.' Note however the Καικίνα mentioned by App. *b.c.* 5.60, with Λεύκιος Κοκκήιος just before the Perusine War as well as the *Caecina quidam Volaterranus* named by Cicero in *Att.* 16.8.2; cf. Broughton MRR, 2.375–376; Syme 1955a, 133.

M. Caelius Rufus (q. 57?) (pr. 48) (RE 35):

Caelius Rufus' quaestorship is not explicitly attested. It is particularly problematic that Cicero, strangely, does not mention it in his speech *Pro Caelio* from 56 (Earl 1966, 306: 'M. Caelius Rufus, about whose career we are well informed because of his connection with Cicero, may well not have held the quaestorship and have come into the senate through holding the tribunate'). Nevertheless, it is highly likely that Caelius Rufus actually held the quaestorship, since this magistracy was the usual access route to the senate in post-Sullan age, unless a special exemption was granted. It has been suggested that Caelius Rufus could have received this exemption as a reward for his successful prosecution of the consular C. Antonius in 59, but there is no evidence for this in Cicero's speech, although the orator mentions the trial several times (see Russell 1953, 75; Lintott 2008, 431: 'it is possibly that he was given quaestorian status through his successful prosecution of C. Antonius'). The *Pro Caelio* gives some hints for the possible date of Caelius' quaestorship. Cicero makes it clear that Caelius was already of an age to be a candidate for a magistracy in 58 (Cic. *Cael.* 18: *Qui cum et ex publica causa iam esset mihi quidem molestam, sibi tamen gloriosam victoriam consecutus et per aetatem magistratus petere posset...*). He also rejects the accusation of *ambitus* against Caelius that the prosecutors seem to have formulated or at least suggested (Cic. *Cael.* 78). This allusion to possible electoral corruption must refer to a recent candidacy for a magistracy, which could only have been the quaestorship. If, as Cicero states, Caelius was in 58 the legal age to be a candidate, it is reasonable to assume that he ran this year for the quaestorship (since he was a praetor in 48, he was probably born no later than 88; Plin. *n.h.* 7.165, asserts that Caelius was born on 28 May 82 like the poet and orator C. Licinius Calvus; Pliny may have been right about the day but not the year; cf. Dyck 2013, 4). Consequently, if he was successful he could have been a quaestor between 5th December 58 and 4th December 57. See Sumner 1971, 248 and n. 11: he leaves it open as to whether Caelius was quaestor in 58 or 57; Sumner 1973, 147; Broughton MRR, 3.44, seems to be inclined to accept that Caelius did hold the quaestorship; Dyck 2013, 5: 'It is plausibly conjectured that he may have handled public monies either in Rome or in a province as quaestor the following year [i.e. 57].'

C. Caepasius (q. before 70) (RE Caepasius):

See **L. Caepasius.** According to Cicero, C. Caepasius and his brother Lucius made themselves known in Rome thanks to their eloquence, and both reached the quaestorship: *Eodem tempore C. L. Caepasii fratres fuerunt, qui multa opera, ignoti homines et repentini, quaestores celeriter facti sunt, oppidano quodam et incondito genere dicendi* (Cic. *Brut.* 242). The two brothers participated as orators in trials during the seventies (Cic. *Cluent.* 57). This makes it plausible that C. and L. Caepasius were quaestors before 70, although a more exact date is impossible to determine. See Sobeck 1909, 76: they were contemporaries of Hortensius; Broughton MRR, 2.475 and 2.540: q. before 70; Sumner 1973, 25: q. before 70; Wiseman 1971, 218–219: q. before 70. Cf. Syme 1964a, 107.

L. Caepasius (q. before 70) (RE Caepasius):
See **C. Caepasius.**

Q. Caerellius M. f. (q. in the late first century, perhaps in the 40s) (RE 2):
Q. Caerellius' political career is recorded in an inscription set up by his son: *Q. Caerellio M. f. Qui(rina) patri tr. milit. quae. tr. pl. praetori leg. M. Antoni procos.* (CIL VI 1364b = ILS 943b). The text of the inscription shows that he was a quaestor, presumably between his military tribunate and and his tribunate of the plebs (Broughton MRR, 2.468: he was a tribune of the plebs before 31). Caerellius later served as a legate under the triumvir M. Antonius in the thirties, and had held the praetorship earlier. This sequence of offices suggests that Caerellius may have been a quaestor in the forties, either before or after 44. See Sobeck 1909, 77: he was quaestor perhaps before Caesar's death; Broughton MRR, 2.475: quaestor of uncertain date.

P. Caesetius (q. 72 and proq. 71, or q. 71 in Sicily) (RE 3):
See **T. Vettius [Chilo?].** P. Caesetius was quaestor of Verres in Sicily and commanded the Sicilian fleet with the legate P. Tadius (Cic. *Verr.* 2.5.63; 2.4.146). The date of his quaestorship is controversial. The year 72 was initially suggested (Sobeck 1909, 44: quaestor in 72 in Syracuse; Broughton MRR, 2.117: quaestor in 72, apparently succeeding Postumius at Syracuse). Subsequently, Marinone 1965–66, has argued in favour of years 72 and 71 (cf. Broughton MRR, 3.44, following Marinone). However, Brennan 2000, 840 n. 95, states that there is no certain attestation for 72, only for 71 (*Verr.* 2.5.63) and for 70 after Verres' departure (*Verr.* 2.4.146). Both these passages suggest, according to Brennan, that Caesetius served at Syracuse. See also Prag 2007b, 306, who dates Caesetius' quaestorship to 71 and states that there is no clear indication of which quaestorship either Caesetius or Vettius held. Like T. Vettius, P. Caesetius may have been quaestor in 72 and proquaestor in 71, or quaestor in 71, at any rate serving under Verres in Sicily.

L. Calpurnius Bestia (q. before 64) (tr. pl. 62) (RE 24):
L. Calpurnius Bestia is mentioned by Sallust as one of the Catilinarians senators in 64 (Sall. *Cat.* 17.3). If this information is correct, he must have been quaestor before 64. See Ryan 1994d, 256 n. 5: 'Bestia might have been a quaestor rather than a senator in 64, but was necessarily a senator in 63,' without further argumentation.

Cn. Calpurnius Piso Cn. f. (q. pro pr. in Hispania Citerior 65–64) (RE 69):
Cn. Calpurnius Piso was sent in 65 as *quaestor pro praetore* to Hispania Citerior by senatorial decree according to Sallust: *Postea Piso in citeriorem Hispaniam quaestor pro praetore missus est* (Sall. *Cat.* 19.1. Cf. CIL I^2 749 = ILS 875 = ILLRP 378: *Cn. Calpurnius / Cn. f. Piso / quaestor pro pr. ex s.c. / provinciam Hispaniam / citeriorem optinuit*). Piso remained in his province in 64, when he was assassinated by horsemen in Hispania (Sall. *Cat.* 19.3). Broughton MRR, 2.159, includes him among the promagistrates of 65 (cf. 2.163 for 64). However, Balsdon 1962, 135, argues that he should be listed as a magistrate that year. According to Balsdon, Piso must have been one of the quaestors of 65, and Hispania Citerior was allocated to him by lot. See also Syme 1960b, 12: Piso was sent in 65 as quaestor to govern Hispania. Cf. Bülz 1893, 6–7; Sobeck 1909, 50; Gruen 1968a, 159–161.

L. Calpurnius Piso Caesoninus (q. urb. 103?) (RE 89):
See **Q. Servilius Caepio.** The quaestorship of L. Calpurnius Piso Caesoninus is known through some denarii in which his name Piso appears together with Caepio and the abbreviation *Q(uaestores)* (PISO · CAEPIO · Q). On the reverse, the abbreviations *AD · FRV· EMV / EX · S·C* must be read as *ad frumentum emundum ex senatus consulto*, that is 'to purchase grain in accordance with a senatorial decree.' According to Crawford RRC 330–331 (see also 313), given that in his opinion only one *quaestor urbanus* seems to have been in charge of the *aerarium*, one of them would be a *quaestor urbanus* and the other a *quaestor Ostiensis*, 'a likely combination for dealing with the corn supply.' Crawford identifies Piso as the quaestor Ostiensis and dates the coins to the year 100 (the dating in 96–95 proposed by Pink 1952, 29, must be discarded). However, the actual position of the two quaestors, as well as the date of their office, is far from clear. First, it appears more likely that both were acting as *quaestores urbani*. This is perhaps the reason why only the abbreviation *Q(uaestores)* was used in the denarii, without needing to specify the supposed different offices of Piso and Caepio, and taking for granted the usual relation between minting and *quaestores urbani* at Rome. Regarding the date of the coinage, it has been suggested that the purchase of corn at the expense of the state was the senatorial response to the attempt of the tribune of the plebs Saturninus to pass a *lex frumentaria* (Rhet.Her. 1.21). If this hypothesis is correct, the issue becomes determining whether the grain law of Saturninus should be dated to his first tribunate in 103 or to his second in 100 (Broughton MRR, 3.21: 'the grain law of Saturninus should more probably be dated to his first tribunate in 103 than to his

second in 100.' In MRR, 3.47, Broughton nevertheless leaves room to doubt the date of Piso's quaestorship: 'Quaestor 103 or 100'; Benness 1991, 38, suggests 103). Schneider 1982–83, 209, rightly argues that the grain law of Saturninus must be connected with the slave war that began in Sicily in 104. The revolt on the island must have provoked a food shortage at Rome. Consequently, the *lex frumentaria* of Saturninus should probably be dated to 103 as a response to the lack of food in the city; likewise, the coinage of the quaestors Piso and Caepio should be assigned the same date, if we understand their coinage as the senatorial response to Saturninus' law. As a result, 103 is a more probable date for the quaestorship of Piso and Caepio.

L. Calpurnius L. f. Piso Caesoninus (q. by 70) (cos. 58) (RE 90):
Cicero states that Piso obtained all magistracies throughout his political career without ever being defeated in an election (*sine repulsa*): *Is mihi etiam gloriabatur se omnis magistratus sine repulsa adsecutum?* (Cic. *Pis.* 1). Scholars have inferred that Piso was elected in the first possible year (*suo anno*) for each magistracy for which he was a candidate (quaestorship, aedileship, praetorship and consulate, this last office the only one for which the year 58 is securely attested). If this assumption is correct, Piso could have been quaestor around 70. See Sobeck 1909, 46; Broughton MRR, 2.128; 2.541; van der Blom 2016, 183.

C. Calpurnius L. f. Piso Frugi (q. 58) (RE 93):
As quaestor in 58, Piso Frugi gave up going to his province of Pontus and Bithynia in order to help Cicero, his father-in-law, return from exile: *C. Piso gener… qui Pontum et Bithyniam quaestor prae mea salute neglexit* (Cic. *p. red. Sen.* 38). He died the following year. See Sobeck 1909, 55–56; Broughton MRR, 2.197. Cf. Gruen 1968a, 162. He is probably the moneyer *C · PISO ·L· F· FRVGI* in Crawford RRC, 419–436, no. 408.

Cn. Calpurnius Cn. f. Piso (Frugi) (q. 49, proq. 48) (cos. suff. 23) (RE 95):
Piso's proquaestorship is attested by some denarii: on obverse we find the inscription *CN · PISO · PRO · Q*, while the reverse has *MAGN* above *PRO · COS*. The coins have been dated to 49 (Crawford RRC 463, no. 446). Grueber, CRRBM 2.361, deduces that Cn. Calpurnius Piso was proquaestor in Hispania Ulterior during the Civil War, but the proposal is conjectural. See Sobeck 1909, 64; Broughton MRR, 2.261. More recently, Woytek 2003, 113–118, has argued that this issue (as well as Crawford RRC no. 447: see **A.? (Terentius) Varro**) was coined in Greece in 48 by the Pompeians. Piso would be, therefore, one of the quaestors of 49 who had fled Rome with Pompey.

Fig. 3: Cn. Pompeius Magnus, 49. AR Denarius. Corcyra? Bare head of Numa Pompilius with diadem inscribed NVMA right, CN. PISO PRO Q. behind. Prow right, MAGN above, PRO COS below. Crawford RRC, no. 446/1.

Canidius (q. 58? and proq. 57?) (RE 1):

Plutarch mentions Canidius on several occasions as a friend of Cato, collaborating with him during his command in Cyprus (Plut. *Cat.min.* 35.1; 37.1–3; *Brut.* 3). Cato did indeed send Canidius in advance to Cyprus in 58 to take charge of the royal treasure and to urge Ptolemy to yield his kingdom without putting up a fight. Even though Plutarch does not give an official title for Canidius, it seems plausible that he was a quaestor in view of his financial and political responsibilities. In addition, Velleius Paterculus asserts that the *lex Clodia* which appointed Cato as *quaestor pro praetore* in 58 to annex Cyprus gave him a quaestor as assistant to carry out his mission: *ut is [Cato] quaestor cum iure praetorio, adiecto etiam quaestore, mitteretur in insulam Cyprum ad spoliandum regno Ptolemaeum...* (Vell. 2.45.4. See Badian 1965, 111 n. 11: 'we do not know the name of the quaestor'). Consequently, Canidius may have been this quaestor in 58, serving under Cato when he was sent to Cyprus. Furthermore, he could have been proquaestor in 57 if he remained on the island with Cato. See Wiseman 1964, 123; Broughton MRR, 3.49. Geiger 1972, 133, proposes the identification of this quaestor Canidius with L. Caninius Gallus (RE 3), tribune of the plebs in 56. Nothing in Plutarch's text suggest this possibility and it is a pure speculation.

Caninius Sallusti(an)us? (q. 51? and proq. 50 in Syria) (RE 1 A.2 1913 and 1919; Caninius 14):

This man is known only through a letter that Cicero sent him in August 50 (Cic. *fam.* 2.17). The salutation is *CANINI SALLUSTIO PRO Q.* The name, however, is corrupt in the preserved manuscripts, so that the name of the quaestor has been a continual subject of debate. His identification with the historian Sallust must be rejected. As Broughton MRR, 2.247 n. 2, rightly argues, it is improbable that the historian, who was a supporter of Caesar, would have served under Bibulus. Münzer (RE Caninius 14) suggests the cognomen Sallustianus as a possible alternative to Sallustius. Wiseman 1971, 258 no 371, asserts that 'perhaps Caninius Sallusti(an)us should be read.' Cf. Syme 1964b, 11 n. 20. However, an adoptive *nomen* could admit the former *nomen* as well (see Shackleton Bailey 1976, 55–57): in such a case, he may have been a Sallustius adopted by one Caninius. Leaving aside the rather insoluble question of his name (Sobeck 1909, 62, called him Cn. (C.) Sallustius [Sallustianus]), it is only sure that this man was proquaestor in 50 in Syria under the command of Bibulus. He may have been quaestor in 51 (Broughton MRR, 2.242; 3.184).

Sp. Carvilius (q. 391) (RE 4):

According to Pliny, the quaestor Spurius Carvilius reproached M. Furius Camillus for appropriating a bronze door from the booty of Veii and having it at home: *Camillo inter crimina obiecit Spurius Carvilius quaestor, ostia quod aerata haberet in domo* (Plin. n.h. 34.13). Carvilius' quaestorship should be dated to 391 (Broughton MRR, 1.93). The verb used by Pliny (*obicere*) does not suggest a formal accusation like the one formulated against Camillus by the tribune L. Appuleius (Plut. *Cam.* 12–13), but rather a moral reproval. Sobeck 1909, 4–5, considers the name of this quaestor to be unhistorical: the story of Camillus' trial and exile could be fictional as well as the quaestor Carvilius (cf. Shatzman 1972, 190).

A. Cascellius A. f. (q. 75 or 74) (RE 4):

A. Cascellius (Αὖλος Κασκέλιος Αὔλου υἱὸς {ὁ υἱὸς} Ῥωμιλία) is one of the senators mentioned in the *SC de Oropiis* of 73 (SIG³ 747 = RDGE 23). The names appear in the list in hierarchical order. Cascellius is one of the *quaestorii* and is mentioned after Cicero, who had been quaestor in 75, Q. Axius and Q. Pompeius Rufus. As a consequence, Cascellius must have held the quaestorship before 73, either in 75 as a colleague of Cicero, or in 74. See Broughton MRR, 2.543: 'Q.? before 73' (cf. 3.50); Wiseman 1971, 222: q. by 73; Ryan 2005. The Digest confirms Cascellius' quaestorship: *Aulus Cascellius... quaestorius fuit nec ultra proficere voluit, cum illi etiam Augustus consulatum offerret* (Dig. 1.2.2.45).

C. Cassius C. f. Longinus (q. 55? proq. 54–53? proq. pro pr.? 53–51? in Syria) (cos. desig. 41) (RE 59):

There is no doubt that C. Cassius Longinus served as quaestor and proquaestor under the command of Crassus in Syria. Velleius Paterculus names Cassius Longinus quaestor in 53 during the disaster in Carrhae and praises him for having saved the rest of the legions and for having preserved Syria in Roman hands: *Reliquias legionum C.*

Cassius, atrocissimi mox auctor facinoris, tum quaestor, conservavit Syriamque adeo in populi Romani potestate retinuit... (Vell. 2.46.4). See also Livy: *C. Cassius, quaestor M. Crassi, Parthos qui Syriam transcenderant, cedicit* (Liv. *per.* 108; cf. Cass.Dio 40.25.4). The sources refer to Cassius as quaestor, but we know that they also frequently use this word to refer to a proquaestor. As we shall see, a proquaestorship in 53 should not be discounted. At any rate, Cassius Longinus was certainly proquaestor in 51, when Cicero sent him a letter from Cilicia with the heading *M. CICERO IMP. S. D. C. CASSIO PROQ.* (Cic. *fam.* 15.14; the letter was written in October 51). It is actually most likely that Cassius was quaestor before 53. The battle of Carrhae took place on 9th June 53. If Cassius was quaestor then, he should have been elected in 54. However, there were no elections in 54 for 53. The elections for the magistrates of 53 were held in the summer of the same year, after Carrhae. Therefore, we can safely deduce that Cassius was a proquaestor at the time of the battle (Linderski 1975, 35 – 37; cf. Ryan 1994b, 598 n. 47). When did he hold the quaestorship? It is known that Cassius was older than Brutus (Plut. *Brut.* 29; 40; App. *b.c.* 4.89), who was certainly born in 85. If Cassius' date of birth was in 86, he was already eligible for the quaestorship of 55 (Sumner 1971, 365). The elections for 55 were delayed, and they took place in that very year. As a result, all the new magistrates entered their office much later than usual, including the quaestors. The consul Crassus left for Syria in November 55 (Cic. *Att.* 4.13.2; cf. Pina Polo 2011, 237). Cassius may have been elected quaestor in 55, and could have remained in Rome until November, before departing for Syria together with his commander Crassus (Syme 1980, 404 – 405; cf. Sobeck 1909, 59: quaestor in Syria in 54; Broughton MRR, 3.51: Cassius was already quaestor in 54, or even in 55). Throughout 54 and until the battle of Carrhae, Cassius was a proquaestor always serving under Crassus (Ward 1977, 80). After Crassus' death at Carrhae, he may have become *proquaestor pro praetore* (even if not properly attested) commanding the troops in Syria until the arrival of the proconsul M. Calpurnius Bibulus in late 51 (Balsdon 1962, 134; Kondratieff 2015, 438 – 439. Cf. Broughton MRR, 2.237; 2.242).

Q. Cassius Longinus (q. and perhaps proq. in any year between 55 and 51 in Hispania Ulterior) (tr.pl. 49; propr. 49 – 47) (RE 70):
Both Cicero and Cassius Dio state that Quintus Cassius Longinus served in the fifties as quaestor under Pompey in Hispania Ulterior: Cic. *Att.* 6.6.4: *Pompeius, eo robore vir, iis radicibus, Q. Cassium sine sorte delegit, Caesar Antonium*; Cass.Dio 41.24.2: πράξας δὲ ταῦτα τὸ μὲν ἔθνος ἐκεῖνο τῷ Λογγίνῳ τῷ Κασσίῳ προσέταξεν, ἐπειδὴ συνήθης αὐτοῖς ἐκ τῆς ταμιείας ἦν ὑπὸ τῷ Πομπηίῳ ἐτεταμιεύκει <ἦν>. According to Cassius Dio, it was because of his previous knowledge of the region that Caesar later appointed Longinus as propraetor of the same province. Cassius Longinus was allocated to Hispania *extra sortem*, that is, he was directly chosen by Pompey as quaestor. Cicero's comparison to Antonius refers exclusively to the method of appointment and does not suggest that they held their quaestorships in the same year. The remaining questions are when Longinus went to Hispania and how long he stayed in the province. In fact,

there is no chronological hint, so he may have been quaestor (and perhaps also proquaestor) in any year between the *lex Trebonia* of 55 and 51. Pompey sent his legates to Hispania as soon as he received his command in 55. Consequently, it is plausible that Cassius Longinus could have been elected quaestor for 55 and gone to Hispania at once or remained in Rome as Pompey's *quaestor consularis*, assuming his provincial nomination as proquaestor in 54. This option is reasonable but unsubstantiated, like his election for 54 or 53 (Linderski 1975, 37–38). It is possible that he was already in Rome in 51 being prosecuted *de repetundis*. See also Bülz 1893, 10–11; Sobeck 1909, 57: quaestor under Pompey in Hispania between 55 and 50; Broughton MRR, 2.236, includes Cassius Longinus among the quaestors of 52 (cf. 2.544: q. ca. 52), but in 3.52 Broughton recognises that his quaestorship could be dated to any year between 55 and 51.

Díaz Ariño 2008b, 102–105 (see also Díaz Ariño 2008a; 2011, 170), proposes identifying Q. Cassius Longinus as the man mentioned as *q(uaestor) pro pr(aetore)* in an inscription from Carthago Nova (CIL 2.3421). Unfortunately, only the final part of his name has been preserved: *–inus* (Koch 2010, suggests the name Sextus Curvius Silvinus, which would date the inscription to the early Principate). Díaz Ariño suggests that, if the identification is correct, the inscription could be dated to 52, the year of Longinus' quaestorship according to Broughton MRR, 2.236. According to the text of the inscription, at his own expense this man paid for the construction, presumably in Carthago Nova, of a temple (*aedes*, if the reading is correct) and some hydraulic structures. Despite the fragmentary nature of the inscription, the hypothetical identification with Longinus is possible from an epigraphical viewpoint. However, neither the office of the individual nor the place in which his actions are recorded encourage an identification with Cassius Longinus. First, Carthago Nova was in Hispania Citerior and not in Hispania Ulterior, the province in which Longinus apparently held his office as quaestor. Why would he be active in Hispania Citerior? On the other hand, as a quaestor Longinus served under Pompey, who was officially the governor of both provinces in Hispania. In fact, Longinus was under the command of Pompey's legate, M. Petreius in the case of Hispania Ulterior. As a consequence, there is no evidence that Cassius Longinus was a *quaestor pro praetore* in Hispania in the period 55–51. Ultimately, the identification with Longinus is uncertain, and the final letters *–inus* could refer to other individuals with *cognomina* ending in *–inus* who held their office in Hispania, such as M. Minatius Sabinus (see below) or others who are unknown to us.

L. Claudius L. f. (q. before 73, perhaps 74) (RE 23):
L. Claudius (Λεύκιος Κλαύδιος Λευκίου υἱὸς Λεμωνία) is one of the senators included in the *SC de Oropiis* of year 73 (SIG^3 747 = RDGE 23). He is one of the *quaestorii* of the *consilium*. Thus, Claudius should have held the quaestorship before 73 (Broughton MRR, 2.115). Since he is cited third from last, and the list is arranged by rank, a quaestorship in 74 is likely. Nevertheless, Taylor suggests that this Claudius may have

been *rex sacrorum* and that he entered this sacerdotal office around this date (Cic. *dom.* 127, mentions an unknown Claudius who bestowed the office of *rex sacrorum*; Taylor 1942b, 398; 1960, 203. Cf. Macrob. *Sat.* 3.13.11). He would be the father of L. Claudius, *rex sacrorum* in 57, who became a member of the college of pontifices at the end of the 60s (Taylor 1942b, 412; Rüpke 2008, 610, no 1160). If this proposal were correct, Claudius would have obtained his place in the senate through his priesthood rather than a quaestorship, given that the *rex sacrorum* was barred from a political or military career (Broughton MRR, 3.54). Even though Taylor's speculation is interesting and possible, Claudius' quaestorship, perhaps in 74, remains the more likely option.

Ap. Claudius C. f. Caecus (q. before 315) (cos. 307 and 296) (RE 91):

Appius Claudius' *elogium* shows that he held the quaestorship presumably after having been military tribune and before his aedileship: *Appius Claudius C. f. Caecus censor cos. bis dict. interrex III pr. II aed. cur. II q. tr. mil. III* (CIL I^2 192 = Incr. Ital. 13.3.79). The date of his quaestorship is, however, completely unknown. Sobeck 1909, 5, simply suggests a date before 315. Broughton 1.156, points to 316 as the latest probable date, if Claudius was a curule aedile before his censorship (he was aedile twice according to his *elogium*). Ferenczy 1965, tries to reconstruct Claudius' political career before his censorship through his *elogium* and a series of interconnected conjectures. Ferenczy refuses to date Claudius' quaestorship to 316, dating his aedileship to this year instead, but he does not give an alternative date for the quaestorship. Most scholars have criticised Ferenczy's utterly speculative reconstruction (so Humm 2005, 114: 'entreprise vaine et méthodologiquement impossible'; cf. Develin ^{2}2005, 311, n. 60). Consistent with the lack of information in the sources, a precise date for Claudius' quaestorship has never been suggested. See Raaflaub, Richards and Samons II 1992, 36–37: 'he may have been quaestor and was probably twice curule aedile before 312.' Cf. Humm 2005, 113–114. In conclusion, it seems evident that Appius Claudius held the quaestorship at some undetermined point before 315, but it is impossible to give a more precise date.

C. (Claudius) Marcellus (proq. 113 in Macedonia?) (not in RE):

An inscription from Samothrace records a proquaestor: *C. Caecilio Cn. Papirio cos. / C. <M>arcello proq.* (CIL I^2 662 a-b = III suppl. I.1. 7367 = *Ephemeris Epigraphica* V no. 222 = IG XII 8, p.38). The inscription is known only through the drawing made by Cyriacus of Ancona, in which the name of the proquaestor appears as *Aarcellus*. The M and A were presumably in ligature, which would explain the mistake in the reading of the name (see Dimitrova 2008, 151–152). The mention of the consuls C. Caecilius Metellus Caprarius and Cn. Papirius Carbo allows us to date Marcellus' proquaestorship exactly to 113, presumably in Macedonia (Bültz 1908, 15–16; Sobeck 1909, 19; Broughton MRR, 1.534 and 536 as well as 2.545 lists him as proquaestor in Macedonia in 114 and 113). He may have been a quaestor in previous years, perhaps in 114. Although the *nomen* of this individual is not mentioned in the inscription, it has been assumed that it was probably Claudius. This C. (Claudius) Marcellus is otherwise unknown. Dimitrova 2008, 152, proposes that the inscription corresponded to the beginning of a list of Roman initiates in the mysteries of Samothrace. If the man mentioned in the inscription really was one of the Claudii Marcelli, his link with the sanctuary in Samothrace could be understood within the family tradition (Plut. *Marc.* 30. Cf. Muscolino 2009–2010, 416 n. 39).

However, this C. Marcellus also has been associated with C. Claudius Marcellus, the praetor of 80 (RE 214). Broughton himself (MRR, 2.47 and 2.55) identifies the man of the inscription with the Marcellus who was praetor in 80, making him quaestor in 87 and proquaestor in 86: 'if the proquaestor of the Samothracian inscription may be identified with the praetor of 80, we may suppose that his career in the period of Sulla roughly paralleled that of Lucullus' (MRR, 2.52 n. 4). On the basis of Broughton's assumption and taking into account that Marcellus was praetor in 80, Badian 1959a, suggests 90 or 89 for his quaestorship, although he adds: 'in any case, such speculation is hardly worth while' (83). Keaveney 1984, 119–120, also identifies the Marcellus of the Samothracian inscription with the praetor of 80. As a consequence, Keaveney places his quaestorship at some point around 93–92, perhaps as quaestor and proquaestor of C. Julius Caesar, praetor in 92 and proconsul in Asia in 91 (Broughton MRR, 2.17 and 22. Cf. Sumner 1978, 148–150: 'we could fit Caesar in as proconsul from some point in 92 to at least January/February of 90').

There is no reason to identify the proquaestor of the Samothracian inscription with the praetor of 80. The proquaestorship of C. Marcellus seems to be securely dated to 113 thanks to the mention of the consuls of this year. An interval of more than thirty years between his proquaestorship and his supposed praetorship seems hardly credible. Therefore, the proquaestor of 113 and the praetor of 80 are two different persons. Dimitrova proposes that the proquaestor could be the father of the praetor. While the temporal sequence may appear suitable, the hypothesis is impossible, because the praetor of 80 was *M.f* and not *C.f.* (Muscolino 2009–2010, 416 n. 39). Finally, C. Claudius Marcellus (RE 214) was in all probability quaestor at some point in the nineties or eighties of the first century, but the dates proposed for his quaestorship by Broughton, Badian or Keaveney are mere speculation.

M. Claudius M. f. Marcellus (q. urb. 64) (cos. 51) (RE 229):
A Marcellus was the colleague of Cato in the quaestorship. According to Plutarch (Plut. *Cat.min.* 18.3–4), on the last day of his term of office Marcellus was forced by influential men to register in the *aerarium* some remission of owed money. His colleague Cato asked for the tablets and erased the entry, while Marcellus himself stood by silently. This story clearly demonstrates that Marcellus and Cato were urban quaestors in the same year. Marcellus was in all probability Marcus Claudius Marcellus, a friend of Cato's from his boyhood, and later consul in 51. If Cato's urban quaestorship is dated to

64, this must also be the year that this Marcellus was urban quaestor. See Sobeck, 49; Broughton MRR, 2.162; Sumner 1973, 138; Fehrle 1983, 76 n. 54.

M. Claudius Marcellus Aeserninus (q. 48) (cos. 22) (RE 232–233):

According to Cassius Dio (42.15.1–5), in 48 Marcus Claudius Marcellus Aeserninus was the quaestor (Μᾶρκον Μάρκελλον Αἰσερνῖνον τὸν ταμίαν) of the propraetor Q. Cassius Longinus in Hispania Ulterior. When the troops rebelled against Longinus, Marcellus took the command, but he tried not to show himself in favour of either Caesarians or Pompeians. Münzer identifies him in RE with the consul of 22 with the same name. See Bülz 1893, 11–12; Sobeck 1909, 66; Broughton MRR, 2.274; Sumner 1973, 91: he was born by 79, since the requirements of the *lex Annalis* should have been in force during the elections held in 49 (cf. Sumner 1971, 257); Welch 1995, 451.

Ti. Claudius Nero (q. 48, proq. 47?) (pr. 42) (RE 254):

Tiberius Claudius Nero was the father of the later emperor Tiberius. During the Alexandrian war, he was in charge of the fleet as Caesar's quaestor (Suet. *Tib.* 4: *pater Tiberi, quaestor Caesaris Alexandrino bello classi praepositus...*; cf. *B. Alex.* 25; Cass.Dio 42.40.6). Claudius Nero was therefore quaestor in 48, and he may have remained at Alexandria as proquaestor in 47. See Sobeck 1909, 66; Broughton MRR, 2.274: 2.288; Sumner 1971, 258.

Ap. Claudius Ap. f. Pulcher (q. urb. 111–110? or 99?) (cos. 79) (RE 296):

See **T. Maloleius.** The interpretation of some coins with the legend *AP · CL · T · MAL · Q · VR* (perhaps *T · MANL*) has been much debated. Mommsen suggests that *Q · VR* was the abbreviation of *Q(uaestores) Vr(bani)*. The previous two names would belong to the urban quaestors who had struck the issue. This explanation appears to be reinforced by the fact that the order of the names is not always the same (appearing sometimes as *AP · CL* and on other occasions as *T · MAL*) but *Q · VR* is always placed at the end of the legend. One of the presumed quaestors was Ap. Claudius Pulcher, the name of the other is uncertain. This generally accepted theory was challenged by Crawford RRC, 312–313 no. 299, who argues that *Q · VR* should be read as a name, specifically Quintus Urbinius, not otherwise known. Crawford's interpretation is based on the questionable assumption that only one urban quaestor was in charge of the *aerarium* at any given time. Therefore, it must be explained why two urban quaestors would have minted these coins and why both of their names would have appeared on them. Crawford concludes that the issue was struck by three moneyers, whose names were recorded in the legend (Sumner 1973, 63, however, states that he did not see any reason 'to invent a *monetalis* Q. Urbinius here'). While Crawford is certainly right to assert that a historical explanation for the unusual joint coinage of the two urban quaestors is needed, Mommsen's explanation remains the easiest and most logical interpretation. As for the chronology, Broughton MRR, 2.2, dates the coins, and consequently the two urban quaestorships, to 99, whereas Crawford prefers 111 or 110. In the case of Appius Claudius Pulcher, the problem concerning Crawford's chronology is the very long interval between this office (moneyer or quaestor) and the higher magistracies, since Pulcher was praetor in 89 and consul in 79, around twenty and thirty years later respectively.

C. Claudius Ap. f. Pulcher (shortly before 110?) (cos. 92) (RE 302):
As seen in his *elogium*, C. Claudius Pulcher began his political career by holding the quaestorship prior to a moneyership, a not unusual combination at the beginning of the *cursus honorum* in that period: *q. III vir a. a. a. f. f. aed. cur. iudex q. veneficis pr. repetundis curator vis sternundis cos. cum M. Perperna* (CIL I^2 200 = ILS 45). Thus, the date of his quaestorship must be determined by the date of his moneyership. The coins minted by Claudius Pulcher are usually dated to around 104, which must place his quaestorship before this year (Sobeck 1909, 23: shortly before 104; Broughton MRR, 1.556 and 1.558 n. 5, includes him tentatively among the quaestors of 105). However, Crawford RRC, 313, no. 300 (issues with the inscription *C · PVLCHER*), moves the date of his coins to 110 or 109. If Crawford's suggestion is correct (Mattingly 1982, 44, prefers 106), Claudius Pulcher's quaestorship should be dated to some point before 110, probably shortly before this year. This dating creates an unusually long but not impossible interval of around twenty years before his quaestorship and his consulship in 92. It must be taken into account that Cicero points out that Claudius Pulcher was not able to hold his magistracies *suo anno* (Cic. *off.* 2.57 and 2.59). See Broughton MRR, 3.57: by 110; Sumner 1973, 100: quaestorship by 113. According to Sumner, his birthday around 141 would be acceptable for a son of Ap. Claudius, consul in 143. Evans 1994, 184 and 211, seems to consider the dates given by both Crawford and Mattingly as plausible for the coins of Claudius Pulcher. As a result, Evans dates his quaestorship to either 112–111 or 108–107. He was quaestor, therefore, aged between twenty-six and thirty. More recently, Ryan 1996 g, 80, suggests placing Claudius Pulcher among the quaestors of 108. Since he was born in 136, he could not, according to Ryan, have been a candidate for the quaestorship before 109.

P. Clodius Pulcher (q. 61 in Sicily) (aed. cur. 56) (RE 48):
Publius Clodius Pulcher held the quaestorship in Sicily in 61 (Ascon. 52–53 C: *significat id tempus, quo P. Clodius, cum adhuc quaestor designatus esset, deprehensus est, cum intrasset eo, ubi sacrificium pro populo Romano fiebat*). His departure for the island was delayed by the Bona Dea trial (Cic. *har.resp.* 43, discredits Clodius' quaestorship as 'fateful for religion, for the courts and for the state': *Exorta est illa rei publicae, sacris, religionibus, auctoritati vestrae, iudiciis publicis funesta quaestura, in qua idem iste deos hominesque, pudorem, pudicitiam, senatus auctoritatem, ius, fas, leges, iudicia violavit*). In Sicily he served under the praetor C. Vergilius Balbus (*Schol.*

Bob. p. 87 Stangl). On his return to Rome, see Cic. *Att.* 2.1.5. See Sobeck 1909, 53; Broughton MRR, 2.180; Sumner 1973, 136; Prag 2007b, 308.

T. Cloelius (Cloulius) (q. 98?) (RE 5):

Some quinarii have the image of Victory with the legend *T · CLOVI* and *Q.* in exergue. Following Crawford (RRC 331–332, no. 332), the type seems to allude to the recent victories of Marius, and T. Cloulius could presumably be identified with T. Cloelius, a Marian legate fighting against Pompey in 83 (Plut. *Pomp.* 7.1–2: Plutarch calls him Κλοίλιος. See Wiseman 1967, 263–264). Crawford dates the coins to 98. The abbreviation *Q.* in the coins presumably does not refer to their value as quinarii, but to the office of quaestor, *Q(uaestor)* (see Pink 1952; cf. Broughton MRR, 2.458). Consequently, T. Cloelius (or Cloulius) was a quaestor in 98 according to Crawford's dating (Broughton MRR, 2.548: by 100; Evans 1994, 214, accepts the date of 98). Nonetheless, a later date for this quaestorship has been proffered by Wiseman 1967, 263–264: quaestor by 95. In addition, Wiseman points out the connection of the family with Tarracina. That had to do with the way in which the T. Cloulii spelt their name. The date of around 95 is accepted by Tatum 1990a, 303. Cf. Broughton MRR, 3.58.

C. Coelius L. f. Caldus (q. 50, proq. pro pr.? 49 in Cilicia) (RE 14):

The evidence for the quaestor C. Coelius Caldus assuming the command of Cilicia from the hands of Cicero in 50 is clear (Cic. *fam.* 2.15.4: *Ego de provincia decedens quaestorem Coelium praeposui provinciae*; cf. *Att.* 6.6.3–4; 7.1.6). He remained in command of Cilicia when Cicero went back to Rome at the end of July, probably becoming proquaestor (perhaps *pro praetore*) in 49 until P. Sestius took charge of the province. See Bülz 1893, 59–61; Sobeck 1909, 63; Broughton 2.250 and 2.261; Balsdon 1962, 134.

M. Coelius M. f. Vinicianus (q. before 54) (pr. 48 or 46? See Broughton MRR, 3.60) (RE 27):

His quaestorship is known through an inscription set up by his wife in his honour: *M. Coelio M. f. Viniciano pr. pro cos. tr. pl. q. Opsilia uxor fecit* (CIL I² 781 = XIV 2602 = ILS 883 = ILLRP 402). M. Coelius Vinicianus' political career is obviously recorded in this case in descending order (Eck 2005, 7). Given that he was a tribune of the plebs in 53, he must have held the quaestorship prior to this date, but the precise year is impossible to determine. The compulsory interval of at least two years between two offices makes 55 the latest possible date for Coelius Vinicianus' quaestorship. See Sobeck 1909, 59; Broughton MRR, 2.210; Wiseman 1971, 225: q. ca. 56?

C. Cornelius (q. 74 and proq. 73 – 71 in Hispania? or q. 70?) (tr. pl. 67) (RE 18):
See **C. Memmius.** C. Cornelius was no doubt a quaestor under Pompey before becoming a tribune of the plebs: *fuerat quaestor Cn. Pompei, dein tribunus plebis...* (Ascon. 57 C. Cf. Ascon. 61 C). Cornelius was a tribune in 67 and therefore held the quaestorship prior to this year under the command of Pompey. This could have been either during Pompey's first consulate in 70 or at any moment during his stay in Hispania fighting against Sertorius in 76 – 71. Both hypotheses are feasible, but neither one is substantiated in the sources.

Pompey remained in Rome with his colleague Crassus throughout his consulship, carrying out intense political and legislative activities, including the restoration of the tribunician powers. Griffin 1973, 203, rejects the notion that Cornelius may have been Pompey's quaestor in 70, arguing that 'he could hardly have avoided the embroilment in politics of which Asconius implies he was innocent until 67' (Ascon. 61 C: *Cornelius... cetera vita nihil fecerat quod magnopere improbaretur*). However, the possibility of Cornelius having held the quaestorship in 70 should not be discarded by any means. Asconius implies that until his tribunate, Cornelius had done nothing that deserved much censure. This assertion is perfectly compatible with a supposed co-operation with Pompey in 70. Pompey was highly regarded in Rome after his recent victories over Sertorius and the rest of Spartacus' troops, and his legislative proposals apparently already enjoyed a general approval when he spoke to the people as a consul designate (Cic. *Verr.* 45). Therefore Cornelius could hardly have been discredited for collaborating with the consul Pompey as his quaestor. In fact, Cornelius' connection with Pompey was his major asset in the trial against him, as Asconius makes clear (Ascon. 61 C).

Alternatively, it is equally plausible to place Cornelius' quaestorship in Hispania, always serving under Pompey. This has been the prevailing opinion in the scholarship since Münzer made this suggestion in RE (see Sobeck 1909, 39; Broughton MRR, 2.122, includes him among the quaestors of 71 as the latest possible year). Pompey was sent by the senate in 77 to fight against Sertorius. Pompey's first quaestor was C. Memmius (Cic. *Balb.* 5), who was killed in battle in 75 (Oros. 5.23.12; Plut. *Sert.* 21.1). As a consequence, Cornelius could only be Pompey's quaestor in Hispania after that year. He may have been quaestor in 74, and could perhaps have remained under Pompey's command until the end of the war in 71. Of course, Cornelius' quaestorship in Hispania also would have created the close connection with Pompey mentioned by Asconius.

Q. Cornelius (q. urb. 44) (RE 5 and 52; cf. 51):
See **Q. Rutilius.** Cicero alludes to someone who was a *scriba* under Sulla's dictatorship and who became an urban quaestor during Caesar's dictatorship: *quam P. Sulla cum vibrasset dictatore propinquo suo... qui in illa dictatura scriba fuerat, in hac fuit quaestor urbanus* (Cic. *off.* 2.29). Cicero does not give the name of the man. Sallust in his *Histories* mentions a powerful *scriba* of the name Cornelius acting in Sulla's time (Sall. *hist.* 1.55.17 M. = McGushin 1992, 1.30 – 31 and 120). It has usually been inferred that the

Cornelius of Sallust is the very *quaestor urbanus* mentioned by Cicero (see Broughton MRR, 2.475; David 2007, 44 n. 37; 2019, 228). There is one more piece of relevant information. According to Josephus, a Quintus Cornelius, who was urban quaestor, was named in a decree of the senate (Ios. *AJ* 14.219: δόγμα συγκλήτου ἐκ τοῦ ταμιείου ἀντιγεγραμμένον ἐκ τῶν δέλτων τῶν δημοσίων τῶν ταμιευτικῶν Κοΐντω Ῥουτιλίω Κοΐντω Κορνηλίω ταμίαις κατὰ πόλιν). Cf. Sobeck 1909, 70; Broughton MRR, 2.325). The senatorial decree dates to 44, which implies that his quaestorship should be dated to this year as well. If Cicero's urban quaestor should be identified with this Q. Cornelius (RE 5 and 52. See Syme 1955a, 134), we would have here a link with the Sullan *scriba*. The only problem is that Cicero uses the word *fuit* when referring to this quaestor. Since Cicero was writing his *De officiis* in 44, this *fuit quaestor urbanus* seems to suggest an earlier date for Cornelius' quaestorship. Nevertheless, Sumner 1971, 368, argues that Cicero wrote *De officiis* in October-November 44 (Cic. *Att.* 15.13a.2; 16.11.4), so that Cornelius could have held the office in this year and then died by October 44 (see Broughton MRR, 3.62). In addition, the possibility remains of identifying this Cornelius with another Cornelius who was a *pontifex minor* by 69 (RE 51; Broughton MRR, 2.135). Through Livy we know that minor pontifices were once termed *scribae pontificii* (Liv. 22.57.3). This would mean that the Sullan *scriba*, the minor pontifex and the urban quaestor of 44 could be one and the same person, as Syme suggests (see above; cf. Broughton MRR, 3.62). Ryan 1996f, 39: the Cornelius mentioned by Cicero was quaestor in one of the years between 49 and 44; since he was born by 95, he was at least forty-five years old when he took up the quaestorship.

In conclusion, it is certain, according to Josephus, that a Q. Cornelius was *quaestor urbanus* in 44. According to Cicero it is likewise sure that one of the urban quaestors under Caesar's dictatorship had been a *scriba* under Sulla more than thirty years earlier. It is possible, but not definite, that Cicero alludes to this very Q. Cornelius. Certainly, Cornelius could be a freedman who made a fortune as a result of the Sullan proscriptions and thrived socially to the point of holding a prominent magistracy like the urban quaestorship, presumably at an advanced age. All in all, there is no indication of a secure connection between the Sallustian Cornelius and the Ciceronian *quaestor urbanus*, as Sobeck 1909, 82, notes.

L. Cornelius P. f. Balbus (q. 44? q. or proq. 43 in Hispania Ulterior) (RE 70):

Lucius Cornelius Balbus was Asinius Pollio's quaestor in Hispania Ulterior, as shown in the letter written by Asinius to Cicero in 43 (Cic. *fam.* 10.32.1: *Balbus quaestor magna numerata pecunia...* Cf. *Att.* 15.13.4: Balbillus). The letter denotes that Balbus was serving in June 43 under Asinius Pollio, who was in charge of Hispania Ulterior in 44. Although he is named quaestor, Broughton MRR, 2.325 (cf. 2.344) points out that Balbus could, rather, have been a proquaestor in 43 and that he may have gone to Hispania with his commander in 44 as quaestor (see MRR, 3.63, as well as Bülz 1893, 13–14; Sobeck 1909, 71; Wiseman 1971, 226–227; Sumner 1971, 368). The use of the word quaestor for a proquaestor is certainly not unusual, so Broughton's suggestion is plausible. Nonetheless, it is also possible that Balbus was actually a quaestor in 43. The question must remain open.

C. Cornelius Cethegus (q. urb. 63?) (RE 89):
C. Cornelius Cethegus was one of the leaders of the Catilinarian conspiracy. He was a senator in 63 according to Sallust (Sall. *Cat.* 17.3), but Appian makes him an urban praetor together with Cornelius Lentulus Sura (App. *b.c.* 2.2). Appian's statement is clearly mistaken, because Cethegus was not an urban praetor in 63 (Broughton MRR, 2.489). However, Ryan 1994d, proposes that Cethegus may have been an urban quaestor instead. This could explain Appian's misunderstanding. It could be objected that there is no evidence of Cethegus being forced to resign from his supposed office. Ryan explains it in the following way: the execution of Cethegus and the other plotters took place on the Nonae of December, and Cethegus would have ceased as quaestor on 4th December. Consequently, a resignation of his office was unnecessary. Ryan's proposal is ultimately speculative and is not buttressed by any supporting evidence.

(Cornelius) Cinna (q. 44 in Asia) (RE 104):
Cinna was quaestor in 44 and served under P. Cornelius Dolabella. The cavalry that he was bringing to Dolabella in Asia fell into the hands of Brutus in Thessaly (Cic. *Phil.* 10.13; Plut. *Brut.* 25.1). See Sobeck 1909, 70; Broughton 2.325. Sumner 1971, 368–369, identified him with L. Cornelius, the *consul suffectus* of year 32.

Cn. Cornelius (L. f. Lentulus) (q. 212) (cos. 201) (RE 176):
The quaestor Cn. Cornelius assumed command of Gracchus' troops in Lucania when he died in 212 (Liv. 25.19.4). Cornelius supposedly received from Hannibal the head of Gracchus and buried it: *in castra Romana ad Cn. Cornelium quaestorem deferret [caput Gracchi]* (Liv. 25.17.7). See Bülz 1908, 4–5; Sobeck 1909, 7–8; Broughton *MRR*, 1.268.

L. Cornelius Ser. f. Lentulus (q. by 102–100 in Asia) (RE 193, suppl. 3.259):
The otherwise unknown quaestor L. Cornelius Lentulus is honoured in a Greek inscription on a statue base from Delos (I. Délos 1694: Λεύκιον Κορνήλιον Σερουίου υἱὸν Λέντελον / ταμίαν Ῥωμαίων, Ἰταλοὶ καὶ Ἕλληνες). The artist Demostratos made the statue, who was also the sculptor of another statue dated securely to the very end of the second century. The quaestorship of this Cornelius Lentulus, therefore, should be placed at the same time. Since he was son of Servius, he might be the brother of Servius Cornelius Lentulus (RE 208b), who was proconsul in Asia by 110 (I. Délos 1845). See Bültz 1908, 22; Sobeck 1909, 25: quaestor 102–101; Broughton MRR, 1.576: quaestor at some date in the late second century (cf. 2.553: q. before 100).

Cn. Cornelius P. f. Lentulus Marcellinus (q. urb. 75?) (cos. 56) (RE 228):
Some denarii bear the legend *CN · LEN · Q · EX S · C*. Other denarii of the same series read *LENT · CVR ·DEN · FL*, that is, *cur(ator) den(ariis) fl(andis)*. There is complete agreement that these coins were issued by Cn. Cornelius Lentulus Marcellinus in the seventies. The question is precisely when. The coins were initially dated to 74, and it was thought that Lentulus Marcellinus was acting as quaestor urbanus (see Babelon 1885, 416–417; Sobeck 1909, 39–40; cf. Broughton MRR, 2.103 and 2.553: quaestor in 74?; Sumner 1973, 133). Crawford RRC, 407 no. 393, dates the denarii to 76–75 in the catalogue, but elsewhere in his book he asserts that the issue 'still very fresh in the Pontecorvo hoard, belongs precisely in 75' (RRC, 82). Hersh and Walker 1984, Table 2, give the same chronology. However, Michiels 1972, ignores the new chronology and insists without new arguments on dating the issue to 74. Crawford assumes that the coins were probably minted in Hispania during the Sertorian War (Grueber already suggested that the coins had been minted by a quaestor of Pompey in Hispania; see Broughton MRR, 3.68). More recently, Hollstein 1993, 65, makes a new proposal. Hollstein draws attention to the fact that in this period it was utterly exceptional to mint coins outside Rome. If these denarii were minted in Hispania, they would be actually the only coins not minted in Rome between 78 and 50. Consequently, Hollstein argues that Marcellinus was *quaestor urbanus* in 76, and immediately after this office he became *curator denariis flandis*. Marcellinus was entrusted by the senate to mint coins for the Sertorian war. When he ended his term of office as quaestor, a part of the silver that had been delivered to him to be minted was left over. To finish his task, he was elected *curator denariis flandis*. This would explain why the denarii with the legend *curator* are more scarce than coins with the word quaestor.

To sum up, it seems more likely that the coins were issued by Marcellinus in Rome as quaestor urbanus than in Hispania as quaestor to Pompey (or to Metellus in Hispania Ulterior). As far as the chronology is concerned, assuming that 76–75 is the most probable date for the denarii, both years could be acceptable for Marcellinus' quaestorship. However, given the development of the war in Hispania, perhaps 75 is preferable. The issue may have been a quick response from the senate to the dramatic letter sent by Pompey (Sall. *hist.* 2.98 M.), in which the *imperator* claimed to have exhausted his resources and requested that new funds for his troops in Hispania be sent at once. As urban quaestor and by order of the senate, Marcellinus would have had the responsibility for minting the coins to improve the situation for the troops in Hispania. As Hollstein suggests, he would have accomplished his task at the beginning of 74, now acting as *curator denariis flandis*. If this reconstruction is correct, Lentulus Marcellinus may have been *quaestor urbanus* in 75, namely the date that Crawford gives for the issue (see above).

P. Cornelius P. f. Lentulus Marcellinus (q. pro pr.? 75 o 74 in Cyrene) (RE 231):
Publius Cornelius Lentulus Marcellinus was the first Roman magistrate in charge of Cyrene. According to Sallust, he was sent to Cyrene in either 75 or 74 as quaestor (Sall.

hist. 2.43 M. = 2.41 McGushin (for a commentary, see McGushin 1992, 1.206–208). Given his duties in Cyrene, it has generally been assumed that he possessed *imperium*. As a consequence, Lentulus Marcellinus may officially have been *quaestor pro praetore* (or maybe *proquaestor pro praetore*), although Sallust just calls him quaestor (Jashemski 1950, 78–79). See Bülz 1893, 70–72; Sobeck 1909, 40: he went to Cyrene at the beginning of 74 as *proquaestor pro praetore*; Broughton MRR, 2.97, 2.103 and 2.554: quaestor *cum imperio* 75 or 74; but MRR, 3.69: 'he was sent in 75, or more probably in 74, to Cyrene as quaestor pro praetore, or perhaps, like Cato to Cyprus in 58, as pro quaestore pro praetore'; Oost 1963, 21; Badian 1965, 119: 'perhaps in 75 and certainly for 74… quite probably as quaestor pro praetore'; Gruen 1974, 194: quaestor in Cyrene ca.75; Brennan 2000, 408–409: 'P. Marcellinus appears to have remained in Cyrene down to late 74 or early 73.'

P. Cornelius Lentulus Marcellinus (q. 48) (RE 232):
As quaestor P. Cornelius Lentulus Marcellinus commanded a part of Caesar's troops at Dyrrachium in 48: *Ad eas munitiones Caesar Lentulum Marcellinum quaestorem cum legione VIIII positum habebat* (Caes. *civ.* 3.62.4; cf. 3.64–65; Oros. 6.15.19). See Bülz 1893, 34; Sobeck 1909, 66; Broughton MRR, 2.274 and 3.69; Sumner 1973, 134: he may be son or nephew of Lentulus Marcellinus consul 56. Cf. Sumner 1971, 257–258.

P. Cornelius P. f. Lentulus Spinther (q. urb. 71?) (cos. 57) (RE 238):
See **L. Plaetorius [Cestianus]**. Some denarii minted in Rome bear the legend *P · LENT · P · F / L · N* (on the reverse) *Q · S · C* (on the obverse). Crawford RRC, 83 and 409 no. 397, identifies the quaestor with the consul of 57, Publius Cornelius Lentulus Spinther, discarding the possible identification with Publius Cornelius Lentulus Marcellinus, the quaestor mentioned by Sallust (*hist.* 2.43 M. Cf. Horsfall 1986, 84). Crawford dates this issue to 74. Lentulus Spinther would have been urban quaestor in 74, a date already suggested by other scholars. See Sobeck 1909, 40; Broughton MRR, 2.103 and 2.554 (cf. 3.69): urban quaestor ca. 74. Nevertheless, the discovery of the Mesagne Hoard has shifted the previously accepted dating of some coins. Hersh and Walker 1984, Table 2, dates these denarii to 71. This date was accepted by Hollstein 1993, 89–95. According to Hollstein, the types on the reverse, *Genius populi Romani* and Victory, should be seen as symbols of the triumph against Sertorius in Hispania. These coins would have been issued to finance the celebration of the triumphs of Metellus and Pompey over Hispania in 71. Hence the special issue ordered by the senate and carried out by an urban quaestor. If this argument is accepted, Lentulus Spinther may have held the urban quaestorship in 71.

Nevertheless, it must be noted that Sumner 1973, 142, proposes 101 as the year of his birth. On the basis of this date, Ryan 1996 g, 83–84, suggests placing Lentulus Spinther's urban quaestorship in 70 or 69, assuming that he could not have been of age earlier than 70. Ryan links the date of Lentulus Spinther's quaestorship to a text of

Diodorus Siculus (40.1.2), in which a senatorial decree in favour of the Cretans was opposed by Lentulus Spinther. His intervention took place during a meeting of the senate, and Diodorus does not allude to any office held by Lentulus at that moment. However, Mattingly 1956, 200 n. 1, suggests that he had acted as urban quaestor: 'Spinther in 70 BC invalidated an *SC de Cretensibus*; he could well do this as *quaestor urbanus*, the official responsible for registering Senatus Consulta at the *aerarium*, by which alone they gained force.' Ryan basically agrees with this thesis: Lentulus, as urban quaestor, had the opportunity to render decrees null, and it would not make sense to place the decree and the quaestorship in different years. Nonetheless, this argument is far from rock solid. First, the date of the Cretan embassy which occasioned the senatorial decree is uncertain (the Cretan legates may have arrived to Rome in 70 or 69; on the subject Marshall 1985, 218; Linderski 1990, 163 and n. 33). Second, there is no evidence to date this episode to the same year that Lentulus Spinther held his quaestorship. Moreover, urban quaestors were certainly responsible for registering *senatus consulta* in the *aerarium*, always following orders given to them by the consuls, who in turn were following instructions of the senate. However, there is no evidence to suggest that the urban quaestors had the power of the veto, and such a notion is highly implausible. Consequently, Lentulus Spinther must have challenged the *senatus consultum* as a senator while it was being debated—not as urban quaestor.

P. Cornelius P. f. Lentulus Spinther (q. 44, proq. pro pr. 43 in Asia) (RE 239):
P. Cornelius Lentulus Spinther served in Asia as quaestor under C. Trebonius. We know from a letter of Cicero that Lentulus Spinther was in Rome in April 44 and about to leave to Asia (Cic. *Att*. 14.11.2: *Lentulus Spinther hodie apud me; cras mane vadit*). When Trebonius was killed, Lentulus Spinther took the command of the province as *proquaestor pro praetore*. This title is attested in the heading of a letter sent in the spring of 43 by Lentulus to the magistrates, senate and people of Rome: *P. Lentulus P. f. proq. pro pr. s. d. coss. pr. tr. pl. senatui populo plebique Romanae* (Cic. *fam*. 12.15). See Bülz 1893, 46–49; Sobeck 1909, 69; Broughton MRR, 2.325 and 2.344; Sumner 1971, 369: he was the son of the consul of 57, and he was two or more years under age for the quaestorship of 44.

P. Cornelius P. f. Lentulus (Sura) (q. urb. 81) (cos. 71) (RE 240):
See **C. (Valerius) Triarius.** According to Cicero, Lentulus (Sura) and Triarius were the urban quaestors of 81: *P. Lentulo L. Triario quaestoribus urbanis res rationum relatarum* (Cic. *Verr*. 2.1.37; cf. Plut. *Cic*. 17.2). See Sobeck 1909, 33–34; Broughton MRR, 2.76; Sumner 1973, 127 and 137: Lentulus (Sura) held the quaestorship two years after reaching the minimum age, and this would explain the unusually short interval between his quaestorship and his consulship (cf. Ryan 1996 f, 39: Lentulus was born in 115–114 and took up the quaestorship at the age of thirty-two or thirty-three). According to Plutarch, Lentulus Sura wasted and lost large amounts of public money during his

quaestorship. As a consequence, the dictator Sulla demanded that he present his accounting to the senate, to which Lentulus Sura answered arrogantly that he would not give any account (Plut. *Cic.* 17.2).

L. Cornelius L. f. Scipio (q. urb. 167) (RE 324):
This Lucius Cornelius Scipio was the son of Scipio Asiaticus. Since he died at the age of 33, he only could be military tribune and quaestor according to his *elogium: L. Corneli. L. f. P. [n.] Scipio quaist. tr. mil. annos gnatus XXXIII mortuos. Pater regem Antioco subegit* (ILS 5). He was presumably urban quaestor in 167. Scipio was sent by the senate to Capua to meet King Prusias, and he was appointed to be his constant attendant while staying in Rome (Liv. 45.44.7 and 17: <L.> *Cornelius Scipio quaestor, qui et Capuam ei obviam missus fuerat… donec ad classem dono datam ei rex pervenisset, L. Cornelius Scipio ne ab eo abscederet sumptumque ipsi et comitibus praeberet, donec navem conscendisset*. Cf. Val.Max. 5.1.1, who mistakenly gives the *praenomen* Publius. See Sobeck 1909, 12–13; Broughton MRR, 1.433.

L. Cornelius P. f. Scipio Asiaticus (q. before 196) (cos. 190) (RE 337):
The quaestorship of Scipio Asiaticus is known only through his *elogium: (L. Corneli)us P.f. S(cipio Asia)ticus (cos. pr. aed. cu)r. q. tr.(mil.)* (CIL I² 194 = Inscr. Ital. 13.3.15). Scipio Asiaticus was aedile in 195 (Broughton MRR, 1.340). Therefore, he must have held the quaestorship at the latest in 196 or earlier. See Sobeck 1909, 10–11; Broughton MRR, 1.336; Beck 2005, 359–360.

Cn. Cornelius Cn. f. Scipio Hispanus (q. by 150) (pr. 139) (RE 347):
The order in which Scipio Hispanus held his offices is known through his *elogium: Cn. Cornelius Cn. f. Scipio Hispanus pr. aid. cur. q. tr. mil. II X vir sl. iudik. X vir sacr. fac.* (CIL I² 15 = ILS 6 = ILLRP 316). In the first stages of his political career, Scipio Hispanus was *decemvir stlitibus iudicandis*, military tribune and quaestor. This is the usual and logical order, but in his case the dating become more complicated because he was military tribune twice. According to Appian, in 149 Scipio Hispanus and Scipio Nasica Serapio were sent to Carthage by the senate in order to take control of weapons from the Carthaginians (App. *Lib.* 80). Appian does not specify the office of both Scipiones, but they were probably military tribunes (Broughton MRR, 1.459 and 460 n. 4). We cannot possibly know whether it was Scipio Hispanus' first or second appointment as military tribune. Given the significance of this task, it seems reasonable to hypothesise that Scipio Hispanus was selected because he already had previous experience as military tribune and perhaps as quaestor too. If this was the case, Scipio Hispanus may have been quaestor shortly before 149 between his first and second military tribunates. See Sobeck 1909, 14, who does not dismiss the posibility of Scipio Hispanus holding the quaestorship in 149 and places this office either in 149 or soon afterwards;

Broughton MRR, 1.456 and 2.556: quaestor ca. 150 (however, Broughton MRR, 1.457, also includes Scipio Hispanus among the possible military tribunes in 150).

P. Cornelius Cn. f. Scipio Nasica (q. between 203 and 199) (cos. 191) (RE 350):
Publius Cornelius Scipio Nasica had yet not been quaestor in 204 (Liv. 29.14.8: *nondum quaestorium*. Cf. Val.Max. 8.15.3). As a consequence, he may have been quaestor in 203 at the earliest. Scipio Nasica held the aedileship in 197, so he must have been quaestor in 199 at the latest. The year 200 should probably be discarded, since he was one of the triumvirs appointed to supplement the colony of Venusia (Liv. 31.49.6). According to the evidence, Scipio Nasica must have held his quaestorship, which is not attested, in 202, 201 or 199. See Broughton MRR, 1.324: after 204 and before 199.

Faustus Cornelius L. f. Sulla (q. 54, proq. pro pr. 49–46) (RE 377):
As Asconius shows, the son of Sulla was quaestor in 54: *post diem autem quartam, quam postulatus erat Scaurus, Faustus Sulla tum quaestor, filius Sullae Felicis, frater ex eadem matre Scauri...* (Ascon. 20 C. Cf. Broughton MRR, 2.223). Sobeck 1909, 57–58, claims that Faustus Sulla was an urban quaestor because some coins minted by him with the legend *FAVSTVS* had initially been dated to 54 (cf. Bülz 1893, 32–34). Nevertheless, Crawford RRC, 88 and 449–451, dates the issue to 56, which has been corroborated by the study of the Mesagne Hoard (Hersh and Walker 1984, Table 2). Therefore, Faustus Sulla should have been a moneyer in 56 and a quaestor in 54, but there is no evidence of his urban quaestorship (see Broughton MRR, 3.73).

A Greek inscription from Elateia in honour of Faustus Sulla names him *proquaestor pro praetore* (ILS 8778 = IG 9.1.143: [ὁ] δᾶμος Ἐλατέων Φαῦστο[ν Κορνήλιον] / [Λευκίου] υἱὸν Σύλλαν Ἐπαφρόδιτον, ἀ[ντιταμίαν καὶ] / [ἀ]ντιστράτηγον, τὸν ἑατοῦ ε[ὐ]/εργέταν). The evidence of his proquaestorship is confirmed by a letter from March 49, in which Cicero refers to him very briefly: *praeter hunc et C. Cassium reliqui legati, Faustus pro quaestore* (Cic. *Att.* 9.1.4). Faustus Sulla apparently kept his title from 49 to 46, being active in different areas of the Mediterranean. While fleeing to Hispania in 46, he was captured and put to death in Africa. See Broughton MRR, 2.261, 2.276, 2.288 and 2.297; Balsdon 1962, 135; Thonemann 2004, 81.

P. Cornelius P. f. Sulla (q. and proq. of Caesar in 48–47?) (RE 387):
This man was the son of the homonymous P. Cornelius P. f. Sulla, consul designate in 65 (RE 386). He was a young man in 54 and was still alive in 46 (Cic. *Q. fr.* 3.3.2; *fam.* 15.17.2. See Broughton MRR, 3.73). Shackleton Bailey *Ep.Att.*, 2.175–176, suggested that the general who was in charge of the Caesarean camp at Dyrrachium and commanded the right wing of Caesar's army at Pharsalus in 48 was actually this man (Caes. *civ.* 3.51; 3.89.2 and 3.99.4; App. *b.c.* 2.76). He was still active in 47, serving Caesar's interests (Cic. *Att.* 11.21.2; 11.22.2). According to Shackleton Bailey, this P.

Cornelius Sulla (RE 387) acted as quaestor and proquaestor in 48 and 47, respectively (cf. Champlin 1989, 57). Broughton, however, identifies the Caesarean commander as the consul designate of 65 (RE 386) (presumably the father of RE 387) and supposes that he was a legate in 48–47 (Broughton MRR, 2.281 and 2.290). The sources do not provide any substantial hint to clarify whether he was the father or the son. If the man was the father, he should have been at least sixty years old in 48. It is not at all impossible that he was commanding a section of Caesar's army at Pharsalus, although his obviously much younger son would also be a good candidate. In any case, there is no way to elucidate whether he was a legate or a quaestor and/or proquaestor. In conclusion, Publius Cornelius Sulla (RE 387) may have become a senator at some point (Broughton MRR, 3.73), but there is no secure evidence of any of his possible offices, including the quaestorship.

L. Cornelius L. f. Sulla Felix (q. 107, proq. 106, proq. pro pr. 105) (cos. 88; 80) (RE 392):

There is no doubt that the later dictator Sulla was a quaestor under Marius in Numidia in 107: *Ceterum, dum ea res geritur, L. Sulla quaestor cum magno equitatu in castra venit* (Sall. *Iug.* 95.1); *in qua re praecipua opera L. Corneli Syllae, quaestoris C. Mari, fuit* (Liv. per. 66. Cf. Diodor. 34.39; Plut. *Sull.* 3.1; *Mar.* 10.3; etc. See Bültz 1908, 17–19; Sobeck 1909, 22–23; Broughton MRR, 1.551; Hinard 1985b, 31; Evans 1994, 211). In Italy Sulla collected a force of cavalry and went to Numidia late in 107 or early in 106. He remained there serving under Marius in 106–105, now as proquaestor (Broughton MRR, 1.554 and 1.556). According to Sallust, in 105 Marius left Sulla in charge of the camp *pro praetore* while he set out to attack a fortress in the desert (Sall. *Iug.* 103.4: *ad Sullam profugiunt, quem consul in expeditionem proficiscens pro praetore reliquerat*). Sulla's title should presumably be understood as *proquaestor pro praetore* in absence of the consul (cf. Kondratieff 2015, 437).

Q. Cornificius Q. f. (q. pro pr. 48–47 in Illyricum, proq.? in Cilicia and Syria 46) (pr. 45) (RE 8):

Q. Cornificius was a Caesarian quaestor in 48 acting *pro praetore* in Illyricum this year and the following: *(in Illyricum) missus aestate cum duabus legionibus Q. Cornificius, Caesaris quaestor, pro praetore…* (*bell. Alex.* 42; cf. 47 for year 47) (see Bülz 1893, 25–26; Sobeck 1909, 66–67; Broughton MRR, 2.274; 2.276; 2.288. Cf. Syme 1955c, 61; Sumner 1971, 258; Rawson 1978, 188). He was probably proquaestor in 46, when he was sent to Cilicia and later in the same year to Syria (Broughton MRR, 3.76).

Q. Curius (q. before 70) (RE 1):

Q. Curius is called a *homo quaestorius* by Asconius: *Q. ve Curium hominem quaestorium* (Ascon. 93 C). Sallust confirms that he had been a senator (Sall. *Cat.* 17.3), and that he was expelled from the senate in 70, most probably as a *quaestorius* (Sall. *Cat.* 23.1; cf. App. *b.c.* 2.3). As a consequence, Curius' quaestorship should be dated before 70, but a more precise date is impossible to determine. See Sobeck 1909, 45; Broughton MRR, 2.122 and 2.558 (cf. 3.78): quaestor? by 71. Marshall 1978, suggests that after his exclusion from the senate in 70 Curius held a second quaestorship by 65. There is, however, no evidence to support this conjecture. Curius is certainly called *quaestorius* in a speech delivered in 64 (*In toga candida*), as the text of Asconius shows, but he could be termed *quaestorius* on the basis of the quaestorship he held before 70 without need of a later second office (see Ryan 1994d, 259–261, with additional arguments).

C. (Curtius) Postumus (q. by 71?) (RE 24):
Broughton MRR, 2.122, suggests that C. (Curtius) Postumus may have held the quaestorship by 71, simply on the basis of his candidature for the praetorship in 63 (Cic. *Mur.* 57). Postumus was certainly quaestor, probably in the seventies, but no source mentions this. There is no way to confirm the date. Broughton's speculation could be applied to any magistrate (aedile or higher magistrate) for whom his quaestorship is not attested, estimating when he may have reached the minimum age to be a candidate for the quaestorship. This would be, however, a completely speculative exercise.

M. Curtius Peducaeanus (q. urb. 61) (pr. 50) (RE 8):
See **P. Sestullius.** According to Cicero, Marcus Curtius was quaestor urbanus with P. Sextilius in the year following the consulship of D. Silanus and L. Murena: *quid? Postero anno nonne M. Curio et P. Sextilio quaestoribus pecunia in classem est erogata?* (Cic. *Flacc.* 30). Consequently, there is no doubt as to his quaestorship in 61. Both urban quaestors were in charge of collecting funds for the fleet. As shown by Cicero, Curtius' cognomen was Peducaenus (Cic. *fam.* 13.59). For his praenomen Marcus, see Cic. *p. red. Sen.* 21. See Sobeck 1909, 53; Broughton MRR, 2.180; 3.79.

C. Decimius (q. by 49? proq. 48–46?) (RE 2):
In 46 C. Decimius was a *quaestorius* in charge of the Pompeian troops on Cercina in Africa. He fled from the island when the praetor Sallustius arrived (*bell. Afr.* 34.1–2: *Per id tempus C. Sallustius Crispus quem paucis ante diebus missum a Caesare cum classe demonstravimus, Cercinam pervenit. Cuius adventu C. Decimius quaestorius qui ibi cum grandi familiae suae praesidio praeerat commeatui, parvulum navigium nactus conscendit ac se fugae commendat*). Consequently, he was a quaestor sometime before 46 (Sobeck 1909, 67, who suggests that this Decimius could be the same person as in Cic. *Att.* 4.16.9; Broughton MRR, 2.475; 2.559). Ryan 1996e, 114–115, argues that Decimius may have been quaestor by 49 and proquaestor afterwards. His argument is based on the fact that the Pompeians in Thessalonica held no elections for 48. That means that all Pompeian leaders were promagistrates in 48. As a consequence, Decimius must

have been quaestor in 49 at the latest. Ryan's argument is convincing. Decimius must have been a quaestor in 49 or shortly before this year. He may have been a proquaestor serving under Pompey throughout the whole Civil War or just in 46, when his command is attested.

L. Domitius Cn. f. Ahenobarbus (q. 66) (cos. 54) (RE 27):
The quaestorship of Lucius Domitius Ahenobarbus is only attested through an emendation made by Manutius to the text of Asconius. According to this correction, Domitius Ahenobarbus strongly opposed the *rogatio de libertinorum suffragiis* submitted by the tribune of the plebs C. Manilius shortly after his entering the office: *constantiam L. Domiti, quam in quaestura (MSS praetura) praestitit, significat* (Ascon. 45 C). Manilius was a tribune of the plebs from 10th December 67 and he introduced his bill on the last day of the year. The *rogatio* was rejected by the senate on the first day of 66 (Cass.Dio 36.42.3). That means that the quarrel between Domitius and Manilius must have taken place between 10th and 29th December 67 (Badian 1959a, 83, rejects the emendation and prefers to maintain the reading *praetura*, which he thinks referred to Cicero's praetorship; however, Badian's assumption, although accepted by Champlin 1989, 57, is not possible: since Cicero entered his office on the first day of 66, he could not have opposed Manilius as a magistrate). If Domitius Ahenobarbus fought against Manilius as a quaestor, he must have entered office on 5th December 67. Marshall 1985, 195, assumes the emendation as correct, but he dates Ahenobarbus' quaestorship to 67, the year in which he reached the minimum age for the magistracy. This date, however, cannot be accepted. If Domitius Ahenobarbus was quaestor in 67, he should have left office on 4th December, and consequently he could not have opposed Manilius' bill as a quaestor. Domitius was probably born ca. 98, so that legally he could already have been elected for the quaestorship of 67. Nevertheless, it was not unusual to hold a magistracy after the minimum age required (Sumner 1973, 140). In short, Lucius Domitius Ahenobarbus was in all probability quaestor in 66 (Broughton MRR, 2.153; 3.83; Ryan 1995a; 1996f, 41). Nothing else is known about his activity.

C. Egnatuleius C. f. (q. 97) (RE 1):
Egnatuleius coined some quinarii at the beginning of the first century. The issues show a laureate head of Apollo and the legend *C · EGNATVLEI C · F · Q* on the obverse, while there is Victory, a trophy and a *carnyx* on the reverse with the letter *Q* placed between Victory and the trophy. According to Crawford RRC, 332 no. 333, the *Q* on the obverse and reverse should be interpreted as an abbreviation of the word quaestor. The reverse type presumably alludes to the victories of C. Marius. Crawford dates Egnatuleius' quaestorship to 97. It is not known whether C. Egnatuleius held any other magistracy. See Broughton MRR, 3.85 (cf. 2.439; 2.458; 2.561): *monetalis* or quaestor; Evans 1994, 214: quaestor in 97 following Crawford. Cf. Wiseman 1971, 229.

Fig. 4: Cn. Egnatuleius, quaestor 97. AR Quinarius. Rome. Head of Apollo right, C. EGNATVLEI C. F. Q behind. Victory standing left with a trophy and *carnyx*, Q in field, ROMA in exergue. Crawford RRC no. 333/1.

L. Egnatuleius (q. 44) (RE 2):

According to Cicero, Lucius Egnatuleius was quaestor under the consul Marcus Antonius in 44: *quarta legio duce L. Egnatuleio quaestore, civi optimo et fortissimo...* (Cic. *Phil.* 3.7; cf. 3.39). Egnatuleius brought the fourth legion from Macedonia to Italy. In November, he transferred it to Octavian. In January Cicero proposed to reward him with the right to be a candidate for another office before the legal time. Nothing else is known about him. See Sobeck 1909, 70; Broughton 2.325–326.

M. Eppius M. f. (q. 53 or 52) (RE 2):

See **L. Ateius Capito** and **C. Scribonius Curio.** Marcus Eppius is included by Caelius in the list of the senators present at the session in which a *senatus consultum* was approved (Cic. *fam.* 8.8.5–6: *C. Scribonius C. f. Pop. Curio, L. Ateius L. f. An. Capito, M. Eppius M. f. Ter.*). We must assume that the senators are cited in hierarchical order. Since Eppius is mentioned in the final place, he would have been among the most recent members of the senate, and consequently he was in all probability a *quaestorius* in 51, when the letter of Caelius was written. C. Scribonius Curio (RE 11), who is mentioned inmediately before Ateius Capito and Eppius, had been quaestor in Asia, perhaps in 55, and proquaestor in 54 and 53. Eppius (and probably Ateius Capito as well) was, therefore, quaestor before 51 and after 54 (or 55), presumably in 53 or 52. See Broughton MRR, 2.236; 2.246–247; 2.561: quaestor by 52; Wiseman 1971, 229.

K. Fabius M. f. Ambustus (q. 409) (tr. mil. c. p. 404, 401, 395, 390) (RE 42, cf. 39):
According to Livy, he was a patrician quaestor in 409, the year in which the first plebeian quaestors were elected (Liv. 4.54.2–3: *Eum dolorem quaestoriis comitiis simul ostendit et ulta est tunc primum plebeiis quaestoribus creatis, ita ut in quattuor creandis uni patricio, K. Fabio Ambusto, relinqueretur locus, tres plebeii, Q. Silius P. Aelius P. Papius, clarissimarum familiarum iuvenibus praeferrentur*). Cf. Sobeck 1909, 4; Broughton MRR, 1.78.

L. Fabius L. f. Hispaniensis (q. by 81 in Hispania) (RE 84):
See **C. Tarquitius.** There is no doubt that Lucius Fabius Hispaniensis was quaestor under the praetor C. Annius (Plut. *Sert*. 7) in Hispania by 81, as some coins show. They bear the legend *C · ANNI · T · F · T· N · PRO · COS · EX · S · C·* on the obverse, and *L · FABI · L · F · HISP Q* on the reverse (Crawford RRC, 381– 386 no. 366). According to Crawford, this issue was struck in Italy, whereas a later one was struck in Hispania by the quaestor C. Tarquitius. The presence of two quaestors serving under Annius can be explained, in his opinion, by the fact that Annius was in charge of Hispania Citerior and Hispania Ulterior. The year 81 has been unanimously accepted for Fabius Hispaniensis' quaestorship, but it should not be discounted that he could already have been quaestor in 82 (Sobeck 1909, 34; Broughton MRR, 2.77 and 3.86; Gabba 1954, 307; Wiseman 1971, 230; Spann 1987, 171). Thanks to Sallust (Sall. *hist*. 3.83 M = McGushin 3.79: *L. Fabius Hispaniensis senator ex proscriptis*), we also know that Fabius Hispaniensis was proscribed and that he fought in the Sertorian ranks. When and why this happened has been controversial, but the answer is connected with the quaestorships in Hispania in 81. Gabba 1954, 307, argues that he was proscribed after Lepidus' rebellion in 78 and believes that Fabius then fled to Hispania with Perpernna to fight on the side of Sertorius (see also Wiseman 1971, 230; Gruen 1974, 203 n. 164; Spann 1987, 171). However, there is another explanation, which was already put forth by Bülz 1893, 3, and later developed by Konrad 1987, 521. According to this interpretation, Fabius Hispaniensis joined Sertorius because he had been proscribed while he was quaestor in Hispania in 81. Fabius Hispaniensis would obviously have been dispossessed of his office, which would have led to the appointment of a new quaestor in his stead, C. Tarquitius. Accordingly, both quaestors did not serve under Annius simultaneously but, rather, in succession (Antela-Bernárdez, 2012, 38 and 2013; see also Díaz Fernández 2015, 538–539, n. 100). Against this interpretation, Hinard 1991, argues that the quaestor and the proscribed Sertorian senator were two different persons with the same name.

Q. Fabius (q. in Sicily in the second century?) (not in RE):
The identification of this Quintus Fabius with one of the known Fabii (not to mention his chronology and even the possibility of his having held the quaestorship) has been very controversial. The starting point is a text of Valerius Maximus, according to which

Fig. 5: C. Annius, proconsul, and L. Fabius, quaestor 81. AR Denarius. Hispania. Draped bust of Anna Perenna right, Caduceus behind, scale in front, C. ANNI. T. F. T. N. PRO COS. EX S. C. above. Victory in quadriga right, Q above, L. FABI. L. F. HISP in exergue. Crawford RRC no. 366/1a.

the consul P. Rupilius was made to leave Sicily and go to his son-in-law Quintus Fabius due to his negligently having lost the citadel of Tauromenium in the western part of the island: *nam P. Rupilius consul <eo bello, quod in Sicilia cum fugitivis gessit, Q. Fabium generum suum, quia neglegentia Tauromenitanam arcem amiserat, provincia iussit decedere>* (Val.Max. 2.7.3). On the other hand, some coins issued in the eastern Sicilian city of Panormus bearing the legend *Q · FAB* (see Bahrfeldt 1904, 393–396 nos. 46–47) have been linked to the text of Valerius Maximus. Interpretations have differed significantly. Sobeck does not associate the text with the coins. He assumes that the coins of Panormus were minted by a quaestor of the name Quintus Fabius, but considers it impossible to identify him with one of the Q. Fabii known in the first century (p. 86). Sobeck identifies the Quintus Fabius in the text of Valerius Maximus as a quaestor in 134, namely as Q. Fabius Maximus Allobrogicus (RE 110; see below) (pp. 16–17). Broughton MRR, 1.491 n. 1 and 1.498 links the text to the coins and suggests identifying the man as Q. Fabius Maximus (Eburnus) (RE 111), later consul in 116. Broughton dates his quaestorship in Sicily to 132, where he served under his father-in-law Rupilius (Stewart 1987, 436–438, identifies without hesitation the man to whom Valerius Maximus refers as the quaestor Q. Fabius Maximus Eburninus and dates his office to 132). Following Broughton, Prag 2007b, 300, records Q. Fabius (Maximus Eburnus?) (RE 111), as a possible quaestor in 132. However, Prag emphasises that neither the identification with Eburnus nor the office of quaestor inferred from the coins of Panormus are certain. Covino 2012, tackles the problem in depth. Nothing in Valerius Maximus allows us to conclude that this Q. Fabius was a quaestor under Rupilius. He could simply have been a legate. Covino assumes that the moneyer of the coins of Panormus was a quaestor. However, he could not be the same man as the Q. Fabius in Valerius Maximus' text, since the coins were issued on the other side of the island, where a second quaestor with no relation with Tauromenium was supposedly in charge. Consequently, they were two different Q. Fabii, and it is impossible to determine who the quaestor Fabius in Sicily was. He may have been Q. Fabius Eburnus or Q. Fabius Labeo, but he could also have been neither of these and instead an otherwise unknown Fabius. Covino goes on to discard the idea that he could have been Q. Fabius Maximus Allobrogicus, who indeed could have been the legate mentioned by Valerius Maximus. Finally, Frey-Kupper 2013, 248–250 and 267, dates all Sicilian issues coined by Roman magistrates to the second century. In most cases we only know the names of the magistrates, but not the offices they held (the Q. Fabius quoted in the coins of Panormus may indeed have been Q. Fabius Maximus Aemilianus, praetor in Sicily in 149; see Pol. 36.5.8). In other words, the coinage does not imply that every moneyer was a quaestor (this provided the starting point of the list of quaestors in Sicily made by Broughton MRR, 2.477–480, who dates the coins to the first century). According to Frey-Kupper, only in the case of coins in which the abbreviation Q was included can it be assumed for sure that the moneyers were quaestors.

The question has by no means been definitively solved. Nevertheless, it must be said that there is no certain evidence of a Quintus Fabius who was quaestor in Sicily in the second century, according to the current state of our knowledge. There is no reason to relate the moneyer of Panormus to the unsuccessful general of Tauromenium and it is not at all certain that the moneyer was a quaestor. If this last circumstance could be proved, this Quintus Fabius could be the same person as one of the otherwise known Q. Fabii (for instance Q. Fabius Maximus Eburnus), but he could also be a completely unknown figure. The identification with Q. Fabius Maximus Allobrogicus should, in any case, be discarded.

Q. Fabius (q. 188, proq. 187–186 in Hispania Citerior) (pr. 181) (RE 32, 58):

A Quintus Fabius held the quaestorship in Hispania Citerior under the command of L. Manlius Acidinus Fulvianus (pr. 188/cos. 179): *L. Manlius proconsul ex Hispania redierat... Tulit coronas aureas quinquaginta duas, auri praeterea pondo centum triginta duo, argenti sedecim milia trecenta, et pronuntiavit in senatu decem milia pondo argenti et octoginta auri Q. Fabium quaestorem advehere* (Liv. 39.29.4). Manlius Acidinus was sent to Hispania Citerior in 188 as praetor (Liv. 38.35.10), but his command was presumably prorogued in 187 and 186, since no successor was sent to this province (Liv. 38.42.5–6; cf. 39.7.6–7). As a promagistrate, Manlius Acidinus won a victory over the Celtiberians (Liv. 39.21.6–10). He is actually named *proconsul* by Livy when he refers to his return from Hispania and to his request to celebrate a triumph. According to Livy, there is no doubt that Q. Fabius was the quaestor of Manlius Acidinus at that time. Although it is not attested, he could also have been his quaestor in 188, and consequently may have accompanied his commander during his whole stay in Hispania, first as a magistrate and then as a promagistrate. If this was the case, Quintus Fabius was quaestor in 188 and proquaestor in 187 and 186. His cognomen could be Buteo, Maximus or even Labeo, all well-known *cognomina* for the Republican Fabii.

See Bültz 1908, 8–9; Sobeck 1909, 12; Broughton MRR, 1.366 (Q. Fabius [Buteo or Maximus]) and 2.562.

Q. Fabius Q. f. Labeo (q. urb. 196) (cos. 183) (RE 91):
See **L. Aurelius.** According to Livy, L. Aurelius and Quintus Fabius Labeo were the *quaestores urbani* in 196. They quarreled with augurs and pontifices about the payment of their contributions during the Hannibalic War (Liv. 33.42.2: *Sed magnum certamen cum omnibus sacerdotibus eo anno fuit quaestoribus urbanis Q. Fabio Labeoni et L. Aurelio*). See Sobeck 1909, 10; Broughton MRR, 1.336.

Q. Fabius Q. Aem. f. Maximus Allobrogicus (q. 134 Hispania Citerior, proq. 133– 132?) (cos. 121) (RE 110):
Quintus Fabius Maximus, later called Allobrogicus, was elected quaestor for 134 with the support of his uncle Scipio Aemilianus: *Aemilianum... cum quaestoriis comitiis suffragator Q. Fabi Maximi, fratris filii, in campum descendisset, consulem iterum reduxit* (Val.Max. 8.15.4. App. *Iber.* 84, wrongly calls him Buteo). Fabius Maximus served as quaestor under the command of Aemilianus in Hispania—perhaps directly appointed by his uncle—where he was in charge of 4,000 volunteers. Fabius probably stayed in Hispania as proquaestor until Aemilianus' return to Rome in 132 to celebrate his triumph over Numantia. See Bültz 1908, 11; Sobeck 1909, 16–17; Broughton MRR, 1.491; Scullard 1960, 72; Astin 1967, 82 n. 4. According to Sumner 1973, 60, Fabius was probably born in 164. Consequently, he held the quaestorship at the age of thirty (Evans 1994, 184).

Q. Fabius Q. f. Maximus Verrucosus (q. II before 238–237) (cos. 233, 228, 215, 214, 209) (RE 116):
We know through his *elogium* that Verrucosus, the Cunctator, was, quite exceptionally, quaestor twice: *(Q. Fabius) Q. f. Maximus dictator bis cos. V ce(n)sor interrex II aed. cur. q. II tr. mil. II pontifex augur primo consulatu Ligures subegit...* (CIL I^2 p. 193 = Inscr. Ital. 13.3.80). Nothing is known about these two quaestorships, whose chronology is impossible to determine. Verrucosus held his first consulship in 233. Earlier he was aedile, but never praetor. If the legal interval between offices was respected, 235 is the last possible year for his aedileship. As a consequence, Verrucosus should have been quaestor before 235, perhaps long before this year, but there is no evidence to support more exact date. At any rate, the date depends upon when he was born. Sumner 1973, 30–32, argues that Verrucosus was not born many years before 265. If this was the case, he seems to have held both quaestorships not long before his first consulship and consequently to have developed his political career in a limited number of years. See Sobeck 1909, 5–6; Broughton MRR, 1.222: quaestor perhaps in 237 and 236, but he may have held this office much earlier (cf. 2.563: Q. before 237 and 236?; 3.88); Beck

2005, 274–275: both quaestorships must be dated at some point before his aedileship, which he held at the latest in 235. However, Fabius Maximus did not necessarily hold both quaestorships before his curule aedileship. At a time in which the *cursus honorum* was not strictly fixed, it must not be discounted that the second quaestorship might have followed the aedileship. In any case, the repetition of the same office does not necessarily signal a regression in his political career. Moreover, it must be taken into account that, according to his *elogium*, he was never praetor. Therefore, the second quaestorship, if he held it after his aedileship, could exceptionally have substituted the praetorship in his *cursus honorum*.

T. Fadius (q. 63) (tr. pl. 57) (RE 9):
Titus Fadius was Cicero's quaestor during his consulship in 63: *iam T. Fadius, qui mihi quaestor fuit* (Cic. *p. red. in sen.* 21). It must be rejected that his cognomen was Gallus, which was added by mistake to the superscription of the Ciceronian letters addressed to him (Cic. *fam.* 7.23–27). See Sobeck 1909, 51, who gives the cognomen Gallus as likely; Broughton MRR, 2.168, also adds Gallus, but later he corrects his mistake (3.89); Shackleton Bailey 1962, 195–196; Syme 1964a, 116; Wiseman 1971, 230 no. 169.

C. Fannius (q. by 61?) (pr. 54 or 50?) (RE 9):
C. Fannius was tribune of the plebs in 59. For this reason, Ryan 1994e, 682, hypothesises that he must have been quaestor by 61. It is mere speculation, which in reality could be applied to almost every politician in the post-Sullan age for whom we do not have a reference to his quaestorship.

M. Favonius (q. 62?) (pr. 49) (RE 1):
See **Q. Caecilius Metellus Pius Scipio Nasica**. Marcus Favonius was a senator in 59, since he swore in the Curia to respect the consul Caesar's law (Plut. *Cat.min.* 32; Cass.Dio 38.7). Then, he was probably a *quaestorius* (Favonius was aedile in 52). This means that Favonius held the quaestorship before 59 (Broughton MRR, 2.190), but the question is exactly when. In May 60 a supplementary election to fill a vacancy in a regular magistracy took place, and Favonius was defeated by Metellus Scipio (Cic. *Att.* 2.1.9). Broughton MRR, 2.189, first thought that this magistracy was the tribunate of the plebs, but later he followed Sumner's arguments in favour of the quaestorship (MRR, 3.41–42). Despite his defeat, Favonius was again a candidate for 59 (Cic. *Att.* 2.1.9). According to Sumner 1973, 112–113, this time Favonius was successful, and he was elected quaestor for 59. As a quaestor, and consequently as a senator, he was able to take the oath in 59. However, it seems more likely that Favonius also lost this second election, probably not for the quaestorship but for the aedileship (Konrad 1996, 108; Pina Polo 2012, 67 and 82 n. 61). This brings us back to the problem of the date of Favonius' quaestorship. Ryan 1994c, 516, argues that Favonius could not have

been a quaestor in 59 when he took the oath, because a quaestor was not yet a senator while holding his office. Nor can he have held the quaestorship in 60. If he had, he could not have been a candidate for the suffect magistracy, nor in the elections for 59. An episode in 61 in the context of the trial against Clodius for *incestum* suggests that Favonius was already a *quaestorius* (Cic. *Att.* 1.14.5; cf. Ryan 1994c, 516). Besides, had he been a quaestor in 61, it seems doubtful that he could have been a candidate for a suffect magistracy the following year. As a result, Ryan proposes 62 as the most probable date for Favonius' quaestorship. At any rate, it seems to be the latest possible date.

C. Flaminius C. f. (q. 210, proq. 209 in Hispania) (cos. 187) (RE 3):
C. Flaminius served as quaestor in Hispania under Scipio Africanus. After the capture of Carthago Nova in 209, Scipio entrusted to him the booty (Liv. 26.47.8: *haec omnia C. Flaminio quaestori appensa adnumerataque sunt*) as well as the oversight of relations with some of the indigenous hostages taken in the city (Liv. 26.49.10: *ceterorum curam benigne tuendorum C. Flaminio quaestori attribuit*). Scipio Africanus probably arrived in Hispania in autumn 210 and remained there until 206 as a promagistrate. Flaminius could have followed the steps of his commander. He was certainly Scipio's (pro) quaestor in 209, as attested by our sources. As Scipio's trustworthy man, Flaminius had in all probability accompanied him to his province in 210. Whether he stayed as proquaestor in Hispania under Scipio until 206 is uncertain, but plausible. See Bülz 1908, 5; Sobeck 1909, 8: quaestor in 210; Broughton MRR, 1.286: quaestor in 209.

C. Flavius Fimbria (q. 86? proq. 85? in Asia) (RE 88):
Flavius Fimbria was involved in an episode of the Mithridatic War in Asia, when the consul *suffectus* L. Valerius Flaccus was killed during a mutiny of the troops under his command. The sources disagree about the office that Flavius Fimbria held at this moment. Most of the sources call him legate (Liv. *per.* 82; *vir.ill.* 70; Oros. 6.2.9; cf. Cass.Dio 30–35 fr. 104.1–4: ὁ ὑποστράτηγος Φλάκκου Φιμβρίας). Velleius Paterculus refers to Fimbria as *praefectus equitum* (Vell. 2.24.1). In a very doubtful version, Appian considers Fimbria to have accompanied Flaccus to Asia as a volunteer. Appian does not give Fimbria a title, but probably thinks of him as a legate who quarreled with Flaccus' quaestor, an incident that took place before the assassination of the consul (App. *Mith.* 51–52). Only Strabo considers Fimbria as Flaccus' quaestor (ταμίας), when he relates the story of the mutiny and how Fimbria took command of the troops (Str. 13.1.27: εἶτ' ἐκάκωσαν αὐτὴν πάλιν οἱ μετὰ Φιμβρίου Ῥωμαῖοι λαβόντες ἐκ πολιορκίας ἐν τῷ Μιθριδατικῷ πολέμῳ. συνεπέμφθη δὲ ὁ Φιμβρίας ὑπάτῳ Ὀυαλερίῳ Φλάκκῳ ταμίας προχειρισθέντι ἐπὶ τὸν Μιθριδάτην).

The scholarship has reflected the diversity of opinion found the ancient sources. Some scholars have accepted that Fimbria was a legate: Broughton MRR, 2.56 (cf. 3.92, where Broughton collects other views); Reinach 1975, 178 (Fimbria was legate and *praefectus equitum*, but not a quaestor); McGing 1986 (in his onomastic index); De Michele 2005, 281; Muñiz Coello 1995 – 96, 268 – 270, identifies Fimbria with the consul of 104 without providing very convincing arguments. Others have preferred to make of Fimbria a *praefectus equitum*, for instance Ballesteros 1996, 161 and n. 41. However, Lintott 1971, gives plausible arguments in favour of Fimbria's quaestorship under Flaccus (Suolahti 1955, 202, takes for granted that Fimbria was quaestor, following Strabo without any supplementary explanation). Fimbria may have been the quaestor of Marius at the beginning of 86. When Marius died and Flaccus was elected consul *suffectus*, Fimbria became Flaccus' quaestor and went to Asia with him. According to Lintott, as a quaestor Fimbria could have presided over the *iudicium populi* against Scaevola before departing for Asia (Cic. *Rosc. amer.* 33; cf. Val.Max. 9.11.2). Consequently, the sources that refer to Fimbria as a legate would be mistaken and only Strabo would be right. Lintott's viewpoint has been accepted by other scholars: Sumner 1973, 124: Fimbria was quaestor in 86 and legate in 85; Weinrib 1968, 43 n. 45, emphasises the role played by Fimbria in the trial of Scaevola and concludes that he was not acting as aedile or tribune of the plebs, but as quaestor; Mastrocinque 1999, 60. On the chronology of the events, Lintott 1976, 491, suggests that the killing of Flaccus did not happen before April-May 85. Only then did Fimbria take the command of the army for the rest of the year.

The office held by Fimbria remains obscure. It is certainly possible that he held the quaestorship in 86, first under Marius and then after his death under the *consul suffectus* Valerius Flaccus. In 85 Fimbria may have remained under Flaccus' command as proquaestor, and as such he may have taken control of the troops after Flaccus was killed. Although it is not impossible that a legate assumed control of the army when the commander died, it seems more probable that the quaestor, second in the hierarchy, did so. Nevertheless, there is no decisive reason to prefer Strabo's version to others, particularly when both Appian (*Mith.* 52) and Cassius Dio (30 – 35 fr. 104.4) record that Fimbria quarreled with Flaccus' quaestor in Asia (διαφορᾶς τινὸς τῷ Φιμβρίᾳ πρὸς τὸν ταμίαν γενομένης). If Fimbria was Flaccus' quaestor, who was the person arguing with him? Given the diversity of the sources, Fimbria's quaestorship must remain an open question.

M. Fonteius (q. urb. 83) (pr. 75?) (RE 12):
See **Hirtuleius (RE 1).** According to Cicero, M. Fonteius was *triumvir monetalis* and quaestor at the beginning of his political career (Cic. *Font.* 5: *Duorum magistratuum, quorum uterque in pecunia maxima tractanda procurandaque versatus est, triumviratus et quaesturae...*). Apparently, Fonteius was a moneyer before holding the quaestorship. Crawford RRC, 361, dates his moneyership before 87. There is no doubt that Fonteius was quaestor after the Valerian law regulating payment of debts was passed in 86 (Cic. *Font.* 1). Likewise, Cicero suggests that Fonteius held his quaestorship before Sulla returned to Italy in 83 (Cic. *Font.* 6). Taking into account all these premises, Sobeck 1909, 31, dates Fonteius' quaestorship between 86 and 84. Broughton MRR,

2.60, tentatively suggests 84 (but see 2.62 n. 2, where Broughton seems to betray some reservation), just like Luce 1968, 31, without ulterior arguments. However, Ryan 1996c, reaches the conclusion that his quaestorship should surely be dated to the year 83. According to Ryan, nothing in Cicero's speech excludes the possibility that Fonteius may have been elected in summer or autumn 84 and may have entered his office on 5th December 84, some months before Sulla's return (nevertheless, it must be noted that nothing proves that the quaestors entered office on 5th December in the pre-Sullan age). Additionally, Ryan interprets the Ciceronian expression *hunc omnium superiorum* (Cic. *Font.* 1: *hunc omnium superiorum, huius autem omnis qui postea fuerint auctoritatem dico secutos*) as evidence that Fonteius had followed all his predecessors in the quaestorship in fulfilling of the requirements of the Valerian law in 86. According to Cicero's statement, at least three quaestors preceded Fonteius holding office in 86, 85 and 84. As a consequence, Ryan concludes, 83 would be the only possible date for Fonteius' quaestorship.

L. Fulcinnius (q. 167? in Macedonia) (RE 2):

See **C. Publilius (RE 10).** The quaestorship of Lucius Fulcinnius is known only through bronze coins that he issued in Macedonia while serving as quaestor. The chronology is controversial, because only stylistic criteria can be used. Gaebler 1902, 152 and 157, suggests 148 as the probable date for Fulcinnius' coins. This chronology is accepted by Sobeck 1909, 14, who thought Fulcinnius had served as quaestor under Caecilius Metellus Macedonicus; it is also accepted by Broughton MRR, 1.461, although he wrongly speaks of Metellus Numidicus instead of Metellus Macedonicus. However, MacKay 1968, who bases his arguments on coin types, rejects Gaebler's date and proposes 167 as an alternative. According to MacKay, Fulcinnius was quaestor in Macedonia under Aemilius Paullus (cf. Broughton MRR, 3.94). This date, which MacKay convincing supports, has been taken up by many scholars, including Boehringer 1972, 113–114; Papazoglou 1979, 307 n. 18; and Morkholm 1991, 166. The year 167 seems to be the most probable date for Fulcinnius' quaestorship. In fact, this date was already proffered by Lenormant 1852, 319–321.

C. Fulvius (q. 218) (RE 10):

See **L. Lucretius (RE 4).** The quaestors C. Fulvius and L. Lucretius were captured by the Boii and given up to Hannibal in order that he might feel confidence in their support: *Venienti in Ligures Hannibali per insidias intercepti duo quaestores Romani, C. Fulvius et L. Lucretius... quo magis ratam fore cum iis pacem societatemque crederet, traduntur* (Liv. 21.59.10). This happened presumably in 218. We do not know whether Fulvius recovered his freedom and consequently whether he held other offices later. See Bülz 1908, 3–4; Sobeck 1909, 6, who adds the cognomen Centumalus to his name; Broughton MRR, 1.239 and 240 n. 6.

Fig. 6: L. Fulcinnius, quaestor 167? AE. Macedonia. Roma wearing winged helmet right. ΜΑΚΕΔΟΝΩΝ | ΤΑΜΙΟΥ ΛΕΥΚΙΟΥ | ΦΟΛΚΙΝΝΙΟΝ within oak wreath.

C. Fundanius (q. urb. 101) (RE 1):

The quaestorship of C. Fundanius is attested in coins in with the legend *C · FVNDAN Q*. The reverse of the denarii shows a triumphator in a quadriga holding a laurel-branch in his left hand, while the quinarii present a victory crowning a trophy and a kneeled captive with hands tied behind his back (Crawford RRC, 328 no. 326). This iconography refers, in all probability, to C. Marius' triumph over Cimbri and Teutons, which was celebrated in 101 (Hollstein 1993, 87–88: the coins were issued to finance Marius' triumph). This has prompted Crawford to date the coins and consequently Fundanius' quaestorship to the year 101. The same is defended by Sobeck 1909, 26, and Broughton MRR, 1.572 (with question mark; cf. 3.96). See also Evans 1994, 213. Mattingly 1982, 41, suggests a later date in the mid-90s. According to Syme 1963, 58 n. 40, this quaestor Fundanius and the C. Fundanius C. f. attested as a senator in 81 (OGIS 441, l. 20–21) were probably the same person (nothing is known about any other office that he held). He was presumably the father of C. Fundanius, who was tribune of the plebs by 68 (Broughton MRR, 2.138). As a quaestor in charge of the mint at Rome, particularly if the issue had to finance the triumph of Marius, Fundanius must have been an urban quaestor.

T. Furfan(i)us Postumus (q. 50? proq. (pro pr.)? 49 in Sicily) (RE 1):

See **L. [or T.?] Postumius (RE 15).** A letter from Cicero to Atticus reveals that a Furfanius (or Furfanus) was in Sicily in February 49 waiting to be replaced by his successor Postumius. However, Postumius refused to go to the island without Cato (Cic. *Att.* 7.15.2: *Postumius autem, de quo nominatim senatus decrevit ut statim in Siciliam iret*

Fig. 7: C. Fundanius, quaestor 101. AR Denarius. Rome. Helmeted head of Rome right. Triumphator holding laurel branch in quadriga right, C. FVNDAN in exergue, Q behind. Crawford RRC, no. 326/1.

Furfanioque succederet, negat se sine Catone iturum...). According to Shackleton Bailey 1976, 25, his name was probably Furfanus, though the form Furfanius is also attested (cf. Cic. *fam.* 6.8.3: *T. Furfanio Postumo, familiari meo, legatisque eius, item meis familiaribus, diligentissime te commendabo, cum venerint*). It is therefore apparent that Furfanus held an office in Sicily in 50 and at least in the first months of 49 while he waited for his substitute. Sobeck 1909, 61, argues that he could not have been the governor in Sicily and suggests that Furfanus was quaestor in 51 and remained as proquaestor in 50. Broughton MRR, 2.241, accepts Furfanus' quaestorship in Sicily in 51 as a possibility (cf. Syme 1964a, 116–117, without other arguments) as well as his quaestorship in 50 and 49, perhaps as *proquaestor pro praetore* (2.250 and 2.262). Balsdon 1962, 134: since no appointments of provincial governors had been made since June 51, at the beginning of 49 most provinces were governed by *proquaestores pro praetore*, such as Furfanus Postumus in Sicily.

Sumner 1971, 268–269, argues that the special distinction of the jury on which Furfanus took part in Milo's trial in 52 (Cic. *Mil.* 74–75, cf. Ascon. 38–39 C; Vell. 2.76.1) implies that he was already a senator in 52. If Sumner was right, Furfanus should have held the quaestorship not in 51, but considerably earlier (see Broughton MRR, 3.96). His command in Sicily in 50 and 49 could not have been as proquaestor, but possibly as an ex-praetor (his praetorship, then, would date to 55 at the latest).

Nevertheless, Sumner's thesis has not won wide acceptance, mainly because its starting point is not solid. Certainly, Asconius describes the members of Milo's jury as persons of prestige (Ascon. 38 C: *Album quoque iudicum qui de ea re iudicarent Pompeius tale proposuit ut numquam neque clariores viros neque sanctiores propositos esse constaret*). However, this does not necessarily imply that they were senators. Furfanus could have had equestrian status. As Brennan 2000, 674–675, has argued, it was clear that at the end of 50 Furfanus had fulfilled the time in Sicily that was assigned to his office and was waiting to be replaced. If Furfanus had had praetorian status, he could have delegated his command and departed for Rome. Furfanus had to wait for his substitute because he was a quaestor in command of Sicily, something that happened at the time in other provinces, such as Syria, Macedonia, Cilicia and Asia. According to Brennan, Furfanus may have been elected quaestor for 51 or even 50.

For his part, Prag 2007b, 308, suggests that Furfanus was a quaestor probably in 50, and a proquaestor (*pro praetore*) or a legate in 49. Furfanus was, in his opinion, most likely a quaestor left in Sicily at the end of 50 with delegated *imperium*.

To summarise, Titus Furfanus (probably better than Furfanius, although this form cannot be discounted) Postumus may have been quaestor in 51 and proquaestor in 50 and 49 (at least at the beginning of this year), or quaestor in 50 and proquaestor in 49, at any case in Sicily. On the basis of Cicero's letter to Atticus, it is certain that he had finished his time in office at the end of 50 and was waiting to be replaced in 49. His office in 50 must have been the quaestorship, and consequently in 49 he could have acted temporarily as proquaestor, probably in command of Sicily.

C. Furius Aculeo (q. 190) (RE 31):

C. Furius Aculeo was quaestor under L. Cornelius Scipio Asiaticus during the war against Antiochus in 190 (Liv. 38.55.4–5: *et C. Furii Aculeonis quaestoris et, ut omnia contacta societate peculatus viderentur, scribae quoque duo et accensus. L. Hostilius et scribae et accensus, priusquam de Scipione iudicium fieret, absoluti sunt, Scipio et A. Hostilius legatus et C. Furius damnati*). He was later condemned for embezzlement (cf. Liv. 38.58.1). See Bültz 1908, 8; Sobeck 1909, 11; Broughton MRR, 1.356.

L. Furius Bibaculus (q. 216) (RE 35):

See **L. Atilius.** Lucius Furius Bibaculus and L. Atilius were quaestors under the consuls C. Terentius Varro and L. Aemilius Paullus in 216 (Liv. 22.49.16: *in his ambo consulum quaestores, L. Atilius et L. Furius Bibaculus...*). Both were killed at the battle of Cannae. See Bülz 1908, 4; Sobeck 1909, 7; Broughton MRR, 1.249.

Furius Crassipes (q. between 54 and 51 in Bithynia) (RE 54):

A Ciceronian letter shows that Crassipes was quaestor in Bithynia (Cic. *fam.* 13.9.3: *a te peto... rem... et utilitatem sociorum (cuius rei quantam potestatem quaestor habeat, no sum ignarus) per te quam maxime defensam et auctam velis*). Cicero asks Crassipes to serve the interests of the Bithynian company taking advantage of his position as quaestor. There is little doubt that this Crassipes must be identified with Furius Crassipes, his son-in-law. He married Tullia in 56–55 and got divorced some time before Cicero's proconsulship in Cilicia. The quaestorship of Furius Crassipes is dated before 50 by Sobeck 1909, 53 (cf. Bülz 1893, 52–53). Broughton MRR, 2.242, suggests the year 51 and that he served under P. Silius. However, Shackleton Bailey 1977, 1.477–478, points out that nothing in Cicero's letter allows us to conclude that it could not have been written before the divorce. As a consequence, Shackleton Bailey tentatively dates it to 54, although he admits that a later or even an earlier year would be also possible. Unfortunately, there is not enough evidence to fix the date of Furius Crassipes' quaestorship in Bithynia, which could have fallen in any year between 54 and 51, if not even earlier.

A. Gabinius (q. 102? proq. 102–100? in Cilicia) (RE 8):

See **C. Norbanus.** The quaestorship of Aulus Gabinius is attested in a Greek inscription from Rhodes, in which Gabinius is mentioned together with the proconsul M. Antonius (IGRP 4.1116, *ll.* 4–5: [Μ]άρκου Ἀντωνίου στραταγοῦ ἀνθυπά/[του καὶ] Αὔλου Γαβεινίου τ[α]μία ʿΡωμαίων ἰς [Κ]ιλικίαν). Sobeck 1909, 41, supposes that this Antonius was Antonius Creticus, who fought against the pirates in 74; consequently, he dates Gabinius' quaestorship to this year. However, this identification has been rejected in the scholarship (Broughton MRR, 1.573 n. 3), which has unanimously associated him with the famous orator M. Antonius (cos. 99, RE 28). Antonius was praetor and afterwards proconsul in Cilicia in 102–100, and it must have been during this time that Gabinius was quaestor under his command. The question to be answered is whether Gabinius accompanied Antonius when he left Rome in 102 and remained with him throughout his stay in Cilicia, or whether he only served under his command during a portion of this time. The problem intensifies if we consider that C. Norbanus was also a quaestor under Antonius, either in Cilicia, or during Antonius' consulship in 99.

Broughton MRR, 1.572, rightly points out that the title of proconsul for Antonius in the Greek inscription (στραταγὸς ἀνθύπατος) suggests 101 rather than 102, when he was a praetor (cf. Broughton 1946, 40). As a consequence, Broughton dates the quaestorship of Gabinius to 101 (Badian 1959b, 86–87, identifies this Gabinius as the legate of 89; cf. Broughton MRR, 2.36 and 3.97). While this seems reasonable enough, the dating of the inscription could also be 100 or Gabinius might already have been quaestor in 102, remaining as proquaestor in Cilicia in 101 and/or 100. In the opinion of Gruen 1966c, Gabinius was actually the only quaestor serving under Antonius in Cilicia, where he remained the whole time from 102 to 100. Norbanus would have been the quaestor of Antonius during his consulship in 99. On the contrary, Badian 1983, 170, dates Gabinius' quaestorship exclusively to 102, since he claims that Norbanus was the quaestor of Antonius in 101. This would mean that Antonius successively had two different quaestors under his command in Cilicia.

It is not easy to provide a clear answer for the problem. However, we are inclined to follow Gruen in supposing that Gabinius was Antonius' quaestor and his right-hand man throughout his stay in Cilicia. If this was the case, Gabinius would have held the quaestorship in 102 (cf. Evans 1994, 212), remaining as proquaestor in 101 and 100.

Granius Petro (q. desig. 46) (RE 9):

According to Plutarch (*Caes.* 16.4), Granius Petro was a quaestor designate, presumably for 46, who was captured in Africa by the Pompeian Q. Caecilius Metellus Scipio Nasica. Scipio offered to spare his life, but Granius Petro killed himself. See Bülz 1893, 76–77; Sobeck 1909, 69; Broughton MRR, 2.296; Wiseman 1971, 234 no 197; Sumner 1971, 271; Townend 1987, 334–335.

M. Herennius M. f. Rufus (q. in 80s first century?) (RE 41):

The quaestorship of Marcus Herennius Rufus is only known through an inscription from Alsium, a city on the coast of Etruria, about 35 km from Rome: *M. Herennius M. f. Mae(cia) Rufus praef(ectus) Cap(uam) Cum(as) q(uaestor)* (CIL I^2 827 = CIL XI 3717 = ILLRP 441). The date of his quaestorship, which was obviously connected with the prefecture of Capua and Cumae, is impossible to determine with any precision. Degrassi argues that such prefects lost their power after the refounding of Capua as a Roman colony in 59 (see his comment in ILLRP 441). Broughton MRR, 2.476 and 2.483, dates it rather vaguely before 90. However, Taylor 1960, 220, rejects such an early chronology for the inscription, given that it was on a piece of high-quality marble. Taylor suggests that the prefecture of Capua and Cumae could have continued after the Social War. Consequently, she dates Herennius Rufus' acceptance to the senate to the 80s, during the domination of C. Marius' allies. Badian 1971a, 376 n. 14, dates Herennius Rufus' quaestorship to some time after the Social War (cf. Broughton MRR, 3.102). According to Badian, this man may have been the son or the grandson of the consul of 93. Deniaux 1979, 628–629, basically follows Taylor's arguments and dates the quaestorship of Herennius Rufus to the 80s. None of these arguments can be considered definitive. A dating in the 80s is possible but hypothetical.

Hirtuleius (q. urb. 86) (RE 1):

See **M. Fonteius.** According to Cicero (Cic. *Font.* 2), Hirtuleius applied the law of the suffect consul L. Valerius Flaccus shortly after it was passed in 86. The law allowed debtors to settle their debts for a quarter of the principal sum. Hirtuleius preceded M. Fonteius in the urban quaestorship, but not immediately. Sobeck 1909, 31, dates his quaestorship to 86 or 85 and wrongly considers this Hirtuleius to be same individual as the quaestor of Sertorius in Hispania (see L. Hirtuleius, RE 3). While Broughton MRR, 2.54, includes him as quaestor in 86 with a question mark, in the index (2.572) he is more cautious and opts to give two possible years: Q. 86 or 85. Ryan 1996c, gives good arguments to date Hirtuleius' urban quaestorship precisely to 86. According to Ryan, the Valerian law was put into practice immediately after the law was approved (i.e. in the year 86). Since Hirtuleius was the first urban quaestor who applied the law, he must have held the office in 86. Cf. Wiseman 1971, 235 no 207: 'possibly identical with the C. Hirtuleius defended by L. Sisenna in the eighties (Cic. *Brut.* 260).'

L. Hirtuleius (q. 83?, proq. 82–76?) (RE 3):
See **M. Marius.** Lucius Hirtuleius is mentioned in the ancient sources as Sertorius' quaestor in Hispania in different circumstances between 79 and 76 (Liv. per. 90: *Q. Sertorius proscriptus in ulteriore Hispania ingens bellum excitavit. L. Manlius procos. et M. Domitius legatus ab Hirtuleio quaestore proelio victi sunt*; Liv. per. 91: *Q. Metellus procos. L. Hirtuleium, quaestorem Sertori, cum exercitu cecidit*; cf. Plut. Sert. 12.3). The sources call him quaestor, but he must have acted as proquaestor under Sertorius, although the Roman senate obviously did not recognise him as such. Sobeck 1909, 31, claims that he was the same man as the quaestor Hirtuleius who was urban quaestor in 86 (see above) (cf. Bülz 1893, 16–17). Konrad 1994, 131–132 and 186–187, considers Sobeck's identification of the Sertorian oficial with the quaestor of 86 to be compelling; he further points out that Hirtuleius was technically proquaestor during his stay in Hispania. Broughton MRR, 2.83, 2.94 and 3.102, makes Hirtuleius the quaestor of Sertorius in 79 and his proquaestor in 78–76. Cf. Wiseman 1971, 235 no. 208.

It does not seem probable that this Lucius Hirtuleius should be identified with the Hirtuleius who was urban quaestor in 86. They are most likely two different persons. There is no doubt that L. Hirtuleius served under Sertorius in Hispania technically as proquaestor. The question is when he held the quaestorship. Since Sertorius was appointed praetor for Hispania Citerior in 83 and, consequently, a quaestor must have accompanied him when he departed for his province, it is plausible that Hirtuleius was quaestor in 83, that he came with Sertorius to Hispania and that he remained there as his proquaestor during the following years.

Q. Hortensius L. f. Hortalus (q. before 78) (cos. 69) (RE 13):
The quaestorship of Q. Hortensius Hortalus, the orator, is attested by Cicero in his *Verrines: nuper, Hortensi, quaestor fuisti...* (Cic. Verr. 2.3.182). The word *nuper* seems to denote that Hortensius had held his quaestorship recently before 70, when Cicero wrote his *Verrines*. However, the use of *nuper* is vague, which makes impossible to determine the date of the magistracy with certainty. Hortensius held the aedileship in 75. As a consequence, he must have been a quaestor in 78 at the very latest, if we take into account the compulsory interval of two years between these offices. But he could also have been a quaestor some years earlier, since he was born in 114 (Cic. Brut. 230). Additionally, his political career could have been altered by the circumstances around the civil war and the dictatorship of Sulla in the 80s. See Sobeck 1909, 30: quaestor between 86 and 78; Broughton MRR, 2.573: q. ca. 80? Broughton's date was uncritically accepted by Sumner 1973, 24, and Arkenberg, 1993. Badian 1959a, 83: as we know that Hortensius was aedile in 75, he cannot in any case have been quaestor later than 77. A more precise date for Hortensius' quaestorship is impossible to determine.

Q. Hortensius Q. f. Hortalus (q. 51–50 Asia?) (RE 8):
The hypothetical quaestorship of Q. Hortensius Hortalus, son of the famous orator (RE 13; his cognomen Hortalus is attested in Catul. 65.2), depends on the interpretation of a letter that Cicero sent to Atticus: *Hortensius filius fuit Laodiceae gladiatoribus flagitiose et turpiter… Is mihi dixit se Athenis me exspectaturum ut mecum decederet* (Cic. *Att.* 6.3.9). If *decedere* is interpreted as a synonym for *deponere* in the sense of *provincia decedere* (see Balsdon 1937, 8), it is possible, according to Broughton, that Hortensius was quaestor in Asia in 51–50, preceding L. Antonius (Cic. *fam.* 2.18). See Broughton MRR, 3.103.

C. Julius C. f. Caesar (q. by 100) (pr. by 97) (RE 130):
He is the father of Julius Caesar the dictator. We know of his quaestorship through his elogium (Inscr. Italiae 13.3.75 = CIL VI 1311; see Frank 1937). A second copy was found in 1925 in the Forum of Augustus. Broughton 1948, 324–325, argues that Caesar was a *decemvir* before holding his quaestorship, and that he led a colony to the island of Cercina either after 103 or in 100 in accordance with a colonization law of the tribune of the plebs Saturninus for Marius' veterans (cf. Broughton MRR, 1.577: Caesar settled colonists on Cercina either after 103 or in 100; cf. MRR, 3.104–105). In his index, Broughton dates Caesar's quaestorship just before 100 (MRR, 2.574). The date of Caesar's quaestorship depends on when we date his activity as a *decemvir* (and ultimately this depends on the date of Saturninus' legislation). If, as seems most probable, Caesar was a *decemvir* before holding the quaestorship, he may have been quaestor by 100, either shortly before or even shortly after this year.

C. Julius C. f. Caesar (q. 69, proq. 68 in Hispania Ulterior) (dict. 49–44) (RE 131):
There is no doubt that Caesar held the quaestorship in Hispania Ulterior under the command of Antistius Vetus (Suet. *Iul.* 7; Vell. 2.43.4; *bell. Hisp.* 42; Plut. *Caes.* 5.3; Cass.Dio 37.52.2). Its date, however, has been a subject of controversy, in part because of disagreement over the year in which Caesar was born. Initially the quaestorship was dated to 68, that is, between 5th December 69 and 4th December 68 (Bülz 1893, 8–10; Sobeck 1909, 47; Rice Holmes 1917, 150). Nevertheless, Taylor 1941, 122–123, compellingly argues in favour of 69. According to Taylor, Caesar entered office on 5th December 70. He remained in Rome during part of his term, since he delivered funeral orations for his aunt Julia and his wife Cornelia from the *rostra*, when he was quaestor (Suet. *Iul.* 6: *Quaestor Iuliam amitam uxoremque Corneliam defunctas laudavit e more pro rostris*; Plut. *Caes.* 5.6: θάψας δὲ τὴν γυναῖκα, ταμίας εἰς Ἰβηρίαν ἑνὶ τῶν στρατηγῶν Βέτερι συνεξῆλθεν). As a consequence, Caesar went to Hispania in the spring or summer of 69. Apparently with the consent of his commander Antistius Vetus, Caesar left Hispania before finishing his term (Suet. *Iul.* 8: *Decedens ergo ante tempus…*), when Antistius was still in charge of the province. In Taylor's opinion, Caesar was back in Rome in early 67, when he supported the Gabinian law (see also Taylor 1942a, 14. Cf.

Badian, 1969, 201 n. 1: Caesar returned from Hispania probably late 68 or early 67). Broughton MRR, 2.132 and 136 n. 7 (see also 3.105–106), follows Taylor: Caesar was quaestor in 69 and proquaestor in 68. He left Hispania sometime in 68. The dates of 69 and 68 respectively for Caesar's quaestorship and proquaestorship in Hispania Ulterior have generally been accepted. See among others Marinone 1970, 273; Etienne 1997, 40–41; Jehne 1997, 23; Tansey 2000, 243; Tatum 2008, 33. See also Sumner 1973, 136.

L. Julius L. f. Caesar (q. 77 in Asia) (cos. 64) (RE 143):

Lucius Julius Caesar is mentioned as quaestor (ταμίαν) in a Greek inscription found in Ilion (OGIS 444 – SEG 4.664, *ll.* 5–6: καὶ ἐπὶ τὸν ταμίαν Λεύκιον Ἰούλιον / Λευκίου υἱὸν Καίσαρα). His quaestorship in Asia has been unanimously dated to 77. See Sobeck 1909, 36; Broughton MRR, 2.89 and 3.110; Magie 1950, 2.1119, n. 24; Nicolet 1980, 118–119.

L. Julius Caesar (q. by 50 or earlier; proq. 47? and 46 in Africa) (RE 144):

In the context of the Civil War, we have information about Lucius Julius Caesar in both 49 and 46. In the year 46, he is called proquaestor under the command of Cato Uticensis at Utica: *[Cato] liberis suis L. Caesari qui tum ei pro quaestore fuerat commendatis...* (*bell. Afr.* 88.3; cf. 89; Plut. *Cat.min.* 66; Cass.Dio 43.12.3. See Bülz 1893, 77–78; Sobeck 1909, 68; Broughton MRR, 2.289 and 2.297: probably a proquaestor in 47 and 46). Although there is no evidence of his quaestorship, it has been assumed that he went to Caesar as an official legate of the senate in January 49, together with Roscius Fabatus (Caes. *civ.* 1.8: *Eo L. Caesar adulescens venit, cuius pater Caesaris erat legatus*). He is called *adulescens* by Caesar, not necessarily because he was very young, but rather in order to distinguish him from his father (cf. Cass.Dio 41.5.3). Because of the presumably official character of this embassy, it has been deduced that Lucius Julius Caesar was a senator in 49 and that he likely held the quaestorship by or before 50 (Willems 1878, 1.538: 'Nous ne savons pas en quelle année il fut questeur; mais il est probable qu'il le fut plusieurs années avant 49'; Sumner 1971, 204 and 258; 1976, 343). However, Shackleton Bailey 1960, 80–83, demonstrates that L. Caesar and Roscius did not act as official senatorial legates (the same conclusion is found in Raaflaub 1975, 251). Nevertheless, this unofficial character of the embassy does not mean that L. Caesar had not yet held the quaestorship. Furthermore, Caesar refers to Roscius as a praetor, but he does not mention an office for L. Caesar. It seems logical to conclude that he was a *privatus* in 49 (otherwise Caesar would have mentioned his office), but he could already have been a senator of quaestorian rank. Such a conclusion is supported by the offices that L. Caesar held after 49 (he was not only proquaestor in 46 and maybe in 47, as we have seen, but also *praefectus classis* in 49 and 48: Broughton MRR, 2.270 and 2.283). This line of argumentation implies that Lucius Julius Caesar might have been quaestor by 50 or perhaps earlier. See Broughton MRR, 3.110–111; Ryan 1996e.

Sex. Julius Sex. f. Caesar (q. 48?, proq. pro pr. in Syria 47–46) (RE 153):
According to Cass.Dio 47.26.3, Sextus Julius Caesar was a quaestor (ταμίας) when he was appointed by Caesar to the command of Syria in the summer of 47. Taking into account that no elections were held in 47 until the autumn, he was probably already quaestor in 48. Therefore, Sextus Julius Caesar was presumably proquaestor in 47 and also in 46, when he was killed in Syria during a rebellion led by the Pompeian Caecilius Bassus. See Sobeck 1909, 68: quaestor in 47–46; Broughton MRR, 2.274 and 2.285 n. 5 (quaestor in 48); 2.289 and 2.297 (probably *proquaestor pro praetore* in 47 and 46); Sumner 1971, 258; 1976, 343 (quaestor in 48).

C. Julius L. f. Caesar Strabo Vopiscus (q. 104–103 in Sardinia? or between 100 and 96?) (RE 135):
The only evidence of the quaestorship of Caesar Strabo Vopiscus is found in his *elogium*: *C. Iulius L. f. Caesar Strabo aed. cur. q. tr. mil. bis Xvir agr. dand. adtr. iud. pontif.* (CIL I².1, p. 198 = Inscr. Ital. 13.3.6). The dates for all of his offices remain uncertain, with the exception of the aedileship, which he held in 90 (Broughton MRR, 2.26 and 2.30 n. 6). Since the offices are presumably mentioned in chronological order, Caesar Strabo must have been quaestor before 90 (Sobeck 1909, 28, does not wager a more specific date), after twice being military tribune and having served as a *decemvir* on an agrarian commission.

Providing a more precise date for his quaestorship is controversial and hypothetical, since any argument must rely on the equally controversial dates of his other offices. On the one side, Gabba 1976, 198–199 n. 157, suggests that Caesar Strabo was quaestor in Sardinia around 104–103. We know that in 103 he defended the interests of the Sardinians in a trial *de repetundis* against T. Albucius, who had been governor on the island around 106–104 (Cic. *div. in Caec.* 63). According to Gabba, Caesar Strabo could have been selected as patron by the Sardinians because of a previous quaestorship on the island. If Gabba is right (Champlin 1989, 58, thinks that Gabba's suggestion is plausible), Caesar Strabo's birth should be dated around 131–130. In this case, he would not have held the aedileship *suo anno*, which is quite possible in light of the rest of his political career.

On the other side, a later date for his quaestorship has been proposed. Sumner 1973, 105: the certain date of his aedileship in 90 establishes a date not later than 127 for his birth. The reconstruction of his career could be as follows: member of the agrarian commission in 103; military tribune in 102 and 101; quaestor sometime between 100 and 96. Broughton MRR, 3.109, also dates the agrarian commission to 103 rather than 100 (MRR, 1.577). Following Suolahti 1955, 312 and 405, Broughton claims that he could have been military tribune twice around 100. Regarding the quaestorship, Broughton reaches a conclusion similar to Sumner's and tentatively suggests the year 96 (MRR, 2.10). Cf. Evans 1994, 187–188: 'his membership of the agrarian commission established by Saturninus in 103, followed by an extended period of service in the army, probably rules out a quaestorship during the period between 104 and 99, by which time the office may no longer have possessed much attraction for him.'

There is not enough evidence to decide whether the earlier chronology of 104–103 or the later dating at the beginning of the first century is more convincing. His possible quaestorship in Sardinia is also hypothetical.

D. Junius D. f. Brutus Albinus (q. 50?) (cos. desig. 42) (RE 55a, suppl. 5):

Although there is no clear evidence, Brutus Albinus' quaestorship has been tentatively dated to the year 50. According to Sumner 1971, 358–359, Brutus Albinus is described as an *adulescens* under the command of Caesar in 56 and 52 (Caes. *Gall.* 7.9.1 and 7.87.1). Since he is not mentioned as a legate, he was probably not yet a senator. However, he reappeared in 49 as a legate, which suggests that he had already become a senator. Sumner concludes that he was presumably elected in 51 for the quaestorship in 50. Syme reaches the same conclusion: Brutus Albinus may have held the quaestorship in 50, when he was paying court to Valeria Polla, the sister of Valerius Triarius (see Syme 1960a, 327; 1980, 406; 1981, 424). These arguments are collected in Broughton MRR, 3.112.

M. Junius M. f. Brutus (q. 54? proq. 53–51? in Cilicia) (cos. desig. 41) (RE 53):

After being adopted by his uncle, he became Q. Servilius Caepio Brutus. It is known that Marcus Junius Brutus was, at the beginning of his career, successively a moneyer and a quaestor. Crawford RRC, 88 and 455–456, dates his coins (with the legend *BRVTVS*) to 54, immediately preceding his quaestorship in 53. Crawford claims that 55 is impossible, since we already know the moneyers for that year. The year 53 has indeed been the favourite date for Brutus' quaestorship. As quaestor he served in Cilicia under the command of his father-in-law Appius Claudius. See Sobeck 1909, 59–60; Broughton MRR, 2.229; Clarke 1981, 11 and 15–16; Mattingly 2004, 259.

However, the year 54 has also been proffered for Brutus' quaestorship. So Sumner 1971, 365–366: Brutus was born in 85 (Cic. *Brut.* 229 and 324). He was therefore eligible in the elections of 55 for the quaestorship of 54. According to *vir.ill.* 82.3–4 (*Quaestor <Caesari> in Galliam proficisci noluit, quod is bonis omnibus displicebat. Cum Appio socero in Cilicia fuit, et cum ille repetundarum accusaretur, ipse ne verbo quidem infamatus est*), Brutus refused to serve under Caesar in Gaul and prefered to go with Ap. Claudius to Cilicia. Claudius was consul in 54 and proconsul in 53–51. Brutus may have been quaestor under Claudius in 54 and proquaestor from 53, or alternatively quaestor in 53. The evidence of *De viris illustribus* allows for either possibility.

Nevertheless, it must also be remembered that the elections for 53 did not take place until July of that year—not in 54. If Brutus was elected quaestor in these elections, he only could have joined Claudius in Cilicia at the end of 53. Since Claudius apparently proceeded to his province at the end of 54 (Cic. *Att.* 4.18.4; *fam.* 1.9.25; *Q.fr.* 3.2.3. Cf. Pina Polo 2011, 235) and must have been accompanied by a quaestor,

Brutus would have had to replace that previous quaestor in 53. It is more reasonable that Brutus was already a quaestor in 54, which is plausible because (1) he had reached the minimum age for office and (2) our main evidence, the text in *De viris illustribus*, is compatible with this interpretation. He must have travelled to Cilicia with Ap. Claudius at the end of 54 and remained in the province as proquaestor, presumably until they returned together in 51. See Broughton MRR, 3.112; Syme 1980, 404; 1987, 324: 'since he was born in 85, it is convenient to assign his quaestorship to 54.' Brutus' quaestorship to 54 obviously challenges the chronology for his moneyership that Crawford proposes. Perhaps this office should be dated earlier.

M. Junius Silanus Murena (q. 89?) (pr. 77?) (RE 170?):

The departure point is a much-debated Greek inscription from Priene (I. Priene 121, ll. 21–24: πρὸς τ[ούς τε ἀπεσταλμέν]ους εἰς τὴν Ἀσίαν ὑπὸ Ῥωμαίων στρατηγοὺς Γάϊον τε Λαβέωνα καὶ Λεύκιον Πείσωνα καὶ Μᾶρκον Ὑψαῖον κ<αὶ Μ>ᾶρκον Σιλανὸν Μυρέναν ταμίαν καὶ πρὸς ἄλλους Ῥωμαίους), in which some Roman στρατηγοί sent to Asia are mentioned. The inscription honours a man who undertook numerous diplomatic missions of behalf of Priene. It is not clear whether the names of the στρατηγοί are sorted into chronological order or according to rank. Among them, a M. Silanus Murena appears, whose name is followed by the word quaestor (ταμίαν). The debate essentially hinges upon the identification of this quaestor. For some scholars, the text should be interpreted as a reference to a M. (Junius) Silanus who was quaestor under Murena (this interpretation requires the amendment of Μυρέναν to a genitive in order to translate 'and M. Silanus the quaestor of Murena'); for others, however, the quaestor was named M. Silanus Murena.

Sobeck 1909, 32, dates M. Junius Silanus' quaestorship in Asia between 84 and 81 and identifies him as the proconsul of 76 in Asia. Broughton MRR, 2.60, 2.64 and 2.69 (cf. 2.577 and 3.114), maintains the same identification. According to Broughton, M. Junius Silanus was quaestor in 84 serving in Asia under Licinius Murena, and he remained in the province as proquaestor in 83 and 82. Gruen 1966c, 106, argues that Silanus had probably served under Murena since 87, and that he was a proquaestor (not a quaestor) in 84. According to Gruen, it is not likely that Rome would have dispatched a quaestor to assist Sulla's lieutenant in 84.

This identification is challenged by Wiseman 1976, 2. Wiseman (following Magie 1950, 1126 n. 43) suggests that Μυρέναν should be accepted as it appears in the stone without any emendation; furthermore, he considers it as an adoptive *cognomen*, hence a (Licinius) Murena adopted by a M. (Junius) Silanus. Consequently, the man mentioned in the inscription would be the quaestor M. (Junius) Silanus Murena. This proposal is accepted by Crawford 1982, 124, and subsequently by most scholars who have dealt with the Priene inscription. Keaveney 1984, 120–121, accepts the existence of a quaestor M. Junius Silanus Murena and further develops this argument. This Silanus could not be the quaestor of Murena, because Murena's quaestor was L. Lucullus; furthermore, a quaestorship in 84–81 would be too late if this man should be identified with the praetor of 77 (RE 170). If he was indeed the praetor in 77, as Keaveney presumes, his quaestorship should fall somewhere around 90 – 89. Taking into account that the ambassador from Priene went to see the quaestor and not the governor, it should be assumed that the latter was absent. Keaveney argues that this picture fits perfectly with the year 89, when the governor was away in Bithynia and Cappadocia. Accordingly, Keaveney proposes that this M. Junius Silanus Murena was quaestor under C. Cassius in 89 and then proconsul in Asia (Broughton MRR, 2.34 and 2.38). The dating of Cassius' governorship in Asia seems to be secure (Sumner 1978, 150: 'A fixed point for the chronology of the governors of Asia is the fact that C. Cassius was proconsul in 89 and 88'). Stumpf 1985, 190, identifies M. Junius Silanus, the consul in 109, as the only possible adoptive father of Silanus Murena and dates the latter's quaestorship to the beginning of the 90s. Also Mackay 2000, 192 n. 98, rejects the emendation of the inscription and consequently the idea that Silanus was Murena's quaestor; however, he does not go any further (cf. Brennan 2000, 558 – 559). There are some other examples of the simple adoption of the former cognomen in the name of the adoptee: Cn. Aufidius Orestes (cos. 71) or A. Terentius Varro Murena (RE 91), who was probably a son of L. Licinius Murena (pr. ca. 88), governor of Asia ca. 84 – 81, adopted by the legate (SIG³ 745) A. Terentius Varro (RE 82); see Shackleton Bailey 1976, 55 – 57 and 76 – 77.

However, Eilers 1996, rejects Wiseman's hypothesis and champions the suggestion made years ago by Wosnik 1963, 1 – 9. According to Wosnik, the name M. Silanus Murena resulted from the stonecutter's mistake. The inscription was supposed to read κ<αὶ Μ>ᾶρκον Σιλαν<ὸν καὶ Λεύκι>ον Μυρέναν ταμίαν. Therefore, they would be two different individuals, a M. Silanus and a Murena (whose *praenomen* is unknown). Eilers argues that this Murena should be identified with the praetor of 88 L. Licinius Murena (RE 122), and that he served in Asia both as quaestor and later as praetorian governor. This <L.> (Licinius) Murena would be praetor ca. 88, governor of Asia ca. 84 – 81 (see Brennan 2000, 556 – 557) and quaestor by 100. It is not possible to know under which commander he served. Eilers points out that he could also have been *quaestor pro praetore*, and could have governed the province in his own right.

As in other cases, we cannot reach a conclusive answer. It now seems clear that the first emendation of the inscription is unnecessary and that this Silanus was not Murena's quaestor. But perhaps the other correction proposed by Wosnik and accepted by Eilers is also unnecessary. The inscription from Priene makes good sense as it is: a M. Junius Silanus Murena seems to have been quaestor in Asia at some point. The chronology of his quaestorship is difficult to determine, but Keaveney's suggestion is both attractive and plausible.

M. Juventius Laterensis (q. by 63 – 62 in Cyrene and Crete) (pr. 51) (RE 16):

Cicero alludes to the presence of M. Juventius Laterensis as quaestor in Cyrene (Cic. *Planc.* 12 and 63) as well as in Crete (Cic. *Planc.* 85), as Schol. Bob. 167 St. seems to confirm this (*constabat enim Laterensem fuisse in Creta provincia*). The context seems to be the Catilinarian plot, which is why Laterensis' quaestorship has been dated around 63–62. Sobeck 1909, 43–44, as always very cautious, argues that he was quaestor in Cyrene and Crete (as a single province) at some point between 73 and 60, since Marcellinus was quaestor in 74 and Laterensis was a candidate to the tribunate of the plebs in 59. Broughton MRR, 2.175 and 2.577, dates his quaestorship to 62, but stressed that the date is uncertain. Perl 1970, 330–331; 1971, 370–373, sticks to a date around 63 and rejects the association of Laterensis with Praeneste or the games of Sulla, which Mattingly 1956, 198–199, proposes (see Broughton MRR, 3.116). Badian 1965, 120, suggests that Laterensis was a proquaestor in Cyrene, although it would be uncertain whether he was the governor or served under one. Badian seems to assume that Laterensis was under the command of a governor. Brennan 2000, 409, following Badian, states that Laterensis was proquaestor in 63.

There is actually no reason to think that Laterensis was proquaestor and not quaestor as Cicero asserts. His quaestorship in Cyrene under the command of a praetor seems to be supported by an inscription which reads [---]τίου Λατερα[νοῦ --] / [--στρα]τηγοῦ (provided that the word [στρα]τηγός does not refer to the quaestor). If this were the case, the text could be reconstructed as [ταμίου καὶ ἀντιστρα]τήγου (see Pugliese Carratelli, 1963, 338, no. 211, *ll.* 16–17). Laterensis was quaestor in Cyrene, probably by 63–62. See Díaz Fernández 2015, 242 and 490–491.

C. Laelius C. f. (q. 202) (cos. 190) (RE 2):

According to Livy, Laelius served as quaestor in 202 under Scipio Africanus. He was appointed by decision of the senate and not by lot: *Laelium, cuius ante legati, eo anno quaestoris extra sortem ex senatus consulto opera utebatur, cum Italico equitatu ab sinistro cornu, Masinissam Numidasque ab dextro opposuit* (Liv. 30.33.2). His service as a cavalry commander at the battle of Zama is well attested (Liv. 30.33–35; Pol. 15.9.8; 15.12.5; 15.14.7; App. *Lib.* 41 and 44; Frontin. *Str.* 2.3.16). See Bülz 1908, 7; Sobeck 1909, 9–10; Broughton MRR, 1.316.

D. Laelius D. f. Balbus (q. 44? (pro?)q. pro pr. 43–42? in Africa) (RE 6):

His quaestorship is attested by an inscription from Korbous (Tunisia) in which D. Laelius D. f. Balbus is honoured as *quaestor pro praetore* (CIL VIII 24016 = ILS 9367: *D(ecimus) Laelius D(ecimi) f(ilius) / Balbus q(uaestor) pro/pr(aetore) assa(m) destrictar(ium) / solariumque / faciundu(m) coerav(it)*); Zucca 1994, 1433–1434. He is the Λαίλιος, ἕτερος τοῦ Κορνιφικίου, who besieged the city of Cirta that was later defeated jointly with Q. Cornificius by T. Sextius in 42; see App. *b.c.* 4.53–56; Cass.Dio 48.21.1–6 (48.21.5: ὁ δὲ δὴ ταμίας ἐπ' ἐκεῖνον). Since Cornificius apparently held the province of Africa Vetus from 44 (see Cic. *fam.* 12.17–27), Laelius Balbus might have been sent to Africa as quaestor in 44, so he could have been *quaestor pro praetore* (as CIL VIII 24016 remarks) then and proquaestor in 43–42.

L. Licinius L. f. Crassus (q. 111 in Asia) (cos. 95) (RE 55):
See **Q. Mucius Scaevola.** Cicero asserts that Lucius Licinius Crassus was quaestor in Asia, but he does not give the date (Cic. *de orat.* 3.75: *Paulum sitiens istarum artium, de quibus loquor, gustavi, quaestor in Asia cum essem, aequalem fere meum ex Academia rhetorem nactus, Metrodorum illum, de cuius memoria commemoravit Antonius; et inde decedens Athenis, ubi ego diutius essem moratus, nisi Atheniensibus, quod mysteria non referrent, ad quae biduo serius veneram, suscensuissem.* Cf. *de orat.* 1.45: *audivi enim summos homines, cum quaestor ex Macedonia venissem Athenas...*; 2.365). Crassus was born in 140 (Cic. *Brut.* 161), and we know that he was tribune of the plebs in 107. Presumably he was quaestor before his tribunate. According to this information, Sobeck 1909, 20, dates Crassus' quaestorship between 112 and 109, which are the earliest and the latest possible dates. Broughton MRR, 1.546, sees 109 as the latest probable date, since he became tribune of the plebs in 107. However, in MRR, 3.118, Broughton argues (following Sumner) that Crassus could have held the quaestorship in 111 or 110. Sumner 1973, 96–97, suggests that Crassus may have succeeded M. Antonius as quaestor in Asia in 111, although he recognises that 110 is also possible. Sumner conjectures that Crassus may have served under a hypothetical command of the praetor M. Aurelius Scaurus (a close relationship between Crassus and Scaurus is evidenced by the coins that they minted in Narbo). Evans 1994, 184 and 210: quaestor in 111 or 110.

In principle both 111 and 110 are acceptable years for Crassus' quaestorship. That he served under Aurelius Scaurus is, however, merely speculative, because there is no indication of this in the sources. Furthermore, there is nothing to support Aurelius Scaurus' command in Asia. Nevertheless, the year 109 is very unlikely. According to Cicero (Cic. *de orat.* 3.75), Crassus spent some time in Athens on his return from Asia and had even wished to stay longer. It seems clear that Crassus had no need to hurry back to Rome, which certainly would have been the case if he had wanted to run for the tribunate of the plebs in the elections of 108. Wisse 2017, 122–127, convincingly argues for the year 111 on the basis of Cicero's texts. One of the philosophers whom Crassus says was active in Athens is Clitomachus the Academic: he was head of the school until he died in the archonship of Polyclitus, which can be dated to 110–109. Furthermore, Crassus arrived just too late for the Eleusinian Mysteries, which implies that his visit cannot be placed very late in the year, since this autumn festival took place around the end of September. Assuming that Crassus left Asia after his first year of service as quaestor, he could not have done so before this first year had actually ended. Consequently, his visit to Athens could not have taken place during his first year of office; it follows that Crassus' Athenian soujourn took place neither in autumn 111 nor in autumn 109 (Clitomachus was already dead by that point), but in autumn 110. Therefore, his quaestorship must be placed in 111.

M. Licinius M. f. Crassus (q. 54, proq. 53 in Gaul) (RE 56):
See **P. Licinius Crassus** (RE 63). Marcus Licinius Crassus served under Caesar in Gaul. Caesar always calls him quaestor: *Tres in Belgis collocavit: eis Marcum Crassum quaestorem et Lucium Munatium Plancum et Gaium Trebonium legatos praefecit* (Caes. Gall. 5.24.3); *...nuntium in Bellovacos ad M. Crassum quaestorem mittit* (5.46.1); *Caesar partitis copiis cum Gaio Fabio legato et Marco Crasso quaestor...* (6.6.1). Sobeck 1909, 58–59: M. Licinius Crassus was quaestor in 54 and 53; he remained in Gaul perhaps in 52, since Caesar does not mention any other quaestor (cf. Bülz 1893, 20–23). Broughton MRR, 2.223 and 2.230, also considers M. Crassus to have stayed in Gaul two years (in 54 as quaestor and in 53 as proquaestor). Syme 1980, 405: both brothers Marcus and Publius Licinius Crassus were in Rome in January 54 (Cic. *fam.* 5.8.2; 5.8.4). At some point during the year, Marcus went to Gaul, where Caesar mentions him as quaestor, also at the beginning of 53. Syme concludes that Marcus Licinius Crassus, the elder brother according to Syme, was probably quaestor in 54, although he may have been quaestor in 55 and proquaestor in 54–53 (see also Syme 1987, 324: quaestor or proquaestor in 54). Marshall 1976b, 10 and 202, does not discuss the question in depth, but dates M. Crassus' quaestorship to 54; Ward 1977, 55–56: quaestor in 54.

It is certain that M. Crassus was a proquaestor in 53. There is no evidence, however, that he stayed in Gaul in 52. It seems likely that he was quaestor rather than proquaestor in 54 and that he departed to meet Caesar at some point during the first months of the year. Nevertheless, the fact that Caesar always refers to him as quaestor should not bear too much weight, since the sources sometimes allude to a proquaestor as quaestor, ignoring the technicalities.

P. Licinius M. f. Crassus (q.?) (RE 63):
See **M. Licinius Crassus** (RE 56). The quaestorship of Publius Licinius Crassus is not attested. The hypothetical dates proposed for it depend on two considerations: (1) whether Publius was the elder or younger son of Marcus Licinius Crassus, the consul of 70 and 55; (2) whether he issued coins as quaestor or as moneyer, and when he did so. Publius Crassus had been generally considered the elder son of the 'triumvir', which would suggest that he could have held the quaestorship before his brother Marcus. However, Syme 1980, 406, has argued that Marcus was actually the elder son and doubted that Publius had quaestorian rank when he joined his father in Syria in 54–53. Syme suggests that Publius was born by 83–82. Broughton MRR, 2.217, dates Publius' quaestorship to 55, with a question mark (cf. 2.580: perhaps quaestor in 55. See MRR, 3.119). Sumner 1973, 149–150, also identifies Publius as the elder brother. According to Sumner, he was born by 86, a date compatible with his quaestorship in 55. Broughton and Sumner base his hypothesis on some coins minted by P. Crassus, perhaps while holding the quaestorship (see Mattingly 1956, 20–21, who makes Publius Crassus an urban quaestor and links the coins with the apparent *ludi Victoriae Sullanae* in Praeneste, which is pure speculation). Crawford RRC, 88 and 454 no. 430, who thinks Publius the younger son, dates these coins to 55, but concludes that he had

issued them as moneyer and not as quaestor (the legend on the reverse is *P · CRASSUS M·F·*, without any allusion to a quaestorship). Ward 1977, 56, proposes an earlier chronology for Publius' quaestorship and dates it to 58, when P. Crassus served in Gaul under Caesar.

The quaestorship of Publius Licinius Crassus is therefore the subject of speculation, since there is no firm evidence in the sources. The year 55 must be discarded, since he was then a moneyer and not a quaestor, following his return from Gaul. It must likewise be rejected that he was quaestor (and proquaestor) during his stay in Gaul under Caesar. Publius Crassus certainly stayed in Gaul under the command of Caesar in 58–56, but Caesar never mentions him as a quaestor, which contrasts with the references to his brother Marcus (Caes. *Gall.* 1.52.7; 2.34; 3.7–9). It seems probable that Syme is right: Marcus was older than his brother Publius. If this was the case and we bear in mind that it was usual to be a moneyer before holding the quaestorship, it appears plausible that P. Crassus was never quaestor, since he followed his father to Syria in 54 and died in the battle of Carrhae in 53 (Plut. *Crass.* 25–26).

P. Licinius P. f. Crassus Dives Mucianus (q. 151) (cos. 131) (RE 72):

The quaestorship of Publius Crassus Dives Mucianus is recorded by Valerius Maximus: *Q. Fabius Maximus... de tertio Punico bello indicendo quod secr<et>o in curia erat actum P. Crasso rus petens domum revertenti in itinere narravit, memor eum triennio ante quaestorem factum, ignarus nondum a censoribus in ordinem senatorium allectum...* (2.2.1). According to Valerius Maximus, Fabius committed an indiscretion when he told Crassus that the senate had decided to declare war on Carthage. Fabius Maximus thought that Crassus was a member of the senate because he had held the quaestorship some years ago, but actually the censors had not yet included him in the *album senatorium*. There were censors in 154–153 and in 147–146 (Broughton MRR, 1.449 and 1.463), which explains why Crassus was not yet a member of the senate. The so-called Third Punic War began in 149, and the vote in the senate took place at the beginning of that year. Valerius Maximus states precisely that Crassus then became quaestor (*quaestorem factum*), rather than that he had already been quaestor three years before the outbreak of war. This implies that he was elected quaestor in 152 for 151 (see the correct argument in Sumner 1973, 52). Sobeck 1909, 13, and Broughton MRR, 1.454, date his quaestorship to 152 (but see MRR, 3.120). Cf. Evans 1994, 183: 'his age as quaestor was between twenty-six and twenty-nine, provided the evidence of Valerius Maximus may be regarded as reliable.'

L. Licinius L. f. Lucullus (q. 87 in Greece, proq. 86–80 in Asia) (cos. 74) (RE 104):

Lucius Licinius Lucullus served under Sulla as quaestor and proquaestor in Greece and in Asia. The date of his quaestorship has, however, proven controversial. Initially, Badian 1959a, 81 n. 10, doubted whether Lucullus was quaestor in 88 or in 87. Nevertheless, when his article was included in the volume *Studies in Greek and Roman*

History in 1964, Badian asserted without any doubt (153 n. 10) that 'L. Lucullus was quaestor in 88,' and added that 'he was almost certainly the 'one quaestor' who followed Sulla in his march on Rome' according to App. *b.c.* 1.57. Badian had already developed this argument in 1962, 54–55: in his opinion, there can be little doubt that the quaestor whom Appian claims remained with Sulla during his march on Rome was Lucullus. Badian adds: 'oddly enough, modern works do not usually recognize this.' The year 88 for Lucullus' quaestorship had previously been defended by Sobeck 1909, 29, which was accepted by Broughton MRR, 3.121 (though he prefers the year 87 in MRR, 2.47), Sumner 1973, 113, and Evans 1994, 185 (he was quaestor in 88 aged thirty).

However, Thonemann 2004, convincingly argues for the year 87. On the one hand, the identification of Lucullus with the quaestor who, according to Appian, accompanied Sulla to Rome is far from evident. On the other hand, some honorific inscriptions for Lucullus from Asia and Greece are known: see, for instance, Hypata (IG 9.2.38: [τὸ κοι]νὸν τῶν Αἰνιάνω[ν] / [Λεύκι]ον Λικίνιον Λευκίου [υἱὸν] / Λεύκολλον ταμίαν εὐεργέ[ταν]), Synnada (*MAMA* 4.52: ὁ δῆμος/ Λεύκιον / Λικίννιον / Λευκίου / υἱὸν / Λεύκολλον / ἀντιταμίαν / πατρῶνα / καὶ / εὐεργέτην), Thyateira (*TAM* 5.2.918: [ὁ δῆ]μος [ἐτείμησεν] / Λεύκιον Λικίνιο[ν Λευκίου υἱὸν] / Λεύκολλον τὸν ἀντι[ταμίαν Ἀσίας] / σωτῆρα καὶ εὐεργέτην καὶ κτ[ίστην] / τοῦ δήμου ἀρετῆς ἕνεκεν κα[ὶ] / εὐνοίας τῆς εἰς ἑαυτόν), Ephesos (*I. Ephesos* 2941: [Λεύκιον] Λικίννιον Λεύ[κολλον] / [τὸν ἀ]ντιταμίαν, [πάτρωνα] / [κ]αὶ εὐεργέτ[ην]) and Rhodes (IG 12.1.48, ll. 7–8: ποτὶ Λεύκιον Λικίνιον Λευκίου υἱὸν Λεύκο[λλον] / ἀντιταμίαν). In all of the inscriptions from the Roman province of Asia, Lucullus is honoured as proquaestor (ἀντιταμίας), but in the Hypata inscription from central Greece he is called quaestor (ταμίας). It is agreed that in 87 Lucullus was in central Greece and went to Asia the following year, where he remained for the rest of the decade. Thonemann's argument is based on the principle that epigraphical terminology is usually very precise, whereas literary texts are often less so (so Cic. *Arch.* 11, mentions Lucullus as quaestor in Asia referring to 86, but Cicero should have written *pro quaestore* instead). As Lucullus is called quaestor (ταμίας) in the Hypata inscription, he must have held this office at that moment. Consequently, Thonemann concludes, Lucullus' quaestorship should be dated to 87.

After his quaestorship in 87, there is no doubt that Lucullus remained in Asia as proquaestor for the following years, as the aforementioned inscriptions show (cf. Cic. *acad.* 1.1: *in Asiam quaestor profectus ibi per multos annos admirabili quam laude provinciae praefuit*; see Ameling 1989). In 86 Lucullus sailed to Cyrene, Alexandria and some other ports to raise a fleet among the allies of Rome; see Plut. *Luc.* 2.2–4; App. *Mith.* 33; 51; *vir.ill.* 74.1–2 (*munus quaestorium*). Broughton MRR, 2.580 and 3.121, suggests that Lucullus acted as proquaestor until the year 80. For Sumner 1973, 113–114, he stayed in Asia at least until 82 (SIG 3.745), and probably until 80. According to Plutarch, *Luc.* 1.6–7, Lucullus delayed his aedileship in order to hold this office in the same year as his brother in 79. Cic. *acad.* 2.1, states that Lucullus was elected aedile when he was absent from Rome. Sumner claims that, although Lucullus could have been candidate in 81 for the aedileship of 80, he preferred to remain for one more year in Asia, being elected *in absentia* in 80 for 79. See also Keaveney 1984, 121.

L. Licinius L. f. Murena (q. 74) (cos. 62) (RE 123):

See **Ser. Sulpicius Rufus.** Lucius Licinius Murena was a legate under Lucullus in Asia after holding the quaestorship, presumably beginning in the year 73 at the latest (Broughton MRR, 2.113). According to Cicero, Murena and Ser. Sulpicius Rufus were colleagues in the quaestorship, with political careers closely parallel to that of Cicero himself (Cic. *Mur.* 18). Sobeck 1909, 38–39, dates Murena's quaestorship to 74, as does Broughton MRR, 2.103 and 2.109 n. 5. To justify this chronology, Broughton argues that neither Murena nor Sulpicius Rufus are mentioned as colleagues of Cicero in 75. Since Murena soon afterwards became legate under Lucullus, the year 74 would be the most probable option for his quaestorship.

The year 74 remains the most likely candidate (see the arguments in favour of this chronology in the entry on Ser. Sulpicius Rufus). Nonetheless, the year 75 cannot be discarded entirely. The outbreak of the Third Mithridatic War took place in all probability in 74 (Keaveney 1992, 204–205). Lucullus may have left Rome towards the middle of August 74 or somewhat later that year (Keaveney 1992, 188–189; Ooteghem 1959, 60–61: September. Cf. Pina Polo 2011, 236–237). If Murena departed Rome with him as a legate, he should have held the quaestorship in 75. Alternatively, he may have been quaestor in 74 and may have joined Lucullus in Asia later in 73. Unfortunately, there is no evidence as to when Murena joined Lucullus' army. Cf. Ryan 1996 f, 40 n. 20: the likeliest date for the quaestorship of Murena (and Ser. Sulpicius Rufus) is 74, but the legateship of Murena does not exclude a quaestorship in 73, since the first datable event with which Murena is connected as legate is the siege of Amisus, which could be placed in the spring of 72 or later.

T. Ligarius (q. urb. by 54) (RE 5):

The urban quaestorship of Titus Ligarius is attested in Cicero's speech in favour of his brother Quintus Ligarius (Cic. *Lig.* 35: *memoria teneo qualis T. Ligarius quaestor urbanus fuerit erga te et dignitatem tuam*). The date of his quaestorship is uncertain, although it should be dated to the time in which Cicero was close to Caesar in the 50s. Willems 1878, 1.526, tentatively proposes the year 56. This date is followed by Sobeck 1909, 63–64, who nonetheless heads the entry of this quaestor with a cautious 'before 49.' Broughton MRR, 2.223, suggests the year 54, which is the date that has generally won acceptance (see Syme 1964a, 118; Wiseman 1971, 237 no. 227; Gruen 1974, 521). More recently, Ryan 1999, 244, has suggested that Ligarius was urban quaestor by 50. This date, however, is unlikely. Cicero says that he personally remembers (*memoria teneo*) what kind of urban quaestor Ligarius was. However, Cicero was away from Rome for most of year 50, since he stayed in Cilicia until July. For the same reason the year 51 must be excluded.

No date currently finds solid support in the sources, so that any proposal remains speculative. Ligarius may have been urban quaestor around 54, as has usually been accepted. But he could also have held the quaestorship somewhat earlier or later in the 50s.

M. Livius M. f. Drusus (q. 97 in Asia?) (tr. pl. 91) (RE 18):
Neither the quaestorship nor the aedileship of Marcus Livius Drusus are mentioned in his *elogium*, an inscription which may not be complete (Inscr. Ital. 13.3.74 = CIL 1².1 p.199 = ILS 49). Because of this, the very fact of him having held the quaestorship has been called into question (Mommsen Röm.St., I 542 n. 3 and 544 n. 2. Cf. Bültz 1908, 13–14; Sobeck 1909, 83, who includes Drusus among those whose quaestorship is uncertain). However, a passage from *De viris illustribus* speaks of Drusus as quaestor in Asia: *quaestor in Asia nullis insignibus uti voluit, ne quid ipso esset insignius* (*vir.ill.* 66.3). Obviously, Drusus' quaestorship (as well as his aedileship) must be dated before his tribunate of the plebs in 91, when he died. The date is controversial, since there is no secure evidence. At any rate, it probably preceded his aedileship (in *De viris illustribus* his aedileship is mentioned before his quaestorship, but this information is not at all decisive, because the author does not always follow a determined order when he cites a series of offices).

Broughton MRR, 1.569 and 1.570 n. 4, dates the quaestorship by 102, and the aedileship tentatively to 94. Broughton argues that the quaestorship should precede or coincide with the censorship of 102, on the grounds that Cicero includes Drusus in the list of senators who fought Saturninus (Cic. *Rab. perd.* 21: *cum omnes praetores, cuncta nobilitas ac iuventus accurreret... M. Drusus*). Nevertheless, as Broughton himself later recognised (MRR, 3.126), this is a mistaken interpretation of the Ciceronian text. Cicero does not include Drusus among the senators but with the *iuventus* who confronted Saturninus in 100 (see Sumner 1973, 110–111; Marshall 1987). As a consequence, if Drusus was not a senator in 100, he could not have been quaestor by 102 or earlier, as Broughton originally supposed. Therefore, a later date is not only possible but preferable, even more so if Drusus was born not before 124, which Sumner 1973, 110–111, points out (Drusus was a *pupillus* when his father died in 109: Sen. *brev.vit.* 6.1).

There is supplementary evidence that seems indirectly to corroborate that Drusus held a quaestorship and that this was in Asia. Pliny asserts that Drusus visited the city of Anticyra in Boeotia in order to obtain there a medication when he was presumably travelling to Asia: *Drusumque apud nos, tribunorum popularium clarissimum... constat hoc medicamento liberatum comitiali morbo in Anticyra insula* (Plin. *n.h.* 25.52). Pliny refers to white hellebore (*veratrum album*), a herb from which a drug was prepared. If Drusus was actually quaestor in Asia, it seems plausible (although certainly hypothetical) that he served there under Scaevola and his uncle Rutilius Rufus (cf. Sumner 1973, 110–111; Marshall 1987, 318). The date of Scaevola's governorship in Asia has also proven controversial, but the year 97 appears to be the most likely, following Scaevola's praetorship and not his consulship (see Balsdon 1937; Marshall 1976a; Pina Polo 2011, 244). Badian 1956, however, is against this date and defends that Scaevola went to Asia in 95–94 after his consulship. But if Drusus had been quaestor in Asia in 94, we would have to eliminate his aedileship, since there would be no place for it between his quaestorship and his tribunate of 91.

To summarise, if these arguments are correct, Livius Drusus may have been quaestor in Asia in 97 preceding his aedileship by 94, as Broughton suggests, and his tribunate in 91.

L. Livius L. f. Ocella (q. in Hispania Citerior in the 40s?) (RE 26):

L. Livius Ocella was a quaestor according to two lost inscriptions (CIL VI 14446a/b) from the via di Largo Argentina in Rome. Since the inscriptions were dedicated by the 'Segobrigenses' and 'Sussetanei' (sic), he was possibly quaestor in Hispania Citerior in the 40s. See *B. Afr.* 89.5; Broughton MRR, 2.476; Díaz Ariño 2011, 175–176. Cf. CIL X 6319.

M. Lollius (q. 64) (RE 9):

According to Plutarch (*Cat.min.* 16.9: καὶ Λόλλιος Μᾶρκος εἷς συνάρχων τοῦ Κάτωνος), Marcus Lollius was one of Cato's colleagues when he was quaestor. Consequently, the year of his quaestorship depends on the date of Cato's office, probably in 64. See Sobeck 1909, 50, who dates Cato's and Lollius' quaestorship to 65; Broughton MRR, 2.162: year 64.

L. Lucretius (q. 218) (RE 4):

See **C. Fulvius.** Two quaestors, L. Lucretius and C. Fulvius, were apprehended by the Boii, presumably in 218, and handed over to Hannibal in order to demonstrate the support of the Boii for the Carthaginians: *Venienti in Ligures Hannibali per insidias intercepti duo quaestores Romani, C. Fulvius et L. Lucretius... quo magis ratam fore cum iis pacem societatemque crederet, traduntur* (Liv. 21.59.10). It is not known whether Lucretius recovered his freedom. In any case, there is no evidence for him holding any subsequent offices. See Bülz 1908, 4; Sobeck 1909, 6; Broughton MRR, 1.239.

Q. Lutatius Cerco (q. 109 or 108?) (RE 14):

The quaestorship of Quintus Lutatius Cerco is known thanks to the coins minted with the legend Q · LVTATI CERCO Q. On the reverse the victory of C. Lutatius Catulus at the Aegates Insulae in 241 is commemorated. The issue is dated to 109 or 108 by Crawford RRC, 315 no. 305. This date has been accepted by Broughton MRR, 3.131 (see also Evans 1994, 210). Other years have also been suggested: Sobeck 1909, 24: by 104; Broughton MRR, 2.27: quaestor in 90 according to Grueber (Sydenham proposed 106). Ryan 1996 g, 85, proposes 106 as the earliest possible date for Lutatius Cerco's quaestorship. Nothing else is known about this man and his political career.

T. Maenius T. f. (q. 75 or 74) (RE 16):
Titus Maenius (Τίτος Μαινίος Τίτου υἱὸς Λεμωνία) is one of the senators mentioned in the *SC de Oropiis* of year 73 (SIG³ 747 = RDGE 23). Maenius is one of the *quaestorii* included in the *consilium*. He must therefore have held the quaestorship before 73 and after 75, when Cicero, the first of the senators of quaestorian rank, was quaestor (Broughton MRR, 2.115; cf. 3.222). Bearing in mind that the senators are recorded according to rank and that he is one of the last mentioned in the list, the year 74 seems more likely.

T. Mallius (or T. Manlius) (see T. Maloleius).
T. Maloleius? (or Mallius? or Manlius?) (q. urb. 111–110? or 99?) (not in RE):
See **Ap. Claudius Pulcher.** The interpretation of some coins with the legend *T · MAL ·* (or *T · MANL ·*) *AP · CL · Q ·VR* has been quite controversial, ever since Mommsen assumed that *Q · VR ·* was an abbreviation for *Q(uaestores) VR(bani)*. The previous two abbreviations would belong to the urban quaestors who had coined the issue. This interpretation was apparently reinforced by the fact that the order of the names is not always the same, appearing first sometimes *AP · CL ·* and on other occasions *T· MAL ·*, but *Q · VR* is always at the end of the legend. One of the supposed quaestors was Ap. Claudius Pulcher, while the name of the other is uncertain. T. Maloleius has been suggested, following the proposal of Cichorius (Suolahti 1955, 127; Badian 1963, 138), along with T. Mallius (Broughton MRR, 2.2) and T. Manlius (Crawford RRC, 312–313 no. 299). While Mommsen's theory has generally been accepted, Crawford RRC, 312–313 no. 299, argues that *Q · VR* should be read as a name, namely Quintus Urbinius (otherwise unknown), perhaps the father of C. Urbinius, quaestor in 74. According to Crawford, only one urban quaestor seems to have been in charge of the *aerarium* at any one time, at any rate down to the time of Sulla. Therefore, it should be explained why, exceptionally, the two urban quaestors issued these coins together and their names appeared on them. Crawford concludes that the issue was struck by three moneyers, whose names were recorded in the legend (Sumner 1973, 63, however, states that there is no reason 'to invent a monetalis Q. Urbinius here'). While Crawford is certainly right to assert that a historical explanation for the unusual joint coinage of the two urban quaestors is needed, Mommsen's explanation remains the easiest and most logical interpretation. As for the chronology, Broughton MRR, 2.2, dates the coins, and consequently the two urban quaestorships, to 99, whereas Crawford prefers 111 or 110. The subsequent career of this T. Maloleius (if this was his name) is utterly unknown, so that both chronologies are equally possible. But in the case of Ap. Claudius Pulcher, it is striking that there would be a such long interval between his office in 111 or 110 and his praetorship in 89 or consulship in 79.

Fig. 8: T. Maloleius or Mallius? and Ap. Claudius Pulcher, urban quaestors 111–110? AR Denarius. Rome. Helmeted head of Roma right. Victory in quadriga right, above, AP. CL. T. MAL. Q. VR in exergue. Crawford RRC, no. 299/1a.

L. Manlius (Acidinus?) (q. urb. 168) (RE 26):

See **L. Stertinius.** According to Livy, the urban quaestor L. Manlius was sent by the senate with a sum of money to meet the son of King Masinissa, Masgaba, who had landed at Puteoli. Manlius had to escort him to Rome (Liv. 45.13.12: *Et Masgabae, regis Masinissae filio, Puteolis nave egresso praesto fuit obviam missus cum pecunia L. Manlius quaestor, qui Romam eum publico sumptu perduceret*). This took place in 168. See Sobeck 1909, 12; Broughton MRR, 1.428.

A. Manlius A. f. [Torquatus] (q. urb. 80) (RE 13, cf. 70 and 76):

Some aurei coined at the mint of Rome bear the legend $A \cdot MANLI\ A \cdot F \cdot Q$ on their obverse, while on the reverse we find an equestrian statue of Sulla together with the inscription *Felix Dictator*. Since Sulla did not take the title *Felix* until the very end of 82, the coins and therefore Manlius' quaestorship should be dated to 81 at the earliest (Sobeck 1909, 34–35). Broughton MRR, 2.77, dates it to 81 and identifies the quaestor as A. Manlius A.f. Torquatus. For Mitchell 1966, 31, who also defends the year 81, this Manlius is the same as the A. Manlius Torquatus who was praetor in 70 (RE 70) and governor of Africa before 68 (RE 76). However, Crawford RRC, 397 no. 381, prefers 80 and argues that the quaestor was not a Torquatus, but rather the eldest son of the A. Manlius who was legate in 107–105 (RE 12. Broughton MRR, 1.552 and 2.585). On this point, Crawford follows the thesis found in Mattingly 1972b, 13. See also Broughton MRR, 3.135.

Since Manlius must have issued the coins as urban quaestor and we know that the *quaestores urbani* in 81 were Lentulus (Sura) and (Valerius) Triarius, Crawford's suggestion of 80 seems like the most likely date for Manlius' quaestorship.

L. Manlius Torquatus (q. 113 or 112?) (RE 78):

Very different chronologies have been proposed for the quaestorship of Lucius Manlius Torquatus, none of which are certain. His quaestorship is known through some coins that he issued following a decree of the senate while quaestor. They bear the legend *L · TORQVA Q EX S · C*. Sobeck 1909, 24, dates his quaestorship by 104, although he admits that it is impossible to determine a year with certainty. Broughton MRR, 2.13, tentatively suggests 94, without any special reasoning. Mitchell 1966, 31, has analysed the quaestor's relations and offers a stemma of the family. He dates his quaestorship to 96, as does Münzer in his article in RE. Crawford RRC, 308 no. 295, always on the basis of the coins, suggests 113 or 112 (he was followed without any additional arguments by Evans 1994, 209; see Broughton MRR, 3.136).

It is only certain that L. Manlius Torquatus was quaestor at the end of the second or at the beginning of the first century: any specific date (113 or 112, around 104, 96 or 94) is speculative. Nothing else is known about his life or whether he held other offices.

L. Manlius L. f. Torquatus (q. and proq. 84–82? in East and Italy) (cos. 65) (RE 79):

There are silver and gold coins with the legends *L · MANLI PRO · Q* on the obverse and *L · SVLLA IMPE* or *IMP* on the reverse. The moneyer has been identified as Lucius Manlius Torquatus, who was later consul in 65. Crawford RRC, 386–387 no. 367, dates the issue to 82 (Sobeck 1909, 33, also dates Manlius' proquaestorship to 82, along with Sumner 1973, 129, while Mitchell 1966, 31, opts for 81). According to the legend on the coins, Manlius Torquatus was therefore proquaestor under Sulla in 82, but he must have been proquaestor for a longer period. Broughton MRR, 2.61, 2.64 and 2.70, proposes that he was Sulla's proquaestor between 84 and 82 in the East and in Italy (but MRR, 2.586: proquaestor 84–81). Keaveney 1984, 119–121, accepts Crawford's chronology for the coins, but argues that L. Manlius Torquatus was originally L. Licinius Murena's quaestor. In his opinion, when Asia was again in Roman hands, Sulla and Murena seem to have swapped quaestors: Torquatus issued Sulla's coins in 82 and Lucullus governed Asia as Murena's proquaestor while the latter was away fighting Mithridates. Keaveney's suggestion is followed by Mackay 2000, 192 n. 98.

To sum up, it is certain that L. Manlius Torquatus served under Sulla as proquaestor as the coins minted by him show, probably in 82. It remains uncertain whether he was Sulla's or Murena's proquaestor in the previous years. Likewise, the year of his quaestorship is unknown.

T. Manlius Torquatus (q. and/or proq. in the 80s or at the beginning of the 70s?) (RE 85):

The political career of this T. Manlius Torquatus is unknown (Broughton MRR, 2.493, includes him among the senators without any known office). Nevertheless, Cicero makes it clear that he could have reached the consulship if he had lived long enough, which suggests that he probably held the praetorship (Cic. *Brut*. 245. Mitchell 1966, 31, dates his praetorship to 69). There is no certain evidence of his quaestorship. Sumner 1973, 130, identifies him with the T. Manlius T.f. who was honoured in an inscription from Delos between 84 and 78 (I. Délos 1660, l. 6: [T]ίτον Μάνλιον Τίτου υἱὸν). This inscription is nearly identical to one that honours the proquaestor Manius Lepidus, the consul of 66 (I. Délos 1659). According to Sumner, the gap after the name Torquatus should be completed with the word ἀντιταμίας (proquaestor) as in Lepidus's inscription. Note that the gap seems to show the letters [---]αιων, perhaps the end of the title [ἀντιταμίας 'Ρωμ]αίων, though other options are also possible. Sumner concludes that this Manlius Torquatus may have been proquaestor under Sulla from 84 to 81, or quaestor by 79 (see Broughton MRR, 3.136–137). Mitchell 1966, 31, dates his quaestorship to 80 without any further arguments.

The chronology of T. Manlius Torquatus' quaestorship or proquaestorship is utterly speculative. There is no evidence to date it to the 80s or the beginning of the 70s.

Marcius Rufus (q. 49 in Africa) (RE 94):

According to Caesar, Marcius Rufus was quaestor of C. Scribonius Curio in Africa in 49: *Hunc secutus Marcius Rufus quaestor navibus duodecim, quas praesidio onerariis navibus Curio ex Sicilia eduxerat...* (Caes. *civ*. 2.23.5. Cf. 2.24.1; 2.43.1). He conducted the troops to Sicily after the defeat and death of Curio. See Bülz 1893, 74–75; Sobeck 1909, 64; Broughton MRR, 2.259.

C. Marius C. f. (q. 123–121?) (cos. 107, 104–100, 86) (RE 14, suppl. 6):

The first question is whether Marius really was quaestor or whether he was tribune of the plebs without ever holding the quaestorship. Marius' elogium makes it clear that he held the quaestorship: *C. Marius C.f. cos. VII pr. tr. pl. q. aug. tr. militum...* (CIL I^2 195 = Inscr. Ital. 13.3.83. The *elogium* is also preserved in a copy found near Arpinum: CIL X 5782. However, Evans 1994, 187, is sceptical about the information contained in the *elogium*: 'this source of information should not be regarded as an infallible guide to all his offices'). Valerius Maximus (6.9.14) asserts that Marius ran for the quaestorship in Rome after being defeated in elections in Arpinum: *Iam C. Marius... Arpinatibus honoribus iudicatus inferior quaesturam Romae petere ausus est*. However, Plutarch (*Mar*. 4.1) states that Marius' first office was the tribunate of the plebs (this is the viewpoint of Evans 1994, 32–35 and 186–187: 'Marius, already in his mid-thirties and with much military experience, may have chosen to avoid the quaestorship and campaign instead...for a tribunate'). Diodorus (35.38.1), vaguely alludes to Marius' difficulties in being elected for the lower offices at the beginning of his career, but he does not specify to which offices he is referring (cf. also *vir.ill.* 67.1; see Sage 1979, 204).

Despite the contradictory sources, it seems likely that Marius actually held the quaestorship after serving as military tribune and before becoming tribune of the plebs in 119. Sobeck 1909, 17, very cautiously dates his quaestorship between 132 and 121. Broughton MRR, 1.521, tentatively places it in 121. Marius's quaestorship should be dated at some point between 123 and 121, 121 being the latest possible year. Carney 1961, 17–18, suggests a proquaestorship (which is not attested) in 121, in which case, Marius would have served under Q. Fabius Maximus in Transalpine Gaul. Cf. Wiseman 1971, 240 no. 248; Broughton MRR, 3.139–140.

(L.) Marius (q. 50 in Syria) (RE 4):
See **Caninius Sallusti(an)us.** There is no doubt that a Marius was the succesor of the proquaestor Caninius Sallusti(an)us in Syria. He was therefore quaestor in 50 (Cic. *fam.* 2.17.5: *Marium quidem successorem tarde video esse venturum, propterea quod senatus ita decrevit ut cum legionibus iret*). However, Cicero does not mention his *praenomen*, which could be Lucius if this Marius should be identified with Scaurus' accuser in 54 of name L. Marius (Ascon. 19 C. RE 20). See Bülz 1893, 69–70; Sobeck 1909, 63; Broughton MRR, 2.250 and 3.139.

M. Marius (q. 78? proq. 77–76 in Hispania) (RE 23):
See **L. Hirtuleius.** This Marcus Marius is mentioned as quaestor of Sertorius in Hispania: *Postero die M. Marium quaestorem in Arvacos et Cerindones misit* (Liv. 91 fr. 21). Plutarch (*Sert.* 24.3) alludes to him as one of the senators who had taken refuge with Sertorius in Hispania. He was sent to the East in 75 as military adviser to Mithridates, who gave him a command in the Third Mithridatic War (cf. Plut. *Luc.* 8.5). Otherwise unknown, Marius' office has been the subject of controversy in the unusual context of the Sertorian War in Hispania. Without providing any further argumentation, Berve 1929, 209 and n. 3, accepts Livy's assertion about Marius' quaestorship. Broughton MRR, 2.93 and 3.140, dates his quaestorship to 76 and adds that Marius had probably come to Hispania with Perperna. Spann 1987, 172, accepts this hypothesis. However, Konrad 1994, 99 and 200–201, argues that Marius must have been quaestor and senator not later than 82. Although Orosius does not explicitly call him one of the proscribed, the context of his death suggests, in Konrad's opinion, that he was (Oros. 6.2.21–22; cf. Hinard 1985a, 404–406: Hinard prefers the name Varius, given by App. *Mith.* 76 and considers him to have been included in the Sullan proscriptions in 82). According to Konrad, Marius may have been a member of Sertorius' original staff and, consequently, he may have come with him in 82 as quaestor, if Sertorius had two quaestors at that point.

Sertorius always considered himself the legal governor in Hispania because he never recognised the Sullan regime (actually he kept the title proconsul, use of which became part of Sertorian propaganda; see Beltrán Lloris 1990). Nevertheless, it seems unlikely that Sertorius himself appointed Marius as quaestor at some point during the war in Hispania. Sertorius gave importance to the appearance of his actions' legality, and it is clear that he was not legally authorised to appoint a quaestor who had not been elected by the people (Schulten 1926, 82, wrongly claims that Sertorius had the ability to designate quaestors). Therefore, it appears more probable that either Marcus Marius came to Hispania as Sertorius' quaestor in 82 and remained with him in the following years, as Konrad suggests, or he was quaestor of M. Aemilius Lepidus in 78 and later joined Sertorius' troops along with Perperna in 77. Konrad's hypothesis rests on the assumption that Sertorius could be the governor of both provinces, Hispania Citerior and Hispania Ulterior, and that consequently he needed two different quaestors, but there is no evidence for that. At any rate, Marcus must have been a proquaestor when he is first attested in 76 while serving under Sertorius in Hispania Citerior (it is not unusual that sources call someone who is technically a proquaestor simply quaestor).

C. Memmius (q. 77? proq. 76–75? in Hispania) (RE 7):

See **C. Cornelius.** The sources connect Memmius' quaestorship to Pompey's activity in Hispania during the Sertorian war: *ut Pompeius in Hispaniam venerit Memmiumque habere quaestorem coeperit...* (Cic. *Balb.* 5); *Memmius, quaestor Pompei idemque vir sororis eius, occisus est* (Oros. 5.23.12). Cf. Plut. *Sert.* 21.2. Sobeck 1909, 36–37, mistakenly identifies him with the praetor of the same name for the year 58 (RE 8). Additionally, Sobeck claims that the Memmius in Orosius was different from the one whom Cicero mentions. His thesis is accepted by Biedl 1930, 105, but rightly rejected by Münzer in RE. According to Cicero (*Balb.* 5), C. Memmius served under Metellus at the beginning of the Sertorian war, probably as military tribune, although the sources give him no title (cf. Bülz 1893, 5–6; Broughton MRR, 2.84 and 2.91). The sources show him later as quaestor under the command of his brother-in-law Pompey, fighting against the Sertorian forces until he was killed in 75 (see Konrad 1994, 175). Broughton MRR, 2.93, 2.96 n. 3, 2.98 and 3.141, dates his quaestorship to 76 (or 77), remaining in Hispania in 75 as proquaestor. The chronology of the Sertorian War is confusing, but Pompey may have arrived in Hispania in the second half of the year 77, probably in the autumn (Konrad 1995, 184–186).

Putting together all this evidence, we can try to reconstruct C. Memmius' career in the following way: he was in southern Hispania under the command of Metellus in 79 and maybe (part of) 78. Upon his return to Rome, he was elected as quaestor for 77. When his brother-in-law Pompey received the command against Sertorius, Memmius was the obvious choice to accompany him as his right-hand man, given his previous experience in Hispania. Memmius went to Hispania as quaestor in 77, and remained there as proquaestor in 76 and 75. Alternatively, but less likely, he could have been elected quaestor for 76 and have joined Pompey at some point that year. In either case, he was proquaestor in 75. After his death he was replaced by the quaestor C. Cornelius.

C. Memmius L. f. (q. by 67 or later?) (pr. 58) (RE 8):

There is no evidence at all for Memmius' quaestorship (he is neither included in Sobeck's list nor recorded by Broughton as quaestor). We know that he was tribune of the plebs in 66, according to Broughton (MRR, 2.153), and praetor in 58 (MRR, 2.194). Broughton's reconstruction has been partially refuted by Ryan 1995c, 296 n. 11: if Memmius was praetor *suo anno* in 58, he could not have been tribune in 66 (Ryan proposes 62 instead) and quaestor before 67. There is no doubt that Memmius held the quaestorship just like the rest of his contemporaries, because the office was compulsory. That said, its date is completely speculative, especially taking into account that we do not know when Memmius was born and whether he really was praetor *suo anno*.

L. Memmius (q. before 112?) (RE 13):

Lucius Memmius was a moneyer in 109 or 108 (Broughton MRR, 2.446 and 2.590: 109; Crawford RRC, 315 no. 304: 109 or 108). Crawford suggests identifying him as the brother of C. Memmius (tribune of the plebs in 111) and as the senator who visited Egypt in 112 (RE 12); see P. Teb. 1.33; Broughton MRR, 1.112 n. 5. If this identification is correct, L. Memmius must have held the quaestorship before being moneyer, at any rate before 112, as a means of gaining access to the senate.

L. Memmius C. f. (q. in the 40s first century?) (RE 15):

The quaestorship of Lucius Memmius is known only through an inscription in which his political career is recorded: *L. Memmius C. f. Gal. q. tr. p(l). frumenti curator ex s. c. praefectus leg. XXVI et VII Lucae ad agros dividundos pontifex Albanus...* (CIL VI 1460 = CIL XIV 2264 = ILS 887). His regular career included the quaestorship and the tribunate of the plebs. Additionally, he was put in charge of the grain supply by senatorial decree, supervised the distribution of land in Luca to veterans of the legions VII and XXVI, and was also *pontifex Albanus* (Rüpke 2008, 1148). The date of his quaestorship depends on whether he held this office before or after being a legionary prefect (cf. Broughton MRR, 2.476: quaestor either before 43 or between 40 and 34). If his political offices are listed in chronological order beginning with the quaestorship, it should be expected that he was quaestor before he was legionary prefect. Since the distribution of land in Luca followed the battle of Philippi in 42 (Keppie 1984, 106–107; Moatti 1993, 17 n. 57: the prefect L. Memmius settled two legions in 42 in Beneventum [an obvious mistake for Luca]), L. Memmius may have been quaestor before 43.

L. Mescinius Rufus (q. 51, proq. 50 in Cilicia) (RE 2):

L. Mescinius Rufus was Cicero's quaestor in Cilicia: *L. Mescinius ea mecum necessitudine coniunctus est, quod mihi quaestor fuit* (Cic. fam. 13.26.1). He sailed for the province along with Cicero in 51 and remained in Cilicia as proquaestor in 50, even after Cicero left in July of that year. See among other references Bülz 1893, 58–59; Sobeck 1909, 61; Broughton MRR, 2.242; Taylor 1941, 123–124; Wiseman 1971, 240 no. 251; Cotton 1979, 39–50, 39 n. 1.

M. Minatius Sabinus (q. by 49? proq. 48–45? or proq. 46–45) (RE 3):
Some coins minted in Hispania present the legend *CN · MAGN IMP* and *M · MINAT SABIN PR(O) · Q*. They have unanimously been dated to 46 and/or 45. For Buttrey Jr. 1960, 75 and n. 2, the year 46 is more likely, since the reverse types suggest the opening of Cnaeus Pompeius' campaign in Hispania and celebrate his initial victories, before Caesar reached the south of Hispania. Crawford RRC, 480, no. 470, dates the *denarii* to 46–45. Therefore, according to the legend on the coins there is no doubt that Marcus Minatius Sabinus served as proquaestor under the elder son of Pompey, also named Cn. Pompeius Magnus (see Bülz 1893, 12–13; Sobeck 1909, 68–69: Minatius may have been proquaestor in 46 and 45; Broughton MRR, 2.298, 2.309 and 3.142; Wiseman 1971, 241 no. 256). Given the development of the war in Hispania, it seems likely that Minatius was proquaestor both in 46 and at the beginning of 45, until the battle of Munda in March. A different question is whether, and when, he held the quaestorship. Cassius Dio (41.43.1–3) states that the Pompeians did not organise elections for 48 in Thessalonica, which means that all their leaders were promagistrates. As a consequence, Minatius should have held the quaestorship at the latest in 49 (see Willems 1878, 1.577–578: '[Minatius] n'a pu gérer la questure postérieurement à 49'; Ryan 1996e). He may have been quaestor in 49 and proquaestor since then, but only his proquaestorship in Hispania in 46–45 is attested.

Fig. 9: Cn. Pompeius and M. Minatius Sabinus, proquaestor ca. 46–45? AR Denarius. Hispania. Head of Pompeius Magnus right; CN. MAGN. IMP. Personification of a city (Corduba?) standing right, holding spear and grasping the hand of a soldier disembarking from a ship; M. MINAT. SABIN in exergue. PR. Q on left. Crawford RRC, no. 470/1a.

L. Minucius Basilus (q. 55 or 54?) (pr. 45) (RE 38):

There is no evidence of Lucius Minucius Basilus' quaestorship in the sources (Sobeck does even not include him in his list of quaestors). He is attested as praetor in 45 (Cass.Dio 43.45.5). Earlier we find him in Gaul fighting under the command of Caesar in 53 and in the following years, probably as a legate (Caes. *B. Gall.* 6.29–30. Broughton MRR, 2.592: legate in 53–48). Sumner 1971, 359, suggests that he may have been quaestor before going to Gaul in 55 or 54, or in 50 after his presumed return to Rome (cf. Broughton MRR, 3.143). That Minucius Basilus held the quaestorship in 55 or 54 is possible but hypothetical.

Q. Minucius M. f. Thermus (q. 89?) (RE 66):

The moneyer who issued coins in 103 with the legend *Q · THERM · M F* (Crawford, RRC, 324–325 no. 319) is presumably the same person as the Q. Minucius M. f. Ter. who appears as a member of Pompeius Strabo's *consilium* in the Bronze of Ascoli (ILS 8888). Cichorius 1922, 142–144, argues that he could have been quaestor during the siege of Asculum in 89 under the command of Pompeius Strabo, given that the members of the council would be mentioned in hierarchical order and Minucius appears in the sixth place. Other scholars have cautiously followed Cichorius' hypothesis: Broughton MRR, 2.34 and 3.144–145; Suohlati 1955, 338; Criniti 1970, 101–102; Evans 1994, 215, Ryan 1995d, 308.

Q. Minucius Q. f. Thermus (q. 75 or 74) (pr. by 58) (RE 67):

Quintus Minucius Thermus (Κόϊντος Μυνύκιος Κοΐντου υἱὸς Τηρηντίνα) is one of the senators mentioned in the *SC de Oropiis* of 73 (SIG³ 747 = RDGE 23). It is generally assumed that the names appear in hierarchical order. Minucius Thermus is a senator of quaestorian rank and is named after Cicero, quaestor in 75, Axius, Pompeius Rufus and Cascellius. Like the other quaestorians in the document, he therefore held the quaestorship before 73, presumably either in 75 or 74. See Broughton MMR 2.115 and 2.592.

This Q. Minucius Thermus of the Greek inscription has long been identified with the tribune of the plebs of 62. However, Ryan 1995d, 306–308, proposes to identify him with the Thermus who ran for the consulship in 65 (Cic. *Att.* 1.1.2). Shackleton Bailey 1976, 78, argues that this Thermus was actually C. Marcius Figulus, one of the consuls in 64. After his adoption, he may have called himself C. Marcius Figulus Thermus. According to Ryan, this man could have begun his political career as Q. Minucius Thermus (as he appears in the *SC de Oropiis*) and later on changed his name to C. Marcius Figulus Thermus, keeping his original *cognomen*. Following his argument, Ryan (308) suggests that the Q. Minucius Thermus who was tribune in 62 could have been the son of the Thermus mentioned in the *SC de Oropiis*. He would have been praetor in 49 and quaestor in 64, a date which is utterly speculative.

Q. Mucius P. f. Scaevola (q. 111) (cos. 95) (RE 22):
See **L. Licinius Crassus.** Cicero makes clear that Q. Mucius Scaevola and L. Licinius Crassus were colleagues in all offices except the tribunate of the plebs and the censorship, which Scaevola did not hold (Cic. *Brut.* 161: *Omnibus quidem aliis, inquam, in magistratibus, sed tribunus anno post fuit eoque in rostris sedente suasit Serviliam legem Crassus; nam censuram sine Scaevola gessit...*). Although there is no other evidence for Scaevola's quaestorship, his office should be dated without doubt to the same year as Crassus. Broughton MRR, 1.546, places Scaevola's quaestorship in 109 together with Crassus (see however MRR, 3.118, where Broughton prefers 111–110 following Sumner 1973, 96–97). However, Wisse 2017, 122–127 and 148, has convincingly argued for the year 111 on the basis of Cic. *de orat.* 1.45; 2.365; 3.75.

Cn. Nerius (q. urb. 49) (RE 3):
Nerius appears as urban quaestor in coins issued with the legend *NERI · Q · VRB* on the obverse. On the reverse, a legionary eagle and the names of the consuls of the year. On the obverse the head of Saturn. The consular dating of the issue leaves no doubt as to the date of Nerius' urban quaestorship in 49 (Sobeck 1909, 64–65; Broughton MRR, 2.259; Crawford RRC, 460 no. 441: 'the head of Saturn alludes to the fact that Cn. Nerius was quaestor urbanus'; Wiseman 1971, 244 no. 270; Gruen 1974, 207). His *praenomen* Cnaeus comes from the identification with the Cn. Nerius Pup., who is mentioned by Cicero in a letter to his brother (Cic. *Q. fr.* 2.3.5). The use of a consular date in coins is exceptional. It certainly provides a political message in the context of the beginning of the Civil War. It was considered necessary to make clear that the coins were minted by order of the legitimate consuls of 49, who were then out of Rome. According to Woytek 2003, 97–100, the issue was coined in Illyria, perhaps in Apollonia, once the Pompeians had left Rome.

M. Nonius Sex. f. Sufenas (q. urb.? or moneyer 57?) (pr. 55?) (RE 52):
Some coins issued by M. Nonius Sufenas depict on their obverse the legend *S·C* and the head of Saturn. It has been debated whether Sufenas, who has usually been identified with the praetor of 55 (?), was *quaestor urbanus* or moneyer. In addition, the issue's chronology has been a matter of discussion. Crawford, RRC, 445–446 no. 421, dates the coins to 59. In his opinion, the legend *S.C.* provides no evidence for Sufenas' quaestorship. Consequently, Crawford claims that Sufenas acted as moneyer (cf. Broughton MRR, 2.175: he minted coins, perhaps as quaestor, perhaps as *monetalis*, probably by 62, since he held the tribunate in 56; but in MRR, 3.148, Broughton, following Crawford, assumes that Nonius Sufenas was quaestor, but at an uncertain date, since his coinage provides no evidence for his quaestorship). Certainly, Crawford is right to assert that not every issue with *S·C* implies that the moneyer was an urban quaestor. However, Crawford, who analyses the head of Saturn on the issues of Cn. Nerius (see above) as a reference to the fact that Nerius was urban quaestor, says

nothing about it in this case. Could the head of Saturn be a symbol of Sufenas' quaestorship? Sobeck 1909, 54, thinks so and dates the coins by 60. Nevertheless, there appears to be an insurmountable problem: Sufenas makes no mention of the office of urban quaestor, as Nerius expressly did in his coins with the legend $Q \cdot VRB$. It seems unlikely that Sufenas would not have signalled his office if he was urban quaestor (the head of Saturn appears on five occasions on Republican coins: Crawford no 313; 330; 349; 421; 441. Only in two cases, no. 330 and 441, are these quaestorian issues). It seems therefore more probable that he was a moneyer.

As for the date of the coins, Hersh and Walker 1984, Table 2, date them to 57, since they are not present in the Mesagne Hoard, which is dated to 58. The coins of Sufenas must therefore have been minted later. Hollstein 1993, 244–248, accepts the year 57, but doubts the identification of the moneyer with the praetor of 55, given the short interval between both offices. Hollstein proposes to identify the moneyer with the tribune of the plebs of 56 and even suggests that his praenomen could be Sextus instead of Marcus.

C. Norbanus C. f. (Balbus?) (q. 99?) (cos. 83) (RE 5):

See **A. Gabinius.** There is no doubt that Norbanus was a quaestor serving under the famous orator M. Antonius, either in 102–100 during his command against the pirates in Cilicia or in 99 during his consulship. This gives the reason why Antonius defended Norbanus in a trial afterwards (Cic. de orat. 2.198–202). Both proposals have had supporters (see a summary in Evans 1987, 123 n. 18). Sobeck 1909, 25–26, who wrongly identifies Norbanus as tribune of the plebs in 105, dates his quaestorship either to 102 or to 99, after providing arguments in favour of each of the two options (cf. Bültz 1908, 20–21). Münzer 1932, favours 102 because Norbanus was exiled to Rhodes twenty years later when he was proscribed by Sulla (Liv. per. 89; Oros. 5.21.3): he fled to Rhodes because he had been there as quaestor under Antonius. However, the dating of Norbanus' quaestorship to 102 must be rejected, since he undoubtedly held the tribunate of the plebs in 103 (Broughton MRR, 1.563 and 565–566 n. 7 and 3.149). If he was a tribune in 103, he left office on 9th December. Consequently, he could not have taken his new office as quaestor on 5th December, since this was legally impossible (Taylor 1964, 21 n. 23. Nonetheless, Taylor takes it for granted that the quaestors entered office on 5th December by the end of the second century, which is far from certain). As a result, if Norbanus was Antonius' quaestor in Cilicia, this could only have happened in 101 or 100. This argument is defended by Badian 1957, 332; 1983: Norbanus was quaestor under Antonius in 101 and 100, succeeding A. Gabinius, who had been his quaestor in 102. Badian's thesis contradicts Gruen 1966c, who argues that Gabinius was serving as a quaestor (or better proquaestor) under Antonius in 101, according to a Greek inscription from Rhodes (IGRP 4.1116). That would make Norbanus' quaestorship in 101 impossible.

The argument put forward by Münzer (and accepted by Badian) seems inconsistent. There is no reason to think that Norbanus was necessarily exiled to Rhodes because he had previously been on the island during his quaestorship. It seems probable that Gabinius was Antonius' quaestor throughout his stay in Cilicia in 102– 100. Consequently, it seems reasonable to date Norbanus' quaestorship to 99, coinciding with the consulship of Antonius (see Wiseman 1971, 245; Evans 1994, 188 and 213). The fact that later on Antonius defended Norbanus in a trial because of their special relationship can be perfectly explained, if we consider their joint work as consul and quaestor in 99.

Q. Numerius Q. f. Rufus (q. in Africa by 60?) (tr. pl. 57) (RE 5):

The quaestorship of Quintus Numerius Rufus is known only through an inscription from Africa, in which he is honoured with a statue by three *pagi*: *Q. Numerio Q. f. Rufo q. stipendiariei pagorum Muxsi Gususi Zeugei* (CIL I^2 2513 = ILS 9482 = ILLRP 388). Numerius Rufus was tribune of the plebs in 57, when he opposed the motion for Cicero's recall (Broughton MRR, 2.201). An inscription from Lissus (CIL I^2 759 = III 3078) records him as legate and *patronus* (*Q. Numerius Q. f. Vel. / Rufus leg. patron.*), probably under Caesar ca. 55 (see Broughton MRR, 2.219). Consequently, he was quaestor in Africa some years earlier, probably around 60 (Broughton MRR, 2.184; Wiseman 1971, 246 no. 282; Zucca 1994, 1446–1447). The date is completely hypothetical.

C. Octavius C. f. (q. before 66?) (pr. 61) (RE 15):

C. Octavius was the father of the future Augustus. His political career is known thanks to his *elogium*: *C. Octavius C. f. C. n. C. pr(on.) pater Augusti tr. mil. bis q. aed. pl. cum C. Toranio iudex quaestionum pr. pro cos. imperator appellatus ex provincia Macedonia* (CIL I^2 1, p. 199 = Inscr. Ital. 13.3.75b = ILS 47). He held the praetorship in 61, but the dates of his previous offices are uncertain. If he was aedile around 64 (Broughton MRR, 2.162), he would have been quaestor by 66 at the latest (Sobeck 1909, 47). Broughton MRR, 2.110 and 2.595, dates Octavius' quaestorship by 73 without further arguments, after he had twice been military tribune (cf. Wiseman 1971, 246 no. 287). There is no real evidence to determine the precise date of C. Octavius' quaestorship.

L. Octavius Cn. f. (q. urb.? by 90–88) (cos. 75?) (RE 26):

See **C. Pomponius.** An inscription, which appears to have been set up on the road from Nursia to Spoletium, records the activity of the quaestors L. Octavius and C. Pomponius. The text makes it clear that they were acting in accordance with the senate's decision (*de senatus sententia*): *C. Pomponius C. f. L. Octavius Cn. f. q. d. s. s* (CIL I^2 832 = IX 4541). Based on the filiation, this Lucius Octavius is probably the consul of 75, so he may have held the quaestorship by 90–88. See Broughton MRR, 2.476 and 2.596: quaestor in the early first century. Since Octavius and Pomponius were acting jointly and their tasks appear to have similar to those of **T. Vibius Temudinus** (see below) and performed around the same time, they may have been urban quaestors.

C. or Cn. Octavius Rufus (q. by 230? or by 250?) (RE cf. 79):

According to Suetonius, he was the first Octavius to obtain a magistracy by popular election: *Primus ex hac magistratum populi suffragio cepit C. Rufus. Is quaestorius Cn. et C. procreavit, a quibus duplex Octaviorum familia defluxit conditione diversa* (Suet. *Aug.* 2.2). His *praenomen* is controversial. Suetonius calls him Caius, but Geer 1934, proposes that either Suetonius or his manuscript changed his name mistakenly and that the right one is Cnaeus. Geer bases his thesis on the assumption that the elder son should bear the father's *praenomen* as well as on the presumption that this Octavius Rufus was the father of Cn. Octavius, the praetor of 205, and the grandfather of Cn. Octavius Cn. f. Cn. n., the consul of 165. Geer's arguments are accepted by Broughton MRR, 1.227, who tentatively dates Cn. Octavius Rufus' quaestorship around 230. While this theory appears reasonable, it should not be taken for granted that Suetonius (or his manuscript) is wrong. As Wardle 2014, 83, emphasises, there is nothing that precludes the possibility that a Caius Octavius Rufus actually existed and that he was the great-grandfather and not the grandfather of the consul of 165. If this is the case, C. Octavius Rufus' quaestorship should be dated to the time of the first Punic war, presumably around 250 (Sobeck 1909, 73–74, does not question the *praenomen* Caius and dates the quaestorship towards the middle of the third century). Of course, the date is purely speculative.

Cn. Octavius Ruso (q. urb.? by 105) (pr. by 91) (RE 82):

Sallust asserts that the quaestor Cn. Octavius Ruso was entrusted to bring money for Marius' troops in Africa. He returned to Rome with the envoys of Bocchus of Mauretania: *Ceterum Mauri impetratis omnibus rebus tres Romam profecti duce Cn. Octavio Rusone, qui quaestor stipendium in Africam portaverat, duo ad regem redeunt* (Sall. *Iug.* 104.3). His quaestorship should be dated by 105, and this date has generally been accepted. See Sobeck 1909, 23 (year 106); Broughton MRR, 1.556; van Ooteghem 1964, 169; Gruen 1966c, 106; Evans 1994, 34 and 211. According to Badian 1990, 406, this Octavius Ruso would be the same as the Cn. Octavius L.f. Aemilia tribu included in the *consilium* of the *S.C. de agro Pergameno*.

Since Sulla was the quaestor serving under the command of Marius in Numidia (see **L. Cornelius Sulla.** Cf. Sall. *Iug.* 95.1; 103.4), Octavius Ruso could not have been Marius' quaestor at the moment he was sent to Africa, as his immediate return to Rome shows. Given that he was sent to Africa on a special mission in relation to the transport of money taken from the *aerarium* as well as his escorting of Bocchus' legates back to Rome, all indications point to Octavius Ruso being an urban quaestor.

L. Opimius Pansa (q. 294) (RE 12):

The only information we have about Lucius Opimius Pansa refers to his quaestorship in 294. With the consul M. Atilius Regulus he went to Samnium, where he was killed during an attack by the Samnites on the Roman camp: *Itaque captum quaestorium quaestorque ibi L. Opimius Pansa occisus* (Liv. 10.32.9). See Bülz 1908, 3; Sobeck 1909, 5; Broughton MRR, 1.180; Oakley 2005b, 354: the whole family is unknown until much later, when the Opimii began to play a more important political role. Nonetheless, nothing indicates that the name is incorrect.

P. Oppius (q. 74, proq. 73 in Bithynia) (RE 17):

Publius Oppius served under M. Aurelius Cotta in Bithynia. Cotta was consul in 74, when he departed for the East before his colleague Lucullus, probably as soon as he received the command of the fleet in Bithynia (Pina Polo 2011, 236). It is very likely that Oppius was Cotta's quaestor in 74 and that he accompanied him to the East. Cotta remained in his province as proconsul until 70, when he returned to Rome after the capture of Heracleia Pontica. Oppius continued to serve under Cotta as proquaestor at least in 73, but it is unclear whether he remained in Bithynia until 70. According to Cassius Dio (36.40.3), Oppius was dismissed by Cotta because of bribery and the suspicion of conspiracy. Sallust speaks of a quarrel between Cotta and Oppius during the siege of Heracleia Pontica (Sall. *hist.* 3.59–60 M.), but this does not imply that Oppius was present during the whole siege of the town. Oppius was tried in 69, probably for extortion, and was defended by Cicero (Quint. *inst.* 5.10.69; 13.20–21 and 30; 11.1.67; Ps. Ascon. p. 236 Stangl. Griffin 1973, 205: Oppius could have been expelled from the senate by the censors of 70; cf. Alexander 1990, no. 187). According to this evidence, it seems probable that Oppius was quaestor in 74 and proquaestor at least in 73, but we do not know exactly when he was expelled from the province (Stewart 1987, 438–441, dates Oppius' dismissal to the year 73). See Bülz 1893, 50–51; Sobeck 1909, 41–42 (Sobeck wrongly asserts that Bülz suggested that Oppius had been urban quaestor in 74); Broughton MRR, 2.103: quaestor in 74; 2.111–112; 2.597: quaestor in 74 and probably proquaestor 73.

C. Papirius (Paperios) Ti. f. (q. between 267 and 241) (not in RE or RE 6):

See **M. Publicius Malleolus** and **L. Quinctius.** Caius Papirius (Paperios) is one of the two quaestors mentioned in three inscriptions on Egadi's *rostra* (no. 4, 6 and 11): *M(arcos) Populicio(s) L(ucii) f(ilios) q(uaestores) p(robaverunt) C(aios) Paperio(s) Ti(beri) f(ilios)* (no. 4); *C(aios) Paperio(s) Ti(beri) f(ilios) M(arcos) Populicio(s) L(ucii) f(ilios) q(uaestores) p(robaverunt)* (no. 6) (Prag 2014b, 41–43; 2014c; 2017; Coarelli 2014, 103–106; cf. Oliveri 2012, 118–119). The rams belonged to ships that would have taken part in the battle of the Egadi Islands in 241 at the end of the first Punic War. This C. Papirius Ti. f. cannot be identified with certainty. A C. Papirius was certainly consul in 231 (RE 57), but he was C(aii) f(ilius) and consequently he cannot be the same person. However, Valerius Maximus mentions an otherwise unidentified Papirius (RE 6) assisting the consul Q. Lutatius in 241 in drawing up the terms of surrender for the Falisci (Val.Max. 6.5.1b). This Papirius has usually been identified with the consul of 231, but he also could be the quaestor who is mentioned on the Egadi *rostra* (Prag

2014b, 51–53. Cf. Coarelli 2014, 104). C. Papirius (Paperios) must have been quaestor at some point between 267 and 241. According to Tusa and Royal, 2012 45 (cf. Prag 2014b, 51), the presence of a number of Latin inscribed *rostra* on the seabed, precisely at the site of the decisive Roman victory that put an end to the first Punic War, could be explained if all these rams came from Roman ships previously captured by the Carthaginians in earlier battles, in particular at the battle of Drepanum in 249, when the Carthaginians overcame 93 Roman ships and took them back to Carthage (Pol. 1.51.12; 1.53.1). Those ships and rams could have been reused by the Carthaginians as part of their emergency fleet of 241, which was sunk by the Romans at the battle of the Egadi Islands. If this explanation is correct, the quaestorship of Papirius should obviously be dated before 249. If this is the case and if he is identified with the Papirius mentioned by Valerius Maximus, he would have been an established senator by 241, perhaps then serving as a *legatus* to the consul Lutatius in the campaign against the Falisci. Nevertheless, it is also possible that the *rostra* belong to ships that were constructed by 242 during the preparations for the Egadi battle, which would date Publicius' quaestorship around that year. As Prag points out, it is implicit that the task completed by the quaestors was the object of the *probation*, to which the inscriptions allude: it seems that the *rostra* themselves were the subject of the *probatio*, since this is where the text was inscribed. Accordingly, the quaestors mentioned would have been in charge of the *rostra*'s production and therefore of their *probatio* (it is probable that the *probatio* extended to the construction of the whole ship). However, the inscriptions do not specify to which quaestors they refer: they could be the urban quaestors, the consular quaestors or the new quaestors created by 267. This last option is particularly attractive.

P. Papius (or Pupius) (q. 409) (RE Pupius *1):

See **P. Aelius and Q. Silius.** According to Livy, Publius Papius was one of the first plebeian quaestors in 409: *Eum dolorem quaestoriis comitiis simul ostendit et ulta est tunc primum plebeiis quaestoribus creatis, ita ut in quattuor creandis uni patricio, K. Fabio Ambusto, relinqueretur locus, tres plebeii, Q. Silius P. Aelius P. Papius, clarissimarum familiarum iuvenibus praeferrentur* (Liv. 4.54.2–3). Their names are suspicious and could be fictitious, but apparently there is no reason to correct Papius for Pupius, as Sobeck 1909, 4, does (Broughton MRR, 1.78, calls him Papius; Ogilvie 1965, 616 prefers Papius to Pupius). Cf. Drummond 2008, 404: 'apart from an obviously fictitious quaestor in 409, Papii are not otherwise known to have held office at Rome before the first century B.C.'

P.? Pavus Tubitanus or Tuditanus (q. in second century in Hispania) (RE Pavus):

Lucilius mentions a quaestor of the name Publius Pavus Tubitanus, who had supposedly served in Hispania in the second century under an unknown governor: *Publius Pavus mihi Tubitanus quaestor Hibera in terra fuit, lucifugus, nebulo, id genus sane* (Lucil. 467–468 M. = 499–500 W. = 472–473 K.). His name has been corrected to Tuditanus, a well known *cognomen* in the *gens* Sempronia (Gruen 1992, 294 n. 117). Actually a C. Sempronius Tuditanus was the praetor of Hispania Citerior in 197. At any rate, given that the mention of this individual must be understood in the context of Lucilius' satire, his real name remains unknown. Lucilius accompanied Scipio Aemilianus in Hispania during the Numantine War. Could he be referring in his text to a quaestor in office at that time? The problem for such an identification is that we know that Q. Fabius Maximus Allobrogicus was the praetor serving in Hispania under the command of Scipio Aemilianus. See Sobeck 1909, 74; Broughton MRR, 2.476; Cichorius 1908, 317–319: Charpin 1979, 2.233.

Q. Petillius C. f. Spurinus (q. by 189) (cos. 176) (RE 4, 11):

Livy shows that Quintus Petillius Spurinus held the quaestorship: *et erat familiaris usus, quod scribam eum quaestor Q. Petilius in decuriam legerat* (Liv. 40.29.10). However, the date is conjectural. Petillius was tribune of the plebs in 187. Assuming that the quaestorship preceded his tribunate, he may have been quaestor by 189. See Sobeck 1909, 12: quaestor before 181, when he was praetor; Broughton MRR, 1.366 and 2.600: quaestor probably by 188; Develin 1978a, 143: that Petellius Spurinus' quaestorship preceded his tribunate of 187 is only conjectural, but very likely.

L. Philo (L. Veturius Philo?) (q. 102 in Sicily) (RE Veturius 21) (or L. Sempronius Pit(h)io?) [RE 74]):

See **M. Aurelius Scaurus** and **Cn. Pompeius Strabo.** Cicero mentions three quaestors who had been barred from prosecuting the men under whom they had served as quaestors: L. Philo against C. Servilius, M. Aurelius Scaurus against L. Flaccus and Cn. Pompeius Strabo against T. Albucius (Cic. *div. in Caec.* 62–63: *neque fere umquam venit in contentionem de accusando qui quaestor fuisset, quin repudiaretur. Itaque neque L. Philoni in C. Servilium nominis deferendi potestas est data, neque M. Aurelio Scauro in L. Flaccum, neque Cn. Pompeio in T. Albucium*). C. Servilius was praetor and governor of Sicily in 102. His trial probably followed his return to Rome in 101 (Gruen 1968b, 177: the charge was apparently *repetundae*). Consequently, Philo's quaestorship in Sicily should be dated to 102 (Bültz 1908, 21–22; Broughton MRR, 1.569; 1.570 n. 5; 3.156; Badian 1984b, 301–306; Evans 1994, 212; Prag 2007b, 301). It has generally been assumed that Cicero gives these three examples in chronological order (so Ps. Ascon. 203 Stangl). Accordingly, Sobeck 1909, 21–22, concludes that Philo's quaestorship should be dated prior to the quaestorships of Scaurus and Pompeius Strabo, before 108. However, if the date of Philo's quaestorship in 102 is correct, the order of Cicero's passage actually seems to be from the most recent to the oldest, Philo's quaestorship being the most recent of the three.

As for his name, since Cicero only mentions his *cognomen*, Lucius Veturius Philo has been suggested (Broughton MRR, 3.156) as well as Lucius Sempronius Pit(h)io after the *monetalis* of 148 (Badian 1984b, 291–296 and 301–306). Cf. Prag 2007b, 301: possibly L. Veturius Philo, or perhaps L. Sempronius Pit(h)io.

C. Plaetorius (q. 48 in Pontus [and Bithynia?]) (RE 5):
C. Plaetorius served under Cn. Domitius Calvinus in Asia Minor in 48: *mittit [Domitius Calvinus] P. Sestium ad C. Plaetorium quaestorem, ut legionem adduceret quae ex tumultuariis militibus in Ponto confecta erat* (*bell. Alex.* 34.5). See Bülz 1893, 51–52; Sobeck 1909, 67; Broughton MRR, 2.274.

L. Plaetorius L. f. (Cestianus) (q. urb. 71?) (RE 14):
See **P. Cornelius Lentulus Spinther.** Cicero mentions a L. Plaetorius, who was a senator in 66, when he delivered his speech *Pro Cluentio: Opportune adest homo summa fide et omni virtute praeditus, L. Plaetorius, senator, qui illius Vibi hospes fuit et familiaris* (Cic. *Cluent.* 165). Consequently, this Plaetorius must have held the quaestorship before 66 (Sobeck 1909, 48; Broughton MRR, 2.173 and 2.601: quaestor 74?; 3.157: quaestor ca. 74–66). Some denarii with the legend *L · PLAETORI · L · F · Q · S · C* allow us to date Plaetorius' quaestorship precisely. Crawford RRC, 408 no. 396, identifies the quaestor of these coins with the senator mentioned by Cicero, for whom there is no evidence of his having held other magistracies (Gruen 1974, 198). The type on the reverse, a victorious boxer holding a *caestus*, would support the cognomen Cestianus, known from other members of the family (Wiseman 1971, 251: he could be the father of L. Plaetorius Cestianus, quaestor in 42 under Brutus). Crawford dates these denarii to 74.

However, the discovery of the Messagne Hoard has forced us to revisit the dating of the issues from the period. Hersh and Walker 1984, Table 2, date the denarii of L. Plaetorius to 71 instead of 74. Following this new chronology, Hollstein 1993, 84–88, identifies Plaetorius as an urban quaestor. The purpose of the issue, ordered by the senate and carried out by the urban quaestor, would have been to finance the celebration of several triumphs at the end of 71: both the triumphs of Pompey and Metellus *ex Hispania*, of M. Terentius Varro Lucullus *de Bessis* as well as the *ovatio* of M. Licinius Crassus *de fugitivis et Spartaco*. The type of Juno Moneta and the legend *MONETA* on the obverse as protecting goddess of the Roman mint were the symbols of this official minting by the urban quaestor.

If the dating of these denarii in 71 is correct, Lucius Plaetorius (Cestianus) may have been a *quaestor urbanus* that year (against Ryan 1996 g, 85, who tentatively dates Plaetorius' quaestorship to ca. 70–69 together with P. Cornelius Lentulus Spinther).

M. Plaetorius (M. f.?) Cestianus (q. by 70?) (pr. 64?) (RE 16):
It has been supposed that Marcus Plaetorius Cestianus had already held the quaestorship when he prosecuted M. Fonteius in 69, and to this end the incomplete be-

ginning of Cicero's speech for Fonteius has been adduced as evidence (Cic. *Font.* 1; see Münzer RE 16, col. 1950, who claims that the quaestorship of Plaetorius Cestianus is implied in the Ciceronian text, though his name is not mentioned). Broughton MRR, 2.128 (cf. 3.157), dates Plaetorius' quaestorship tentatively to 70. According to Crawford RRC, 414–418 no. 405, Plaetorius issued coins as *monetalis* in 69. Crawford argues that there is no room in Plaetorius' career for his quaestorship after the moneyership. Consequently, he must have been quaestor before 69. Crawford's arguments are probably right, and Broughton's proposal of by 70 for Plaetorius' quaestorship is feasible. However, the lacunose text of Cicero does not provide evidence for his quaestorship. Since the office was compulsory after Sulla, Plaetorius was no doubt quaestor, but neither his quaestorship nor his dates are actually attested (Sobeck does not include Plaetorius in his list of Republican quaestors). The year 70 is pure speculation; in fact, he may have been quaestor earlier. More recently, Ryan 1996d, 352, has argued that the date given by Crawford for Plaetorius' moneyership should not be taken as incontrovertible; accordingly, Ryan dates his quaestorship to 69 and claims that Plaetorius could not have been quaestor later (he was an aedile in 67), but he could certainly have held this office before 69. It has usually been assumed that the prosecutor of Fonteius was the same man who was later aedile and praetor (Wiseman 1971, 251 no. 320). However, see the cautious note in Gruen 1974, 268 n. 28: the prosecutor in the trial against Fonteius, Plaetorius, remains unknown, although a Plaetorius, perhaps the same man, is mentioned in other sources (Cic. *fam.* 1.8.1; *Att.* 5.20.8). He might be the governor of Macedonia mentioned in an inscription from Delphi (Delph. 4.45: ...μετὰ τοῦ στρατηγοῦ Πλαιτωρίου...); see Syme 1955a, 130.

Cn. Plancius (q. 58 in Macedonia) (RE 4):

According to Cicero, Cn. Plancius was quaestor in 58 in Macedonia under L. Appuleius: *in Macedonia tribunus militum fuit, in eadem provincia postea quaestor* (Cic. *Planc.* 28. Cf. *Planc.* 24; 60; 98–99; *p. red. Sen.* 35; Schol. Bob. 153 Stangl). Plancius protected Cicero during his exile (Cic. *Att.* 3.14 and 3.22; *fam.* 14.1.3). See Bülz 1893, 28–30; Sobeck 1909, 56; Broughton MRR, 2.196; Syme 1987, 323: quaestor in 59 or 58; Wiseman 1971, 251 no. 321; Ryan 1996f, 41: Plancius was at least thirty-two at the beginning of this quaestorship.

P. Plautius Hypsaeus (q. 67 or 66, proq. 66–61 or 65–61? in the East) (pr. by 55) (RE 23):

See **M. Aemilius M. f. Scaurus**. According to Asconius, P. Plautius Hypsaeus was quaestor of Pompey: *Milo misisse ad Cn. Pompeium dicebatur, quod Hypsaeo summe studebat, quod fuerat eius quaestor, desistere se petitione consulatus, si ita ei videretur* (Ascon. 35 C). The exact date of Plautius' quaestorship is not attested. It has been accepted that Plautius Hypsaeus was Pompey's quaestor during his command in the East against Mithridates. Under the Manilian law Pompey received the command of the war in 66. Consequently, Plautius Hypsaeus would have been his quaestor in that year and he could have served under Pompey as proquaestor throughout his whole command between 65–61, when Pompey returned to Rome. See Bülz 1893, 70; Sobeck 1909, 49: quaestor between 66 and 63; Broughton MRR, 2.153: quaestor in 66; 2.602: proquaestor since 65. Cf. Gruen 1974, 107; Marshall 1985, 160. We know that Marcus Aemilius Scaurus was Pompey's quaestor in 66 (or perhaps already in 67) and that was probably under his command in Syria this same year. Scaurus remained in Pompey's service during the following years as proquaestor. When Pompey returned to Rome in 63, Scaurus took charge of Syria as *proquaestor pro praetore*. These conclusions do not exclude Hypsaeus from having been Pompey' quaestor in the East, since Plutarch states that Pompey, according to the *lex Gabinia* of 67, was authorised to have two quaestors during his campaigns in the Mediterranean (Plut. *Pomp.* 26.2). Consequently, Plautius Hypseus may have been one of Pompey's quaestors already in 67 and may have remained with him once the *lex Manilia* was passed in 66. See Ioannidopoulos 2017.

A. Pompeius A. f. (q. before 80? Triumviral period?) (RE 4):

An inscription from Interamna Nahars honours the quaestor A. Pompeius as patron: *A. Pompeio A. f. Clu. q. patrono municipi…* (CIL I² 2510 = XI 4213 = ILS 6629 = ILLRP 364). Broughton MRR, 3.160, dates his quaestorship probably before 80, if the alleged dangers from which he saved the town can be identified as the confiscation of land by Sulla (*municipium ex summis pereiculeis et difficultatibus expeditum et conservatum est*). RE: he was quaestor certainly before 74, when he accompanied his younger brother Q. Pompeius Bithynicus to Bithynia. Neither the information contained in the inscription nor its palaeography are definitive. However, the floral decoration seems to date it to the very end of the Republic or even to the early Empire (Badian 1968b, 241–242). Consequently, this Aulus Pompeius could be a son of Q. Pompeius Bithynicus' brother, also named A. Pompeius. If this is the case, his quaestorship could be better dated to the triumviral period (cf. Sumner 1977, 15: 'it is clear that the inscription can hardly be earlier than 49 and probably belongs to the period of the Triumvirate, not to the Sullan period… The easy solution is to identify this quaestor as the son of Q. Bithynicus' brother Aulus'). As Taylor 1960, 245, already observed, it is not necessary to postulate that A. Pompeius rescued Interamna Nahars from a peril dating to the Sullan period. The Perusine War during the triumviral age should also be considered.

Q. Pompeius Bithynicus (q. or proq. by 75? in Asia) (RE 25):

The quaestorship of Pompeius Bithynicus is not expressly attested. Broughton MRR, 2.100, includes him among the legates of 75, but asserts: 'probably served under M. Iuncus [proconsul in Asia], either as quaestor or as legate, and was active in organizing Bithynia in late 75 or early 74.' He brought to Rome the royal treasure of Bithynia, according to Festus p. 320 L.: *quod signum Pompeius Bithynicus ex Bithynia supel-*

lectilis regiae Romam deportavit. Nevertheless, in the index (MRR, 2.603) Broughton gives three different options: legate, lieutenant or proquaestor in 75, and in MRR, 3.161, he seems to lean towards legate. However, Sumner 1973, 129, suggests that Bithynicus could have been quaestor in 77 or 76 on the basis of his age. Kunkel and Wittmann 1995, 360, n. 210, proffer that he was sent to Bithynia by the senate as *quaestor pro praetore*, a rank which could explain the *agnomen* Bithynicus.

There is no evidence to decide whether Pompeius Bithynicus acted in Bithynia around 75 as either quaestor or proquaestor, though it is possible.

T. Pompeius Longinus (q. 49 in Asia?) (RE 29):
See **Q. Raesius.** Josephus lists T. Pompeius Longinus in fourth place among the members of the *consilium* of the consul L. Cornelius Lentulus Crus in 49 in Asia (Ios. *AJ* 14.229; 14.238). Suolahti 1955, 340; 1958, 157, argues that Longinus could have been either quaestor or military tribune, but in his opinion the former seems more probable. Broughton MRR, 3.160, outlines Suolahti's argument without judging in its favour or against it. Suolahti's hypothesis is speculative but feasible. At any rate, Longinus' quaestorship is not expressly attested.

Q. Pompeius Q. f. Rufus (q. 75 or 74) (pr. 63) (RE *8):
Quintus Pompeius Rufus (Κόϊντος Πομπήϊος Κοΐτου υἱὸς Ἀρ[νιή]σσης Ῥοῦφος) appears as one of the senators in the *SC de Oropiis* of year 73 (SIG^3 747 = RDGE 23). The names are presumably cited in order of rank. Pompeius Rufus is one of the *quaestorii* and is mentioned immediately after Cicero, who was quaestor in 75, and Q. Axius. Consequently, Pompeius Rufus must have held the quaestorship before 73, either in 75 as Cicero's colleague, or in 74. See Broughton MRR, 2.604: 'Q. before 73'; Ryan 2005. Cf. Wiseman 1964, 125 n. 3: he was probably the adopted son of the consul of 88.

Cn. Pompeius Sex. f. Strabo (q. 106? in Sardinia) (cos. 89) (RE 14):
See **M. Aurelius Scaurus** and **L. Philo.** After his quaestorship under T. Albucius in Sardinia, Cn. Pompeius Strabo attempted to prosecute his former commander but was barred from doing so (Cic. *div. in Caec.* 62–63: *neque fere umquam venit in contentionem de accusando qui quaestor fuisset, quin repudiaretur. Itaque neque L. Philoni in C. Servilium nominis deferendi potestas est data, neque M. Aurelio Scauro in L. Flaccum, neque Cn. Pompeio in T. Albucium.* Cf. Ps. Ascon. p. 203 Stangl; Cic. *off.* 2.50). Pompeius Strabo' quaestorship is usually dated to 104 (Bültz 1908, 19–20; Sobeck 1909, 23; Broughton MRR, 1.560; Rowland Jr. 1968; Douglas 1966, 303 n. 19, prefers the year 105). However, Gruen 1964, 100–103; 1968b, 171–172, comprehensively demonstrates that the trial against Albucius must have been held in 105 or 104 and that Strabo's quaestorship consequently cannot be dated to 104 and must be dated earlier, probably to 106. Badian 1984b, 306–309, gives additional arguments in favour of the year 106,

although he does not exclude 107 or 105. According to Badian, Strabo was a tribune of the plebs in 104. As tribune, he prosecuted Q. Fabius Maximus Eburnus before the people for putting his son to death. The traditional date of 104 for Strabo's quaestorship would therefore be impossible. His attempt to prosecute Albucius could be dated to 105. The date of 106 for Strabo's quaestorship has since been generally accepted (see Broughton MRR, 3.165–166; Evans 1994, 184 and 211: he was quaestor aged twenty-six to twenty-nine. Cf. Sumner 1973, 104–105: 106 would be the earliest possible date, since Pompeius Strabo was born by 132 or a few years earlier).

C. Pomponius C. f. (q. urb.? by 90–88) (not in RE):

See **L. Octavius.** The joint activity of the quaestors C. Pomponius and L. Octavius is mentioned in an inscription that appears to refer to the road from Nursia to Spoletium. The text evidences that the quaestors were acting at the bequest of the senate (*de senatus sententia*): *C. Pomponius C. f. L. Octavius Cn. f. q. d. s. s.* (CIL I^2 832 = IX 4541). C. Pomponius is otherwise unknown. If his colleague was the consul of 75, L. Octavius, he may have been quaestor by 90–88. See Broughton MRR, 2.476 and 2.604: quaestor in early first century. Given that L. Octavius and C. Pomponius were acting jointly and the parallel nature of their duties with those carried on by Temudinus (see **T. Vibius Temudinus**) around the same time, they may have been urban quaestors.

A. Pomp(onius) Vic(tor) (q. 49? proq. 48–46?) (not in RE):

Pomp(onius) Vic(tor) was identified by Grant 1946, 20–21, as a Pompeian in Africa in 47 or 46 who was *Q(uaestor ad) A(erarium?)* (see Broughton MRR, 2.287. However, Sumner 1971, 263, rejects Grant's view, arguing rightly that no Pompeian quaestor was elected to office after 50. As a result, Pomp(onius) Vic(tor) must have held the quaestorship in 49 and continued in the following years as proquaestor (cf. Broughton MRR, 3.167).

M. Porcius M. f. Cato (q. 204) (cos. 195) (RE 9):

Cicero asserts clearly that Marcus Porcius Cato was quaestor during the consulship of M. Cornelius Cethegus and P. Sempronius Tuditanus: *At hic Cethegus consul cum P. Tuditano fuit bello Punico secundo quaestorque his consulibus M. Cato modo plane annis CXL ante me consulem* (Cic. Brut. 60); *Quaestor deinde quadriennio post factus sum, quem magistratum gessi consulibus Tuditano et Cethego...* (Cic. de senec. 10) (see also Liv. 29.25.10: Cato is mentioned with C. Laelius on the left wing of Scipio's fleet as it sets out for Africa. The reference to Africa confirms that Livy refers to the year 204). As a result, it has been almost unanimously assumed that Cato was quaestor in 204 (Bülz 1908, 5–7; Sobeck 1909, 8–9; Broughton MRR, 1.307; Della Corte ^{2}1969, 19; Ruebel 1977, 162; Astin 1978, 12–13; Prag 2007b, 291). As quaestor, Cato served under P. Cornelius Scipio, the future Africanus. When Scipio embarked for Africa, Cato went with him. Nepos introduces a discrepancy, however, since he asserts that Cato was quaestor when Scipio Africanus was consul: *Quaestor obtigit P. Africano consuli; P. Scipio Africanus, consul iterum, cuius in priori consulatu quaestor fuerat* (Nep. *Cat.* 1.3 and 2.2). This would date Cato's quaestorship to 205. Astin 1978, 12, dismisses Nepos' information, which he considers to be an incorrect interpretation of the historical facts. But Kienast 1954, 16–19 and 38, accepts Nepos' evidence and concludes that Cato was probably quaestor in 205 and proquaestor in 204. Kienast's suggestion remains, however, an exception within the scholarship. On one hand, Nepos could use the word *consul* loosely for *proconsul*; on the other, Cicero's evidence seems more conclusive, favouring the year 204 for Cato's quaestorship. Nevertheless, it is uncertain whether Cato only served under Scipio Africanus in 204 or whether he may have remained under his command as proquaestor in the following years (this is suggested by Ruebel 1977, 162: 'perhaps he remained in Africa till after Zama'). Plutarch tells a dubious story according to which Cato quarrelled with Scipio about his conduct in Sicily and as a result returned to Rome to denounce him (Plut. *Cat.mai.* 3.5–8). See Broughton MRR, 1.310 n. 4: the chronology of Plutarch's account can hardly outweigh against the testimony of Cicero and Livy.

M. Porcius M. f. Cato (Uticensis) (q. urb. 64, proq. pro pr. 58–56 in Cyprus) (pr. 54) (RE *20):

The year 64 is the most probable date for the quaestorship of Marcus Porcius Cato, which has been generally accepted in the scholarship (Plut. *Cat.min.* 16.3–6; Cass.Dio 47.6.4). Nonetheless, the year 65 has also, exceptionally, been proposed (Sobeck 1909, 49). The evidence that he was born in 95 (Plut. *Cat.min.* 3 and 73; Liv. *per.* 114) favours the year 64, according to the legal age for the quaestorship in the post-Sullan period (Broughton MRR, 2.163; Sumner 1973, 138; Fehrle 1983, 76 n. 53; Syme 1987, 322; Bellemore 1996, argues conclusively that the quaestorship of Cato and the tribunate of Memmius coincided in 64). Plutarch (*Cat.min.* 16.4) implies that Cato was a quaestor at the same time as Q. Lutatius Catulus was censor (together with M. Licinius Crassus). This seems to point to the year 65 rather than 64 for Cato's quaestorship. However, the censors may have been in office when Cato entered his quaestorship on 5th December 65, and they could have resigned shortly afterwards (Broughton MRR, 3.170–171).

Some years after his quaestorship, in 58, Cato was designated with *imperium* under Clodius' law to annex Cyprus. His official title was not *quaestor pro praetore* (Broughton MRR, 2.198), but *proquaestor pro praetore* (Balsdon 1962, 135; Broughton MRR, 3.171; Badian 1965, 110–111). As on other occasions, the sources use the term *quaestor* for *proquaestor* inaccurately: *P. Clodius in tribunatu sub honorificentissimo ministerii titulo M. Catonem a re publica relegavit: quippe legem tulit, ut is quaestor cum iure praetorio, adiecto etiam quaestore, mitteretur in insulam Cyprum...* (Vell. 2.45.4); *Quaestor Cyprum missus ad vehendam ex Ptolomaei hereditate pecuniam cum summa eam fide perduxit...* (*vir.ill.* 80.2). As Velleius Paterculus implies, he was given a quaestor to assist him, whose name is unknown (however, see **Canidius**). See also Bülz 1893, 56–58.

L. (or T.?) Postumius (appointed q. 49 in Sicily?) (RE 15):
See **T. Furfan(i)us Postumus.** According to Cicero, this Postumius was appointed by the senate to replace the quaestor T. Furfan(i)us Postumus in 49 in Sicily: *Postumius autem, de quo nominatim senatus decrevit ut statim in Siciliam iret Furfanioque succederet, negat se sine Catone iturum...* (Cic. *Att.* 7.15.2). However, he did not end up going to Sicily, because he refused to do so without M. Cato. The other option for the senate to supersede Furfan(i)us was C. Fannius, but there is no evidence that he arrived on the island. Therefore, Postumius may have been appointed as quaestor for 49, although he never held the office. Nevertheless, it is also possible that he was ordered to take charge of Sicily as a legate, as Broughton points out (MRR, 2.269): 'he was a senator of some influence, and so probably a praetorian legate.' See Prag 2007b, 309: 'the statement of Cicero that he was to succeed Furfanus and his refusal to go out without Cato both imply a subordinate position and perhaps suggest that he was assigned to Sicily as quaestor.'

M. Postumius (q. 73 in Sicily) (RE 19):
See **Q. Caecilius Niger.** The otherwise unknown Marcus Postumius was quaestor under Verres in Sicily in 73: *Deinde ceteras dicas omnis illo foro M. Postumius quaestor sortitus est* (Cic. *Verr.* 2.2.44). Since Postumius was trying cases in the Syracuse area, he was presumably the eastern quaestor on the island. See Sobeck 1909, 42; Broughton MRR, 2.110 and 3.173; Marinone 1965–66, 252; Prag 2007b, 306.

L. Postumius Tympanus (q. 194) (RE 24):
Lucius Postumius Tympanus served in 194 as quaestor under the consul Ti. Sempronius Longus in North Italy. He died during an attack on the Roman camp carried out by the Boii (Liv. 34.47.1: *in portam quaestoriam inruperant Galli resistentesque pertinacius occiderant L. Postumium quaestorem, cui Tympano fuit cognomen...*). See Bültz 1908, 7; Sobeck 1909, 11; Broughton MRR, 1.344.

Q. Publicius Q. f. (proq. pro pr. in Asia in the 70s) (pr. 67?) (RE 13?):
An inscription from Ephesus mentions a Q. Publicius as *proquaestor pro praetore* (AE [1983] 920: [Κό]ϊντον Ποπλίκιον Κοΐντου υἱ[ὸν] / [ἀ]ντιταμίαν καὶ ἀντιστράτηγο[ν] / [ἀ]νδραγαθο(ῦ)ντα ἀρετῆς ἕνεκε[ν] / [κ]αὶ τῆς εἰς ἑαυτὸν εὐεργεσίας). He is likely the praetor Q. Publicius (ca. 67) quoted by Cic. *Cluen.* 126; accordingly, his quaestorship could be dated early in the seventies.

C. (Publicius) Malleolus (q. 80 in Cilicia) (RE *14):
According to Cicero, a Malleolus served as quaestor in 80 under Cn. Dolabella in Cilicia, where he was killed: *C. Malleolo, quaestore Cn. Dolabellae, occiso duas sibi hereditates venisse arbitratus est, una quaestoriae procurationis, nam a Dolabella statim pro quaestore iussus est esse...* (Cic. *Verr.* 2.1.41). He should probably be identified with C. Publicius Malleolus and could be the same moneyer who issued coins possibly in 96 (RE 18. See Crawford RRC, 333–336 no. 335). See Bülz 1893, 53–54; Sobeck 1909, 35: quaestor in 80 or 79; Broughton MRR, 2.80; 3.176; Gruen 1966b, 395; Luce 1968, 31.

M. Publicius (Populicios) L. f. Malleolus (q. between 267 and 241) (cos. 232) (RE 22):
See **C. Papirius (Paperios)** and **L. Quinctius.** Marcus Publicius is one of the quaestors mentioned in three inscriptions on the Egadi *rostra* (no. 4, 6 and 11): *M(arcos) Populicio(s) L(ucii) f(ilios) q(uaestores) p(robaverunt) C(aios) Paperio(s) Ti(beri) f(ilios)* (nº 4); *C(aios) Paperio(s) Ti(beri) f(ilios) M(arcos) Populicio(s) L(ucii) f(ilios) q(uaestores) p(robaverunt)* (no. 6) (Prag 2014b, 41–43; 2014c; 2017; Coarelli 2014, 103–106; Oliveri 2012, 118–119). The rams belonged to ships that would have participated in the decisive battle of the Egadi Islands in 241 at the end of the First Punic War. We know of a Marcus Publicius Malleolus who was consul in 232. He also held the aedileship together with his brother L. Publicius in either 241 or 238 (Vell. 1.14.8, dates him to 241; Plin. *n.h.* 18.286, to 238). He may be identified with the M. Publicius (Populicios) of the ram's inscription and consequently he probably held the quaestorship before the aedileship in the 240s (Coarelli 2014, 104–105). However, it would also be possible to date Publicius' quaestorship to the late 250s. The presence of Latin inscribed *rostra* on the seabed, at the site where a Roman victory took place, would be explained if these rams were all from Roman ships that had previously been captured by the Carthaginians in earlier battles. The most obvious option would be the battle of Drepanum in 249, when the Carthaginians captured 93 Roman ships and took them back to Carthage (Pol. 1.51.12; 1.53.1). According to Tusa and Royal (2012 45. Cf. Prag 2014b, 51), those ships and rams could have been reused by the Carthaginians as part of their emergency fleet of 241, which was sunk by the Romans at the battle of the Egadi Islands. If this explanation is correct, the quaestorship of Publicius should be dated before 249. At any rate, it cannot be discarded that the *rostra* belong to ships that were constructed by 242 in preparation for the Egadi battle, which would date Publicius' quaestorship around that year. The object of the *probatio* to which the inscriptions allude is implicit: as Prag points out, it seems reasonable that the *rostra* themselves were the subject of the *probatio*, since this is where the text was inscribed. Consequently, the quaestors appear to have taken responsibility for the production of the *rostra* (it is probable that the *probatio* extended to the construction of the whole ship as well). The inscriptions do not specify to which quaestors they refer: they could be the urban quaestors, the consular quaestors or the new quaestors created by 267. This last option is very attractive.

M. Publicius M. f. Scaeva (q. 75 or 74) (not in RE):
Marcus Publicius Scaeva (Μάαρκος Ποπλίκιος Μαάρκου υἱὸς Ὁρατία Σκαίουας) is one of the senators of quaestorian rank mentioned in the *consilium* of the *SC de Oropiis* of 73 (SIG³ 747 = RDGE 23). He must therefore have held the quaestorship before 73 and after 75, when Cicero, the first of the *quaestorii*, was quaestor (Broughton MRR, 2.115; cf. 3.222). Publicius Scaeva was quaestor either in 75 or 74.

C. Publilius (q. 168? in Macedonia) (RE 10):
See **L. Fulcinnius.** We know of C. Publilius' quaestorship thanks to coins minted in Macedonia, in which Publilius appears as quaestor (Μακεδόνων ταμίου Γαΐου Ποπλιλίου). The dating of these coins and consequently of his quaestorship has been a subject of controversy. Lenormant 1852, 319–321, dates them to the very beginning of the Roman presence in Macedonia, after the battle of Pydna. However, Gaebler 1902, 158–159, suggests that Publilius was the successor of Fulcinnius, whose coins Gaebler dates to 148. Sobeck 1909, 14, accepts this chronology and considers Publilius to be quaestor in 147 or 146, still under Metellus Macedonicus or already under the command of Mummius. Broughton MRR, 1.466, also takes up this later chronology and dates Publilius' quaestorship to 146 under Mummius. Nevertheless, MacKay 1968, returns to the old dating proposed by Lenormant and discards Gaebler's chronology. MacKay suggests 168 as date for Publilius' quaestorship, who had served under the command of Aemilius Paullus, just like Fulcinnius (cf. Broughton MRR, 3.176). MacKay's conclusion has been generally accepted by the scholarship (see for instance Boehringer 1972, 113–114; Papazoglou 1979, 307 n. 18; Morkholm 1991, 166). Consequently, if the dating of Publilius' issues in 168 is correct, these would be the first series of bronze coinage struck in Macedonia after the Roman victory in Pydna.

M. Pupius M. f. Piso Frugi (Calpurnianus) (q. 83) (cos. 61) (RE 10):
The quaestor M. Piso Frugi (on his name see Shackleton Bailey 1976, 126–127) was allocated by lot to serve under the command of the consul L. Cornelius Scipio Asiagenus in 83, but he refused to join him: *M. Piso. Quaestor cum L. Scipioni consuli obtigisset, non attigit pecuniam, non ad exercitum profectus est* (Cic. *Verr.* 2.1.37). See Bültz 1908, 24; Sobeck 1909, 32–33; Broughton MRR, 2.63; Badian 1962, 60; Gruen 1968a, 169.

Sex. Quinctilius Varus (q. 49) (RE 17):
Sextus Quinctilius Varus was quaestor in 49. He served under L. Domitius Ahenobarbus at Corfinium, and later under Attius Varus in Africa (Caes. *civ.* 1.23.2: *erant quinque ordinis senatorii... Sex. Quintilius Varus quaestor*; *civ.* 2.28: *Erat in exercitu Vari Sextus Quintilius Varus, quem fuisse Corfinii supra demonstratum est... ne primam sacramenti, quod apud Domitium atque apud se quaestorem dixissent, memoriam de-*

ponerent...). See Bülz 1893, 75–76; Sobeck 1909, 65; Broughton MRR, 2.259. He may have held other offices in the following years (Broughton MRR, 3.178: he perhaps held the praetorship at some point between 49 and 42; Gruen 1974, 194; Rawson 1978, 195).

L. Quinctius C. f. (q. between 267 and 241) (not in RE):

See **C. Papirius (Paperios)** and **M. Publicius (Populicios) Malleolus.** A L. Quinctius C.f. is mentioned as quaestor in three inscriptions on the Egadi's *rostra* (no. 7, 8 and 10: *L(ucios) Quinctio(s) C(aii) f(ilios) quaistor probavet* (Prag 2014b, 36–41; Coarelli 2014, 103–106). The rams belonged to ships that would have taken part in the battle of the Egadi Islands in 241 at the end of the first Punic War. This L. Quinctius could be the grandfather of C. Quinctius Flamininus, praetor *peregrinus* in 177. He may have been a quaestor in the 240s, or perhaps in the late 250s, in any case between 267 and 241. Prag suggests that the presence of several Latin inscribed *rostra* on the seabed, at the site where the decisive Roman naval victory occurred, could be explained if all these rams originally came from Roman ships previously captured by the Carthaginians in earlier battles. This may have happened at the battle of Drepanum in 249, when the Carthaginians took hold of 93 Roman ships and took them back to Carthage (Pol. 1.51.12; 1.53.1). According to Tusa and Royal (2012 45. Cf. Prag 2014b, 51), those ships and rams could have been reused by the Carthaginians as part of their emergency fleet of 241, which was sunk by the Romans at the battle of the Egadi Islands. Provided that this explanation is correct, the quaestorship of Quinctius should be dated before 249. It cannot be ruled out, however, that the rams belong to ships that were constructed ca. 242 in preparation for the Egadi battle. This would date Quinctius' quaestorship around that year. The object of the *probatio* to which the inscriptions allude remains implicit: as Prag points out, it seems reasonable that the *rostra* themselves were the subject of the *probatio*, since the text was inscribed on them. The quaestor L. Quinctius appears, therefore, to have been in charge of the production of the rams and their *probatio* (the *probatio* probably extended to the construction of the whole ship). The inscriptions do not specify to which kind of quaestors they refer: they could be either the urban quaestors, the consular quaestors or the new quaestors created by 267. The latter option is attractive.

T. (Quinctius?) Crispinus (q. by 69) (not in RE):

The quaestorship of Titus (Quinctius) Crispinus is only attested in the Ciceronian discourse in favour of Fonteius: *quaestore usque ad T. Crispinum quaestorem aliter neminem solvisse* (Cic. *Font.* 1). Nothing else is known about him. It has been assumed that Crispinus was quaestor shortly before the trial against Fonteius, which was presumably held in 69. Crispinus' quaestorship has accordingly been dated by 70 (Sobeck 1909, 46: shortly before 69; Broughton MRR, 2.128 and 2.611: quaestor before 69. Cf. Syme 1955c, 68). However, Ryan 1996d, 351–352, thinks it preferable to date Crispinus' quaestorship to 69, which would mean that he was a quaestor when the trial against Fonteius was held. This proposal is not new at all. Münzer 1920, 121–122, already claimed that Crispinus was a quaestor in 69, and Willems 1878, 1.508, slightly more cautiously dated his office 'vers 69.' There is no conclusive evidence to determine with certainty the date of Crispinus' quaestorship, which at any rate should be placed by 69.

T. Quinctius T. f. Flamininus (q. 199) (cos. 198) (RE *3):
The quaestorship of Flamininus is mentioned by Livy: *quae ipsa per M. Fulvium et M'. Curium tribunos plebis impediebantur, quod T. Quinctium Flamininum consulatum ex quaestura petere non patiebantur: iam aedilitatem praeturamque fastidiri nec per honorum gradus, documentum sui dantes, nobiles homines tendere ad consulatum, sed transcendendo media summa imis continuare* (Liv. 32.7.8–10). From Livy it can be deduced that Flamininus held the consulate in the year 198 after the quaestorship. The exact meaning of the expression *consulatum ex quaestura petere*, however, has proven controversial. It seems evident that Flamininus did not hold the aedileship and the praetorship after being a quaestor, but did he hold the consulate immediately after the quaestorship? Sobeck 1909, 10, concludes that *ex quaestura* would indicate that Flamininus was quaestor presumably shortly before his consulship of 198, but he did not suggest any specific date. Broughton MRR, 1.328 and 329 n. 2, includes Flamininus among the quaestors of 199, the latest possible date. Broughton asserts that *ex quaestura* could indicate that Flamininus was quaestor in 199 and proceeded immediately to the consulship, but this expression could also be used when some time elapsed between two offices. Accordingly, Broughton concludes, Flamininus may have been quaestor between 203, when he ceased to be in command *pro praetore* at Tarentum, and 199. Badian 1971b, considers that *ex quaestura* does not mean 'straight after the quaestorship.' He then goes on to provide a rather speculative reconstruction of Flamininus' career before his consulship: according to Badian, Flamininus may have been quaestor after his military tribuneship under the consul Marcellus in 208 and before he was placed in command at Tarentum in 205. Consequently, Badian dates Flamininus' quaestorship to 206 (see also Broughton MRR, 3.179–180). More recently, Pfeilschifter 2005, 34–36, has argued in favour of 199 for Flamininus' quaestorship (Pfeilschifter describes Badian's hypothesis as 'ebenso brillant wie abenteuerlich'). In his opinion, from Livy's text it must be deduced that Flamininus moved directly from the quaestorship to the consulship. In particular the sentence *transcendendo media summa imis continuare* seems to imply, in his opinion, a continuation between the two magistracies.

The year 199 certainly seems to be the best option for Flamininus' quaestorship (in 200 he was one of the *triumviri* in charge of the recruitment of new settlers for Venusia: Liv. 31.49.6; in 201 he was one of the *decemviri* elected to assign land to veterans who had served under Scipio in Africa: Liv. 31.4.1–3 and 49.5; see Broughton MRR, 1.322 and 325). The expression *ex quaestura* appears to indicate the exceptional continuation between quaestorship and consulate, and this is why the tribunes of the plebs opposed his candidature and why Livy highlights the episode. In any case the senate judged Flamininus' candidacy for the consulship to be legal, although he had not held either of the intermediate magistracies (the aedileship and the praetorship).

Q. Raesius Q. f. (or Caesius?) (q. 49 in Asia?) (not in RE):

See **T. Pompeius Longinus.** Josephus includes Q. Raesius (Κόιντος Καίσιος Κοΐντου) in third place among the members of the *consilium* of the consul L. Cornelius Lentulus Crus in 49 in Asia (Ios. *AJ* 14.229; 14.238). Suolahti 1958, 157, argues that Longinus could have been either quaestor or military tribune, although he favoured the quaestorship. Broughton MRR, 3.45, outlines Suolahti's argument without coming down one way or another. As in the case of T. Pompeius Longinus, Suolahti's hypothesis is speculative but feasible. At any rate, Raesius' quaestorship is not expressly attested. As for his name, Suolahti opts for Raesius, although Caesius also appears in manuscripts of Josephus.

Q. Rancius Q. f. (q. before 73, maybe 74) (RE 1):

Quintus Rancius (Κόϊντος 'Ράγκιος Κοΐντου υἱὸς Κλαυδία) is a member of the *consilium* of senators included in the *SC de Oropiis* of year 73 (SIG³ 747 = RDGE 23). He is one of the *quaestorii*. Consequently, Rancius must have held the quaestorship before 73 (Broughton MRR, 2.115; 2.612; cf. Wiseman 1971, 256 no. 355; Gruen 1974, 204). Given that the senators are ordered by rank and Rancius is mentioned next to last, he was probably quaestor in 74.

Q. Rutilius (q. urb. 44) (RE 11):

See **Q. Cornelius.** Josephus quotes a decree of the senate from 44 in which Quintus Rutilius is mentioned as urban quaestor (Ios. *AJ* 14.219: δόγμα συγκλήτου ἐκ τοῦ ταμείου ἀντιγεγραμμένον ἐκ τῶν δέλτων τῶν δημοσίων τῶν ταμιευτικῶν Κοΐντω 'Ρουτιλίω Κοΐντω Κορνηλίω ταμίαις κατὰ πόλιν). See Sobeck 1909, 70; Broughton MRR, 2.325.

P. Rutilius P. f. Nudus (q. in Macedonia by 87?) (pr. by 74?) (RE 30):

P. Rutilius Nudus is honoured by the Italian *negotiatores* of Aigion in Achaea: *Italicei quei Aegei negotiantur P. Rutilium P. f. Nudum q(uaestorem)* (ILLRP 370). He was quaestor in Macedonia under C. Sentius, perhaps as early as 87, if he was praetor around 74 (Badian 1961, 492–493; Broughton MRR, 3.182). However, the date of his praetorship is controversial. He was the father-in-law of L. Calpurnius Piso, the consul of 58 (Ascon. 5 C).

C. Sallustius Crispus (q. 55? and 48?) (pr. 46) (RE 10):
Sallust was expelled from the senate in 50. Before this date, we only know that he held the tribunate of the plebs in 52. Since Sallust was born in 86, it has been suggested that he was probably a quaestor in 55 (Sobeck 1909, 56–57: quaestor in 56 or 55; Broughton MRR, 2.217). This date, however, is purely speculative, because nothing is known about Sallust's early life and his quaestorship is not actually attested. See the scepticism of Syme 1964b, 28: 'Nothing, it must be repeated, can be recovered of Sallust's career and vicissitudes before he stood for the tribunate in the summer of 53.' Earl 1966, 306, holds a similar view: he could have become a member of the senate through the tribunate of the plebs.

Sallust recovered his senatorial rank after his expulsion in 50 in the context of the Civil War. The question is how. According to Ps. Cic. *invect. in Sall.* 17 and 21, Sallust held the quaestorship again, perhaps in 48 (Broughton MRR, 2.274. Sobeck 1909, 56–57, dated his second quaestorship to 49). This is far from being certain. According to Cassius Dio (42.52.2), Sallust was praetor designate in 47 and praetor in 46, in order to become a member of the senate again. Nothing is said about a second quaestorship (see Sumner 1971, 259, who rejects the statement in the invective against Sallust. Cf. Broughton MRR, 3.184). To sum up, Sallust was probably a quaestor before holding the tribunate in 52, perhaps in 55, and he may have held the quaestorship again after 50, perhaps in 48, but there is no concrete evidence for either quaestorship

Q. Sanquinius Q. f. (q. of uncertain date, perhaps in the 40s) (RE 3):
The career of this Quintus Sanquinius is detailed in an inscription: *Q. Sanquinius Q. f. Stel. q. tr. pl. pr. pro cos.* (CIL I² 837 = CIL VI 1323 = ILS 905). We know of a M. Sanquinius Q.f. who was moneyer by the year 15. This Q. Sanquinius could be his father (but he could likewise be his brother). If this is the case, he should have carried out his political career throughout the last decades of the first century. Consequently, his quaestorship could be dated tentatively to the 40s, although not necessarily before 44. See Sobeck 1909, 78; Broughton MRR, 2.476: late Republic or early Augustan period. Cf. Wiseman 1971, 259 no 377.

Cn. Saturninus (q. 68?) (RE 27):
There is no evidence of Cnaeus Saturninus' quaestorship. He is mentioned several times by Cicero in his speech *Pro Plancio* (Cic. *Planc.* 19, 27 and 29). From these references, Broughton MRR, 2.488, concludes that he was probably a senator in 54, the date of Cicero's speech. Syme 1964a, 121–122, goes further. On the basis of the references in *Pro Plancio*, Syme does not think that his name was Appuleius Saturninus, as had been proposed through comparison with other men with these *nomen* and *cognomen*, but just Saturninus. As a consequence, Syme does not accept that he was the son of L. Appuleius, the praetor in 59. He would not be the same man as the Cn. Saturninus mentioned in Cic. *fam.* 8.14.1, who would in fact be his son. Finally, from

Cic. *Planc.* 27 (*fuit in Creta postea contubernalis Saturnini, propinqui sui, miles huius Q. Metelli*), Syme suggests that Saturninus was presumably legate or quaestor in 68. As can be seen, the date of Cn. Saturninus' quaestorship is merely conjecture.

C. Saufeius (q. 100 or 99) (RE 3):
According to App. *b.c.* 1.32, C. Saufeius was one of the supporters of the tribune of the plebs L. Appuleius Saturninus. Saufeius was killed during the riots on 10th December of the year 100 (cf. Cic. *Rab. perd.* 20; Oros. 5.17.8). Appian calls him quaestor. Hinrichs 1970, 482, identifies Saufeius as an urban quaestor for year 100, although there is no evidence of his supposed urban quaestorship (see Sobeck 1909, 27: quaestor in 100). Broughton MRR, 2.2, initially proposed the date of 99. However, in MRR, 3.22, Broughton seems inclined to date Saufeius' quaestorship to 100, on the basis of not accepting Appian's date for Saturninus' death (see Badian 1984a; Gruen 1966a, 33 n. 6), which could be placed earlier in the year; this is, nevertheless, far from being certain (see the convincing arguments of Seager 1967). Cf. Wiseman 1971, 259 no. 383; Evans 1994, 213: quaestor 100.

We do not know exactly when the quaestors took office at the time, and in particular whether they did so on 5th December, as was usual in the post-Sullan period. Assuming that Saufeius was a quaestor in office when Saturninus was killed, as Appian states, and that Saturninus died on 10th December 100, Saufeius may have been quaestor in 100 (and in this case he was in the last days of his magistracy) or in 99, provided in this case that he entered office on 5th December 100. If the assassination of Saturninus took place earlier in 100, the only possible date for Saufeius' quaestorship would be that year.

C. Scribonius C. f. Curio (q. 55?, proquaestor 54–53 or early 52? in Asia) (RE 11):
See **L. Sestius (Pansa?)**. The quaestorship of C. Scribonius Curio is not specifically attested in the ancient sources. Nevertheless, it has generally been assumed that he served as quaestor and then as proquaestor in Asia under C. Claudius Pulcher. He may have been quaestor in 54, and we know that he was not in Rome in the autumn of 53, when Cicero was designated augur in Curio's absence (Cic. *fam.* 2.5.1; 2.6.1; *Phil.* 2.4). See Bülz 1893, 42–44; Sobeck 1909, 58: quaestor in 54; Broughton MRR, 2.224, quaestor in 54, Curio may have served this year and until the end of 53 or early 52 under Claudius Pulcher; Douglas 1966, 301: 'Curio quaestor 54, therefore born by 85...'; Sumner 1973, 148. Later on, however, Broughton MRR, 3.186, changed his mind slightly and dated his quaestorship tentatively to 55 (Claudius Pulcher was proconsul in Asia since 55, and he was praetor in 56: MRR, 2.218). Cf. Lintott 2008, 171: 'his quaestorship is perhaps of 55'; Linderski 1972, 184 n. 12. An honorary inscription from Caunus of Caria mentions him without title as well as his son (Bean 1954, 89–90, nos. 23–24: Curio, quaestor of Asia in 55–54; I. Kaunos 107–108; 108: [ὁ δῆμος ὁ] Καυνίων ἐπαινεῖ κ[αὶ στεφανοῖ] / [χρυσῷ σ]τεφάνῳ, τιμᾷ δὲ καὶ εἰκό[νι χαλκῇ] / [(?)Μεμμ]ίαν, Γαΐου Μεμμίου

θυγ[ατέρα, γυναῖκα] / [δὲ Γαΐο]υ Σκριβωνίου Γαΐου υἱ[οῦ Κουρίωνος] / [δ]ιὰ τὰς γεγενημένας εὐεργ[εσίας ὑπὸ Γαΐου] / [Σκρ]ιβωνίου Γαΐου υἱοῦ Κουρίωνος εἰς [ἑα]υτόν).

Consequently, there is no sure evidence for Curio's quaestorship. It is certainly striking that his official title is not mentioned in the inscriptions of Caunus. Yet it continues to be probably that Curio accompanied Claudius Pulcher to Asia as quaestor. Therefore, he may have been quaestor in 55 and proquaestor in 54 and 53, or he could even have remained in Asia until early 52. However, his quaestorship is not completely certain. See McDermott 1972, 387, who emphasises the fact that neither the letters of Cicero nor the inscriptions of Caunus mention Curio's title; therefore, he concludes that Curio may have not held the quaestorship. According to McDermott, Curio may have been born in 82 or 81, and his tribunate in 50 may have been his first elective office. He may have been *tribunus militum* or *praefectus* under Claudius in Asia.

L. Scribonius L. f. Libo (q. 61? in Hispania Ulterior, proq. 60?, proq. pro pr. mid-60 to spring 59?) (cos. 34) (RE 20):

An inscription found in Espera (province of Cádiz, Spain) at the end of the nineteenth century (now lost) mentions a *proquaestor pro praetore* in Hispania Ulterior: *[L(ucio) Scribonio] L(ucii) f(ilio) Liboni pr[o] q(uaestore) pro pr(aetore) apsen[ti]*. Hübner, Ephemeris Epigraphica 8.502 no. 277, identifies him as Lucius Scribonius Libo, the consul of 34 (cf. Broughton MRR, 2.481). González 1982, 68 no. 99, follows Hübner's reconstruction without any further commentary. If the identification with the consul of 34 is correct, the question is when Libo was quaestor and proquaestor. A letter dated to 13th January 56 from Cicero to Lentulus Spinther presents Libo as a member of Pompey's inner circle in the senate (Cic. *fam.* 1.1.13: *Libonis et Hypsaei non obscura concursatio et contentio omniumque Pompeii familiarium studium in eam opinionem rem adduxerunt, ut Pompeius cupere videatur...*). That Libo was a member of the senate in 56 should mean that he had previously held the quaestorship, presumably in Hispania Ulterior according to the aforementioned inscription. Ferriès 2007, 462–463, proposes the year 59 for his quaestorship and 58–57 for his proquaestorship. More recently Kondratieff 2015, 434–439, has reasonably argued that Libo may have served under Caesar as quaestor in Hispania Ulterior in 61 and that he continued in this province as proquaestor from 5th December 61 to mid-60, when Caesar, desiring a triumph and the consulship, returned to Rome without waiting for the arrival of his successor, as Suetonius records (Suet. *Iul.* 18: *pacataque provincia pari festinatione, non expectato successore ad triumphum simul consulatumque decessit*). As shown in the inscription, Libo might have stayed for some months more in Hispania Ulterior as *proquaestor pro praetore* in Caesar' absence (*q. pr[o] pr. apsen[ti]*), until the arrival of the next governor.

L. Sempronius Asellio? See Asullius.

M. Se[---] (q. of uncertain date in Asia?) (not in RE):
See **M. Servilius**. A Marcus Se[---] is mentioned as quaestor (ταμίας) in an inscription from Delos (I. Délos 1844: Μάρκον Σε[---]/ ταμίαν Ῥωμ[αίων]); Broughton MRR, 2.476). Nothing else is known about his name or the date of his quaestorship, but he may have been quaestor in Asia. According to the beginning of Σε[---], the *nomen* could be Sempronius, Septimius, Sergius or Servilius. He might be the quaestor M. Servilius (RE 20) accused of *repetundis* in 51 (Cic. *fam.* 8.8.2; *Att.* 6.3.10); see below.

Ti. Sempronius Blaesus (q. 217) (RE 32):
According to Livy (22.31.5), the quaestor Tiberius Sempronius Blaesus was killed in Africa in 217, when the consul Cn. Servilius Geminus' troops were surrounded by the enemy. Sobeck 1909, 6–7, takes him as the quaestor under the consul Servilius (cf. Bülz 1908, 4). However, Broughton MRR, 1.244 and 1.246 n. 8, argues that he might not be the consul's regular quaestor, since Servilius' forces were not drawn from the consular legions.

C. Sempronius Ti. f. Gracchus (q. 126, proq. 125–124 in Sardinia) (tr.pl. 123–122) (RE 47):
C. Sempronius Gracchus was quaestor in 126 (Plut. *C.Gr.* 1.4–2.3; Cic. *Brut.* 109; *vir.ill.* 65.1). He served under the consul L. Aurelius Orestes in Sardinia and remained on the island under his command in 125 and 124 as proquaestor. Gracchus returned to Rome in 124, before his commander, in order to become a candidate for the tribunate. See Bültz 1908, 12–13; Sobeck 1909, 17–18; Broughton MRR, 1.508; 1.511 and 1.512. C. Gracchus held the quaestorship at the age of twenty-seven or twenty-eight (Sumner 1973, 70; Evans 1994, 184).

Ti. Sempronius Ti. f. Gracchus (q. 137 in Hispania Citerior) (tr.pl. 133) (RE 54):
Tiberius Sempronius Gracchus was quaestor in 137 in Hispania Citerior under the command of the consul C. Hostilius Mancinus (Plut. *Ti. Gr.* 5–7; Cic. *har. resp.* 41 and 43; *Brut.* 103; Gell. 6.9.12; Flor. 2.2.2; Vell. 2.2.1; *vir.ill.* 59.5 and 64.1). He took part in the Numantine war. See Bültz 1908, 10–11; Sobeck 1909, 15–16; Broughton MRR, 1.485; Bernstein 1978, 57. Since Ti. Gracchus was born in 163 or 162 (Sumner 1973, 58, on the basis of Plut. *C.Gr.* 1.2.), he was twenty-six when he was quaestor in Hispania (Evans 1994, 183).

C. Sempronius C. f. Tuditanus (q. 145) (cos. 129) (RE 92):
Cicero asserts that Sempronius Tuditanus was quaestor the year after the consulship of Mummius. He therefore held the quaestorship in 145: *Et quidem <de Tuditano idem> puto. Nam filius anno post quaestor fuit quam consul Mummius* (Cic. *Att.* 13.4.1. Cf. *Att.* 13.32; 13.33). See Sobeck 1909, 14–15; Broughton MRR, 1.470. Sumner 1973, 46–47, considers it very probable that he was born in 172. Evans 1994, 183, is more sceptical and claims that 'Cicero's evidence cannot be used to confirm a normal age for the quaestorship in the second century.'

P. Septimius (q. in the 70s in Illyricum?) (RE 11):
Publius Septimius was quaestor under M. Terentius Varro (RE 84), according to Varro himself: *e quis tris scripsi P[o]. Septumio, qui mihi qu<a>estor fuit...* (Varr. *l.l.* 7.109). The relationship between the two men must have been close, since Varro dedicates to Septimius three books of his work *De lingua latina*. The date of Septimius' quaestorship is, however, uncertain (see Sobeck 1909, 50: quaestor between 65 and 60; Broughton MRR, 2.477: quaestor of uncertain date. Cf. Wiseman 1971, 260 no. 390). Varro reached the praetorship, but we know nothing about it, not even the date. He served under Pompey in Hispania against Sertorius in 75 (Sall. *hist.* 2.69), later on in the Ionian sea as *legatus pro praetore* during Pompey's campaign against the pirates in 67 (Flor. 1.41.9; Plin. *n.h.* 3.101; App. *Mith.* 95) and finally again in Hispania Ulterior in the years before the outbreak of the Civil War as well as during the beginning of the conflict (Broughton MRR, 2.625). Since he was born in 116, he may have been praetor after returning from Hispania in the 70s (soon after 76 according to Broughton MRR, 2.466, and 75 according to Brennan 2000, 920–921, n. 399) with P. Septimius as quaestor in any province. However, there is no direct evidence for this. Pseudo-Asconius (p. 193 Stangl) mentions one Varro as *reus ex Asia apud L. Furium praetorem primo de pecuniis repetundis* in 75, and once again *apud P. Lentulum Suram* in 74, who was finally absolved by his cousin (*consobrinus*) Q. Hortensius in 72. Stangl identifies him with M. Terentius Varro; accordingly, P. Septimius may have been quaestor in Asia with Varro. But Magie 1950, 1125, n. 42, rejects this option convincingly: the *reus ex Asia* is probably A. Terentius Varro (RE 82) (see Arkenberg 1993, 332–333). A better option is probably to think that Varro visited Liburnia, as he comments in *r.r.* 2.10.7–9 (*cum in Liburniam venisses*; see also Plin. *n.h.* 3.142), after his praetorship, and that he may have held, with Septimius as quaestor, the province of Illyricum in the 70s; C. Cosconius was indeed fighting in Illyricum ca. 78–76, so Varro may have succeeded him some years later.

M'. Sergius M'. f. (q. of uncertain date) (RE 18):
This Manius Sergius is only known through a brief reference in Varro: *...sed etiam quaestores, Commentarium indicat vetus Anquisitionis M'. Sergii, Mani filii, quaestoris, qui capitis accusavit Trogum* (Varr. *l. l.* 6.90). Varro gives no hint about the chronology

of his quaestorship in his Commentarium Anquisitionis. The word vetus may suggest a very ancient time in archaic Rome, but the mention of praetores in the plural implies that Sergius must have been quaestor after 242, when the second praetorship was introduced. There is no real evidence to determine even approximately the date of Sergius' quaestorship. See Sobeck 1909, 73; Broughton 2.477: the date is after 242 but otherwise remains uncertain.

M. Sergius Silus (q. urb. 116 or 115?) (RE 42):
The only evidence of this Marcus Sergius Silus is found in some coins that he minted as quaestor, in all probability as urban quaestor. They include the legend *M' · SERGI SILVS Q*. The date of his quaestorship has been controversial. Sobeck 1909, 24, dates it to 104, following the suggestion made by Babelon for the coins. Broughton MRR, 2.13, prefers 94, although he adds a question mark. Crawford RRC, 302 no. 286, dates the coins to 116 or 115 (cf. Broughton MRR, 3.192). According to Crawford, he was not the father of Catilina, who was a Lucius, but rather belonged to a different branch of the *gens* Sergia. We do not have any other information about his political career. The date of his quaestorship remains hypothetical.

Fig. 10: M. Sergius Silus, quaestor 116–115. AR Denarius. Rome. Helmeted head of Roma right; around ROMA EX S. C. Horseman galloping left with sword and severed head aloft; below Q and M. SERGI. SILVS in exergue. Crawford RRC, no. 286/1.

Q. Sertorius (q. 91? proq. 90?) (RE 3):
We have evidence of Quintus Sertorius' quaestorship through Plutarch, who states that Sertorius was elected quaestor after returning from Hispania (Plut. *Sert*. 4.1: ἐκ τούτου Σερτώριος ἐν τῇ Ἰβηρίᾳ διεβοήθη, καὶ ὅτε πρῶτον ἐπανῆκεν εἰς Ῥώμην, ταμίας ἀποδείκνυται τῆς περὶ Πάδον Γαλατίας ἐν δέοντι), where he had served under T. Di-

dius. Didius was consul and then proconsul in Hispania Citerior between 98 and 93 (Broughton MRR, 2.559). Upon his return to Rome, Didius celebrated his triumph on 10th June 93 (Inscr.Ital. 13.1.85, p. 562). On the basis of this evidence, Sertorius' quaestorship was initially dated to 90 (Bültz 1908, 23; Sobeck 1909, 28–29; Broughton MRR, 2.27; Berve 1929, 218 n. 1; Evans 1994, 215). However, the year 91 is preferable. According to Plutarch, the Sertorius' election as quaestor took place promptly after his return from Hispania. This statement seems to point to his election in 92 rather than in 91 (Sumner 1973, 107–108. Cf. Spann 1987, 20–24; Broughton MRR, 3.193). Plutarch continues by saying that Sertorius was assigned to Cisalpine Gaul at a critical time, since the *Bellum Sociale* was threatening (Mommsen Röm.St., II 572 with nn. 1–2, suggests the existence of a *provincia Gallica* with capital in Ravenna in which Sertorius had served; this hypothesis has no basis). In Cisalpine Gaul, Sertorius levied troops and procured arms. If Sertorius' quaestorship is dated to 91, this means that it coincided with the tribunate of Drusus, whose death precipitated the outbreak of war. In all likelihood, Sertorius remained in Cisalpine Gaul as proquaestor, at least at the beginning of the war. We do not know the name of the general under whose command he served.

Servaeus (q. before 51) (RE 3):
In a letter sent to Cicero Caelius calls Servaeus *tribunus plebis designatus* (Cic. fam. 8.4.2). He was then a *quaestorius*. The letter was written in August 51. Consequently, this Servaeus was elected tribune in 51 for 50. He must have been quaestor before 51, but any date is speculative. Cf. Wiseman 1971, 260 no. 395.

L. Serveilius L. f. (q. of uncertain date) (RE 17):
The political career of this Serveilius is recorded in an inscription from Rome: *L. Serveili L. f. L. n. q. III (vir)*... (CIL I² 841 = CIL VI 31616). Sobeck 1909, 79, only dares to affirm that the inscription dates to the Republic. Broughton MRR, 2.477, dates it to the late Republic. It is impossible to give even a hypothetical date for Serveilius' quaestorship.

M. Servilius (q. 56? in Asia?) (RE 20):
See **M. Se[---]**. Marcus Servilius (he is different from the tribune of the plebs in 43) was accused of *repetundis* in 51, because he had supposedly received money illegally extracted by C. Claudius Pulcher, the proconsul in Asia in 55–53 (Cic. fam. 8.8.2; Att. 6.3.10). From these references, Broughton MRR, 2.496, rightly concludes that Servilius was probably a senator in 51. Consequently, he must have been quaestor earlier, but there is no evidence of when he held the office. Sumner 1973, 146, reasonably supposes that Servilius belonged to Claudius Pulcher's staff in Asia, probably as a legate, since C. Scribonius Curio and L. Sestius Pansa were his quaestors thro-

ughout his stay in the province. It follows that 55 was the latest date for Servilius to enter into the senate, and that therefore he may have held the quaestorship in 56. See Broughton MRR, 3.193: the latest probable date for his quaestorship is 56. If he held the quaestorship in Asia, he could be the Marcus Se[---] mentioned in an inscription from Delos (I. Délos 1844).

Cn. Servilius Cn. f. Caepio (q. end second century in Macedonia) (RE 47):
A Greek inscription from Thessalonica mentions Cnaeius Servilius Caepio as ταμίας 'Ρωμαίων (IG X 2,1 135, *ll*. 1–3: ἡ πόλις Γναῖον Σερουίλιον / Γναίου υἱὸν Καιπίωνα / ταμίαν 'Ρωμαίων). Münzer identifies him in RE with the father of Servilia, wife of Ap. Claudius Pulcher, consul in 54, who died in a shipwreck while still young (Cic. *Att*. 12.20.2). Münzer suggests 104 as the date of Servilius' death. This has led Broughton MRR, 1.556, to date his quaestorship tentatively to 105 (see also Sarikakis 1971, 173; Evans 1994, 211), which is a rather speculative date. In any case, Servilius Caepio's quaestorship should be dated to the end of the second century (Broughton MRR, 1.558 n. 6 and 2.618. Cf. Bülz 1893, 38–39; Sobeck 1909, 79: Servilius' quaestorship is impossible to date).

Q. Servilius Caepio (q. urb. 103?) (pr. 91?) (RE 50):
See **L. Calpurnius Piso Caesoninus.** As *quaestor urbanus*, Quintus Servilius Caepio opposed the grain law that L. Appuleius Saturninus intended to pass as tribune of the plebs: *Cum Lucius Saturninus legem frumentariam...laturus esset, Q. Caepio, qui per id temporis quaestor urbanus erat, docuit senatum aerarium pati non posse largitionem tantam. Senatus decrevit, si eam legem ad populum ferat, adversus rem publicam videri ea facere: Saturninus ferre coepit, conlegae intercedere; ille nihilominus sitellam detulit. Caepio ut illum contra SC intercedentibus conlegis adversus rem publicam vidit facere, cum viris bonis impetum facit, pontes disturbat, cistas deiecit, impedimento est, quo setius feratur; arcessitur Caepio maiestatis* (*Rhet. Her.* 1.21; cf. 2.17). Caepio's quaestorship is also known through some denarii in which his name appears together with that of Piso and the abbreviation *Q*(uaestores). On the reverse, the abbreviations *AD · FRV · EMV / EX · S · C* must be understood as *ad frumentum emundum ex senatus consulto* ('to purchase grain in accordance with a senatorial decree'). On these coins see Crawford RRC, 330–331. Leaving aside whether the other quaestor, Piso Caesoninus, was the quaestor Ostiensis as proposed by Crawford, there is no doubt that Caepio issued the coins as quaestor urbanus. The date of Caepio's quaestorship is more problematic. It has been suggested that the purchase of grain by the state was the senatorial response to the attempt of the tribune Saturninus to introduce his *lex frumentaria*. Indeed, this is the bill to which Caepio was opposed, as shown by the *Rhetorica ad Herennium*. Therefore, the date of Caepio's quaestorship depends on the date of Saturninus' grain law. Although this bill has sometimes been dated to the second tribunate of Saturninus in 100 (and as a consequence Caepio's quaestorship

has been placed in the same year: Sobeck 1909, 27; Broughton 1.576; Sumner 1973, 116; Evans 1994, 213), there are good reasons to move it to his first tribunate in 103. Gruen 1966a, 44 n. 71, 57 n. 151, considers 103 a more appropriate date for Saturninus' *lex frumentaria* and dates Caepio's quaestorship to this year. Before Gruen, other scholars had already reached the same conclusion: Last 1932, 165; Passerini 1934, 113–115; Badian 1964, 63 n. 9. Broughton MRR, 3.21, follows Gruen: 'the grain law of Saturninus should more probably be dated to his first tribunate in 103 than to his second in 100' (the same conclusion in Benness 1991, 38). Schneider 1982–83, 209, provides further arguments. He rightly argues that Saturninus' grain law must be connected with the revolt of the slaves that began in Sicily in 104. The rebellion on the island must have resulted in a food shortage at Rome. As a result, the *lex frumentaria* of Saturninus should be dated to 103 as a response to the shortage of food in the city. Consequently, the coinage of the quaestors Piso and Caepio should have the same date, if this is understood as a senatorial reaction to Saturninus' law. The year 103 is therefore the most probable date for Piso and Caepio's quaestorships. Caepio was no doubt *quaestor urbanus*.

Q. Servilius Caepio (q. 67?) (RE 40–42):
The date of Quintus Servilius Caepio's quaestorship is hypothetical. He died at Aenus (Thrace) in 67, when he was on his way to Asia (Plut. *Cat.min.* 11.1: ὁ ἀδελφὸς εἰς τὴν Ἀσίαν βαδίζων ἐνόσησε περὶ Θρᾴκην ἐν Αἴνῳ). Florus gives a list of those who served under Pompey's command in the war against the pirates, in which a Caepio is mentioned as being in charge of Asia (Flor. 1.49.9–10). On the basis of this evidence, Badian 1957, 327, suggests that this Caepio (Cato Uticensis' half-brother) was quaestor under Pompey in 67. This hypothesis is taken up by Broughton MRR, 2.194 and 3.193, as well as Syme 1987, 323: perhaps a quaestor in 68 or 67.

C. Servilius Glaucia (q. before 108) (pr. 100) (RE 65):
C. Servilius Glaucia was a senator in 102 (App. *b.c.* 1.28). This means that the censors of 108 had included him in the list of senators (the following censors were elected for 102). Although his quaestorship is not attested, he may have been quaestor before 108 at an uncertain date. Broughton MRR, 1.546, dates Glaucia's quaestorship tentatively to 109 as the latest year before the censorship of 108, but obviously he may have been quaestor earlier than this. Cf. Sumner 1973, 121. See, however, Evans 1994, 187 and 210–211: Glaucia might not have held the quaestorship and instead could have been a senator in 102 as a *tribunicius*.

P. Servilius P. f. Isauricus (q. before 61) (cos. 48 and 41) (RE 67):
Cicero describes a senatorial session in which Publius Servilius Isauricus spoke among the quaestorians at the end of the debate: *Et ita factum est a P. Servilio filio, qui*

in postremis sententiam dixit, sed immutari hoc tempore non potest (Cic. *Att.* 1.19.9). The meeting of the senate took place in March 60. He had therefore held the quaestorship in 61 or earlier in order to become a member of the senate. The actual date is unknown. See Broughton MRR, 2.184 and 2.619: quaestor by 60. However, Broughton MRR, 3.196: his quaestorship should be dated in or before 61. Cf. Badian 1959a, 83.

Servius Cordus (q. 49? proq. 48 in Cyprus?) (RE 3):
Lucan mentions a Cordus who as quaestor had supposedly accompanied Pompey to Egypt. According to Lucan, this Cordus was the one who burnt Pompey's corpse: *Cordus / quaestor ab Icario Cinyreae litore Cypri / infaustus Magni fuerat comes* (Lucan. 8.715–717). However, other sources unanimously allude to Philippus, a freedman of Pompey, as the one responsible for the cremation (see Plut. *Pomp.* 80; Val.Max. 1.8.9; Cass.Dio 42.5.6; App. *b.c.* 2.86). Only a passage in *De viris illustribus* presents some resemblance to Lucan's text, but it refers to a Servius Codrus instead of Cordus and it does not mention whether he held an office (*vir.ill.* 77.9: *Truncus Nilo iactatus a Servio Codro rogo inustus humatusque est inscribente sepulcro: Hic positus est Magnus*). The quaestor Cordus of Lucan is otherwise unknown and he has generally been thought to not really have existed. See Brennan 1969, 103–104; Seager ²2002, 168; Noy 2000, 190; Losehand 2008, 207–209: Lucan implicitly wanted the reader to relate this invented Cordus with someone well known of the same name, such as Aulus Cremutius Cordus or perhaps C. Mucius Cordus Scaevola. Nonetheless, if this Servius Cordus (or Codrus) really existed, the evidence we have would make him a quaestor in 48 in Cyprus (Broughton MRR, 3.197: quaestor or proquaestor 48; Syme 1955c, 69; Wiseman 1971, 261 no. 396: 'q. Cypr. 48'). According to Cass.Dio 41.43.1–3, the Pompeians did not organise elections in Thessalonica for the year 48, so that all men with offices were actually promagistrates. This means that Cordus would have been a proquaestor in 48. We do not know whether 48 was his first year as a promagistrate. He may have been quaestor in 49, but the year 50 is also possible. See Ryan 1998b, 254: the year 49 would be the *terminus post quem* for his quaestorship.

P. Sestius (q. 414) (RE 15):
The quaestorship of Publius Sestius in 414 is known thanks to Livy: *Itaque cum fremitus aperte esset, et quaestor P. Sestius eadem violentia coerceri putaret seditionem posse qua mota erat...* (Liv. 4.54.2. Cf. Zon. 7.20). Sestius served under the military tribune with consular power P. Postumius Albinus Regillensis in the war against the Aequi. In the middle of a riot, Postumius died, stoned by his own soldiers, and his quaestor Sestius was also injured. The episode is of doubtful authenticity, especially when we consider the similarities with the death of A. Postumius Albinus (consul of 99) in 89 who was also killed by his own troops. See Bülz 1908, 3; Sobeck 1909, 3–4; Broughton MRR, 1.75; Ogilvie 1965, 610.

P. Sestius L. f. (q. 63, proq. 62–61 in Macedonia) (pr. by 54) (RE 6):
Publius Sestius was assigned by lot as quaestor to C. Antonius in 63: *quaestor hic C. Antonii, collegae mei, fuit sorte, sed societate consiliorum meus* (Cic. *Sest.* 8; cf. 11–12). He fought under Antonius against Catilina in Etruria and went to Macedonia as proquaestor in 62, also under the command of Antonius. See Bülz 1893, 26–27; Sobeck 1909, 51–52, who makes Sestius an urban quaestor in 63; Broughton MRR, 2.168, 2.176 and 2.181.

L. Sestius (Pansa?) (q. in the 60s or 50s? in Asia) (RE 10):
See **C. Scribonius Curio.** An inscription from Pergamum mentions a quaestor of the name Lucius Sestius (OGIS 452: ὁ δῆμος ἐτ[ί]μησεν / Λεύκιον Σήστ[ι]ον τὸν τα/μίαν, τὸν ἑαυτ[οῦ] πάτρωνα / καὶ εὐε[ργέτη]ν). It has usually been identified with the L. Sestius Pansa to whom Cicero alludes (Cic. *Q. fr.* 2.9.2). According to the inscription, he was quaestor in Asia, but the date is uncertain. Broughton MRR, 2.224, dates his quaestorship to 54 on the basis of Cicero's letter to his brother. In this letter, written in 54, Cicero speaks of L. Sestius Pansa, who had opposed the wishes of Magnesia under Sipylus to honour Quintus with a *mentio honorifica*. However, C. Scribonius Curio may have been the quaestor or the proquaestor in Asia in 54 under the command of C. Claudius Pulcher (pr. 56). Sobeck 1909, 79–80, draws attention to this circumstance and consequently concludes that L. Sestius Pansa was quaestor in Asia in the first century, before Q. Cicero was governor between 61 and 58. It is impossible to know exactly when.

If the year 54 does not seem feasible for L. Sestius Pansa's quaestorship in Asia, we must analyse Cicero's reference differently and not identify the L. Sestius mentioned in the inscription from Pergamum with the L. Sestius Pansa from the letter. Consequently, as Sobeck points out, Sestius was certainly quaestor or/and proquaestor in Asia in the first century and he may have held this office in the sixties, or perhaps in the fifties, but the date remains uncertain.

L. Sestius P. f. Quirinalis Albinianus (proq. 44–42 in Macedonia) (cos. suff. 23) (RE 3):
As proquaestor, L. Sestius Quirinalis (on his name see Broughton MRR, 3.197; he is the son of P. Sestius RE 6) provided in 44 a fleet for Brutus and Cassius (Cic. *Att.* 16.4.4. Cf. Broughton MRR, 2.326). The following two years he served as proquaestor under the command of Brutus in Macedonia. From this time, we know of some coins that he minted and that bear the legend *L · SESTI · PRO · Q* on the obverse and *Q · CAEPIO · BRVTVS · PRO · COS* on the reverse (Crawford RRC, 515, no. 502, dates them to 43–42. Cf. Woytek 2003, 518–519). See Bülz 1893, 34–37; Sobeck 1909, 72; Broughton MRR, 2.362–363. Sumner 1971, 369, dates Sestius' quaestorship to year 44. Sestius was, according to Sumner, several years under age for the quaestorship.

Fig. 11: Q. Caepio Brutus, proconsul, and L. Sestius Quirinalis, proquaestor ca. 44–42. AR Denarius. Rome. Draped head of Libertas right; L. SESTI. PRO Q. Tripod between sacrifica laxe and simpulum; around Q. CAEPIO BRVTVS PRO COS. Crawford RRC, no. 502/2.

P. Sestullius (q. urb. 61) (RE Sextilius 13):

See **M. Curtius Peducaenus.** Cicero is clear about who held the urban quaestorship in the year 61: M. Curtius and a man supposedly called P. Sextilius (Cic. *Flacc.* 30: *quid? Postero anno nonne M. Curio et P. Sextilio quaestoribus pecunia in classem est erogata?*) (Sobeck 1909, 53; Broughton MRR, 2.180; cf. 3.198). However, Mitchell 1979, demonstrates that the correct reading of the manuscripts of Cicero's *Pro Flacco* is Sestullius instead of Sextilius. Mitchell's emendation is followed by Badian 1980, 472: the quaestor of 61 turns out to be a Sestullius; he was clearly the father of the senator in the *SC de Panamareis*, dated to the year 39.

C. Sextilius Rufus (q. 49? in Cyprus) (RE 23):

We have evidence of the quaestorship of C. Sextilius Rufus in a letter that Cicero addressed to him: *M. Cicero C. Sextilio Rufo quaestori sal. d.* (Cic. *fam.* 13.48). He was quaestor in Cyprus, a territory that belonged to the province of Cilicia. The date is uncertain, but must be after Cicero's proconsulship in Cilicia in 51–50 and before Caesar returned Cyprus to the Ptolemies in 47 (Cass.Dio 42.35.5), as a consequence very probably in 49. The first scholars who tackled the topic provided different answers: Sobeck 1909, 65: quaestor in 49 or 48 (cf. Bülz 1893, 61–62); Broughton MRR, 2.287 and 2.620: quaestor in 47; Marshall 1964: 48 or 47. Nevertheless, Broughton has rectified this first view in favour of the year 49 (Broughton MRR, 3.198). Broughton follows Badian 1965, 113–115 (see also Sumner 1971, 263). According to Badian, Cicero's letter should be dated to the beginning of 49. If the letter was sent in 48, Cicero could not have written it without reference to politics or war in that troubled year. Sextilius was not one of Caesar's appointees, but one of the last quaestors elected before the outbreak of the Civil War. He may have been sent to Cyprus as a special quaestor, or may have been the regular quaestor in Cilicia appointed to the island by the governor of the province, P. Sestius. Note that Cicero apparently points to Sextilius as the first quaestor sent to Cyprus (*quum primus in eam insulam quaestor veneris*).

C. Sextius Calvinus (q. 111 in Numidia) (pr. by 92) (RE 1 and 21):
A quaestor of the name Sextius (RE 1) served in 111 under the command of the consul L. Calpurnius Bestia in the war against Jugurtha: *Ceterum interea fidei causa mittitur a consule Sextius quaestor in oppidum Iugurthae Vagam* (Sal. *Iug.* 29.4). Sallust does not give his *praenomen*. This Sextius has been identified with Publius Sextius (RE 9), the praetor-designate who was convicted of bribery by 90 (Cic. *Brut.* 180). See Bültz 1908, 17; Sobeck 1909, 21; Broughton MRR, 1.541 and 1.543 n. 4; Evans 1994, 210. However, it seems more likely that he should be identified with C. Sextius Calvinus (RE 21), an elegant orator of the same age as C. Flavius Frimbria and M. Junius Brutus mentioned by Cicero (Cic. *Brut.* 130), son of the consul of 124 (RE 20). He was later praetor by 92 (Broughton MRR, 2.18). See Sumner 1973, 76–77. Broughton MRR, 3.198–199, accepts this thesis. Cicero calls him C. Sextius (*de orat.* 2.246) or just Calvinus (*de orat.* 2.249).

C. Sicinius (q. 74?) (RE 7):
See **C. Visellius Varro.** According to Cicero, C. Sicinius died as a senator of quaestorian rank: *C. Sicinius igitur Q. Pompei illius, qui censor fuit, ex filia nepos quaestorius mortuus est* (Cic. *Brut.* 263). We also know that Sicinius was a contemporary of C. Visellius Varro. Sumner 1973, 138: if Sicinius was born in the same year as Visellius (i.e. 105), his quaestorship should also be dated to the same year, by 74. See Sobeck 1909, 80: quaestorship at the beginning of the first century; Broughton MRR, 2.128: quaestor in 70?

Q. Silius (q. 409) (RE 10):
See **P. Aelius** and **P. Papius.** According to Liv. 4.54.2–3, Silius was one of the three first plebeians to be elected quaestors (Sobeck 1909, 4; Broughton MRR, 1.78). For the doubts about their historicity see Ogilvie 1965, 616.

C. Sosius (q. 66) (pr. 49) (see RE 2: this man is mistaken with C. Sosius cos. 32):
Cicero claims that C. Sosius was the quaestor of the consul M'. Aemilius Lepidus in 66: *C. Sosius praetor in Formianum venit ad M'. Lepidum vicinum nostrum quoius quaestor fuit* (Cic. *Att.* 8.6.1). See Sobeck 1909, 48; Broughton MRR, 2.154 and 2.257: he should be distinguished from Marcus Antonius' legate who became consul in 32. Cf. Wiseman 1971, 262 no. 407.

C. Staienus. See C. Aelius Paetus Staienus.

L. Stertinius (q. urb. 168) (RE 6):
See **L. Manlius [Acidinus?]**. The urban quaestor Lucius Stertinius was sent by the senate to Brundisium in order to bring one of Masinissa's sons, Misagenes, to Rome and accommodate him in the city: *haud ita multo post de altero Masinissae filio Misagene litterae adlatae sunt... <ad> eum cum isdem muneribus, quae data Romae fratri eius erant, L. Stertinius quaestor Brundisium missus <iussus>que curare, ut aedes hospi<tio>...* (Liv. 45.14.9. Cf. Val.Max. 5.1.1). See Sobeck 1909, 12; Broughton MRR, 1.428.

P. Sulpicius (q. 69) (RE 15):
According to Cicero, Publius Sulpicius was one of the jurors in the trial against Verres, a position that he had to leave on the Nones of December when he began his quaestorship (Cicero does not mention the quaestorship expressly, but this was the only magistracy which began on that date every year): *P. Sulpicius, iudex tristis et integer, magistratum ineat oportet Nonis Decembribus* (Cic. Verr. 1.30). There is no doubt, therefore, that Sulpicius held the quaestorship in 69 (Sobeck 1909, 46–47; Broughton MRR, 2.132). His name, however, has been controversial. Although Cicero just names him Sulpicius, he has been identified with P. Sulpicius Rufus (RE 93), one of the praetors in 48 (Broughton MRR, 2.132 and 2.624; Sumner 1971, 249–250: he must be the brother of the well-known jurist Ser. Sulpicius Rufus). This identification is, nonetheless, highly unlikely, because of the long interval between the quaestorship in 69 and the praetorship in 48 (Broughton MRR, 3.202). P. Sulpicius (RE 15) and P. Sulpicius Rufus (RE 93) are, therefore, two different individuals. Also, he should not be identified as P. Sulpicius Galba (RE 55), which has been recently suggested by Daguet-Gagey 2015, 308–310: the defendant disqualified P. Galba as a juror (Cic. Verr. 2.1.18: *qui cum P. Galbam iudicem reiecisset*). It has usually been assumed that Galba held the curule aedileship in 69 (Broughton MRR, 3.201; Crawford RRC, 418 no. 406) and the praetorship in 66. Following Ryan 1994a, Daguet-Gagey dates Galba's aedileship to 68, after his supposed quaestorship in 69. This concentration of offices in such a short period of time seems unlikely; consequently it seems more probable that Cicero was speaking of two different people, P. Sulpicius (RE 15) and P. (Sulpicius) Galba (RE 55) in the aforementioned passages.

An interesting additional issue still remains. Since he was a juror, Sulpicius was certainly a senator at the time. However, he had not yet held his first magistracy, the quaestorship, which gave access to the senate. This circumstance could be explained if he was one of the new senators appointed directly by Sulla during his dictatorship (Broughton MRR, 3.200; cf. Nicolet 1966–1974, 585). Or, alternatively, he could have become a senator immediately after being elected quaestor in the elections of 70 for the year 69, that is, as quaestor designate (Box 1942).

Ser. Sulpicius Q. f. Rufus (q. Ostiensis 74) (cos. 51) (RE 95):
See **L. Licinius Murena.** Cicero asserts that Servius Sulpicius Rufus was the colleague of L. Licinius Murena in the quaestorship and calls him *quaestor Ostiensis* (Cic. Mur. 18: ...*tu illam cui, cum quaestores sortiuntur, etiam adclamari solet, Ostiensem, non tam gratiosam et inlustrem quam negotiosam et molestam*). The date of Sulpicius Rufus' quaestorship consequently depends on the year assigned to Murena's as well as on the chronology of the outbreak of the Third Mithridatic War. Although both 75 and 74 are theoretically possible, Broughton MRR, 2.103 and 2.109 n. 5, argues convincingly for 74: given that Sulpicius Rufus and Murena are not named as colleagues of Cicero and Murena soon became a legate under Lucullus, Sulpicius Rufus should be included among the quaestors of 74. See Sobeck 1909, 38–39; Cébeillac Gervasoni 2002, 64. Ryan 1996f, 40 n. 19: as Cicero describes Sulpicius' *provincia Ostiensis* as 'busy and annoying,' he could not have spoken this way if he had been quaestor at a time of abundant supplies. It is therefore relevant to note that Q. Creticus was beset by rioters during a food shortage while campaigning for the praetorship in 75 (Sall. *hist.* 2.45 M.) and that M. Seius provided grain to the people as curule aedile in 74 (Cic. *off.* 2.58). Consequently, Ryan dates Sulpicius' quaestorship to 74.

Ser. Sulpicius Rufus (q. 50 or 49?) (RE 96):
He was the son of the famous jurist. His presumed quaestorship is not attested. Actually, he does not appear in Sobeck's book nor in Broughton' list of magistrates (but Broughton MRR, 3.203: he was perhaps a senator in 43). However, Syme conjectures that Servius Sulpicius Rufus may have been quaestor in 50 or 49, without really providing evidence for his proposal. See Syme 1955c, 69–70; 1981, 424 n. 14; 1987, 325: 'a quaestorship c. 50 will cause no discomfort.'

C. Tarquitius P. f. (q. 81 in Hispania) (RE 1):
See **L. Fabius Hispaniensis.** C. Tarquitius was quaestor under C. Annius (Plut. *Sert.* 7) in Hispania in 81, as the coins struck by him show. They bear the legend $C \cdot ANNI \cdot T \cdot F \cdot T \cdot N \cdot PRO \cdot COS \cdot EX \cdot S \cdot C$ on the obverse, and $C \cdot TARQVITI \cdot P \cdot F \cdot Q$ on the reverse (Crawford RRC, 381–386 no. 366). According to Crawford, these coins were struck in Hispania after a first series that was issued in Italy by the quaestor L. Fabius Hispaniensis, also for Annius. The presence of two quaestors serving under Annius should be explained, in Crawford's opinion, by the fact that he was in charge of both Hispanian provinces. This last point has been much debated. If it is accepted that Fabius Hispaniensis deserted to Sertorius because he was proscribed by Sulla (Bülz 1893, 3; Konrad 1987, 521. *Contra* Hinard 1991), we can assume that Tarquitius substituted Fabius when he was dispossessed of his office. Consequently, both quaestors did not serve in Hispania under Annius simultaneously but in succession (Antela-Bernárdez, 2012, 38 and 2013). This C. Tarquitius P.f. is not the same as C. Tarquitius Priscus (Heurgon 1953, 407–408, and Spann 1987, 173, consider both individuals to be the

same person; cf. Wiseman 1971, 264 no. 420), who fought in the ranks of Sertorius as legate and conspired against him at the end of his life (Sall. *hist.* 3.81 and 83 M. = McGushin 3.77 and 79; the distinction between the two individuals is already emphasised in Cichorius 1922, 167–168). As for the date of Tarquitius' quaestorship, the year 81 has been unanimously accepted, but we cannot dismiss the possibility that he may already have come to Hispania with Annius in 82. See also Bülz 1893, 3–4; Sobeck 1909, 34; Broughton MRR, 2.77 and 3.203.

Terentius Varro (q. 154 in Hispania) (RE 77):
According to Appian, the quaestor Terentius Varro was killed in battle by the Lusitanians in 154 (App. *Ib.* 56: οἳ Λυσιτανοὶ καλοῦνται, Πουνίκου σφῶν ἡγουμένου, τὰ Ῥωμαίων ὑπήκοα ἐλῄζοντο καὶ τοὺς στρατηγοῦντας αὐτῶν, Μανίλιόν τε καὶ Καλπούρνιον Πείσωνα, τρεψάμενοι κτείνουσιν ἑξακισχιλίους καὶ ἐπ' αὐτοῖς Τερέντιον Οὐάρρωνα ταμίαν). His *praenomen* is unknown. He may have been Calpurnius Piso's quaestor (cf. Richardson 2000, 151; on the identity of this Calpurnius Piso, Díaz Fernández 2015, 536, n. 87. See Bültz 1908, 9; Sobeck 1909, 13; Broughton MRR, 1.450; Arkenberg 1993, 331–332: he could be the father of the M. Terentius Varro who adopted M. Licinius Lucullus (cos. 73).

A.? (Terentius) Varro (q. 49, proq. 48) (RE 78):
See **M. Terentius Varro** (RE 84, suppl. 6). We know some coins that bear the legend *VARRO · PRO Q* on the obverse and *MAGN · PRO COS* on the reverse. Crawford RRC, 463 no. 447, dates them to 49. According to Crawford, there was a military mint that travelled with Pompey and these coins were struck in Greece in preparation for the campaign that ended at Pharsalus. He is not the same man as M. Terentius Varro (Reatinus) (RE 84, suppl. 6), the *legatus pro praetore* of 49 in Hispania, as was thought decades ago (in favour of this option without new arguments, see Amela Valverde 1990–1991, 181–183; see Broughton MRR, 2.100 n. 7, 2.264 and 3.204). More recently Woytek 2003, 113–118, has argued that the issue was coined in Greece in 48 (as well as Crawford RRC no. 446: see **Cn. Calpurnius Cn. f. Piso [Frugi]**) and he identifies the proquaestor as the Aulus Varro who is mentioned fighting on the Pompeian side in Illyria during the Civil War (Caes. *civ.* 3.19.4). He would be one of the quaestors of 49 who had fled Rome with Pompey.

A. Terentius A. f. Varro (q. 88 or 87?) (RE 82):
Broughton MRR, 2.72 (cf. 2.625) includes A. Terentius Varro among the legates of Licinius Murena in Asia in 82. His conclusion is based on two inscriptions dedicated to Varro as πρεσβευτής (SIG³ 745 = IG 12.1.48 – ILS 8773 – ILLRP 369; see also IGRP 1.843). A fragmentary inscription from Delos (I. Délos 1698 = CIL I² 738: *A. Terentium A. f. Varro[nem leg.] / Italicei et Graecei quei Ḍelei negoti[antur] /* [Α]ὖλον Τερέντιον Αὔλου

υἱὸν Οὐ[άρρωνα πρεσβευτὴν] / [ʿΡ]ωμαίων, Ἰταλικοὶ καὶ Ἕλληνες οἱ κατ[οικοῦντες ἐν Δήλωι]) has also been linked with Varro's *legatio* under Murena's command. However, in his review of Degrassi's ILLRP (*JRS* 58, 1968, 245–246), Badian reconstructs this inscription in the following way: *A. Terentium A. f. Varro[nem q.]*. According to Badian, Varro may have been quaestor in 88 or 87 in one of the provinces in the East, before being a legate under Murena. Badian's hypothesis, therefore, provides the only possible evidence for Varro's quaestorship. Díaz Fernández, 2015, 559–560, n. 210, has recently proposed that Varro could have been proconsul of Asia after a praetorship in 78; hence his later prosecution *de pecuniis repetundis ex Asia* in 75–74 (Ps. Ascon. 193 Stangl). Since the Delos' inscription is only partially preserved, it could also be reconstructed *A. Terentiuṃ Ạ. f. Varro[nem pro cos.] / Italicei et Graecei quei Ḍelei negoti[antur]*.

C. Terentius C. f. Varro (before 222) (cos. 216) (RE 83):

C. Terentius Varro was praetor in 218 and consul in 216 (Broughton MRR, 1.238 and 1.247). Earlier he held the quaestorship and was aedile twice: *quaesturaque et duabus aedilitatibus, plebeia et curuli, postremo et praetura, perfunctus, iam ad consulatus spem cum attolleret animos* (Liv. 22.26.3). Sobeck 1909, 6, dates his quaestorship before 220. Broughton MRR, 1.233 and 2.625, places this office by 222, considering this year the latest possible date (the same date is given by Arkenberg 1993, 327). Since Varro held three offices before his praetorship of 218 (the plebeian and the patrician aedileships as well as the quaestorship), it seems unlikely, though not impossible, that he did so in consecutive years. As a consequence, he should have been quaestor before 222, at a date impossible to determine (see Sumner 1973, 33; Develin 1979, 70).

M. Terentius Varro (q. 85?) (pr. in 70s?) (RE 84, Suppl. 6):

See **A.? (Terentius) Varro** (RE 78). This Marcus Terentius Varro is the intellectual. Since Varro was thirty years old in 86 (Varr. *Sat. Men.* 478B: *inde caballum reduxi ad censorem*), he may have been quaestor in 85, although there is no evidence for it (Broughton MRR, 2.57; 3.204; Arkenberg 1993, 335–336). Badian 1962, 60, conjectures that Varro was quaestor in 85 under the command of Cinna. It was at that time that he may have been in Liburnia on the northeastern Adriatic coast (Varr. *r.r.* 2.10.7–9: *cum in Liburniam venisses*). Varro could have crossed with the advanced party to organise the landing of the rest of the army. However, it is difficult to accept Varro as quaestor under Cinna, since he conducted his political career under Sulla's right-hand man, Pompey (see above on P. Septimius). Immediately after his quaestorship, Varro went to Athens, where we find him studying philosophy between 84 and 82. He must not be identified (so Sobeck 1909, 37) with the proquaestor Varro (RE 78) to whom some coins allude (Crawford RRC, 463 no. 447; Woytek 2003, 113–116).

M. Terentius Varro Gibba (q. 46 in Cisalpine Gaul) (RE 89):
We know, thanks to a letter of Cicero, that Marcus Varro Gibba was in 46 the quaestor of M. Junius Brutus in Cisalpine Gaul: *cum ad te [M. Iunium Brutum] tuus quaestor, M. Varro, profisciceretur...* (Cic. *fam.* 13.10.1). See Bülz 1893, 18–19; Sobeck 1909, 68; Broughton MRR, 2.296; Sumner 1971, 271: Varro Gibba had probably reached the legal age when he was elected quaestor for 46.

M. Terentius M. f. Varro Lucullus (q. and proq. 86–83? in the East) (cos. 73) (RE Licinius 109):
He served in the East under the command of Sulla, probably as quaestor (Plut. *Luc.* 37.1: ὁ δὲ Λεύκολλος ἀναβὰς εἰς Ῥώμην, πρῶτον μὲν κατέλαβε τὸν ἀδελφὸν Μᾶρκον ὑπὸ Γαΐου Μεμμίου κατηγορούμενον ἐφ' οἷς ἔπραξε ταμιεύων Σύλλα προστάξαντος). However, Plutarch also refers to him as one of Sulla's commanders (Plut. *Sull.* 27.7: ἔτι δὲ Μᾶρκος Λεύκολλος, εἷς τῶν ὑπὸ Σύλλα στρατηγούντων). As a consequence, Broughton MRR, 2.65, concludes that he was quaestor or legate in 83 (cf. Arkenberg 1993, 333), but the two texts are certainly compatible: as Sulla's quaestor, M. Terentius Varro Lucullus was one of his commanders. Additionally, some coins circulating widely in Greece during the Sullan war against Mithridates, the so-called Lucullan coins, have been attributed to him instead of to his brother L. Licinius Lucullus (Thompson 1961, 437–438). According to Thompson, M. Terentius Varro Lucullus may have issued these coins in Athens as quaestor or proquaestor, at Sulla's orders, at some point between 86 and 84. The Greek monograms on the coins have been read as ΜΑΡ(κου) ΤΑΜ(ίου), that is, 'of quaestor Marcus,' which seems to allude to Marcus Lucullus (see Kroll 1997, 140).

The quaestorship of M. Lucullus has generally been taken for granted in the scholarship. So Keaveney 1984, 119 and 121: it is beyond dispute that L. Lucullus was Sulla's quaestor. However, when L. Lucullus went to collect a fleet, Sulla picked a replacement and his choice was his brother M. Lucullus. In the absence of L. Lucullus, the treasure which Sulla confiscated in Greece was coined by M. Lucullus as quaestor (cf. Keaveney 1992, 129–130: M. Lucullus was prosecuted by the tribune of the plebs C. Memmius in 66 for his deeds from around twenty years earlier when he was Sulla's temporary quaestor in the First Mithridatic War). Of the same opinion is Santangelo 2007, 142, who considers the quaestor M. Lucullus to have been a prominent figure among the Sullans. Santangelo proffers 83 as the year of M. Lucullus' quaestorship (142 n. 29).

More recently, Ryan 1995b, has suggested a completely different reconstruction of M. Lucullus' political career. In his opinion, it is quite possible that M. Lucullus was responsible for the minting in the East under Sulla, but there is no evidence that he did this as quaestor. Nevertheless, Plutarch must not be wrong when he alludes to M. Lucullus as quaestor. According to Ryan, he may have been Sulla's quaestor at Rome in 81, and may have collaborated with the implementation of the Sullan proscriptions (Ryan 1996f, 39: Lucullus was born in 117 and took up the quaestorship at the age of thirty-five). This would provide the reason why M. Lucullus was later prosecuted by the tribune Memmius.

Ryan's reconstruction seems too speculative. There is enough evidence (literary sources and coins) to place the probable quaestorship of M. Lucullus in the context of the Mithridatic War under Sulla's command. The date is, however, controversial. Broughton suggests 83 as the latest possible date before he became propraetor in Cisalpine Gaul. But an earlier date is obviously feasible, and even more likely, as Thompson proposes in an analysis of the numismatic evidence. M. Lucullus may have been quaestor and proquaestor in all or a part of the period 86–83.

C. Toranius (or Thoranius) (q. 73? proq. 72?) (RE 4):

C. Toranius was quaestor under the command of the praetor P. Varinius during the war against Spartacus (Sall. *hist.* 3.96 M.; cf. Flor. 2.8.5). Ryan 1996a, 208–209, argues that Varinius' operations began in the autumn of 73 and probably continued into 72. As a consequence, Ryan suggests that Toranius could have been quaestor either in 73 or in 72. However, it seems more likely that Toranius was already quaestor under Varinius in 73 at the beginning of the war and that perhaps he could have continued as proquaestor in 72. See Sobeck 1909, 42–43; Broughton MRR, 2.110. See a recent discussion on the chronology of P. Varinius' command against Spartacus in Vervaet 2015, 412–414. As to his name, the spelling Thoranius in Sallust and Florus should be corrected to Toranius on basis of ILS 47 = Incr. Ital. 13.3.75b (cf. Broughton MRR, 2.115 n.4).

C. Trebonius C. f. (q. urb. 58?) (cos. suff. 45) (RE 6):

Cicero speaks of C. Trebonius as quaestor: *Nam, ut illa omittam, quae civitate teste fecisti, cum mecum inimicitias communicavisti, cum me contionibus tuis defendisti, cum quaestor in mea atque in publica causa consulum partes suscepisti, cum tribuno plebis quaestor non paruisti, cui tuus praesertim collega pareret...* (Cic. *fam.* 15.21.2). The date of Trebonius' quaestorship depends on the interpretation of this passage. It could be the year 60, if Cicero refers to the opposition to Clodius' attempt to transfer himself to the plebs (Willems 1878, 1.496: quaestor by 60; Sobeck 1909, 54; Broughton MRR, 2.184; Wiseman 1971, 267 no 444). However, it could also have been in 58, as Broughton MRR, 3.207, suggests, if the consuls Trebonius opposed were Piso and Gabinius and if the tribune of the plebs to whom Cicero alludes was Clodius himself. According to Ryan 1997a, the key lies in the correct explanation of the sentence *consulum partis suscepisti*. It has been usually interpreted as 'you [Trebonius] sided with the consuls' (so the Loeb edition). If this is right, the quaestorship of Trebonius should be dated to 60, as Cicero would never have praised somebody who was on the side of his great enemies, the consuls of 58. Nevertheless, Shackleton Bailey, who nonetheless opt for the year 60, prefers to explain the sentence otherwise: 'Trebonius as quaestor took upon himself the duties of the consuls' (Shackleton Bailey 1977, 2.367). Shackleton Bailey adds: 'How Trebonius as quaestor took upon himself the duties of the consuls is beyond a guess.' Ryan argues that Trebonius did not assume the duties of the consuls, since this was legally impossible, but rather acted openly in that political scenario as the consuls should have done. According to Ryan, this necessarily places the date of Trebonius' quaestorship in 58. Additionally, Cicero refers to consuls in the plural. The consuls in 60 were Metellus Celer and Afranius. While the latter could be seen as one of Cicero's adversaries, this is certainly not the case with Metellus Celer, who was frequently praised by Cicero.

As a result, it seems more likely that Trebonius was quaestor in 58 than in 60. Finally, Cicero's mention of Trebonius' colleague suggests that he was one of the two urban quaestors that year.

Cn. Tremellius Flaccus (q. before 205) (RE 4):
See **M. Valerius Falto.** In 205 M. Valerius Laevinus was sent to King Attalus in order to bring the Magna Mater to Rome. Among the Roman envoys were the quaestorians Cn. Tremellius Flaccus and M. Valerius Falto: *Legatos ad eum [Attalum] decernunt... duos quaestorios Cn. Tremellium Flaccum et M. Valerium Faltonem* (Liv. 29.11.3). Consequently, Tremellius was quaestor before 205, 206 being the latest possible date. See Sobeck 1909, 8; Broughton MRR, 1.299; Develin 1979, 68.

Cn. Tremellius Scrofa (q. by 87?) (pr. by 77 or 72?) (RE 5):
See next item **Cn. Tremellius Scrofa** (q. 71). This is Cn. Tremellius Scrofa the agronomist. Münzer combines the political careers of two different individuals under the same name and number in RE 5. Brunt 1972, and Perl 1980, show that they are, in fact, two different people. The senior one is the agronomist, interlocutor in the first two books of Varro's *De re rustica*. He was a grandson of L. Tremellius Scrofa (RE 6). According to Perl (p. 99), he may have been born between 120 and 118 and consequently may have held the quaestorship by 87 (see however Díaz Fernández 2014, 93–94: Scrofa may have been praetor by 82). This date is highly speculative, on the basis of his possible date of birth and his later career. See also Broughton MRR, 3.207–208.

Cn. Tremellius Scrofa (q. 71) (pr. by 60?) (RE 5):
See previous item **Cn. Tremellius Scrofa** (q. by 87?). As explained in the previous item, Münzer confuses the careers of two different individuals in RE 5. This is the younger one, who was born around 101. According to Plutarch (*Crass*. 11.4), this Cn. Tremellius Scrofa was quaestor under M. Licinius Crassus in 71, during the war against the slaves. He was defeated and wounded at Petelia. In 70 he was a juror, and therefore a senator, in the trial against Verres (Cic. *Verr.* 30). See Sobeck 1909, 44–45; Broughton MRR, 2.122; 3.208.

L. Tremellius Scrofa (q. 143 or 142, or q. 143 and proq. 142, in Macedonia) (pr. by 136) (RE 6):

According to Livy, Lucius Tremellius Scrofa served as quaestor under the command of Licinius Nerva in Macedonia. He defeated an usurper, to whom Livy refers as a Pseudophilippus: *Alter Pseudophilippus in Macedonia a L. Tremellio quaestore cum exercitu caesus est* (Liv. *per.* 53). See also Eutrop. 4.15: *Iterum in Macedonia Pseudoperses, qui se Persei filium esse dicebat, collectis servitiis rebellavit et, cum sedecim milia armatorum haberet, a Tremellio quaestore superatus est*. Note that Var. *r.r.* 2.4.2, points to the fact that Licinius Nerva was called imperator thanks to Varro's victory (*ut eo Nerva, praetor imperator sit appellatus*). He was the grandfather of the agronomist, and the first to take the *cognomen* Scrofa (Varr. *r.r.* 2.4.1). The order of events in Livy's *Periocha* allows us to conclude that Scrofa was quaestor in either 143 or 142. Licinius Nerva could also have been in command of Macedonia in both 143 and 142. In that case, Scrofa may have been quaestor in 143 and proquaestor in 142. There is no evidence to settle the matter with absolute certainty. See Bültz 1908, 9–10; Sobeck 1909, 15: quaestor in 142; Broughton MRR, 1.472; 1.475; 2.627: quaestor in 143 or 142; and 3.208: quaestor in 143; Brunt 1972, 306: quaestor in 142 (cf. Brunt 1973, 295); Perl 1980, 99: quaestor in 143 (or 142).

M. Tullius M. f. Cicero (q. 75 in Sicily) (cos. 63) (RE 29):

Marcus Tullius Cicero held the quaestorship in 75 at Lilybaeum in Western Sicily under the command of Sex. Peducaeus (see among other references Cic. *Brut.* 318: *Unum igitur annum, cum redissemus ex Asia, causas nobilis egimus, cum quaesturam nos, consulatum Cotta, aedilitatem peteret Hortensius. interim me quaestorem Siciliensis excepit annus...*). See Sobeck 1909, 38; Broughton 2.98; Prag 2007b, 304.

Q. Tullius M. f. Cicero (q. before 66?) (pr. 62) (RE 31):

See **L. Valerius Flaccus.** There has been speculation as to when Quintus Cicero held the quaestorship. The only apparent evidence is found in a letter written by Marcus Cicero to Atticus in November 68, which makes it clear that Quintus was not in Rome at the time (Cic. *Att.* 1.5.2 and 8: *Quintum fratrem cotidie exspectamus*). Marcus Cicero does not inform us where his brother was or how long he had been absent. On the basis of this scarce information, Münzer (RE 1287) conjectures that Quintus Cicero held his quaestorship during this period. Broughton MRR, 2.139, accepts Münzer's conjecture and adds the possibility that Quintus Cicero was quaestor in 68 ('he was absent from Rome in this and perhaps previous years'). McDermott 1971, rejects Quintus' quaestorship in 68, 'because the reference in the letter to Atticus is so vague that we cannot draw conclusions from it,' but he does suggest an alternative: according to McDermott, Quintus Cicero was probably not in Rome in the year 70. Otherwise he would surely have accompanied his brother Marcus to Sicily as did L. Cicero. Quintus may then have held an office far from Rome, perhaps as quaestor or proquaestor. McDermott argues that he might have been quaestor in Hispania under M. Pupius Piso Frugi Calpurnianus. He may have been assigned to him as quaestor in 70, as the substitute of L. Valerius Flaccus, and he may have stayed in Hispania as proquaestor until Piso's return to Rome to celebrate his triumph in 69. As McDermott himself recognises, this reconstruction is utterly speculative, and Quintus may have served his quaestorship earlier or in another area.

As Badian 1959a, 83, rightly points out, Münzer's conjecture should be abandoned, because we do not even know how long Quintus had been away at the time when Cicero wrote his letter nor, for that matter, how far away he was. Likewise, McDermott's conjecture should be rejected. There is no evidence in the sources of Quintus Cicero's quaestorship in Hispania Citerior in 70–69. Actually, the quaestor in this province in those years seems to have been Flaccus. As a matter of fact, there is no evidence at all for Quintus Cicero's quaestorship. Certainly he must have been quaestor before becoming aedile in 65, but we have no clue as to when—or if—he served outside Rome. Taking into account the necessary interval between two offices, the year 67 seems to be the latest possible date for his quaestorship.

Tullius Rufus (q. before 46) (RE 49):
The Caesarian Tullius Rufus was killed at the battle of Thapsus in 46: *in quo numero fuit Tullius Rufus quaestorius qui pilo traiectus consulto a milite interiit* (*bell. Afr.* 85.7–8). There is no other evidence about his life. Consequently, the date of his quaestorship is impossible to determine. See Sobeck 1909, 67; Broughton 2.477.

D. Turullius (q. 44, proq. 43 in Bithynia) (RE 1):
According to Cassius Dio (51.8.2), Publius (*sic*) Turullius was one of the assassins of Caesar and he is described as a senator. In a letter written in 43, Cicero speaks of Turullius as quaestor: *nos illa relicta, quod et in castra pervenire satius esse putabamus et sequebatur classis altera, quam anno priore in Bithynia Tillius Cimber compararat, Turullius quaestor praeerat, Cyprum petivimus* (Cic. *fam.* 12.13.3). Turullius was, therefore, quaestor in 44 and he went to Bithynia with the praetor L. Tillius Cimber. Although Cicero calls him quaestor, Turullius was in all probability proquaestor in 43. As for his name, the coins minted in 31 for M. Antonius with the legend *D · TVR(ullius)* make it clear that his *praenomen* was not Publius as Cassius Dio states (Πούπλιον Τουρούλλιον; Crawford RRC, 542 no. 545). See Sobeck 1909, 70–71; Broughton MRR, 2.326; 2.350 and 3.210; Wiseman 1971, 268 no. 450; Syme 1964a, 123–124: it is very unlikely that there were two different Turulli, the one mentioned by Cassius Dio and the man who issued the coins under Antonius.

C. Urbinus (or Urbinius) (q. 74 in Hispania Ulterior) (not in RE):

Sallust provides evidence for C. Urbinus' quaestorship: *Eum quaestor C. Urbinus aliique cognita voluntate...* (Sall. *hist.* 2.59, McGushin 1992, vol. 1 p. 53 = 2.70 M.). He served as quaestor under the command of Metellus Pius in Hispania Ulterior, during the Sertorian War. The most probable date for his quaestorship is 74 (Spann 1987, 126; Frassinetti 1975, 387–388, proposes 75). It is unknown whether he stayed in Hispania as proquaestor for a longer period. See Bülz 1893, 8; Sobeck 1909, 41; Broughton MRR, 2.103, prefers the name Urbinius, likewise Gruen 1974, 203. Cf Wiseman 1971, 269 no. 453.

M. Valerius Falto (q. before 205) (RE 153):

See **Cn. Tremellius Flaccus.** An embassy headed by M. Valerius Laevinus was sent in 205 to King Attalus in order to bring Magna Mater to Rome. Among the Roman envoys were the quaestorians M. Valerius Falto and Cn. Tremellius Flaccus: *Legatos ad eum [Attalum] decernunt... duos quaestorios Cn. Tremellium Flaccum et M. Valerium Faltonem* (Liv. 29.11.3). Therefore, Valerius Falto was quaestor before 205, 206 being the latest possible date for his quaestorship. See Sobeck 1909, 8; Broughton MRR, 1.299; Develin 1979, 70.

L. Valerius L. f. Flaccus (q. 71 and proq. 70–69, or q. 70 and proq. 69, in Hispania Citerior) (pr. 63) (RE *69, 179):

See **Q. Tullius Cicero.** Lucius Valerius Flaccus was, according to Cicero, quaestor in Hispania: *fuit M. Pisoni quaestor in Hispania; vox de quaestura missa nulla est* (Cic. *Flacc.* 6). He served under the command of M. Pupius Piso Frugi Calpurnianus, who was praetor probably in 71 and proconsul in Hispania Citerior until 69, when he celebrated a triumph in Rome (Cic. *Pis.* 62; Ascon. 15 C; see Díaz Fernández 2015, 545 n. 128). Flaccus may have accompanied Piso as his quaestor in 70, or even at the end of 71, and may have remained in Hispania as proquaestor in 69, or in 70–69, until the arrival in the province of the new governor. See Bülz 1893, 14–16; Sobeck 1909, 46: quaestor in 70; Broughton MRR, 2.123: quaestor in 71; 2.129: probably proquaestor in 70 (however, MRR, 2.629: quaestor 71 or 70, and proquaestor? under Piso in Hispania); Ryan 1996f, 41. The hypothesis of McDermott 1971, 713, who suggests that Quintus Cicero may have been assigned to Piso as quaestor in 70 as substitute of Flaccus and then may have remained in Hispania as proquaestor in 69 must be rejected. Q. Cicero would have returned to Rome with Piso in 69. As McDermott himself asserts, this reconstruction is highly speculative and finds no basis in the sources.

M. Valerius M. f. Messala (not q. but moneyer 53) (cos. suff. 32) (RE *97):

On the basis of coins issued by M. Valerius Messala in 53 (curule chair, legend *PATRE · COS* and *S · C*), Sobeck 1909, 60, suggests that he was urban quaestor that year. Nevertheless, nothing indicates this. In fact, everything points to Messala as moneyer. The inscription was dedicated to his father, who was consul in 53. See Broughton MRR, 2.454; Crawford RRC 457 no. 435.

M. Valerius M. f. Messalla Niger (q. by 73) (cos. 61) (RE 266):

The political career of Messalla Niger has been preserved in his *elogium: M. Valerius M. f. M. (n.) Messalla pontife(x) tr. mil. II q. pr. urb. co(s) V vir a. d. a. interr(ex) III censor* (CIL I² 1, p. 201 = Inscr. Ital. 13.3.77). Sobeck 1909, 42, dates his quaestorship to 73, following Mommsen's suggestion, who considers Messalla to have held the quaestorship *suo anno*, like Cicero. Accordingly, Messalla should have been born in 104 and held the consulship in 61 and the quaestorship by 73. See Broughton MRR, 2.110: the interval between the year 73 and Messalla's consulship is the same as that between Cicero's quaestorship and consulship. Cf. Sumner 1973, 131. It is certain that Messalla was a quaestor. The date of his quaestorship may have been around 73.

M'. Valerius Messala Potitus (q. in Asia in the 40s?) (RE 267):

A Greek inscription discovered at Claros (SEG 37.959) honoured Manius Valerius Messala Potitus as quaestor (ταμίας): ὁ δῆμος / Μάνιον Οὐαλέριον / Μεσσάλαν Ποτῖτον / ταμίαν ἀρετῆς ἕνε/κα καὶ πάτρωνα ὄντα τῆ[ς] / πόλεως. Syme 1955b, 156– 159 and 1956, 206 considers that this Messala Potitus could be the praetor of 32 (CIL VI 37075) and *consul suffectus* of 29, if he changed his *praenomen*. This is far from certain. See also Broughton MRR, 3.214: Messala Potitus should be listed among quaestors of uncertain date.

L. Valerius Poplicola Potitus (q. 446) (cos. 449) (RE 304):

See **Mam. Aemilius [Mamercinus]**. In accordance with Tacitus, Lucius Valerius Poplicola Potitus was one of the first two quaestors elected by the people in 446: *Creatique primum Valerius Potitus et Aemilius Mamercus sexagesimo tertio anno post Tarquinios exactos, ut rem militarem comitarentur* (Tac. ann. 11.22). See Sobeck 1909, 3; Broughton MRR, 1.51.

C. (Valerius) Triarius (q. urb. 81) (RE 363, 366):

See **P. Cornelius Lentulus [Sura]**. Cicero makes it clear that the urban quaestors in 81 were P. Cornelius Lentulus (Sura) and a Triarius: *P. Lentulo L. Triario quaestoribus urbanis res rationum relatarum* (Cic. Verr. 2.1.37). The *nomen* of this Triarius must be Valerius, but his *praenomen* has been controversial. Some manuscripts give L(ucius), and this *praenomen* was initially accepted in the scholarship. So Sobeck 1909, 33; Broughton MRR, 2.77 and 2.631. Broughton identifies this individual with the praetor of 78 (*contra* Badian 1959a, 83–84). However, Shackleton Bailey 1976, 71–72, demonstrates that the manuscript tradition strongly favours the *praenomen* C(aius), and consequently he suggests the identification of this individual with the C. Valerius Triarius who was in charge of Sardinia as propraetor and opposed Lepidus in 77. This identification is accepted by Broughton MRR, 3.214–215: the urban quaestor of 81, C. Valerius Triarius, was the same as the propraetor in 77 in Sardinia and the legate under Lucullus in 73–67.

P. Vatinius P. f. (q. 63) (cos. 47) (RE *2):

Publius Vatinius was quaestor in 63 during the consulship of Cicero: *quaesturam petisti cum P. Sestio, cum hic nihil loqueretur nisi quod agebat, tu de altero consulatu gerendo te diceres cogitare* (Cic. *Vat.* 11). According to Cicero, the so-called *aquaria provincia* was allocated to Vatinius by lot; the consul Cicero sent him to Puteoli to prevent the export of precious metals (Cic. *Vat.* 12). See Sobeck 1909, 52; Broughton MRR, 2.168; Wiseman 1971, 270 no. 467.

C. Vergilius C. f. Balbus (q. 69? proq. 68? in Sicily) (pr. 62) (RE 3):

C. Vergilius Balbus was honoured by the people of the city of Halaesa in Sicily (IG 14.356 = IGRP 1.508: Γάιον Οὐεργίλιον Γαίου υἱὸν Βάλβον / ἀντιταμίαν <ὁ> δᾶμος τῶν Ἀλαισίνων / εὐνοίας ἕνεκεν). In the inscription, Balbus is named as proquaestor (ἀντιταμίας). He has been identified as the praetor of 62, governor of Sicily in 61–58. The date of his quaestorship should presumably be placed in the early 60s (Sobeck 1909, 52, cautiously dates it before 62; Broughton MRR, 2.128: quaestor? in 70; 2.133: proquaestor in 69). Prag 2007a, 86 n. 96; 2007b 307, argues that the inscription from Halaesa may reflect the victory of L. Metellus, the successor of Verres on the command of the island, against the pirates, presumably with the support of Sicilian troops. As a result, Prag suggests that Vergilius Balbus may have been quaestor under L. Metellus' command in 69 and he may have remained on the island as proquaestor in 68, always under Metellus' command. Alternatively, Balbus could have taken over Metellus' role after his departure (cf. Badian 1983, 158).

C. Verres C. f. (q. 84, proq. 83–82?) (pr. 74) (RE 1):

Cicero alludes to Verres' political career in the Verrines: *quaestor Cn. Papirio consuli fuisti abhinc annos quattuordecim* (Cic. *Verr.* 2.1.34); *quibus probemus istum in quaestura pecuniam publicam Cn. Carboni consuli datam avertisse...* (Cic. *Verr.* 2.1.11). Verres was, therefore, quaestor under the consul Cn. Papirius Carbo fourteen years before the trial against him. Although Bülz 1893, 55 (cf. Bültz 1908, 23–24), and Sobeck 1909, 33, date his quaestorship in 82 during the third consulate of Carbo, Cicero's testimony is clear: since the trial against Verres took place in 70 and he held the quaestorship fourteen years earlier, the date must be 84, during the second consulate of Carbo. Verres may have continued in 83 as proquaestor under Carbo in Gaul, and then deserted him for Sulla in 82, still as proquaestor (Cic. Verr. 2.1.34–40). See Bülz 1893, 55–56; Broughton MRR, 2.61; 2.64 and 2.69; Gruen 1966b, 396; Luce 1968, 31.

P. (Vettius?) Sabinus (q. 99?) (RE Sabinus 30; Vettius 15):

Some coins bear the legend *P · SABIN Q*. Crawford RRC, 331 no. 331, dates them to 99. His *nomen* Vettius is conjectural. Nothing is known about a possible later office. Evans 1994, 213, names him P. Sabinius, quaestor in 99.

T. Vettius (Chilo?) (q. 72 and proq. 71, or q. 71 in Sicily) (pr. 59) (RE *9, 11 and 14):

See **P. Caesetius**. T. Vettius has been identified as the moneyer T. Vettius Sabinus, who issued coins in 70 and was later praetor in 59 (Crawford RRC, 414; cf. Syme 1955c, 71; Broughton MRR, 3.219). However, Cicero notes that T. Vettius, quaestor under C. Verres in Sicily, was the brother of both Verres' wife and P. Vettius Chilo, a wealthy Roman *eques* (Cic. Verr. 2.3.168: *Vettius, tuus familiarissimus, Vettius, tuus adfinis, cuius sororem habes in matrimonio, tuae frater uxoris, Vettius, frater tui quaestoris*); see Gruen 1974, 203, n. 161. Both the date and location of his quaestorship are controversial (Sobeck 1909, 43: quaestor in 73 at Lilybaeum; Broughton MRR, 2.110: quaestor in 73). Cicero confirms that Vettius was quaestor at the time of the trial of the Sicilian navarchs in 71 (Cic. Verr. 2.5.114: *Condemnat omnis de consili sententia; tamen neque iste in tanta re tot hominum T. Vettium ad se arcessit, quaestorem suum, cuius consilio uteretur...*). The passage may be taken to imply that he was based in Syracuse, but there is no clear evidence for this. Marinone 1965–66, argues that Vettius' quaestorship should be dated to 72–71 at Syracuse (cf. Broughton MRR, 3.219, following Marinone). However, Brennan 2000, 840 n. 95, gives arguments in favour of Vettius' quaestorship in 71 as well as identifies his location in the west at Lilybaeum. Prag 2007b, 306, also dates his quaestorship to 71. The year 73 must be discarded, since we know the names of the two quaestors in Sicily that year, Q. Caecilius Niger and M. Postumius. Likewise as P. Caesetius, T. Vettius may have been quaestor in 72 and proquaestor in 71, or quaestor in 71, at any rate serving under Verres in Sicily.

T. Vibius Temudinus (q. urb. 80s?) (not in RE):

Titus Vibius Temudinus is mentioned in an inscription found in Rome not far from the Porta Collina: *ope[r(is)] [magistro? cur(atore)] viar(um) T(ito) Vibio Temuudino [sic] q(uaestore) urb(ano)...* (CIL VI 31603 = CIL I² 808 = ILS 5799 = ILLRP 465). The inscription alludes to the repair of the Via Caecilia. Vibius Temudinus was in charge of the project as urban quaestor and *curator viarum*. The letters of the inscription suggest a chronology in the Sullan period, that is, in the 80s. See Sobeck 1909, 80; Broughton MRR, 2.477; Wiseman 1970, 145; Duncan-Jones 1974, 225 n. 455; Giovagnoli 2012, 207–208; Dillon and Garland ²2015; Kolb 2015, 658–659.

C. Visellius C. f. Varro (q. before 73, probably in 74) (RE 3):

C. Visellius Varro (Γάϊος Οὐσέλλιος Γαΐου υἱὸς Κυρίνα Οὐάρρων) is one of the senators mentioned in the *SC de Oropiis* of year 73 (SIG³ 747 = RDGE 23). He was Cicero's cousin, who describes him as a *vir doctus* (Cic. *Verr.* 2.1.71; *Brut.* 264). Visellius is one of the *quaestorii* of the *consilium*. Therefore, Visellius must have held the quaestorship before 73 (Broughton MRR, 2.115; cf. 3.222). Taking into account that the senators are recorded in order of rank and that Visellius is cited in last place, he was very probably quaestor in 74 (cf. Sumner 1973, 138–139).

L. [---] (*nomen* unknown) (q. in unknown date):

CIL I² 3153: *L. [---] f. / quaestor//es / dedere*.

M. [---] (*nomen* unknown) (q. pro pr. late second century) (not in RE):

A Marcus of unknown *nomen* is mentioned in an inscription from Delos as quaestor pro praetore: (I. Délos 1843: Μ̣άαρ<κ>[ον --] / ταμίαν <καὶ> ἀντιστρ<άτηγον> / Ῥωμαίω<ν>). Nothing is known about the identification of the magistrate, but he may have held his office in the last quarter of the second century according to the name of the man who dedicated the inscription. See Broughton MRR, 2.481: *quaestor pro praetore*, late second century.

M. [---] (*nomen* unknown) (q. in Asia first century) (not in RE):

A Marcus appears as quaestor in a Greek inscription from Magnesia (I. v. Magnesia 155: [Μ]ᾶρκο[ν --] / ταμίαν [---] / τον ἀρε[τῆς ἕνεκα καὶ εὐνοίας τῆς] / πρὸς τὸ[ν δῆμον]). His *nomen* is utterly unknown. Sobeck 1909, 81: the inscription could be dated to the first century; Broughton MRR, 2.476: quaestor in Asia, at some point in the first century.

P. [---]nius (proq. before 88) (not in RE):

A Publius [---]nius is known through an inscription from Delos, in which he appears as proquaestor (I. Délos 1846: Πόπ>[λιον --]νιον ἀγ[τι]/[τα]μίαν Ῥωμαίων / Αὖλος Φάβιος Λευκίου [---] / τὸν ἑαυτοῦ φίλον). The date of his proquaestorship is uncertain, at any rate before 88. See Broughton MRR, 2.481.

Anonymous (q. 211 in Sicily):

According to Livy, in 211 Marcellus put an unnamed quaestor together with an escort in charge of Syracusan royal treasure (Liv. 25.31.8: *inde quaestor cum praesidio ad Nassum ad accipiendam pecuniam regiam custodiendamque missus*). See Prag 2007b, 291.

Anonymous (q. ca. 147–146 in Hispania Ulterior):
According to Appian, in 146 Viriathus slew four thousand soldiers and the praetor C. Vetilius in an ambush near the city of Tribola, in Hispania Ulterior. However, C. Vetilius' unnamed quaestor managed to escape with six thousand Roman soldiers to the unknown city of Καρπησσός (sic), where they remained waiting for help from Rome; cf. App. *Ib.* 63; Broughton MRR, 1.464; Richardson 2000, 155.

Anonymus (q. by 107–106 in Asia):
See **C. Billienus.** An inscription from Delos (I. Délos 1632: ὁ δῆμος [ὁ Ἀθηναίων] / καὶ οἱ τὴν ν[ῆσον κατοικοῦντες --] / Βιλλιῆνον [---] / ταμίαν [Ῥωμαίων — πρες] / βεύσαντ[α —εὐ]/εργεσίας [ἕνεκεν --] / ἐπὶ ἐπιμελητ[οῦ --]) was dedicated by the Athenians and the inhabitants of the islands to a Billienus, probably C. Billienus C. f. (RE 4), proconsul of Asia according to I. Délos 1854 (CIL I² 815), and presumably his quaestor (ταμίας), whose name is not preserved. C. Billienus was also legatus in Asia (I. Délos 1710), but the inscription seems most likely to relate to his proconsulship, given the allusion to the quaestor. Billienus' praetorship and later Asian command is usually dated around 107–106, since he was consular candidate during C. Marius' consulships (Cic. *Brut.* 175); see Brennan 2000, 547–548; Díaz Fernández, 2015, 444–445.

Anonymous (q. 88 in Sicily):
On his flight from Italy to Africa in 88, C. Marius was compelled to land at Erycina in western Sicily when the supply of fresh water failed. The unnamed quaestor of the island nearly captured him (Plut. *Mar.* 40.2–3). See Prag 2007b, 303.

Anonymous (q. 86 in Asia):
See **C. Flavius Fimbria (RE 88).** According to Appian and Cassius Dio, C. Flavius Fimbria, L. Valerius Flaccus' legate in Asia, had a tense dispute with Flaccus' quaestor about their lodgings (App. *Mith.* 52: 'ὡς δ' ἔν τινι καταγωγῇ περὶ ξενίας ἔριδος αὐτῷ καὶ τῷ ταμίᾳ γενομένης ὁ Φλάκκος διαιτῶν οὐδὲν ἐς τιμὴν ἐπεσήμηνε τοῦ Φιμβρίου, χαλεπήνας ὁ Φιμβρίας ἠπείλησεν ἐς Ῥώμην ἐπανελεύσεσθαι'; cf. also Cass.Dio 30–34 fr. 104.4–5). While neither historians includes the quaestor's name, we cannot dismiss the possibility that he was the Thermus whom Flaccus left in charge of the Roman troops at Byzantium when the consul sailed to Chalcedon. On Thermus, cf. Broughton MRR, 2.56; see **Q. Minucius Thermus (RE 66).**

Anonymous (q. 74–71?):
According to a fragment of Cassius Dio (30–35 fr. 111), the Cretans sent an embassy to Rome hoping to renew the old treaty. This happened some time after the death of M.

Antonius Creticus. The Cretan legates expected to get some consideration 'for saving the quaestor and his soldiers.' Cassius Dio provides no further information, but it seems evident that he is referring to the quaestor of Antonius Creticus, who was praetor in 74 and proconsul in 73–71 during his command against the pirates. Apparently a section of Antonius' army led by a quaestor was trapped or apprehended by the Cretans, who later released the Romans, perhaps after coming to an agreement with Antonius. Nothing is known about the name of the quaestor. See Linderski 1990, 163–164.

Anonymous (q. 70 in Sicily):
Cicero refers to L. Caecilius Metellus' quaestors present in Syracuse in the first part of 70. He gives no names (Cic. *Verr.* 2.2.11). Prag 2007b, 307.

Anonymous (q. pro pr. in Sicily in late Republic?):
There is evidence of a Sicilian *quaestor pro praetore* in an inscription from Eryx (CIL I² 843 = ILLRP 446: *[q(uaestor)] pro pr(aetore)...*). His name has not survived. He should probably be dated to the late Republic. See Prag 2007b, 309.

Appendix 2:
Chronological list of quaestors in the Roman Republic

446	Mam. Aemilius (Mamercinus) (RE 16, 97)
	L. Valerius Poplicola Potitus (RE 304)
414	P. Sestius (RE 15)
409	P. Aelius (RE 9)
	K. Fabius Ambustus (RE 42, cf. 39)
	P. Papius (RE Pupius *1)
	Q. Silius (RE 10)
391	Sp. Carvilius (RE 4)
before 315	Ap. Claudius (Caecus) (RE 91)
Third century	C. An(n)ius (RE 8)
Third century?	Aemilius (not in RE or RE 66?)
294	L. Opimius Pansa (RE 12)
between 267 and 241	C. Papirius (Paperios) (not in RE or RE 6)
	M. Publicius (Populicios) Malleolus (RE 22)
	L. Quinctius (Quinctios) (not in RE)
by 230? (or by 250?)	C. or Cn. Octavius Rufus (RE cf. 79)
before 238–237	Q. Fabius Maximus Verrucosus (q. II) (RE 116)
before 222	C. Terentius Varro (RE 83)
218	C. Fulvius (RE 10)
	L. Lucretius (RE 4)
217	Ti. Sempronius Blaesus (RE 32)
216	L. Atilius (RE 13)
	L. Furius Bibaculus (RE 35)

214	L.? Caecilius Metellus (RE 73)
212	Cn. Cornelius (Lentulus) (RE 176)
210	C. Flaminius (RE 3)
before 205	Cn. Tremellius Flaccus (RE 4) M. Valerius Falto (RE 153)
204	M. Porcius Cato (RE 9)
202	C. Laelius (RE 2)
second century P.?	Pavus Tubitanus or Tuditanus (RE Pavus)
between 203 and 199	P. Cornelius Scipio Nasica (RE 350)
199	T. Quinctius Flamininus (RE *3)
before 196	L. Cornelius Scipio Asiaticus (RE 337)
196	L. Aurelius (RE 18) Q. Fabius Labeo (RE 91)
195?	L. Aemilius Paullus (RE 114)
194	L. Postumius Tympanus (RE 24)
190	C. Furius Aculeo (RE 31)
by 189	Q. Petillius Spurinus (RE 4, 11)
188	Q. Fabius (RE 32, 58)
168	L. Manlius (Acidinus?) (RE 26) L. Stertinius (RE 6)
168?	C. Publilius (RE 10)
167	L. Cornelius Scipio (RE 324)
167?	L. Fulcinnius (RE 2)

154	Terentius Varro (RE 77)
151	P. Licinius Crassus Dives Mucianus (RE 72)
by 150	Cn. Cornelius Scipio Hispanus (RE 347)
second century in Sicily	M'. Acilius (RE 11)
	L. Alp(ius)? De(-) (not in RE)
	Q. Fabius?
145	C. Sempronius Tuditanus (RE 92)
143 or 142	L. Tremellius Scrofa (RE 6)
137	Ti. Sempronius Gracchus (RE 54)
before 136?	M'. Aquillius (RE 10)
134	Q. Fabius Maximus Allobrogicus (RE 110)
by 130	Asullius (not in RE)
126	C. Sempronius Gracchus (RE 47)
123–121?	C. Marius (RE 14, suppl. 6)
120	P. Albius (RE 2)
120–119	M. Annius (not in RE)
by 120–115?	C. Billienus (RE Bellienus 3–4)
116 or 115?	M. Sergius Silus (RE 42)
113	M. Antonius (RE 28)
	C. (Claudius) Marcellus (not in RE)
113 or 112?	L. Manlius Torquatus (RE 78)
before 112?	L. Memmius (RE 13)
111	L. Licinius Crassus (RE 55)

	Q. Mucius Scaevola (RE 22)
	C. Sextius Calvinus (RE 1 and 21)
111–110? (or 99?)	Ap. Claudius Pulcher (RE 296)
	T. Maloleius? (or Mallius? or Manlius?)
shortly before 110?	C. Claudius Pulcher (RE 302)
before 108	C. Servilius Glaucia (RE 65)
109 or 108?	Q. Lutatius Cerco (RE 14)
107	L. Cornelius Sulla Felix (RE 392)
106?	Cn. Pompeius Strabo (RE 14)
105?	L. Appuleius Saturninus (RE 29)
by 105	Cn. Octavius Ruso (RE 82)
104–103? (or between 100 and 96?)	C. Julius Caesar Strabo Vopiscus (RE 135)
by 103?	M. Aurelius Scaurus (RE 215)
103?	L. Calpurnius Piso Caesoninus (RE 89)
	Q. Servilius Caepio (RE 50)
by 102–100	L. Cornelius Lentulus (RE 193, suppl. 3.259)
102	L. Philo (L. Veturius Philo?) (RE Veturius 21)
	(or L. Sempronius Pit(h)io?) (RE 74)
102?	A. Gabinius (RE 8)
101	C. Fundanius (RE 1)
by 100	C. Julius Caesar (RE 130)
end second century	Cn. Servilius Caepio (RE 47)
100 or 99	C. Saufeius (RE 3)

99?	C. Norbanus (Balbus?) (RE 5)
	P. (Vettius?) Sabinus (RE Sabinus 30; Vettius 15)
98?	T. Cloelius (Cloulius) (RE 5)
beginning of first century	Q. Baebius (RE 20a, suppl. 1.236 / 53, suppl. 3.192)
97	C. Egnatuleius (RE 1)
97?	M. Livius Drusus (RE 18)
95–94?	Aesillas (not in RE)
91?	Q. Sertorius (RE 3)
80s	M. Herennius Rufus (RE 41)
80s?	T. Vibius Temudinus (not in RE)
by 90–88	L. Octavius (RE 26)
	C. Pomponius (not in RE)
89?	M. Junius Silanus Murena (RE 170?)
	Q. Minucius Thermus (RE 66)
88 or 87?	A. Terentius Varro (RE 82)
by 87?	P. Rutilius P.f. Nudus (RE 30)
	Cn. Tremellius Scrofa (RE 5)
87	L. Licinius Lucullus (RE 104)
by 86?	Q. Anicius (not in RE)
86	C. Flavius Fimbria (RE 88)
	Hirtuleius (RE 1)
86?	M. Terentius Varro Lucullus (RE Licinius 109)
85?	M. Terentius Varro (RE 84, suppl. 6)
84	C. Verres (RE 1)

84–82?	L. Manlius Torquatus (RE 79)
84–78	M'. Aemilius Lepidus (RE 62)
83	M. Fonteius (RE 12)
	M. Pupius Piso Frugi (Calpurnianus) (RE 10)
83?	L. Hirtuleius (RE 3)
shortly before 82?	C. Caecilius Metellus (RE 71)
81	P. Cornelius Lentulus (Sura) (RE 240)
	C. Tarquitius (RE 1)
	C. (Valerius) Triarius (RE 363, 366)
by 81	L. Fabius Hispaniensis (RE 84)
80	A. Manlius [Torquatus] (RE 13, cf. 70 and 76)
	C. (Publicius) Malleolus (RE *14)
80s or beginning 70s?	T. Manlius Torquatus (RE 85)
before 80? Triumviral period?	A. Pompeius (RE 4)
70s	M. Aurelius Scaurus (RE 216)
	Q. Publicius (RE 13?)
	P. Septimius (RE 11)
before 78	Q. Hortensius Hortalus (RE 13)
78	C. Aelius Paetus Staienus (RE Staienus 1)
78?	M. Marius (RE 23)
77	L. Julius Caesar (RE 143)
77?	C. Memmius (RE 7)
by 75?	C. Annaeus (not in RE)
	Q. Pompeius Bithynicus (RE 25)

75	P. Autronius Paetus (RE 7)
	M. Tullius Cicero (RE 29)
75?	Cn. Cornelius Lentulus Marcellinus (RE 228)
75 or 74	Q. Axius (RE 4)
	A. Cascellius (RE 4)
	P. Cornelius Lentulus Marcellinus (RE 231)
	T. Maenius (RE 16)
	Q. Minucius Thermus (RE 67)
	Q. Pompeius Rufus (RE *8)
	M. Publicius Scaeva (not in RE)
74	Q. Ancharius (RE 3)
	L. Licinius Murena (RE 123)
	P. Oppius (RE 17)
	Ser. Sulpicius Rufus (RE 95)
	C. Urbinus (or Urbinius) (not in RE)
74?	L. Claudius (RE 23)
	Q. Rancius (RE 1)
	C. Sicinius (RE 7)
	C. Visellius Varro (RE 3)
74 or 70	C. Cornelius (RE 18)
by 73	M. Valerius Messalla Niger (RE 266)
73	Q. Caecilius Niger (RE 101)
	M. Postumius (RE 19)
73?	C. Toranius (or Thoranius) (RE 4)
72 or 71	P. Caesetius (RE 3)
	T. Vettius (Chilo?) (RE *9, 11 and 14)
by 71?	C. (Curtius) Postumus (RE 24)
71	Cn. Tremellius Scrofa (RE 5)
71?	P. Cornelius Lentulus Spinther (RE 238)
	L. Plaetorius (Cestianus) (RE 14)

Appendix 2: Chronological list of quaestors in the Roman Republic — 343

71 or 70	L. Valerius Flaccus (RE *69, 179)
before 70	C. Caepasius (RE 1)
	L. Caepasius (RE 1)
	Q. Curius (RE 1)
by 70?	L. Aquillius Florus (not in RE)
	L. Calpurnius Piso Caesoninus (RE 90)
	M. Plaetorius Cestianus (RE 16)
60s or 50s?	L. Sestius (Pansa?) (RE 10)
by 69	T. (Quinctius?) Crispinus (not in RE)
69	C. Julius Caesar (RE 131)
	P. Sulpicius (RE 15)
69?	C. Vergilius Balbus (RE 3)
68?	Cn. Saturninus (RE 27)
67?	Q. Servilius Caepio (RE 40–42)
by 67 or later?	C. Memmius (RE 8)
before 66?	C. Octavius (RE 15)
	Q. Tullius Cicero (RE 31)
67 or 66	M. Aemilius Scaurus (RE 141)
	P. Plautius Hypsaeus (RE 23)
66	L. Domitius Ahenobarbus (RE 27)
	C. Sosius (see RE 2)
65–64	Cn. Calpurnius Piso (RE 69)
before 64	L. Caecilius Rufus (RE 110)
	L. Calpurnius Bestia (RE 24)
by 64?	C. Alfius Flavus (RE 7)
64	M. Claudius Marcellus (RE 229)
	M. Lollius (RE 9)

	M. Porcius Cato (Uticensis) (RE *20)
63	Sex. Atilius Serranus Gavianus (RE 70) T. Fadius (RE 9) P. Sestius (RE 6) P. Vatinius (RE *2)
63?	C. Cornelius Cethegus? (RE 89)[1]
by 63–62	M. Juventius Laterensis (RE 16)
62?	Q. Caecilius Metellus Pius Scipio Nasica (RE 99) M. Favonius (RE 1)
by 62?	A. Allienus (RE 1)
before 61	P. Servilius Isauricus (RE 67)
61	P. Clodius Pulcher (RE 48) M. Curtius Peducaeanus (RE 8) P. Sestullius (RE Sextilius 13)
61?	L. Scribonius L. f. Libo (RE 20)
by 61?	C. Fannius (RE 9)
60	L. Aemilius (Lepidus) Paullus (RE 81)
by 60?	Q. Numerius Rufus (RE 5)
59	Caecilius (RE 1)
58	C. Calpurnius Piso Frugi (RE 93) Cn. Plancius (RE 4)
58?	Canidius (RE 1) C. Trebonius (RE 6)
57?	M. Caelius Rufus (RE 35)

---

[1] Ryan 1994d, proposes that C. Cornelius Cethegus, one of the leaders of the Catilinarian plot, was urban quaestor in 63. Ryan's proposal is ultimately a speculation without evidence to support it.

	M. Nonius Sufenas (q. or moneyer?) (RE 52)
56?	M. Servilius (RE 20)
55?	C. Cassius Longinus (RE 59) C. Sallustius Crispus (and 48?) (RE 10) C. Scribonius Curio (RE 11)
between 55 and 51?	Q. Cassius Longinus (RE 70)
55 or 54?	L. Minucius Basilus (RE 38)
before 54	M. Coelius Vinicianus (RE 27)
by 54?	T. Ligarius (RE 5)
54	Faustus Cornelius Sulla (RE 377) M. Licinius Crassus (RE 56)
54?	M. Junius Brutus (RE 53)
between 54 and 51	Furius Crassipes (RE 54)
53 or 52	L. Ateius Capito (RE 9) M. Eppius (RE 2)
by 52?	L. Caecilius Metellus (RE 75)
before 51	Servaeus (RE 3)
by 51?	M. Aquinius (or Aquinus) (RE Aquinius 2; cf. Aquinus 5)
51	M. Antonius (RE 30) L. Mescinius Rufus (RE 2)
51?	C. Antonius (RE 20) Caninius Sallusti(an)us? (RE 1 A.2 1913 and 1919; Caninius 14)
51–50?	Q. Hortensius Hortalus (RE 8)
by 50 or earlier	L. Julius Caesar (RE 144)

50	T. Antistius (RE 22)
	L. Antonius Pietas (RE 23)
	C. Coelius Caldus (RE 14)
	(L.) Marius (RE 4)
50?	T. Furfan(i)us Postumus (RE 1)
	D. Junius Brutus Albinus (RE 55a, suppl. 5)
50 or 49?	Ser. Sulpicius Rufus (RE 96)
by 49?	C. Decimius (RE 2)
	M. Minatius Sabinus (RE 3)
49	Cn. Calpurnius Piso (Frugi) (RE 95)
	Marcius Rufus (RE 94)
	Cn. Nerius (RE 3)
	L. (or T.?) Postumius (RE 15)
	Sex. Quinctilius Varus (RE *10)
	A.? (Terentius) Varro (RE 78)
49?	T. Pompeius Longinus (RE 29)
	A. Pomp(onius) Vic(tor) (not in RE)
	Q. Raesius (or Caesius?) (not in RE)
	Servius Cordus (RE 3)
	C. Sextilius Rufus (RE 23)
48	M. Claudius Marcellus Aeserninus (RE 232–233)
	Ti. Claudius Nero (RE 254)
	P. Cornelius Lentulus Marcellinus (RE 232)
	C. Plaetorius (RE 5)
48?	P. Cornelius Sulla? (RE 387)
	Sex. Julius Caesar (RE 153)
	C. Sallustius Crispus (and 55?) (RE 10)
48 or 47	P.? Appuleius (RE 2? 15?)
48–47	Q. Cornificius (RE 8)
before 46	Tullius Rufus (RE 49)
46	Granius Petro (q. desig.) (RE 9)
	M. Terentius Varro Gibba (RE 89)

46?	Q. Aelius L. f. Tubero (RE 156)
45?	M. Appuleius (RE 13)
45–44?	C. Antistius Vetus (RE 47)
44	Q. Cornelius (RE 5 and 52; cf. 51)
	(Cornelius) Cinna (RE 104)
	P. Cornelius Lentulus Spinther (RE 239)
	L. Egnatuleius (RE 2)
	Q. Rutilius (RE 11)
	D. Turullius (RE 1)
44?	P. Aemilius Lepidus (not in RE)
	L. Cornelius Balbus (RE 70)
	D. Laelius D. f. Balbus (RE 6)
44–42	L. Sestius Quirinalis Albinianus (RE 3)
late first century, maybe in the 40s	M. Ampudius (RE 1)
	C. Appuleius Tappo (RE 31)
	L. Caecina (not in RE)
	Q. Caerellius (RE 2)
	L. Livius Ocella (RE 26)
	L. Memmius (RE 15)
	Q. Sanquinius (RE 3)
	M'. Valerius Messala Potitus (RE 267)
of uncertain date	M' Sergius (RE 18)
	L. Serveilius (RE 17)
	M. Se—(not in RE)

Bibliography

Abbreviations
Broughton MRR
Crawford RRC
Mommsen Röm. St.
Shackleton-Bailey, *Ep.Att.*
Sherk, RDGE

Afzelius, A. (1946) "Lex Annalis", *Classica et Mediaevalia* 8, 263–278.
Alexander, M.C. (1990) *Trials in the late Roman Republic, 149 BC to 50 BC*, Toronto.
Alföldi, A. (1959) "Hasta Summa Imperii", *AJA* 63, 1–27.
Amela Valverde, L. (1990–1991) "La amonedación pompeyana en Hispania. Su utilización como medio propagandístico y como reflejo de la clientela de la *gens Pompeia*", *Faventia* 12–13, 181–197.
Ameling, W. (1989) "Lucius Licinius in Chios", *ZPE* 77, 98–100.
Antela-Bernárdez, B. (2012) "The coinage of C. Annius Luscus", in F. López Sánchez (ed.) *The City and the Coin in the Ancient and Early Medievals Worlds*, Oxford, 37–47.
Antela-Bernárdez, B. (2013) "Los cuestores de C. Annio y el gobierno provincial en Hispania", *L'Antiquité Classique* 82, 263–265.
Arkenberg, J.S. (1993) "Licinii Murenae, Terentii Varrones, and Varrones Murenae: I. A Prosopographical Study of Three Roman Families", *Historia* 42, 326–351.
Astin, A.E. (1958) *The Lex Annalis before Sulla*, Bruxelles.
Astin, A.E. (1967) *Scipio Aemilianus*, Oxford.
Astin, A.E. (1978) *Cato the Censor*, Oxford.
Babelon, E. (1885) *Description historique et chronologique des monnaie de la République romaine vulgairement appelées monnaies consulaires*, Paris.
Badian, E. (1954) "*Lex Acilia repetundarum*", *AJPh* 75, 374–384.
Badian, E. (1956) "Quintus Mucius Scaevola and the Province of Asia", *Athenaeum* 34, 104–123.
Badian, E. (1957) "Caepio and Norbanus: Notes on the Decade 100–90 B.C.", *Historia* 6, 318–346.
Badian, E. (1959a) "Caesar's Cursus and the Intervals between Offices", *JRS* 49, 81–89.
Badian, E. (1959b) "The Early Career of A. Gabinius (Cos. 58 B.C.)", *Philologus* 103, 87–99.
Badian, E. (1961) "Review to Broughton, T. R. S., *Supplement to the Magistrates of the Roman Republic*", *Gnomon* 33, 492–498.
Badian, E. (1962) "Waiting for Sulla", *JRS* 52, 1962, 47–61.
Badian, E. (1963) "Notes on Roman Senators of the Republic", *Historia* 12, 129–143.
Badian, E. (1964) *Studies in Greek and Roman history*, New York.
Badian, E. (1965) "M. Porcius Cato and the Annexation and Early Administration of Cyprus", *JRS* 55, 110–121.
Badian, E. (1968a) [1970] "The Sempronii Aselliones", *Proceedings of the African Classical Association* 11, 1–6.
Badian, E. (1968b) Review of Degrassi, ILLRP, *JRS* 58, 240–249.
Badian, E. (1969) "Two Roman non-entities", *CQ* 19, 198–204.
Badian, E. (1971a) "Roman Politics and the Italians (133–91 B.C.)", *Dialoghi di Archeologia* 4–5, 373–421.
Badian, E. (1971b) "The family and early career of T. Quinctius Flamininus", *JRS* 61, 1971, 102–111.
Badian, E. (1971c) "Two More Roman Non-Entities", *Phoenix* 25, 134–144.

Badian, E. (1974) "The Quaestorship of Tiberius Nero", *Mnemosyne* 27, 160–172.
Badian, E. (1979) Review of H. Kloft, *Prorogation und außerordentliche Imperien 326–81 v. Chr.*, *Gnomon* 51, 792–794.
Badian, E. (1980) "A fundus at Fundi", *AJPh* 101, 470–482.
Badian, E. (1983) "The Silence of Norbanus: A Note on Provincial Quaestors under the Republic", *AJPh* 104, 156–171.
Badian, E. (1984a) "The Death of Saturninus", *Chiron* 14, 101–147.
Badian, E. (1984b) "Three Non-Trials in Cicero: Notes on the Text, Prosopography and Chronology of *Divinatio in Caecilium* 63", *Klio* 66, 291–309.
Badian, E. (1986) "Two notes on *senatus consulta* concerning Pergamum", *LCM* 11, 14–16.
Badian, E. (1990) "The Consuls, 179–49 BC", *Chiron* 20, 371–413.
Bahrfeldt, M. (1904) "Die römisch-sicilischen Münzen aus der Zeit der Republik", *Revue Suisse de Numismatique* 12, 331–445.
Ballesteros Pastor, L. (1996) *Mitrídates Eupátor, rey del Ponto*, Granada.
Ballesteros Pastor, L. (2009) "Quinto Pompeyo Bitínico y el testamento de Nicomedes IV", *Habis* 40, 127–133.
Balsdon, J.P.V.D. (1937) "Q. Mucius Scaevola the Pontifex and *ornatio provinciae*", *CR* 51, 8–10.
Balsdon, J.P.V.D. (1962) "Roman History, 65–50 B.C.: Five Problems", *JRS* 52, 134–141.
Bandy, A.C. (1983) *Ioannes Lydus, On Powers or the Magistracies of the Roman State*, Philadelphia.
Barrandon, N. and Hurlet, F. (2009) "Les gouverneurs et l'Occident romain (IIe siècle av. J.-C. – IIe siècle ap. J.-C.", in F. Hurlet (ed.), *Rome et l'Occident (IIe siècle av. J.-C. – IIe siècle apr. J.-C.). Gouverner l'Empire*, Rennes, 35–75.
Bastien, J.-L. (2007) *Le triomphe romain et son utilisation politique à Rome aux trois derniers siècles de la République*, Rome.
Bauslaugh, R.A. (2000) *Silver coinage with the types of Aesillas the quaestor*, Numismatic Studies 22, New York.
Bean, G.E. (1954) "Notes and inscriptions from Caunus (continued)", *JHS* 74, 85–110.
Beck, H. (2005) *Karriere und Hierarchie: Die römische Aristokratie und die Anfänge des cursus honorum in der mittleren Republik*, Berlin.
Beck H. and Walter, U. (2001 and 2004) *Die frühen römischen Historiker*, 2 vols. Darmstadt.
Bellemore, J. (1996) "The quaestorship of Cato and the tribunate of Memmius", *Historia* 45, 504–508.
Beltrán Lloris, F. (1990) "La *pietas* de Sertorio", *Gerión* 8, 211–226.
Beness, J.L. (1991) "The Urban Unpopularity of Lucius Appuleius Saturninus", *Antichton* 25, 33–62.
Bengtson, H. (1977) *Marcus Antonius. Triumvir und Herrscher des Orients*, Munich.
Bernstein, A.H. (1978) *Tiberius Sempronius Gracchus. Tradition and Apostasy*, Ithaca.
Berrendonner, C. (2014) "Pour administrer, faut-il-savoir compter? Les questeurs provinciaux et la tenue des comptabilités publiques (IIe-Ier siècles av. J.-C.)", in J. Dubouloz, S. Pittia and G. Sabatini (eds.), *L'imperium Romanum en perspective. Les savoirs d'empire dans la République romaine et leur héritage dans l'Europe médiévale et moderne*, Besançon, 173–191.
Berve, H. (1929) "Sertorius", *Hermes* 64, 199–227.
Biedl, A. (1930) "De Memmiorum Familia", *WS* 48, 1930, 98–107.
Blasi, M. (2008) "...*Publico funere censuit efferendum:* sul supposto *funus publicum* per Siface e sul modello Perseo", *Ziva Antika* 58, 71–85.
Blasi, M. (2012) *Strategie funerarie: onori funebri pubblici e lotta politica nella Roma medio e tardorepubblicana, 230–27 a.C.*, Roma.
Blom, H. van der (2016) *Oratory and Political Career in the late Roman Republic*, Cambridge.

Blösel, W. (2016) "Provincial Commands and Money in the Late Roman Republic", in H. Beck, M. Jehne and J. Serrati (eds.), *Money and Power in the Roman Republic*, Brussels.
Boehringer, C. (1972) *Zur Chronologie Mittelhellenistischer Münzserien 220–160 v. Chr.*, Berlin.
Box, H. (1942) "Ciceron, in Verrem I.30", *Classical Review* 56, 72.
Braund, D. (1983) "Royal Wills and Rome", *PBSR* 51, 16–57.
Braund, D. (1985) "The Social and Economic Context of the Roman Annexation of Cyrenaica", in G. Barker, J. Lloyd and J. Reynolds (eds.), *Cyrenaica in Antiquity*, Oxford, 319–325.
Brennan, D.B. (1969) "Cordus and the burial of Pompey", *CPh* 64, 103–104.
Brennan, T.C. (2000) *The Praetorship in the Roman Republic*, Oxford.
Broughton, T.R.S. (1946) "Notes on Roman magistrates. I. The command of M. Antonius in Cilicia. II. Lucullus' commission and Pompey's acta", *TAPhA* 77, 35–43.
Broughton, T.R.S. (1948) "The *elogium* of Julius Caesar's father", *AJA* 52, 323–330.
Broughton, T.R.S. (1951–1952, 1986) *The Magistrates of the Roman Republic*, 3 vols. Atlanta (abbreviation MRR).
Brunt, P.A. (1972) "Cn. Tremellius Scrofa the Agronomist", *Classical Review* 22, 304–308.
Brunt, P.A. (1973) "Corrigendum Cn. Tremellius Scrofa", *Classical Review* 23, 295.
Brunt, P.A. (1988) "*Tabula Bantina*", in P.A. Brunt, *The Fall of the Roman Republic and Related Essays*, Oxford, 139–143.
Bülz, M. (1893) *De provinciarum romanarum quaestoribus qui fuerunt ab a.u.c. 672 usque ad a.u.c. 710*, Diss. Chemnitz.
Bülz, M. (1908) *Fasti quaestorum qui ab urbe condita CCCXXXX ad ab urbe condita DCLXXI extra Romam fuerunt*, Zittau.
Buttrey, Jr., T.V. (1960) "The Denarii of Cn. Pompeius Jr. and M. Minatius Sabinus", *American Numismatic Society. Museum Notes*, 9, 75–94.
Buttrey, Jr., T.V. (1987) "Crete and Cyrenaica", in A. M. Burnett and M. H. Crawford (eds.), *The Coinage of the Roman World in the Late Republic. Proceedings of a colloquium held at the British Museum in September 1985*, Oxford, 165–174.
Caimi, J. (1984) *Burocrazia e diritto nel 'de magistratibus' di Giovanni Lido*, Milan.
Campbell, B. (2000) *The Writings of the Roman Land Surveyors*, London.
Canali de Rossi, F. (2001) *Il ruolo dei 'patroni' nelle relazioni politiche fra il mondo greco e Rome in età repubblicana ed augustea*, Munich.
Carney, T.F. (1961) *A Biography of C. Marius*, Proceedings of the African Classical Associations, Supplement 1, Assen.
Castillo Pascual, Mª J. (1996) *Espacio en orden: el modelo gromático-romano de ordenación del territorio*, Logroño.
Cébeillac Gervasoni, M. (2002) "Les rapports institutionnels et politiques d'Ostie et de Rome de la République au IIIe siècle ap. J.-C.", *MEFRA* 114, 59–86.
Cébeillac Gervasoni, M. (2014) "Quaestor Ostiensis: une fonction ingrate?", in M. Chiabà (ed.) *Hoc quoque laboris praemium. Scritti in onore di Gino Bandelli*, Trieste, 53–62.
Chamoux, F. (1986) *Marc Antoine, dernier prince de l'Orient grec*, Paris.
Champlin, E. (1989) review of T.R.S. Broughton, *The Magistrates of the Roman Republic*, vol. 3: Supplement, *CPh* 84, 51–59.
Chandler, D.C. (1978) "Quaestor Ostiensis", *Historia* 27, 328–335.
Charpin, F. (1979) *Lucilius: Satires*, Paris.
Churchill, J.B. (1999) "*Ex qua quod vellent facerent*: Roman Magistrates' Authority over *Praeda* and *Manubiae*", *TAPhA* 129, 85–116.
Cichorius, C. (1908) *Untersuchungen zu Lucillius*, Berlin.
Cichorius, C. (1922) *Römische Studien. Historisches, Epigraphisches, Literargeschichtliches aus vier Jahrhunderten Roms*, Leipzig – Berlin.
Clark, J.H. (2014) *Triumph in Defeat. Military Loss and the Roman Republic*, Oxford.

Clarke, M.L. (1981) *The Noblest Roman. Marcus Brutus and his Reputation*, Ithaca, New York.
Cloud, D. (1971) "*Parricidium:* From the *lex Numae* to the *lex Pompeia de parricidiis*", *Zeitschrift der Savigny-Stiftung für Rechtsgeschichte* 88, 1–66.
Cloud, D. (1998) "A pattern of error in Ioannes Lydus: the parricide quaestors", in M. Humbert and Y. Thomas (eds.), *Mélanges à la memoire de André Magdelain*, 91–108.
Cloud, D. (2003) "Motivation in Ancient Accounts of the Early History of the Quaestorship and its Consequences for Modern Historiography", *Chiron* 33, 93–120.
Coarelli, F. (1999) s.v. Pons Aemilius, in E.M. Steinby (ed.), *LTUR*, vol.4 Rome, 106–107.
Coarelli, F. (2014) "I *quaestores classici* e la battaglia delle Egadi", in M. Chiabà (ed.) *Hoc quoque laboris praemium. Scritti in onore di Gino Bandelli*, Trieste, 99–114.
Corbier, M. (1974) *L'Aerarium Saturni et l'Aerarium Militare. Administration et prosopographie sénatoriale*, Rome.
Cornell, T.J. (1995) *The Beginnings of Rome. Italy and Rome from the Bronze Age to the Punic Wars (c.1000–264 BC)*, London – New York.
Cornell, T.J. (ed.) (2013) *The Fragments of the Roman Historians*, 3 vols. Oxford.
Cotton, H.M. (1979) "Cicero, Ad familiares XIII, 26 and 28: Evidence for *Revocatio* or *Reiectio Romae/Romam?*", *JRS* 69, 39–50.
Coudry, M. (1994) "Sénatus-consultes et *acta senatus* rédaction, conservation et archivage des documents émanant du Sénat, de l'époque de César à celle des Sévères", in C. Nicolet (ed.) *La mémoire perdue. À la recherche des archives oubliées, publiques et privées, de la Rome antique*, Paris, 65–102.
Coudry, M. (2004) "Contrôle et traitement des ambassadeurs étrangers sous la République romaine", in C. Moatti (ed.), *La mobilité des personnes en Méditerranée de l'Antiquité à l'époque moderne. Procédures de contrôle et documents d'identification*, Rome, 529–565.
Coudry, M. (2009) "Partage et gestion du butin dans la Rome républicaine: procédures et enjeux", in M. Coudry and M. Humm (eds.), *Praeda. Butin de guerre et société dans la Rome républicaine*, Stuttgart, 21–79.
Covino, R. (2011) "The fifth century, the Decemvirate, and the Quaestorship", *Australasian Society for Classical Studies* 32.
Covino, R. (2012) "On the Identity of the 'Q. Fabius' of Val. Max. 2.7.3", *Studia Humaniora Tartuensia*, 13, A.4 (available in http://sht.ut.ee/index.php/sht/article/view/13.A.4).
Covino, R. (2013) s.v. Quaestor, in R.S. Bagnall, K. Brodersen, C.B. Champion and A. Erskine (eds.), *The Encyclopedia of Ancient History*.
Crawford, M.H. (1969) "Saturninus and the Italians", *Classical Philology* 64, 37–38.
Crawford, M.H. (1974) *Roman Republican Coinage*, Cambridge (abbreviation RRC).
Crawford, M.H. (1982) "M. Silanus Murena", *LCM* 7, 124.
Crawford, M. H. (1985) *Coinage and Money under the Roman Republic*, Berkeley – Los Angeles.
Crawford, M.H. (ed.) (1996) *Roman Statutes*, 2 vols., London.
Crawford, M.H. and Coleman, R.G. (1996) "*Lex Osca Tabulae Bantinae*", in M.H. Crawford (ed.), *Roman Statutes*, London, I 271–292.
Criniti, N. (1970) *L'epigrafe di Asculum di Gn. Pompeo Strabone*, Milan.
Cuomo, S. (2011) "All the proconsul's men: Cicero, Verres and account-keeping", in A. Roselli and R. Velardi (eds.) *L'insegnamento delle technai nelle culture antiche: atti del convegno, Ercolano, 23–24 marzo 2009 AION. Quaderni* 15, 165–185.
Daguet-Gagey, A. (2015) *Splendor aedilitatum. L'édilité à Rome (Ier s. avant J.-C. -IIIe s. après J.-C.)*, Rome.
Dalla Rosa, A. (2015) "Il concetto di *provincia*", in C. Letta and S. Segenni (eds.) *Roma e le sue province. Dalla prima guerra Punica a Diocleziano*, Rome, 19–22.
Dart, C. (2012) "*Duumviri navales* and the navy of the Roman Republic", *Latomus* 71, 1000–1014.

David, J.-M. (2007) "Ce que les *Verrines* nous apprennent sur les scribes de magistrats à la fin de la République", in *La Sicile de Cicéron: lecture des Verrines. Actes du colloque de Paris (19–20 mai 2006)*, Besançon, 35–56.

David, J.-M. (2019) *Au service de l'honneur. Les appariteurs de magistrats romains*, Paris.

De Callataÿ, F. (1996) "Les monnaies au nom d'Aesillas", in *Italiam fato profugi Hesperinaque uenerunt litora. Numismatic Studies Dedicated to Vladimir and Elvira Eliza Clain-Stefanelli*, Louvain, 113–151.

De Callataÿ, F. (1998) "The Coins in the Name of Sura", in A. Burnett, U. Wartenberg and R. Witschonke (eds.), *Coins of Macedonia and Rome: Essays in Honour of Charles Hersh*, London, 113–117.

De Francisci, P. (1959) *Primordia civitatis*, Rome.

De Martino, F. (1960) *Storia della costituzione romana*, Naples.

De Michele, L. (2005) "Fimbria e Sertorio: *proditores reipublicae?*", *Athenaeum* 93, 277–289.

De Sanctis, G. (1907) *Storia dei romani*, Milan-Turin.

De Souza, P. (1999) *Piracy in the Graeco-Roman World*, Cambridge.

Della Corte, F. (^{2}1969) *Catone Censore. La vita e la fortuna*, Florence.

Dementyeva, V.V. (2009) "The Functions of the Quaestors of Archaic Rome in Criminal Justice", *Diritto @ Storia* 8.

Deniaux, E. (1979) "À propos des Herennii de la République et de l'époque d'Auguste", *MEFRA* 91, 623–650.

Dettenhofer, M.H. (1992) *Perdita iuventus: zwischen den Generationen von Caesar und Augustus*, Munich.

Develin, R. (1978a) "The Atinian plebiscite, tribunes, and the senate", *CQ* 28, 141–144.

Develin, R. (1978b) "Tradition and the Development of Triumphal Regulations in Rome", *Klio* 60, 429–438.

Develin, R. (1979) *Patterns in Office-Holding, 366–49 BC*, Bruxelles.

Develin, R. (^{2}2005) "The integration of plebeians into the political order after 366 B.C.", in K.A. Raaflaub, ed., *Social Struggles in Archaic Rome. New perspectives on the conflict of the orders*, Oxford, 293–311.

Di Stefano Manzella, I. (1982) in *Epigrafia e Ordine Senatorio*, Rome, vol. 1, 521–525.

Díaz Ariño, B. (2008a) "Un *quaestor pro praetore* republicano en Carthago Nova", *JRA* 21, 255–263.

Díaz Ariño, B. (2008b) *Epigrafía Latina Republicana de España*, Barcelona.

Díaz Ariño, B. (2011) "Epigrafía y gobernadores provinciales en Hispania durante la época republicana", *Chiron*, 149–179.

Díaz Fernández, A. (2014) "A propósito de M. Porcio Catón y su presencia en la *Gallia Narbonensis* (Gel., 13.10.12)", *DHA*, 75–96.

Díaz Fernández, A. (2015) *Provincia et Imperium. El mando provincial en la República romana (227–44 a.C.)*, Seville.

Díaz Fernández, A. (2017a) "A Survey of the Roman Provincial Command from Republican Epigraphy: The Cases of Sicily and Sardinia", in J. Velaza (ed.), *Insularity, Identity and Epigraphy in the Roman World*, Cambridge, 69–92.

Díaz Fernández, A. (2017b) "*Asullius*: A Missing Roman *Nomen?*", *Latomus* 76, 961–974.

Díaz Fernández, A. (2019) "Military Disasters, Public Opinion, and Roman Politics during the Wars in Hispania (153–133 B.C.)", in C. Rosillo-López (ed.), *Communicating Public Opinion in the Roman World*, Stuttgart, 107–133.

Dillon, M. and Garland, L. (^{2}2015) *Ancient Rome: Social and Historical Documents from the Early Republic to the Death of Augustus*, London – New York.

Dimitrova, N.M. (2008) *Theoroi and Initiates in Samothrace: The Epigraphical Evidence*, Princeton.

Dittenberger, W. – Purgold, K. (eds.) (1896) *Die Inschriften von Olympia*, Berlin.

D'Orta, M. (1993) "Trebazio Testa e la questura. A proposito di D. l. 13.1.1 (Ulp. *l. sing. de officio quaestoris*)", *Studia et Documenta Historiae et Iuris* 59, 279–297.
Douglas, A.E. (1966) "*Oratorum aetates*", *AJPh* 87, 290–306.
Dreyer, B. and Smarczyk, B. (2009) "*Res publica ut aliena*. Zur Funktion der republikanischen Verfassungsexkurse bei Tacitus", *Gymnasium* 116, 135–168.
Drogula, F. K. (2015) *Commanders and Command in the Roman Republic and Early Empire*, Chapel Hill.
Drummond, A. (1989) "Rome in the fifth century II: The citizen community", in *The Cambridge Ancient History*, 2nd edition, vol. 7, part 2, Cambridge, 172–242.
Drummond, A. (2008) "The ban on gentiles holding the same priesthood and Sulla's augurate", *Historia* 57, 367–407.
Dubuisson M. (1991) "Jean le Lydien et les formes de pouvoir personnel à Rome", *Cahiers du centre Gustave Glotz* 2, 55–72.
Dubuisson M. (1992) "Jean le Lydien et le latin: les limites d'une compétence", *Serta Leodiensia Secunda*, Liège, CIPL, 123–131.
Dubuisson, M. and Schamp, J. (eds.) *Jean le Lydien. Des magistratures de l'État romain*, 3 vol., Paris.
Duncan-Jones, R. (1974) *The Economy of the Roman Empire. Quantitative Studies*, Cambridge.
Dyck, A.R. (2013) *Cicero: Pro Marco Caelio*, Cambridge.
Dzino, D. (2010) *Illyricum in Roman Politics, 229 BC – AD 68*, Cambridge.
Earl, D.C. (1966) "The early career of Sallust", *Historia* 15, 302–311.
Eck, W. (2005) "Der Senator und die Öffentlichkeit – oder: wie beeindruckt man das Publikum?", in W. Eck and M. Heil (eds.), *Senatores populi Romani. Realität und mediale Präsentation einer Führungsschicht*, Stuttgart, 1–18.
Eckstein, A.M. (2012) "Rome Dominates the Mediterranean", in A. Erickson, L. Goldstein and C. Lord (eds.), *China Goes to Sea Maritime Transformation in Comparative Historical Perspective*, Annapolis, 63–92.
Eilers, C. (1996) "Silanus <and> Murena (I. Priene 121)", *CQ* 46, 175–182.
Eilers, C. (2002) *Roman Patrons of Greek cities*, Oxford.
Engels, J. (1998) *Funerum sepulcrorumque magnificentia*, Stuttgart.
Erdkamp, P. (2005) *The Grain Market in the Roman Empire. A Social, Political and Economic Study*, Cambridge.
Etienne, R. (1997) *Jules César*, Paris.
Evans, R.J. (1987) "Norbani Flacci: The consuls of 38 and 24 B.C.", *Historia* 36, 121–128.
Evans, R.J. (1994) *Gaius Marius: A Political Biography*, Pretoria.
Evans, R.J. and Kleijwegt, M. (1992) "Did the Romans Like Young Men? A Study of the *lex Villia Annalis:* Causes and Effects", *ZPE* 92, 181–195.
Fallu, E. (1973a) "La Questure de Ciceron. Examen de la fonction questorienne dans le domain de la fiscalité en Sicile", *CEA* 2, 31–53.
Fallu, E. (1973b) "Les *rationes* du proconsul Cicéron. Un exemple de style administratif et d'interprétation historique dans la correspondance de Cicéron", *ANRW* 1.3, 209–238.
Fallu, E. (1979) "Les règles de la comptabilité publique à Rome à la fin de la République", in H. van Effenterre (ed.), *Points de vue sur la fiscalité antique*, Paris.
Famerie, E. (1999) "La transposition de *quaestor* en grec", *L'Antiquité Classique* 68, 211–225.
Fazio, A. (1891–1892) "Sull'origine dei quaestores", *Annuario dello Istituto di Storia del Diritto Romano. Università Catania* 2, 62–65.
Fehrle, R. (1983) *Cato Uticensis*, Darmstadt.
Ferenczy, E. (1965) "La carrière d'Appius Claudius Caecus jusqu'à la censure", *AAntHung* 13, 379–404 = "The career of Appius Claudius Caecus to the censorship", *From the Patrician State to the Patricio-Plebeian State*, Budapest 1976, 120–143.

Ferone, C. (2003) "Lido, *De Magistratibus* I 27 e la politica navale di Roma nel III sec. a.C.", *Klio* 85, 70–81.

Ferrary, J.-L. (1984) "L'archéologie du *de re Publica* (2,2,4–37,63): Cicéron entre Polybe et Platon", *Journal of Roman Studies* 74, 87–98.

Ferrary, J.-L. (2000a) "Les inscriptions du sanctuaire de Claros en l'honneur de Romains", *BCH* 124, 331–376.

Ferrary, J.-L. (2000b) "Les Gouverneurs des provinces romaines d'Asie Mineure (Asie et Cilicie), depuis l'organisation de la province d'Asie jusqu'à la première guerre de Mithridate (126–88 av. J.-C.)", *Chiron*, 30, 161–193.

Ferrary, J.-L. (2010) "La législation comitiale en matière de création, d'assignation et de gouvernement des provinces", in N. Barrandon and F. Kirbihler (eds.), *Administrer les provinces de la République romaine. Actes du colloque de l'université de Nancy II. 4–5 juin 2009*, Rennes, 33–44.

Ferrary, J.-L. (2014) "Loi Acilia *de pecuniis repetundis* (pl. sc.)", in J.-L. Ferrary and Ph. Moreau (eds.), *Leges Populi Romani* (online), Paris, http://www.cn-telma.fr/lepor/notice3/ (last updated 17th September 2014).

Ferriès, M.-C. (2007) *Les partisans d'Antoine (des orphelins de César aux complices de Cléopâtre)*, Bordeaux.

Flach, D. (1994) *Die Gesetze der frühen römischen Republik*, Darmstadt.

Flower, H. (2010) *Roman Republics*, Princeton.

Forsythe, G. (2005) *A Critical History of Early Rome. From Prehistory to the First Punic War*, Berkeley.

Frank, T. (1937) "The new *elogium* of Julius Caesar's Father", *AJPh* 58, 90–93.

Frassinetti, P. (1975) "I fatti in Spagna nel libro II delle *Historiae* di Sallustio", *Studi Urbinati* 49, 381–398.

French, D.H. (1995) "Milestones from the Izmir region 1994", *Epigraphica Anatolica* 25, 95–102.

Frey-Kupper, S. (2013) *Die antiken Fundmünzen vom Monte Iato 1971–1990. Ein Beitrag zur Geldgeschichte Westsiziliens*, Lausanne.

Gabba, E. (1954) "Le origini della Guerra Sociale e la vita politica romana dopo l'89 A.C.", *Athenaeum* 32, 41–114 and 293–345.

Gabba, E. (1976) *Republican Rome, the Army, and the Allies*, Oxford (^{1}Florence 1973).

Gabba, E. (1983) "Lineamenti di un commento alla *Lex Cornelia de XX quaestoribus*", *Athenaeum* 61, 487–493.

Gabrielli, Ch. (2012) *Moneta e finanza a Roma in età repubblicana*, Roma.

Gaebler, H. (1902) "Zur Münzkunde Makedoniens", *Zeitschrift für Numismatik* 23, 141–189.

Gagliardi, L. (2009) "La *lex Iunia Licinia* e le procedure di pubblicazione e di conservazione delle leges nella Roma tardo-repubblicana", *Diritto@Storia* 8, www.dirittoestoria.it/8/Tradizione-Romana/Gagliardi-Lex-Iunia-Licinia.htm.

Galsterer, H. (1971) "Die *lex Osca tabulae Bantinae*. Eine Bestandsaufnahme", *Chiron* 1, 191–214.

García Morcillo, M. (2005) *Las ventas por subasta en el mundo romano: la esfera privada*, Barcelona.

García Riaza, E. (2002) *Celtíberos y lusitanos frente a Roma: diplomacia y derecho de guerra*, Vitoria.

Garnsey, P. (1988) *Famine and Food Supply in the Graeco-Roman World*, Cambridge.

Garofalo, L. (1985) "La competenza giudiziaria dei 'quaestores' e Pomp. D. 1,2,2,16 e 23", *Studia et Documenta Historiae et Iuris* 51, 409–423.

Gasperini, L. (1967) "Due nuovi apporti epigrafici alla storia di Cirene romana", *QAL* 5, 53–64.

Geer, R.M. (1934) "Suetonius, Augustus, II, 2", *AJPh* 55, 337–339.

Geiger, J. (1972) "Canidius or Caninius?", *CQ* 22, 130–134.

Giovagnoli, M. (2012) "Il capitolato d'appalto della Via Cecilia', in R. Friggeri, M.G. Granino Cecere and G.L. Gregori (eds.), *Terme di Diocleziano. La collezione epigrafica*, Milan, 207–208.

Giovannini, A. (1984) "Les origines des magistratures romaines", *Museum Helveticum* 41, 15–30.
Gnoli, T. (2012) *Navalia: guerre e commerci nel Mediterraneo romano*, Rome.
González Fernández, J. (1982) *Inscripciones romanas de la provincia de Cádiz*, Cadiz.
Grant, M. (1946) *From Imperium to Auctoritas. A Historical Study of the Aes Coinage in the Roman Empire, 49 B.C. – A.D. 14*, Cambridge.
Greenidge, A.H.J. (1901a) *Roman Public Life*, London.
Greenidge, A.H.J. (1901b) *The Legal Procedure of Cicero's Time*, Oxford.
Gregori, G.L. (2007–08) "*Loca sepulturae publice data* e *funera publica* nel Lazio d'età romana: qualche considerazione sulla documentazione epigrafica", in G. Bartoloni and M.G. Benedettini (eds.) *Sepolti tra i vivi. Buried among the living. Evidenza ed interpretazione di contesti funerary in abitato. Scienze dell'Antichità* 14, 1067–1079.
Griffin, M. (1973) "The tribune C. Cornelius", *JRS* 63, 196–213.
Gruen, E.S. (1964) "Politics and the courts in 104 B.C.", *Transactions and Proceedings of the American Philological Association* 95, 99–110.
Gruen, E.S. (1966a) "Political prosecutions in the 90's B.C.", *Historia* 15, 32–64.
Gruen, E.S. (1966b) "The Dolabellae and Sulla", *AJPh* 87, 385–399.
Gruen, E.S. (1966c) "The Quaestorship of Norbanus", *Classical Philology* 61, 105–107.
Gruen, E.S. (1968a) "Pompey and the Pisones", *California Studies in Classical Antiquity* 1, 155–170.
Gruen, E.S. (1968b) *Roman Politics and the Criminal Courts, 149–78 B.C.*, Cambridge Mass.
Gruen, E.S. (1974) *The Last Generation of the Roman Republic*, Berkeley – Los Angeles.
Gruen, E. S. (1984) *The Hellenistic World and the Coming of Rome*, Berkeley – Los Angeles – London.
Gruen, E.S. (1992) *Culture and National Identity in Republican Rome*, Cornell.
Ioannidopoulos, G. (2017) "M. Aemilius Scaurus et P. Plautius Hypsaeus: Pompée et ses questeurs entre 67 et 61", *L'Antiquité Classique* 86, 97–113.
Hamilton, Ch.D. (1969) "The *Tresviri Monetales* and the Republican *Cursus Honorum*", *Transactions and Proceedings of the American Philological Association* 100, 181–199.
Harmand, J. (1957) *Un aspect social et politique du monde romain: le patronat sur les collectivités publiques, des origines au Bas-Empire*, Paris.
Harries, J. (2007) *Law and Crime in the Roman World*, Cambridge.
Harris, W.V. (1976) "The Development of the Quaestorship, 267–81 B.C.", *CQ* 26, 92–106.
Harris, W.V. (1979a) *War and Imperialism in Republican Rome, 327–70 BC*, Oxford.
Harris, W.V. (1979b) "Lydus, *De Magistratibus* I 27. A Reply", *BASP* 16, 199–200.
Harris, W.V. (2006) "A Revisionist View of Roman Money", *JRS* 96, 1–24.
Harris, W.V. (2017) "Rome at Sea: The Beginnings of Roman Naval Power", *Greece & Rome* 64, 14–26.
Haussoullier, B. (1899) "Un nouveau milliaire au nom de Manius Aquillius", *Rev.Phil.* 23, 293–299.
Head, B. V. (1911) Historia Numorum. *A Manual of Greek Numismatics*, Oxford.
Hermon, E. (1997) "M'. Curius Dentatus et les ventes questoriennes au IIIe siécle av. J. C.", *Scripta Classica Israelica* 16, 32–42.
Hersh, C. and Walker, A. (1984) "The Mesagne Hoard", *ANSMusN* 29, 103–134.
Herzog, E. von (1884) *Geschichte und System der römischen Staatsverfassung*, vol.1, Leipzig.
Heurgon, J. (1953) "Tarquitius Priscus et l'organisation de l'ordre des haruspices sous l'empereur Claude", *Latomus* 12, 402–417.
Heuss, A. (1944) "Zur Entwicklung des Imperiums der römischen Oberbeamten", *Zeitschrift der Savigny-Stiftung für Rechtsgeschichte* 64, 57–133.
Hinard, F. (1985a) *Les proscriptions de la Rome républicaine*, Rome.
Hinard, F. (1985b) *Sylla*, Paris.

Hinard, F. (1991) "Philologie, prosopographie et histoire à propos de Lucius Fabius Hispaniensis", *Historia* 40, 113–119.

Hinrichs, F.T. (1970) "Die Lateinische Tafel von Bantia und die '*lex de piratis*", *Hermes* 98, 471–502.

Hollstein, W. (1993) *Die stadtrömische Münzprägung der Jahre 78–50 v. Chr. zwischen politischer Aktualität und Familienthematik*, Munich.

Horsfall, N. (1986) "Fast. Cons. Cap. fr. XXXIX: A problematic grandfather", *ZPE* 65, 84.

Humm, M. (2005) *Appius Claudius Caecus. La république accomplie*, Rome.

Hurlet, F. (2010) "Recherches sur la *profectio* de la dictadure de Sylla à la *lex Pompeia* (82–52). Le cas des gouverneurs de rang prétorien", in N. Barrandon and F. Kirbihler (eds.), *Administrer les provinces de la République romaine. Actes du colloque de l'université de Nancy II. 4–5 juin 2009*, Rennes, 45–72.

Hurlet, F. (2012) "*Pro consule uel pro praetore?* À propos des titres et des pouvoirs des gouverneurs prétoriens d'Afrique, de Sicile et de Sardaigne-Corse sous la République romaine (227–52 av. J.-C.)", *Chiron* 42, 97–108.

Ilari, V. (1974) *Gli italici nelle strutture militari romane*, Milan.

Jashemski, W. (1950) *The origins and history of the proconsular and propraetorian imperium*, Chicago.

Jaworski, P. (2012) "Roman Republican coins found in Ptolemais", in J. Żelazowski (ed.) *Ptolemais in Cyrenaica. Studies in Memory of Tomasz Mikocki*, Warsaw, 285–291.

Jehne, M. (1987) *Der Staat des Dictators Caesars*, Cologne.

Jehne, M. (1997) *Caesar*, Munich.

Jehne, M. (2012) "Statutes on Public Powers and their Relationship to *mos*", in J.-L. Ferrary (ed.) *Leges publicae. La legge nell'esperienza giuridica romana*, Pavia, 405–428.

Jones, A.H.M. (1972) *The Criminal Courts of the Roman Republic and Principate*, Oxford.

Kallet-Marx, R. (1995) *Hegemony to Empire. The Development of the Roman Imperium in the East from 148 to 62 B.C.*, Berkeley – Los Angeles – Oxford.

Karlowa, O. (1885) *Römische Rechtsgeschichte*, vol.1, Leipzig.

Keaveney, A. (1984) "Who were the Sullani?", *Klio* 66, 114–150.

Keaveney, A. (1992) *Lucullus. A Life*, London – New York.

Keil, J. (1902) "Zur *lex Cornelia de viginti quaestoribus*", *Wiener Sudien* 24, 548–551.

Keppie, L. (1984) *The Making of the Roman Army: From Republic to Empire*, London.

Kienast, D. (1954) *Cato der Zensor: Seine Persönlichkeit und seine Zeit*, Heidelberg.

Koch, M. (2010) "Warum nicht Curvius Silvinus? Eine Hypothese!", *Madrider Mitteilungen* 51, 360–367.

Kolb, A. (2015) "Communications and Mobility in the Roman Empire", in C. Bruun and J. Edmondson (eds.), *The Oxford Handbook of Roman Epigraphy*, Oxford, 649–670.

Kolodko, P. (2014) "The Genesis of the Quaestorship in the Ancient Rome. Some Remarks", *Legal Roots: The International Journal of Roman Law, Legal History and Comparative Law*, 269–280.

Kondratieff, E. (2015) "Finding Libo: Epigraphic and Topographic Evidence for the *cursus honorum* of L. Scribonius L.F. Libo, cos. 34 B.C.E.", *Historia* 64, 428–466.

Konrad, C.F. (1987) "Some friends of Sertorius", *AJPh* 108, 519–527.

Konrad, C.F. (1994) *Plutarch's Sertorius. A Historical Commentary*, Chapel Hill – London.

Konrad, C.F. (1995) "A New Chronology of the Sertorian war", *Athenaeum*, 83, 1995, 157–187.

Konrad, C.F. (1996) "Notes on Roman Also-Rans", in J. Linderski (ed.), *Imperium sine fine: T. Robert S. Broughton and the Roman Republic*, Stuttgart, 103–143.

Koptev, A. (2005) "Three Brothers' at the Head of Archaic Rome: The King and his 'Consuls'", *Historia* 54, 382–423.

Kretschmer, P. (1919) "Pontifex", *Glotta* 10, 212.

Kroll, J.H. (1997) "Coinage as an Index of Romanization", in M.C. Hoff and S.I. Rotroff (eds.), *The Romanization of Athens*, Oxford, 135–150.
Kunkel, W. (1962) *Untersuchungen zur Entwicklung des römischen Kriminalverfahren in vorsullanischer Zeit*, Munich.
Kunkel, W. (1963) s.v. quaestio, *RE* XXIV, 720–786.
Kunkel, W. and Wittmann, R. (1995) *Staatsordnung und Staatspraxis der römischen Republik. 2. Die Magistratur*, Munich.
Lacey, W.K. (1985) "Antony's quaestorship: the evidence of Cicero, Phil. 2.48–50", *LCM* 10, 82.
Laronde, A. (1988) "La Cyrénaïque romaine, des origines à la fin des Sévères (96 av. J.-C. – 235 ap. J.-C.)", *ANRW* 2.10.1, 1006–1064.
Last, H. (1932) "The Enfranchisement of Italy", in *Cambridge Ancient History* 9, Cambridge, 158–210.
Latte, K. (1936) "The Origin of the Roman Quaestorship", *Transactions and Proceedings of the American Philological Association* 67, 24–33 = (1968) *Kleine Schriften*, Munich 359–366.
Leigh, M. (2004) *Comedy and the Rise of Rome*, Oxford.
Lengle, J. (1933) "Die Auswahl der Richter im römischen Quaestionsprocess", *ZSS* 66, 275–296.
Lenormant, F. (1852) "Mémoire sur les monnaies des questeurs romains de Macédoine", *Revue Numismatique* 17, 317–333.
Letta, C. and Segenni, S. (eds.) (2016) *Roma e le sue province. Dalla prima guerra púnica a Diocleziano*, Rome.
Lewis, R.G. (2006) *Asconius. Commentaries on Speeches by Cicero*, Oxford.
Linderski, J. (1972) "The Aedileship of Favonius, Curio the Younger and Cicero's Election to the Augurate", *HSCP* 76, 181–200.
Linderski, J. (1975) "Two quaestorships", *CPh* 70, 35–38.
Linderski, J. (1990) "The surname of M. Antonius Creticus and the *cognomina ex victis gentibus*", *ZPE* 80, 157–164.
Linderski, J. and Kaminska-Linderski, A. (1974) "The Quaestorship of M. Antonius", *Phoenix* 28, 213–223.
Lintott, A. (1971) "The offices of C. Flavius Fimbria in 86–5 B.C.", *Historia* 20, 696–701.
Lintott, A. (1976) "Mithridatica", *Historia* 25, 489–491.
Lintott, A. (1978) "The *quaestiones de sicariis et veneficiis* and the Latin *Lex Bantina*", *Hermes* 106, 125–138.
Lintott, A. (1981a) "What was the *Imperium Romanum?*", *G&R* 28, 53–67.
Lintott, A. (1981b) "The *leges de repetundis* and Associate Measures Under the Republic", *ZSS* 98, 162–212.
Lintott, A. (1992) *Judicial reform and land reform in the Roman Republic: A new edition, with translation and commentary, of the laws from Urbino*, Cambridge.
Lintott, A. (1993) *Imperium Romanum. Politics and Administration*, London.
Lintott, A. (1999) *The Constitution of the Roman Republic*, Oxford.
Lintott, A. (2008) *Cicero as Evidence: A Historian's Companion*, Oxford.
Longpérier, H. de (1868) "Recherches sur les insignes de la questure et sur les récipients monétaires", *Revue Archéologique* 18, 58–72.
Loreto, L. (1993) "Sull'introduzione e la competenza originaria dei secondi quattro questori (ca.267–210 a.C.)", *Historia* 42, 494–502.
Losehand, J. (2008) *Die letzten Tage des Pompeius. Von Pharsalos bis Pelusion*, Vienna.
Luce, T.J. (1968) "Political Propaganda on Roman Republican Coins", *AJA* 72, 25–39.
Lundgreen, Chr. (2011) *Regelkonflikte in der römischen Republik. Geltung und Gewichtung von Normen in politischen Entscheidungsprozessen*, Stuttgart.
Luzzatto, G. I. (1985) *Roma e le province. I. Organizzazione, economia, società*, Bologna.

Mackay, C.S. (2000) "Sulla and the Monuments: Studies in his Public Persona", *Historia* 49, 161–210.
MacKay, P.A. (1968) "Bronze Coinage in Macedonia, 168–166 B.C.", *ANSMuN* 14, 5–13.
Madvig J.N. (1881) *Verfassung und Verwaltung des römischen Staates*, Leipzig.
Magdelain, A. (1968) *Recherches sur l'imperium, la loi curiate et les auspices d'investiture*, Paris.
Magie, D. (1950) *Roman Rule in Asia Minor*, Princeton.
Manganaro, G. (1989) "Iscrizioni latine della Sicilia", *Epigraphica* 51, 161–196.
Mantovani, D. (2009) "*Quaerere*', '*quaestio*'. Inchiesta lessicale e semantica", *Index* 37, 25–67.
Marinone, N. (1965–66) "I questori e i legati di Verre in Sicilia", *Atti dell'Accademia delle Scienze di Torino* 100, 219–252.
Marinone, N. (1970) "Il banchetto dei pontefici in Macrobio", *Maia* 22, 271–278.
Marshall, A.J. (1964) "Cicero's letter to Cyprus", *Phoenix* 18, 206–215.
Marshall, A. J. (1972) "The *Lex Pompeia de Provinciis* (52 B.C.) and Cicero's *Imperium* in 51–50 B.C.: Constitutional Aspects", *ANRW* 1.1, 887–921.
Marshall, B.A. (1976a) "The date of Q. Mucius Scaevola's governorship of Asia", *Athenaeum* 54, 117–130.
Marshall, B.A. (1976b) *Crassus, a Political Biography*, Amsterdam.
Marshall, B.A. (1978) "Q. Curius, *homo quaestorius*", *AC* 47, 207–209.
Marshall, B.A. (1985) *A Historical Commentary on Asconius*, Columbia.
Marshall, B.A. (1987) "The Career Pattern of M. Livius Drusus", *RFIC* 115, 317–324.
Marsura, S. (2015) "Nummi Luculliani: Lucio Licinio Lucullo, quaestor di Silla", in T.M. Lucchelli and F. Rohr Vio (eds.) *Viri militares. Rappresentazione e propaganda tra Repubblica e Principato*, Trieste, 43–59.
Mason, H.J. (1974) *Greek Terms for Roman Intitutions. A Lexicon and Analysis*, Toronto.
Mastrocinque, A. (1999) *Studi sulle guerre Mitridatiche*, Stuttgart.
Mateo, A. (1999) *Manceps, redemptor, publicanus. Contribución al estudio de los contratistas públicos en Roma*, Santander.
Mattingly, H.B. (1956) "The Denarius of Sufenas and the Ludi Victoriae", *NC* 16, 189–204.
Mattingly, H.B. (1957) "The Victoriate", *The Numismatic Chronicle* 17, 97–119.
Mattingly, H.B. (1969) "Suetonius *Claud.*, 24,2 and the 'Italian Quaestors'", in *Hommages Renard*, vol.2, Brussels, 505–511.
Mattingly, H.B. (1972a) "The date of the Senatus Consultum *de agro Pergameno*", *AJPh* 93, 412–423.
Mattingly, H.B. (1972b) "The Numismatic Evidence and the Founding of Narbo Martius", *Revue Archéologique de Narbonnaise* 5, 1–19.
Mattingly, H.B. (1977) "Coinage and the Roman State", *The Numismatic Chronicle* 17, 199–215.
Mattingly, H.B. (1979) "L. Julius Caesar, Governor of Macedonia", *Chiron* 9, 147–167.
Mattingly, H.B. (1982) "The Management of the Roman Republican Mint", *Annali dell'Istituto Italiano de Numismatica* 29, 9–46.
Mattingly, H.B. (2004) *From Coins to History. Selected Numismatic Studies*, Ann Arbor.
McDermott, W.C. (1971) "Q. Cicero", *Historia* 20, 702–717.
McDermott, W.C. (1972) "Curio Pater and Cicero", *AJPh* 93, 381–411.
McGing, B.C. (1986) *The Foreign Policy of Mithridates VI Eupator King of Pontus*, Leiden.
McGushin, P. (1992) *Sallust. The Histories*, Oxford.
Meiggs, R. (^{2}1973) *Roman Ostia*, Oxford.
Merkelbach, R. (1975) "Drei Texte des Jahres 49 v. Chr. aus Thyateira", *ZPE* 16, 39–42.
Meyer, E. (^{2}1961) *Römischer Staat und Staatsgedanke*, Zurich – Stuttgart.
Michels, A. (1967) *The Calendar of the Roman Republic*, Princeton.
Michiels, A. (1972) "Trois *Cornelii Lentuli* de la première moitié du Ier siècle av. J.-C. et leurs deniers", *RBN* 118, 7–27.

Mitchell, J.F. (1966) "The Torquati", *Historia* 15, 23–31.
Mitchell, S. (1979) "A Roman family in Phrygia", *Anatolian Studies* 29, 13–22.
Moatti, C. (1993) *Archives et partage de la terre dans le monde romain (IIe siècle avant – Ier siècle après J.-C.)*, Rome.
Mommsen, Th. (1858) "Sui modi usati da' Romani nel conservare e pubblicare le leggi ed i senatusconsulti", in *Annali dell'Istituto di corrispondenza archeologica* 39, 181–212 = Th. Mommsen, *Gesammelte Schriften*, Berlin – Dublin – Zurich (1965) (first edition 1907) III, 290–313.
Mommsen, Th. (1859) *Die Römische Chronologie bis auf Caesar*, Berlin.
Mommsen, Th. (1876–1888) *Römisches Staatsrecht*, 3 vols. in 5, Leipzig (abbreviation Röm.St.).
Moreau, Ph. (1982) *Clodiana religio. Un procès politique en 61 av.J.-C.*, Paris.
Morgan, M. (1974) "Cornelius and the Pannonians: Appian, *Illyrica*, 14, 41 and Roman History 143–138 BC", *Historia* 23, 183–216.
Morgan, M. (1977) "Calendars and Chronology in the First Punic War", *Chiron* 7, 89–117.
Morkholm, O. (1991) *Early Hellenistic Coinage. From the Accession of Alexander to the Peace of Apamea*, Cambridge.
Morrell, K. (2017) *Pompey, Cato, and the Governance of the Roman Empire*, Oxford.
Münzer, F. (1920) *Römische Adelsparteien und Adelsfamilien*, Stuttgart.
Münzer, F. (1932) "Norbanus", *Hermes* 67, 220–236.
Muñiz Coello, J. (1982) *Empleados y subalternos de la administración romana. I. Los* scribae, Huelva.
Muñiz Coello, J. (1983) "Empleados y subalternos de la administración romana. II. Los *praecones*", *Habis* 14, 117–146.
Muñiz Coello, J. (1995–96) "C. Flavius Fimbria, consular y legado en la provincia de Asia (86–84 a. de C.", *Studia Historica. Historia Antigua* 13–14, 257–276.
Muñiz Coello, J. (1998) *Cicerón y Cilicia. Diario de un gobernador romano del siglo I a.C.*, Huelva.
Muñiz Coello, J. (2014) "Los cuestores republicanos. Origen, funciones y analogías", *Klio* 96, 500–536.
Muscolino, F. (2009–2010) "I monumenti di Olympis e di C. Claudio Marcello a Taormina", *Atti della Pontificia Accademia Romana di Archaeologia*, 82, 407–460.
Nicolet, C. (1966–1974) *L' ordre équestre à l'époque républicaine, 312–43 av. J-C.*, 2 vols., Paris.
Nicolet, C. (ed.) (1980) *Insula Sacra: La loi Gabinia-Calpurnia de Délos (58 av. J.-C.)*, Rome.
Nicoletti, A. (1967) s.v. quaestores, *Novissimo Digesto Italiano* 14, Turin, 615–617.
Niemeyer, K. (1854) "Ein Beitrag zur Geschichte der Quaestur", *Zeitschrift für die Altertumswissenschaft* 12, 515–531.
Noy, D. (2000) "Half-Burnt on an Emergency Pyre': Roman Cremations which went Wrong", *Greece & Rome* 47, 186–196.
Ñaco del Hoyo, A. (2003) Vectigal incertum. *Economía de guerra y fiscalidad republicana en el occidente romano: su impacto en el territorio, 218–133 a.C.*, Oxford.
Oakley, S.P. (2005a) *A commentary on Livy, Books VI-X, vol.3: Book IX*, Oxford.
Oakley, S.P. (2005b) *A commentary on Livy, Books VI-X, vol.4: Book X*, Oxford.
Ogilvie, R.M. (1965) *A commentary on Livy, Books 1–5*, Oxford.
Oliveri, F. (2012) "Bronze Rams of the Egadi Battle. Epigraphic evidences on the rams Egadi 4 and 6", *Skyllis* 12, 117–124.
Oost, S.I. (1963) "Cyrene, 96–74 B.C.", *CPh* 58, 11–25.
Ooteghem, J. van (1959) *Lucius Licinius Lucullus*, Brussels.
Ooteghem, J. van (1964) *Caius Marius*, Brussels.
Papazoglou, F. (1979) "Quelques aspects de l'histoire de la province de Macédoine", *ANRW* 2.7.1, 302–369.

Pasquinucci, M. (1979) "La transumanza nell'Italia romana", in E. Gabba – M. Pasquinucci (eds.), *Strutture agrarie e allevamento transumante nell'Italia romana (III-I sec. A.C.)*, Pisa, 79–182.
Passerini, A. (1934) "Caio Mario come uomo politico", *Athenaeum* 12, 10–44, 109–143, 257–97, 348–80.
Paul, G.M. (1984) *A historical commentary on Sallust's Bellum Jugurthinum*, Liverpool.
Perl, G. (1970) (1971) "Die römischen Provinzbeamten in Cyrenae und Creta zur Zeit der Republik", *Klio* 52, 319–354; 53, 369–380.
Payne, M. J. (1984) *Ἀρετᾶς ἕνεκεν: Honors to Romans and Italians in Greece from 260 to 27 B.C.*, Diss. Michigan State University.
Perl, G. (1980) "Cn. Tremellius Scrofa in Gallia Transalpina. Zu Varro, RR 1,7,8", *AJAH* 5, 97–109.
Pfeilschifter, R. (2005) *Titus Quinctius Flamininus. Untersuchungen zur römischen Griechenlandpolitik*, Göttingen.
Pina Polo, F. (1989) *Las contiones civiles y militares en Roma*, Zaragoza.
Pina Polo, F. (1995) "Procedures and Functions of Civil and Military *contiones*", *Klio* 77, 1995, 203–216.
Pina Polo, F. (2001) "Die Freunde des Scipio Aemilianus im numantinischen Krieg: Über die sogennante *cohors amicorum*", in M. Peachin (ed.), *Aspects of Friendship in the Graeco-Roman World*, Portsmouth, 89–98.
Pina Polo, F. (2011) *The Consul at Rome. The Civil Functions of the Consuls in the Roman Republic*, Cambridge.
Pina Polo, F. (2012) "*Veteres candidati*: Losers in the Elections in Republican Rome", in F. Marco, F. Pina Polo and J. Remesal (eds.), *Vae Victis! Perdedores en el mundo antiguo*, Barcelona, 63–82.
Pina Polo, F. (2013) "The Political Role of the *consules designati* at Rome", *Historia* 62, 420–452.
Pina Polo, F. (2016) "SPQR. Institutions and Popular Participation in the Roman Republic", in P.J. du Plessis, C. Ando and K. Tuori (eds.), *The Oxford Handbook of Roman Law and Society*, Oxford, 85–97.
Pink, K. (1952) *The Triumviri Monetales and the Structure of the Coinage of the Roman Republic*, New York.
Pinzone, A. (1979) "*Maiorum sapientia* e *lex Hieronica*: Roma e l'organizzazione della provincia Sicilia da Gaio Flaminio a Cicerone", *AAPel* 55, 165–194.
Pinzone, A. (2000) "La 'romanizzazione' della Sicilia occidentale in età Repubblicana", in *Terze Giornate Internazionali di Studi sull'area Elima (Gibellina – Erice – Contessa Entellina, 23–26 ottobre 1997). Atti*, II, Pisa-Gibellina, 849–878.
Potter, D. (2004) "The Roman Army and Navy", in H. Flower (ed.), *The Cambridge Companion to the Roman Republic*, Cambridge, 66–88.
Prag, J.R.W. (2007a) "*Auxilia* and *Gymnasia*: A Sicilian Model of Roman Imperialism", *JRS* 97, 68–100.
Prag, J.R.W. (2007b) "Roman Magistrates in Sicily, 227–49 BC", in J. Dubouloz and S. Pittia (eds.), *La Sicile de Cicéron, Lectures des Verrines*, Besançon, 287–310.
Prag, J. R. W. (2013) "Sicily and Sardinia-Corsica: The First Provinces", in D. Hoyos (ed.), *A Companion to Roman Imperialism*, Leiden-Boston, 53–65 .
Prag, J.R.W. (2014a) "The Quaestorship in the Third and Second Centuries BC", in J. Dubouloz, S. Pittia, and G. Sabatini (eds.), *L'imperium Romanum en perspective. Les savoirs d'empire dans la République romaine et leur héritage dans l'Europe médiévale et moderne*, Besançon, 193–209.
Prag, J.R.W. (2014b) "Bronze *rostra* from the Egadi Islands off NW Sicily: the Latin inscriptions", *JRA* 27, 33–59.
Prag, J.R.W. (2014c) "Inscribed Bronze *rostra* from the Site of the Battle of the Aegates Islands, Sicily, 241 BC", in W. Eck and P. Funke (eds.), *Öffentlichkeit – Monument – Text. XIV.*

Congressus Internationalis Epigraphiae Graecae et Latinae, 27.–31. Augusti MMXII. Akten, Berlin, 727–729.
Prag. J.R.W. (2017) "A Revised Edition of the Latin Inscription on the Egadi 11 Bronze *rostrum* from the Egadi Islands", *ZPE* 202, 287–292.
Pugliese Carratelli, G. (1963) "Supplemento epigrafico cirenaico", *ASAA* 39–40, 219–375.
Purcell, N. (1983) "The *apparitores*: A Study in Social Mobility", *PBSR* 51, 125–173.
Purcell, N. (1996) s.v. vigintisexviri, in S. Hornblower and A. Spawforth (eds.), *The Oxford Classical Dictionary* (third edition) 1598–1599.
Raaflaub, K.A. (1975) "Caesar und die Friedensverhandlungen zu Beginn des Bürgerkrieges von 49 v.Chr.", *Chiron* 5, 247–300.
Raaflaub, K.A., Richards, J.D., and Samons II, L.J. (1992) "Rome, Italy, and Appius Claudius Caecus before the Pyrrhic Wars", in T. Hackens, N.D. Holloway, R.R. Holloway and G. Moucharte (eds.), *The Age of Pyrrhus*, Providence – Louvaine, 13–50.
Rafferty, D. (2019) *Provincial Allocations in Rome, 123–52 BCE*, Stuttgart.
Raggi, A. (2001) "*Senatus consultum de Asclepiade Clazomenio sociisque*', *ZPE* 135, 73–116.
Rankov, B. (1987) "M. Iunius Congus the Gracchan", in M. Whitby and P. Hardie (eds.), *Homo Viator: Classical Essays for John Bramble*, Bristol, 89–94.
Rawson, E. (1978) "The identity problems of Q. Cornificius", *CQ* 28, 188–201.
Reinach, Th. (1975) *Mithridates Eupator König von Pontos*, Hildesheim – New York (^{1}Leipzig 1895).
Revillout C.-J. (1865) "Les questeurs urbains", *Mémoires de la Societé des Sciences Morales*, Versailles.
Reynolds, J. M. (1962) "Cyrenaica, Pompey and Cn. Cornelius Lentulus Marcellinus", *JRS* 52, 97–103.
Reynolds, J.M. (1982) *Aphrodisias and Rome*, London.
Rice Holmes, T. (1917) "Was Caesar born in 100 or in 102 B.C.?", *JRS* 7, 145–152.
Richardson, J.S. (1996) "*Lex Latina Tabulae Bantinae*", in M.H. Crawford (ed.), *Roman Statutes*, London, I 193–208.
Richardson, J.S. (2000) *Appian. Wars of the Romans in Iberia*, Warminster.
Richardson, J.S. (2008) *The Language of Empire. Rome and the Idea of Empire from the Third Century BC to the Second Century AD*, Cambridge.
Rickman, G. (1980) *The Corn Supply of Ancient Rome*, Oxford.
Rögler, G. (1962) "Die *Lex Villia Annalis*. Eine Untersuchung zur Verfassungsgeschichte der römischen Republik", *Klio* 40, 76–123.
Rolfe, J.C. (1915) "The so-called Callium Provincia", *AJPh* 36, 323–331.
Romanelli, P. (1943) *La Cirenaica romana (96 a.C.–642 d.C.)*, Verbania.
Roselaar, S. (2010) *Public Land in the Roman Republic: A Social and Economic History of the* ager publicus*, 396–89 BC*, Oxford.
Rosenstein, N. (1986) "*Imperatores Victi:* The Case of C. Hostilius Mancinus", *ClAnt* 5, 230–252.
Rosenstein, N. (1990) Imperatores Victi. *Military Defeat and Aristocratic Competition in the Middle and Late Republic*, Berkeley – Los Angeles – Oxford.
Rosenstein, N. (1995) "Sorting out the Lot in Republican Rome", *AJPh* 116, 43–75.
Rosillo-López, C. (2010) *La corruption à la fin de la république romaine (IIe-Ier s. av. J.-C.: aspects politiques et financiers*, Stuttgart.
Rosillo-López, C. forthcoming, "Strategies of Prorogation in the Roman Republic", in A. Díaz Fernández (ed.), *Provinces, Commanders, and Allies in the Roman Republic*.
Rotondi, G. (1966, ^{1}1912) Leges publicae populi Romani. *Elenco cronológico con una introduzione sull'attivita legislativa dei comizi romani*, Hildesheim (^{1}Milan).
Rowland Jr., R.J. (1968) "The date of Pompeius Strabo's quaestorship", *CPh* 63, 213–214.
Ruebel, J.S. (1977) "Cato and Scipio Africanus", *Classical World* 71, 161–173.

Rüpke, J. (2008) *Fasti Sacerdotum: A Prosopography of Pagan, Jewish, and Christian Religious Officials in the City of Rome, 300 BC to AD 499*, Oxford – New York.
Russell, H.E. (1953) *Advancement in Rank under the Republic as a Reward for the Soldier and the Public Prosecutor*, Diss. Bryn Mawr College.
Ryan, F.X. (1994a) "The Aedileship of P. Sulpicius Galba", *Eos* 82, 55–65.
Ryan, F.X. (1994b) "The Praetorship of Favonius", *AJP* 115, 587–601.
Ryan, F.X. (1994c) "The Quaestorship of Favonius and the Tribunate of Metellus Scipio", *Athenaeum* 82, 505–521.
Ryan, F.X. (1994d) "The Quaestorship of Q. Curius and C. Cornelius Cethegus", *Classical Philology* 89, 256–261.
Ryan, F.X. (1994e) "The Meaning of 'Consularis Auctoritas' in Cicero", *Mnemosyne* 47, 681–685.
Ryan, F.X. (1995a) "The date of the Quaestorship of L. Domitius Ahenobarbus", *Athenaeum* 83, 270–274.
Ryan, F.X. (1995b) "The Early Career of M. Terentius Varro Lucullus", *Eos* 83, 141–145.
Ryan, F.X. (1995c) "The Tribunate of C. Memmius L.F.", *Hermes* 123, 293–302.
Ryan, F.X. (1995d) "Two Senators in 73 B.C.", *ZPE* 108, 306–308.
Ryan, F.X. (1996a) "Four Republican Senators", *Classica et Mediaevalia* 47, 207–215.
Ryan, F.X. (1996b) "The Quaestorship and Aedileship of M'. Aquillius (Cos. 129)", *Hermes* 124, 115–116.
Ryan, F.X. (1996c) "The Quaestorships of Hirtuleius and M. Fonteius", *Hermes* 124, 250–253.
Ryan, F.X. (1996d) "The Quaestorships of T. Crispinus and M. Plaetorius", *Philologus* 140, 351–352.
Ryan, F.X. (1996e) "Three Quaestorships: C. Decimius, M. Minatius Sabinus, and L. Iulius Caesar", *Hermes* 124, 113–115.
Ryan, F.X. (1996f) "The Minimum Age for the Quaestorship in the Late Republic", *MH* 53, 37–43.
Ryan, F.X. (1996g) "Ten Ill-Starred Aediles", *Klio* 78, 68–86.
Ryan, F.X. (1997a) "The Quaestorship of Trebonius", *RhM* 140, 414–416.
Ryan, F.X (1997b) "C. Alfius Flavus", *Historia* 46, 377–379.
Ryan, F.X. (1998a) "Die Quäestur des L. Aemilius Paullus (Konsul 50)", *Hyperboreus* 4, 399–400.
Ryan, F.X. (1998b) "The Quaestorship of Servius Cordus", *Historia* 47, 254.
Ryan, F.X. (1998c) *Rank and Participation in the Republican Senate*, Stuttgart.
Ryan, F.X. (1999) "The Quaestorships of T. Ligarius and Q. Aelius Tubero", *L'Antiquité Classique* 68, 243–245.
Ryan, F.X. (2005) "Three More Senators in 73 B.C.", *ZPE* 153, 269–270.
Ryan, F.X. (2015) "The Supposed Quaestorian Stool on Provincial Coins of the Republican and Imperatorial Periods" (https://independent.academia.edu/ FXRyan).
Sage, M.M. (1979) "The elogia of the Augustan Forum and the 'viris illustribus'", *Historia* 28, 192–210.
Salinas de Frías, M. (1995) *El gobierno de las provincias hispanas durante la República romana (218–27 a.C.)*, Salamanca.
Santalucia, B. (1989) *Diritto e processo penale nell'antica Roma*, Milan.
Santalucia, B. (1999) "Cic. Pro Rosc. Am. 3.8 e la scelta dei giudici nelle cause di parricidio", *Iura* 50, 143–151.
Santangelo, F. (2007) *Sulla, the Elites and the Empire: A Study of Roman Policies in Italy and the Greek East*, Leiden – Boston.
Sarikakis, Th. Ch. (1971) Ῥωμαῖοι ἄρχοντες τῆς ἐπαρχίας Μακεδονίας. Μέρος Ά. Ἀπὸ τῆς ἱδρύσεως τῆς ἐπαρχίας μέχρι τῶν χρόνων τοῦ Αὐγούστου (148–27 π.Χ.), Tessaloniki.
Sartre, M. (2005) *The Middle East under Rome*, Harvard.
Schäfer, T. (1989) *Imperii Insignia. Sella curulis und Fasces. Zur Repräsentation römischer Magistrate*, Mainz.

Schneider, H. (1982–83) "Die politische Rolle der *plebs urbana* während der Tribunate des L. Appuleius Saturninus", *Ancient Society* 13–14, 193–221.
Schulten, A. (1926) *Sertorius*, Leipzig.
Scullard, H.H. (1960) "Scipio Aemilianus and Roman politics", *JRS* 50, 59–74.
Seager, R. (1967) "The Date of Saturninus' murder", *The Classical Review* 17, 9–10.
Seager, R. (^{2}2002) *Pompey the Great*, Oxford.
Seguí Marco, J. J. (2001) "La trama hispana de la Primera Conjuración de Catilina", *Gerión* 19, 391–423.
Serrati, J. (2000) "Garrisons and Grain: Sicily between the Punic Wars", in C. Smith and J. Serrati (eds.), *Sicily from Aeneas to Augustus. New Approaches in Archaeology and History*, Edinburgh, 115–133.
Shackleton Bailey, D.R. (1960) "The Credentials of L. Caesar and L. Roscius", *JRS* 50, 80–83.
Shackleton Bailey, D.R. (1962) "Two tribunes, 57 B.C.", *CR* 12, 195–197.
Shackleton Bailey, D.R. (1965–70) *Cicero: Epistulae ad Atticum*, Cambridge (abbreviation *Ep.Att.*).
Shackleton Bailey, D.R. (1976) *Two Studies in Roman Nomenclature*, New York.
Shackleton Bailey, D.R. (1977) *Cicero: Epistulae ad familiares*, Cambridge.
Shackleton Bailey, D.R. (1992) *Onomasticon to Cicero's Speeches*, Stuttgart – Leipzig.
Shatzman, I. (1972) "The Roman General's Authority over Booty", *Historia* 21, 177–205.
Sherk, R.K. (1969) *Roman Documents from the Greek East*, Baltimore.
Sherwin-White, A. N. (1977) "Roman Involvement in Anatolia, 167–88 B.C.", *JRS* 67, 62–75.
Siber, H. (1952) *Römisches Verfassungsrecht in geschichtlicher Entwicklung*, Lahr.
Sigonius, C. (1555) *T. Livii Patavini historiarum ab urbe condita libri qui extant XXXV: cum universae historiae epitomis*, Venice.
Skydsgaard, J.E. (1974) "Transhumance in Ancient Italy", *Analecta Romana Instituti Danici* 7, 7–36.
Smith, M. (1978) "Lydus, *De Magistratibus* 1.27 and the Quaestors of 267 B.C.", *BASP* 15, 125–126.
Sobeck, F. (1909) *Die Quästoren der römischen Republik*, Diss. Trebnitz.
Souza, P. de (2015) "Polybius on Naval Warfare", in T. Howe, E Garvin and G. Wrightson (eds.), *Greece, Macedon, and Persia*, Oxford, 181–197.
Spann, P.O. (1987) *Quintus Sertorius and the Legacy of Sulla*, Fayetteville.
Staveley, E.S. (1954–55) "*Provocatio* during the fifth and fourth centuries B.C.", *Historia* 3, 412–428.
Steinby, Ch. (2007) *The Roman Republican Navy: From the sixth century to 167 B.C.*, Helsinki.
Steel, C. (2014) "The Roman Senate and the post-Sullan *res publica*", *Historia* 63, 323–339.
Stewart, R. (1987) *Sors et provincia: Praetors and Quaestors in Republican Rome*, Ph.D. Duke University.
Stewart, R. (1998), *Public Office in Early Rome. Ritual Procedure and Political Practice*, Ann Arbor.
Stockton, D. (1979) *The Gracchi*, Oxford.
Stumpf, G. (1985) "C. Atinius C.f. praetor in Asia 122–121 v. Chr., auf einem Kistophor", *ZPE* 61, 186–190.
Sumner, G.V. (1971) "The Lex Annalis under Caesar", *Phoenix* 25, 246–271; 357–371.
Sumner, G.V. (1973) *The Orators in Cicero's Brutus: Prosopography and Chronology*, Toronto.
Sumner, G.V. (1976) "A Note on Julius Caesar's Great-Grandfather", *CPh* 71, 341–344.
Sumner, G.V. (1977) "The Pompeii in their Families", *AJAH* 2, 8–25.
Sumner, G.V. (1978) "Governors of Asia in the Nineties B.C.", *GRBS* 19, 147–153.
Suolahti, J. (1955) *The Junior Officers of the Roman Army in the Republican Period*, Helsinki.
Suolahti, J. (1958) "The Council of L. Cornelius P.f. Crus in the year 49 B.C.", *Arctos* 2, 152–163.
Syme, R. (1955a) "Review of Broughton, *The Magistrates of the Roman Republic (1951–1952)*", *CPh* 50, 127–138.

Syme, R. (1955b) "Review of A. E. Gordon, *Potitus Valerius Messalla Consul Suffect 29 B.C.*, Berkeley and Los Angeles, 1954", *JRS* 45, 155–160.
Syme, R. (1955c) "Missing Senators", *Historia* 4, 52–71.
Syme, R. (1956) "Missing Persons (*P-W* VIII A)", *Historia* 5, 204–212.
Syme, R. (1960a) "Bastards in the Roman Aristocracy", *Proceedings of the American Philosophical Society*, 104, 323–327.
Syme, R. (1960b) "Piso Frugi and Crassus Frugi", *JRS* 50, 12–20.
Syme, R. (1963) "Ten tribunes", *JRS* 53, 55–60.
Syme, R. (1964a) "Senators, Tribes and Towns", *Historia* 13, 105–125.
Syme, R. (1964b) *Sallust*, Berkeley – Los Angeles.
Syme, R. (1980) "The Sons of Crassus", *Latomus* 39, 403–408.
Syme, R. (1981) "A Great Orator mislaid", *CQ* 31, 421–427.
Syme, R. (1987) "Marriage Ages for Roman senators", *Historia* 36, 318–332.
Tan, J. (2008) "*Contiones* in the Age of Cicero", *Classical Antiquity* 27, 163–201.
Tanner, J. (2000) "Portraits, Power, and Patronage in the Late Roman Republic", *JRS* 90, 18–50.
Tansey, P. (2000) "The Inauguration of Lentulus Niger", *AJPh* 121, 237–258.
Tarpin, M. (2009) "Les *manubiae* dans la procédure d'appropriation du butin", in M. Coudry and M. Humm (eds.), *Praeda. Butin de guerre et société dans la Rome républicaine*, Stuttgart, 81–101.
Tatum, W.J. (1990a) "P. Clodius Pulcher and Tarracina: *Publi Progenies Appi Cognomine Pulchri Occubit letum*", *ZPE* 83, 299–304.
Tatum, W.J. (1990b) "The *lex Clodia de censoria notione*", *CPh* 85, 34–43.
Tatum, W.J. (2008) *Always I am Caesar*, Malden MA – Oxford.
Taylor, L.R. (1941) "Caesar's Early Career", *Classical Philology* 36, 113–132.
Taylor, L.R. (1942a) "Caesar and the Roman nobility", *TAPhA* 73, 1–24.
Taylor, L.R. (1942b) "Caesar's colleagues in the pontifical college", *AJPh* 63, 385–412.
Taylor, L.R. (1960) *The Voting Districts of the Roman Republic*, Rome.
Taylor, L.R. (1964) "Magistrates of 55 B.C. in Cicero's Pro Plancio and Catullus, 52", *Athenaeum* 42, 12–28.
Taylor, L.R. and Scott, R.T. (1969) "Seating Space in the Roman Senate and the Senatores Pedarii", *TAPhA* 100, 529–582.
Thiel, J.H. (1954) *A History of Roman Sea-Power before the Second Punic War*, Amsterdam.
Thompson, L.A. (1962a) "The Relationship between Provincial Quaestors and Their Commanders-in-Chief", *Historia* 11, 339–355.
Thompson, L.A. (1962b) "The Appointment of Quaestors *Extra Sortem*", *PACA* 2, 17–25.
Thompson, L.A. (1965) "Cicero's Succession Problem in Cilicia", *AJPh* 86, 375–386.
Thompson, M. (1961) *The New Style Silver Coinage of Athens*, New York.
Thonemann, P. (2004) "The date of Lucullus' quaestorship", *ZPE* 149, 80–82.
Thonemann, P. (2015) *The Hellenistic World: Using Coins as Sources*, Cambridge.
Timmer, J. (2005) "Zwischen Militär und Recht: Altersgrenzen politischer Partizipation in der römischen Republik", in Chr. Gusy and H.-G. Haupt (eds.), *Inklusion und Partizipation. Politische Kommunikation im historischen Wandel, Historische Politikforschung* 2, Frankfurt – New York.
Timmer, J. (2008) *Altergrenzen politischer Partizipation in antiken Gesellschaften*, Berlin.
Townend, G.B. (1987) "C. Oppius on Julius Caesar", *AJPh* 108, 325–342.
Toynbee, A.J. (1965) *Hannibal's Legacy*, Oxford.
Trisciuoglio, A. (1998) *Sarta tecta, ultrotributa, opus publicum faciundum locare. Sugli appalti relative alle opere pubbliche nell'età repubblicana e augustea*, Naples.
Tusa, S. and Royal, J. (2012) "The Landscape of the Naval Battle at the Egadi Islands (241 B.C.)", *JRA* 25, 7–48.

Urso, G. (1995) "Prigionia e morte di Perseo di Macedonia", *RIL* 129, 343–355.
Urso, G. (2005) *Cassio Dione e i magistrati. Le origine della repubblica nei frammenti della Storia Romana*, Milan.
Varvaro, M. (1995) "Per una interpretazione della *Lex de XX quaestoribus*", *A.S.G.P.* 43, 577–588.
Venturini, C. (1979) *Studi sul 'crimen repetundarum' nell'età repubblicana*, Milan.
Verboven, K. (2009) "Currency, Bullion and Accounts. Monetary Modes in the Roman World", *Revue Belge de Numismatique et de Sigillographie* 155, 91–121.
Vervaet, F.J. (2006) "The Scope of the *lex Sempronia* Concerning the Assignment of the Consular Provinces (123 BCE)", *Athenaeum* 94, 627–656.
Vervaet, F.J. (2012) "The Praetorian Proconsuls of the Roman Republic (211–52 BCE). A Constitutional Survey", *Chiron* 42, 45–96.
Vervaet, F.J. (2014) "Erratum to: Crassus' Command in the War against Spartacus (73–71 BCE): His Official Position, Forces and Political Spoils", *Klio* 97, 405–442.
Vervaet, F.J. (2017) *The High Command in the Roman Republic. The Principle of the* Summum Imperium Auspiciumque *from 509 to 19 BCE*, Stuttgart.
Walbank, F.W. (1970) *A Historical Commentary on Polybius*, vol.1, London.
Waldherr, G. (2002) "Das System der *calles* (Herdenwanderwege) im römischen Italien: Entstehung und infrastrukturelle Bedeutung", in E. Olshausen and H. Sonnabend (eds.), *Stuttgarter Kolloquium zu Historischen Geographie des Altertums 7. Zu Wasser und zu Land: Verkehrswege in der antiken Welt*, Stuttgart, 429–444.
Walter, U. (2013) *Cicero. Zweite Rede an das Volk gegen den Volkstribunen Publius Servilius Rullus über das Ackergesetz*, Bielefeld.
Ward, A.M. (1977) *Marcus Crassus and the Late Roman Republic*, Columbia – London.
Wardle, D. (2014) *Suetonius: Life of Augustus*, Oxford.
Weigel, R D. (1978) "A Note on P. Lepidus", *CPh* 73, 42–45.
Weinrib, E.J. (1968) "The Prosecution of Roman Magistrates", *Phoenix* 22, 32–56.
Welch, K. (1995) "The career of M. Aemilius Lepidus 49–44 B.C.", *Hermes* 123, 443–454.
Wesch-Klein, G. (1993) *Funus Publicum. Eine Studie zur öffentlichen Beisetzung und Gewährung von Ehrengräbern in Rom und den Westprovinzen*, Stuttgart.
Wesener, G. (1963) s.v. quaestor, in *RE* 47, 801–827.
Wikander, O. (1976) "Caius Hostilius Mancinus and the *Foedus Numantinum*", *ORom* 11, 85–104.
Willems, P. (1878) *Le sénat de la République romaine*, Louvain.
Wiseman, T.P. (1964) "Some Republican Senators and Their Tribes", *CQ* 14, 122–133.
Wiseman, T.P. (1967) "T. Cloelius of Tarracina", *CR* 17, 263–264.
Wiseman, T.P. (1970) "Roman Republican Road-Building", *PBSR* 38, 122–152.
Wiseman, T.P. (1971) *New Men in the Roman Senate, 139 B.C.–14 A.D.*, Oxford.
Wiseman, T.P. (1976) "Factions and Family Trees", *LCM* 1, 1–3.
Wisse, J. (2017) "Philosophers and Gentlemen: The Orator Crassus's Quaestorship, Philosophers' Deaths, and Historical Realities in Cicero's *De oratore*", in A.H. Groton (ed.), *Ab omni parte beatus: Classical Essays in Honor of James M. May*, Mundelein, IL, 121–159.
Wosnik, B. (1963) *Untersuchungen zur Geschichte Sullas*, Diss. Würzburg.
Woytek, B. (2003) *Arma et Nummi. Forschungen zur römischen Finanzgeschichte und Münzprägung der Jahre 49 bis 42 v.Chr.*, Vienna 2003.
Woytek, B.E. (2016) "The Denarius Coinage of the Roman Republic", in W.E. Metcalf (ed.) *The Oxford Handbook of Greek and Roman Coinage*, Oxford, 315–334.
Zucca, R. (1994) "*Inscriptiones latinae liberae rei publicae Africae, Sardiniae et Corsicae*", *L'Africa romana* 11, 1425–1489.
Zucchelli, Z. (1975) "Un antiquario Romano contro la nobilitas: M. Giunio Congo Graccano", *Studi Urbinati* 49, 109–126.

Index of names

Names marked in bold have their own entry in the prosopography.

Acilius (RE 11), **M'.** 168, 205, 211, 338
Acilius Caninus, M. 205
Acilius Glabrio, M'. 89
Aebutius, P. 97
Aelius (RE 9), **P.** 24, 205, 251, 293, 319, 336
Aelius Paetus Staienus (RE Staienus 1), **C.** 54, 206, 320, 341
Aelius Tubero, L. 206
Aelius Tubero (RE 156), **Q.** 206f., 347
Aemilius (not in RE) 207f., 336
Aemilius Lepidus (RE 66), **M.** 207
Aemilius Lepidus, M. 134, 207
Aemilius Lepidus, M. 73, 101f., 114, 206f., 284
Aemilius Lepidus (RE 62), **M'.** 207, 319, 341
Aemilius Lepidus (not in RE), **P.** 207, 347
Aemilius Lepidus Paullus (RE 81), **L.** 54, 208, 344
Aemilius Lepidus Porcina, M. 72
Aemilius (Mamercinus) (RE 16, 97), **Mam.** 330, 336
Aemilius Mamercus 7f., 26, 208, 330
Aemilius Paullus, L. 220, 261
Aemilius Paullus (RE 114), **L.** 57f., 100, 104, 145, 208, 258, 303, 337
Aemilius Scaurus, M. 47, 216
Aemilius Scaurus (RE 141), **M.** 132, 159, 187, 190f., 208f., 296f., 343
Aesillas (not in RE) 167, 209f., 340
Afranius 326
Albius (RE 2), **P.** 171, 209f., 338
Albucius, T. 209, 267, 294, 298f.
Alfius Flavus (RE 7), **C.** 210, 343
Allienus (RE 1), **A.** 210, 344
Alp(ius) (not in RE), L. 168, 205, 211, 338
Ampudius (RE 1), **M.** 211, 347
Ancharius (RE 3), **Q.** 211, 342
Anicius Gallus, L. 132, 145
Anicius (not in RE), **Q.** 212, 340
Annaeus (not in RE), **C.** 212, 341
Anneius, M. 173
Annius, C. 167, 251f., 321f.
Annius (not in RE), **M.** 139, 187f., 191, 203, 212, 338
Annius, T. 68

Annius Milo, T. 64, 117, 260
An(n)ius (RE 8), **C.** 212, 336
Antiochus III 86, 89, 93, 96, 99, 175, 261
Antiochus XII Asiaticus 159
Antistius (RE 22), **T.** 186, 213, 346
Antistius Vetus 138, 140, 192, 213, 265
Antistius Vetus (RE 47), **C.** 213, 347
Antonius (RE 20), **C.** 214f., 345
Antonius (RE 28), **M.** 61, 75, 214f., 262, 272, 289f., 338
Antonius Creticus, M. 149, 154, 157, 211, 335
Antonius (RE 30), **M.** 54, 70f., 74f., 103, 112, 132, 150, 214f., 227, 232, 250, 319, 328, 335, 345
Antonius Hybrida, C. 77, 141, 226, 317
Antonius Pietas (RE 23), **L.** 139, 186, 191, 214, 265, 346
Apollonius 96, 99
Appuleius, L. 231
Appuleius (RE 13), **M.** 215, 347
Appuleius (RE 2? 15?), **P.?** 174, 215f., 346f.
Appuleius, Sex. 215
Appuleius Saturninus, L. 296, 307
Appuleius Saturninus (RE 29), **L.** 33, 47, 62, 111, 216, 308, 314, 339
Appuleius Tappo (RE 31), **C.** 217, 347
[Appuleius] Saturninus, Cn. 216
Aquillius Florus (not in RE), **L.** 218, 343
Aquillius (RE 10), **M'.** 217f., 338
Aquillius, M'. 218
Aquinius (RE 2), **M.** 218f., 345
Asclepiades 73, 101f.
Asinius Pollio, C. 175, 240
Asullius (not in RE) 219, 310, 338
Ateius Capito (RE 9), **L.** 219f., 250, 345
Atilius (RE 13), **L.** 220, 261, 336
Atilius, L. 146
Atilius Regulus, M. 27, 37, 291
Atilius Serranus Gavianus (RE 70), **Sex.** 220, 344
Atinius, C. 134, 190
Attalus I of Pergamum 326, 329
Attalus III of Pergamum 91, 152f., 179
Augustus 48f., 53, 74, 103, 150, 158f., 163, 231, 250, 265, 290

Aurelius Cotta, C.   149, 155, 166
Aurelius Cotta, M.   77, 175, 194, 292
Aurelius Orestes, L.   71, 119, 137 f., 140 f., 148, 166, 310
Aurelius (RE 18), L.   95, 123, 220 f., 254, 337
Aurelius Scaurus (RE 215), M.   220 f., 272, 294, 298, 339
Aurelius Scaurus (RE 216), M.   220 f., 341
Autronius Paetus (RE 7), P.   54, 222, 342
Axius (RE 4), Q.   222, 231, 287, 298, 342

Baebius (RE 20a, suppl. 1.236), Q.   222 f., 340
Billienus (RE 3–4), C.   223, 334, 338
Bocchus of Mauretania   81, 97, 165, 192, 291

Caecilius (RE 1)   223, 344
Caecilius Bassus   267
Caecilius Metellus (RE 71), C.   224, 341
Caecilius Metellus, L.   331, 335
Caecilius Metellus (RE 75), L.   224, 345
Caecilius Metellus (RE 73), L.?   55, 224, 337
Caecilius Metellus Caprarius, C.   234
Caecilius Metellus Celer, Q.   326
Caecilius Metellus Creticus, Q.   149, 157, 159, 321
Caecilius Metelus Macedonicus, Q.   258, 303
Caecilius Metellus Nepos, Q.   117
Caecilius Metellus Pius, Q.   109, 149, 169, 242 f., 264, 284, 295, 329
Caecilius Metellus Pius Scipio Nasica (RE 99), Q.   224 f., 255, 263, 344
Caecilius Niger (RE 101), Q.   138, 176, 194, 225, 301, 332, 342
Caecilius Rufus (RE 110), L.   225, 343
Caecina (not in RE), L.   225 f., 347
Caelius Rufus (RE 35), M.   53, 158, 219, 226, 250, 313, 344
Caepasius (RE Caepasius), C.   226 f., 343
Caepasius (RE Caepasius), L.   226 f., 343
Caerellius (RE 2), Q.   227, 347
Caesetius (RE 3), P.   138, 150, 182, 227, 332, 342
Callistratus   87
Calpurnius Bestia, L.   165, 319
Calpurnius Bestia (RE 24), L.   228, 343
Calpurnius Bibulus, M.   139, 142, 169, 186, 188, 231 f.
Calpurnius Piso, C.   190
Calpurnius Piso (RE 69), Cn.   70, 189, 228, 343

Calpurnius Piso Caesoninus, L.   184, 322
Calpurnius Piso Caesoninus (RE 89), L.   83, 110, 123, 228, 314, 339
Calpurnius Piso Caesoninus (RE 90), L.   229, 306, 343
Calpurnius Piso Frugi (RE 93), C.   229, 344
Calpurnius Piso (Frugi) (RE 95), Cn.   229 f., 322, 346
Camillus, M.   13, 17, 231
Canidius (RE 1)   162, 230, 301, 344
Caninius Gallus, L.   230
Caninius Rebilus, C.   64
Caninius Sallusti(an)us (RE 14)   72, 90, 142, 169 f., 183, 230 f., 283, 345
Canuleius, C.   10 f., 18, 22
Carvilius (RE 4), Sp.   231, 336
Cascellius (RE 4), A.   231, 287, 342
Cassius, Sp.   10, 13, 17
Cassius, C.   270
Cassius Longinus (RE 59), C.   54, 139, 142, 156, 158, 188 f., 191, 203, 231 f., 317, 345
Cassius Longinus (RE 70), Q.   75, 232 f., 236, 345
Cassius Parmensis, C.   207
Claudius   27, 48
Claudius (RE 23), L.   233, 342
Claudius Caecus (RE 91), Ap.   56 f., 234, 336
Claudius Caudex, Ap.   36
Claudius Marcellus (RE 214), C.   235
Claudius Marcellus (RE 217), C.   108
Claudius Marcellus, M.   126, 129, 144 f., 176, 178, 182
Claudius Marcellus (RE 229), M.   82, 124, 235, 343
(Claudius) Marcellus (not in RE), C.   234 f., 338
Claudius Marcellus Aeserninus (RE 232–233), M.   236, 346
Claudius Nero, Ti.   182, 346
Claudius Nero (RE 254), Ti.   236
Claudius Pulcher (RE 295), Ap.   237
Claudius Pulcher (RE 296), Ap.   111, 123, 236 f., 279 f., 339
Claudius Pulcher (RE 297), Ap.   75, 77, 268 f., 314
Claudius Pulcher (RE 302), C.   62, 152, 237, 339
Claudius Pulcher, C.   308 f., 313, 317
Claudius Sabinus Inregillensis, Ap.   123

Clodius Pulcher (RE 48), **P.**   54, 57, 117, 119 f.,
  159–162, 215, 237, 256, 300, 325, 344,
Cloelius (RE 5), **T.**   238, 340
Coelius Caldus (RE 14), **C.**   72 f., 173, 186,
  194, 238, 346
Coelius Vinicianus (RE 27), **M.**   238, 345
Congus   6 f.
Cornelia   120, 265
Cornelius (RE 18), **C.**   112, 132, 239, 284, 342
Cornelius (RE 5 and 52), **Q.**   54, 124, 239,
  306, 347
Cornelius Balbus (RE 70), **L.**   175, 240, 347
Cornelius Cethegus, C.   146
Cornelius Cethegus (RE 89), **C.**   124, 241, 344
Cornelius Cethegus, M.   299
Cornelius Cinna, L.   323
Cornelius (Cinna), L.   241
(Cornelius) Cinna (RE 104)   182, 241, 347
Cornelius Dolabella, Cn.   138, 161, 166, 174 f.,
  185, 302
Cornelius Dolabella, P.   190, 241
Cornelius Lentulus, Cn.   112
Cornelius Lentulus (RE 193, suppl. 3.259), **L.**
  241, 339
Cornelius Lentulus, Ser.   241
Cornelius (Lentulus) (RE 176), **Cn.**   57, 187,
  241, 337
Cornelius Lentulus Crus, L.   108, 298, 306
Cornelius Lentulus Marcellinus (RE 228), **Cn.**
  109, 124, 155, 242 f., 342
Cornelius Lentulus Marcellinus (RE 231), **P.**
  151 f., 154–159, 161, 178 f., 180, 185, 189,
  191, 203, 242 f., 342
Cornelius Lentulus Marcellinus (RE 232), **P.**
  182, 190, 243, 346
Cornelius Lentulus Spinther (RE 238), **P.**   54,
  108, 113, 124, 163, 243 f., 295, 309, 342
Cornelius Lentulus Spinther (RE 239), **P.**   190,
  244, 347
Cornelius Lentulus (Sura) (RE 240), **P.**   54, 86,
  90, 123, 168, 209, 241, 244 f., 330, 341
Cornelius Scipio (RE 324), **L.**   61, 100 f., 123,
  245, 337
Cornelius Scipio Aemilianus, P.   60, 75, 182–
  184, 219, 254, 294
Cornelius Scipio Africanus, P.   72, 75, 85–87,
  97, 105, 131 f., 182, 195, 256, 271, 299 f.
Cornelius Scipio Asiagenus, L.   70, 76, 303
Cornelius Scipio Asiaticus (RE 337), **L.**   57 f.,
  83, 85–87, 93, 175, 245, 261, 337

Cornelius Scipio Hispanus (RE 347), **Cn.**   61,
  245, 338
Cornelius Scipio Nasica (RE 350), **P.**   58, 246,
  337
Cornelius Scipio Nasica, P.   153
Cornelius Sulla (RE 377), **Faustus**   246, 345
Cornelius Sulla, P.   246
Cornelius Sulla (RE 387), **P.**   246 f., 346
Cornelius Sulla Felix (RE 392), **L.**   26, 30,
  33 f., 42 f., 48, 51–54, 61, 63, 65, 67–71,
  89 f., 97, 104 f., 121, 125, 128–130, 134,
  136–138, 141–143, 145, 151 f., 161, 165,
  167 f., 183 f., 187–193, 197, 200, 203, 224,
  235, 239 f., 245–247, 257, 264, 269, 271,
  274 f., 279–282, 289, 291, 296 f., 320 f.,
  323–325, 332, 339
Cornificius (RE 8), **Q.**   247, 271, 346
Cosconius, C.   311
Curius (RE 1), **Q.**   247 f., 343
Curtius Peducaeanus (RE 8), **M.**   39, 124, 248,
  318, 344
(Curtius) Postumus (RE 24), **C.**   248, 342

Decimius (RE 2), **C.**   248 f., 346
Democritus of Sicyon   210
Didius, T.   312–313
Domitius Calvinus, Cn.   295
Domitius Ahenobarbus (RE 27), **L.**   54, 249,
  303, 343

Egnatuleius (RE 1), **C.**   249 f., 340
Egnatuleius (RE 2), **L.**   182, 250, 347
Epigonus, tyrant of Colophon   183
Eppius (RE 2), **M.**   219 f., 250, 345

Fabius (not in RE), **Q.**   77 f., 194, 251–253,
  338
Fabius (RE 32, 58), **Q.**   129 f., 176–178, 253,
  337
Fabius Ambustus (RE 42), **K.**   251, 336
Fabius Buteo, N.   146
Fabius Hispaniensis (RE 84), **L.**   167, 251, 321,
  341
Fabius Labeo (RE 91), **Q.**   58, 95, 123, 220,
  254, 337
Fabius Maximus, Q.   64
Fabius Maximus Aemilianus, Q.   253, 274
Fabius Maximus Allobrogicus (RE 110), **Q.**   75,
  182, 184, 252–254, 283, 338
Fabius Maximus Eburnus, Q.   45, 252, 299

Fabius Maximus Verrucosus (RE 116), Q.   56 f., 254 f., 336
Fabius Vibulanus, K.   10
Fadius (RE 9), T.   255, 344
Fannius (RE 9), C.   255, 301, 344
Favonius (RE 1), M.   224 f., 255 f., 344
Flaminius (RE 3), C.   58, 132, 134, 176 f., 256, 337
Flavius Fimbria, C.   319
Flavius Fimbria (RE 88), C.   181, 256, 334, 340
Fonteius (RE 12), M.   62, 85, 123, 257 f., 263, 295 f., 304 f., 341
Fulcinnius (RE 2), L.   258 f., 303, 337
Fulvius (RE 10), C.   258, 278, 336
Fulvius Nobilior, M.   207
Fundanius (RE 1), C.   109, 123, 259, 339
Furfan(i)us Postumus (RE 1), T.   186, 259 – 261, 301, 346
Furius Aculeo (RE 31), C.   83, 87, 93, 175, 261, 337
Furius Bibaculus (RE 35), L.   220, 261, 336
Furius Camillus, M.   231
Furius Crassipes (RE 54)   174, 261 f., 345

Gabinius, A.   160, 325
Gabinius (RE 8), A.   262, 289 f., 339
Gentius, king of Illyria   132, 145
Granius Petro (RE 9)   263, 346

Hannibal   241, 258, 278
Helvius, M.   146
Herennius Rufus (RE 41), M.   263, 340
Hiero of Syracuse   127, 176, 178
Hirtius, A.   74, 103 f.
Hirtuleius (RE 1)   123, 257, 263 f., 340
Hirtuleius, C.   263
Hirtuleius (RE 3), L.   182, 264, 283, 341
Hispala Fecenia   97
Hortensius Hortalus (RE 8), Q.   265, 345
Hortensius Hortalus (RE 13), Q.   150, 221 f., 227, 264, 311, 341
Hostilius Cato, A.   83, 87, 93, 175, 261
Hostilius Mancinus, C.   170, 192, 310

Julia   265
Julius Caesar (RE 130), C.   235, 265, 339
Julius Caesar (RE 131), C.   42 f., 54, 70 f., 75, 77, 104, 119 f., 131 f., 138, 140, 143, 156, 163, 172, 192, 205 f., 211, 213 – 215, 227, 231 f., 236, 239 f., 243, 246 f., 265 – 268, 273 f., 276, 282, 286 f., 290, 309, 318, 328, 343
Julius Caesar, L.   209
Julius Caesar (RE 143), L.   209, 266, 341
Julius Caesar (RE 144), L.   266, 345
Julius Caesar (RE 153), Sex.   267, 346
Julius Caesar Strabo Vopiscus (RE 135), C.   267, 339
Julius Libo, L.   27, 37
Junius Brutus, D.   72
Junius Brutus, L.   7
Junius Brutus, M.   319
Junius Brutus Albinus (RE 55a, suppl. 5), D.   268
Junius Brutus (RE 53), M.   54, 75, 77, 162, 207, 215, 232, 241, 268 f., 295, 317, 324, 345
Junius Gracchanus   6 – 9, 14, 20, 22
Junius Juncus, M.   178
Junius Pennus, M.   119
Junius Silanus, D.   114
Junius Silanus, M.   188
Junius Silanus Murena (RE 170?), M.   269 f., 340
Juventius Laterensis (RE 16), M.   155 – 157, 159, 270 f., 344

Laelius Balbus (RE 6), D.   271, 347
Laelius (RE 2), C.   58, 70, 72, 75, 131 f., 182, 184, 195, 271, 299, 337
Lars Porsenna   9
Licinius Calvus, C.   226
Licinius Crassus, M.   69, 77, 109, 139, 142, 188, 231 f., 239, 295, 300, 326
Licinius Crassus Dives Mucianus, P.   153, 217 f.
Licinius Crassus Dives Mucianus (RE 72), P.   61, 274, 338
Licinius Crassus (RE 55), L.   62, 272, 288, 338
Licinius Crassus (RE 56), M.   77, 273, 345
Licinius Crassus (RE 63), P.   273 f.
Licinius Geta, C.   45
Licinius Lucullus (RE 102), L.   183
Licinius Lucullus (RE 103), L.   135
Licinius Lucullus (RE 104), L.   47, 54, 152, 167, 183, 189, 274 f., 324, 340
Licinius Murena (RE 122), L.   269 f., 281, 322 f.

Licinius Murena (RE 123), **L.** 47, 54, 71, 114, 248, 269, 276, 321, 342
Licinius Nerva 185, 193, 203, 327
Ligarius, Q. 206
Ligarius (RE 5), **T.** 124, 276, 345
Livius Drusus (RE 18), **M.** 277f., 340
Livius Ocella (RE 26), **L.** 278, 347
Livius Salinator, C. 134
Lollius (RE 9), **M.** 278, 343
Lucretius Ofella, Q. 51
Lucretius (RE 4), **L.** 258, 278, 336
Lutatius Catulus, C. 278
Lutatius Catulus, Q. 73, 121, 300
Lutatius Cerco, Q. 292f.
Lutatius Cerco (RE 14), **Q.** 278, 339

Maelius, Sp. 92
Maenius, Q. 114
Maenius (RE 16), **T.** 279, 342
Maloleius (not in RE), **T.** 111, 123, 236, 279f., 339
Manilius, C. 249
Manlius (Acidinus?) (RE 26), **L.** 61, 74, 80–82, 99, 123, 280, 320, 337
Manlius Acidinus Fulvianus, L. 129, 134, 176, 178, 253
Manlius Torquatus (RE 70, 76), A. 280
Manlius Torquatus (RE 78), **L.** 281, 338
Manlius Torquatus (RE 79), **L.** 281, 341
Manlius Torquatus, T. 90
Manlius Torquatus (RE 85), **T.** 282, 341
Manlius [Torquatus] (RE 13), **A.** 112, 124, 280, 341
Manlius Volso, L. 146
Manlius Vulso, Cn. 65, 89, 96
Marcius Figulus, C. 54, 287
Marcius Philippus, L. 159, 209
Marcius Rufus (RE 94) 182, 189, 282, 346
Marius (RE 14 suppl. 6), **C.** 62, 81, 97, 109, 130, 135f., 142, 165, 183, 187f., 190, 192f., 203, 223, 238, 247, 249, 257, 259, 263, 265, 282f., 291, 334, 338
Marius, L. 116
Marius (RE 4), **(L.)** 72f., 283, 346
Marius (RE 23), **M.** 264, 283f., 341
Masgaba 80f., 99f., 280
Masinissa, king of Numidia 74, 80f., 99f., 104, 280, 320
Memmius (RE 7), **C.** 132, 182, 239, 284f., 341

Memmius (RE 8), **C.** 285, 300, 324f., 343
Memmius (RE 13), **L.** 62, 285, 338
Memmius (RE 15), **L.** 285, 347
Menenius Agrippa 104
Meniskos 73, 101f.
Mescinius Rufus (RE 2), **L.** 88, 130, 170–173, 177, 186, 285, 345
Micipsa, king of Numidia 166
Minatius Sabinus (RE 3), **M.** 233, 286, 346
Minucius Basilus (RE 38), **L.** 287, 345
Minucius Rufus, Q. 146
Minucius Thermus (RE 66), **Q.** 62, 287, 334, 340
Minucius Thermus (RE 67), **Q.** 138f., 186, 191, 214, 287, 342
Misagenes 81, 100, 320
Mithridates VI, king of Pontus 89, 132, 149, 155, 157, 161, 167, 281, 283, 296, 324
Mucius Scaevola Augur, Q. 171, 209, 257
Mucius Scaevola (RE 22), **Q.** 62, 219, 272, 277, 288, 339
Mummius, L. 112, 303, 311

Neoptolemus 183
Nerius (RE 3), **Cn.** 107f., 110, 124, 288f., 346
Nicomedes IV Philopator 149, 151, 178f.
Nonius Sufenas (RE 52), **M.** 108, 288, 345
Norbanus (Balbus?) (RE 5), **C.** 62, 75, 212, 262, 289f., 340
Novius Ofalius 48
Numa Pompilius 6f., 10f., 22
Numerius Rufus (RE 5), **Q.** 167, 290, 344

Octavius (RE 15), **C.** 208, 290f., 343
Octavius (RE 26), **L.** 107, 123, 149, 155, 166, 290f., 299, 340
Octavius Rufus (RE 79), **C.** 291, 336
Octavius Ruso (RE 82), **Cn.** 81, 97, 123, 165, 291, 339
Opimius Pansa (RE 12), **L.** 291f., 336
Oppius (RE 17), **P.** 77f., 175, 194, 292, 342
Orodes, king of Parthia 188

Papirius Carbo (RE 37), Cn. 234
Papirius Carbo (RE 38), Cn. 70, 132, 138, 161, 168f., 171, 174, 180, 193, 331
Papirius (not in RE), **C.** 38f., 292f., 302, 304, 336
Papius (RE Pupius *1), **P.** 205, 293, 319, 336
Pavus Tubitanus (RE Pavus), **P.?** 293, 337

Peducaeus, Sex.   138, 142, 144, 148, 327
Perperna (RE 4), M.   91
Perperna (RE 6), M.   161, 251, 283 f.
Perseus of Macedonia   100, 104 f., 114, 145, 185
Petillius Spurinus (RE 4, 11), **Q.**   56, 294, 337
Petreius, M.   233
Philo (L. Veturius Philo?) (RE Veturius 21), **L.**   144, 220, 294 f., 298, 339
Phylargirus   88, 179
Plaetorius (RE 5), **C.**   182, 295, 346
Plaetorius (Cestianus) (RE 14), **L.**   108 f., 124, 243, 295 f., 342
Plaetorius Cestianus (RE 16), **M.**   295 f., 343
Plancius (RE 4), **Cn.**   54, 296, 344
Plautius, C.   187, 296 f.
Plautius Hypsaeus (RE 23), **P.**   132, 208, 296 f., 343
Polystratos   73, 101 f.
Pompeius (RE 4), **A.**   297, 341
Pompeius, Sex.   139, 187, 212
Pompeius Bithynicus (RE 25), **Q.**   151, 161, 178–180, 297 f., 341
Pompeius Longinus (RE 29), **T.**   298, 306, 346
Pompeius Magnus, Cn.   286
Pompeius Rufus (RE *8), **Q.**   231, 287, 298, 342
Pompeius Strabo (RE 14), **Cn.**   220, 222, 287, 294, 298 f., 339
Pompey   43, 69, 75, 77, 89 f., 108, 110, 132 f., 148–150, 155–157, 159, 161, 173, 187, 190, 208 f., 213, 229, 232 f., 238 f., 242 f., 249, 284, 286, 295–297, 311, 315 f., 322 f.
Pomponius   11 f., 14, 62
Pomponius (not in RE), **C.**   107, 123, 290, 299, 340
Pomp(onius) Vic(tor) (not in RE), **A.**   299, 346
Pomptinus, C.   186
Porcius Cato (RE 9), **M.**   57, 169, 299 f., 337
Porcius Cato (Uticensis) (RE *20), **M.**   79, 82, 84, 88 f., 116, 120 f., 124, 133, 156, 158–163, 179, 185, 191, 230, 235, 243, 259, 266, 300 f., 315, 344
Postumius (RE 15), **L.**   259, 301, 346
Postumius (RE 19), **M.**   138, 225, 227, 301, 332, 342
Postumius Albinus, A.   140, 186
Postumius Albinus (RE 33), A.   316
Postumius Albinus (RE 44), Sp.   97

Postumius Albinus (RE 45), Sp.   140, 186
Postumius Albinus Regillensis, P.   316
Postumius Tympanus (RE 24), **L.**   301, 337
Prusias of Bithynia   100 f., 104, 245
Ptolemy Apion   149, 152, 154, 156, 178 f.
Ptolemy of Cyprus   159, 179, 230
Ptolemy VI Philometor   101
Ptolemy XII Auletes   159 f., 162
Publicius Malleolus (RE 22), **M.**   38 f., 292 f., 302, 304, 336
(Publicius) Malleolus (RE *14), **C.**   161, 302, 341
Publicius (RE 13?), **Q.**   301, 341
Publicius Scaeva (not in RE), **M.**   303, 342
Publilius (RE 10), **C.**   258, 303, 337
Punicus   184
Pupius Piso Frugi (RE 10), **M.**   70, 76, 303, 328 f., 341

Quinctilius Varus (RE 17), **Sex.**   303, 346
Quinctius Capitolinus, T.   10, 55
(Quinctius?) Crispinus (not in RE), **T.**   304, 343
Quinctius Flamininus (RE *3), **T.**   58, 305, 337
Quinctius (not in RE), **L.**   38 f., 292, 302, 304 f., 336

Raesius (not in RE), **Q.**   298, 306, 346
Rancius (RE 11), **Q.**   306, 342
Romulus   6 f., 10, 21 f.
Roscius Fabatus   266
Rupilius, P.   77 f., 194, 252
Rutilius (RE 11), **Q.**   112, 124, 239, 306, 347
Rutilius Nudus (RE 30), **P.**   174, 306, 340
Rutilius Rufus, P.   277

Sallustius Crispus (RE 10), **C.**   248, 307, 345 f.
Sanquinius (RE 3), **Q.**   307, 347
Saturninus (RE 27), **Cn.**   216 f., 307 f., 343
Saufeius (RE 3), **C.**   118 f., 308, 339
Scribonius Curio, C.   149
Scribonius Curio (RE 11), **C.**   54, 182, 189, 219 f., 250, 282, 308 f., 313, 317, 345
Scribonius Libo (RE 20), **L.**   309, 344
Se[---] (not in RE), **M.**   310, 313 f., 347
Seius, M.   48, 150, 321
Sempronius Asellio, L. (see Asullius)   219, 310
Sempronius Blaesus (RE 32), **Ti.**   310, 336

Sempronius Gracchus (RE 47), C.   7, 60, 71, 119f., 137f., 140f., 148, 166, 310, 338
Sempronius Gracchus, Ti.   95, 97, 187
Sempronius Gracchus (RE 54), Ti.   60f., 170, 192f., 310, 338
Sempronius Longus, P.   190
Sempronius Longus, Ti.   301
Sempronius Pit(h)io, L. (see L. Philo)   294f., 339
Sempronius Tuditanus, C.   146, 294
Sempronius Tuditanus (RE 92), C.   61, 311, 338
Sempronius Tuditanus, P.   299, 311
Sentius, C.   209, 306
Septimius (RE 11), P.   311, 323, 341
Sergius (RE 18), M'.   311f., 347
Sergius Catilina, L.   312, 317
Sergius Silus (RE 42), M.   112, 123, 312, 338
Sertorius (RE 3), Q.   29, 49, 109, 132, 149, 182f., 239, 243, 251, 263f., 283f., 311–313, 321f., 340
Servaeus (RE 3)   313, 345
Serveilius (RE 17), L.   313, 347
Servilia   314
Servilius, C.   144, 294
Servilius (RE 20), M.   310, 313f., 345
Servilius Caepio (RE 47), Cn.   314, 339
Servilius Caepio (RE 40–42), Q.   315, 343
Servilius Caepio (RE 49), Q.   177
Servilius Caepio (RE 50), Q.   83, 110, 117, 123, 228, 314, 339
Servilius Caepio Brutus, Q. (see M. Junius Brutus)
Servilius Geminus, Cn.   310
Servilius Glaucia (RE 65), C.   62, 315, 339
Servilius Isauricus (RE 67), P.   315, 344
Servilius Vatia Isauricus, P.   89
Servius Cordus (RE 3)   316, 346
Servius Tullius   10
Sestius (RE 6), P.   141, 163, 173, 238, 317, 319, 344
Sestius (RE 15), P.   316, 336
Sestius (Pansa?) (RE 10), L.   308, 313, 317, 343
Sestius Quirinalis Albinianus (RE 3), L.   139, 161, 317f., 347
Sestullius (RE Sextilius 13), P.   39, 124, 248, 318, 344
Sextilius, P. (see P. Sestullius)

Sextilius Rufus (RE 23), C.   163, 174, 318f., 346
Sextius, T.   271
Sextius Calvinus (RE 1 and 21), C.   165, 319, 339
Sicinius (RE 7), C.   319, 342
Silius, P.   261
Silius (RE 10), Q.   205, 293, 319, 336
Sosius (see RE 2), C.   319, 343
Spartacus   132, 150, 239, 325
Stertinius (RE 6), L.   81, 100, 123, 280, 320, 337
Sulpicius (RE 15), P.   66, 320f., 343
Sulpicius Galba, P.   320
Sulpicius Rufus, P.   320
Sulpicius Rufus (RE 95), Ser.   47–49, 54, 71, 73f., 83, 103, 151, 276, 320f., 342
Sulpicius Rufus (RE 96), Ser.   83, 321, 34
Syphax   104f.

Tadius, P.   150, 183, 227
Tarquinius Superbus   9
Tarquitius (RE 1), C.   167, 251, 321f., 341
Tarquitius Priscus, C.   321
Terentius Culleo, Q.   83, 93
Terentius Varro (RE 77)   184, 322, 338
Terentius Varro (RE 82), A.   270, 311, 322f., 338
Terentius Varro, C.   220
Terentius Varro (RE 83), C.   58, 261, 323, 336
Terentius Varro (RE 84, suppl. 6), M.   311, 322, 323, 340
(Terentius) Varro (RE 78), A.?   229, 322, 323, 346
Terentius Varro Gibba (RE 89), M.   324, 346
Terentius Varro Lucullus (RE Licinius 109), M.   54, 109, 149, 295, 322, 324, 340
Tiberius   236
Tigranes, king of Armenia   89f.
Tillius Cimber, L.   328
Titius (Mutto), Q.   71
Titius, Sex.   71
Toranius (RE 4), C.   132, 325, 342
Trebatius Testa, C.   42
Trebonius (RE 6), C.   119f., 124, 190, 244, 325f., 344
Tremellius Flaccus (RE 4), Cn.   57, 326, 329, 337
Tremellius Scrofa (RE 5), Cn.   326, 340, 342

Tremellius Scrofa (RE 6), L.   185, 189, 326 f., 338
Tullia   261
Tullius, M.   88, 172
Tullius Cicero, L.   327
Tullius Cicero (RE 29), **M.**   6, 39, 43–49, 53 f., 56, 62, 64, 66, 70–77, 79, 83, 85–90, 92, 94, 98 f., 103, 112, 115, 119 f., 130 f., 138–144, 148, 150 f., 158–163, 166, 168–177, 180, 183, 185 f., 188 f., 191, 193 f., 199, 204, 206, 208, 210, 212–217, 220–223, 226, 229–232, 237–240, 244, 246, 248–250, 255, 257–259, 261, 263–265, 270–272, 275–277, 282–288, 290, 292, 294–296, 298–304, 307–309, 311, 313, 315, 317–321, 324–333, 335, 342
Tullius Cicero (RE 31), **Q.**   210, 317, 327, 329, 343
Tullius Rufus (RE 49)   328, 346
Tullus Hostilius   6 f., 19, 21 f.
Turullius (RE 1), **D.**   328, 347

Urbinus (not in RE), **C.**   279, 329, 342
Urbinius, Q.   111, 236, 279

Valeria Polla   268
Valerius, L.   10
Valerius, P.   172
Valerius Falto (RE 153), **M.**   58, 326, 329, 337
Valerius Flaccus, L.   181, 220 f., 256–257, 263, 294, 334
Valerius Flaccus (RE *69, 179), **L.**   39, 54, 98, 223, 327–329, 343
Valerius Laevinus, M.   326, 329
Valerius Messala, M.   134
Valerius Messala (RE *97), **M.**   329
Valerius Messala Niger (RE 266), **M.**   330, 342
Valerius Messala Potitus (RE 267), **M'.**   330, 347
Valerius Messalla Rufus, M.   64
Valerius Poplicola Potitus (RE 304), **L.**   7 f., 26, 55, 208, 330, 336, 347
Valerius Publicola, L.   8 f., 21
Valerius Triarius, L.   268
(Valerius) Triarius (RE 363, 366), **C.**   124, 244, 281, 330, 341
Varinius, P.   132, 325
Vatinius (RE *2), **P.**   43–47, 54, 71, 74, 199, 331, 344
Vergilius Balbus (RE 3), **C.**   119, 237, 331, 343
Verres (RE 1), **C.**   66, 70, 72, 86 f., 89, 97, 132, 138, 148, 150 f., 161, 166–169, 171 f., 174–176, 180, 182 f., 185, 191, 193 f., 221 f., 225, 227, 301, 320, 326, 332 f., 340
Vetilius, C.   185, 187 f., 334
(Vettius?) Sabinus (RE Sabinus 30), P.   332, 340
Vettius (Chilo?) (RE *9, 11 and 14), **T.**   138, 192, 227, 332, 342
Veturius, P.   8
Veturius Philo, L. (see L. Philo)
Vibius Pansa, C.   74, 103 f.
Vibius Temudinus (not in RE), **T.**   105 f., 123, 290, 299, 332, 340
Viriathus   185, 187, 334
Visellius Varro (RE 3), **C.**   319, 333, 342
Volscius, M.   13
Volscius Fictor, M.   10, 17
Volusius, Q.   172 f.

Index of subjects

accomodation 99
aerarium 11–16, 19–24, 34, 39, 55, 66, 73 f., 79–93, 95–99, 102, 104, 106, 108–118, 120–122, 129, 131, 134, 137, 139, 141, 143, 146 f., 151, 168 f., 171–173, 175–180, 184, 196 f., 201 f., 224, 228, 235 f., 244, 279, 291, 314
Africa 42, 72, 75, 81, 97, 100, 126, 128, 140 f., 145, 150, 158, 165, 167, 182, 187, 189, 195, 218, 246, 248, 263, 266, 271, 280, 282, 290 f., 299 f., 303, 305, 310, 334
Africa Vetus 271
ager quaestorius 93 f.
apparitores 65 f., 79, 84 f., 96, 201
Asia 42, 57, 65, 86, 91, 126, 134, 138 f., 141, 149, 152 f., 158, 166 f., 169, 171, 174 f., 178, 181, 184, 186, 190 f., 207, 209 f., 214–216, 218–223, 235, 241, 244 f., 250, 256 f., 261, 265 f., 269 f., 272, 274–278, 281, 295, 297 f., 301, 306, 308–311, 313–315, 317, 322 f., 327, 330, 333 f.
auction 91–95, 162, 177–179, 202

Bithynia 76–78, 143, 149, 151, 158, 161, 174 f., 178 f., 182, 194, 229, 261 f., 270, 292, 295, 297 f., 328
bonorum sectio 92
booty 86, 88–91, 116, 129, 169, 176–178, 202, 231, 256
Bronze of Ascoli 287

calles 27–30, 32, 50, 199
Cilicia 72 f., 75, 77, 87 f., 126, 128, 130, 138, 140, 142, 149, 155, 158, 160 f., 163, 166, 169, 171–174, 185 f., 194, 232, 238, 247, 261 f., 268 f., 276, 285, 289 f., 302, 318 f.
Cimbri and Teutons 109, 259
Cisalpine Gaul 28 f., 31 f., 49, 168, 172, 183, 313, 324 f.
cohors praetoria 168
conservation of roads 105, 107
consilium 163, 181, 186, 192, 210, 212, 222, 233, 279, 287, 291, 298, 303, 306, 333
consul 6–11, 13, 15–24, 27, 33 f., 36, 39, 41–47, 50 f., 55–59, 64–74, 76 f., 85, 91, 96–98, 101–104, 107 f., 113 f., 117, 119, 121, 123, 125 f., 128, 130–135, 137–142, 144, 146, 148–150, 152–155, 157, 160 f., 164–166, 168–170, 175, 180–183, 185–187, 192–194, 196–200, 203, 206 f., 209, 213, 215, 217 f., 220 f., 232, 234–237, 239, 241, 243 f., 246 f., 250, 252, 254–257, 261, 263, 268, 270, 273, 281 f., 287 f., 290–293, 298–303, 305 f., 309–311, 313 f., 316, 319, 323, 325 f., 330 f., 334
consular quaestors 30, 33, 39 f., 42 f., 69, 72 f., 84, 126, 128, 131, 137, 198, 200, 293, 302, 304
creation of the quaestorship 5, 9, 20 f.
Crete 149, 158 f., 183, 207, 270 f.
curator viarum 80, 105 f., 332
cursus honorum 2 f., 51, 55–57, 59, 62–64, 121 f., 129, 193, 199 f., 217 f., 225, 237, 255
Cyprus 88, 133, 139, 143, 156, 158–164, 174, 179 f., 183, 191, 230, 243, 300, 316, 318 f.
Cyrenaica 139, 143, 149, 151–159, 161, 164, 178 f., 183–185, 189, 191, 242 f., 270 f., 275

diplomacy 98, 191
duumviri navales 27, 36, 40 f.

Early Republic 2–5, 9–11, 18, 23 f., 26, 34, 55, 67, 91, 197, 200
Egadi's *rostra* 3, 25, 38–41, 55, 83, 103, 198, 265, 292 f., 302, 304
Egypt 159, 183, 285, 316
Eleusinian Mysteries 272
elogium 56 f., 62, 123, 208, 234, 237, 245, 254 f., 265, 267, 277, 282, 290, 330
extra sortem 69 f., 72, 75–77, 131 f., 182, 195, 201, 213, 215, 232, 271

financial audits 86
First Punic War 3, 33, 35 f., 38, 40–42, 68, 127, 145, 198, 291–293, 302, 304
fleet 27 f., 30, 32, 36–42, 100 f., 150, 162, 182 f., 198, 207, 227, 236, 248, 275, 292 f., 299, 302, 304, 317, 324
foreign ambassadors 99
funerary honours 103, 202
funus publicum 103–105

Gaul 75, 77, 97, 128, 134, 138, 142, 158, 186, 213–215, 268, 273f., 283, 287, 331
Greece 222f., 229, 274f., 322, 324

Hispania 49, 70, 75, 109f., 120, 126, 129–135, 137, 141, 146f., 149, 158, 167, 178, 182, 184, 187, 189f., 192, 228, 232f., 239f., 242f., 246, 251–254, 256, 263–266, 283f., 286, 293–295, 310–313, 321f., 328f.
Hispania Citerior 42, 70, 75, 128f., 134, 146f., 170, 176, 183, 192f., 228, 233, 251, 253f., 264, 278, 284, 294, 310, 313, 328f.
Hispania Ulterior 75, 129, 134–136, 138, 140, 146f., 169, 175, 184, 187, 189f., 192, 213, 229, 232f., 236, 240, 242, 251, 265f., 284, 309, 311, 329, 334

Illyricum 108, 132, 145, 186, 247, 288, 311, 322
imperator 75f., 89, 91, 104, 110, 115f., 125, 132, 149, 162, 177, 185, 191–193, 199, 203, 242, 290, 327
imperium 11, 13, 35, 37, 42f., 49, 125, 128–130, 132f., 139–141, 145, 149, 153–156, 158, 160, 162, 164, 180f., 184f., 188–191, 193, 195, 198, 203, 243, 261, 300

Judaea 188
Jugurthine War 140, 165
jurors 66, 116f., 202, 320

lex Cornelia de XX quaestoribus 42, 51, 65f., 68, 79f., 84, 128, 136, 142, 197
lex frumentaria 110, 118, 160, 228f., 314f.
lex Gabinia 148, 208, 297
lex Iulia de repetundis 87f., 172
lex Iunia Licinia 114
lex Manilia 209, 297
lex Sempronia 134f., 137
lex Terentia et Cassia frumentaria 150
lex Titia 44, 70f.
lex Trebonia 233
lex Villia 59–61, 63, 199f., 217
Lucullan coins 324

Macedonia 77, 114, 126, 139, 141, 145, 149, 158, 161, 167, 174, 185–187, 189, 191, 203, 208–213, 222, 234, 250, 258f., 261, 272, 290, 296, 303, 306, 314, 317, 327

Magna Mater 326, 329
Mesagne Hoard 108, 243, 246, 289
Middle Republic 25, 30, 32, 34, 54, 57, 69
milestones 218
Military tribunate 20, 22, 49, 51f., 56–59, 61–63, 120, 219, 222, 227, 234, 245f., 267, 283f., 290, 298, 306, 316
minimum age 2, 53f., 59–61, 63, 199f., 222, 244, 248f., 269
minting of coins 107, 109, 111, 202, 216
Mithridatic War 132, 154, 167, 183, 256, 276, 283, 321, 324f.
monarchy 7–9, 12, 14–16, 19–21, 196
mos 52, 76, 88, 172, 193

necessitudo 75, 138, 176, 193f., 204
negotiatores 154, 174, 306
Nones of December 65f., 84f., 133, 136f., 200, 320
Numantine War 182, 219, 294, 310
Numidia 104f., 130, 140, 142, 165f., 183, 187f., 190, 192, 203, 247, 291, 319

oaths 115f.
origin of the quaestorship 2, 5–10, 12f., 15, 18, 196

patricians 10, 24, 54f., 61, 197
plebeian quaestors 24, 34, 64, 197, 205, 251, 293
plebeians 10, 22, 24, 34, 42, 54f., 61, 197, 199, 319
pons Aemilius 207
Pontecorvo Hoard 109, 242
praeda 83, 90–92, 169, 177f.
prisoners of war 83, 91, 95, 202
probatio 38–40, 293, 302, 304
prorogatio 33, 126, 128, 131, 133f., 137, 140f., 143, 199
provincia 3, 28–30, 33, 35, 38f., 41–50, 64–66, 69–75, 77, 79, 84f., 106, 125f., 128f., 131–135, 137–139, 141, 143–147, 152f., 155–162, 164f., 167f., 171f., 175, 178, 181, 185f., 188–192, 194, 198–201, 203, 213, 223, 225, 228, 238, 252, 265, 270, 275, 290, 296, 309, 313, 331
provincia aquaria 32, 43–48, 71, 74, 128, 199, 331
provincia Ligures 134

provincia Ostiensis 27–31, 35, 40, 43f., 46–49, 72, 128, 137, 139, 143, 151, 231, 321
publicani 166
public expenses 84, 87, 95–97, 99, 101–104, 106, 154, 165, 167, 169, 201f.
public funds 8f., 39, 62, 90, 105f., 165, 169, 171, 177, 183, 202, 215, 331
public income 84, 95f., 107, 201f.
public notaries 90f., 112, 202

quaerere 6, 9, 12f., 15, 20
quaesitor 6, 13, 19, 27
quaestor Lilybitanus 127, 144
quaestor Ostiensis 28, 32f., 35, 46–49, 110f., 199, 216, 223, 228, 314, 321
quaestor urbanus 3, 17, 23f., 29f., 33, 39f., 42f., 66f., 72–74, 79–88, 90–99, 101–114, 116–119, 122f., 131, 137, 139, 143, 146f., 156, 160, 165, 168, 171, 196, 198, 200–202, 220, 228, 235f., 239f., 242, 244, 248, 254, 276, 279–281, 288, 290, 293, 295, 299, 302, 304, 314f., 326, 330
quaestores aerarii 13f., 16, 18
quaestores classici 3, 27f., 36f., 40f., 72, 198
quaestores Italici 2f., 25, 28f., 31–33, 35, 43f., 48–50, 197, 199
quaestores parricidii 2, 6, 11–20, 196

rationes 86–89, 168, 170–172, 178, 203

Sardinia 30f., 35, 41f., 71, 90, 119, 125f., 128f., 131, 134, 136f., 140f., 146–148, 150, 158, 166, 169, 181, 198, 267f., 298, 310, 331

scribae 66f., 74, 79f., 82, 84f., 87f., 102, 120, 122, 173, 201, 240, 261
Second Punic War 25, 30, 36, 41, 50, 55f., 58, 68, 95, 145f., 197, 212, 220, 254
senatus consultum 45, 53, 70–72, 97, 99, 102, 112f., 158, 160, 173, 219, 244, 250
senatus consultum de agro Pergameno 209f., 291
senatus consultum de Asclepiade 73, 101
senatus consultum de Oropiis 212, 222, 231, 233, 279, 287, 298, 303, 306, 333
senatus consultum de Panamareis 318
Sertorian War 109, 132, 167, 242, 283f., 329
Sicily 3, 28, 30f., 33, 35–37, 41f., 48, 52, 77, 89, 118f., 125–129, 131, 134f., 138, 141–148, 150f., 158, 161, 166f., 176, 181f., 186, 194, 198, 205, 211f., 219, 224f., 227, 229, 237, 251–253, 259–261, 282, 294, 300f., 315, 327, 331–335, 338
signa 11, 23, 85f., 89, 132
Slave War 144, 168, 194, 219, 229
Social War 101, 183, 263
sortitio 68–72, 74f., 131–137, 141, 143, 147, 182, 201

tabulae publicae 93, 96, 112, 115, 122, 170, 201
Temple of Saturn 8, 14f., 18, 21f., 98, 108, 115
Third Punic War 274
tributum 96, 201
triumviri monetales 30, 62f., 71, 85, 107, 199, 202, 236, 249, 257, 279, 288, 295f.

Via Caecilia 105f., 202, 332

www.ingramcontent.com/pod-product-compliance
Lightning Source LLC
Chambersburg PA
CBHW081823230426
43668CB00017B/2359